Also by Stephan Thernstrom

Poverty and Progress: Social Mobility in a Nineteenth Century City
The Other Bostonians:
Poverty and Progress in the American Metropolis 1880–1970
Harvard Encyclopedia of American Ethnic Groups (ed.)
A History of the American People, Vols. 1 & 2

Also by Abigail Thernstrom

Whose Votes Count?: Affirmative Action and Minority Voting Rights
A Democracy Reader: Classic and Modern Speeches, Essays, Poems,
Declarations and Documents on Freedom and Human Rights Worldwide
(with Diane Ravitch)

America in Black and White

ONE NATION, INDIVISIBLE

STEPHAN THERNSTROM
AND ABIGAIL THERNSTROM

SIMON & SCHUSTER

SIMON & SCHUSTER
Rockefeller Center
1230 Avenue of the Americas
New York, NY 10020

SIMON & SCHUSTER and colophon are registered trademarks
of Simon & Schuster Inc.

Designed by Irving Perkins Assoc., Inc.

Maps by Jeffrey L. Ward

Manufactured in the United States of America

1   3   5   7   9   10   8   6   4   2

Library of Congress Cataloging-in-Publication Data
Thernstrom, Stephan.
America in black and white: one nation, indivisible /
Stephan Thernstrom and Abigail Thernstrom.
p.   cm.
Includes bibliographical references and index.
1. Afro-Americans—Civil rights—History—20th century.   2. Afro-
Americans—Social conditions.   3. United States—Race relations.
4. Racism—United States—History—20th century.
I. Thernstrom, Abigail M., date.   II. Title.
E185.61.T45   1997   97-14078   CIP
305.896′073—dc21
ISBN 0-684-80933-8

Acknowledgments

ABIGAIL THERNSTROM is a senior fellow at the Manhattan Institute, and for the extraordinary freedom to write full-time, she could not be more grateful. For their unwavering commitment to this seemingly endless project, particular thanks is owed to two remarkable men: Lawrence Mone, the Institute's president, and Roger Hertog, chairman of the board of trustees. They have provided a warm and nurturing home for an academic who chose to leave the academy.

The John M. Olin Foundation, the Lynde and Harry Bradley Foundation, the Smith Richardson Foundation, the Earhart Foundation, and the Carthage Foundation have also generously funded our research. Harvard University gave Stephan Thernstrom sabbatical leave in the academic year 1992–1993, and in the spring of 1993 Abigail Thernstrom was a visiting scholar at the Woodrow Wilson Center in Washington, D.C., a wonderful academic retreat that owes much to its director, Charles Blitzer.

Many friends and colleagues read the manuscript in whole or part. Douglas Besharov, Martha Derthick, Howard Husock, Morton Keller, Randall Kennedy, Andrew Kull, Stephen J. Markman, Walter Olson, Diane Ravitch, Charles Shanor, Ricky Silberman, Alex Von Hoffman, and James Q. Wilson all offered critical advice about specific chapters. Mary Ash, Henry Fetter, William Guenther, Edward Lev, and Stephen Teles stared at every page and provided highly detailed, invaluable feedback. We learned much from their painstaking reviews. Finally, perhaps our greatest debt is to our son, Samuel Thernstrom, whose editorial skills are daunting and whose wise counsel on many matters of substance made us think and think again.

We were blessed with wonderful research assistants: Michael Burgmaier, Andrew Hazlett, Kevin Marshall, Todd Molz, Joel Pulliam, and Romney Resney. As a Harvard undergraduate, Joel worked for us part-time throughout his college career; for more than a year Andrew devoted his life to our project. Gina Hewes tabulated unpublished survey data that were important to our analysis. We owe a special thanks to them. Our warmest thanks as well to our literary agents, Glen Hartley and Lynn Chu, who have guided the book in countless small ways, and to our superb editor at Simon & Schuster, Robert Bender, who handled both book and authors with a firm and deft touch.

Inevitably, readers will wonder who wrote which chapters. This was truly a collaborative project; every chapter was a joint effort. The order of our names on the jacket has no significance; it resulted from the toss of a coin.

A.T.
S.T.
Lexington, Massachusetts

TO MELANIE AND SAM

Contents

PART THREE
Equality and Preferences: The Changing Racial Climate

Introduction

"An American Dilemma," Gunnar Myrdal called the problem of race in his classic 1944 book. He saw a painful choice between American ideals and American racial practices. But in 1944, ten years before *Brown v. Board of Education,* most white Americans were not actually in much pain. Indeed, when asked in a survey that same year whether "Negroes should have as good a *chance* as white people to get any kind of job," the majority of whites said that "white people should have the first chance at any kind of job."[1] Blacks belonged at the back of the employment bus, most whites firmly believed.

"Are they relatives of yours?" a white asks the protagonist in Ralph Ellison's 1952 novel, *Invisible Man.*

> "Sure, we're both black," I said, beginning to laugh.
> He smiled, his eyes intense upon my face.
> "Seriously, are they your relatives?"
> "Sure, we were burned in the same oven," I said.[2]

Burned in the same Jim Crow oven, in the heat generated by overwhelming racial hostility. That brutal world is gone, but some of the scars remain. Both points are easy to forget but essential to remember. On both left and right, writers too often distort the picture for political ends, clouding our understanding of the nation's most important domestic issue. On the right, they frequently dismiss the persistence of racial animus, suggesting, indeed, that "those who look carefully for evidence of racism . . . are likely to come up short."[3] On the left, critics such as Derrick Bell allude to the "bogus freedom checks" that "the Man" will never honor.[4] An enslaved people remains enslaved.

There is no racism; there is nothing but racism. The issue of race sends people scurrying in extremist directions. And thus there is almost no overlap between opposing views, and little sympathy and understanding across the lines of political battle. In October 1994 the Court of Appeals for the Fourth Circuit struck down the University of Maryland's blacks-only Banneker Scholarship program. "I can't get over the irony of the rising African American jail population and then taking away a program like this that tries to bring African Americans into the university," the president of the university remarked.[5] The Fourth Circuit had seen the issue quite differently: "Of all the criteria by which men and women can be judged," the court had said, "the most perni-cious is that of race."

Americans committed to racial justice were not always so divided. In 1963, when the Reverend Martin Luther King, Jr., stood at the Lincoln Memorial and spoke of his dreams, blacks and whites marching together pictured the "beautiful symphony of brotherhood" that treating blacks and whites alike would surely create. But that shared vision quickly faded, as many came to believe that race consciousness was the road to racial equality. "In order to get beyond racism, we must first take account of race," Justice Harry Black-mun said in the *Bakke* case in 1978. In the civil rights community, by the late 1970s, that much-quoted aphorism had come to seem indisputably right.

Today we argue without a common language. University of Pennsylvania law professor Lani Guinier, a much sought after presence in the media, has repeatedly called for "a national conversation on race." We have not exactly fallen silent on the subject. We talk endlessly, obsessively about the issue, but across linguistic barricades. "Equal opportunity" is a much-used phrase with a much-disputed meaning. In the battleground of ideas, language is part of the territory each side seeks to capture. And thus, while advocates of race-neutral policies equate such equality with basic access—an absence of closed doors —their critics look for outcomes. "As a general matter, increases in the num-bers of employees, or students or entrepreneurs from historically underrepre-sented groups are a measure of increased opportunity," Christopher Edley and George Stephanopolous, advisors to President Clinton, argued in 1995. No opportunity without results.

Definitional quarrels are only the start of the problem. Opposing sides in the debate over race start from different premises, and see American society through very different lenses. The topic of race raises fundamental questions about who we are, where we're going, how we get there. To talk about race is to talk about America—and vice versa. The question pops up everywhere; one can't escape it. Try to name a significant domestic issue that has nothing to do with the status of African Americans: it's a challenge. Crime, family, education, housing, the environment, even foreign military entanglements and border control. Immigration is a good example. Newcomers, immigration advocates say, are good for the country; they contribute to its economic vitality. But are they good for *black* America? And if not, how much does that matter? What do we owe those who arrived on our shores in 1619 and remained members of an oppressed caste for more than three centuries? A relatively narrow question—immigration policy—is hopelessly entangled with the cen-tral issue in American life.

As authors, we have no easy answers to such policy questions. We offer instead a framework for debate—a map. Or rather a book of maps, in the hope that if we understand the territory we can better decide the direction in which to head. Thus, we start with six historical chapters dealing with developments that climaxed in the 1960s and fundamentally altered the place of African Americans in American society and altered American society itself. We open with a detailed account of the development and nature of segregation in the Jim Crow South, drawing a dark picture too often forgotten. Until World War II three-quarters of the black population lived in the South, where they were a subordinate caste in a society dedicated to white supremacy. Chapter 2 traces the first Great Migration of blacks from South to North and describes the life blacks found upon arriving in Chicago and other northern cities. The contrast between the two regions was real, but not as stark as some have made it out to be. In the North, the pervasive threat of white violence that defined southern black lives was absent. But discrimination in the labor market and elsewhere was rampant.

In Chapter 3 we turn to the impact of World War II on the status of African Americans—the major social, economic, and demographic changes that occurred in the 1940s and 1950s. Once again, in large numbers blacks boarded trains and buses for northern cities where the money was (relatively) good; in the war and immediate postwar years, black earnings rose dramatically—more dramatically than they have in any subsequent two decades. The military was segregated, but southern and northern blacks served together, and the exposure of those from the South to northern racial attitudes was subversive. Ten years after the end of the war, the Montgomery bus boycott would begin —a peaceful mass protest that led straight to the great civil rights legislation of the mid-1960s.

In Chapter 4 we trace the breakdown of that amazing patience that African Americans had so long displayed. We open with a discussion of *Brown v. Board of Education,* look at the quiet revolution in racial attitudes that began in the 1940s, and then go on to the opening chapters of the civil rights revolution itself: Montgomery; the rise of the Southern Christian Leadership Conference; the use of federal troops to force the desegregation of Little Rock's Central High School; and the sit-ins that began in 1960. Chapter 5 opens with a discussion of presidential politics and civil rights, and closes with the making of the 1964 Civil Rights Act; in the intervening pages it describes the Freedom Rides, the crashing failure of the demonstrations in Albany, Georgia, and the stunning success of those in Birmingham, Alabama; the revolution in white racial attitudes; the 1963 March on Washington; and the political timidity of President John F. Kennedy. In the last chapter of this first section, we treat the murder of student civil rights workers in Mississippi, the passage of the crucial Voting Rights Act of 1965, the emergence of the black power movement, and the eruption of race riots in the nation's cities.

We linger over what might seem, to some, ancient history (although within our lifetime, as authors) for two reasons. Much has changed, and we want to make that clear. Too often, the voices of racial pessimism depict a caste society in the 1990s not fundamentally different from that in which Richard Wright grew up in the Jim Crow South—or that which he found in the North when he migrated at the end of the 1920s. The racial problems of today are in fact not the same as those of yesterday, and we cannot address them with a clear head unless we understand the difference.

There is another point to the historical chapters, however. We have not only come a long way; we began our travels well before the civil rights movement of the 1950s and '60s. As important as that movement was, led by Dr. King, it would not have succeeded if white racial attitudes had not already begun to change. By the time of the Montgomery bus boycott, at the end of 1955, a great many whites had already come to acknowledge the truth of Myrdal's charge that Americans did not practice what they preached.

From the historical section we move on to a group of chapters that examine social, economic, and political trends since the civil rights revolution. How many African Americans work in professional jobs? How many black families have middle-class incomes? How many now live in suburbia? How many black students are graduating from high school and attending college? Are whites voting for black politicians? We do a lot of counting in this book; how to measure social change reliably is one of our main concerns. We supply the reader with more than seventy statistical tables, making it possible to judge whether or not our conclusions are grounded in the evidence.

The third section is devoted to public policy and the changing racial climate. It's indisputably different to be black than white in America; race does matter. But how should Congress, federal agencies, courts, school boards, and others engaged in shaping our public life respond to the continuing importance of race? We trace the evolution of that response over the last thirty-five years and weigh the costs and benefits of race-conscious legislative districting, busing to integrate public schools, set-asides that reserve public dollars for minority-owned firms, affirmative action in university admissions, and related policies.

We end Part III with a chapter that explores the current racial climate: the racial divide that the O. J. Simpson trial made so evident; the seeming alienation of the black middle class; the conspiracy theories that have a surprising life across the lines of social class in the black community; the beliefs and social interaction of ordinary blacks and whites (as revealed in survey data); and the politics of racial grievance. And finally, in a conclusion that wraps up the book, we consider the status of blacks today, compare the black experience with that of other racial and ethnic groups, consider the general question of group differences, and outline our hopes for the future. As two authors for whom the 1960s were formative years, we remain committed to race-neutral policies. Not simply because they are morally right; in a society already deeply divided along lines of race, we see divisive race-conscious programs as dangerous.

This is a long book that provides a great deal of information about a wide range of matters related to the problem of race. But we cannot pretend to have examined every important facet of this enormous topic. Both of the authors are social scientists with a strong interest in public policy, and we have naturally devoted much of our attention to the issues that social scientists and policymakers have argued about most. We have neglected other dimensions of race and race relations not because we think them unimportant but because we know too little about them to feel that we have something significant to add. For example, it would undoubtedly be illuminating to trace the changing role of African Americans in American popular culture over the span of years considered here, from the days when two white radio performers played Amos and Andy, stereotypical black characters, to the era of Oprah, Michael Jackson, and Magic Johnson. Today disproportionate numbers of blacks rank among the highest-paid entertainers and athletes. Although we do not analyze this remarkable shift here, we believe that central arguments of the book will help to explain it.

The picture we draw is both heartening and sobering. Heartening because real progress has been made—more progress than those who put their lives on the line in the 1960s probably imagined. Sobering because some of that progress has had negative unintended consequences; because civil rights strategies have not ameliorated the problems that grip the rural poor and the urban underclass; because some of those problems have actually worsened over time; and because old worries have now been joined by new and unexpected ones.

The signs of progress are all around us, although we now take that progress for granted. "Thirty-three years ago, I could not have come in here to have a cup of coffee and talk with my friends," Franklin McCain, Jr., the son of a participant in the first Woolworth's sit-in in Greensboro, North Carolina, noted in 1993 on the occasion of the closing of that store. "Today, I know my money is as good as any other man's. This means a lot."[6] Andrew Young, among others, has also marveled at the pace of change. Delivering a sermon in 1983, he recalled his fear when driving through Georgia in the early 1960s. "It was the worst place in the world," he said. "If someone had told me that I would be a congressman in Georgia, an ambassador to the United Nations, and a mayor of Atlanta, what I would have replied cannot be said in a church."[7]

In 1940 there was not a single African-American policeman in the five Deep South states, although those states contained almost 5 million black people, close to 40 percent of the nation's total black population. In that year the poverty rate for black families was a staggering 87 percent. Traveling in the South at about that time, Gunnar Myrdal was appalled to learn that any white could "strike or beat a Negro, steal or destroy his property, cheat him in a transaction and even take his life, without much fear of legal reprisal."[8] Black people, he discovered, were "excluded not only from the white man's society but also from the ordinary symbols of respect."[9] It would have been a major violation of the social order to address a black woman as "Mrs. Washington"—"Mrs." being a term reserved for whites. Few African Americans could vote, and blacks and whites were kept apart in all public places.

In the North, restaurants, hotels and other public accommodations were not segregated by law. Blacks could cast a ballot and run for office, use the local hospital and the public library, sit at the front of a bus, share a lunch counter—and even shake hands—with whites. Perhaps most important, they had rights that whites had to respect. But a color line kept them out of the best-paid and most desirable jobs, the better restaurants, most "white" neighborhoods, and therefore "white" schools. In fact, some states allowed local communities to operate dual educational systems; *Brown v. Board of Education,* it may be recalled, involved segregated schools in Topeka, Kansas.

The curtain came down on the Jim Crow South in the 1950s and 1960s. In the North, too, the status of blacks began to improve dramatically—the consequence of judicial decisions, the congressional action that followed civil rights protests, and a revolution in racial attitudes that began in the 1940s. In 1942, half of all northern whites believed that blacks were not as intelligent as whites, that they could not "learn things just as well if they [were] given the same education and training." Four years later the skeptics were down to less than 40 percent, and by 1956 their numbers had dropped to 17 percent. Asked whether they would object to a black "with the same income and education" moving into their block, in 1942 almost two-thirds of the nation's whites said yes. By 1956 the figure was down to 49 percent, and to 42 percent among northern whites.

Those were questions asked before sickening scenes of German shepherds and water from high-pressure hoses, used to quell peaceful demonstrations, had flashed across American television screens in the early 1960s. The civil rights revolution changed hearts and minds, as well as the law. By 1972 there was almost no dissent—even in the South—from the notion that whites and blacks should have an equal opportunity to get "any kind of job"; moreover, 84 percent of whites agreed that black and white students should attend the same schools.

Today almost three-quarters of black families are above the poverty line. In 1940, 87 percent of black families were in poverty; the figure was down to 47 percent in 1960 and 26 percent in 1995. The black college population has grown from 45,000 in 1940 to over 1.4 million today, a thirtyfold increase. Sixty percent of employed black women were domestic servants in 1940; today very few are. A majority, in fact, hold white-collar jobs. The number of black men in professional occupations has also risen impressively. Power and influence, in fact, were exclusively white prerogatives in 1940; there was no Vernon Jordan and no Michael Jordan.

That's the good news—too little acknowledged or even understood. But there is much that is bad as well—as anyone who has paid cursory attention to the news reports knows. The proportion of blacks in poverty is still triple that of whites. The unemployment rate for black males is double the white rate, the rate of death from homicide six times higher. Two-thirds of all black infants are now born to unmarried women, and only 35 percent of black children live with two parents—dramatic changes that are of recent origin.

There are some discouraging—as well as many encouraging—signs on the educational front. Today's typical black twelfth-grader scores no better on a reading test than the average white in the eighth grade, and is 5.4 years behind the typical white in science. Blacks from families earning over $70,000 a year have lower average SAT scores than whites from families taking in less than $10,000; blacks with a parent who graduated from college on average score below whites whose parents never finished high school. In a 1992 test of adult literacy and numeracy, the typical black college graduate performed only a shade better than the typical white high school graduate with no college, and far below white college dropouts.[10]

Some of the bad news is familiar (the black poverty rate, for instance), its high visibility in part a consequence of the great expectations—inevitably frustrated—that the civil rights revolution properly raised. And then, too, there is grave and legitimate concern in the mainstream media about the appalling condition of much life in the black urban ghettos. We have quarrels with the pictures drawn by the media but not with the concern expressed.

That quarrel centers on the lack of analytic rigor that so often characterizes media discussions of white racism. Take, for example, a July 1994 report in the *New York Times* on the "lagging" recruitment of black police officers in that city.[11] Despite two black police commissioners, the last holding office from 1990 to 1992, the number of black men in the NYPD remained low, the article pointed out; in 1994 the city was 29 percent black, while its police force was only 11.6 percent African American.

In 1993 the police department had tried hard to recruit minority officers, and the number of test-takers had risen. But while the written tests had been purged of most supposedly discriminatory features, the *Times* reported, those who passed the entry exams were also screened for psychological, medical, and character problems. That more-subjective testing still favored white males, black officers charged. Although no direct quotation was provided, the president of an organization of black police and corrections personnel complained that white psychiatrists, physicians, and interviewers assessed minority candidates by "white, middle-class values." Subtle and not so subtle discrimination kept the NYPD disproportionately white, said such "experts" and "advocates."

Other cities had done better—for instance, Los Angeles. In 1994 the LAPD, like the city itself, was 14 percent black. Did that mean that its recruitment processes were more racially fair? The *Times* did not suggest that possibility, perhaps because the LAPD suffered a national reputation for racism even before anyone had heard of Mark Fuhrman. The applicant pools may have been different. The job market differs from city to city; in New York perhaps better-paying work was more available. The *Times* ignored these and other possibilities. Over the previous two decades, it reported, the proportion of black men in the police force had actually declined (from 7.7 percent to 7.5 percent). Had either the city or those who ran the NYPD become more racist since the early 1970s? It is difficult to believe.

Racism is serious, but such uncritical stories—with their unsubstantiated charges and casual assaults on standards disparagingly labeled white and middle-class—invite indifference. Worse still, such assaults encourage dangerous conclusions about the significance of skin color and reinforce the perception that blacks in general have "underclass" values, such that the "character testing" used to screen whites was inappropriate for them. In a very long article the *Times* quoted no one who questioned the notion that blacks should not be judged by the same criteria as whites. Racist assumptions crop up in unexpected quarters.

What counts as racism? And what to do when we find it? Two questions, and no consensus on the answers. On the policy issue, in fact, there is increasing disagreement within the civil rights community itself. As the problems have grown more complex, the solutions have become more controversial. More than forty years down the civil rights road, the terrain has turned hazardous.

Take the issue of persistent segregation in higher education. In 1992 the U.S. Supreme Court found that the State of Mississippi was still separating white and black college students.[12] There were no WHITES ONLY signs, of course. But the majority of whites and blacks attended different schools, in part because African Americans who applied to the University of Mississippi and other historically white institutions faced a hurdle that whites more easily surmounted. Those schools relied heavily (by no means exclusively) on American College Test scores in selecting students for admission, and although they set the bar low, fewer blacks than whites met the standard.

The use of the ACT "fostered" segregation, Justice Byron White argued in *U.S. v. Fordice,* speaking for a majority of eight on the Court. Although neutral on their face, the admissions criteria and other policies were declared to have their roots in the Jim Crow era and were thus constitutionally suspect. "That college attendance is by choice and not by assignment does not mean that a race-neutral admissions policy cures the constitutional violation of a dual system," he wrote.[13]

The past is always present, the Court had suggested. " 'Everything in Alabama' . . . is influenced by past segregation," Kenneth Tollett, a law professor at Howard University remarked in response to a related ruling.[14] But what, precisely, was that "influence"? In 1962, when James Meredith broke the color barrier at "Ole Miss," it was clear why the school was 100 percent white; that's the way the whites wanted it. But thirty years later the Court in *Fordice* was reduced to talking about admissions criteria, institutional "mission assignments," and programmatic duplications that conceivably influenced to an unknown extent the decisions students made about which school to attend.

Elusive definitions of racism that fail to pinpoint actual harms invite remedies that provide no genuine relief. In 1954 in *Brown v. Board of Education,* the Court had spoken of the irrevocable damage to the "hearts and minds" of the black children condemned by the state to segregated schools, but were the college students who had elected to attend Mississippi Valley State University more than three decades later similarly affected? And if not, what exactly—if anything—was wrong with majority-black MVSU?

Nothing, was the conviction of those who had brought the Fordice suit; they had wanted more money for historically black schools. But increased funding was unacceptable to the Court, which saw in that remedy the ghost of "separate but equal"—a return to the infamous 1896 *Plessy v. Ferguson,* a walk backward into a dark past. Only this time the misleadingly labeled "exclusively black enclaves" (they weren't all-black) would be created "by private choice": an important difference that made no difference to the High Court.[15] Thus, the district court, in whose hands the question of a remedy rested, proposed instead closing all but one of the traditionally black colleges, forcing African-American students to attend largely white schools. Those forced choices, Justice White had already intimated, would be "truly free." [16]

That wasn't how the black leadership saw it, however. In the summer of 1994, the NAACP (at first thrilled by the Supreme Court's ruling) organized a civil rights march to preserve Mississippi Valley State University, an historically black institution founded in the Jim Crow era. An allegedly "segregated" institution had become a black cause. The march was the culmination of two years of outrage. "The mood runs from anger to disgust to disbelief," MVSU president William Sutton had said in the fall of 1992. No one wants a repeat of *Brown v. Board of Education,* which led to the closing of black schools, an assistant counsel for the NAACP Legal Defense Fund had added.[17] "It's important . . . for blacks to hang onto something and call it their own," an MSVU student remarked when in 1995 the district court judge finally said okay, the "black enclaves" that had so offended the Supreme Court's integrationist sensibilities would remain.[18]

Ironies abound. *Brown v. Board of Education* was by far the most important case the NAACP ever won; thirty-eight years later that same organization spoke of that landmark decision with regret. The Supreme Court had attempted to draw a straight analytical line from *Brown* to *Fordice,* but in fact much had changed between 1954 and 1992. Laws such as that which barred Linda Brown from school had vanished; desegregation had come to mean the busing of students to achieve racial balance; the status of blacks had improved dramatically; white racial attitudes had been transformed; and black views on many issues had shifted. Changing black sensibilities in a different America, courts and other public institutions caught in shifting civil rights winds, troubling definitions of racism, a racial climate created in part by the unintended consequences of well-meaning remedies—these themes, so apparent in the Mississippi higher education case, run as a leitmotif through our book.

Much has changed, but the racial divide has not disappeared. The trial of black celebrity O. J. Simpson, accused of murdering his white ex-wife and Ronald Goldman, was a particularly vivid reminder of that sobering fact. Blacks and whites were equally absorbed by the trial, but from the outset their views were radically different. Most whites concluded Simpson was guilty; most blacks believed his professed innocence. And in the days that followed the October 3, 1995, not-guilty verdict, unforgettable images flitted across the nation's television screens: of cheers, hugs, and high fives among black crowds; of downcast whites and racist graffiti in Brentwood, the traditionally white, liberal, upscale neighborhood in which O.J. and Nicole Brown Simpson both lived. "Whites v. Blacks" was the title *Newsweek* gave its post-verdict story.[19] "Will the Verdict Split America?" *Time* magazine asked.[20] Are we two nations or one? The question assumed still greater urgency when Louis Farrakhan led a Million Man March in Washington, D.C., just thirteen days after the O.J. verdict.

Questions that had moved to the periphery of the civil rights debate have now returned to center stage. How culturally important is skin color? Are blacks a group like no other and likely to remain quite separate? If so, does the drive for integration remain important? "When I got my law degree, I didn't check my blackness at the door," Leonardo Knight, a lawyer living on Capitol Hill, remarked in 1994.[21] "There is very little difference between black Americans and white Americans when you go to the bottom of it. But what little there is, is very important," the literary critic Gerald Early had written a year earlier.[22] Black and white, much more equal, but still separate. It wasn't the vision we once had.

"We cannot walk alone," Dr. King said in his 1963 "I Have a Dream" speech. The destiny of whites and blacks is inextricably entwined. But how to walk together? That question has lost none of its urgency in the fifty years since Gunnar Myrdal wrote *The American Dilemma*. Myrdal's work was full of hope; he believed fervently in the potential for racial decency in most Americans. Our book, too, rests on that optimistic premise.

PART ONE

History

CHAPTER ONE

Jim Crow

In 1962, COLIN and Alma Powell, recently married, packed all their belongings into his Volkswagen and left Fort Devens in Massachusetts for a military training course in Fort Bragg, North Carolina. "Driving through Dixie with a new wife was . . . unnerving," General Powell wrote in his 1995 autobiography. "I remember passing Woodbridge, Virginia," he went on, "and not finding even a gas station bathroom that we were allowed to use. I had to pull off the road so that we could relieve ourselves in the woods."[1]

In 1962—not so long ago—no bathroom that a man, serving his country and about to leave for Vietnam, could use. Filling stations that sold black customers gas would not let them use the restroom. A minor indignity? No. And only one of many that southern blacks faced every day less than four decades ago.

That world is gone—gone and often seemingly forgotten. Scholars casually refer to the "new slavery" in describing the condition of black America today. Or they talk of "segregation" and "hypersegregation," as if the residential clustering of the mid-1990s were equivalent to the "Jim Crow" laws and customs that once rigidly mandated black and white separation in the South.[2] Have we really just been spinning our wheels, going nowhere since the civil rights revolution of the mid-1960s? It's a fundamental question. We cannot understand the present without an accurate picture of the past. We need to know how far we've traveled and by what road.

Discussions of the status of blacks today are often laced with historical references. In the 1990s the end of Reconstruction is repeating itself, it is often charged; once again, white America is abandoning blacks.[3] Do the two periods in fact resemble one another? Racism is said to be "worse now than it's ever been."[4] Worse than in 1910? In December 1995 black employees at the Library of Congress forced the closing of an exhibit about slave life on southern plantations. "I was so upset I couldn't look at the rest of the exhibit," reported an employee who had glanced at an 1895 photograph depicting an armed white man on a horse looking down on black cotton pickers. "It reminded me of the white overseers here at the Library . . . looking down over us to make sure we're in the fields doing our work."[5]

Past and present, one and the same? An odd denial of historical change, it seems to us. Especially odd when, at the same time, the past is said to be too painful to contemplate.[6] Thus, in October 1994, protesters from civil rights organizations and a local college objected to the reenactment of a slave auction in historic Williamsburg, Virginia. "The story of slavery needs to be remembered, not necessarily retold," a local newspaper publisher argued.[7] Slave auctions represent such a wrenching chapter in black history that people "don't want to see it rehashed again," Salim Khalfani of the NAACP said, summing up the message of callers to the organization's Richmond office. A black man laying bricks in Colonial Williamsburg was disturbed to learn of the reenactment. "Blacks around here don't want to be reminded," he said. "It bothers people. People think it's very insensitive to dig it all up again."[8] Six of the demonstrators who objected to the auction pushed through the audience and began singing "We Shall Overcome," the song from the 1960s that symbolized the fight against the Jim Crow South.[9]

In such emotionally stormy seas, navigation isn't easy. And yet, as James Baldwin wisely observed in 1955, "the Negro problem in America" cannot "even be discussed coherently without bearing in mind its context; its context being the history, traditions, customs, the moral assumptions and preoccupations . . ."[10] In the next few chapters we explore the historical context that Baldwin insisted we know. Our starting point is the South, the home of the overwhelming majority of the nation's blacks until after World War II. Our objective is to draw a picture of the separate and unequal life that African Americans were forced to live in the white man's South.

THE BACKDROP

African Americans today are city people. When Gunnar Myrdal wrote his monumental report on the state of black America half a century ago, they were predominantly rural, not city folk, and certainly not big-city folk. In 1940 fewer than half (49 percent) lived in communities with as many as 2,500 inhabitants.[11] African Americans were a mere 6 percent of the population in New York City; in Chicago they totaled 8 percent, in Detroit 9 percent, as compared with 29 percent, 39 percent, and 76 percent respectively today.[12]

Blacks lived on the land and in the South. Until World War II three-quarters of the black population resided south of the Mason-Dixon line (along the Pennsylvania-Maryland border), where they were a quarter of the total population. In the Deep South the black concentration was even greater: more than a third of the residents were the descendants of slaves. In Mississippi about half the population was black, and the figure for South Carolina was almost as high (see map). No state outside the South had concentrations of African Americans remotely approaching those levels. In 1940 blacks were less than 5 percent of the population in New York, Pennsylvania, Michigan, Ohio, and Illinois.[13]

Historical circumstances as old as the nation itself made the South home to the vast majority of the nation's African Americans. Blacks were originally brought to America in chains to work as slaves cultivating cotton, tobacco, rice, and other crops that were the foundation of the southern agricultural economy. Although the institution of slavery existed in all of the British colonies in North America, it was marginal to the economies of those north of Delaware and Maryland, and was abolished there in the aftermath of the American Revolution. But that revolution—despite its stirring egalitarian rhetoric—abolished slavery only where it was not economically vital. In the South itself its eradication required a bloody civil war. Halfway through the war Lincoln issued an Emancipation Proclamation that freed the slaves in those parts of the Confederacy still in rebellion, and in 1865, with the passage of the Thirteenth Amendment to the Constitution, the "peculiar institution" finally died.

The Thirteenth, Fourteenth, and Fifteenth Amendments abolished slavery and gave full citizenship to African Americans. Only temporarily, however. Basic civil rights were enforced in that brief period known as Reconstruction, but the effort to remake the South failed. Southern whites had always thought of blacks as an inferior breed of person, less than fully human. Yankees could insist that all men were created equal and endowed by their Creator with inalienable rights, but the white South thought otherwise. Conquest had not changed hearts and minds; indeed it had created fierce resentments—against both those who came to conquer and those whom they liberated.

In addition, the slave system under which African Americans had been forced to live had not been designed to produce the independent, self-reliant citizens celebrated in nineteenth-century American democratic political thought. Quite the contrary: it aimed to control every aspect of the lives of its black victims in order to extract maximum profits from their toil. The African Americans suddenly released from bondage by the defeat of the Confederacy were thus impoverished, illiterate, and despised by most of the whites with whom they came into contact.[14]

Moreover, the high-blown democratic, egalitarian rhetoric of the Yankees sounded hypocritical, and that perception further fanned the flames of white southern resentment. Had the northern architects of Reconstruction truly wanted the best for blacks, they would have rolled out the welcome mat, inviting them to join the thousands of immigrants from foreign lands who were coming to their job-rich, rapidly industrializing region. But northerners were generally hostile to the tiny numbers of free blacks who already lived in

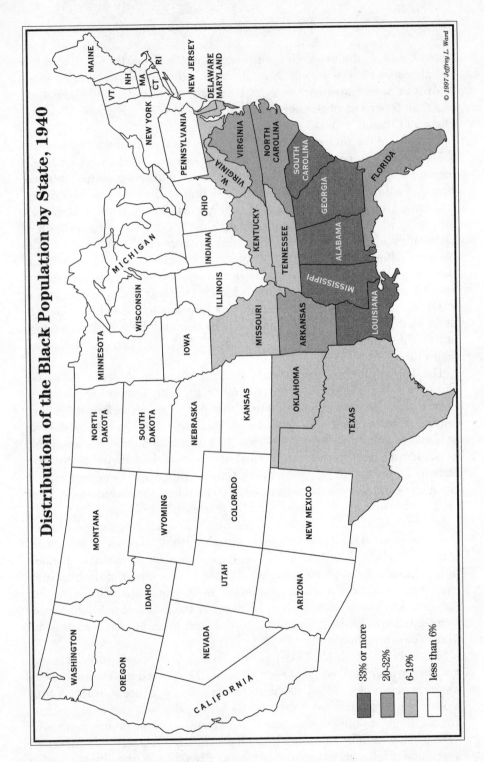

Distribution of the Black Population by State, 1940

33% or more
20-32%
6-19%
less than 6%

© 1997 Jeffrey L. Ward

their midst, and they were certainly averse to an influx of many more. Not even Charles Sumner of Massachusetts, one of the most progressive members of the Senate, could swallow a proposed plan to stimulate black migration northward; "utterly untenable," he called it.[15]

Sumner and his allies did push to win new political rights for blacks in the southern states in the hope of putting that region in the Republican column in national elections. That strategy, however, had an important flaw: African Americans were only 42 percent of the population in the eleven states that had joined the Confederacy.[16] Republicans thus still came up short, especially because the new black vote predictably drove southern whites into the Democratic camp. As a result, once federal troops were withdrawn from the South, blacks were left at the mercy of the party that opposed the basic civil rights that the war had, in theory, ensured.

The black population was numerically strong, but it could not organize and fight to sustain those rights. It was too poor and thus too economically vulnerable. The planters had lost their slaves but not their lands, and without their own land, the freedmen had no alternative but to work for their former masters as tenants or sharecroppers. In a position of economic dependency, they were politically impotent as well. If they dared to try to vote, they could be starved into submission.

In case that point was lost on some African Americans, dozens of organizations also sprang up with the aim of driving blacks (and white Republicans) from politics by any means necessary. These groups had begun to form immediately after the end of the war; for instance, the Ku Klux Klan was started by Confederate veterans in Tennessee in 1866. Even before the end of Reconstruction their impact was apparent. After a wave of black murders by vigilante groups on the eve of the 1876 elections in Mississippi, the Republican vote in six heavily black counties plunged from over 14,000 to a mere 723.[17] Federal troops were still stationed in the South, but their numbers were too small to suppress such a powerful grassroots movement; in Mississippi in 1875 only 596 soldiers were available to protect black voting and other civil rights.[18]

Northern zeal for Reconstruction waned. Quelling southern white resistance began to seem impossible without a more or less permanent occupation and thus a totally unprecedented suspension of democratic self-government. Furthermore, Republicans soon discovered their party could be competitive in national politics without the southern black vote. By the time the last federal troops were withdrawn from the South in 1877 and Democratic opponents of the Reconstruction governments had seized control in every southern state, "the solid South" was reliably Democratic. Eleven and only eleven of the states in the union failed to go Republican more than twice in the presidential elections from 1876 to 1944, and they were the states that had seceded to form the Confederacy.[19] Republican strength in other regions sufficed to offset that electoral advantage, however, allowing that party to capture the

White House in three out of every four presidential elections between the Civil War and the Great Depression of the 1930s.

DISFRANCHISEMENT

Reconstruction ended in 1877, but southern whites, with their eye on northern opinion and the possibility of renewed intervention, still felt some need to be cautious in their treatment of blacks. By the 1890s, though, that danger seemed remote, and two powerful movements swept the South: a campaign to drive black people from the polling booth and public life altogether, and a parallel drive to separate the races and force African Americans to use racially segregated "Jim Crow" institutions and facilities.

"The right of citizens of the United States to vote shall not be denied or abridged . . . on account of race, color, or previous condition of servitude" the Fifteenth Amendment stated. To write a law that explicitly stripped blacks of their right to vote would violate a clear constitutional right—one of the basic rights guaranteed in the aftermath of the Civil War. The Supreme Court might well avert its gaze from disfranchisement that took a more subtle form, however, and thus in the 1890s the South began to enact a variety of measures that indirectly kept blacks from the polls. The two most important were the poll tax and the literacy test; neither were novel southern inventions, but both had a devastating effect. The demand that voters pay a poll tax affected more blacks than whites; black farming families, on average, earned an annual income of under $100 in the 1880s and 1890s, making the tax of even a dollar too high to pay. And literacy tests for voting were difficult hurdles for citizens who had no schooling before 1865, and only the most inferior education thereafter.

In fact, not even educated blacks could pass a literacy and "understanding" test administered by racist registrars. The view of southern Democrats was summed up fifty years later when a Mississippi white told the eminent scholar of southern politics V. O. Key, "right or wrong, we don't aim to let them vote. We just don't aim to let 'em vote."[20] Fraudulent tests that illiterate whites passed but fully literate blacks failed decimated the African-American vote. Thus, Louisiana's 1896 registration law cut the proportion of black adult males on the electoral rolls from 93 percent to 9 percent, and a new state constitution two years later whittled the proportion down further, to just 3 percent.[21] By 1904 the number of black voters in the state had plunged from 130,000 to just 1,342. By 1906, Alabama managed to purge all but 2 percent of its adult black males from the voting rolls.[22]

Several southern states added a "grandfather clause" to their state constitutions. Uneducated southern whites would not support the imposition of literacy tests if they, too, might fail. They would be reassured, however, if all voters whose grandfathers had been eligible to vote before Reconstruction were exempt from the new requirements. That exemption, of course, would affect only whites, since blacks had been disfranchised. Not until 1915 did the Supreme Court strike that blatant evasion of the Fifteenth Amendment down, and its decision affected neither literacy tests nor the poll tax. A 1909 article in the *Harvard Law Review* asked: "Is the Fifteenth Amendment Void?" The answer was clearly yes.[23] The most basic of constitutional guarantees had been abandoned, but not even the North objected. "The experience of some thirty-five years," said the editor of *Harper's Weekly* in 1905, "has shown that the colored people, considered as a whole, . . . are not qualified to possess the franchise."[24]

The long-run effect of the destruction of slavery, ironically, was to give southern whites increased power in national politics, once blacks had been driven from the polls. Article I, Section 2 of the Constitution allowed states to count slaves as only three-fifths of a person, a rule designed to limit the political influence of the South. But with Emancipation, ex-slaves became whole persons, and the South—the politically white South—gained. In 1860 Mississippi's 437,000 slaves added only 262,000 to the state's total in determining the number of congressmen and presidential electors to which it was entitled ($437,000 \times \frac{3}{5} = 262,000$). After the passage of the Thirteenth Amendment (permanently barring the holding of slaves), the state's black citizens counted as a full 437,000. And yet by the end of the nineteenth century, African Americans in Mississippi and elsewhere in the South had no more political rights than a slave—which is to say, none at all.

THE ORIGINS OF SEGREGATION

As southern states moved to deprive blacks of any political voice, they also built a system of racial segregation in all public facilities. The private lives of black and white people were often intertwined; black women, for example, did the cooking and cared for the children in the typical white middle-class home. But the public realm was different. The races were strictly separated by law on streetcars, buses, and railroads; in schools; in waiting rooms, restaurants, hotels, boardinghouses, theaters, cemeteries, parks, courtrooms, public toilets, drinking fountains, and every other public space. The mania for separation went to such lengths that Oklahoma required separate telephone booths for the two races; Florida and North Carolina made it illegal to give white pupils textbooks that had previously been used by black students. Macon County, Georgia, took the prize for absurdity by seriously debating a proposal that the county maintain two separate sets of public roads, one for each race, and rejecting the idea only because of the prohibitive cost.[25] By the early twentieth century the two races were as rigidly separated by law in the South as they later would be under apartheid in South Africa. In fact, South

African whites closely followed what was happening in the American South, and used it as a model in devising their own segregation codes.[26]

The Jim Crow codes were new in the 1890s, but before that, it need hardly be said, the two races in the South were not happily integrated. The public schools that had first been created during Reconstruction were racially segregated from the outset.[27] There was little racial separation in public facilities other than schools before the 1890s, but that is mainly because there were few public facilities of any kind in the overwhelmingly rural South. Forcing blacks to sit in a separate section at the back of the streetcar was not an urgent issue in a region in which there were hardly any streetcars.

By the last decade of the nineteenth century, though, the urban population of the South had grown to over four million—a fourfold increase since the Civil War. There were thus more streetcars and other similarly anonymous settings for interracial contact, settings in which blacks might not behave as if they knew their "place" and where violence might break out as a result. And by then most African-Americans had never experienced the harsh discipline of slavery and were not inclined to defer automatically to whites, a necessary survival skill in the antebellum South. Southern lawmakers responded by drawing the line between the races very clearly, just as it had been drawn previously in public education.

It might seem that laws preventing black people from riding in the same railroad car as whites were patent violations of their constitutional rights. The Fourteenth Amendment, passed in 1868, had barred states from denying "to any person within its jurisdiction the equal protection of the law." But by the 1890s the Supreme Court had lost all enthusiasm for supervising the South's treatment of its black citizens, as its 1896 decision in *Plessy v. Ferguson* made crystal clear. A Louisiana statute mandating separate cars for blacks and whites on railroads operating within the state was constitutional, the Court held.

Although the specific phrase did not appear in the opinion, *Plessy* was the source of what became known as the "separate but equal" doctrine, and it gave a green light to a flood of state and local segregation measures that were enacted soon after. With only one dissent the Court held that legally mandated separation of the races in public transportation did not violate the Constitution *if* the segregated accommodations were "equal." The plaintiffs who challenged Louisiana's statute had argued a point that was clear to anyone with eyes to see —that such legislation placed "a badge of inferiority" on black people in plain violation of the commitment to equality contained in the Fourteenth Amendment, and indeed that it could also be seen as "a badge of servitude" that violated the Thirteenth Amendment. With breathtaking obtuseness, the majority responded that "if this be so, it is not by reason of anything found in the act, but solely because the colored race chooses to put that construction on it." "If one race be inferior to the other socially, the Constitution of the United States cannot put them upon the same plane," said the Court.[28]

Justice John Marshall Harlan wrote the sole dissent in *Plessy,* insisting quite correctly that the decision would one day be regarded as no less "pernicious" than *Dred Scott,* the 1857 ruling in which the Court had declared African Americans noncitizens. "Our Constitution is color-blind, and neither knows nor tolerates classes among citizens," Harlan argued. Laws that were obviously "conceived in hostility to, and enacted for the purpose of humiliating, citizens of the United States of a particular race" were "inconsistent not only with that equality of rights which pertains to citizenship but with the personal liberty enjoyed by every one within the United States."[29]

Justice Harlan's was a lonely voice in 1896, and decades would pass before the Supreme Court or any other branch of the federal government would begin to act to secure the promises contained in the Fourteenth and Fifteenth Amendments.[30] By the end of the nineteenth century the position of black people in the United States had been fixed for half a century to come. Although the long span of years between the *Plessy* decision and World War II saw sweeping changes in virtually every aspect of American life, the basic situation of African Americans altered remarkably little. In the South, where the vast majority continued to live throughout the period, they were both disfranchised and forcibly segregated from whites.

THE JIM CROW ECONOMY

The prosperous "Sunbelt" states of today were not always so well off. From the Civil War until World War II, the South was economically the most backward part of the United States; it had remained an agrarian backwater in an increasingly urban and industrial age. Even its agriculture was behind the times. In 1940 more than half of the nation's farmers lived in Dixie, but the farms of the region turned out little more than a quarter of the nation's agricultural output.[31] On the average, they were only about half as productive as those in Iowa and Nebraska.

The South was poor. And the black people who lived there were, for the most part, the poorest of the poor. After carefully examining the evidence, Gunnar Myrdal concluded flatly that "the economic situation" of African Americans in the southern states half a century ago was "pathological."

Except for a small minority enjoying upper or middle class status, the masses of American Negroes, in the rural South and in the segregated slum quarters in Southern cities, are destitute. They own little property; even their household goods are mostly inadequate and dilapidated. Their incomes are not only low but irregular. They thus live from day to day and have scant security for the future. Their entire culture and their individual interests and strivings are narrow.[32]

In 1940, according to one estimate, no fewer than 71 percent of all African Americans in the United States had incomes below the poverty line. Another calculation, based on a less stringent definition of what qualifies as being poor, puts the black poverty rate in 1940 at a staggering 87 percent.[33] Both of these studies estimated the white poverty rate at about half the black level. It is indisputable that all but a "small minority" of African Americans, as Myrdal said, had incomes at the bare subsistence level.

These figures are for the nation as a whole. They would look even worse, much worse, if available for the South alone. Poverty levels were generally much higher in the southern states, and the black-white income gap was considerably greater there as well. The median income of black husband-wife families in Atlanta in 1935–36 was 34 percent of that which white married couples earned; the figure was the same for Mobile, Alabama, and slightly lower (31 percent of the white average) in Columbia, South Carolina.[34] The vast majority of southern blacks were poor because they were confined to ill-paid, insecure, menial jobs—jobs that few whites would take. As a subordinate caste in a society dedicated to white supremacy, blacks were treated as a lesser breed suitable only for certain kinds of work: toiling in the fields, doing the cooking and laundry, collecting the garbage, and the like.

Agriculture was still the main source of livelihood for almost half of southern blacks.[35] In Mississippi, the most agrarian as well as the most heavily black state, over two-thirds of African Americans were agricultural workers.[36] They toiled on farms, but few of them were "farmers" as the term was understood in other parts of the country. Only one of eight southern black farmworkers owned the land on which he worked, as compared with over 40 percent of the whites who worked in southern agriculture. Most blacks employed in agriculture were either "sharecroppers" or "laborers." Sharecroppers rented the land they cultivated, but lacked the cash to pay the rent in advance or to obtain food, clothing, or other necessities. In return for providing these, the landlord took a share of the crop when it was harvested. What was due the landlord at year's end was often more than the crop was worth, so that the cropper ended up another year older and deeper in debt.

Southern black sharecroppers and farm laborers probably worked harder for less money than any other occupational groups in America. In 1937 sharecropping families in the southern Cotton Belt had annual incomes of just $73 per person, a mere one-eighth of what the average family in the nation took in that year. Farm laborers were paid even less than that, hard though it is to imagine that anyone could live on so little.[37]

By the 1930s the southern economy was no longer entirely agricultural. Alabama, for example, had a great complex of steel mills in Birmingham. North Carolina had tobacco factories and lumber mills, and much of America's textile industry had moved from New England to the South because of lower labor costs there. Some optimists expected that the urbanization and industrialization of the South would undermine Jim Crow, but that did not happen. From the employer's point of view, segregation in the labor market was ineffi- cient and irrational. To refuse to hire perfectly competent blacks (or members of any other group) is to pay a wage premium to the white workers hired in their place.[38] Southern employers, though, did not act in accord with the logic of the market, picking those who could do the job best, regardless of race. Many doubtless accepted the notion of black inferiority so deeply ingrained in southern white culture, and would thus have been too blinded by prejudice to assign challenging tasks to a black employee. But they could not, in any case, break the color bar without risking a strike by their workers and ostra- cism by their neighbors.

By 1940, African Americans were thus more strongly segregated, and even further behind whites in the competition for well-paying work than they had been decades earlier.[39] One out of seven southern white males had a skilled job of some kind in 1940; the figure for blacks, on the other hand, was one in twenty-five. Another 18 percent of whites, but only 11 percent of blacks, held "semiskilled" positions.[40] It was a dismal economic situation that put heavy pressure upon black women to work for wages, too. Married white women— even working-class white married women—didn't generally work in 1940; just one out of seven were employed outside the home. But black women were different: more than a third had to work for wages.[41]

Black women might seem to have been, in this limited sense, uniquely liberated. But in fact they were driven by desperation. High rates of out-of- wedlock births, divorce, desertion, and widowhood meant that a substantial number of black women had no husband living with them—18 percent, compared to 10 percent for whites.[42] And even those who did have a husband were under unusual economic pressure because black men's earnings were so low and irregular.

The presence of a huge pool of black women desperate for work did much to make life easier for southern white women, and gave them a strong stake in the maintenance of the caste system. Elsewhere in the nation, middle-class Americans had long complained of "the servant problem," their inability to find reliable domestic help at wages they could afford to pay. The picture in the South was quite different. The financial need of black women was so great, and their employment opportunities so few, that most white families could afford a black servant. A 1935 survey revealed that in southern cities more than 60 percent of white families with incomes above the poverty line employed household help; in northern cities, the figure was less than a third of that.[43]

The black women who did such work toiled amazingly long hours for a pittance. In North Carolina black domestics put in six twelve-hour days to earn from $3.00 to $8.00 a week; in Georgia they got from $2.75 to $6.00, in Alabama $2.50 to $5.00 for toiling from dawn till dark, with only Sunday off.[44]

Inflation has eroded the purchasing power of the dollar approximately tenfold since the Great Depression, but even multiplied by ten these are pathetically low earnings.[45] That plenty of African-American women were nevertheless available for such jobs is compelling testimony to the absence of any alternative for them.

SCHOOLS IN THE CASTE SYSTEM

Slaves had been given no formal education at all. Indeed, it had been a crime to teach a slave to read; ignorance made for a more docile and tractable labor force. It took the better part of a century to wipe out the mass illiteracy that was one of slavery's most crippling legacies. In the opening year of this century almost half—45 percent—of the nation's black adults were unable to read and write, and in 1940 the proportion was still a sizable one out of nine.[46]

Although sheer illiteracy was becoming uncommon by 1940, the educational level of the black population was exceedingly low. It was not very high for southern whites either; the South lagged well behind the rest of the nation in education, as it did in virtually every other aspect of economic and social development. Nevertheless, even by the standards of an educationally backward region, blacks were deprived. The average African-American adult in the South in 1940 had spent just five years in school, three and a half years less than the average white (Table 1). Blacks who had gone through high school were a much smaller elite group than black college graduates today. Only one in twenty had a high school diploma, as compared with one in four whites.[47]

The schools black children attended were not only inferior; they were segregated—by law. Because that had been true during Reconstruction as well, the 1896 decision in *Plessy*, which sanctioned segregation, had little impact on education. It simply ratified the status quo. And indeed, while the

Table 1
Years of School Completed by Race for Residents of the South Aged 25 or More, 1940

	BLACK	WHITE
Percent with less than 5 years	49	16
Percent with 4 years of high school or more	5	25
Median years of school completed	5.0	8.5

Source: U.S. Bureau of the Census, Current Population Reports, Special Studies, P-23-80, *The Social and Economic Status of the Black Population in the United States: An Historical View, 1790–1978* (Washington, D.C.: U.S. Government Printing Office, 1979), 93.

Supreme Court had specified that the separate facilities for the two races must be "equal," it was not a serious demand. But in the late 1930s the Supreme Court did begin to look critically at whether the educational opportunities provided blacks were indeed equal, and to put pressure upon southern states to devote far more funds to schools for African Americans. From then until 1954, when it abandoned the "separate but equal" formula in *Brown v. Board of Education,* substantial progress was made toward eliminating the gross funding inequities that had been so common.

The poverty of the South and the blindness of its planter-dominated leadership to the need for an educated labor force made the region the educational backwater of the country. School expenditures per pupil in Georgia in 1940, for example, were 42 percent of the national average; they were even lower in Alabama, Arkansas, and Mississippi.[48] Those were figures for both black and white students; blacks of course fared worse than whites. Thus, in 1940, Alabama spent 3.2 times as much per pupil on whites as on blacks; Georgia 3.3 times as much; South Carolina 3.8 times as much; Mississippi a staggering 7.2 times as much.[49] In the most heavily black counties of the Black Belt (so-called because of the exceptionally rich dark soil), per-pupil expenditures for black children were less than one one-thirteenth of what was spent on whites.[50] A pamphlet documenting such inequalities issued by the National Conference on Fundamental Problems in the Education of Negroes in 1934 observed wryly that "if we assume the democratic principle of equal educational opportunity for all children, it would appear that it takes seven times as much to teach a white child as a Negro. As Booker T. Washington used to say, it is too great a compliment to the Negro to suppose that he can learn seven times as easily as his white neighbor."[51]

Although educational spending is hardly a perfect measure of school quality, the Jim Crow schools of the South were clearly dreadful. Gunnar Myrdal paid a visit to one in the Georgia countryside in the late 1930s. Students ranging in age from six to seventeen were crowded into a single classroom, taught by a twenty-year-old with only a high school education. None of the pupils knew who the president of the United States was or even what the president did. One hesitantly suggested, in response to a question about Booker T. Washington, the most eminent black American in the nation at the turn of the century, that he was "a big white man." Not one had ever heard of the National Association for the Advancement of Colored People or of W. E. B. Du Bois, Washington's successor as the country's most prominent African-American leader. A question about what the Constitution of the United States was and its significance for them provoked a long silence, until someone volunteered that it was "a newspaper in Atlanta."

Myrdal considered this particular Georgia school even more dismal than most Jim Crow institutions, but he concluded that "a large portion of rural Negro schools are at, or near, this cultural level."[52] For the most part, the teachers, whose own schooling had of course been in inferior segregated institutions, were not equipped to provide a solid education. In the school Myrdal visited, the teacher at least had a high school diploma; that was not the case for a third of the teaching staff in southern black schools in the 1930s.[53] When the distinguished black educator Horace Mann Bond administered the Stanford Achievement Test not to students, but to 306 African-American teachers in Alabama's black public schools in 1931, he found that their scores averaged below the national norm for ninth-graders.[54]

That blacks without even a high school diploma or the equivalent skills were employed as teachers is not surprising; most southern states had little interest in educating the children of their black citizens beyond the primary grades. Whites believed, as one educator put it, that "the colored race is only capable of receiving and profiting by an elementary education, which costs comparatively much less than that suitable for the white race in its more advanced stages of civilization."[55] Thus it was that eighty-seven southern counties with 46,000 black students of high school age provided only primary education for African-American pupils in the 1938–1939 school year, and in another 115 counties with over 100,000 black children of that age, the segregated "high schools" they were eligible to attend stopped short of twelfth grade. These were not counties with such small black populations as to give white racists an excuse to ignore black educational needs. Forty-five, in fact, were majority-black.[56]

Opportunities for black children to receive an education would have been even more restricted if the matter had been left entirely to those white authorities. It is a bizarre and revealing fact that a great many of the schools attended by black pupils were not built as a result of public initiative; nor were they paid for by tax dollars, although black families of course paid taxes. Black children went to school because liberal northern philanthropists made it possible. Between 1914 and 1932 the Julius Rosenwald Fund subsidized the construction of some 5,000 schools for African Americans in the southern states.[57] The Fund typically picked up 15 percent of the bill. Local governments, charitable whites, and the impoverished black community itself had to raise the remainder.[58]

Other northern philanthropic organizations also poured money into the South to build black schools and to train teachers for them.[59] The extreme stinginess of the southern states in providing schools for black children was rooted in the deep ambivalence of the whites who held an absolute monopoly of political power. In his classic 1937 study, *Caste and Class in a Southern Town*, John Dollard described the picture in Indianola, Mississippi. On the one hand, southern whites shared the commitment to mass education that was integral to American culture.[60] Since Americans saw schools as the solution to almost every problem that ailed the society, Mississippi whites found it hard to suggest that black children should go educationally hungry. But they worried that educating African Americans did more harm than good. If blacks were literate, who would pick the cotton? "When they learn to spell dog and cat," warned a Virginia newspaper, "they throw away the hoe."[61]

Partly for this reason, it was late before either whites or blacks were compelled to attend school in the South.[62] The region's large black population cast doubt on the whole educational enterprise. When North Carolina's commissioner of labor polled white farmers in 1905 about a proposal for a compulsory school attendance law, nine out of ten respondents said that the requirement would be all right for white children but not for blacks, because "educated Negroes, in nearly all cases, become valueless as farm laborers."[63] Many whites thought that an educated Negro was a contradiction in terms. In 1909 one of the most vocal of the South's many demagogic white politicians, Mississippi governor James K. Vardaman, spelled out a view that was still common a generation later:

> Money spent today for the maintenance of public schools for negroes is robbery of the white man, and a waste upon the negro. You take it from the toiling white men and women, you rob the white child of the advantages it would afford him, and you spend it upon the negro in an effort to make of the negro what God Almighty never intended should be made, and which men cannot accomplish.[64]

If blacks were incapable of learning, it was odd to fret about their taste for picking cotton once they had more schooling. But the views of southern whites were not logical. Exposed to education, ineducable blacks (they worried) would fast pick up dangerous political ideas. The void in the students' knowledge of elemental facts about American government and history that Myrdal discovered was not coincidental. Those were supersensitive subjects in a segregated society. For southern blacks to know the rights of American citizens that were guaranteed by the Constitution would doubtless have had a subversive effect on the caste system. What would they have made of the Fifteenth Amendment, which explicitly guaranteed their right to vote? Incredible as it may seem, in 1940 the Mississippi State Senate debated a proposal to purge all references to voting, elections, and democracy in civics texts used in the black public schools. It was defeated by a slim margin.[65]

Who knew where political ideas might lead? "Education," a leading Alabama attorney said in 1946, "causes the Negro to seek political equality because political equality leads to social equality and social equality leads to intermarriage."[66] He reasoned that schooling would stimulate black desires for a political voice, and a political voice would lead to sexual mixing, contaminating the "purity" of "white blood." Given such fears, it is perhaps surprising that Jim Crow schools were not even worse than Myrdal found them.

BADGES OF INFERIORITY

There was nothing innately degrading about segregation, the Supreme Court had maintained in *Plessy*. If critics saw Jim Crow laws as "badges of inferiority," they were deluded. At the end of the Great Depression, after half a century's experience with separate "equality," the inequality should have seemed evident. African Americans were barred from virtually all of the better jobs available in the southern economy. Their children were confined to second-class schools. And the caste system provided constant reminders that they were considered a lesser breed, precisely as it was designed to do.

Consider, for example, the laws and customs that dictated how black passengers had to behave while riding a bus. In all the southern states African Americans were required to sit at the back of the bus and to stand while riding if there were no empty seats in the designated "colored" section; a vacant seat up front was out of bounds. That the section reserved for blacks was at the rear was hardly coincidental. The *back* is where the once-enslaved belonged. What is more, in many communities blacks had to board the bus at the front in order to give the fare to the driver, but then—amazingly—go back down the stairs, walk outside to the rear door, and climb back up again.[67] Was the arrangement bizarre and irrational? Not when one understands that such rules conveyed an important message: the inferiority of blacks, the superiority of whites. As Dollard observed after his prolonged stay in Indianola, Mississippi, northerners could derive social prestige from wealth or education. Southerners needed neither; just being white sufficed. Whites had "an automatic right to demand forms of behavior from Negroes which serve[d] to increase [their] own self-esteem."[68]

Jim Crow speech codes revealed the racial hierarchy clearly. In a small southern city, Gunnar Myrdal repeatedly asked the whites he met how to find Mr. Jim Smith, the African-American principal of the black high school, and was met with blank stares. When Smith was finally located, Myrdal was told that he should have just asked the whereabouts of "Jim."[69]

The most aggressive and demeaning term whites used in addressing black people was, of course, "nigger." As Dollard noted, this racial slur had "the effect of isolating the Negro from human society and establishing him as an inferior, animal-like being," and it clearly gave "a sadistic satisfaction to the user."[70] "Nigger" was only the tip of the iceberg of the intricate vocabulary of caste. Blacks who were known to the white speaker were at least called by their first name; those who were not were normally addressed as "boy," a term freely applied to adult black men until they were obviously of such an advanced age that "uncle" was used instead. Young African-American women were referred to as "girl," and older ones as "auntie."[71]

When the black person being addressed was someone of such standing in the community that using his or her first name was thought to be too offensive, a title like "professor," "doctor," or "reverend" was employed, even when the individual in question was nothing of the sort.[72] This small gesture of ostensible respect was thus undercut by an element of ironic mockery. White schoolteachers were never called "professor," while black teachers very often were. Clearly this did not mean that whites respected black teachers more than white ones. (In sly retaliation some blacks addressed whites with no claims to the title as "judge," or "colonel" in similar fashion, stroking their egos while laughing behind their backs.)[73]

What's in a name? A great deal. Charles S. Johnson, a distinguished black scholar who investigated African-American reactions to Jim Crow on the eve of World War II, found that resentment about the seemingly small matter of forms of address was expressed so often by the blacks he interviewed that "this offense to personal self-esteem might be considered more acute than the fact of segregation itself."[74] Such patterns of etiquette were an obvious holdover from the antebellum South; slaves, of course, never called their masters "George." And slaves had no last names by which they could be addressed. More than seven decades after slavery had been abolished from the land, blacks were still, as Myrdal noted, "excluded not only from the white man's society but also from the ordinary symbols of respect."[75] No Negro could aspire to them, and no white would be allowed to offer them. So great was white aversion to dignifying African Americans with "Mr." or "Mrs." that postal officials in some southern towns actually crossed those titles out on envelopes addressed to African-American residents until they were forced to stop the practice by orders from Washington.[76]

Breaking bread with whites was another "ordinary symbol of respect" denied to blacks. Restaurants and lunch counters were never open to both races. Moreover, interracial dining in private homes was equally out of the question. After his extensive travels in the South, Gunnar Myrdal concluded that "the taboo against eating together" was "the main symbol of social inequality between the two groups."[77] Myrdal himself broke this taboo a few times by dining with Ralph Bunche, a black scholar working on his staff who went on to a distinguished career as a diplomat and the first African-American winner of the Nobel Peace Prize. Perhaps because of Myrdal's obvious foreign accent, Bunche's light skin, or both, the two were served without incident, but Bunche was apparently rather irritated that Myrdal had so cavalierly run the risk of a humiliating public incident.[78]

Sharing a meal seemed to whites an irresistible invitation to other forms of social equality, a fatal first step down the road to perdition. One scholar has attributed the extreme phobia of southern whites over interracial dining to "the post-prandial non-sequitur," the delusion that "if a Negro eats with a white man he is assumed to have the right to marry his daughter."[79] And marriage was even worse than *rape*, since it meant that a white female had consented of her own free will to what white society considered the ultimate degradation. A psychoanalyst could doubtless go on at great length about what might explain this extraordinary phobia about sexual relations between members of the two races; the historian can only note the fact.

The phobia was really about sexual relations between black males and white females, of course. Under slavery many white masters took advantage of their female slaves, who were powerless to say no. After Emancipation, it was not uncommon for white men to have black mistresses, though the custom seems to have been dying out in the South as more puritanical attitudes towards marital fidelity took hold in the twentieth century. There was a strict double standard, though. White females did not have similar latitude to cross the color line in search of a sexual partner. Southern white women were on a pedestal. To "protect" them was the highest duty of the southern white man, and there was no danger greater than that posed by the supposedly lustful, insatiable black man. The southern white woman and "her blue-eyed, golden-haired little girl" were "the loveliest and purest of God's creatures, the nearest thing to an angelic being that treads this terrestrial ball. . . ."[80] Presumably it was panic at the "threat" to such "angelic beings" that led otherwise rational men to lapse into very strange logic when confronted at the prospect of the "mixing of . . . blood." One white minister asked: "Do black birds intermingle with the blue birds? Does the redwing fly with the crows? Would it make sense . . . to mix Black Angus cattle with . . . pure-bred Herefords?"[81] The real aim of all critics of racial segregation, said an Alabama state senator flatly, was "to open the bedroom doors of our white women to black men."[82]

Fears of sexual contact between whites and blacks were a major reason that racial integration in the schools was seen as monstrous, and likewise why racially integrated municipal swimming pools and dance halls were regarded as so abhorrent. All of these forms of social intimacy, at least in the minds of southern whites, held out the promise of intolerable sexual intimacy.

Two other rigid rules of social intercourse under the caste system deserve mention. Blacks who came to the residence of a white, whatever the reason, could not enter through the front door.[83] In one Mississippi town, a northern observer reported in amazement, some residents were in the habit of locking the back door against thieves but not the front door when they went out. Apparently they assumed both that all potential burglars were black, and that even blacks determined to commit a crime would not dare to come in the front door![84]

In addition, whites never shook hands with blacks. For a handshake, like walking through the front door, suggested equality. The taboos, on the other hand, were powerful reminders that the two racial groups were ranked, the basic organizing principle of the caste system. As Myrdal noted, the "thousand and one precepts, etiquettes, taboos, and disabilities" inflicted upon blacks in the Jim Crow South had "a common purpose: to express the subordinate status of the Negro people and the exalted position of the whites."[85]

Whites were able to do things that were simply off-limits to blacks. Thus, public libraries in the South were not really *public* libraries; the black public was not welcome, except in the branch libraries for "colored" residents that could only be found in a few large cities. As a teenager, Richard Wright, who would become the first black novelist to reach a wide national audience, hungered for books; he was able to take them out of the Memphis Public Library by claiming that he was fetching them for his white employer. "You're not using these books, are you?" the librarian suspiciously asked young Richard of the H. L. Mencken volumes he was clutching. "Oh, no, ma'am. I can't read," he answered.[86]

Public parks were likewise parks for white members of the public only; just a few cities had separate parks that blacks were allowed to use. Houston was unusually liberal in opening the park that contained its zoo to African Americans on certain special days each year.[87] Such recreational facilities as roller-skating rinks, bowling alleys, municipal swimming pools, and public tennis courts were for whites only. The first public swimming pool open to blacks in the entire state of Mississippi was built in the tiny all-black town of Mound Bayou during World War II.[88] Arthur Ashe, born in Richmond, Virginia in 1943, had to learn tennis on segregated courts in the public park and could not compete in the tournaments in which whites played. The state university was also out of bounds.[89]

The color line applied as strictly in sickness as it did in health. In the rural and small-town South, hospitals were for whites. Some institutions might examine black patients in the emergency room, but would provide them only with what was essentially first aid. A seriously ill black person had to travel to a city, where there would be a hospital that had a "colored" ward. Even in Baltimore, far from the Deep South, the University of Maryland hospital had "Colored" and "White" entrance signs chiseled into the stone doorways.[90] In Mississippi in 1938 there were 0.7 hospital beds per 1,000 African Americans in such segregated facilities, but more than three times as many for whites (2.4 per 1,000).[91]

The picture was more varied and confusing in stores, but that fact was a mixed blessing, since it meant that blacks could only determine whether they could make a purchase by subjecting themselves to the potential humiliation of finding out that they could not. In stores that did serve blacks as well as whites, clerks customarily waited on white customers first. Blacks were automatically at the back of the line, even if they arrived first, just as they were automatically at the back of the bus. In small towns and rural areas, though not in the larger cities, this was even true at the U.S. Post Office. Blacks could buy stamps or pick up mail only when there were no white customers. And when it came to buying personal items like clothing, hats, and gloves, they could never try them on, since their touch was regarded as contaminating.

The coming of the automobile to the South in the 1920s posed a challenge to the caste order. Blacks as chauffeurs was one thing, but the idea that black people might own automobiles and go where they chose was another. And yet whites could not stop African Americans from buying cars. Thus, there were efforts to impose a "racial right-of-way"—a rule of black deference to white drivers, especially white women drivers, without regard to which car arrived first at an intersection. It was an unworkable rule, soon abandoned, although in Mississippi as late as World War II, there were towns open only to white motor traffic.[92]

On the other hand, gas stations (although not their rest rooms) were open to blacks and whites alike even in the most rabidly segregationist areas of the Jim Crow South. Filling up the tank was such a transitory and impersonal experience that service station operators would not sacrifice profits in order to indulge their prejudices. But motels and hotels for the weary auto traveler were strictly segregated by race, of course, and in most of the South those open to blacks were few and far between.

These are the best generalizations that can be made about the etiquette of race relations in the Jim Crow South. But they are only generalizations. Exactly how black people were expected to conduct themselves vis-à-vis whites in fact varied considerably from place to place. Indeed, this variability was one of the worst aspects of the caste system. Behavior that was regarded as routine and perfectly acceptable in one town might be interpreted elsewhere as a violation of the caste order. Thus, it was very dangerous for African Americans to travel into unknown territory, since they would not know the precise rules of the local game. They would know only that all the caste rules, constraints, and taboos conveyed the same very clear and very ugly message. It was well summed up by a Mississippi undertaker who was interviewed by Charles S. Johnson on the eve of World War II:

> In this part of the country a Negro can only go so far. I know that, and that's the reason I am able to stay out of trouble. They know you are a Negro and I know I am a Negro, and I know that there is a certain way white people are going to treat a Negro. They want you to stay in your place, and if you get out of it too much they are going to put you back in it. I mean by this that the white man is the boss in the South and you got to talk to him like he is the boss. It don't make any difference how much money you have or how much education you have, he won't look at you as his equal, and there is no use in you acting like you're his equal if you want to stay here.[93]

LYNCH LAW AND WHITE SUPREMACY

The ultimate sanction upholding the caste system was a lynching—death at the hands of a mob. In the years between 1883 and 1927, more than 3,000 African Americans were lynched. Mississippi was the leader, but Georgia,

Arkansas, Alabama, South Carolina, and Texas were not far behind in the body count.[94]

The lynch mob sometimes sent its victims to a speedy death at the end of a rope or with a bullet to the brain. Often, though, lynchers displayed a savagery that most Americans today may find difficult to believe. They dragged blacks to death tied to the bumper of a car; they tortured the life out of them with a blowtorch or a hot iron; they burned them to cinders in bonfires a Mississippi paper called, with sickening humor, "Negro barbeques." One black couple accused of murdering a planter had their fingers and ears chopped off one by one, their eyes gouged out, and their bodies ripped open with corkscrews before they were tossed into a roaring fire.[95]

The number of lynchings in the South averaged over a hundred a year in the 1890s, and then began to fall off (Table 2). By the second decade of this century the figure had been cut in half, and it continued to decline sharply in the 1920s and 1930s. In the entire depression decade, 1931–1940, there were fewer lynchings than in a typical *year* in the 1890s. But it still did not take many outrages as monstrous as a lynching to terrorize the population that was its target. The lynch mob delivered a message that was unforgettable. In 1968 an investigator who was attempting to study a lynching that had occurred in the town of Rocky Ford, Georgia, more than *forty years* before found the task impossible because local blacks were still too traumatized to say a word about it. Not one was even willing to mention the victim's name.[96]

It is tempting to regard such monstrous crimes as aberrant—irrational outbursts by redneck hoodlums, without larger significance. In fact, lynchings were only the most extreme expressions of the determination of southern whites to uphold the foundation of the southern caste system—the principle of white supremacy and black subordination. They were not usually the furtive work of masked men wearing sheets, as is sometimes thought. Rather they were highly public events; the perpetrators were not only known to the community but sometimes even posed for "before" and "after" photographs in the local paper first with their victim and then with their victim's corpse!

Lynchings were a communal ritual designed to reaffirm white solidarity in

Table 2
Annual Lynchings of Blacks, Average by Decade

1891–1900	104
1901–1910	75
1911–1920	55
1921–1930	25
1931–1940	10

Source: U.S. Bureau of the Census, *Historical Statistics of the United States: Colonial Times to 1970,* 2 vols. (Washington, D.C.: U.S. Government Printing Office, 1975), 422.

support of the view that, as one newspaper put it, the South was "a white man's country to be ruled by white men as white men see fit." They were an unmistakably vivid warning to blacks that whites would feel no inhibitions about taking the most drastic repressive measures against any African Americans who sought "social and political equality."[97] A white resident of Oxford, Mississippi, put the point bluntly when he said in 1938 that it was "about time to have another lynching. When the niggers get so that they are not afraid of being lynched, it is time to put the fear in them."[98]

THE UNEQUAL PROTECTION OF THE LAWS

Traveling in the South in the late 1930s, Gunnar Myrdal was at first puzzled that the black men and women he met were so obviously afraid of him. "The Southern Negro," he observed, "seems to suspect a possible danger to himself . . . whenever a white stranger approaches him."[99] In fact, blacks displayed the same fear around whites whom they knew, he soon discovered.

That fear, Myrdal soon realized, was not paranoia. In the Jim Crow South, he was appalled to learn, blacks were frightened of whites for the very good reason that whites seemed to have a license to treat them without any regard for law or morality whenever they wished:[100]

> The Negro cannot claim the protection of the police or the courts, and personal vengeance on the part of the Negro usually results in organized retaliation in the form of bodily injury (including lynching), home burning or banishment. Practically the only check on white maltreatment of Negroes is a rather vague and unformulated feeling on the part of Southern public opinion that a white man should not be "mean" to a Negro except where he "deserves" it. But unless a white man acquires a reputation for being mean and unjust, his occasional violation of a Negro's legal rights is felt to be justified or—at most—"his own business."[101]

To be black in the South was to live without the most elemental personal security. Your freedom, your property, your very life might be snatched away if you made a misstep. This, of course, was an outrageous violation of the right to "the equal protection of the laws" guaranteed by the Fourteenth Amendment, but the Supreme Court was not prepared to take on the enormous task of ensuring that southern law enforcement authorities—no more racially enlightened than the white community they served—provide equal justice for blacks.

In one sense the southern justice system was "democratic"; judges, prosecuting attorneys, sheriffs, and police chiefs were either elected directly or picked by elected officials who had to answer to the voters. But the electorate that chose them was all white, since blacks had been completely excluded from political participation by the end of the nineteenth century. And thus in any conflict between enfranchised whites and disfranchised blacks, the rights of the latter inevitably counted for little. The blatant injustice of the "justice" blacks received made for strongly negative attitudes toward the law and law enforcement officials, an alienation that was one of the worst and most enduring legacies of Jim Crow. A middle-class black woman from Cleveland who came South for a long visit in the 1930s noted "the strangest feeling . . . the policeman on the corner was not there to protect me." [102]

The policeman was almost invariably white. The five Deep South states of Alabama, Georgia, Louisiana, Mississippi, and South Carolina had populations more than a third black in 1940, and were the home of almost 40 percent of the nation's black population; none had a single African-American police officer. Likewise, in Arkansas and Virginia, with populations more than a quarter black, only whites enforced the law. The entire state of North Carolina had just one black officer; Florida had five.[103] The city of Houston was positively enlightened: it had five black police officers. Their exclusive beat, though, was the ghetto, and they were not empowered to arrest whites! [104]

Whites on a police force had not been selected on the basis of standards that blacks, who had attended inferior Jim Crow schools, could not meet. Little in the way of education or special skill was required to qualify for a badge. The typical policeman was just a "poor white with a legal sanction to use a weapon," and with views even more racist than those of other southern whites, Myrdal thought.[105] Certainly the uninhibited sadism of police officers toward the blacks they arrested suggested that was the case. "The badge of police authority," observed a black scholar after careful investigation, "gives lower-class whites freedom to bolster their socially impoverished egos, which has contributed, perhaps more than any other factor, to the generalized hostility of southern Negroes. . . ." [106] Moreover, it was a freedom unconstrained by the array of legal rules that today protect the criminally accused.

Blacks were no better represented in other parts of the criminal justice system. There were no black judges in the South, of course, and virtually no attorneys. In 1940 there were but eight African-American lawyers in the entire state of Georgia, which had a million black residents. There were five for the 800,000 blacks in South Carolina, and just three for the million in Mississippi. As late as 1947, Louisiana—with about 800,000 African Americans—had but one black attorney.[107] The only law school in the South that admitted blacks was at Howard University, in Washington, D.C., and until the 1930s it was an unaccredited night school. Most of the tiny number of blacks in the nation with law degrees naturally avoided the South, where some judges would not admit them to the courtroom, where juries were almost invariably all white, and where they had great difficulty getting clients unless they had an arrangement with a white attorney who would front for them. Of course the criminally accused did need counsel, but black defendants had reason to fear that having a black attorney might be a liability in a judicial system already stacked against them. In any case, neither poor blacks nor poor whites could afford an attorney, and except in the case of capital crimes, criminal defendants did not have a constitutional right to legal representation until the 1960s.

Juries were all white because blacks were excluded from them. Laws explicitly limiting jury service to white males had been struck down by the Supreme Court as early as 1880, but the decision had very limited impact, in part because black defendants who wished to challenge the composition of a jury had to prove deliberate, intentional discrimination in a southern court. In addition, the law was often irrelevant; in rural areas and small towns blacks were simply left off the jury lists. Only in a few large cities—and even there, mainly in the federal courts—were African Americans occasionally allowed to sit in the jurors' box.

In 1935 an important Supreme Court decision allowed defendants in criminal cases to establish a prima facie case of discrimination by showing a marked disparity between the number of blacks serving as jurors and the black population. But, again, its impact and that of other decisions interpreting the holding was quite limited. Southern jurisdictions considered using black jurors only when the defendants were black and the charges were serious (the only circumstances in which a challenge to the jury composition was likely), and even capital cases often had all-white juries unless the prosecution thought that an appeal was likely.[108]

Although many blacks in the South complained of aggressive and brutal treatment by the police, others objected to the lax law enforcement and insufficient police protection.[109] These were not contradictory views. Southern police officers and southern courts were extremely harsh and punitive in their treatment of blacks convicted of crimes against whites or the white-dominated caste order. But they were extremely lenient with blacks whose victims were "only" other African Americans. Whites in Indianola, Mississippi, John Dollard reported, thought "Negroes . . . [were] a mysterious lot, impulsive and primitive; and they should not be held accountable by white standards."[110] Unless, of course, they harmed a white person. "We have very little crime," said a white resident of Natchez, Mississippi. "Of course, Negroes knife each other occasionally, but there is little *real* crime. I mean Negroes against whites, or whites against each other."[111] A Mississippi newspaper editor estimated that only a third of blacks who murdered other blacks were ever arrested. "It is like dog chewing on dog and the white people are not interested in the matter. Only another dead nigger—that's all."[112]

This laxity in dealing with black-on-black crime was especially pronounced when the accused happened to be the employee of some powerful local white willing to appear for him as a character witness. Judges sometimes asked

"Whose nigger is this?" when the defendant first appeared, and if a prominent resident claimed him, it affected the outcome. In the rural and small-town South, where most blacks still lived, a social pattern rooted in slavery survived as late as World War II—a paternalistic bond between powerful whites and their powerless black employees. Dollard thought that this patron-client relationship had a "feudal" character, and noted that it meant that some blacks had "extraordinary liberty to do violent things to other Negroes."[113] Myrdal likewise reported that many African Americans in the South were disturbed that "criminal and treacherous Negroes . . . secure immunity from punishment because they are fawning and submissive toward whites."[114]

Southern apologists sometimes claimed that the protection provided black defendants accused of black-on-black crime was proof of white goodwill. Blacks should be pleased, one argued, that "the weaknesses of a child-race are accorded only an amused indifference or a patient tolerance by their stronger neighbors."[115] This glaring double standard, Dollard saw, "made life dangerous in the Negro group." The "lack of adequate legal protection of the Negro's life and person," he suggested, was "itself an incitement to violence."[116] Treating blacks with special leniency when they committed crimes against fellow blacks was no less discriminatory than treating them with special harshness for crimes against whites.

The statistics on crime and punishment seem to confirm Dollard's observations, though we must remember that the evidence was all compiled by a highly racist, white-dominated criminal justice system.[117] Thus, a study of all murders committed in Richmond, Virginia, and six North Carolina and Georgia counties in the 1930s found that 83 percent of the 645 victims were black, though blacks were only 29 percent of the population of those communities.[118] The racial disproportion was almost three to one. There may well have been other murders of blacks by whites that did not get registered as such. (Only six whites were indicted for killing blacks.) Quite possibly, too, white indifference about yet "another dead nigger" resulted in some black killers of blacks not being apprehended and prosecuted. Both of these biases, though, would work in the same direction, suggesting that the disproportionate representation of blacks as murder victims was even greater than the reported three to one.

Blacks were both victims and perpetrators—as they are in inner cities today. All but 6 of the 532 accused murderers of blacks in the study of Richmond and six counties were themselves black, and 408 of the 411 persons actually convicted of these crimes were black. But there was a clear racial double standard in the treatment of those convicted of homicide. Black defendants were not routinely given far tougher sentences than whites, as is sometimes assumed. The picture was the more complex one that Dollard described. The severity of the sentence depended not only on the race of the offender but the race of the victim. Only 3 percent of the blacks convicted of killing other blacks were executed; whites who killed whites were five times as likely to receive the death penalty. (Part of this seeming racial difference may have been that more of the black murders grew out of disputes between friends or family members, which the law has always treated less harshly than killing store clerks, bank guards, or other strangers, but the disparity seems too large for that to be the sole explanation.) Whites who murdered their fellow whites were also three times as likely to be put away for life as were blacks who murdered their fellow blacks. The 22 blacks convicted of killing whites, though, were treated more severely than white killers of whites. Six out of 10 of them were executed or locked up for life, as compared with only a quarter of the whites who murdered other whites. (Again, this could in part reflect differences in the character of the crimes, with more of the white-on-white murders involving kin or friends.)

Thus, whatever the cause of the very high rate of black-on-black violence —the experience of racial subjugation and the laxity of police enforcement are the obvious explanations—one fact was clear: the law provided very little protection for black citizens, either from lawless whites or lawless blacks.

UNDUE PESSIMISM

What was the legacy of the Jim Crow South? The impact of segregation and white supremacy, Gunnar Myrdal believed, could be seen in the "distorted" and "pathological" nature of black communal life. Myrdal's discussion of that life was actually the least satisfactory part of his great survey of the "American Dilemma" half a century ago, and indeed he devoted only two of his forty-five chapters to the institutions and culture that defined "the Negro Community."[119]

The emphasis on "pathology" made a powerful political point. By hammering away throughout his massive volume on the terrible damage that racial subjugation had inflicted, and by giving hardly any sympathetic attention to the life black Americans had made for themselves within the severely circumscribed limits set by white society, Myrdal sought to awaken the national conscience and thus to persuade his readers of the urgent need for major reform to promote racial justice. To have provided a more positive picture would have weakened the force of his stinging moral indictment of American racism.

It is thus not surprising that *An American Dilemma* was a main source of ammunition for the NAACP when it argued that the Supreme Court should strike down racially segregated public schools. Nor is it surprising that Myrdal's volume was cited favorably in the Court's unanimous opinion in *Brown v. Board of Education.* Thurgood Marshall, leader of the NAACP's legal team, had told his staff that they should try the case "just like any other one in which you would try to prove damages to a client. If your car ran over my client, you'd have to pay up, and my function as an attorney would be to put experts on the stand to testify how much damage was done." [120] *An American Dilemma* was used to provide that proof of damage; white America had been a runaway car that had crushed black citizens under its wheels, and it was time to "pay up." [121]

One of Myrdal's most enthusiastic supporters was Richard Wright, author of the best-selling novel *Native Son* (1940), the first work by a black writer to be made a Book-of-the-Month Club selection. Wright called *An American Dilemma* "monumental," and argued that it demonstrated that "the Negro's conduct, his personality, his culture, his entire life flow naturally and inevitably out of the conditions imposed upon him by white America." [122] That was the assumption that underlay *Native Son*, his searing tale of racial oppression. None of Wright's black characters in the novel had a shred of personal autonomy and independence; they belonged to no culture or ethnic community from which they could draw strength. [123]

One of the few dissenting voices in this chorus of approval was that of a younger black writer just beginning his career. Ralph Ellison's novel *Invisible Man* (1951) displayed a very different sensibility. The *Antioch Review* had asked the relatively unknown Ellison to review *An American Dilemma* but failed to publish his critique, perhaps because it ran counter to prevailing white liberal orthodoxy. Although Ellison found the book impressive in many ways, he also expressed serious doubt about the core proposition upon which Myrdal and Richard Wright agreed: the view that the most important characteristics of black Americans were largely "marks of oppression." "Can a people," Ellison asked, "live and develop for over three hundred years simply by *reacting*? Are American Negroes simply the creation of white men, or have they at least helped to create themselves out of what they found around them? Men have made a way of life in caves and upon cliffs, why cannot Negroes have made a life upon the horns of the white man's dilemma?" [124]

Myrdal's view, as Ellison saw it, robbed blacks of all dignity. But there were good political reasons for ignoring Ellison's point until segregation was in retreat and the need to stress its damage consequently diminished. There was indeed a black American cultural style, as Ellison later put it, that could be discerned in "jazzmen and prize fighters, ballplayers and tap dancers; in gesture, inflection, intonation, timbre and phrasing . . . in all those nuances of expression and attitude which reveal a culture." [125] And there was a black communal life, centered in large part around the church. Myrdal seems to have been tone deaf to religion; Richard Wright, reacting to the overdose of religion he had been given as a boy, was similarly unperceptive. Nothing in either *Native Son* or *An American Dilemma* prepared readers for the role that the black church would play in the civil rights struggle of the 1950s and '60s. In fact, the accounts given in these books provided no clue as to how a group

whose communal life was so "distorted" and "pathological" could produce a
disciplined and powerful mass movement that destroyed Jim Crow.

The notion of blacks as putty in the hands of white racists, their culture
entirely shaped by whites, did not die with Myrdal or the civil rights revolution
of the 1960s. It lives in the arguments of those who attribute all the social
problems that seem particularly evident in inner-city black communities (a
high crime rate, low levels of educational attainment, and the like) directly to
the "lingering effects" of slavery and the Jim Crow South.[126] And it lives on in
the widely believed notion that blacks are helpless against a variety of white
conspiracies—that drugs in poor black neighborhoods, for instance, are a
consequence of a deliberate government decision to make them available, a
topic to which we will return in later chapters.

White conspiracies and black helplessness have been important themes in
a number of contemporary autobiographies by black writers. Whites have "a
master plan that leaves little to accident, that [means] most of the ugliest
things happening to black people are not accidental but the predictable results
of the working of the plan," John Edgar Wideman wrote in *Brothers and
Keepers*. His brother had refused to play by white "rules"; he was into "rebellion"—or rather "what little is left in us." He paid a high price, landing in
prison convicted for murder.[127] In *Makes Me Wanna Holler*, Nathan McCall
painted much the same portrait. He described "two distinct worlds": one for
blacks, "dark and limited," and one for whites, full of promise. When a white
teacher reached out to him, he wondered how he could possibly " 'make
something' of [himself] in the fucking white man's world?"[128]

"Blacks aren't accepted because whites believe they can't succeed," Derrick
Bell has said.[129] In fact, it is Nathan McCall, John Edgar Wideman, and
Derrick Bell himself—three black writers—who seem to believe that blacks
cannot succeed. If Myrdal's pessimism—his picture of blacks as totally
crushed by racism—was useful at the time, Ellison's optimism was much
closer to the truth. Black life in America has changed profoundly in the
decades since Myrdal wrote, and blacks themselves have had much to do with
the course of that change, we hope subsequent chapters will show.

CHAPTER TWO

The Promised Land

IN 1927 THE young Richard Wright boarded a train for Chicago in search of the "dignity" he had never found as a "black boy" in the South.[1] The trip was not his alone. In two "Great Migrations," each triggered by the outbreak of world war, a great many African Americans moved from South to North and from country to city. And in doing so, they transformed the issue of race—largely a southern "dilemma"—into a national question.

"Harlem was as close to Heaven as we were going to find on this Earth," the Delany sisters wrote in *Having Our Say*. They were describing their arrival in New York toward the end of World War I.[2] In fact, the North was no racial paradise, as the two sisters acknowledge. But by the standards of the South, it was the land of freedom. "Would you speak to a white girl up there?" a white factory worker asked Richard Wright upon learning he was moving North. And when Wright answers, "Oh, no, sir . . . ," his interrogator replies, "You'll change. Niggers change when they go north."[3] That was of course precisely the point for Wright: the chance to change.

Upon his arrival in Chicago he saw a difference immediately. In the train station, he later wrote, "I looked about to see if there were signs saying: FOR WHITE—FOR COLORED. I saw none. Black people and white people moved about, each seemingly intent upon his private mission. There was no racial fear."[4] That was the difference that made all the difference. In the North, blacks were shut out of "white" neighborhoods, restaurants, beaches, and even some schools, but Wright could speak to those white girls who were first and foremost on the mind of his white interrogator on the factory floor in Memphis. Working in a Chicago restaurant, in fact, he was astonished to feel the body of a white waitress pressed closely against his as she drew a cup of coffee. In the South

the work of the hot and busy kitchen would have had to cease for the moment so that I could have taken my tainted body far enough away to allow the southern white girl a chance to get a cup of coffee. There lay a deep, emotional safety in knowing that the white girl who was now leaning carelessly against me was not thinking of me, had no deep vague, irrational fright that made her feel that I was a creature to be avoided at all costs.[5]

For Wright and the other southern blacks who left the South in two great waves, it was that relative "emotional safety" that made the North so very different.

THE GREAT MIGRATION

With the end of slavery, African Americans acquired that most elementary and American of rights—the freedom to pick up stakes and settle elsewhere. And yet in the half century that followed the Civil War, despite assaults by lynch mobs, disfranchisement, and the tightening bonds of segregation, surprisingly few blacks actually left the South. Fully 89 percent of the nation's 10 million blacks still resided in the southern states in 1910, a mere 3 points lower than the figure at the time of the Census of 1860.

They stayed because they had a place in the southern economy. A place on the bottom of the heap, to be sure, but nonetheless a place. In both the farming and industrial sectors, employers were accustomed to using black labor, mainly at jobs that whites would not take. In the North, on the other hand, European immigrants were flocking to New York, Chicago, Philadelphia, and other cities in numbers sufficient to meet the needs of industry. Few employers had any experience with black workers; moreover, hiring them risked bitter resistance from white workers and their unions.

War changed the picture. The outbreak of fighting in Europe in 1914 cut off the flow of immigration, creating an acute labor shortage—a shortage that became even greater after the United States entered the war in early 1917. The young men who had worked in the factories left for the battlefields at the same time that wartime orders created a booming economy and thus plenty of work. Needing laborers, for the first time northern industrial employers opened the factory gates to black workers, who heard the call and came from the South. And while the supply of fresh laborers from Europe was temporarily restored when the war ended, restrictive legislation in the 1920s once again cut the supply of immigrants and increased the demand for indigenous labor.

Close to half a million blacks had left the South by 1920, and they were joined by another three-quarters of a million by the end of the 1920s.[6] From 1910 to 1930, the African-American population in New York City soared from 92,000 to over a third of a million, producing the outpouring of literary and musical creativity known as the Harlem Renaissance.[7] In 1930, Chicago had over 200,000 black residents, almost six times as many as twenty years before; Detroit had a stunning twenty-four times as many.[8]

This "Great Migration" was not very great in terms of sheer numbers; it was great mainly by contrast with the remarkable immobility of southern blacks in the half century between Emancipation and World War I. In 1930 the vast majority of the nation's African Americans—almost four out of five— still lived in the region in which their parents and grandparents had been born. The picture was little different in 1940.

A CHANCE TO BE A MAN

Mary Antin, a young Russian-Jewish immigrant who came to the United States with her parents at the end of the nineteenth century, titled her poignant 1912 autobiography *The Promised Land.* Blacks who moved to Chicago, Cleveland, and Detroit during the Great Migration likewise thought in Old Testament terms; they had escaped bondage in the South and entered a promised land—although without a Moses to lead them. The *Chicago Defender,* the nation's leading black newspaper, exhorted southern blacks to join in "The Flight Out of Egypt," and printed the lyrics of songs titled "Bound for the Promised Land" and "Going into Canaan."[9]

In some respects the North was indeed a promised land—a place where blacks would find freedom from systematic racial subordination and oppression. After the intensive investigations he conducted at the end of the 1930s, Myrdal concluded that the "most striking" difference between the regions was the relative freedom from constant fear; northern blacks did not need to display "the submissive and guarded manners of the Southern Negro."[10] A sensitive black scholar who wrote a volume on segregation practices as part of the Myrdal project made the same point; "aggressive self-assertion," he noted, could often be seen in blacks living in Harlem and on the South Side of Chicago, while "subservience and apology" were far more common in the South.[11]

African Americans in northern communities encountered plenty of prejudice and discrimination, as Richard Wright discovered soon after his arrival in Chicago in 1927. What he did not find in Chicago was a system of racial social control designed to inspire terror. In the South from which Wright had come, "the whites had drawn a line over which we dared not cross," he later wrote. A "latent sense of violence" underlay every contact between blacks and whites; the ever-present threat of violent sanctions ensured general compliance with that racial line.[12] Life in Chicago was not easy for blacks, but African Americans had an elementary sense of personal security. They did not have to worry about being "uppity niggers" who did not know "their place." In the North, said one African-American newcomer, you had "a chance to be a man regardless of [your] color."[13]

The freedom to sit next to a white in the front of the bus or to use the same drinking fountain: these seemed matters of relatively minor importance. But the point of those proscriptions in the Jim Crow South was to remind blacks who was boss, to underscore the fact of "white supremacy." In that respect the North was fundamentally different.[14] The elaborate code of racial etiquette that defined and preserved caste boundaries in the South was absent in the North. Whites did not habitually refer to black men by their first names or as "boy" or "uncle." Conversely, as a migrant to Philadelphia noted with pleasure, blacks did not have to "mister every little white boy [who came] along."[15] The notion that blacks should only enter white homes by the back door was unheard of. For members of the two races to dine together was not taboo, nor was the simple act of shaking hands. Black people were not automatically at the back of any line that formed. Richard Wright at first found it startling to stop at a busy newsstand and to find that he was able to buy a paper before all the whites crowding around it were served.[16] The newcomer to Philadelphia similarly marveled that "if you are first in a place here shopping you don't have to wait until the white folks get through trading . . ."[17]

The radical difference between North and South was equally evident in the realm of politics. Black people could run for office, and they were actually encouraged to vote. Not because politicians were passionately committed to egalitarian ideals, but because they were realists and knew how to count. As *Black Metropolis,* the classic sociological account of black life in a northern city, put it, Chicago's politicians realized that "the Negro had a commodity in which they were interested—the vote."[18]

The strenuous competition for the black vote meant that African Americans flocked to the polls. In 1930 the turnout rate in one of Chicago's most heavily black wards was 77 percent, nine points above the city average, despite the fact that rates of political participation are generally lower in neighborhoods with low income and educational levels.[19] Several black candidates won seats on the Chicago City Council in the 1920s and, even though blacks were less than 7 percent of the population, an African American was elected to a municipal judgeship in a citywide contest. Whites did not find it unthinkable to vote for a black candidate. By 1928 five African Americans from Chicago were sitting in the lower house of the Illinois state legislature, one was in the state senate, and one was in the U.S. House of Representatives. In addition, blacks held important appointive offices—six assistant corporation counsels, five assistant city prosecutors, and an assistant state's attorney.[20]

Political power must have had some impact on the delivery of services in the city. And perhaps that impact, combined with relatively low expectations on the part of blacks, explains the almost complete absence of any discussion of police brutality in *Black Metropolis.*[21] In 1945, the same year the work was published, managers of a large cotton plantation in the Mississippi Delta came to Chicago to meet with some former black employees. The plantation was hard up for workers, and hoped to persuade the black migrants to return to the South. But the managers' arguments fell on deaf ears in part because the black workers believed they got better protection from the law in the Windy City.[22]

New Economic Opportunities

The prospects of finding a reasonably well-paid job were far better for blacks in the North than in the South. It was precisely the opening up of better jobs for African Americans in northern industry that set the Great Migration in motion. Until the labor shortages that started with World War I, however, the prejudices of white employers, workers, and customers kept northern blacks locked into a few traditional "Negro jobs," working as unskilled laborers, servants, waiters, janitors, porters, or elevator operators. The industrial semi-skilled and skilled positions that gave millions of immigrants the chance to climb out of poverty were off-limits.

Thus, in 1910 only 3,000 African-American men worked in Chicago's factories, and most of them were doing traditional "black" jobs like sweeping the floor. By 1920, as a result of the labor-hungry war economy, their numbers had risen to 15,000 and most were in occupations previously restricted to whites. By then a third of the city's African-American men were working for large manufacturers such as International Harvester, Pullman, Swift, and Armour, pulling down "white" wages that averaged about $25 a week at a time when black farm laborers in the South earned as little as 75 cents a day.[23] The cost of living was higher in northern cities, of course, but not nearly high enough to erase the huge difference in wages.

The advances made during the World War I decade were impressive, but a large racial disparity in occupations remained. In Chicago in 1920 only 9 percent of African-American men were professionals, business proprietors, clerks, or salesmen, less than a third the proportion among whites. Only a tenth had skilled jobs, as compared to over a quarter of the whites. Four out of five black men were unskilled or semiskilled laborers of some kind, and were usually found in the dirtiest, most dangerous, least secure, and lowest-paid jobs.[24] Two decades later, in 1940, the racial gap in occupations had narrowed only a little. The proportion of black men holding white-collar jobs had edged up from 9 to 16 percent, but it was still well below the 40 percent of white males who were white-collar workers.[25] The fraction doing skilled manual work had not risen at all. Changes on the job front for black women are much simpler to describe: there was no change at all. In 1940, 64 percent worked as domestic servants, precisely the same proportion as in 1920.[26]

The lowly position of black workers was in good part due to their very few years of education in the South's rotten Jim Crow schools; they lacked the training required for many white-collar and skilled jobs. In addition, most were rural folk unfamiliar with the rhythms of urban, industrial society. Relatively uneducated European immigrants from peasant backgrounds also had to settle for jobs on the bottom rungs of the ladder when they first arrived in the American city.[27]

These background handicaps, though, were not the sole reason blacks were rarely doctors, certified public accountants, or tool and die makers. The children of African Americans who were living in the North before the Great Migration were, after all, familiar with city ways. They had much more education than southern migrants, and they had attended racially integrated schools. But such northern-born blacks did not fare dramatically better in the job competition than black migrants from the South. There was a color line in the labor market, a job ceiling that kept them out of many of the more attractive occupations. That ceiling was not nearly as low as in the South, and the color line was less rigid. But racial barriers to getting many of the best-paid and most desirable jobs were nonetheless real.[28]

Labor unions were a particularly important barrier to black occupational advancement. It is often assumed that discrimination in the labor market is largely the work of prejudiced employers who find it profitable to treat members of minority groups unfairly. In fact, to discriminate against minority labor was economically irrational from the employer's vantage point, since black laborers were often willing to work for a lower wage.[29] It was white workers who profited from the exclusion of nonwhites; they acquired protection by virtue of being the "right" color.

The workers' instrument of exclusion was the labor union, already strong by the time blacks arrived on the industrial scene. If it was in the interest of white workers to restrict the competition for jobs to whites, it was natural that the organizations that represented those white workers—trade unions— should exclude African Americans from membership and limit their employment options to the menial positions that whites did not want.[30] And it was equally natural for blacks to work as "scabs"—strikebreakers—when unions went out on strike.

When black exclusion was impossible because African Americans already had a solid foothold in an industry, unions did seek to bring them within their ranks. But when the Amalgamated Meat Cutters and Butcher Workmen launched a major drive to organize blacks working at the Chicago stockyards in 1919, no more than a third of the African Americans signed up. On the basis of long and bitter experience, blacks were deeply suspicious of labor unions.[31] With very few exceptions, until World War II American unions were antiblack, and American blacks were antiunion.

NEIGHBORHOOD SEGREGATION

The color line was even clearer in the housing market than in the labor market. After the Great Migration, neighborhood segregation in the North was as pronounced, or even more pronounced, than in the South. Before the war, however, the residential patterns of blacks resembled those of various European immigrant groups, and historians refer to this as the period "before the ghetto."[32] In Cleveland in 1910, for example, blacks were less strongly segregated from native whites than were both Italian and Romanian immigrants, and not much more segregated than Russian and Hungarian newcomers from abroad.[33]

But the immigrant ghetto was not imposed upon its inhabitants by the hostility of others. Not many native whites were horrified at the prospect of living next door to an Italian or Romanian. "Poletown" was an ethnically identifiable neighborhood by choice; immigrants unpacked their bags where relatives and friends already lived. Moreover, neither they nor those who had arrived before them stayed long; "Little Italy" was a temporary way station, not a permanent abode. As Italians learned the language, became citizens, and traded their ditch-digging jobs for fruit stands, grocery stores, and other businesses, they dispersed into more ethnically mixed neighborhoods.[34]

The contrast with blacks was striking. Black migrants to northern cities also went where their friends and family already were; they, too, wanted a neighborhood church in which they felt at home. But the black ghetto was fundamentally different from European immigrant neighborhoods. Whites did not want blacks next door. Even before the Great Migration, when the African-American population was too small to seem truly threatening, a color line had begun to be drawn. Thus, in Chicago's Hyde Park, a middle-class area surrounding the University of Chicago, the neighborhood improvement association launched a drive in 1909 to insure that "the districts which are now white . . . remain white." In fact, they wanted not only to preserve all-white neighborhoods but to roll back the black "invasion" by expelling African Americans from some blocks that were already integrated. The association thus bought up property owned by blacks in "white" blocks, and offered cash bonuses to black renters who agreed to give up their leases and move out. It boycotted local merchants who served those black customers who insisted on remaining in places the association thought should be 100 percent white.[35]

In the years of the Great Migration, the residential color line hardened. The residential concentration of European immigrant groups dropped, while the clustering of African Americans very sharply increased. That was in part due to the shift in migration patterns. Immigration from abroad had ended, cutting off the supply of the newcomers to the Little Italys and their counterparts. At the same time, long-settled, prospering members of these groups moved out of immigrant neighborhoods. Conversely the sudden growth in the number of black city-dwellers brought a rapid rise in population in areas where blacks already lived.

This was only part of the story, however. White fear of black neighbors also became more acute. Although earlier influxes of impoverished and culturally different immigrants into neighborhoods had often provoked hostility and fear, the arrival of large numbers of African Americans provoked a more intense reaction.[36] Racially restrictive real estate covenants were devised to preserve the "ethnic purity" of neighborhoods; written into real estate deeds, they prohibited the rental or sale of property mainly to blacks, but sometimes to members of other minority groups as well. But such formal legal restrictions were cumbersome; they could only be enforced by a court of law. Informal, often illegal action was swifter and surer. Ostracism, intimidation, and, if necessary, violence kept blacks on the "right" side of the color line. Chicago alone was the site of some fifty-eight racially inspired bombings in the years 1917–1921, with the targets being black-occupied homes in neighborhoods resisting racial transition, real estate businesses who rented to blacks, and banks that loaned them mortgage money. The terrible Chicago race riot of 1919, which resulted in the death of twenty-three blacks and fifteen whites, grew out of these vicious turf wars.[37]

African Americans who wanted to escape the ghetto thus generally could not. Chicago was quite typical of northern cities in this respect. The first major national public opinion poll of American racial attitudes, conducted by *Fortune* magazine in 1939, asked whether blacks "should be allowed to live wherever they want to live, and there should be no laws or social pressure to keep them from it." Not exactly a radical notion. And yet only 19 percent of the residents of New England and the Middle Atlantic states endorsed it. Even more striking were the responses from the Midwest, into whose cities much of the Great Migration had flowed. Just 12 percent of Midwestern whites believed that black people should be free to live wherever they pleased; the difference between the responses in the Midwest and South was too small to be statistically significant.[38]

While white northerners worked hard at keeping blacks from living next door, the rapidly multiplying African-American population could not simply cram itself into the same space at ever-higher levels of density; the boundaries of the ghetto had to expand. "White" property had to become "black." And by the simple mechanism of supply and demand, it did. Despite restrictive covenants and concerted white resistance, the housing market was, in fact, a market. The decisions of thousands of individual property owners governed residential patterns. When the highest bidder for a house or an apartment was black, the temptation to accept the offer was often too strong to resist. The huge pent-up demand for housing adjacent to the black community often meant that desperate blacks would pay more than whites for comparable space—a "color tax" that burdened a group whose earning power was already depressed by prejudice in the labor market.

Black penetration into previously white areas usually resulted merely in larger ghettos, not more racially integrated neighborhoods. White fear that the arrival of one African American would soon "tip" the entire block proved to be a self-fulfilling prophecy. The first white to capitulate to market pressures became a "block-buster." Whites fled in panic, believing that where one black gained entry, others would quickly follow, property values would drop, and the neighborhood would become a slum. But white panic at black faces was not the whole story. Blacks needed housing, and yet most of the city was off-limits. The market operated only at the edge of the ghetto, and thus, even without white flight, near-ghetto neighborhoods were likely to turn all-black. Stable, racially integrated neighborhoods could not be maintained as long as black dollars could buy nothing in most residential areas.

OTHER FORMS OF SOCIAL DISCRIMINATION

Public space, too, was racially earmarked. Blacks in the North were not legally banned from public parks, as they were in the South, but their formal right to have a picnic on the public grass in a white neighborhood was not always secure. In some cities it might have been unpleasant, even dangerous, to exercise that right. In Chicago, the authors of *Black Metropolis* observed, "the very existence of a Black Belt leads the public to feel that Negroes should have their own schools and public recreational facilities, and should not 'invade' those in other sections of the city."[39]

White opposition to "racial mixing" in public swimming pools and beaches was especially pronounced, perhaps because of the sexual undertones of activities conducted in a state of partial undress. Chicago's 1919 race riot began when a black youth drowned at such a hot spot, a public beach on Lake Michigan. Swimming off an informally designated "white" part of the beach, he had been assaulted by a white mob throwing stones. Northern cities did not have signs reading FOR WHITES and FOR COLORED, but the difference in practice was not as sharp as it was in theory.

Phobia about sexual contact between the races was less acute in the North, but it was strong everywhere. In fact, that phobia was explicitly written into the law in many states that did not otherwise make invidious legal distinctions between the races. Indiana, Nebraska, Oregon, and California were among the nineteen states outside the South that outlawed interracial marriages. Only eighteen did not attempt to enforce racial segregation in the most intimate of human relationships, and these were generally states in which the black population was very small. Moreover, in those states that did not legally bar racially mixed marriages, it was socially unacceptable in both the white and black communities and thus extremely rare.[40] Tellingly, none of the public opinion polls taken in the 1930s and 1940s included any questions on attitudes toward interracial marriage; it was so widely condemned it wasn't a question even worth asking until 1958, when just 4 percent of white Americans indicated approval.[41]

Other forms of social discrimination were common in the North as well. Although "mixed" dining was not everywhere taboo, as it was throughout the South, many restaurants would not serve black customers. Large, impersonal establishments that were part of national chains rarely discriminated, but many others did.[42] Hotels often refused accommodations to African Americans. The great singer Marian Anderson was able to stay at the best hotel in Dayton, Ohio, when she was in town for a performance, but only because it was arranged so that "she didn't register or come anywhere near the desk. She went right up the elevator to her room," said the manager, "and no one knew she was around."[43] Barber shops and beauty parlors rarely served both black and white patrons.

The fact that blacks and whites lived apart meant, of course, that neighborhood public schools were predominantly of one race or the other. And while no northern states required segregation, some did allow local communities to establish racially separate schools. (Hence the segregated schools in Topeka, Kansas, that Linda Brown challenged in *Brown v. Board of Education,* which by the 1950s were actually anomalous.)[44] But while most black pupils in the North attended schools with few or no whites, they unquestionably received a far better education than children south of the Mason-Daxon line. No northern community spent several times as much money on white pupils as on black ones, the common pattern in the South, and none offered black students only an elementary school education. Asked why they chose to move North, participants in the Great Migration often pointed to the greater educational opportunities for their children. African Americans living in the North in 1940 had an average of 8.7 years of school, two and a half years more than those in the South, and this figure actually understates the regional difference, since it includes many "northerners" who grew up in the South.[45]

THE GREAT DEPRESSION AND THE NEW DEAL

The move to the promised land subsided during the 1930s. With the collapse of the economy and the beginning of the Great Depression in 1929, job openings in the North dried up and the flood of southern migrants slowed to a trickle. Over the Depression decade the share of the black population living in the southern states thus dropped a mere two points, from 79 to 77 percent.

In 1932, when Franklin D. Roosevelt was first elected president, more than a third of all nonagricultural workers were unemployed, and a great many others were working only part-time for reduced wages. The garbage dumps in most cities were swarming with people hungry enough to eat scraps of stale bread and moldy potatoes. Farm prices had plunged, and hundreds of thousands of farms were on the auction block because their owners were unable to keep up with their mortgage or tax payments. From one perspective, however, blacks were hit less hard than whites; they were already very poor, and had remained so through the boom years of the 1920s. As an eminent black journalist noted, "the Depression didn't have the impact on the Negroes that it had on the whites [because] the Negroes had been in the Depression all the time."[46]

If blacks had less far to slip economically, they were still desperately in need of help, and the Roosevelt administration did break decisively with the past in making national prosperity the responsibility of the federal government. But a number of key New Deal economic programs had harmful effects on black workers. In agriculture, where most blacks were employed, the New Deal's farm subsidy program benefited only those who owned the land—in other words, mostly whites. Worse yet, the Agricultural Adjustment Administration paid farm owners to remove land from cultivation so as to reduce output and thus lift prices, and with less land, they needed fewer tenants and laborers—who were mostly black. Furthermore, many farmers used the subsidy payments they received to invest in tractors and other labor-saving equipment, and in fertilizer, pesticides, and herbicides, further reducing their dependence on black tenants and sharecroppers.[47]

The economic boom that began with World War II would create jobs that triggered a Second Great Migration into northern cities, but through the 1930s, when the unemployment rate for nonagricultural workers remained at crisis levels, displaced black tenants and croppers had nowhere to go. They were stuck not only in the South but on the land—reduced to farm laborers, in circumstances of increasing misery. That misery would have been less if New Deal relief programs had been designed and administered in a manner that was fairer to African Americans. However, southern congressmen (all of them white, of course) were an indispensable partner in the New Deal coalition, and they made sure that federal economic assistance did nothing to interfere with the planters' labor needs. Measly "handouts from Washington" —$3 a month in Mississippi in 1933, for example—kept blacks toiling in the cotton fields. As did the rule that relief could not be given to anyone to whom a planter had offered work—whatever the wage.[48]

Southern congressmen also used their clout to make sure that agricultural workers were denied the old-age pensions and unemployment insurance protection provided by the Social Security Act of 1935, perhaps the most important piece of social legislation enacted during the New Deal. (Twenty years later agricultural workers were finally covered.) The fact that providing such a social safety net would have made blacks less dependent on planters was an important reason for the exclusion.[49] Likewise, although the majority of black women holding jobs were domestic servants, the Social Security Act did not cover them—an exclusion that again benefited the extraordinarily large number of southern white families who enjoyed the services of a black cook, maid, or baby-sitter at rock-bottom prices.

The exclusion of both agricultural and domestic service workers meant that only a third of the nation's African-American employees were covered by Social Security, as compared with nearly two-thirds of the nation's foreign-born workers.[50] Even when New Deal legislation did protect blacks, it did not always work to their benefit. The Roosevelt administration, through such measures as the National Industrial Recovery Act of 1933 and the Fair Labor Standards Act of 1938, sought to improve the condition of American workers by setting minimum wages and hours, and yet a minimum wage that seemed fair in other parts of the country was still well above prevailing levels in the South. Likewise, hours thought reasonable were short by southern standards. New Deal legislation raised the living standards of those who were employed, but it put a damper on further industrial development in the region by removing the most important advantage southern employers had over their northern competitors.[51] It thus took jobs away from blacks in the region in which most lived.[52]

In addition, forcing employers to pay their black help the same minimum rate as whites had the perverse effect of eliminating the incentive to hire black workers who would accept lower wages than whites. Compelled to pay the same wages to blacks and whites, employers responded by dumping those who were black. For example, 68 percent of the workers in the southern tobacco factories had been black in 1930. When the National Recovery Administration began its work, these firms petitioned for a separate and lower wage scale for black workers. The administration resisted the blatantly racist proposal, but the black workers paid a price: whites got their jobs, with the result that by 1940 the proportion of African Americans in the tobacco factories had dropped to 55 percent, with steady declines thereafter. The NRA codes, one estimate has it, threw 500,000 blacks out of work—making it, in the view of the black press, a "Negro Removal Act."[53] The NRA was not a singular story. Later New Deal reform measures had similar effects.[54] Requirements that on their face might seem to have the effect of equalizing the races by putting a uniform floor under wages actually deprived many blacks of a job, and thus widened the racial gap.

New Deal agricultural policies accelerated changes that in time doubtless would have happened anyway. The South could not remain forever an island of inefficient, labor-intensive agriculture while farms elsewhere in the nation became ever more productive and profitable by using fewer workers and more tractors, weed killers, and commercial fertilizers. Under the best of circumstances a more rational and efficient mode of agriculture would have had no use for millions of people—most of them black—who lived in poverty in the southern countryside in the 1930s. They would have had to find a means of livelihood elsewhere, as the surplus farm population in other regions of the country had done earlier. Moreover, in the long run, the demise of the sharecropping economy liberated southern blacks from a hopelessly cramped, oppressive, impoverished way of life.

Through the 1930s black agricultural workers continued to work on southern soil, but World War II once again created a shortage of workers in the manufacturing plants producing war equipment and other northern industries. And once again southern blacks in search of jobs boarded trains and buses, creating the Second Great Migration, which lasted through the mid-1960s. Almost three-quarters of a million black families were tenants or croppers in the South in 1930. By 1950 the number was down to barely half that, and a decade later it had become less than a fifth of its 1930 level, with the end of the fall not yet in sight.[55] In 1940, 33 percent of all black men and women were employed in agriculture; by 1960 the figure was down to 9 percent—a drop of 73 percent.[56]

LIBERALS VERSUS SOUTHERN DEMOCRATS

The Great Depression, the New Deal, the drift of blacks off the land and into northern cities: these were changes with inevitable political consequences. Until the Depression, black Americans—that is, those who lived in the North and could vote—had remained loyal to the party of Lincoln. Republican zeal for protecting basic civil rights had largely vanished with the end of Reconstruction; nevertheless, the GOP remained far more appealing than the Democrats, the voice of the white supremacist South. The sole Democrat to occupy the White House in the first third of the twentieth century was Woodrow Wilson, and although he was an ardent Progressive, a liberal reformer who spoke passionately of "the common man," he was a Virginian with the racial views typical of southern whites. His administration (spanning the years 1913 to 1921) tightened the lines of segregation in federal offices and facilities in Washington and purged blacks from all but the most menial federal jobs.[57]

Until the New Deal, therefore, a black Democrat was almost as rare as an Irish-Catholic Republican. Even in 1932, despite the fact that the black unemployment figures were even worse than those for whites, more than two-thirds of African Americans voted for Herbert Hoover; it was the highest support he got from any demographic group.[58] But black loyalty to the Republicans declined precipitously thereafter; in fact, of all the groups that switched to the Democratic party in the 1930s, none moved as dramatically as blacks, 76 percent of whom cast their ballots for FDR in 1936.[59]

African Americans were attracted to the New Deal not only because Roosevelt promised jobs, but also because prominent members of the administration had strongly liberal views on racial issues.[60] In 1938, Eleanor Roosevelt, the president's wife, attended meetings in Birmingham, Alabama, sponsored by the Southern Conference for Human Welfare, a biracial liberal group. On the opening day of the conference everyone sat where they pleased, defying a city ordinance mandating racially segregated seating at all public events. When news of this audacious challenge to Jim Crow reached Police Commis-

sioner Eugene "Bull" Connor (who twenty-five years later would become a
national symbol of brutal viciousness when civil rights protests erupted in
Birmingham), he threatened arrests, and the conference organizers reluctantly complied with his orders. Mrs. Roosevelt, however, refused to sit on
the "white" side of the hall, and placed a chair in the aisle between the
white and the black delegates.[61] A year later the Daughters of the American
Revolution owned the only concert hall in the nation's capital but would not
allow Marian Anderson to perform in it. Mrs. Roosevelt resigned from the
organization in protest, and, along with Interior Secretary Harold Ickes, arranged for the concert to be held on the steps of the Lincoln Memorial.[62]

The Public Works Administration was headed by the secretary of the interior, and Ickes, a white liberal who had earlier served as president of the
Chicago chapter of the NAACP, took the lead in insisting that black workers
receive a decent share of the jobs on all federal work projects he funded.
Other New Deal agencies also took pains to hire African Americans.[63] Fewer
than 50,000 blacks were federal employees when FDR took office; by 1941
the number had more than tripled and thus roughly matched the proportion
of the nation's population that was black. The increase was partly due to the
dramatic growth in the total federal payroll during the New Deal, but the
black gain was particularly great.[64]

Most blacks added to the payroll in the New Deal years held only low-level
positions. In the National Recovery Administration, for example, all but one
of nearly a thousand black employees worked as messengers. However, most
federal agencies followed the lead of Ickes in the Interior Department and
also appointed African Americans as advisors who were supposed to monitor
how new programs affected black interests. By 1936 there were approximately
three dozen such people, who comprised an informal "Black Cabinet."[65]

Though the president's charisma and compassion, along with the racially
liberal views of his wife, Ickes, and others, pulled a large majority of registered
black voters into the Democratic Party, the political influence of African
Americans was nonetheless very limited. Not only were blacks but a tenth of
the population; more than three out of four lived in the South, where the
electoral "reforms" put in place at the end of the nineteenth century had
stripped them of the right to vote. No more than 80,000 to 90,000 of the
more than 3.5 million adult blacks in nine southern states voted in the 1940
presidential election, a little under 3 percent.[66] A majority of that handful of
black voters were in Texas, which had no literacy test and a somewhat less
rigid caste order than such states as Alabama, South Carolina, and Mississippi;
in the Deep South black political participation was largely confined to the
larger cities, such as Atlanta. Even these pathetically small numbers do not
convey the full extent of southern black disfranchisement. From the end of
Reconstruction until after World War II, the South was a one-party region,
and the November general elections mere formalities. The real political

choices were made earlier in the Democratic Party primaries, in which (except in a few counties in North Carolina, Florida, and Tennessee) blacks could not participate.[67] White primaries would seem to have been a clear violation of the Fifteenth Amendment, but the Supreme Court did not rule that they were unconstitutional until 1944.

During the 1930s, ironically, blacks left the party of Lincoln for the party of white supremacy. In 1938 nearly 40 percent of the Democrats elected to the House of Representatives were from the eleven states of the Old Confederacy, and another 15 percent were from Border states that placed barriers in the way of black political participation.[68] Moreover, those numbers only partially tell the story of white southern strength within the Democratic Party. Until the 1960s, power in both houses of Congress was based entirely on seniority, and since there was little political competition in the one-party South, southern congressmen typically held on to their seats much longer than those from other regions. Thus, they controlled key committees and could block measures that did not serve the interest of their constituents, all of them white.

Without strong support from Democrats in Alabama, Georgia, and Mississippi, Roosevelt could never have gotten his ambitious legislative program through Congress. In return, the administration did nothing to disturb the racial status quo. As political scientist V. O. Key noted, the principal aim of southern politics was "to assure locally a subordination of the Negro population and, externally, to block threatened interferences from the outside with these local arrangements."[69] With Jim Crow deeply entrenched in the South, with northern whites unconcerned and northern blacks still politically weak, in the 1930s no major "interference" from Washington on behalf of African-American citizens was taken.

A top priority of the NAACP was federal protection against lynching, and a bill had actually been passed by the House in 1922, only to be killed by a southern filibuster in the Senate.[70] Similar bills, removing lynching cases from the jurisdiction of southern white officials who often sided with the mob, were filed several times thereafter, but President Roosevelt refused to back the legislation. Moreover, his staff was so anxious to avoid offending the South that it would not schedule a meeting between FDR and Walter White, chief spokesman for the NAACP, to discuss the matter.

Although Eleanor got around the staff, the president would not support an antilynching law. "I just can't do it," he said; "I did not choose the tools with which I must work."[71] In 1937, after two black men were tortured to death by blowtorch in Mississippi, a new antilynching bill finally did get through the House with an almost two-to-one margin; Roosevelt, who needed southern votes to appropriate funds for emergency relief, still failed to support it.[72]

By 1937 lynchings had become such rare events that it might seem that federal legislation against them was only of symbolic significance. Indeed, several southern states enacted strict antilynching laws of their own, partly to stave off this threat. Federal action on the matter, from the southern white point of view, would be a camel's nose under the tent, creating a dangerous precedent that might then be used to justify federal interference with other southern customs and practices, including the whole array of mechanisms by which black people were kept disfranchised and subordinate.

The South could not remain sealed off from "outside interference" for much longer, though. The crisis created by the Great Depression had begun to erode traditional local attachments, producing a heightened sense that Americans were one people, and enhancing the power of the federal government over the economy and the society. The nationalizing and centralizing impulses embodied in the New Deal became notably stronger after the United States became embroiled in a great world war against Nazi Germany and Japan. America's entry into World War II set in motion the forces that would destroy the Jim Crow system over the course of the next quarter century.

CHAPTER THREE

Remarkable Change

IN 1940, W. E. B. Du Bois, the nation's most eminent black intellectual, looked back on his half century of service in the cause of civil rights. His autobiography, *Dusk of Dawn,* was far from optimistic about the future. All the major strategies for black advancement had failed miserably, he concluded. Booker T. Washington had thought black leaders talked too much about rights and not enough about education. His turn-of-the-century message had soothed the sensitivities of southern whites and brought funds from northern philanthropists to the Tuskegee Institute and other black schools in the South, but the price blacks paid—the acceptance of second-class citizenship—had been much too great, Du Bois was convinced. On the other hand, the NAACP's fight for equal rights and an end to segregation, in which Du Bois himself had taken a leading role, had produced pitifully few results, while the ardent black nationalism of Marcus Garvey had yielded even less. The bitter truth, Du Bois reluctantly concluded, was that "for many years, perhaps many generations," the racial scene would not change.[1] In 1903 he had seen "the problem of the color line [as] the problem of the twentieth century."[2] Four decades later he peered sixty years down the road and saw a new century in which—for blacks—there would be nothing new.

It was a bleak and pessimistic view, and it could not have been more wrong. In 1943, four years after they had barred her from their concert hall, the Daughters of the American Revolution opened the doors of Constitution Hall to Marian Anderson, who appeared before a racially mixed audience in a wartime fund-raiser.[3] That performance was a small symbol of the momentous changes that World War II set in motion.

During the 1940s and 1950s millions of blacks left the South for the freer environment provided by the cities of the North. At the same time, millions of others moved from the southern countryside to southern cities, where opportunities for organization and action were much greater, providing the impetus for a civil rights movement that would eventually awaken the nation's conscience and destroy the southern caste system.

These huge gains by black Americans occurred in a time of buoyant economic expansion and spreading affluence, which felt all the more remarkable following on the heels of the worst economic catastrophe in American history. Blacks not only shared in the rising prosperity of the war and the immediate postwar years; they advanced more rapidly than whites. In the 1940s and 1950s, the economic gap between the races narrowed with greater speed than in any comparably short span of years since then. The number of African Americans living in poverty plunged. It is not an overstatement to say that no ethnic group in American history has ever improved its position so dramatically in so short a period, though it must be said in the same breath that no other group had so far to go.

The importance of these two decades must be underscored, because it is too often assumed that the significant advances blacks have made in modern times all occurred in the 1960s and after, and that they were the result of civil rights protest and federal legislation provoked by that protest. This common view, we shall see, is wrong both about the timing of change and about the causes of the change.

WAR FOR FREEDOM OR WHITE MAN'S WAR?

World War II was an ideological struggle as well as a military conflict. Nazi racism was pitted against the forces of freedom and democracy. To many blacks, however, common beliefs about the eternal superiority of the white race and the inferiority of the Negro race bore more than a passing resemblance to the doctrines preached by Hitler. The lofty rhetoric about the great war for freedom and democracy thus rang hollow. That rhetoric, however, gave black Americans new moral leverage to demand their democratic rights.

Even before the Japanese attack on Pearl Harbor in December 1941, some African Americans had called attention to the contradiction between American rhetoric and reality. A columnist for the nation's largest black newspaper, the *Pittsburgh Courier,* had put the point bluntly a year earlier. "Our war," said George S. Schuyler, "is not against Hitler in Europe, but against the Hitlers in America. Our war is not to defend democracy, but to get a democracy we never had."[4] The official journal of the NAACP, *Crisis,* was unmoved by "the hysterical cries of the preachers of democracy in Europe." Obtaining "democracy in Alabama and Arkansas" had higher priority in its eyes.[5]

Skepticism in the black community about wartime rhetoric about American "democracy" was fed by bitter memories of World War I. In 1917, Du Bois and other NAACP leaders had loyally urged that blacks "close ranks" and suspend all protest activities, subordinating racial grievances for the greater good of winning a war whose goal was to "make the world safe for democracy."[6] But by the war's end it was evident that Woodrow Wilson's crusade had done nothing at all to make American democracy more of a reality for blacks at home. While a third of a million African Americans had worn uniforms, they had been strictly confined to Jim Crow units, and almost all had been assigned not to combat but to labor duties.[7] Moreover, most returned to live in communities in which their status as second-class citizens was unchanged.

"Closing ranks" once again was thus not an option black leaders were willing to entertain. In response to the official war slogan "V for Victory," the *Pittsburgh Courier* called for a "Double V" campaign—victory in campaigns both abroad and at home.[8] But while the Roosevelt administration knew it needed black support for the impending war, that support could carry a politically unacceptable price: the estrangement of the powerful southern wing of the Democratic party, and thus a split in the New Deal coalition.

The president won some black gratitude without too many howls from the South a few days before the 1940 elections with a couple of token black appointments.[9] But these gestures were not enough for A. Philip Randolph, founder and president of the all-black Brotherhood of Sleeping Car Porters and the nation's top black trade union leader. Randolph spent the early months of 1941 organizing a major protest march on Washington scheduled for June. He wanted both the integration of the armed services and an assurance that blacks would not be barred from the new jobs that wartime production would inevitably create. Randolph insisted upon the core principle that had been articulated in Justice Harlan's *Plessy* dissent nearly half a century before—that public policy must be color-blind. "In the interest of national unity," Randolph called for "the abrogation of every law which makes a distinction in treatment between citizens based on religion, creed, color, or national origin."[10]

Randolph's planned march down Pennsylvania Avenue was aimed at embarrassing the White House into action. "Negro America," he announced, would "bring its power and pressure to bear upon the . . . Federal Government.[11] It was in fact a credible threat. FDR was convinced that "you can't bring 100,000 Negroes to Washington. Somebody might get killed."[12] And indeed violence against peaceful black protesters would have been very bad political news for an administration leading a democratic nation in a global struggle against totalitarianism. Randolph, though, was adamant. His minimum price for calling the demonstration off was that Roosevelt commit the federal government to a ban on "discrimination in the employment of workers in defense industries or government because of race, creed, color, or national origin."

It would have been impossible to get such a bill through a Congress dominated by Republicans and conservative southern Democrats. But in order to persuade Randolph to cancel the march, Roosevelt met his demand by issuing Executive Order 8802, which created a Fair Employment Practices Committee (FEPC) to hear complaints of discrimination and take "appropriate steps to redress grievances."[13] It was a turning point in civil rights strategy. Randolph had accomplished what traditional attempts at persuading white judges, businessmen, or politicians could not: the federal government had been forced to make its first major gesture toward ensuring black rights since Reconstruction. But it was a gesture, and fell far short of what the March on Washington movement had originally demanded—a series of antidiscrimination executive orders. Those orders would have banned the signing of federal contracts with any firm that discriminated, barred discrimination in government defense training courses, forbade segregation and discrimination in all departments of the federal government, and integrated the U.S. armed forces. Randolph had also hoped that the president would ask for legislation that would deny the protection of the National Labor Relations Act to labor unions that kept blacks from joining.[14]

FDR instead established a committee whose powers were mainly exhortatory, with the result that the FEPC was a dismal failure.[15] The remarkable economic gains that were made by African Americans in the war years—to be described below—were the result not of FEPC pressures but of an acute labor shortage that made it more difficult for employers to indulge in the luxury of refusing to hire qualified workers who had the "wrong" skin color. Southern whites generally opposed the FEPC as unwelcome federal meddling in their affairs, and southern congressmen carried on guerrilla warfare against the committee to keep its appropriations low. But, without much difficulty, they also lived with it. Its powers were slight, and its policies assumed that it was possible to fight employment discrimination without attacking segregation itself.

BLACKS IN UNIFORM

"Equal integration" of blacks in the U.S. armed services had been just as important to A. Philip Randolph as ending employment discrimination in defense plants and government agencies. The goal of desegregating the armed forces, though, had quietly disappeared from his agenda by the time he abandoned the protest, and for good reason. Today the U.S. military is seen as a major avenue of social mobility for African Americans, and something of a model for the larger society in its race relations. But in 1941 the armed forces were in the rear guard of social change. The military was deeply conservative in its ways, particularly on racial matters, partly because the top brass was drawn disproportionately from the South. As Randolph understood, abolishing segregation in an organization that would soon mushroom to include over 10 million Americans, one upon whose performance the fate of the nation depended, would have been a far more radical and politically explosive step than merely appointing a committee with a vague mandate to combat discrimination in government agencies and private firms with defense contracts.

Change was particularly difficult because the generals were not mossbacks out of touch with public opinion; in fact, they reflected that opinion reasonably well. And not just in the South. In the 1940s the study of public opinion was in its early stages, and few questions tapping racial attitudes were asked, but that omission was in itself suggestive—reflecting prevailing white complacency that race relations were not a cause for much concern.[16] Nevertheless, the fragmentary information that is available suggests broad national support for racial segregation in many areas of life, making it highly likely that the segregated military offended few whites. Only 46 percent of whites opposed having separate Jim Crow sections for blacks on streetcars and buses, for example, and 86 percent said that blacks should live in separate sections in cities and towns. Just 42 percent of whites polled in 1944 professed to believe that "Negroes should have as good a chance as white people to get any kind of job"; a clear majority thought that whites should get the "first chance" at jobs and were not ashamed to say so.[17]

Thus, it is not surprising that as the nation mobilized for World War II, the separate and unequal status of African Americans in the U.S. armed services was not seriously questioned by those in positions of power. Black leaders like Randolph might argue that the impending crisis required dramatic change so that democracy would at last become a reality for black citizens, but a large majority of whites simply refused to believe that African Americans had legitimate grievances. In fact, those in the military thought that blacks themselves were perfectly satisfied with their status. A 1943 survey of soldiers serving in the U.S. Army found that only a tenth of southern white servicemen and a seventh of northern whites in uniform said they believed that "most Negroes in this country . . . [were] dissatisfied," even though the black troops polled in the same survey displayed considerable resentment that they remained a subordinate racial caste.[18] Segregation allowed whites to remain ignorant of that black resentment; it thus served to keep intact white illusions about how African Americans felt about the racial status quo.

Roosevelt's view was that the U.S. had to win the war before it planned the future.[19] The leaders of the armed forces were even more dubious than the president about taking the lead in racial change. Judge William Hastie, an African American and chief advisor on black affairs to the secretary of war, prepared a long and thoughtful report calling for "the integration of the Negro soldier into the Army," but Chief of Staff General George Marshall dismissed it as an effort to solve "a social problem which [had] perplexed the American people throughout the history of this nation." The War Department, he went on, could not "ignore the social relationships between negroes and whites which have been established through custom and habit." Nor could it ignore the fact that "either through lack of educational opportunities or other causes the level of intelligence and occupational skill of the negro population is considerably below that of the white. . . ." "Experiments within the Army," he concluded, "in the solution of social problems are fraught with danger to efficiency, discipline, and morale."[20] Judge Hastie would soon resign in frustration over the Air Corps's insistence on racial segregation in all of its training.

More than a million black Americans served in the military during World War II, and yet the proportion of blacks who wore a uniform was well below that for whites. African Americans were almost 10 percent of the population recorded in the 1940 Census, but under 6 percent of the troops in the U.S. Army in 1942, and an even lower fraction of the personnel in the Navy.[21] By the war's end the proportion had risen, to 8.4 percent in the Army and 4 percent in the Navy. But it remained appreciably beneath the black proportion of military-age males in the general population.

African Americans were underrepresented in the armed forces, and those who did serve were generally consigned to unskilled tasks such as loading and unloading trucks, building roads, washing dishes, and working in the laundry. World War II, in this respect, was not different from World War I.[22] In part, poor education was the reason. Before the war the U.S. military required its personnel to have fourth-grade reading, writing, and math skills—hardly a stringent standard but one that affected a disproportionately high proportion of blacks, especially southern blacks. Among those who took the Army General Classification Test between March 1941 and December 1942, a staggering 49 percent of blacks scored in the bottom group, Class V, almost six times the proportion among whites. Six out of seven blacks but only a third of whites ranked in the bottom two classes, the category the Army believed suitable only for the most routine and undemanding tasks.[23]

The AGCT was not a test of raw "intelligence"; the ability of blacks to perform well was a direct function of where they went to school and for how many years. Those educated in the South's Jim Crow schools scored well below blacks with the same amount of education in a northern school.[24] But the officers who relied upon the tests in making assignments "consistently referred to AGCT scores as indexes of intelligence," and the tests served to reinforce very old stereotypes about the capability of black servicemen.[25] As manpower needs grew, recruiting standards were relaxed to allow 10 percent of the needed quota to be filled by men who were classified illiterate, but that small step was not sufficient to equalize the proportion of blacks and whites accepted.

Poor education did not entirely explain the concentration of blacks in lowly "black" jobs. In March 1945, 11 percent of the whites in the Army were officers but less than 1 percent of the blacks, a disparity that was much greater than that which separated white and black test scores.[26] A quarter of all the whites with a grade of I or II on the AGCT actually became officers, while only a tenth of the black top scorers attained that rank.[27] The Jim Crow constraints under which the military operated set severe limits on the number of black officers who could be absorbed. Officers unwilling to challenge caste prejudices refused to put blacks in positions in which they would be giving orders to white troops, fearing that it might provoke racial turmoil and even insubordination—clearly a possibility with respect to southern whites.[28] In addition, with both black and white officers eligible for assignment to black units, the number of slots available for African Americans eager for promotion was further limited.

The U.S. Army was still a Jim Crow institution in 1945 when the war ended, but there were a few small signs of impending change. Black and white liberals had suggested that the military experiment with integrated units, and while their advice was ignored in the early phases of the war, it was finally adopted when the need for infantry replacements in Europe became desperate.[29] In 1944, the Army deployed some platoons of black volunteers in white companies, a decision that worked out well, and helped pave the way for sweeping changes down the road.[30]

Even as a segregated institution, the military opened doors. The training in basic skills laid the foundation for further education. More important, southern blacks—pulled from the closed world of Cotton Belt plantations and small towns—had been exposed to the views of their northern brethren, who had entered the military with stronger expectations of fair treatment. The regional contrast in this regard was striking; to a remarkable degree African Americans from Dixie initially accepted the racial status quo. Surveyed in 1943, 61 percent of black soldiers from the North, but only 40 percent of those from the South rejected the official policy of racial separation. (More than 80 percent of white soldiers said that they favored segregation.)[31] Did 60 percent of southern blacks positively approve of segregation? Surely not, but they were apparently resigned to it. These African-American soldiers, it should be noted, were interviewed by black pollsters, so the results cannot be dismissed on the grounds that black respondents were lying to white interviewers.

Attitudes toward segregation varied as much with education as they did with the region from which the men came. Two-thirds of the southern blacks in the Army had not gone beyond grade school; only a third of this relatively uneducated group expressed opposition to segregation in the military. By contrast, 58 percent of southern black high school graduates objected. It was a difference that had important implications for the future. As levels of educational attainment continued to rise, so, too, would discontent with the

Jim Crow status quo. This was of course precisely what southern whites feared, which is why they tried to keep black education to a minimum.

For many northern blacks, being in the service was educational in a different and more distressing sense. Only 22 percent of blacks lived outside the South in 1940, but they were better able to meet the educational standards, and thus made up almost a third of the African Americans who served.[32] Although they had certainly encountered discrimination before in civilian life, being part of an institution organized on a segregated basis was unfamiliar and unwelcome. The problem was aggravated by the location of most training camps and military bases in the South, where the climate was more suitable for year-round outdoor activity. For many northern blacks this was their first exposure to southern mores. Wearing a uniform did not confer immunity from Jim Crow restrictions, as a young lieutenant named Jackie Robinson, who would go on to shatter the color line in professional baseball when he joined the Brooklyn Dodgers in 1947, found out. Robinson, who had grown up in California and was an all-American athlete at UCLA, was not prepared to obey meekly when a driver in Fort Hood, Texas, in 1944 ordered him to "get to the back of the bus where the colored people belong." He was court-martialed for his refusal but not convicted.[33] Not many northern blacks were willing to run the risk of actually defying segregation laws or customs like Robinson, although the experience of enduring their sting while serving their country produced a sense of outrage that would not be forgotten.

A surprising degree of optimism, however, accompanied the outrage. Asked whether black servicemen would be better or worse off in the long run after they got out of the military, 42 percent of the black soldiers polled in 1943 said "better off," and only 11 percent expected to be worse off. A broader question about whether "after the war Negroes in this country will have more rights and privileges or less rights and privileges than they had before the war" yielded almost identical responses. Forty-three percent said "more rights and privileges"; only 6 percent anticipated a diminution. A distinctly lower proportion of whites—29 percent—expected blacks to be better off. (A still lower fraction of whites—just 20 percent—thought that African Americans *should* have more rights and privileges.)[34]

The optimism expressed by these young black soldiers in the middle of the war stands in striking contrast to the fatalistic attitudes that John Dollard and other observers had found so pervasive in southern black communities in the 1930s. New ideas had been planted in the minds of many: that change was possible and that blacks had certain "rights and privileges." The ground had been laid for the revolution in race relations that would begin to unfold before long.[35]

ON THE HOMEFRONT

The war finally put an end to the Great Depression. The flood of orders for war matériel from Britain and France provided the first stimulus. America's own rearmament program supplied an even greater one. After the Japanese attack on Pearl Harbor in December 1941, the United States was at war in both Europe and Asia. War plants went on twenty-four-hour shifts, and 16 million men left the civilian labor force for the armed services, a number that amounted to almost 40 percent of the total number of men at work or seeking work in 1940.[36] The unemployment rate for nonfarm workers plunged from 25 percent in 1939 to 7 percent by 1942, and then to less than 2 percent by 1944, well below what economists consider the minimal "frictional" level caused by workers voluntarily shifting from one job to another.[37] Detroit's auto factories, now feverishly turning out planes, tanks, and jeeps, were even more desperate to find workers than they had been in the boom period of World War I and the 1920s, and so, too, were employers in other cities and other sectors of the economy.

The superheated war economy and the very tight labor market triggered a resumption of the northward migration of African Americans, this time on an even larger scale than before. A backlog of potential migrants in the South had built up during the 1930s, as landowners took acres out of production in exchange for New Deal subsidies and reorganized their operations so as to require less labor. The war created jobs outside the South—in the steel mills of Cleveland, the auto plants of Detroit, and the aircraft factories of Southern California. Southern cities were booming as well, and large numbers of African Americans left the southern countryside for destinations closer at hand. The farm population of the South plunged 20 percent between 1940 and 1945, while the number of southern city-dwellers grew by almost 30 percent, a rate of urban growth unparalleled elsewhere in the country in those years.[38] Manufacturing employment in the South rose by 50 percent, and wages soared.[39] Jim Crow racial bars remained strong in southern industry, and blacks were hired only as a last resort. But in such a labor-hungry economy employers often had no choice.

The tremendous growth of the black population in southern cities laid the foundation for the emergence of an aggressive civil rights movement with an urban base in the postwar years. In the meantime, however, many southern whites were dismayed at the sudden improvement in the position of black workers. It was startling that black men were no longer "available at will to do whatever work the white man wanted done at whatever price."[40] Nor were they as docile and submissive in other ways. Southern whites were shocked to find, a 1943 book reported, that blacks would sometimes come into a store, expecting to be waited on just as quickly as whites.[41]

The departure of black women from white kitchens was especially unset-tling. A plaintive letter in a small-town newspaper declared that "I just can't wait for this war to end" so that the servants would "come crawling back." (That few would ever "come crawling back" to such domestic jobs was incon-ceivable.) One white woman was in a rage because her cook, who had worked for her for twenty years for weekly wages under $5, had up and quit; the cook's two sons were supporting their mother with their Army wages.[42] The flight of such women from domestic service irrevocably changed the southern way of life.

Anxiety over this unprecedented development was at the root of a remark-able fantasy that flourished in southern white circles during the war. The servants, it was rumored, were all joining "Eleanor Clubs." These secret organizations were engaged in a plot to force white women back into the kitchen, to obtain much higher wages for domestics, and to make employers admit servants through the front door and call them Miss or Mrs. instead of using their first names. Members of "Eleanor Clubs" allegedly would not work for any family that criticized President Roosevelt or his wife.[43] This was all a delusion, but that it was widely believed may suggest that many southern whites sensed the new fragility of the Jim Crow system.

Other fantasies flourished. Local hardware stores were said to have run out of ice picks, blacks having purchased the entire supply to use against whites in an air-raid blackout.[44] Like the legend of the Eleanor Club, the Great Ice Pick Scare had not the slightest foundation in fact, but it is striking that such nightmare visions of black collective resistance to racial oppression were widespread more than a decade before large scale collective protest action actually began.

THE POSTWAR BOOM AND THE SECOND GREAT MIGRATION

Many Americans were convinced that at the end of World War II the economy would plunge back into depression, but their fears proved unfounded. Busi-ness continued to boom in the latter half of the 1940s and through much of the 1950s; wages rose steadily, and unemployment remained low. In the worst year of this period (1958), the jobless rate was less than half its level in 1940.[45]

In the South rapid industrial growth continued into the postwar period, and each year the region's economy more closely resembled that of the rest of the country.[46] In 1940 per capita personal income in the South was only 55 percent of the level in the rest of the United States. Two decades later it was up to almost three-quarters (73 percent) of the level elsewhere.[47] The back-ward South was at last catching up—quite rapidly. The "sleepy South" was giving way to the dynamic Sunbelt.

Southern blacks, though, were doing precious little catching up, and most of the nation's black population still lived in the South. In 1940, African-American men living in the southern states earned incomes that averaged just 43 percent of those of their white counterparts. Twenty years later the figure was a mere four points higher—47 percent.[48] The wartime labor shortage in agriculture that had benefited black workers turned into a peacetime surplus, pulling wages down again. The trend toward mechanized production that had begun during the Depression accelerated. Newly developed chemical herbicides reduced the need for stoop labor to kill the weeds. Mechanical cotton pickers—first put on the market by International Harvester in 1941 but not in general use until the 1950s—made it possible to do with few hired hands even at harvesttime. And yet another factor worked to break the old tie between black people and the cotton fields: in the postwar years cotton production throughout the South plunged in the face of competition from western states and from Africa, Asia, and South America.[49]

The results of these changes were fewer jobs and lower wages for black farm laborers, and less land that large owners were willing to put out to cash tenants and sharecroppers. Blacks who owned and operated their own farms were also displaced, because the new style of farming required capital they did not have. Some 3.5 million blacks lived on farms in the South on the eve of World War II; two decades later the figure had dropped to only 1.3 million.[50]

Black men and women displaced from farming in the course of this massive transformation did not have many alternatives close at hand. Although the southern economy was flourishing, the region's employers were as reluctant as ever to hire blacks except in the worst-paid jobs.[51] But only a day's ride away by train or bus, greater opportunities were available. In 1950 relatively uneducated young black men living in the North earned 55 percent more a year than African Americans in the South. Of course wages in general were higher in the more industrially developed North, but the difference between paychecks in the North and in the South was much greater for blacks than for whites. The regional wage differential for black men was two to three times as large as that for white men. For black women the difference between what they could earn in the North and in the South was even greater.[52]

Thus, the annual income of the typical African-American family, which usually included a working wife, was nearly twice as high (93 percent more) in the North as in the South in 1953, and in 1959 it was more than double (116 percent more). Family incomes were higher overall in the North, and the black income as a proportion of white incomes was also higher—75 percent in 1953, for example, as compared with only 49 percent in the South.[53] No wonder that huge numbers of African Americans pulled up stakes and made the short and relatively inexpensive journey.

Between 1940 and 1960 over 3 million African Americans moved north, and another 1.4 million followed during the 1960s. The Second Great Migration came to a halt by the end of the 1960s, and thereafter the current of black migration gradually reversed itself, with moves from the Snowbelt to the Sunbelt becoming more common than movement from southern to northern states.[54] Altogether, the Second Great Migration was *four times* the size of the earlier Great Migration, though it has received much less attention from historians. During the decade of the 1940s alone more than one-third of all the young blacks living in the Deep South states of Alabama, Georgia, Mississippi, and South Carolina left for the North.[55] For the South as a whole, 26 percent of African Americans aged twenty to twenty-four headed North between 1940 and 1950, and another 25 percent did so in the 1950s.[56] The black population of Michigan rose 113 percent in the 1940s and another 62 percent in the 1950s. For Illinois the rise was 67 and 61 percent; for the state of New York 61 and 55 percent.[57]

The migration northward by African Americans was one of three interrelated demographic shifts of the war and postwar decade (Table 1). Both the proportion of blacks living in the South and the fraction living on farms dropped dramatically; the fraction residing in urban areas soared. By 1960 the black population had become more urbanized than the white population, a striking reversal of the historic pattern that would become even more pronounced thereafter. A decade later 81 percent of African Americans lived in cities, as compared with only 72 percent of whites. By then the black farm population had virtually disappeared, having dropped to a mere 2 percent.[58] The association of blacks with big cities that we take for granted today is

Table 1
Residential Distribution of Blacks and Whites, 1940–1960

	BLACK	WHITE
Percent living in the South		
1940	77	27
1960	60	27
Percent living on farms		
1940	35	22
1960	8	7
Percent living in urban areas		
1940	49	57
1960	73	70

Source: U.S. Bureau of the Census, Current Population Reports, Special Studies, P-23-80, *The Social and Economic Status of the Black Population in the United States: An Historical View, 1790–1978* (Washington, D.C.: U.S. Government Printing Office, 1979), 13–14. The urban and farm populations together do not total 100 percent because some people were in a third category not included here—the "rural non-farm" population.

a phase of our history that began with changes set in motion during World War II.

Economic Progress

The Second Great Migration brought about an enormous improvement in the kinds of jobs held by African Americans and in the incomes they earned. In many respects the pace of progress was more rapid before the civil rights legislation of the early 1960s and the affirmative action policies that began in the late 1960s than it has been since. In 1940 more than four in ten black men (43 percent) worked in agriculture, and few of them were prosperous yeomen farm owners; they were mainly tenants, sharecroppers, or farm laborers whose incomes were pathetically low. By 1960 only one out of seven (14 percent) African American men still labored on the land, an immense change in a period of only twenty years. The huge black agricultural proletariat was well on the way to vanishing, and it would vanish altogether before many more years passed. Conversely, in 1940 only one out of ten black men had any kind of white-collar or skilled manual job, a rough but reasonably good indicator of what it means to be "middle class." By 1960 this middle-class group had expanded to include almost one in four (23 percent) African American males. The proportion of African-American men working as factory operatives almost doubled in these years as well, rising from 13 to 24 percent.[59] Semiskilled factory work, though often dirty and dangerous, meant membership in the stable urban working class, and was plainly a big step up from weeding a cotton patch.

The economic position of black women improved equally dramatically. In 1940 six out of ten were in a miserably paid, menial occupation: domestic service. By 1960 the proportion of African American women working as servants had been cut by almost half, to 35 percent. Some had taken factory jobs, but significant numbers had found more attractive options as clerical or sales workers. Such white-collar work had been almost completely closed to black women before World War II; only 1.4 percent held such jobs, as compared with over a third of employed white women. Two decades later the clerical or sales figure for black women was one out of nine, and another 6 percent were professionals, chiefly schoolteachers.[60]

In the boom times of the 1940s and 1950s, even those who did not move up into higher-ranked jobs managed to obtain much fatter paychecks. The incomes of both male and female black workers rose spectacularly. Between 1940 and 1950 the earnings of the average black man, in real dollars adjusted for inflation, went up a stunning 75 percent. They increased another 45 percent in the 1950s. In 1960 African-American men earned, on the average, a staggering two and a half times what they had earned on the eve of World

War II. Their incomes rose from $6,648 a year (in 1995 dollars) in 1940 to $16,851 twenty years later.[61] Black women matched these gains almost precisely. In 1960 their incomes were 2.3 times as high as they had been in 1940.[62]

Much of this progress, of course, was attributable to the healthy overall state of the economy. White workers were doing well in the period, too. But not nearly as well as blacks. The earnings of white men rose at only half the black rate in the 1940s (37 versus 75 percent) and at a somewhat lower rate in the 1950s as well. Thus, the racial gap in earnings narrowed considerably. Black male annual wages averaged 43 percent of those of white workers in 1940. By 1950 they were 55 percent as much, and by 1960 58 percent as much.[63] Black females made similar progress. At the end of the Great Depression they earned only 40 percent of what their white female counterparts took in; by 1960 that figure had risen to 61 percent.[64]

The incomes of black families rose equally impressively, which might seem inevitable if individual incomes for men and women were rising, but is not.[65] The median income of black families rose from just 41 percent of the white average in 1940 to 56 percent by 1960, and some of the remaining difference was due to the higher proportion of black single-parent families, mainly headed by mothers.[66] (Already in 1960 almost a quarter of black families had only one parent, triple the proportion for whites.)[67] Thus, although the income of the average black family was still well below the white average, the more significant fact was that it had more than doubled in the two decades from 1940 to 1960. The economic circumstances in which the typical black American lived were no longer "pathological," as Myrdal had found them to be in the late 1930s. More dollars meant better housing and clothing, better diets, greater access to medical care—a variety of material comforts previously far out of the reach of most black Americans. The shift from sharecropper or farm laborer to factory worker also meant shorter hours, less sheer drudgery, and much greater freedom to engage in social and political activity. It was the equivalent of being liberated from serfdom.

One of the simplest and clearest indicators of what these gains meant was that, in 1940, African Americans had a life expectancy at birth of just 53.1 years, 11 years less than whites. Over the next two decades black life expectancy rose by 10.5 years, while the figure for whites advanced by little more than half that much.[68] The gains were apparent, too, in the large numbers of African Americans who were finally able to realize the American dream of owning a home. At the end of the Great Depression, fewer than one in four (23 percent) of the dwellings occupied by blacks were owner-occupied; by 1960 the figure had jumped to almost four in ten (38 percent). The proportion of white homeowners was increasing, too, in this affluent period (from 46 to 65 percent), but at a considerably slower pace, and thus, while the black homeownership rate had been only half that of whites in 1940, by 1960 the figure had risen to almost two-thirds.[69] Home ownership is a vital sign of arrival in the middle class, and by this measure the black middle class was swelling rapidly.

While the African-American middle class was expanding, the proportion of blacks stuck on the very bottom rung of the social ladder was shrinking. The 1940s and 1950s saw a striking decline in black poverty, well before the federal government launched a War on Poverty, outlawed discrimination in employment, and mandated affirmative action in employment and education. Three out of four black families in the United States had incomes below the poverty line in 1940, and by some poverty measures the rate was even higher than that. During the World War II decade the black poverty rate fell by 17 points, and in the 1950s it plunged to 39 percent. By 1960 the proportion of black families who had incomes below the poverty line had fallen from three out of four to four out of ten—from the great majority to a distinct (though still large) minority. For African-American families consisting of two parents living together, the poverty rate in 1960 was 33 percent—significantly lower than the overall rate of 39 percent.[70] About half of the previously impoverished black population climbed out of the ranks of the poor in these two decades, a more rapid advance in the struggle to combat poverty than that made in subsequent years.

Amid all these signs of progress, there was one seeming turn for the worse: a steep rise in black unemployment relative to that of whites. But it was somewhat deceptive. The overall jobless rate fell precipitously with the end of the Great Depression, of course—more so for whites than blacks, however. In 1940 the unemployment rate for blacks was only 15 percent higher than it was for whites. A decade later it was 84 percent higher, and by 1960 it was more than double the white rate (10.2 percent versus 5 percent).[71] Unemployment rates in this case, though, are not a very good measure of well being. Desperate black men in the Depression years could usually find someone to take them on as a farmhand, and black women could count on a few dollars a week if they were willing to cook and clean from dawn till dark for a white family. That kept the unemployment rate for African Americans down, but the jobs were so unattractive that classifying those who held them as "employed" seems overly generous.[72]

Progress over the two decades from 1940 to 1960 was thus impressive, by almost every significant measure. And yet blacks remained far behind whites economically. Their earnings in 1960, for example, were about 40 percent less, on the average, and they were more than three times as likely to live in families with incomes below the poverty line (39 versus 12 percent). They were still twice as likely to be unemployed. Why the continuing disparity? Part of the explanation is education, which we discuss below. But discrimination in the labor market played a part as well. That was especially true in the South, where community custom, worker resistance, and their own prejudices kept employers from hiring and promoting people solely on the basis of merit. The situation was better in the North, where the racial gap in earnings (always smaller) shrank further in the years 1940 to 1960. Black men living in the midwestern states earned 67 percent as much as whites in 1940 and 77 percent as much by 1960, while those in the South made much smaller gains.[73]

EDUCATIONAL ADVANCES AND PROBLEMS

The better picture in the North was still not good, in great part as a consequence of the inadequate education blacks received. In 1940 the average African American aged twenty-five to twenty-nine had only gone through seven years of school, 3.6 years less than the typical white (Table 2). More than a quarter had less than five years of schooling, compared to a mere 3 percent of whites. Fewer than one in twelve blacks had completed four years of high school, as opposed to four out of ten whites. For blacks in their early working years, this obviously was a huge handicap in the job market. For example, most white-collar jobs required at least a high school diploma; the supply of black workers who could meet that criterion was very small. In fact, the huge differential for people in this age group in 1940 would continue to

Table 2

Years of School Completed by Race, for Persons 25–29, 1940–1960

	BLACK	WHITE
Percent with less than 5 years		
1940	27.0	3.4
1950	16.1	3.3
1960	7.2	2.2
Percent with 4 years of high school or more		
1940	12.3	41.2
1950	23.6	56.3
1960	38.6	63.7
Median years of school completed		
1940	7.1	10.7
1950	8.7	12.2
1960	10.8	12.3

Source: National Center for Educational Statistics, *Digest of Educational Statistics: 1995* (Washington, D.C.: U.S. Department of Education, 1995), 17. These census tabulations on educational achievement are for "Negroes and other races." But the number of Asians and American Indians in the country in these years was too small to distort the picture very much.

pull down average wages for blacks for decades to come, since these workers would typically remain in the labor force until at least the 1970s.

The next two decades brought striking educational advances for blacks. The proportion in the twenty-five to twenty-nine age bracket with less than five years of schooling shrank dramatically, and the proportion completing high school more than tripled. Whites gained an average of an additional 1.5 years in median schooling between 1940 and 1960; blacks gained no less than 3.7 years, which cut the racial gap by more than half, to just 1.5 years.

This remarkable change reflected the heavy investment southern states suddenly decided to make in their Jim Crow schools. Between 1940 and 1954, per-pupil expenditures on instruction in black schools (in constant dollars) almost *tripled* (they rose by 288 percent), while spending on white schools increased by only 38 percent.[74] Southern whites had not become conscience-striken. The economic boom and the Second Great Migration created labor shortages, and spending on schools for blacks was seen as a way of stemming the flow of black workers out of the region.[75] In addition, southerners were afraid—properly so—that courts would intervene if educational opportunities were not made more equal. In the early 1930s the NAACP had launched a series of legal challenges to Jim Crow education, and in a 1938 decision involving segregation in higher education, the Supreme Court had indicated that it would look more closely at the equality in "separate but equal."[76] By the 1940s minimally prescient public officials saw the scary possibility of *Brown* on the legal horizon. The spending spree on black schools was designed to avert it.

The gains registered by young blacks in these years were auspicious, but they revealed changes in the quantity of schooling, not in the quality. The question of real interest to an employer is not how many *years* a job applicant spent in school but how much they *learned* while they were there. How did the education received by the average African American stack up against that of the average white? Systematic evidence is lacking for the 1940s and '50s, but the results of a major 1965 study by sociologist James S. Coleman doubtless apply for these years as well. Coleman conducted a massive national test of how much American students at various grade levels knew for the U.S. Department of Health, Education, and Welfare. The Coleman report examined pupils in the first, third, sixth, ninth, and twelfth grades. It found that racial inequalities in facilities, teacher salaries, and the like were not as large as most observers had assumed, but that the racial gap in basic reading and mathematics skills was enormous (Table 3). For example, southern black twelfth-graders who lived in small towns or rural areas scored nearly *four years* behind white youths living in similar places in reading, and almost *five years* behind them in mathematics. After twelve years of school, they performed at the level of white pupils in the seventh or eighth grade. Black twelfth-graders from southern metropolitan areas were about a year ahead of

Table 3

Educational Performance of Black Twelfth-Graders in 1965:
Grade Levels Behind Whites, by Region and Metropolitan Status

	READING	MATHEMATICS
Nonmetropolitan South	3.9	4.8
Metropolitan South	3.5	4.4
Metropolitan Northeast	2.9	5.2

Source: James S. Coleman et al., *Equality of Educational Opportunity,* U.S. Department of Health, Education, and Welfare, Office of Education (Washington, D.C.: U.S. Government Printing Office, 1965), 274–275.

their black rural and small-town counterparts in reading and half a year ahead in math; metropolitan schools were thus clearly better. But these students were also far behind whites. Even black pupils attending the much better schools in the cities of the Northeast were almost three years behind their white peers in reading competence and more than five years behind in math, though they scored well ahead of southern blacks.

The racial gap in the incomes of black and white workers will not be closed as long as there remains a large racial gap in the education of the two groups, with education measured not in terms of years spent in a classroom but in terms of mastery of basic educational skills. We will look in detail at how much has been accomplished on this front in Chapter 13.

THE EXPANDING GHETTO

In 1940 blacks were not big-city dwellers. Only 13 percent lived in the nation's largest urban centers. Of the ten biggest cities, only Baltimore, St. Louis, and Philadelphia had a substantially higher fraction of black residents than the 10 percent figure for the nation as a whole (Table 4).

With few exceptions, however, the African Americans who moved north during the Second Great Migration headed for the biggest cities. By 1960 more than a sixth of all American blacks were clustered in New York, Chicago, Philadelphia, Detroit, and Los Angeles. Only in Boston was the black proportion of the population lower than in the United States as a whole. In fact, at the time of the riots of the 1960s, the black big-city population had been growing so dramatically that many observers predicted black majorities in the near future—a prediction that proved unfounded for reasons explored in Chapter 8.

The influx of blacks into Chicago and other large urban centers did not erase the color line that had been drawn during the initial Great Migration of

Table 4
Growth of the Black Population of the Ten Largest Cities in 1940, 1940–1960 (numbers in thousands)

	1940		1960		
	Number	*Percent*	*Number*	*Percent*	*Percent increase*
New York	458	6.1	1,089	14.0	+138
Chicago	277	8.2	813	22.9	+194
Philadelphia	251	13.0	529	26.4	+111
Detroit	150	9.2	483	28.9	+222
Los Angeles	64	4.2	335	13.5	+423
Cleveland	85	9.6	251	28.6	+195
Baltimore	166	19.3	326	34.7	+96
St. Louis	109	13.3	215	28.6	+97
Boston	24	3.1	63	9.1	+163
Pittsburgh	62	9.3	101	16.7	+63

Sources: U.S. Bureau of the Census, *Sixteenth Census of the United States: 1940: Population,* vol. 2, 114; U.S. Bureau of the Census, *Statistical Abstract of the U.S.: 1974* (Washington, D.C.: U.S. Government Printing Office, 1974), 22–24.

the World War I era, although the precise location of that line was still constantly shifting. As had been true earlier, the newcomers were too numerous to be packed into neighborhoods already designated as black turf, but their movement into "white" areas led not to racial integration but to a quick tipping from white to black. The boundary between white and black simply moved; the "Black Belt" became larger, but it stayed about as black as ever. The pattern of racial segregation by neighborhood—described in Chapter 2 —remained pretty much unchanged from the 1920s through the 1950s.

Thus, in a period of rapid change there were also elements of depressing continuity. If a few black families did manage to slip into a "white" neighborhood, panic would set in, with the result that many whites would put their homes on the market at once, hoping to sell before prices declined drastically. In the ensuing white flight, such fears were realized: prices did often plunge. For ordinary working families, their house was the largest investment they would ever make, and they were understandably concerned to protect it. Tragically, that concern led most of them to assume that people with a different skin color should be confined to "their own" neighborhoods, far from where whites resided.

Blacks and whites lived separately; nevertheless, the arrival of blacks fueled racial tensions. Conflict was particularly acute in Detroit, whose factories required many new workers to produce the tanks, jeeps, and airplanes needed to win World War II. More than 250,000 migrants crowded into Detroit in the early years of the war, with virtually no new housing to accommodate them. Many were black; many of the rest were southern whites, who had no experience dealing with blacks in the absence of Jim Crow rules. In February 1942, city officials announced that a new federally funded public housing project, located in a largely white neighborhood far from the ghetto, would be reserved for black tenants. A crowd of angry whites determined to keep blacks out of the project—the Sojourner Truth Homes—threw bricks at incoming tenants, overturned moving vans, and attacked the young black men who gathered on the scene.[77] The police broke up the melee before it became a full-scale race riot, arresting over two hundred blacks but only a few whites, even though most of the violence had plainly been white-initiated. Detroit policemen (virtually all of them white) acted as if they believed their duty was to protect whites from blacks rather than to preserve the peace. The Sojourner Truth Homes did open for black occupancy a few months later, but only with the aid of a formidable armed guard of local police and state troops.

The racial tensions that boiled up in this turf war took a more destructive form in the Detroit race riot of June 1943, the bloodiest racial clash in the United States from the time of the Chicago riot of 1919 to the 1965 Watts uprising.[78] Fighting between small groups of blacks and whites broke out on a hot Sunday evening at a park on Belle Isle, an island in the Detroit River. It then spread into the city, accompanied by the looting of stores and burning of buildings. Crowds of blacks dragged whites from their cars and beat them; white mobs did the same to blacks. Six thousand federal troops had to be called in before order was restored. As had been the case in the battle at the Sojourner Truth Homes, the Detroit police sided with the white rioters. A photograph in the Detroit Free Press showed an elderly black man in the grip of two police officers while a white rioter punched him in the face. Seventeen of the twenty-five African Americans killed in the disturbance were shot by the police; not one of the nine white victims was cut down by a police bullet.

The Detroit story, fortunately, was unique. The only other violent racial incident remotely comparable to it in these years was a much smaller riot in Harlem the same year, which left six people dead. It is impressive that World War II did not see a repeat of the bloody race riots that had broken out in the World War I era in Chicago, East St. Louis, Omaha, Knoxville, Philadelphia, Tulsa, and Washington. White racial attitudes had become more civilized in this elemental respect. Not until the 1960s would large-scale riots reoccur, and as we shall see, by then their character had radically changed.

The Growing Black Influence in Politics

The black migrants who fled the South in the 1940s and 1950s came from communities that had prevented most of them from voting, running for office, or serving on juries. Public life was for whites only. Although African Americans often encountered racial hostility and discrimination in the big northern cities in which they settled, they were not similarly excluded from politics. Quite the contrary. Politicians competed for their votes.

As it happened, black votes were of growing importance in national politics in these years, because the vast majority of African-American migrants who fled the South in the Second Great Migration (87 percent of them) settled in just seven key states—New York, New Jersey, Pennsylvania, Ohio, Illinois, Michigan, and California. These seven states combined had populations large enough to give them almost three-quarters of the number of electoral votes needed to win a presidential election. What is more, the political balance in those strategic states was exceptionally close.[79] The switch of even a relatively small voting bloc could thus make a decisive difference in the outcome. In the 1948 presidential race, for example, the margin of victory was a mere 7,000 votes in Pennsylvania, 18,000 in California, 34,000 in Illinois, and 36,000 in Michigan. In 1960 the margin in Illinois was just 9,000 votes, in New Jersey 22,000, in California 36,000.[80] In the North blacks suddenly found themselves with political leverage they had never had before.

Even in the South, African Americans were gradually beginning to make their voices heard in politics, despite the barriers designed to keep them silent. Professors at the college founded by Booker T. Washington at Tuskegee, Alabama, were not "literate" enough to impress the chairman of the local Board of Registrars that they were qualified to vote. "If a fella makes a mistake on his questionnaire," he said with a grin, "I'm not gonna discriminate in his favor just because he's got a Ph.D."[81] The registrar in another Alabama community did not even pretend to impartiality in administering the law; he declared bluntly that "there ain't a fuckin' nigger in this end of the county who'd so much as go near a ballot box."[82]

The social-control mechanisms that kept blacks from the polls were strongest in rural areas and small towns, though, and stronger in the Deep South than in the Rim South and the Border states. In urban environments the threat of economic coercion against those who dared to appear at a registrar's office was less effective. Residents were too anonymous and institutions too numerous and varied to allow a system of intimidation in which "uppity" blacks would lose their jobs and their credit. The migration of blacks into southern cities during the World War II decade thus did much to spur their political participation. Well under 100,000 voted in the 1940 elections; in 1952 the number of voters was over a million.[83] By 1956, 1.24 million African Americans were registered in the South, about a quarter of the black voting-age population. One-quarter was far below the white registration rate of 60 percent, of course, but it was a giant step forward.[84] In a few instances, black voters were even electing African Americans to office. Two won seats on the Nashville city council in 1948, for example, and another was elected to the city council in Richmond, Virginia.[85]

The entry of southern blacks into politics was also facilitated by a crucial 1944 Supreme Court decision, *Smith v. Allwright*, which forced states to allow blacks to vote in primary elections. As noted in Chapter 2, the Democratic primary in the one-party South was in fact the only meaningful election; the general election in November simply ratified its results. In 1935 the Court had ruled that political parties were private associations, to which constitutional constraints did not apply.[86] But *Smith v. Allwright* abandoned the fiction that a political party was no different from a church or a social club, and signaled a new willingness on the part of the Court to interpret more expansively the constitutional guarantees extended to black Americans by the Civil War Amendments.

The legal challenge to the white primaries had been conducted by attorneys working for the Legal Defense Fund of the NAACP, an organization whose following expanded dramatically in the war and immediate postwar years. In 1940, the NAACP had 355 local chapters and 50,000 members; by 1946 it had three times as many chapters and nine times as many members.[87] The organization's national office concentrated its efforts on fighting discriminatory policies and practices in the courts, but its local branches also organized picket lines, protest demonstrations, and letter-writing campaigns aimed at influencing public opinion.

Although a large majority of its members were African American, the NAACP was a biracial organization, and its impressive membership gains symbolized the new centrality of the civil rights cause to American liberalism as it developed in the war and postwar years. The NAACP continued to follow its tradition of having a white president, a practice that it continued until the 1970s. Moreover, a substantial portion of the NAACP's operating funds had always come from contributions provided by liberal whites.

Blacks drew political strength as well from their new association with the labor movement. Organized labor was making dramatic gains in membership in these years; between 1935 and 1945, union membership rose from 3.5 million to over 14 million, the greatest advance for labor organization in American history.[88] The traditional craft unions in the American Federation of Labor (with rare exceptions) had barred blacks from membership and viewed them as potential scabs who might be hired by employers seeking to break a strike. But the Congress of Industrial Organizations (CIO), organized during the Great Depression, was different. Its leadership was eager to attract black members, even though rank-and-file whites were not equally eager to have them. Employers who gave good jobs to African Americans could thus expect trouble from their white employees. In the early years of the war tens of thousands of white union members in Detroit's defense plants staged massive spontaneous "hate strikes" to protest the promotion of black workers, seriously disrupting war production.[89] But the leaders of the United Auto Workers backed the employers in these conflicts and refused to countenance racist wildcat strikes. Their courage improved the image of organized labor in the black community. The number of black labor-union members rose from 600,000 in 1940 to 1,250,000 by the war's end.[90] This penetration of organized labor by black workers not only advanced the economic interests of the group; it also gave African Americans increased political leverage within the emerging liberal wing of the Democratic Party.

That wing became an increasingly important political force in the postwar years. It lacked the votes in Congress to keep alive the federal Fair Employment Practices Commission; southern Democrats, who controlled key committees in Congress, were able to kill the FEPC off as soon as the war ended. But several northern states created their own antidiscrimination agencies, with New York taking the lead. By 1960 such bodies existed in no fewer than 17 states.[91] What is more, most cities of any size (except in the South) established citizens' committees on race relations; more than two hundred were in existence as early as 1945.[92]

Franklin Roosevelt's successor, Vice President Harry S. Truman, was a Border-state Democratic politician who had shown some courage in backing antilynching legislation (not a cause popular with Missouri whites), but was otherwise an unknown quantity on civil rights issues. While Roosevelt could attract black votes without advocating civil rights policies that would alienate large numbers of southern whites, Truman could not. Lacking FDR's charisma, he was forced to make a painful choice between placating the white South with its attachment to states' rights, or courting blacks and other members of the liberal coalition. He chose the latter, knowing he needed the northern black vote, and that it could not be had without a strong civil rights record. Blacks, after all, had not one, but two other choices: a return to the party of Lincoln or defection to the Progressive Party of Henry Wallace, with its strong civil rights voice.

After six blacks were lynched in Georgia and Tennessee and a black veteran was blinded by a policeman in South Carolina, Truman appointed a group of eminent liberals to a President's Committee on Civil Rights, picking up on an idea that FDR had considered but rejected. The committee's 1947 report, *To Secure These Rights*, adopted the analytical framework and endorsed the conclusions set forth in Gunnar Myrdal's *An American Dilemma*, published just three years earlier.[93] Racial segregation and discrimination were inconsistent with what the report called "traditional American morality" and what Myrdal had termed "the American Creed." It was time for the nation to live up to its ideals.[94] Glossing over three centuries of slavery, disfranchisement, and Jim Crow, the authors concocted an American moral tradition by reading the past selectively, emphasizing things that fit with contemporary racial liberalism and ignoring all those that did not. Its fictitious history aside, the report did persuasively argue that racial discrimination was immoral, and that the federal government should do more to combat it.

In early 1948, Truman laid out a civil rights program based on the recommendations in the 1947 report. He announced that he would soon issue executive orders to eliminate segregation in the armed forces and to secure equal opportunity in federal employment, and asked Congress for a federal antilynching law, an end to discrimination in interstate transportation, a ban on poll taxes, and a permanent FEPC. The legislative requests were symbolic gestures. The Republicans controlled both houses of Congress, and no bold new legislative initiative on civil rights could survive the opposition of a coalition of conservative Republicans and southern Democrats. In fact, after backing these proposals, Truman got cold feet and did nothing to advance them.

Since any federal effort to protect black civil rights was completely unacceptable to southern whites, the 1948 Democratic convention was the scene of a furious battle over the platform.[95] The northern liberal wing of the party, led by Minneapolis Mayor Hubert Humphrey, demanded an endorsement of the program Truman had announced but failed to pursue. Adding weight to the liberal demand was another threatened protest, again organized by A. Philip Randolph, against Jim Crow practices in the military. He would urge young black men to defy the draft, about to be reintroduced. Blacks should "refuse to fight as slaves for a democracy they cannot possess and cannot enjoy."[96] As in 1941, it was not a threat to be taken lightly. The Cold War was escalating, and the United States was claiming the role of leader of the free world, mobilizing its resources for a great ideological and military struggle against Communism. If significant numbers of black youths had actually chosen to go to jail rather than serve in a largely segregated army, the nation's enemies could claim a huge propaganda victory.

At the convention Democratic Party liberals got the civil rights planks they wanted, but the price of victory was a split in the party. The delegates from Mississippi and half of those from Alabama walked out, and formed the new States' Rights Democratic (Dixiecrat) Party. With the South in revolt, Truman moved to shore up his support in the white liberal and black communities by issuing his long-awaited executive orders barring discrimination in federal employment and the armed services. In October he gave a major speech in Harlem, the first president ever to speak there. The gamble paid off. Although the Dixiecrat candidate, South Carolina governor Strom Thurmond took 39 electoral votes from Alabama, Louisiana, Mississippi, and South Carolina, Truman still eked out a victory in November, winning 69 percent of the black vote.

The Truman order directed at the armed forces called for equality and led to the appointment of a presidential committee; it did not explicitly mandate the elimination of segregation in the military. And yet it was strong enough to provoke criticism from General Omar Bradley, the chairman of the Joint Chiefs of Staff. Echoing the arguments advanced by General Marshall at the beginning of the war, Bradley insisted that the armed services were no place to conduct social experiments. Desegregation would come to the military when it came to the rest of the United States and not before.[97] Although military officials continued to drag their feet for more than a year, by 1950 civilian officials in the Department of Defense prevailed. Immediate steps were taken to integrate all military units.[98] Integration thereafter proceeded quickly and smoothly, and the armed services were transformed into perhaps the most thoroughly integrated American institution.

THE INTEGRATION OF PROFESSIONAL SPORTS

Racial barriers to black participation in professional sports—still firmly in place at the close of World War II—quickly collapsed soon after the war. By far the most popular spectator sport was professional baseball, and the American and National Leagues were for white players only. It was perhaps a sign of progress that the baseball commissioner denied that the sport was segregated; at an earlier time he might have felt free to admit it. But in 1942 he asserted that "there is no rule, formal or informal, or any understanding—unwritten, subterranean, or sub-anything—against the hiring of Negro players by the teams of organized ball."[99] It was transparently obvious, though, that there was some sort of gentleman's agreement on the matter, because there were star black players in the Negro leagues who certainly looked as skillful as white major-leaguers. African-American baseball players who could have made the major leagues were having to settle for one of the all-black teams, where both the salaries and the level of competition were lower.[100]

The owners of American and National League teams refused to avail themselves of the opportunity to pick the best ballplayers regardless of race, out of fear that putting blacks on the field would offend white fans and players. Most white players were happy to be protected from competition with black athletes who might take their jobs away from them. And as long as all ball clubs abided by the white-only custom, racist hiring policies placed none at a competitive disadvantage. About a third of the players in organized baseball (the baseball system organized by whites, that is) were from the South, and might well have gone on strike had the unwritten racial rules changed.

Unless it is imposed by law, employment segregation can only be maintained as long as no employers decide that tapping the hitherto unused talent of people from the excluded group would be to their competitive advantage.[101] In baseball the solid front was broken by Branch Rickey, the general manager of the Brooklyn Dodgers, who had a hunch that adding exceptional black athletes to his team would draw additional black spectators to Ebbets Field. He believed, too, that if any of the team's white fans were bigoted enough to boycott the games, they wouldn't stay away long; with its new black players the Dodgers would win more games, and winning teams were what the public came to see.

Jackie Robinson was Rickey's choice to break the color line. Robinson had been a prodigiously gifted athlete in college. In addition to starring in baseball at UCLA, he had been an all-American football player, twice the top-scoring basketball player in the Pacific Coast Conference, and the NCAA champion in the broad jump. He even won the Pacific Coast intercollegiate golf championship![102] His refusal, while in the Army, to follow a bus driver's order to "get to the back of the bus where the colored people belong," demonstrated that he had the guts and determination to be able to run the gauntlet of racist insults that would be hurled at him when he became the only African-American player in major-league baseball.[103]

Before Jackie Robinson played his first game as a Dodger, in 1947, some of his teammates did their best to prevent it, circulating a petition protesting the use of a black player. Manager Leo Durocher exploded when he learned of the protest. "I don't care if a guy is yellow or black, or has stripes like a fuckin' zebra," he told his players. "I'm the manager of this team, and I say he plays." He advised the dissidents to "wipe your ass" with the petition, because Robinson was "going to put money in your pockets and money in mine."[104]

Robinson quickly became an all-star, and the Dodgers moved to recruit other outstanding black players as well, including Roy Campanella and Don Newcombe. Integrating the team did indeed "put money" in the pockets of both the players and the owners. In the ten seasons Robinson played for the Dodgers, they won six National League titles, a record to which the black members of the team significantly contributed. African-American players won five Most Valuable Player awards and four Rookie of the Year awards.[105] In 1959 the last all-white baseball team—the Boston Red Sox—acquired a black player and completed the integration of the major leagues.

The color line crumbled in other sports as well. The National Football League actually was ahead of baseball in making the change; in 1945 the Los Angeles Rams signed two black players, Kenny Washington and Woody Strode. But professional football had much less of a following in the pre–television age than it now does, and the break with tradition received far less publicity than the Jackie Robinson story. In basketball, the sport most dominated by black players today, none of the teams in the two professional leagues that merged to form the National Basketball Association in 1949 had any black players. The NBA opened the doors almost immediately, and by the 1950–1951 season had three African-American players.[106]

Robinson and other black pioneers in professional sports encountered vicious attacks and slurs on and off the field. But they persevered and emerged triumphant from the struggle. Demonstrating great courage as well as athletic skill, they did much to shatter invidious white stereotypes about African Americans. That it "was only a game" may have made their examples all the more persuasive. "By applauding Robinson," one sportswriter observed, "a man did not feel that he was taking a stand on school integration or on open housing. . . . [Nevertheless,] to disregard color even for an instant [was] to step away from old prejudices."[107] In the ensuing years many white youths would grow up with posters portraying black sports stars on their bedroom wall, making it hard to endorse racist claims about the inferiority of blacks; they knew the superior accomplishments of a Jackie Robinson, a Willie Mays, or a Hank Aaron.

REMARKABLE CHANGE

No one in the 1930s predicted the remarkable change in the status of black Americans about to take place. The unprecedented progress of the 1940s and 1950s was not, for the most part, the product of deliberate decisions by government officials or by the leaders of organizations seeking to change public policy. Hundreds of thousands of African Americans uprooted themselves from the land of their birth and headed north in response to painful pressures and tempting new opportunities, transforming the southern "dilemma" into a national issue. The ideological imperatives of a war against Nazi racists contributed to popular acceptance of Gunnar Myrdal's optimistic view that racism was inconsistent with the American Creed. Overt white racial prejudice was gradually waning, and doors that had long been closed to blacks were beginning to open. The black poverty rate plunged; the black homeownership rate soared.

We emphasize these facts about the postwar years because too many discussions of current racial issues draw a misleading picture. Discussions of race are drenched in history—historical references frequently lace discussions of current policy. In fact, history—it is fair to say—is a striking preoccupation in civil rights circles, where some spokesmen equate term limits for officeholders and opposition to busing with the terror and violence of the KKK in the Jim Crow South.[108] History is an obsession and yet the historical record is too often distorted.

Take the issue of affirmative action. Almost all advocates assume that the status of blacks changed very little until the 1960s, and that most black economic advance is the result of the race-concious, preferential policies that have been widely adopted by public authorities, private businesses, and universities over the past quarter of a century. "Everybody who is a person of color in this country has benefited from affirmative action," the mayor of Atlanta said in June 1996. "There's not been anybody who's gotten into a college on their own, nobody who's gotten a job on their own, no one who's prospered as a businessman or businesswoman on their own without affirmative action," he went on.[109] But that is not the case. Immense progress was made by black Americans before the idea of racial preferences was seriously entertained by anyone. By some measures, in fact, the pace of black progress was more rapid in the 1940s and 1950s than it has been since.

This is not to imply, of course, that public policy was irrelevant to the condition of black people. The racial segregation that was the organizing principle of southern society had largely been created by law—by Jim Crow codes. African Americans had been stripped of the right to vote by law—and by discriminatory enforcement of the law. The Supreme Court had allowed Jim Crow to become embedded in the legal fabric by persuading itself, in *Plessy*, that the Fourteenth Amendment did not preclude racially separate public institutions and facilities as long as they were "equal." Policies mandating segregation had made enormous differences in the lives of ordinary people. And so, too, did the reversal of those policies in the 1950s and 1960s.

CHAPTER FOUR

Amazing Patience

ON JANUARY 9, 1961, Charlayne Hunter and Hamilton Holmes broke the color line at the all-white University of Georgia. Six and a half years after the Supreme Court had declared segregated schooling unconstitutional, two students (as Charlayne Hunter-Gault later put it) dared to define their rightful place, indifferent to white wishes. Charlayne had flown in from Detroit, where she had started her college education. At the airport she "could see in the eyes and on the faces of Black skycaps and porters, maids and janitors . . . prideful brightness. . . . *Our time has come,*" they knew.

> It would be the last time that whites could demand of me or any other Black person what they had demanded of Blacks since slavery—that we diffidently accept the secondary and inferior role they had consigned us to, under the paternalistic assurance that everything would be all right as long as we stayed 'in our place.' "[1]

It would not, of course, be the last time that whites would tell blacks to stay in their white-assigned place, but by 1960 that demand had begun to fall on less receptive ears. Their time—one of psychological as well as institutional transformation—had indeed come. The Supreme Court's unanimous decision on May 17, 1954, in the case of *Brown v. Board of Education* had been a true watershed moment. It began a process of irrevocable change in the South, changing white lives, of course, as well as black. "I have sometimes been asked whether, as a white child in the South of the late '40s and early '50s, I thought segregation was wrong," the constitutional scholar Walter Dellinger wrote on the fortieth anniversary of the Court's historic ruling. But it wasn't a question that made much sense before the spring of 1954. "Segregation was a fact about my universe," Dellinger recalled; "it seemed no more 'right' or 'wrong' than the placement of the planets in the solar system. It simply was."[2]

No legal decision in American history has had greater impact on the life of the nation, and none has provoked more controversy. Nine justices, as Dellinger noted, "turned Jim Crow from a social fact into an inescapable and powerful moral question."[3] The Court was not alone; other players would soon appear on the civil rights stage. But in the beginning was *Brown*.

BROWN

Brown v. Board of Education declared state-imposed, de jure segregation in the public schools a violation of the Fourteenth Amendment. Separating children on the basis of race denied black pupils "equal educational opportunities" and hence deprived them of the "equal protection of the laws."[4] It was a ruling that applied to more than 10 million children who were enrolled in single-race schools in twenty-one states and the District of Columbia. They made up roughly 40 percent of the nation's public school students, and more than two-thirds of all African-American pupils.[5] In the long run, the impact of the decision would be even greater than these figures would suggest; later judicial interpretation extended the concept of illegal segregation to cover schools that had never segregated pupils by law.

The students who were immediately affected by *Brown* lived mainly, but not entirely, south of the Mason-Dixon line, as the map makes clear. The Court's decision was the fruit of two decades of effort on the part of lawyers working for the NAACP. Since the early 1930s they had focused their energies on proving that Jim Crow schools did not meet the legal test set forth in *Plessy v. Ferguson*—that they were separate but far from "equal." The legal arm of the NAACP, its Legal Defense and Education Fund, won a long series of such cases, obtaining court orders to increase the salaries of black teachers and to build new schools for black children.[6] But such victories only chipped away at extraordinarily hard rock; plaintiffs in every suit had to prove specific inequities—the lack of adequate funding, for instance, in particular all-black schools.

As Chapter 3 suggested, these decisions—and the fear of worse yet to come—were enough to persuade racist southern legislators that major changes were needed. Perpetuating the glaring inequality, they began to understand, could imperil the very principle of separate schools. But their efforts at reducing that inequality by spending more money on black schools came too late to rescue the *Plessy* doctrine. There was a brief stay of execution in 1950, when two key decisions involving graduate education stopped short of simply throwing out "separate but equal." But it was clear that *Plessy's* days were numbered.

The Court's 1896 decision was particularly vulnerable to attack in the realm of graduate education, since southern states often failed to establish any publicly funded institution of higher education open to blacks. When the

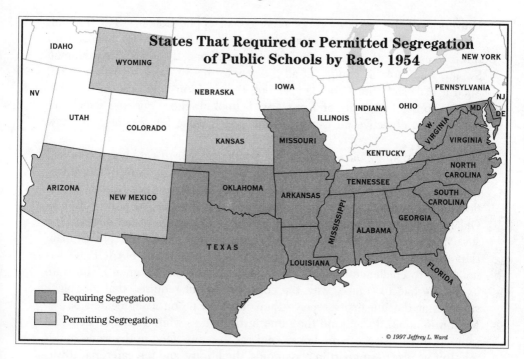

States That Required or Permitted Segregation of Public Schools by Race, 1954

Requiring Segregation

Permitting Segregation

© 1997 Jeffrey L. Ward

Note: Black and white children were required to attend separate schools by state law in all of the southern and border states, and by an edict of Congress in the District of Columbia, which was then governed by Congress. Arizona, Kansas, New Mexico, and Wyoming were in another category. Although they did not mandate racial segregation in the public schools of the state, they allowed local authorities to establish single-race schools if they so wished. No school district in Wyoming was operating segregated schools in 1954. Topeka, Kansas, the residence of Linda Brown, the plaintiff in the *Brown* case, had racially separate elementary schools, but its secondary schools were integrated. Until 1949, Indiana was like Arizona, Kansas, New Mexico, and Wyoming in allowing segregation as a local option. Sixteen states had laws forbidding school segregation and in the remaining eleven the law was silent on the matter; Gerald N. Rosenberg, *The Hollow Hope: Can Courts Bring About Social Change?* (Chicago: University of Chicago Press, 1991), 42; J. Harvie Wilkinson III, *From Brown to Bakke: The Supreme Court and School Integration, 1954–1978* (New York: Oxford University Press, 1979), 194.

University of Texas Law School received an application in 1946 from an African American, the state created a new law school just for blacks, with three rooms and three part-time faculty members. It didn't satisfy Heman Sweatt, who took his complaint all the way to the Supreme Court and won. Such a makeshift Jim Crow law school, the decision held, was inescapably inferior to the University of Texas Law School in "those qualities which are incapable of objective measurement but which make for greatness in a law school."[7]

From the point of view of the white South, the *Sweatt* case was a very bad omen. If the equality promised in *Plessy* was to be strictly interpreted, it was doubtful that any school for blacks only could pass muster. Another case decided the same day reinforced that doubt. Because no black institution in Oklahoma offered a doctorate in education, a district court had ordered the state university to accept George McLaurin, a sixty-eight-year-old black man. (His advanced age was a distinct advantage in the eyes of the NAACP; he was not likely to challenge the caste system by dating white women.) The state legislature had to comply with the court order, but required that any black students at the university receive their instruction "on a segregated basis." McLaurin could thus attend the same institution as white students, hear the same lectures, use the same books, and eat the same food in the same building. But he was to sit apart in classrooms, the library, and the cafeteria. It was a ludicrous definition of equality, and the Supreme Court declared the whole arrangement unconstitutional.[8]

Brown v. Board of Education was one of four cases challenging the constitutionality of segregated public schooling—from Kansas, Virginia, South Carolina, and Delaware—that were consolidated by the High Court. The Court chose the Topeka case to focus on. Eight-year-old Linda Brown had been barred from attending the all-white elementary school just four blocks from her home in Topeka. Her parents and the local branch of the NAACP sued on Fourteenth Amendment, equal-protection grounds. They struck out in the federal district court that first heard the case; the Kansas law segregating students was plainly constitutional under the *Plessy* rule. But was the 1896 decision still good law? Not in the context of public education, the Supreme Court held. For all intents and purposes, "separate but equal" was dead.

Brown broke dramatically with earlier rulings. In this instance, the Court said, "the Negro and white schools involved have been equalized, or are being equalized, with respect to buildings, curricula, qualifications and salaries of teachers, and other 'tangible' factors."[9] That satisfied the *Plessy* test. But, the Court concluded, "in the field of public education the doctrine of 'separate but equal' has no place. Separate educational facilities are inherently unequal."[10]

Surely that was the case, and it is hard to imagine the Court having reached any other conclusion. To have upheld the Kansas law that forced Linda Brown to attend an all-black school across town was out of the question. But, as many critics have argued, Chief Justice Earl Warren's opinion was brief, bland, and ambiguous. Some commentators—thinking wishfully—hailed the decision as a historic vindication of Justice Harlan's magnificent dissent in *Plessy*, which declared the Constitution "color-blind." But the *Brown* Court made no mention of Harlan. The NAACP had explicitly argued that "the Fourteenth Amendment has stripped the state of power to make race or color the basis for governmental action," but the Court refused to make that the controlling principle.[11] The attorneys for Linda Brown (and other children) got the decision they wanted, but not the reasoning they urged. As one scholar has noted, "The Court was prepared to announce new law for a new day but not to justify its doing so."[12]

Brown remains the most important Supreme Court decision in this century. It marked the beginning of the end of the Jim Crow South. But it was not the end of all laws separating the races, and indeed the Court was clearly aware of the limits of its power. To have barred racial classifications as a basis for governmental action—as the NAACP had urged—would have meant, for instance, that state laws forbidding interracial marriages were also unconstitutional. Neither in 1954, nor for thirteen years thereafter, was that an issue the Court was willing to take on. *Brown* was ahead of the public opinion curve, but not way ahead. School desegregation was one thing; black-white weddings quite another. The first national survey on interracial marriage, conducted in 1958, found that no more than 4 percent of whites approved.[13]

Declaring the Constitution "color-blind" would likely have had another long-term effect: later race-conscious policies would have run into constitutional trouble.[14] No court could have approved race-based hiring at the Kaiser Aluminum & Chemical Corporation; in Boston, Judge Arthur Garrity could not have ordered busing to achieve racial balance in the public schools. Both involved racial classifications, of which Justice Harlan (it seems safe to say) would not have approved. In his view, the right of individuals to be treated without regard to race was a moral and political end in itself.

The view of the *Brown* Court was quite different. Segregated public schools were unconstitutional, Chief Justice Warren said, not because racial classifications in the law were in themselves pernicious, but because school segregation was psychologically harmful to black children. Separating black pupils "from others of similar age and qualifications solely because of their race generates a feeling of inferiority as to their status in the community that may affect their hearts and minds in a way unlikely ever to be undone." "Separate educational facilities" were "inherently unequal" and thus violated the guarantees set forth in the Fourteenth Amendment.

In 1954 many Americans were not convinced that segregation positively harmed black pupils. The Court said they were wrong, resting its argument on what Warren called "modern authority"—specifically the authority of recent scholarly writings by social scientists, including Myrdal's *An American Dilemma*. The research the Court cited was well regarded by most social scientists of the day, but Warren took a decided risk in grounding a fundamental reinterpretation of the Constitution on sociological work that might not withstand the test of time. What, for example, if later scholarship suggested that black children scored higher on standardized tests when taught in black-run schools that hired only black teachers? Would such a sociological finding require still another rereading of the nation's fundamental law—indeed perhaps a return to pre-*Brown* separatism?

THE VERDICT IN THE COURT OF PUBLIC OPINION

Brown has often been credited with opening the eyes of white America to the evils of Jim Crow and awakening the conscience of the nation. The Court, Walter Dellinger has said, turned Jim Crow "into an inescapable and powerful moral question." But not one that immediately took ordinary Americans by moral storm, it is important to note. On the basic question of whether there should be separate schools for blacks and whites, the country was split right down the middle. Only half of the nation's whites, and a mere 14 percent of those living in the South, wanted an end to separate Jim Crow schools (Table 1). Even in the North, only six out of ten residents believed in schools open to both races. That was up substantially from the 40 percent figure recorded in 1942, to be sure, but it nonetheless indicated considerable resistance to the idea even in parts of the country in which black and white children did in fact routinely attend the same schools.

Another 1956 poll provided a more nuanced understanding of public opinion on the issue. It found that no more than 11 percent of whites could be characterized as impatient liberals, people who thought that racially separate schools in all parts of the country could be and should be eliminated immediately.[15] Another 24 percent could be called patient liberals; they favored making "every attempt" to do away with separate schools, but felt that "a

Table 1

Percent of Whites Who Believed That "White Students and Negro Students Should Go to the Same Schools," 1942–1956

	ALL	SOUTH	NORTH
1942	30	2	40
1956	49	14	61

Source: Herbert H. Hyman and Paul B. Sheatsley, "Attitudes Toward Desegregation," *Scientific American* 211 (July 1964), 18.

reasonable time" had to be allowed to work out the problem. The liberal 35 percent of the white public (the two groups together) was thus pretty solidly in favor of abolishing legally mandated separate schools, though divided about how quickly it might be accomplished.

At the other end of the spectrum was a somewhat larger fraction of the white population—40 percent—that was adamantly opposed to *Brown*. Four out of five southerners were in this "segregation forever" camp. They believed that the decision was "a mistake," and felt that white and black students should "never be forced to go to the same schools." That left a quarter of the population in the middle, convinced that "the time may come" when children of both races would attend the same schools, but that it would "take years in some places and it shouldn't be pushed." They vaguely endorsed the elimination of schools for one race only but did not regard it as a burning moral imperative.

One bright spot was to be found in white responses to another question concerning race and education—whether blacks had the same intellectual potential as whites. If African Americans lacked the necessary genes to perform at a high intellectual level, separate schools for them might make sense. Thus, it was particularly striking and important that the proportion of whites who believed that blacks had the same intellectual potential as whites rose dramatically in the war and postwar years (Table 2). Between 1942 and 1956, the fraction of whites who viewed blacks as endowed with equal intelligence rose from only four out of ten to three out of four. The liberalization of opinion in the North was impressive, but the shift in southern white opinion was most remarkable. In 1942, only one southerner in five believed that the two races were equal in intellectual capability; just fourteen years later it was a solid majority, three out of five.

This quiet revolution in attitudes attracted little attention at the time, but it was of great significance. Southern whites still continued to favor segregated schools, and many did their best to frustrate the Supreme Court's efforts to put an end to them. But well before that battle was lost, a majority had lost faith in a key tenet upon which the case for segregation rested. If black pupils truly could "learn things just as well if . . . given the same education and training," it was hard to see why local governments should go to all the extra trouble and expense of running an entirely separate school system for them.

Surprisingly, black support for *Brown* was not wholehearted either. The Reverend Martin Luther King, Jr., and his close associate, Rev. Ralph Abernathy agreed on the indispensability of the *Brown* decision, which "had altered forever the conditions on which the continuing struggle would be predicated."[16] But their view was not shared by all African Americans. A great many southern blacks—the people in whose name the NAACP had been conducting its legal crusade against Jim Crow—had serious reservations.[17] A November 1955 poll showed that only a bare majority—53 percent—of the African Americans living in the South approved of the Supreme Court's his-

Table 2

Percent of Whites Who Believed That Blacks "are as intelligent as white people—that is, can . . . learn things just as well if they are given the same education and training," 1942–1956

	ALL	SOUTH	NORTH
1942	41	21	47
1946	52	30	61
1956	77	59	83

Source: Hyman and Sheatsley, "Attitudes Toward Desegregation," 35–39.

toric ruling.[18] These results mesh with the evidence from World War II noted earlier, which indicated that a majority of southern black soldiers were not opposed to segregation in the military.[19] On the other hand, the decision was strongly backed by those in the younger age brackets, by the more educated, and by those living in cities—precisely those elements of the black population that would soon become active in building a mass movement to destroy Jim Crow.[20]

The lukewarm backing for *Brown* among both whites and blacks was reflected in the cautious reactions of the other two branches of the federal government. President Eisenhower refused to make a public statement backing the decision. He claimed that it would "lower the dignity of government" for a president to affirm or attack Supreme Court decisions. But in private Eisenhower expressed the belief that *Brown* was wrong, that forcing change too quickly would "set back progress in the South at least fifteen years."[21]

The leader of the Democratic Party and Eisenhower's opponent in the 1952 and 1956 presidential races—former governor of Illinois Adlai Stevenson—was no more positive. Indeed, he tried harder than Eisenhower to placate southern whites, speaking out against using federal troops to enforce school desegregation and opposing a bill that would have made eligibility for federal aid to education contingent upon a district's having complied with *Brown*. In private correspondence Stevenson worried about the "extremism" of "Negro leaders" and fumed about "NAACP stubbornness."[22]

The sentiments of Eisenhower and Stevenson were those of the majority in Congress, which failed to demonstrate any leadership in support of the decision. And thus the high Court found itself all alone, occupying what it felt to be the moral high ground but with very little company.

BROWN II AND THE BACKLASH

The nine justices may not have studied the public opinion polls, but they knew that their decision would not have much long-run impact unless it was ratified in the court of public opinion. In their deliberations about the case they spoke as if they were reflecting public opinion rather than leading it, referring frequently to such advances as the recent integration of the armed services as evidence that white attitudes toward blacks were becoming more liberal.[23] But they did understand that the racial integration of every public school could not be achieved suddenly by the mere wave of a judicial wand. Thus, they took a full year to mull over how to implement their very general ruling before issuing a second opinion in the case.[24]

Brown I stated the principle; *Brown II* was a guide to implementation, and it sent a signal of extreme patience and considerable flexibility. To begin with, the task of determining what desegregation remedy was appropriate in each community and of setting a realistic timetable for implementing that remedy was left to local federal district judges. As a result, individual black parents had to bring complaints on a case-by-case basis when local authorities were indifferent to the law. In the course of the prolonged struggle that followed, the NAACP had to assume the burden of initiating desegregation suits in more than two thousand southern school districts.[25]

In addition, the Court ordered districts operating single-race schools to proceed toward dismantling their dual school systems "with all deliberate speed." "With . . . speed" would seem to have meant expeditiously, but in fact the permission to proceed at a "deliberate" pace was the more important message. In the Border states, where black population concentrations were smaller and the caste system was not as rigidly enforced, desegregation did proceed with some dispatch and little conflict. But in the eleven ex-Confederate states "deliberate" meant not slow but stop. There, a full decade after *Brown,* a mere 1.2 percent of black public school students attended schools that had *any* white pupils at all.[26] Desegregation, one observer remarked, was proceeding with "the pace of an extraordinarily arthritic snail."[27]

The overwhelming majority of southern whites were outraged at the Court's order to revamp their school systems. A few optimists who favored the decision predicted that opposition would soften with the passage of time, but it did not. To the contrary. Five years after *Brown,* resistance had actually increased; the proportion of white southerners who said they approved of desegregating the schools had actually *fallen,* from 15 percent to 8 percent.[28]

With so many southern white voters firmly committed to school segregation (and with few blacks allowed to vote at all), it was not surprising that the political leaders of the region were almost unanimous in condemning the Court's ruling. Most had held their fire when the decision was first announced, since it was only a statement of principle and included no timetable for enforcement. In March 1956 though, three-quarters of the southern members of the U.S. House of Representatives and all but three southern senators endorsed the "Southern Manifesto," a public statement that denounced *Brown* as an exercise of "naked power" with "no legal basis."[29]

This gesture of defiance by a large majority of southerners holding national office reflected the power of a new grassroots organization that had spread like wildfire in the wake of *Brown*—the white Citizens' Councils. The inspiration for their formation came from a pamphlet denouncing the *Brown* decision by Mississippi Judge Tom Brady. Brady's *Black Monday* displayed the obsessive sexual fear that the specter of integration had always triggered in the South. In his superheated imagination, racially integrated schools somehow threatened the purity of white womanhood. It would be far better to abolish the public school system altogether, Brady contended, than to submit to plans that would endanger "blue-eyed, golden-haired little girls" by putting them in the same classroom with African-American children.[30] Some followers of Brady claimed to have evidence of a sinister plot to put black dolls in the nurseries of white churches, a move that would brainwash the innocent white children who played with them into thinking that race-mixing was natural. The chief justice of the Florida Supreme Court declared that "fish in the sea segregate in schools of their own kind," and that people of different races naturally preferred separate schools for the same reason.[31]

For all of the fiery rhetoric in *Black Monday*, it made a shrewd tactical point. Brady insisted that opponents of *Brown* should not attempt to revive the dormant Ku Klux Klan, and should instead form an entirely new organization to resist racial change—an organization less violent, more respectable, and thus more likely to attract a broad following. The first Citizens' Council chapter was formed in Indianola, Mississippi, in July 1954, and hundreds of others emerged soon after.[32] The Councils were as committed to white supremacy as the KKK, but less crude in their methods. Their strategy, as one of their leaders in Selma, Alabama, put it, was to "make it difficult, if not impossible, for any Negro who advocates desegregation to find and hold a job, get credit, or renew a mortgage." Thus, in Selma, after twenty-nine blacks signed a petition protesting Jim Crow, sixteen were quickly thrown out of work. In Yazoo City, Mississippi, fifty-three African Americans endorsed an antisegregation statement; forty-seven withdrew their names after local Citizens' Council leaders informed them of the price they would be made to pay.[33] Economic pressure was more effective than running around at night wearing white sheets and burning crosses, and it was perfectly legal.

Not every southern white was a die-hard segregationist, but all were under enormous pressure to rally round the flag. Roy Harris, president of the Citizens' Councils of America, declared bluntly that "if you're a white man, then it's time to stand up with us, or black your face and get on the other side."[34] The Councils demanded "absolute conformity from whites and abject submission from Negroes."[35] Even the great novelist William Faulkner was thrown off-balance by the powerful emotional currents swirling around him. Although Faulkner conceded that "the Negroes are right" and southern whites were "wrong" on civil rights issues, his southern patriotism and his rage at what he considered Yankee meddling drove him to say that if he had to make a choice, he would follow the path taken by Robert E. Lee—who resigned from the U.S. Army to take command of the military forces of the Confederate States of America when the Civil War began.[36]

THE MONTGOMERY BUS BOYCOTT

Although white defenders of "the southern way of life" had formidable power and few scruples about using it, by the 1950s they no longer held all the cards. Ever since blacks were driven from the polls and subjected to Jim Crow laws at the turn of the century, the voice of African Americans in the South had been ruthlessly silenced. The occasional rebels who dared to complain of racial injustice were easily squelched. The system seemed impervious to pressures for change from within. John Dollard's *Caste and Class in a Southern Town* made the pattern of black-white relations in Indianola, Mississippi, look strikingly similar to the caste system of traditional India, a system which had lasted thousands of years. Dollard suggested that the forces that ensured white supremacy and black subordination in the South were so deeply rooted that change could happen only at a glacial pace, if at all. It was inconceivable to Dollard, and indeed to almost all American social scientists in those years, that within two decades tens and tens of thousands of southern black people would rise up in resistance.[37]

Dollard's book would not have provided a reader anything that would have proved very useful in understanding the chain of events that began unfolding in the Alabama state capital, Montgomery, on 1 December 1955. Rosa Parks, a forty-two-year-old black woman, boarded a bus after finishing work as a seamstress in a downtown department store.[38] She took a seat that—according to the local segregation ordinance—could be used by a black person only when no white passenger wanted it. It was neither in the front (reserved for whites) nor in the back (assigned to blacks), but in the "no-man's-land" middle, where blacks could sit when all the whites had already been seated. If additional whites boarded the bus, however, blacks who had ventured forward into no-man's-land were required to surrender their places and stand in the rear aisle.[39]

After a white man boarded the bus on that December evening and found no vacant seat in the front section reserved for whites, the driver turned to Rosa Parks and the other three black passengers seated in the row just behind the white section and asked them to get up and move to the rear, where there was standing room only.

Three of the four blacks seated in the row that the driver ordered cleared did comply with his demand, but Mrs. Parks refused, and the driver had her arrested for violating the segregation ordinance. Contrary to legend, Rosa Parks was not an ordinary, anonymous working woman who ran afoul of the law one day simply because she happened to feel too tired to give up her seat. Although her defiance of the driver's orders on that particular day was apparently not planned, she was a veteran political activist who had often been involved in discussions of how the segregation ordinances might be challenged.[40] She had been the secretary of the Montgomery chapter of the NAACP for a dozen years, secretary of the statewide Alabama State Conference of NAACP branches, and an active member of the Women's Political Council, a group organized after the Montgomery League of Women Voters refused to admit black women as members. In fact, December 1, 1955, was not the first time that Montgomery blacks had chosen to defy Jim Crow rules on the buses. Mrs. Parks herself had objected to giving up her seat to a white several times before, although in the past she had been kicked off the bus rather than arrested. The driver who removed her on one of those earlier occasions was the same one who finally had her arrested.[41]

The arrest of Rosa Parks was designed to send a clear message to other blacks who might be tempted to disobey when ordered to turn over their seats to whites. The news that Mrs. Parks was behind bars (a dangerous place for a southern black person to be), did not have its intended effect, however. In one of those fascinating and mysterious moments in history, the system of social control that had worked effectively for many decades suddenly broke down. Instead of intimidating Montgomery's African Americans into compliance with the law once again, the arrest of Rosa Parks was the catalyst for a defiant, determined, and disciplined mass movement.

The leaders of the multitude of churches and civic organizations in black Montgomery had not displayed much unity in the past. Just a few months before the arrest of Mrs. Parks, an effort to form a "Citizens Coordinating Committee" that would bring the city's black leadership together had collapsed as a result of what a dismayed newcomer to the community called "crippling factionalism." The Montgomery black community "was marked by divided leadership, indifference, and complacency."[42] It was an inauspicious setting for the extraordinary action soon to follow. But the chairman of the local branch of the NAACP, trade union leader E. D. Nixon, helped to persuade Mrs. Parks to fight the case in court. And the Women's Political Council, led by faculty members at the local black college, quickly printed fifty thousand flyers announcing a boycott of all Montgomery's buses on December 5.[43]

Montgomery's black community could never have been mobilized behind the boycott of municipal buses without the backing of most of the African-American churches, traditionally the chief source of leadership for the group. In the past black clerics had often been criticized for stressing the other-worldly consolations of religion, overlooking social injustice in the here and now. Whatever the merits of that charge in previous circumstances, it was not one that could be made this time around. In 1955, Montgomery's African-American ministers showed themselves eager to demonstrate that religion could be a powerful force for social change.

Among the black clergymen who joined in the debate on how to respond to the jailing of Rosa Parks was a twenty-six-year-old graduate of the Boston University Divinity School who had recently taken up the pulpit at the Dexter Avenue Baptist Church—the Reverend Martin Luther King, Jr. When an organization to carry out the bus boycott was formed—the Montgomery Improvement Association—King was named its head. He was a newcomer to Montgomery, but that seeming liability was in fact an asset. He had not been in town long enough to have made many friends—or many enemies.[44]

Under King's leadership, what started as a one-day gesture of protest against the mistreatment of black people on local buses became a major long-term commitment, supported by almost the entire black community, which accounted for 37 percent of the city's population and about three-fourths of its regular bus patrons. When the initial boycott produced no response from local authorities, the Montgomery Improvement Association pledged (from its position of extraordinary strength) that it would continue until black passengers were assured of better treatment. The sight of empty buses rolling through black neighborhoods led one woman to remark gleefully that the buses that went by her door were "as naked as can be."[45] Car pools were organized to take care of those in desperate need of a ride, but most of the boycotters simply walked to their destinations. The Montgomery police did their best to put the car pools out of business by arresting drivers for petty, sometimes altogether imaginary, traffic violations. King himself was hauled off to jail on one occasion for allegedly driving at thirty miles an hour in a twenty-five-mile-an-hour zone.[46] But these efforts at harassment were ineffective.

At a mass meeting called to decide whether to continue the boycott, King warned whites that a new day was dawning—that blacks would no longer tolerate being treated as second-class citizens. And he told his fellow blacks that change would never come unless they had the courage to stand up for their rights, regardless of the cost. "We are here this evening," he declared,

> to say to those who have mistreated us so long that we are tired—tired of being segregated and humiliated; tired of being kicked about by the brutal feet of oppression. We had no alternative but to protest. For many years we have shown amazing patience. . . . But we come here tonight to be saved from that patience that makes us patient with anything less than freedom and justice.[47]

Although this was a radical and unflinching challenge to the principle of white supremacy, the concrete changes the organizers of the boycott sought at the outset were remarkably modest. King spoke passionately of the need to obtain "justice on the buses of this city," but by "justice" he did not mean an entirely desegregated bus system. The principal demand of the boycotters at this point was only that Montgomery adopt the somewhat milder form of segregation that was used on the buses in Mobile, Alabama.[48] In Mobile your race determined where you were allowed to sit when you first boarded, but no African American was required to move after having settled into a seat.[49]

The boycott began, then, as a call for better treatment within the framework of "separate but equal." Its organizers launched no principled attack against the whole notion of assigning seats on a bus on the basis of race. In fact, it could even be argued that their demands, by making the system seem a bit more fair, would have given the segregation some additional life.[50] That is precisely why the NAACP refused at first to help with Mrs. Parks's appeal. The organization would not intervene in a case that seemed to be "asking merely for more polite segregation."[51]

The mildness of the initial demands is particularly striking in light of the fact that by December 1955 the principle of segregation in public facilities was being challenged across the South in a variety of ways. *Brown*, after all, had recently sounded the death knell for state-imposed segregation in public education, and its basic message—separate is not equal—could not be confined to schooling. Thus, a week after its 17 May decision, the Court made clear the applicability of *Brown* to a case involving the admission of black patrons to a theatrical performance. Other decisions quickly followed giving blacks access to public beaches and bathhouses, municipal golf courses, and other facilities.[52] Furthermore, just six days before Rosa Parks defied the Montgomery ordinance, the Interstate Commerce Commission, endorsing arguments made by the NAACP, had outlawed racial segregation on all trains and buses traveling across state lines, and in the waiting rooms of the stations they used.[53] Given this trend, the initial demands in Montgomery were remarkably moderate and restrained. It was a "lowest common denominator" strategy. To unite the previously fragmented black community, the movement would push only those demands that hardly anyone could object to.

The protest escalated into a fight for the complete abolition of bus segregation only after two months of futile negotiations with city authorities made their intransigence all too clear. The bus company itself might have welcomed a settlement; with 75 percent of its patrons walking to work, it was running in the red. Privately owned, it was dedicated not to the cause of segregation but to its financial bottom line. (Similarly, the railroad involved in the *Plessy* case opposed segregation; it was a costly nuisance forced upon the company by the politicians.) But the politicians didn't care about the company's balance sheet. They cared about votes—that is, white votes. And whites, with few exceptions, had no sympathy for black demands. In fact, the mayor, all three members of the city commission, and several other public officials belonged to the local chapter of the Citizens' Council, whose membership quickly reached 12,000, more than a quarter of Montgomery's adult white population. Not surprisingly, these officials were determined not to give an inch.

The possibility of reaching a negotiated settlement vanished altogether after a grand jury issued criminal indictments against no fewer than eighty-nine of

Montgomery's black citizens (twenty-four of them ministers) for conspiring to boycott in violation of a 1921 statute.[54] But again, the attempt at repression only strengthened the protest effort. For the first time, the Montgomery story became front-page news in several national newspapers, which in turn increased the flow of outside contributions to the movement.[55]

Once it was agreed that the objective was to abolish segregation, not to make it a little more comfortable, the NAACP's lawyers were happy to do the necessary legal work. Shifting the struggle into a federal courtroom was a momentous and revealing development. Southerners had always insisted that they were capable of resolving racial conflict without the interference of outsiders—judges, in this instance. But the surge of white rage that led to the mushrooming of Citizens' Councils poisoned the political climate; the South, in fact, did not have the capacity to save itself.[56]

It was during the Montgomery boycott that Martin Luther King first articulated the principle of nonviolent resistance so integral to the success of the civil rights movement. And yet it is important to recall that King was not fully committed to nonviolence when the Montgomery struggle began. Although he had been attracted to Gandhian ideas in his student days, in 1955 he apparently believed that "the only way we could solve our problem of segregation was an armed revolt."[57] Painfully aware that black men who defied southern racial mores could expect to be the victims of violence, he had armed guards to protect his residence, and kept a gun at home.

King became a convinced advocate of nonviolence only after experiencing violence directed against his wife and infant daughter. On January 30, 1956, just a few hours after the Montgomery Improvement Association decided to sue the city in federal court, a stick of dynamite exploded on his front porch. No one was hurt, but a furious crowd of blacks, many of them armed, quickly gathered outside the house. King, who had been off at a meeting, arrived on the scene to hear one of his supporters tell a policeman, "You got your .38 and I got mine, so let's battle it out."[58] The incident drove home the obvious point that "an armed revolt" would mean blacks pitted against a white population that outnumbered them ten to one. Rejecting violence as an instrument not only gave civil rights advocates the moral high ground; it was a pragmatic necessity. King calmed the angry crowd that night by warning that "he who lives by the sword will perish by the sword"; "love your enemies," "meet hate with love," he urged. He disarmed his own guards and got rid of his gun.[59]

The boycott finally came to an end after 381 days, but not because either side had lost its will to fight. In June 1956 a three-judge federal panel ruled that the racial segregation of Montgomery's buses was unconstitutional, and in November the Supreme Court affirmed the decision. The boycott officially continued until December 21, 1956, when the court order took effect and King and other supporters of the movement, black and white, boarded a bus and occupied the front seats.[60]

The rage that the boycott had stirred up did not suddenly evaporate with the legal decision. Two days after integrated buses started running, in the middle of the night, someone fired a shotgun through King's front door. A few days later snipers fired upon three buses. More than a dozen prominent blacks had their cars splashed with acid. In early January 1957 four black churches and the homes of both Ralph Abernathy and Robert Graetz (the leading local white minister in the Montgomery Improvement Association) were bombed. Two men were eventually arrested and tried for the bombings. But despite overwhelming physical evidence and their own confessions, a jury refused to convict them.[61]

Montgomery's blacks had won a great victory, of course. But the victory could not be credited to the boycott. The courts would have rendered precisely the same verdict even if there had been no mass protest movement. From one perspective, a boycott in Baton Rouge, Louisiana, three years earlier had been much more successful. The city held out only ten days, and then decided to adopt a Mobile-style, first-come first-served segregation plan.[62] But the Montgomery protest was of far greater historical significance. Not only did it achieve real desegregation; it started a movement that, in King's words, "would gain national recognition; whose echoes would ring in the ears of people of every nation; a movement that would astound the oppressor, and bring new hope to the oppressed."[63]

Montgomery was where King happened to live, and that, too, heightened the boycott's significance. His charismatic presence and exceptional oratorical skills were vital in keeping the spirits of his followers in Montgomery high enough to continue their sacrifices month after month; that it endured so long made the Montgomery struggle much more dramatic and newsworthy than the brief spasm of protest in Baton Rouge. Most important, his personal magnetism and radiance made for intensive coverage in the national and international press. In 1956, *Time, Life,* and *Newsweek* tripled their coverage of civil rights topics, with most of the rise in the number of articles due to the Montgomery protest.[64] The media's fascination with King was greater than a number of other movement leaders thought justified.[65] He had become a national celebrity, the subject of a cover story in *Time* and the focus of a long article in *The New York Times Magazine.* He went on *Meet the Press,* only the second African American ever to appear as a guest on that show.[66] Every move he made thereafter generated publicity. His ability to keep the press corps following him, to make headline news, to fill churches and lecture halls, and to inspire contributors made him the civil rights movement's most important single asset until his assassination a dozen years later.

As the news of what was happening in Montgomery spread, donations came in from as far away as India and Japan. But the bulk of the money came from church groups around the United States, particularly black churches.[67] African Americans throughout the land were inspired to see so many of their brethren refusing to be "kicked about by the brutal feet of oppression," enduring great personal hardship in hopes of obtaining racial justice. "There is a new Negro in the South," King declared, "with a new sense of dignity and destiny."[68]

BIRTH OF A MASS MOVEMENT

The victory in Montgomery increased King's determination to struggle. Just three weeks after he rode triumphantly down that city's streets seated at the front of a bus, he was off to Atlanta for a meeting with other southern black clergymen and veteran northern civil rights activists from the NAACP and CORE (the Congress of Racial Equality). It resulted in the formation of an important new civil rights organization, the Southern Christian Leadership Conference (SCLC), with King at its head.[69]

SCLC was quite unlike existing civil rights organizations. Although local chapters of the NAACP often engaged in social and political action, the national office focused its main efforts on defending and advancing black rights through the courts. The NAACP had provided indispensable legal aid to the Montgomery Improvement Association, once the MIA had decided to raise the stakes and fight for something more than a kinder and gentler segregation. But NAACP leaders were distinctly cool to the idea of pursuing the struggle for equal rights in the streets. CORE, a largely white organization of radical pacifists founded in Chicago in 1942, was keen on direct action of the kind carried out in Montgomery. But CORE had only a tiny membership and virtually no support at all from southern blacks.

The Southern Christian Leadership Conference was the first civil rights organization led by black residents of the South, and the first to concentrate all of its attention on fighting Jim Crow within the region. Defenders of the "southern way of life" had often tried to minimize the significance of civil rights protests by claiming that local black citizens were not unhappy and that the apparent trouble had been stirred up by "outside agitators." That charge was much less plausible when directed against an activity organized by SCLC. Whatever criticisms might be made of SCLC, it was plainly not controlled by northern interlopers.

SCLC was also very different from other civil rights organizations in being firmly rooted in the black churches of the South, which meant that its potential constituency was the huge population of African-American churchgoers. All but one of the nine top leaders of SCLC, and thirteen of the sixteen in the second echelon, were ministers.[70] SCLC was "the decentralized political arm of the black church," a "preacher organization."[71] Its founders grasped that the church was "the most stable social institution in Negro culture," and built their movement upon that foundation.[72] No secular political group could draw crowds that would begin to compare with those that flocked to the churches Sunday morning. Community gatherings sponsored by SCLC were more like revival meetings than political meetings, with fiery sermons and an abundance of hymns.

SCLC conducted a wide variety of programs at the local level. It ran workshops that trained citizens in the tactics of nonviolent protest. It organized campaigns to combat segregation on buses and in other public facilities. It orchestrated voter registration drives. It assisted parents considering school segregation complaints to ensure the enforcement of *Brown*. All of its activities had the larger aim of liberating southern blacks from the fatalistic belief that they were powerless, and of creating what King had called "a new Negro . . . with a new sense of dignity and destiny." Although there is no way to measure how many "new Negroes" developed as a result of its efforts, the massive waves of civil rights protest that swept through the South in the late 1950s and early 1960s were powerful testimony that the psychological transformation that SCLC sought was actually taking place, and on a large scale.

SCLC was born just in time to fill a leadership vacuum that was developing as a result of an aggressive new campaign state officials waged to put the NAACP out of business. The campaign seems shocking, because the freedom of citizens to form voluntary associations and to petition their government for a redress of grievances is central to American democracy. But blacks living in the southern states in the 1950s had no such freedom, and the NAACP was viewed by whites in power as an "outside" organization whose subversive aims deprived it of constitutional protection. Blaming the NAACP for the *Brown* decision, the Montgomery bus boycott, and the general assertiveness of the "new Negro," southern state officials sought to force the organization to turn over its membership lists, exposing members to reprisals from the Citizens' Councils. Judges in Louisiana and Texas issued injunctions that temporarily barred the NAACP from operating in those states. South Carolina made it illegal for any teacher to be a member.[73]

Alabama's repressive efforts were the most determined and most successful. The attorney general, John Patterson, obtained a sweeping court order banning NAACP activities anywhere in the state, on the mistaken premise that the NAACP had been responsible for planning and executing the boycott of the buses in the state capital. (Patterson's anti-NAACP crusade brought this obscure young politician so much favorable publicity that he went on to win election as governor, his only claim to fame being that he was "the man who had run the NAACP out of the state."[74] His predecessor in the governor's chair had been a racial moderate, who had made the fatal mistake of saying that "when the Supreme Court speaks, that's the law.") The Alabama injunction against the NAACP was eventually overruled by the Supreme Court, but it took *eight years*—from 1956 to 1964—for the organization to win the legal battle for its right to exist.[75] In the meantime, its membership in the South had dropped from 130,000 in 1955 to 80,000 in 1957, the opening two years of the battle.[76] But the emergence of SCLC helped to fill the void. The result was a shift from a strategy that emphasized litigation to one focused on the mobilization of masses of people to carry out acts of nonviolent civil disobedience.

Legal attacks upon the organizers of the Montgomery boycott and the NAACP were one tool used by defenders of the racial status quo. Sheer violence was another. Sometimes it was effective, sometimes not. Dynamiting the homes and churches of the leaders of the Montgomery bus boycott did nothing to stop that mass movement. On the other hand, violent resistance worked at the University of Alabama in 1956. The first black student to attend the University of Alabama, Autherine J. Lucy, was admitted by court order. She didn't last long. At first, a rampaging mob kept her from entering. After she did manage to enroll, the university suspended her, on the grounds that her presence on campus would provoke further mob action. (To reward a violent crowd in this way, of course, only incited further violence.) After a federal court ordered her reinstatement, university authorities found another pretext for expelling her. By then the strain had impaired Lucy's health, and she dropped out.

The Autherine Lucy case demonstrated that a determined mob could nullify a federal court order. It would be a long time—seven years—before another black student would set foot in the University of Alabama. Defiant members of the Alabama Senate felt so emboldened by this victory that they thumbed their noses at the outside world by passing an absurd resolution demanding that the Congress appropriate the funds necessary to transport the entire black population of Alabama out of the state.[77] There was not the slightest possibility of this happening, but it did remind black citizens—if any needed reminding—that the whites who ran the state regarded them as unwelcome foreigners in their midst.

A similar clash in Little Rock, Arkansas, the next year had a different outcome. Little Rock authorities had agreed to accept nine black students at Central High School for the 1957–1958 school year, as a result of a court-approved integration plan. Nine was seen as a big number, and the governor of the state, Orval Faubus, decided to use the Arkansas National Guard to keep the African-American pupils out. Faubus claimed that his only aim was to protect the defenseless black children from mob violence, but he had no evidence that any violence had been planned. His decision was pure politics. He had actually been relatively progressive on racial issues, but his chances of reelection were looking poor, and obstructing a plan to integrate the schools seemed like a sure vote-getter. He was right: he smashed his opponent in the next election by a margin of more than four to one.[78]

Faubus was grandstanding; he knew he could not stop school integration in Little Rock. And, indeed, he was forced by a federal court order to withdraw the National Guard and allow the black students to begin school. But his prophecy of violence had been self-fulfilling: a mob too large to be controlled by the Little Rock police showed up at the school, provoking an angry President Eisenhower to send in federal troops. The Autherine Lucy case demonstrated that violent resistance to a federal court order could halt integration for many years. The Little Rock clash showed that defiant mob action could persuade the executive branch of the federal government of the need to use force to make sure the law was enforced.

Even with the U.S. armed forces on the scene, the racial turmoil at Central High was so great that the Little Rock School Board decided to ask judicial permission to postpone desegregation for another two and a half years. Why the scene could be expected to be any more tranquil a couple of years later was not clear. Meeting in a rare special session, the Supreme Court ruled unanimously that the constitutional rights of the Little Rock black students could not be denied them because officers of the state had encouraged and provoked mob violence.[79]

BUSINESS INTERESTS AND THE CIVIL RIGHTS STRUGGLE

Governor Faubus tried other delaying tactics after the Supreme Court decision, but then began to back down. It had become evident that last-ditch resistance on this issue would alienate many of his backers from the state's business community. In Little Rock and elsewhere in the South, business interests exerted considerable influence on the outcome of civil rights struggles. The Old South was giving way to a New South. The cotton fields and the black sharecroppers and laborers who tilled them were moving off center stage, and new factories were taking their place. In 1938, President Roosevelt had called the economic stagnation and backwardness of the South "the Nation's No. 1 economic problem." Though the term would not be used until later, by the 1950s the South was part of the dynamic "Sunbelt," and was attracting more new industry than the Northeast and Midwest.[80] This economic transformation destabilized the Jim Crow system.

The Old South was an economic backwater that had been allowed to go its own peculiar way since the end of Reconstruction. That way entailed white supremacy and black subordination. By the 1950s, though, new businesses independent of the old planter-dominated power structure were proliferating in the region, bringing rising prosperity and whetting appetites for further economic gain. Southern states competed vigorously to attract firms from outside the region by offering tax breaks, public financing of plant construction, and other incentives to locate within their boundaries. They also worked energetically to attract the federal dollars that came with Defense Department and other contracts.[81] "Our economy is no longer agricultural," said William Faulkner in 1959. "Our economy is the federal government."[82]

Although many southern whites were slow to grasp the point, the growing integration of the region into the national economy subjected southern racial patterns to new critical scrutiny. The character of race relations began to exert important influence on the South's ability to attract the business it wanted. Companies would open branch plants in the South only if it appeared that the region's towns and cities were "safe, civilized communities," with decent schools and labor forces that were "well behaved and eager for work."[83] If the South was still a primitive, unreconstructed place in which cross-burnings and lynching parties were a popular form of recreation, they were inclined to stay away. When it took the 101st Airborne Division of the U.S. Army to keep the peace in a high school, Little Rock no longer appeared very safe or civilized.

It is ironic that Orval Faubus, before he meddled in the school desegregation case, had been a pioneer in the effort to attract outside capital to the South, having initiated a major industrial development plan for Arkansas with the help of the wealthy newcomer Winthrop Rockefeller. By 1957 the plan had brought eight major new plants to the state. The Little Rock crisis brought it to a screaming halt. Over the next four years no other major firms took up residence in the state. On the other hand, those Sunbelt communities that managed race relations successfully benefited economically. Atlanta, for example, desegregated its schools and public facilities without violence in 1961. It attracted national attention as the "city too busy to hate" and enjoyed an influx of new investment as a result.[84]

Adamant resistance to racial change could yield rich short-term political rewards to demagogues like Orval Faubus. But when developmental opportunities were lost, politicians who were more willing to compromise on racial issues came increasingly to the fore.[85] It would take a great deal of external pressure from the federal government in the years ahead to force the South to abandon Jim Crow. But accomplishing that task would have been even more difficult if southern whites had been truly united in defense of "segregation now—segregation tomorrow—segregation forever."[86] Overwhelming majorities of whites could be incited temporarily to rally round the Confederate flag, and to vote into power nonentities whose chief qualification for high office was having "run the NAACP out of the state." When it became increasingly evident that segregation was bad for business, though, that simple formula began to lose its political potency.

THE CIVIL RIGHTS ACT OF 1957

Congress was the last of the three branches of the federal government to join in the struggle for civil rights. Segregation in the armed services was eliminated in the wake of President Truman's executive order. The Supreme Court put an end to racial segregation in the public schools of Topeka and on the buses of Montgomery, and President Eisenhower dispatched troops to Little

Rock to ensure that federal court orders were carried out. But Congress, where the South had disproportionate power, watched from the sidelines. As Chapter 2 noted, with southern blacks disfranchised and the chairmanship of congressional committees awarded on the basis of seniority, civil rights legislation was inevitably in for a tough ride. The South's veto power was particularly great in the Senate, where it took a two-thirds majority vote to stop a paralyzing filibuster.[87]

Nevertheless, a civil rights bill did pass in 1957, the first since Reconstruction. It was a bipartisan effort, proposed by the Eisenhower administration and pushed through the Senate by Lyndon B. Johnson, a Texas Democrat who was the majority leader and had ambitions for the White House. Texas was not a typical southern state, and Johnson was not a typical southern senator; he had been one of only three who refused to sign the "Southern Manifesto" denouncing the *Brown* decision. As majority leader, he said, he could take no stand against a ruling that stated the law of the land.[88] It was a public excuse, aimed at placating white southerners, and it won him no friends among black and white liberals whose support he would need in a race for the presidency. Johnson's push for passage of the 1957 Civil Rights Act was thus an effort to acquire the liberal credentials he would need to be a credible candidate for national office.

The new law focused on the denial of voting rights to southern blacks. Thirteen years earlier, in *Smith v. Allwright,* the Supreme Court had thrown out the white primary, but many other barriers to black political participation remained. With the 1957 statute the Justice Department acquired the right to prosecute anyone who interfered with a citizen's right to register or vote—chiefly southern local officials. A new Civil Rights Division was created in the Justice Department to enforce the act, and a U.S. Civil Rights Commission was established to investigate discrimination.[89]

The act did not eliminate the most important obstacles to black voting in the South—which is doubtless why it was not filibustered to death by senators committed to white supremacy. In fact, the South won an important concession: juries, not judges, had been given the power to decide the fate of those accused of violating the act. Racist registrars would be judged by whites who were generally equally keen on keeping blacks from the polls. The result was an act with a decidedly modest impact. The year before the bill was passed, 25 percent of southern blacks of voting age were actually registered to vote, double the 12.2 percent figure of a decade before and eight times as high as in 1940. In 1960, three years after the law was signed, 29 percent of African-American adults living in the South were registered, and this small gain was almost all in the cities.[90] The failure of the bill to effect significant change led supporters to try again in early 1960, but the balance of forces in Congress had not altered, and the Civil Rights Act of 1960 was barely distinguishable from the 1957 measure.[91]

THE SIT-INS

On February 1, 1960, four black seventeen-year-olds, freshmen at the segregated North Carolina Agricultural and Technical School in Greensboro, paid a visit to the local Woolworth's. After purchasing some school supplies, they sat down at the lunch counter and asked the startled waitress for coffee and doughnuts. When she said "I'm sorry, we don't serve you here," one of the students pointed out that they had been served just a minute earlier at the cash register at which they had paid for their purchases. Why could they buy a notebook and not a cup of coffee? The waitress was not sufficiently well versed in the metaphysics of segregation to explain the difference between allowing blacks to purchase items to take out of the store and permitting them to sit down and consume food on the premises, rubbing shoulders freely with white people while doing so. To serve food in racially mixed company violated one of the central taboos in the bizarre world of Jim Crow, although in Greensboro no local ordinance forced the store to engage in practices that the students viewed as absurd, immoral, and impossible to reconcile with true Christianity. While the four were "scared as hell" at first, they were determined to put their bodies on the line to fight for social justice.[92]

Thus began the civil rights movement's version of the Boston Tea Party, "the Greensboro coffee party." While the four sat politely at the counter, a few whites made the hostile racist remarks they anticipated, but others unexpectedly told them that they were doing "a good thing" and "should have done it ten years ago." To their dismay the sharpest criticism came from a black woman washing dishes behind the counter, who denounced them as "rabble-rousers" and "troublemakers."[93] When the store closed, they left. But they were back the next day, along with twenty-three of their classmates. The day after that, black students occupied sixty-three of the sixty-five seats at the counter. By the weekend several hundred students, including the A&T football team, crowded the downtown demanding an end to segregated lunch counters and restaurants. When the football players were challenged with "Who do you think you are?" they responded, "We the Union Army."[94] For six months the Greensboro Woolworth's endured students tying up the seats at its lunch counters and picketing on the sidewalk outside, which discouraged customers. After losing an estimated $200,000 worth of business, the store capitulated.[95]

Sit-in fever spread quickly to other communities. By the end of the year some 70,000 students had occupied Jim Crow lunch counters and restaurants, hotels, public libraries, swimming pools, and other facilities in about a hundred southern cities. The year before, the *New York Times* took note of just 10 civil rights demonstrations in the entire country; in 1960 it registered no fewer than 414.[96] More often than not, the protests succeeded. When a student sit-in leader asked the mayor of Nashville whether he believed that it was "wrong to discriminate against a person solely on the basis of race or color," he had to concede that it was not "morally right" for a store to sell goods to African Americans but not the food and drink it offered to white customers. Three weeks later there were no more segregated lunch counters to be found in Nashville.[97]

The teenagers who boldly occupied forbidden ground at Woolworth's in Greensboro in February 1960 did not invent the sit-in. It was a tactic that had been used before on many occasions. CORE, for example, had organized similar protests against discrimination in Chicago's restaurants as early as 1942.[98] The next year Howard University students occupied eating establishments that refused service to blacks in Washington, D.C., and succeeded in integrating some of them.[99] The tactic was rediscovered and used with increasing intensity after the Montgomery bus boycott. In the late 1950s sit-ins took place in at least sixteen cities, including St. Louis, Miami, Nashville, Louisville, Oklahoma City, and Atlanta. Nine of them were organized by local chapters of the NAACP, usually through its Youth Councils, and CORE was involved in seven.[100]

It was the Greensboro sit-in that made history, however. It caught on across the South, and it stimulated the formation of a new civil rights organization —the Student Nonviolent Coordinating Committee (SNCC, pronounced "Snick"). The organizational meeting in Raleigh, North Carolina, in April 1960, had been called by Ella Baker, acting executive director of SCLC. It was attended by students mainly from southern black colleges, and featured Martin Luther King as the key speaker. College students were the ideal troops for a movement that planned to violate local and state segregation codes in the name of a higher law. As King said, they had high ideals, and did not share "the apathy and complacency of adults in the Negro community."[101] Unlike adults with jobs to lose and family responsibilities, students could spend a few days in jail and have their name appear in the newspaper as a lawbreaker without worrying too much about it, and it was very hard to bring economic pressure to bear upon them.[102]

AMAZING PATIENCE

"For many years we have shown amazing patience," Dr. King said in 1955. In fact, it is hard to decide which was more amazing: the decades of patience or the sudden impatience. In the 1950s the caste system that seemed so rock-solid began to crumble. Why then and not before? Revolutions inevitably contain some element of mystery, but two points implicit in the foregoing narrative can be noted.

First, southern whites had long been fearful of the consequences of educating blacks, and for good reason. It had been illegal to teach slaves to read, because access to the written word might expose them to the dangerous idea that slavery was not divinely ordained. Reading H. L. Mencken's devastating attacks on the backwardness and barbarism of the southern states strengthened Richard Wright's contempt for the doctrine of white supremacy. The Mississippi Senate could debate how to purge the schoolbooks used by the black pupils of references to voting, elections, and democracy, but Mississippi was not an independent nation that could seal off its borders and keep out all subversive ideas. All the studies of black attitudes toward segregation to which we have referred found that the least educated displayed attitudes of passive acceptance, and hostility toward the system increased sharply with rising educational levels. The average black resident of the South in the 1950s had three to four more years of schooling than his or her parents a generation before, and that was a recipe for growing protest against white supremacy.

Second, the role of creative leadership was important. Martin Luther King put his stamp on the movement, set the tone, and was part of the reason for its remarkable success. But he did not work alone. The civil rights movement created genuine American heroes and heroines: Rosa Parks, Charlayne Hunter, Autherine Lucy, and others whose names and faces have long been forgotten. Seventy thousand students participated in sit-ins in 1960. For them and countless others, it was the psychologically transforming experience that Charlayne Hunter-Gault describes so well in her autobiography.

The moral simplicity of the struggle in those years has long since disappeared, but it is important to remember. In the fall of 1994, Rosa Parks, who had moved to Detroit, was beaten and robbed by a young black man who broke into her house. "Many gains have been made," she said. "But as you can see, at this time we still have a long way to go and so many of our children are going astray."[103] Urban children astray are a different problem from the one she sought to solve. That difficult and discouraging terrain lay ahead does not detract from the success of the earlier journey of which she was such an important part.

In 1963, Dr. King spoke of his "dream that one day this nation [would] rise up and live out the true meaning of its creed." He had in mind whites, but in fact, blacks rose up and whites joined in, and together they fulfilled much of what King barely dared to imagine. Myrdal had placed his hopes exclusively on whites, who would one day live up to their true egalitarian creed, he thought. He was wrong to have confidence only in whites, but he was right to believe in America. As the 1960s made clear.

CHAPTER FIVE

We Shall Overcome

ON MARCH 7, 1965—a day that came to be known as "Bloody Sunday"—Alabama state troopers used electric cattle prods, nightsticks, and tear gas to suppress a peaceful Selma-to-Montgomery voting rights march. The troopers had not acted on their own; the governor of Alabama, George C. Wallace, had been just offstage, out of sight but certainly in charge. Thirty years later, when the march was reenacted, Wallace, who had promised "segregation today, segregation tomorrow, segregation forever," was holding hands with black citizens and singing "We Shall Overcome." "My friends," he said, "I have been watching your progress this week as you retrace your footsteps of 30 years ago and cannot help but reflect on those days that remain so vivid in my memory. Those were different days and we all in our own ways were different people."[1]

Thirty years ago, "different days" and "a different people." If so, the change can be traced directly back to the dedication of those who risked their lives in a conscious effort to transform the nation. They made demands that, by 1964, the nation could not refuse. German shepherds, fire hoses, and cattle prods: the violent resistance of the white South—in marked contrast to the nonviolence of those who marched and sang—tipped the scales. Nineteen hundred sixty-four was the year the great Civil Rights Act was passed; a year later the Voting Rights Act was enacted. These historic measures committed the full power of the federal government to the task of wiping out Jim Crow and securing equal rights for black Americans.

CIVIL RIGHTS ON THE NEW FRONTIER

For voters who cared deeply about civil rights, the choice in the 1960 presidential race was tough. African Americans had leaned toward the Democrats since the New Deal, but that was because they saw the party as more attuned to the interests of poor and working-class Americans, not because Democrats were clearly preferable to Republicans on questions involving race. Southern Democrats were still very powerful in the party. Throughout the 1950s the Republicans were more sympathetic to new civil rights legislation than the Democrats were. Eisenhower won a respectable one-out-of-four share of the black vote in 1952 and a very impressive four out of ten in 1956.[2]

In the 1960 presidential contest between John Kennedy and Richard Nixon, civil rights policy was not a burning issue. In fact, the party platforms were indistinguishable, and neither candidate had a well-defined record in this area.[3] Kennedy and Nixon both attempted to strike the same delicate balance, seeking to attract votes from blacks and northern white liberals without suffering offsetting losses among whites in the South. In 1956, when Kennedy had made a bid for the vice presidential nomination, he had been so pleased at his success in wooing southern political leaders that he confided to a friend that "I'm going to sing Dixie for the rest of my life."[4] Choosing Lyndon Johnson of Texas as his running mate in 1960, of course, was one way of singing "Dixie."

With his southern flank well covered, JFK needed to do more to appeal to liberals. When he was battling for the nomination, Kennedy had assured a delegation of black and white liberals from Michigan that civil rights was "of overwhelming moral significance" to him, and that, if elected president, he would use "the full prestige and weight of his office to completely eliminate second-class citizenship in America."[5] In his first speech of the campaign, he spoke in a similar vein, calling upon Congress to "prepare a comprehensive civil rights bill, embodying our platform commitments," at the beginning of its next session.[6] But he had little grasp of the issues. While driving to his Senate office one day, he asked an aide with ties to the civil rights community to take "five minutes" to list "the ten things a President ought to do to clean up this goddamn civil rights mess."[7] Judging from his campaign, JFK learned just one thing rather than ten things from the conversation: discrimination in housing supported with federal funds could be banned by executive order. To accomplish this would take the mere "stroke of a presidential pen," he said repeatedly. It was his campaign mantra whenever he had to respond to a question about civil rights.

Kennedy met with Martin Luther King to solicit his support, but King felt that the SCLC should not become involved in partisan politics, and in any event could not see "that there was much difference between Kennedy and Nixon."[8] King's father, an eminent Atlanta preacher, did see a difference, a difference that favored Nixon. The senior King had always been a Republican and Kennedy was a Democrat. Kennedy was also a Catholic, and in those days that was a serious obstacle in the mind of a dedicated Baptist like Martin Luther King, Sr.[9]

At the last minute, though, Kennedy's advisors came up with a brilliant public relations gesture. Two weeks before the election a Georgia judge threw King in jail for a traffic violation. JFK called King's wife Coretta to express sympathy, and his brother Robert persuaded the judge to let King out on bail. Jackie Robinson, who was active in Republican affairs, tried to get Nixon to say something in support of King, but Nixon remained silent, most likely counting votes: southern whites against blacks and white liberals. Although many of JFK's advisors made the same calculation, their views lost out; the campaign spread the news in black neighborhoods. Quietly, however. Those in charge were eager to get the word out where it would do the candidate some good; they were not equally eager to see the story in the national press.[10]

On election day Martin Luther King, Sr., voted for Kennedy, and so did hundreds of thousands of other African Americans. It's impossible to say whether JFK's intervention on behalf of the younger King was the chief reason, but the proportion of black votes going Democratic rose substantially, from 61 percent in the previous presidential contest to 70 percent.[11] Those nine points were more than enough to carry the election, which Kennedy won by a hair. Nineteen hundred and sixty was the closest election since 1888, with JFK receiving only 119,000 more ballots than Nixon, out of a total of almost 69 million—a difference of less than a quarter of 1 percent. A switch of 5,000 ballots in Illinois and 11,000 in Minnesota, and Kennedy would have lost the electoral college count.[12]

Kennedy had needed African-American support, but almost every vote, black and white, was make-or-break in 1960, so paper-thin was the margin of victory. And thus black votes, in the first two years of the Kennedy administration, had little policy impact. The pen that he had promised to use to end discrimination in federally assisted housing stayed safely in his desk. His first State of the Union address devoted precisely one sentence (a vague statement deploring restrictions on the franchise) to civil rights.[13] The president does not "think it necessary at this time to enact civil rights legislation," embarrassed White House officials said after congressional liberals introduced the very civil rights bill that candidate Kennedy had advocated. In truth, he believed it silly to antagonize the southern congressional establishment over a lost cause.[14]

The president also appointed a number of southern whites with records of support for segregation to the federal bench. But none of these actions should have been surprising. Kennedy was a professional politician, and he did have compelling political reasons for being cautious. More than half of the standing committees in Congress were chaired by southerners.[15] And to get reelected in 1964—surely one of his priorities—he would once again need a great many white southern votes. The once-solid Democratic South—a crucial component of the Democratic Party's electoral base since the Civil War—could no longer be taken for granted. A century after the Civil War, competitive, two-party politics was at last developing in the South; the GOP was shedding its image as the party of the occupying enemy during Reconstruction. Florida, Tennessee, Texas, and Virginia went to Eisenhower in 1952; in 1956, Louisiana, too, defected. Democrats who argued that Ike's successes were attributable only to his charisma rather than his party's appeal were proven wrong in 1960, when Nixon, too, carried Florida, Tennessee, and Virginia, and narrowly missed taking Texas as well.[16]

Freedom Riders

It soon became apparent that Kennedy would assume some leadership on civil rights issues only if a shift in public opinion made it seem politically right. As the national director of CORE remarked, that would happen only in the context of a crisis.[17]

That crisis was not long in coming. By 1961 segregation in public transportation had been outlawed by several rulings of federal courts and the Interstate Commerce Commission, most recently in a December 1960 Supreme Court decision. But little effort had been devoted to the difficult task of enforcing those rulings in the most ardently segregationist states.[18] CORE decided to act. Hoping to make "bus desegregation a reality instead of merely an approved legal doctrine," it organized a "Freedom Ride," which left Washington, D.C., on 4 May 1961, bound for the heart of the Deep South. The departure of the buses, on which a tiny band of seven blacks and six whites sat, was covered by only three reporters, all of them from black publications. The riders (one of whom was John Lewis, who later became a member of Congress from Georgia) planned to travel by day and speak at meetings at night. If arrested for violating segregation codes, they would stay in jail rather than pay fines or put up bail.[19]

The announced aim of the riders was to test the routinely ignored court orders desegregating interstate transportation facilities. But they had an additional goal: provoking violence to demonstrate the need for further federal action to secure basic rights.[20] If the Freedom Riders sought martyrdom in the service of their cause, their wishes were quickly granted. When the buses crossed into Alabama, one was attacked by a mob and destroyed with a firebomb. The other reached the terminal in Birmingham, from which the police were conspicuously absent, although the police station was only two blocks away and the authorities knew the bus was coming. For fifteen minutes whites were left free to wield baseball bats and bicycle chains, and they seriously injured nine of the passengers. Public Safety Commissioner Eugene "Bull" Connor, whose brutal treatment of civil rights demonstrators two years later would make an invaluable contribution to the cause, explained that, while police would normally have been on hand, on this occasion they were off visiting their moms. It was Mother's Day.

This "lapse" in law enforcement was clearly planned. Worse yet, the FBI knew what was coming. A paid informant within the Birmingham Ku Klux Klan had told the agency of a deal to allow the Klan fifteen or twenty minutes in which to pound on the demonstrators until "it looked like a bulldog got a hold of them." Then the police would move in—to arrest the riders, not their attackers. FBI Director J. Edgar Hoover, who was sure that the civil rights movement was controlled by Communists and Communist-sympathizers, was doubtless not unhappy to see the demonstrators roughed up. In any event, he did nothing to prevent it.[21]

In the newspaper headlines the next morning, however, the melee looked exceedingly bad, a fact that greatly irritated the president, who was about to leave for a crucial summit with Soviet Premier Khrushchev in Vienna. Domestic discord like this, he felt, could weaken him in dealing with the Russians. Revealing his profound ignorance of social protest movements, he ordered Harris Wofford, his civil rights advisor, to "tell them to call it off! Stop them! Get your friends off those buses."[22] But the administration could not stop the riders. It could not even force the police in Alabama to do their job; law enforcement was the responsibility of state and local officials. Robert Kennedy, the attorney general, asked the governor of Alabama to guarantee the safety of the Freedom Riders; Alabama could not "guarantee the safety of fools" was the response.[23]

The brutal response to the ride was more than CORE had bargained for, but SNCC came aboard, supplying fresh young volunteers who headed for Montgomery. At the same time, a team of administration officials descended on the state in the naïve hope that a visible federal presence would shame local officials into providing better security. But when the bus reached Montgomery, it was Birmingham all over again: a mob was there and the police were not.[24] This time twenty Freedom Riders, newsmen, and bystanders were injured. Thugs broke one rider's leg, smashed in the teeth of another, and set afire the clothing of a third. The state highway patrol finally stepped in to restore order. The chief contribution of the Montgomery police was to arrest a white couple who had aided some injured blacks on charges of disorderly conduct and failure to obey an officer.[25]

This second Alabama outrage compelled the administration to act with greater vigor. The Justice Department obtained a federal court injunction preventing the Klan from obstructing interstate bus travel, and it flew six hundred U.S. marshals into Montgomery to accompany the Freedom Riders to Jackson, Mississippi, which was their final destination. In Jackson, James Farmer and twenty-six other riders were arrested for violating the segregation code, refused to pay their fines, and started serving jail terms. At this point Robert Kennedy called for a "cooling-off period," but Farmer refused on the ground that "we had been cooling off for 100 years. If we got any cooler we'd be in a deep freeze."[26] In Farmer's view, filling up the jails of Alabama and Mississippi with people asserting their constitutional rights could only dramatize their cause.

King was no more receptive than Farmer. It was "a matter of conscience and morality," he said; the demonstrators would "use their lives and bodies to right a wrong." They would not accept bail. It was a classic dialogue between the hard-boiled political operative and the leader of a moral crusade. The administration would not be pushed around by the martyrdom of those who stayed in jail, Kennedy warned. King replied that he was "deeply appreciative" of what the administration was doing, but that "we've made no gains without pressure"; "moral, legal, and peaceful" efforts would go on. "They don't understand the social revolution going on in the world, and therefore they don't understand what we're doing," King said to Ralph Abernathy.

Jackson, Mississippi, was the final destination for the first Freedom Riders, but it was not the end of such trips. Hundreds of other volunteers boarded buses over the next few months, spreading out across the South. By the end of the summer over three hundred riders had been arrested in Jackson alone, about half of them black (mostly from the South) and about half white (almost all from the North). They attained their immediate goal: the Interstate Commerce Commission, under pressure from the White House, moved vigorously to enforce the ban on segregated transportation and terminal facilities. A year and a half later even CORE conceded that Jim Crow in the realm of public transportation was dead.[27]

The immediate goal of the Freedom Riders had been met, but the crisis failed to achieve the real objective: shifting public opinion in the desired direction. Indeed, the general public seems to have been more irritated with the victims than with the villains. Former President Harry Truman, who had been an effective supporter of civil rights while in the White House, was sharply critical, denouncing the riders as "meddlesome intruders" who "should stay at home and attend to their own business."[28] The *New York Times* blamed the riders for inviting attack, and charged that "nonviolence that deliberately provokes violence is a logical contradiction."[29] Similar sentiments were voiced by a large majority of those polled a month after the Birmingham and Montgomery clashes. Only 24 percent of the respondents who had heard of the rides approved of them, and 64 percent disapproved.[30] Whatever moral outrage they may have felt at southern violence, most Americans were more struck by the fact that those who participated in the rides had gone out of their way looking for trouble.

THE VOTER EDUCATION PROJECT

When the president told the Freedom Riders to quit and no one paid the slightest attention, the Kennedy administration was greatly disconcerted.

Moreover, the governor of Alabama and the police chiefs in Birmingham and Montgomery were apparently equally indifferent to orders from Washington. Clearly, the president, if he hoped to get reelected, would need a new strategy —one that would channel the moral energy of the civil rights movement while retaining the loyalty of those southern whites who could bolt in a Dixiecrat direction.

Thus, the Voter Education Project (VEP) was born—in the corridors of power in Washington. Robert Kennedy met with the representatives of civil rights groups, and together they devised a foundation-funded organization through which the NAACP, CORE, the Urban League, the SCLC, and SNCC would conduct a massive drive to register southern blacks. The attorney general not only concocted the scheme; he arranged for the Internal Revenue Service to give the VEP tax-exempt status, on the specious ground that it was an educational project that would conduct research on the causes and consequences of black disfranchisement.[31]

Robert Kennedy made a special effort to persuade SNCC and CORE activists, most of them still students, to put an end to the continuing Freedom Rides and concentrate on black enfranchisement. Agitation for the vote, he argued, was likely both to encounter less immediate white resistance and to promise greater long-run social change. It was the key to every other right: "From participation in elections [would] flow . . . all of what they wanted to accomplish in education, housing, jobs and public accommodations."[32] He promised protection to registration workers and to the people they signed up, and he even supplied the phone numbers of key officials who would accept collect calls. And he made another confidential promise: those students who dropped out of college to work for the VEP would not lose their draft exemption.[33]

It seemed an inspiration. Especially because the idea was to target unregistered blacks in southern cities like Nashville and Shreveport where registration would be relatively easy, given the black population concentration and the greater racial tolerance of urban whites. The administration was offering a trade-off: the civil rights activists could do good work without risking their lives, and the president could globe-trot in a crusade against Communism without having to deal with embarrassing headlines. The attorney general undoubtedly had one further thought: the newly registered blacks would be strongly predisposed in favor of the Democratic Party.

Between 1962 and 1964, when the VEP was in full swing, the number of southern blacks on the voting lists jumped by almost 700,000. About half of this gain was attributable to the organization. The black registration rate rose from 29 to 42 percent of the voting-age population, a big change although far from parity.[34] But some of those who had joined in the Voter Education Project—especially the young and impatient students from SNCC—were not entirely happy. "I felt that what they were trying to do was kill the Movement, but to kill it by rechanneling its energies," one SNCC worker reported.[35] These young warriors wanted to revolutionize the social order, and they regarded the concentration on voter registration as a concession to the forces for law and order in the lawless Jim Crow South.[36] Especially if that registration effort was confined to relatively safe cities. Thus, bent on challenging white supremacy in its stronghold, they broke partially free of the VEP and, using funds they had raised themselves, headed for the hard-core rural Black Belt counties of Mississippi and Georgia.

The administration had promised help when trouble came; it wasn't forthcoming. In September 1962, for example, a black man in Amite County, Mississippi, who had aided SNCC volunteers was murdered, and his killer got off on a plea of self-defense. A SNCC worker on the scene phoned Robert Kennedy to say he had found witnesses whose testimony would puncture the self-defense argument, but that they couldn't come forward without adequate protection. Kennedy barked: "What do you expect us to do, put guards around them for 24-hour protection for the rest of their lives?" Before long, the Justice Department (under pressure from southern congressmen) ceased even to accept collect calls from VEP workers.[37] It was a recipe for radicalization, and SNCC in succeeding years did become increasingly militant, drifting toward eventual self-destruction, a story to which we will return.

FAILURE IN ALBANY, GEORGIA

In the fall of 1961, Albany, Georgia, was a major target of SNCC's organizing activities. Along with the local chapter of the NAACP, SNCC volunteers formed the Albany Movement to desegregate all public facilities in the town and staged sit-ins and prayer meetings to protest the mass arrests of those involved in the sit-ins. With hundreds of demonstrators in jail and no money to bail them out, the desperate leaders called on Martin Luther King for help. King led a group in prayer on the steps of the City Hall, and ended up in jail.[38] But he accepted bail and left town in exchange for vague promises from local officials.

The Albany protests soon resumed, because the bargain King had arranged proved meaningless. The renewed efforts went on for several more months to no avail. The civil rights revolution is often depicted as an inexorably triumphant march forward. In fact, as the Albany story makes plain, the outcome was often touch-and-go. Divisions within the black community and organization rivalries were part of the problem. SNCC workers, always purists, resented King's efforts to negotiate with the authorities, while more conservative local leaders were not happy about the prominent role being played by outside activists. The NAACP was angry at both SNCC and SCLC for hogging the limelight.

Most important, in Albany law enforcement officials handled the demonstrators shrewdly. Police Chief Laurie Pritchett had taken the trouble to read King's writings for clues as to how to handle him, and had figured out what the police had done wrong in dealing with the civil rights movement in other southern communities.[39] There would be no televised pictures and no front-page stories of Albany police bashing protesters with their nightsticks—none of the crude brutality and blatant racism evident elsewhere. It wouldn't become national news and the subject of discussions in the White House.

The Albany police went by the book, and were firm but polite. Once arrested, demonstrators were not charged with violations of the segregation ordinances, to preclude inevitably successful legal appeals like that which settled the Montgomery bus boycott. They were charged instead with simple breaches of the peace and unlawful assembly. Although the local jail had only enough cells for 30 prisoners and as many as 750 people were arrested in just one week at the peak of the campaign, Pritchett arranged to ship overflow prisoners to other facilities nearby, and had buses lined up to carry them off as soon as they were booked. As a SNCC worker confessed later, the demonstrators had thought they could fill up the jails, but "Pritchett was hep to the fact that we couldn't. We ran out of people before he ran out of jails."[40]

Albany was a defeat for the movement in general, and a wounding personal loss for Martin Luther King, who returned to the town six months later, was arrested again, and was then cleverly manipulated into leaving jail despite his public promise to remain there as a witness to the evils of Jim Crow.[41] In fact, even a victory for the Albany Movement in federal court changed nothing, at least in the short run. After Albany's segregation ordinances were found to be unconstitutional, city officials simply shut down all public facilities rather than allow them to serve both races. They closed the public library; they shut the public parks; they even cut down the nets at the tennis courts to prevent blacks and whites from playing together.[42]

In Albany, King had been outmaneuvered, and stumbled badly; it was a disaster for the movement. Just before his final trip to the Albany jail, another mini-riot had been touched off by the police beating of a black woman at a county jail used to hold the overflow of prisoners. Although Chief Pritchett's men were pelted with beer bottles, rocks, and bricks, they responded in a disciplined, professional way, clearing the streets without resorting to guns or even nightsticks. Pritchett boasted that he was the true practitioner of nonviolence. "Did you see them nonviolent rocks?" he asked reporters. Throughout the Albany struggle Pritchett was able to say with some justice that he had met "nonviolence" with "nonviolence." In this instance he could even claim that he had met violence with nonviolence.[43]

The events in Albany lacked the clarity of a morality play. Pritchett had intelligence and charm, and was no obvious villain. Even the *New York Times* treated the struggle as if both sides were on the same moral plane.[44] But nonviolent repression was still repression, and the repression was in the service of an unjust, racist social arrangement. That central fact was for the moment lost.

INTEGRATING OLE MISS

In September 1962, a month after Martin Luther King departed from Albany, disturbances erupted in Oxford, Mississippi. A federal district court had ordered the University of Mississippi to admit the first African-American student in its history, James Meredith, when the 1962–1963 school year began. Governor Ross Barnett, though, chose to follow the obstructive path taken by Orval Faubus in Little Rock five years earlier. Barnett had his state troopers block Meredith (accompanied by a group of U.S. marshals and Justice Department attorneys) from entering the campus, while the town filled up with fervent segregationists, some of them equipped with rifles.

President Kennedy was desperate to avoid sending in troops; in the 1960 campaign he had accused Eisenhower of laxity for having allowed the situation in Little Rock to drift to the point at which federal intervention had been necessary. But he was naïve in dealing with Barnett. The president put the Mississippi National Guard under federal control, sent in three hundred federal marshals, and delivered an address to the nation explaining that a federal court had ordered Meredith's admission and that he would ensure that the order was carried out. Unwilling to send in a contingent of real soldiers, however, he counted on Barnett to abide by his pledge to keep state troopers on the scene. Barnett reneged on his promise, and left a well-armed mob free to carry out a no-holds-barred attack on the outnumbered marshals.[45]

The result was a melee that lasted all night and left 166 of the federal marshals wounded and two bystanders dead. Twenty-eight of the marshals, who were under strict orders not to fire except to save Meredith's life, were hit by bullets. As morning approached, the first U.S. Army troops (airlifted into Oxford) arrived on the scene; soon there would be 23,000 of them—approximately six times as many as Eisenhower had sent to Little Rock.

Thanks to advances in the speed of mass communications, the bloody events in Oxford had a greater and more immediate impact on public opinion than equally dramatic civil rights struggles just a year or two earlier. Dan Rather of the Dallas office of CBS was there at Ole Miss along with a cameraman, and his pictures and commentary showed up in everyone's living room the very next evening. It was a first. The development of videotape (which could be processed much more rapidly than regular film) and of communications satellites made such dispatch possible. Until 1962, the most provocative pictures to reach the public eye usually appeared several days after the event, in the next week's issue of *Life*.[46]

BIRMINGHAM: THE TRIUMPH OF NONVIOLENT PROVOCATION

Stung by his humiliating defeat in Albany, a conflict he had impetuously entered without weighing the prospects for success, King thought very carefully about where and how to fight the next major battle against Jim Crow. He chose Birmingham, Alabama. If he wanted to attack his enemy where it looked most vulnerable, Birmingham was not an obvious choice. The city was sometimes referred to as "the Johannesburg of North America," sometimes as "Bombingham," a nickname inspired by the eighteen racial bombings that had taken place in the previous six years.[47] Nine years after *Brown,* Birmingham's Jim Crow code was still in place, and its notorious public safety commissioner, Bull Connor, was ready to enforce it by any means necessary. Connor was not only a potent figure in local politics, he was the Democratic Party's national committeeman from Alabama. He had demonstrated his regard for law and order two years earlier, when he had allowed Klansmen to attack Freedom Riders.

But, with the memory of Albany still fresh, these were the very reasons why Birmingham was an inviting target. When the SCLC leaders were debating their choice, one argued tellingly that "we've got to have a crisis to bargain with." The elaborate plan developed for the Birmingham campaign was named Project C, with the *C* standing for Confrontation.[48] This notion of deliberately creating a crisis marked a major shift in King's thinking. He had initially believed in nonviolent persuasion: changing the hearts and minds of his opponents by a peaceful display of Christian love. After Albany he gravitated toward what might be called coercive nonviolence, nonviolent provocation, or passive aggression.[49] Birmingham was the perfect setting in which to test the revised strategy. Albany's Chief Pritchett had been a polite, professional, and unyielding segregationist with brains. Bull Connor would be different. He would make headline news.

Birmingham had a few other advantages. In Albany, the SCLC had been handicapped by rivalries with other civil rights groups. In Birmingham the only black protest group on the scene was the local branch of King's organization: the Alabama Christian Movement for Human Rights (ACMHR). It was founded by the Reverend Fred Shuttlesworth, an officer of the local branch of the NAACP until 1956, when Alabama's legal onslaught closed down the organization for seven years. Shuttlesworth's authoritarian and overbearing leadership style had not made him uniformly popular in the black community, but his organization, which held weekly mass meetings in churches, supplied a useful base upon which to build.[50]

The divisions within Birmingham's white community (absent in Albany) were another consideration. Bull Connor did not speak for all whites. Indeed, he had run for mayor in the April 1963 elections, just before the SCLC campaign started, and had lost by a substantial margin. (As a result of a complex legal dispute, though, the defeated Connor would remain in charge of the police and practically the de facto mayor for another two months.) Connor had a very strong following among Birmingham's rednecks, but was opposed by most members of the local elite—the Chamber of Commerce and the newspapers, for example—as well as by labor unions and black organizations. Progressive-minded businessmen abhorred the bad national press that the beating of the Freedom Riders had brought the city; an article in the *Saturday Evening Post,* for instance, was titled "A City in Fear"—a marked contrast with the image of Deep South rival Atlanta as "too busy to hate."

These businessmen were thus a logical target of protest—ripe for concessions. Indeed, the year before, Birmingham's merchants had made a deal with Fred Shuttlesworth. ACMHR would not stage protests if merchants would remove the "colored" and "white" signs from the restrooms and drinking fountains in their stores. They had done so temporarily, but had been forced to back down, because they were violating the local ordinances that Bull Connor was determined to enforce.[51]

Although carefully thought through, the Birmingham campaign got off to a disappointingly feeble start on April 3, 1963, the day after Connor lost his bid to become mayor. It began with sit-ins at lunch counters in five downtown stores. All but one of the stores responded not by calling the police but by closing the lunch counters. It hurt their pocketbooks a bit but was more painful to protesters, who were rendered irrelevant. The organizers then directed marches at City Hall, where at least they could count on being arrested. But ACMHR was not able to deliver very many volunteers willing to go to jail; of the seventy-five who signed up for the mission at a mass meeting one evening, no more than four showed up the next day and actually managed to get themselves arrested. Over the first eight days of what was supposed to be a massive campaign against Jim Crow in a city with 140,000 black residents, an average of under twenty people per day had been jailed. Part of the difficulty may have been a sense on the part of potential protesters that the protest was precipitous—that the new mayor should be given a little time to prove that he was more enlightened than Connor.

With few participants, the Birmingham campaign seemed to be failing. Worse yet, the police were not responding to provocation in the expected manner. They were on their best behavior. Connor had consulted with Laurie Pritchett, whose message seemed to have gotten through. As a consequence, the campaign was getting little coverage in the national press, and the coverage it did receive was not very pleasing to the organizers. The story was relegated to the back pages of the *New York Times,* which gave it the headline, "Demonstrations Fail to Develop."[52]

The floundering movement was dealt another blow when Connor secured an injunction barring King and 132 others from parading, picketing, or conducting any other protest activity in Birmingham. King would have felt compelled to honor a federal court order, but this came from a state court, whose commands he believed were not binding when they clashed with those of the Constitution. King chose to ignore the order, marched on City Hall, and ended up in a cell on April 12.[53]

During the nine days he spent there, King wrote his eloquent twenty-page "Letter from a Birmingham Jail." It was a response to an attack by a group of the more liberal white ministers of the city, who charged that the protest was "untimely" and "extreme." It was easy for "those who have never felt the stinging darts of segregation to say, 'Wait,' " but African Americans had already waited "more than 340 years for our constitutional and God-given rights," King replied. "You express a great deal of anxiety over our willingness to break laws," he went on. But

> an unjust law is no law at all. . . . [It is] a code that is out of harmony with the moral law. . . . An individual who breaks a law that conscience tells him is unjust, and willingly accepts the penalty by staying in jail to arouse the conscience of the community over its injustice, is in reality expressing the very highest respect for our law. . . . The time is always ripe to do right. Now is the time to make real the promise of democracy, and transform our pending national elegy into a creative psalm of brotherhood. Now is the time to lift our national policy from the quicksand of racial injustice to the solid rock of human dignity.[54]

Those who worked for racial change were "co-workers with God," King said. They stood up "for the best in the American dream," and drew from "the great wells of democracy which were dug deep by the Founding Fathers." King's beautiful "letter" remains deeply moving more than thirty years later, but in the short run eloquence would change nothing in Birmingham. It was back to the drawing board. "Having scraped the bottom of the barrel of adults who would go" to jail, one of its leaders explained, "we needed some new something."[55] The bold "new something" was a "children's crusade." In desperation, the SCLC started to recruit students from the local high schools and to train them in methods of nonviolent resistance. A thousand teenagers showed up to march on 2 May, and six hundred ended up in jail.

That was newsworthy, but in this first encounter the police continued to act with restraint and did their jobs unobtrusively. It was a different story the next day, when another thousand youths gathered at a church for a briefing and then headed off for the main business district, singing "We Shall Overcome." With the jail already filled to overflowing, the police wanted to avoid making further arrests, and sought instead to steer demonstrators away from downtown, where their presence would disrupt business. In attempting to control the crowd, Bull Connor had what he thought was a bright idea: He called out the fire department, and ordered it to disperse student marchers with blasts of water from fire hoses and "monitor guns," sophisticated fire-fighting devices that shot streams of water with enough force to blow the bark off trees at a distance of a hundred feet. Youths who didn't get out of the way fast enough were knocked flat by the water guns, and rolled down the street like rag dolls. Some in the crowd retaliated by throwing rocks and bricks at those wielding the hoses.

When many of the protesters managed to skirt the area within range of the monitor guns and continued on, Connor made another bad mistake. He let his men use their nightsticks on the children. And, even worse, he also brought out teams of dog-handlers with German shepherds on leashes, and used them to drive the students back. The plan to avoid arresting demonstrators was abandoned, and another seven hundred ended up in jail. It turned out that only three young people that day received bites bad enough to require medical treatment. But the ABC, CBS, and NBC cameras were there, and the spectacle transfixed the nation. "In marching only one block," said a Birmingham white leader, the demonstrators "could get enough news film to fill all the newscasts of all the television stations in the United States."[56] As a veteran journalist observed, "a newspaper or television picture of a snarling police dog set upon a human being is recorded in the permanent photo-electric file of every human brain."[57]

Here was precisely the "crisis" that the planners of the campaign had sought. Most Americans were revolted. President Kennedy expressed a common sentiment when he said that the sight of the pictures from Birmingham had "made him sick," and that he well understood "why the Negroes of Birmingham are tired of being asked to be patient."[58]

Finally, the protest had momentum, and the demonstrations continued on an even larger scale. Over a thousand protesters went to jail on 6 May alone, a new national record. Sales receipts at downtown stores fell by a third, partly because of a boycott by blacks and partly because white shoppers wanted to avoid the disturbances going on downtown. The Birmingham white elite was distressed at the disorder, and even more distressed at the possibility that the Kennedy administration might send federal troops into their city, as it had done in Mississippi the year before.[59]

Intense negotiations ensued. With Justice Department officials on hand to serve as intermediaries, Birmingham's business leaders and the incoming city administration reached an agreement with the SCLC. The protesters won practically all of their demands: the desegregation of public facilities, a promise of new jobs and promotions without racial discrimination in employment, a biracial committee to work out other unresolved issues. The two main concessions made by the SCLC were a phase-in of the changes, and an agreement that not all charges against the two thousand demonstrators behind bars would be dismissed. They would be released on bond for later trial.[60]

All was not quite well, however. King's great victory provoked a violent response from some of Bull Connor's most rabid backers. After a thousand hooded members of the Ku Klux Klan held a rally to denounce the agreement, bombs exploded at the home of Martin Luther King's brother, a Birmingham minister, and at the motel that had housed the SCLC office. The news of these attacks triggered a riot by angry blacks who shouted "eye for an eye, tooth for a tooth," turned over cars, set stores afire, and threw bottles and rocks at the police when they appeared to try to put the lid on. A combination of speeches urging nonviolence by King and other SCLC leaders and rough police tactics against the rioters by George Wallace's state troopers eventually cleared the streets, and the settlement between the SCLC and the city remained in effect.[61] But the riot following the bombings gravely endangered the whole campaign, and it was fortunate for the SCLC that it was snuffed out so quickly. The movement depended, for its ultimate triumph, on the support of white Americans who had no taste for violence. Wallace's interests might have been better served by letting the riot continue.

Protest that "Could Not, Would Not, Go Away"

The events in Birmingham inspired many African Americans to assert their grievances in their own communities with a new sense of confidence and urgency, and prompted many whites to join in the effort. "Freedom now" began to seem within reach for those willing to put their bodies on the line. Over the next ten weeks, by one count, no fewer than 758 civil rights demonstrations occurred in 186 cities.[62]

Some of these actions were repressed by methods that made Bull Connor look restrained; the police in the small Virginia city of Danville, for example, managed to put forty-eight of sixty-five protesting blacks in the hospital. The mayor of Jackson, Mississippi, ordered the construction of barbed-wire pens large enough to hold 10,000 demonstrators on the Mississippi State Fairgrounds. Even Roy Wilkins, the executive secretary of the staid, legalistic NAACP, got thrown into jail in Jackson when he appeared to show his support for protesters there.[63]

The record of success was nevertheless impressive. During the summer of 1963 some fifty cities in southern or border states agreed to desegregate their public facilities.[64] (Just a few protests took place in northern communities.) Civil rights groups were energized as never before, and had more money to carry out their activities. Contributions poured in from an expanding circle of sympathizers. The total income of the six leading civil rights groups rose from $3.3 million in 1962 to $5.5 million in 1963, a gain of 67 percent, compared with increases of 25 to 30 percent over the three preceding years. The treasury of the Southern Christian Leadership Conference nearly quadrupled in the year of the battle over Birmingham.[65]

The ink was still drying on the Birmingham settlement when Alabama was back in the headlines for another reason. In 1956 a federal court order had gotten Autherine Lucy into the University of Alabama, but the turmoil surrounding her presence had sapped her spirit and driven her out. Now, seven years later, two black students were knocking at the door with another court order. By 1963 the University of Alabama was the last holdout, the only state university in the country that still barred applicants on the basis of race. George Wallace, elected governor on the strength of his commitment to "segregation now, segregation tomorrow, segregation forever," was determined to keep the campus lily-white. If a federal court mandated integration, Wallace promised to "stand in the schoolhouse door" to prevent it.

On 11 June 1963 the two students appeared to register for the summer session, accompanied by the deputy attorney general of the United States. Wallace went through the charade of proclaiming "I hereby denounce and forbid this illegal and unwarranted action by the central government," but, unwilling to get himself arrested for refusing to abide by a federal court order, he had to step aside. Having already gone through a dress rehearsal for this particular drama the year before at Oxford, Mississippi, the president displayed a steadier and firmer hand this time. He put the Alabama National Guard under his command and dispatched a contingent to the campus immediately, keeping 1,600 standing by in reserve. To be supersafe, Kennedy had an additional 400 regular U.S. Army troops loaded in helicopters sitting on the airstrip at Fort Benning, Georgia, a short flight away. With so much force available so quickly, none was needed.[66]

George Wallace's last-ditch stand at the schoolhouse door crystallized a major shift in the administration's civil rights policy. Kennedy was well into his third year in office, but had failed to deliver on his campaign promise to press for new civil rights legislation, convinced that the effort would be futile and politically costly. A Democratic administration needed southern Democratic support. But the troubles in Birmingham, the rapid spread of racial unrest elsewhere, and the popularity of Wallace's demagoguery among southern whites changed the political equation. The president was convinced that the nation was confronted by a racial problem that "could not, would not, go away"; at the same time, most northerners viewed the administration's inaction as morally weak.[67] The combination was politically worrisome. The Republican Party had no powerful southern wing demanding to be appeased, and it was getting mobilized to fight for new civil rights initiatives, a strategy that might win over significant numbers of northern voters.[68]

The administration in fact had two concerns: Republicans and foreign policy. Asserting American leadership in the world, winning the fight against Soviet Communism, had from the start been the president's highest priority, and he viewed the Freedom Rides and Bull Connor through the lens of that preoccupation. U.S. intelligence reports had informed him that in one two-week period the Soviet Union had broadcast no fewer than 1,420 items about Birmingham as proof that capitalism and racism went hand in hand.[69] If America was to win the Cold War, the racial fires had to be cooled.

It was against this background that on the day of the showdown with Governor Wallace at the University of Alabama, Kennedy delivered a major speech promising to submit a comprehensive civil rights bill to Congress within seven days. The nation was confronted "primarily with a moral issue," one that was "as old as the Scriptures and as clear as the American Constitution," he said. The great principle at stake was that every American should be able to "enjoy the privileges of being an American without regard for his race or color." Kennedy went on to pledge that he would immediately ask the Congress to "make a commitment . . . to the proposition that race has no place in American life or law." With this speech a president of the United States had finally endorsed the central objectives of the civil rights movement. The fence-sitting pitch to southern white moderates stressing the need for law and order had been abandoned—replaced by a call for public policies resting on the principle that "our Constitution is color-blind."[70]

Within hours of Kennedy's address, a terrible reminder of how difficult the struggle was likely to be came from Jackson, Mississippi. Medgar Evers, the state field secretary for the NAACP, returned home after a meeting, parked his car in the driveway, picked up a pile of NAACP sweatshirts proclaiming "Jim Crow Must Go," and walked toward his front door. Before he reached it, a rifle bullet smashed into his back, and he bled to death in front of his wife and three children.[71]

The Revolution in White Racial Attitudes

The dramatic and traumatic events of the spring and summer of 1963 gave racial issues a greater salience across the nation than at any preceding moment in American history since Reconstruction. Since the 1930s the Gallup poll has regularly asked Americans what they thought was "the most important problem facing our country today." Before 1963, racial issues had never ranked very high on the list. The one time that anything related to race or civil rights was mentioned by more than a tenth of the public was in the summer of 1956, during the Montgomery bus boycott, when the figure reached 18 percent. Even then, over twice as many people (48 percent) rated foreign policy concerns as the most important problem.[72] Consciousness of racial issues dropped off quickly after the boycott. A typical result for the 1950s and early 1960s was the February 1958 poll in which "integration" was considered the most important problem by a mere 4 percent of the public.[73]

It would be natural to expect that the drama of the sit-in movement, the Freedom Rides, the Albany protest, and the riot that brought the U.S. Army to the campus of Ole Miss would have changed all that. But these events did not register much on the average American. An April 1963 poll, taken just before the battle over Birmingham, showed that 24 percent of the public rated Cuba as the most important problem, 39 percent mentioned some other international issue, and 4 percent—the same proportion as in 1958—specified "racial problems."[74] Birmingham, however, was a turning point. By July 1963, Bull Connor, George Wallace, and Medgar Evers had become household names, and race suddenly became the number-one issue in the minds of nearly half of the population. By October the figure was over half—52 percent.[75] For the next two years civil rights retained its very high visibility, with at least 35 percent of those polled consistently naming it America's most important problem.

Americans were also becoming persuaded that Washington should take further action to protect the rights of African Americans. Despite a persisting Jeffersonian-Jacksonian tradition of hostility to a powerful central government —a tradition by no means confined to the South—by 1963 a majority of the public was convinced that southern racial practices were so intolerable that federal intervention was required (Table 1). In July 1963, 49 percent of the public (and 55 percent of northern whites) said they favored legislation forbidding racial discrimination in hotels, restaurants, and other public accommodations, while 42 percent opposed it. Support rose substantially over the next few months. By February 1964, proponents of federal antidiscrimination legislation outnumbered opponents by two to one (61 versus 31 percent). Among northern whites the ratio was more than three to one (71 versus 21 percent).[76]

Table 1

Opinions of a Federal Law That Would Give "all persons, Negro as well as white, the right to be served in public places such as hotels, restaurants, and similar establishments"

	TOTAL POPULATION	SOUTHERN WHITE	NORTHERN WHITE
July 1963			
Favor	49	12	55
Oppose	42	82	34
September 1963			
Favor	54	NA	NA
Oppose	38	NA	NA
February 1964			
Favor	61	20	71
Oppose	31	72	21

Source: George H. Gallup, *The Gallup Poll: Public Opinion, 1935–1971* (New York: Random House, 1972), 1827, 1837–1838, 1863.

Events in Birmingham and elsewhere raised public consciousness about civil rights issues, and that new awareness could have carried the American public in any one of a number of different policy directions. The social disorder could have led, for instance, to hard-line calls for law and order. It did not. Instead, the majority of white Americans in 1963 sympathized with the aims of the protests—that is, with color-blind treatment before the law. It is tempting to think that the demonstrations themselves changed hearts and minds, but in fact, white racial attitudes had been undergoing a radical trans-formation for at least two decades. (See Table 2.) In 1944 only 42 percent of whites believed that blacks should have an equal chance at getting a job; 52 percent said frankly that whites should "have the first chance." By 1963 five out of six whites had come to accept the principle that employment opportuni-ties should not be restricted by race. Similarly, support for school integration jumped from 30 to 62 percent between 1942 and 1963, for integrated public transportation from 44 to 79 percent, and for neighborhood integration from 35 to 64 percent. It has sometimes been suggested that federal civil rights legislation in the 1960s was responsible for the huge shift of white racial attitudes, but that puts the cart before the horse. Deep attitudinal changes created the political pressures responsible for the enactment of new law.

Attitudes were considerably more liberal in the North than in the South, of course. This is evident not only from responses to the pollsters but from the public policies pursued in the typical northern state. By 1963 thirty states with two-thirds of the nation's population had laws against discrimination in public accommodations. It is no accident that not one was south of Maryland. Nearly that many states also had statutes to combat discrimination in employ-ment, but again, none in the South.[77] Although racial discrimination could certainly be found everywhere, most northerners believed that it was wrong, so wrong that it should be made illegal in public places and in the job market.

No southern state had laws to combat racial discrimination in 1963; most, indeed, still had laws that required discrimination, in that they mandated the classification of citizens by race and regulated their conduct on the basis of which racial category they belonged to. Even so, southern white opinion was changing in a liberal direction with remarkable speed. Over the two decades from the early 1940s to the early 1960s, acceptance of school integration by white southerners jumped from 2 percent to 31 percent, of integrated public transportation from 4 percent to 52 percent, and of neighborhood integration from 12 percent to 51 percent. The white supremacist South of old was rapidly dying by the 1960s, even though figures of reaction like George Wallace and Orval Faubus were still riding high. The Citizens' Councils did their best to stigmatize as "race traitors" whites who were not prepared to join in a last-ditch defense of segregation, and were politically successful in the short run. But southern white solidarity on the race question was gradually crum-bling.

Table 2
Percent of Whites Giving Pro-Integration Responses, 1942–1963

	TOTAL	SOUTH	NORTH
"Negroes should have as good a chance as white people to get any kind of job"			
1944	42	NA	NA
1963	83	NA	NA
"White students and Negro students should go to the same schools"			
1942	30	2	40
1956	49	15	61
1963	62	31	73
There should not be "separate sections for Negroes on streetcars and buses"			
1942	44	4	57
1956	60	27	73
1963	79	52	89
Would not make any difference to them if "a Negro with the same income and education as you have moved into your block"			
1942	35	12	42
1956	51	38	58
1963	64	51	70

Sources: William G. Mayer, *The Changing American Mind: How and Why American Public Opinion Changed Between 1960 and 1988* (Ann Arbor: University of Michigan Press, 1993), 366; Paul B. Sheatsley, "White Attitudes Toward the Negro," *Daedalus* 95 (Winter 1966), 219, 222.

The racial attitudes of southern whites were changing because the economic and social development of the region had eroded its historic isolation and altered the character of its population. Two wise analysts have noted that, in the 1940s, "no particular kind of white Southerner was less likely to support" segregation than any other kind. Virtually all southern whites were committed to separation of the races and white supremacy. By the 1950s, however,

support for segregation had become less common among educated Southerners, less common among urban Southerners, less common outside the conventionally defined "Deep" South, less common among those who had lived outside the South or were often exposed to the mass media—less common, in short, among the kinds of Southerners being produced in ever larger numbers by urbanization and economic development.[78]

Responses to questions asking southern whites their expectations about race relations in the future show similar changes. As late as 1957, less than half (45 percent) of whites in the South believed—or at least were willing to admit that they believed—that integration of schools, restaurants, and public accommodations would ever come to the South. A mere four years later, though, three of four southern whites (76 percent) were ready to concede that racial integration was bound to come; by July 1963 the figure was up to five out of six.[79] In the very year that George Wallace promised "segregation forever," all but a handful of southern whites thus knew that segregation was on its way out. The politicians of the region would continue to keep up a defiant charade for a while longer; most people knew that it was only a charade.

Racial attitudes were shifting, and in the face of deep social unrest, Americans had not embraced those who used brutal tactics to restore order. And yet there was surprisingly weak support for those who took to the streets in defense of basic civil rights. In a July 1963 poll, for example, 60 percent of the public expressed the view that "demonstrations by Negroes" did the civil rights cause more harm than good; only 27 percent believed they did more good than harm.[80] At the end of that year, 59 percent of northern whites and 78 percent of those in the South said that they disapproved of "actions Negroes have taken to obtain civil rights."

White opposition to the protests was partly due to the perception that "the Negro protest movement has been generally violent rather than peaceful." Although it is hard to grasp how the nonviolent demonstrators could have been considered violent, that was the view of nearly half (47 percent) of northern whites, and of 63 percent of their southern counterparts. Furthermore, surveys disclosed a pervasive and bizarre skepticism about whether the civil rights movement reflected the true feelings of typical African Americans. It might not be surprising that a majority of southern whites in December 1963 held the conspiratorial view that "others" were "really behind the Negro protest movement." That calumny, after all, was one of the chief refrains of the Citizens' Councils. But it is startling to find that nearly four out of ten of their northern counterparts agreed. Fully half of those who thought "others" were "behind" the movement—a total of about a quarter of the white population—said that the "others" they had in mind were Communists.[81] Thus, even before the outbreak of race riots in the nation's cities and the radicalization of the civil rights movement in the black power days of the late 1960s, a great many northern as well as southern whites were turned off by marching and demonstrating, even though most supported the general aims of the protesters.

Mobilizing Support for a Civil Rights Bill

The draft civil rights bill that President Kennedy submitted to Congress after his June 1963 speech went further to protect the civil rights of African Americans than any other measure that had passed Congress since Reconstruction. It focused on discrimination in public accommodations, the main target of the sit-ins, the Freedom Rides, and other protests that had swept the South. Other provisions of the bill gave the president the authority to withhold federal grants to state and local programs that operated in a racially discriminatory manner, and made it easier for the Justice Department to file school desegregation suits.[82]

This was a bold departure from the cautious course Kennedy had steered on civil rights until then, but it was still much too cautious for many. The most important omission in the bill, its critics thought, was a strong fair-employment-practices provision. The measure did nothing more than authorize the president to create a new commission that would have a vague mandate to prevent job discrimination by federal contractors and firms in programs financed by the federal government."[83] The section authorizing a cutoff of federal funds to discriminatory programs left the decision to the president; critics urged that the cutoff should be mandatory whenever discrimination was evident. In addition, the bill did almost nothing to protect the voting rights of African Americans. Even the public accommodations section, the centerpiece of the whole measure, was limited in coverage. It applied only to firms with a "substantial" involvement in interstate commerce, and the enforcement mechanism it provided was weak.[84]

There was ample reason for the administration's caution. It was obvious that southern Democrats were not going to vote for any federal civil rights bill. Although many southern whites no longer held the views that were being advanced so vigorously by George Wallace, few politicians in the South were willing to expose themselves to criticism for being in league with black protesters and "damn Yankees" who were allegedly egging them on. The only hope of actually passing a civil rights bill, therefore, was to get very substantial support from liberal and moderate Republicans.

The bill would be especially difficult to get through the Senate, where it would take a two-thirds majority to break the filibuster that southern senators would inevitably employ to block it. In the previous dozen years no proposal to cut off debate on an issue in the Senate had even gotten a simple majority behind it.[85] Too weak a bill would make civil rights activists and liberals mad. Too strong a bill would alienate too many centrists to pass at all. From the administration's point of view, there was no doubt about which direction in which to err; half a loaf was much better than none at all.

In fact, in the end, Congress bought the whole loaf, and it did so largely in response to events in the late summer of 1963. The civil rights forces mounted an extraordinary campaign that drew strength from the already mounting public support for antidiscrimination legislation. The centerpiece of that campaign was the 1963 March on Washington, best remembered for Martin Luther King's "I Have a Dream" speech. It was an occasion of rare solidarity among the civil rights groups, whose aims, operational styles, and ideologies differed in important respects. Those differences would resurface again after 1963, but on 28 August, the date of the march, the NAACP and the Urban League put on a show of unity in support of the direct-action tactics favored by the SCLC, SNCC, and CORE, while those organizations in turn exercised enough restraint upon their more radical elements to keep them from alienating the Kennedy administration and the white public in general.[86]

The president was at first unhappy about the prospect of a massive black march—a specter much feared in the mid-1960s. Hundreds of thousands of African Americans would descend on Washington, possibly provoking fights just by their presence. And thus Kennedy met with King, A. Philip Randolph, and other leaders in an attempt to persuade them to call it off, warning that the protest would imperil his proposed civil rights program, giving congressmen the "chance to say, 'Yes, I'm for the bill, but I'm damned if I'll vote for it at the point of a gun.' " King responded that he had never been engaged in any civil rights action "which did not seem 'ill-timed.' " "Some people," King said, "thought Birmingham ill-timed." "Including the Attorney General," the president added.[87]

Kennedy could not stop the march, any more than he had been able to stop the Freedom Rides two years earlier. But he was able to co-opt it—to use it for his own ends. His staff worked closely with the civil rights groups—to "make sure it was a success and that it was organized right," as the head of the civil rights division put it.[88] A "success" and "organized right" as the administration defined it. Much of the basic planning was the government's —for instance, the idea of the Lincoln Memorial as the site, as well as the date and time of day, all designed to speed the demonstrators in and out of the city. The Justice Department even rented the public address system, which meant that a trusted employee of the federal government could have his finger on a switch that would instantly silence a speaker who got out of line. Malcolm X, the fiery black nationalist orator from the Nation of Islam, was close to the truth when he charged that the march had been "taken over by the government."[89]

Partly as a result of pressures from the administration, any thoughts of disrupting normal life in the capital through sit-ins or other direct action tactics were shelved. The march would be a time for calm, reasoned speeches that would not offend mainstream America, and for inspirational music from gospel singer Mahalia Jackson and folksinger Joan Baez. Although the official title of the event remained the March on Washington for Jobs and Freedom, little was heard from the podium about jobs. Only mild and muted criticism of the Kennedy civil rights program were offered by the speakers. The administration wanted cheerleaders, not critics.

What the march might have looked like without manipulation by the Kennedy forces is apparent from the text of the speech that John Lewis, the twenty-year-old head of SNCC, wrote but did not deliver unexpurgated. The original version demanded "radical social, political, and economic changes," a "revolution," to be brought about by "the masses." It pronounced the Kennedy civil rights bill worthless, too feeble to support. SNCC workers, Lewis planned to say, would march "through the heart of Dixie the way Sherman did." They would "pursue [their] own 'scorched earth' policy and burn Jim Crow to the ground—nonviolently." (If Lewis thought that the adverb tacked on at the end of this incendiary sentence would mollify anyone who found it troubling, he was naïve.) The administration wanted the speech toned down, and at the very last moment delivered a copy edited by the president himself. With Randolph, King, and pretty much everyone else urging Lewis to give in, and perhaps mindful of the Kennedy official with his finger on the loudspeaker switch, he agreed to go with a relatively tame version.[90] It doubtless was fortunate, if the objective was to generate the widest possible backing for the aims of the demonstration.

Nobody, of course, edited Martin Luther King's speech, covered live on all three national television networks. Its singing phrases to this day define the event for most Americans. As Coretta King later said, "At that moment it seemed as if the Kingdom of God appeared. But it only lasted for a moment." King himself called it "the greatest demonstration for freedom in the history of our nation," and it was. Those who gathered at the Lincoln Memorial had come "to dramatize a shameful condition," he said. "The Negro is still sadly crippled by the manacles of segregation and the chains of discrimination, and finds himself "in exile in his own land." "In his own land": African Americans were Americans—indeed, keepers of the flame lit by the Declaration of Independence and the Constitution. There was nothing wrong with America that living up to its founding principles would not cure. "I still have a dream. It is a dream deeply rooted in the American dream that one day this nation will rise up and live out the true meaning of its creed. . . ." This was the message to whites, but there was one as well to blacks: "We must forever conduct our struggle on the high plane of dignity and discipline"—using not "physical force," but "soul force." "Unearned suffering is redemptive." Freedom would only be won by a "biracial army. We cannot walk alone."[91]

King had cast a vote of confidence in white America—in its willingness to join "a beautiful symphony of brotherhood." But he had also issued a warning: "The whirlwinds of revolt will continue to shake the foundations of our nation until the bright day of justice emerges." Whites were nearly 90 percent of the population and occupied far more than 90 percent of the seats in Congress.[92]

Were they to turn a deaf ear, King knew, the march would be for naught. They did not, and the support it mobilized for national civil rights legislation in turn swelled the membership of organizations like the Leadership Conference on Civil Rights, a biracial organization. The LCCR had been founded in the late 1940s as a coordinating body for organizations with civil rights concerns, and while in 1957 it had only two dozen members, by June 1963 some fifty groups had signed up. By 28 August the number had risen to seventy-nine.[93]

In the South the civil rights movement was rooted in the black church. The SCLC was an organization of black ministers. In the campaign for new civil rights legislation, white church groups also played a critical role. The March on Washington had been endorsed by the National Council of Churches, the American Jewish Congress, the National Catholic Conference for Interracial Justice, New York's Cardinal Spellman, and the Catholic archbishop of Washington.[94] While the political struggle was unfolding, the clergy and lay church leaders had a particularly great influence upon members of Congress who came from overwhelming white districts and were thus free of pressure from groups like the NAACP and the Urban League, as well as from whites driven by strong racial fears and resentments. The fall of 1963 brought many delegations of ministers, priests, and rabbis to Washington, where they lobbied their congressional representatives and held prayer meetings on Capitol Hill.[95]

Such efforts were helped by the moral outrage produced by more bad news from Birmingham, this time in mid-September. Racial tension had been rising in the city once again, with the public schools reopening under court orders to integrate and George Wallace again attempting to obstruct the order. Another bomb had exploded at the home of a local black leader, and another night of rioting in ghetto areas had been suppressed, leaving one of the rioters dead and twenty-one others in the hospital. Something even worse happened on the morning of Sunday, 15 September, when a dozen sticks of dynamite exploded at the Sixteenth Street Baptist Church, the staging ground for the children's marches that had turned the tide in the battle over Birmingham four months earlier. Sunday School was in session, and the blast wounded dozens of children and killed four girls. In the ensuing turmoil in the city two black teenage boys were shot dead.[96]

As public opinion swung more in favor of the bill, the House committee that first took up the measure moved to toughen it considerably. At the urging of the Leadership Conference, committee liberals added a section providing strong protection against racial discrimination in employment. The coverage of the public accommodations provisions was expanded to include all state-licensed businesses, not just those with a "substantial" involvement in interstate commerce. Initially the president was given discretionary power to deny federal funding to programs that practiced discrimination; that cutoff was made mandatory.[97]

Robert Kennedy was furious at the committee liberals; they had moved so far beyond public opinion as to have blown their chance of getting any legislation through, he believed. The "sons of bitches" were obviously "in love with death."[98] But Robert Kennedy's customary skill at counting votes had deserted him on this occasion. Those who wanted a tougher bill had grasped the changing public mood. The list of groups that backed the tougher committee bill kept lengthening, and no organized opposition came from anywhere but the South. The customary prudential rules of politics had turned out not to apply in this case. As it moved through Congress, the bill had become tougher, not weaker. It was a smashing victory for the civil rights forces.

WE SHALL OVERCOME

Martin Luther King, Jr., was politically shrewd. The switch of tactics from persuasion to provocation in 1963 was a brilliant maneuver, and he knew how to use the national stage to play his southern drama. In the southern context the civil rights movement was of course radical; the SCLC, CORE, SNCC and other participants were engaged in civil disobedience. But they managed to package their effort as a deeply conventional revolt against lawless public authorities. It was important that King would not disobey federal court orders; he maintained his allegiance to the Constitution and to core American political and religious values. Leaders of later protests against the Vietnam War delivered a message that flirted with anarchy; King's was quite different.

The appeal to core religious values was integral to the movement's success, although that part of the story is often neglected. CORE had been formed in 1942 as an outgrowth of a Christian pacifist organization, the Fellowship of Reconciliation, a group of conscientious objectors prepared to go to jail rather than participate in the Second World War. CORE's leaders were passionate Christians dedicated to using Gandhian methods to achieve racial change. The SCLC had its base in the black church. King and many of his closest allies were preachers. Without a deep religious commitment to the cause, it is unlikely that James Farmer and other Freedom Riders could have boarded those buses for their voyage into violence.

The participants in the protests—from Montgomery to Birmingham—were people of enormous courage. They put their lives on the line with no assurance that they would succeed. How little it would have taken to kill the movement: more shrewd police chiefs like Laurie Pritchett, no bull-headed Bull Connor. Had Birmingham turned out differently, it's not so clear where King could have gone; two strikes and he might have been out. King was lucky in his friends and lucky in his enemies.

Although the 1964 Civil Rights Act dealt a mortal blow to Jim Crow, it left one major issue untouched—the denial of voting rights to black people in many southern states. That omission would be remedied the next year, with the passage of the Voting Rights Act of 1965, the story we take up next. Immediately after that second great legislative victory for civil rights, however, things took a dramatic turn for the worse, as the first of the great riots of the 1960s exploded in the Watts section of Los Angeles.

CHAPTER SIX

Coming Together— and Apart

"THERE WILL BE neither rest nor tranquillity in America until the Negro is granted his citizenship rights," Martin Luther King had said, speaking at the Lincoln Memorial on 28 August 1963. Nevertheless, he saw a day when "little black boys and black girls will be able to join hands with little white boys and white girls as sisters and brothers."[1] The prediction of unrest was the more prescient. For just a few years in the mid-1960s, Americans of goodwill had faith. "We *shall* overcome," President Lyndon Johnson had told a joint session of Congress on 15 March 1965.[2] Legislation the previous year and legislation to come promised a color-blind America—not tomorrow, but certainly down the road. But within five days of the passage of the great Voting Rights Act of 1965, the Los Angeles ghetto known as Watts blew up. The intelligentsia was sympathetic; black violence was authentic, even chic. On 24 August 1967 the cover of the *New York Review of Books* would feature a diagram illustrating how to make a Molotov cocktail, sanctioning the series of deadly riots that had begun with Watts. But for ordinary Americans it was the beginning of the end of a great deal of hope. Hope, indeed, that has never quite returned.

THE TRIUMPH OF THE "MARCH ON WASHINGTON" COALITION

By the time of John F. Kennedy's death on 22 November 1963, his civil rights bill—actually, a considerably strengthened version of it—was moving through the legislative process on schedule. Kennedy's successor in the White House, Lyndon B. Johnson, was at least as eager as Kennedy had been to see the measure enacted. Johnson had been in Congress since 1938, and, like virtually all successful southern politicians in the 1940s and 1950s, showed more devotion to states' rights than to civil rights. But as he began thinking seriously of running for the presidency in 1960, Johnson realized that an out-and-out segregationist (Woodrow Wilson, for example) could no longer win a national election in the United States. By the time of Kennedy's death, Vice President Johnson sounded as keen on having a civil rights bill as the president himself.[3]

The day after Kennedy's assassination the new president told his advisors that the Civil Rights Act was his "first priority." A few days later, before a joint session of Congress, he argued that passing the bill would be the most fitting way to honor Kennedy's memory. Johnson had truly come to believe that forceful federal action would help to lift the curse of racism off his native region. But he also knew that civil rights was the number-one issue for liberals, and that his presidential prospects in 1964 rested on his ability to woo northern Democrats who had not liked his presence on the ticket in 1960.[4]

The Civil Rights Act passed the House of Representatives easily in February 1964. Only six out of ten Democrats voted in the affirmative, because of massive defections from the South. (Just seven southern Democrats backed it.) Their loss was more than made up for by overwhelming support from House Republicans, four out of five of whom voted yes.[5] The battle in the Senate was prolonged. The measure was debated there for eighty-two days, the longest congressional debate in American history. It produced an estimated 10 million words that filled 6,300 pages of the *Congressional Record.* The outcome, however, was the same. In June the Senate voted 71 to 29 to invoke cloture and end the filibuster mounted by the South. The measure passed 73 to 27. Again, the defection of southern Democrats was more than made up for by Republican votes; all but 6 of the 33 Republican senators backed the bill, but only 44 of the 67 Democrats. Within the year, the Democrats would come to be known as the party of civil rights, but in 1964 a considerably higher proportion of Republicans than Democrats voted for the most important piece of civil rights legislation in this century.[6]

The legislation, in its final form, outlawed segregation in every facility designed to serve the general public: buses and streetcars, restaurants and lunch counters, hotels and motels, public libraries, swimming pools, movie theaters, bowling alleys, and dance halls. It forbade discrimination in employment and in public education, and barred the use of federal funds in programs that operated in a discriminatory manner, a provision that would soon have an important impact on the ongoing struggle to implement the *Brown* decision. The statute has by now become such a fixed part of the American legislative landscape, it is hard to remember how radical a break with the past it represented. Before 1964, privately owned restaurants were just that—private (except in those northern states that had laws forbidding racial discrimination in public accommodations). They were regulated by state and local health codes but could serve whom they pleased. No longer. The long arm of the federal government now reached Ollie's Barbecue, a small Birmingham restaurant that served a local clientele.[7]

Coming into the 1964 elections, the Civil Rights Act was the Johnson administration's main legislative achievement. The president's Republican opponent, Arizona's ultraconservative senator Barry Goldwater, was one of only six Republican senators to vote against the civil rights bill. The outcome in November was a smashing victory for civil rights proponents. Other issues swayed voters, of course, the most important of which involved foreign policy and the nuclear threat. Still, it was very significant that the candidate who endorsed "states' rights" won a mere 38.5 percent of the popular vote and carried only his own state and five others—all in the Deep South.

The 1964 election brought the Democrats an additional thirty-seven seats in the House and one more in the Senate, giving them majorities of more than two-thirds in both chambers. It was a partisan imbalance the likes of which has not been seen since. Indeed, the Democratic margin was one of the most lopsided in American history.[8] Even if all the conservative white Democrats from the South sided with the Republican opposition, as had often been the case since 1938, northern Democrats of more or less liberal disposition were now in the majority. "The 1964 elections marked a turning point in American politics," Bayard Rustin, a close advisor to Martin Luther King and the chief tactician for the March on Washington, exulted at the time.[9]

The 1964 elections, however, did not prove to be the "turning point" that Rustin thought he saw. Within two years it was evident that 1964 marked not the beginning of an extended era of reform but the beginning of the end for postwar American liberalism. In the congressional elections of 1966, the Democrats suffered a startling defeat; the "Negro-labor-liberal axis" (as Rustin described it) was falling apart. And while an unpopular war in Southeast Asia was part of the reason, the issue of race played a significant part. Riots, a skyrocketing crime rate, ugly black power rhetoric, a marked increase in the number of welfare dependents: all of these discredited the liberal cause in the eyes of ordinary working people.

MURDER IN MISSISSIPPI

The 1964 Civil Rights Act had met the main demands of the civil rights movement. Jim Crow was not dead, but the full force of the federal government had been committed to destroying every residue of state-enforced segregation. And yet the fundamental right of political participation was not secure. In fact, the mild voting rights provision in the original Kennedy bill was the only part that was actually weakened in the lengthy congressional infighting that preceded passage of the act.[10]

Since World War II, black participation in politics had been rising gradually and inexorably (Table 1). In 1940 barely 3 percent of southern blacks of voting age had managed to register. By 1960 the figure had risen to 29 percent, and by 1964 it was up to 42 percent. The surge in the total black vote between

Table 1
Percent of Southern Blacks of Voting Age Registered to Vote

1940	3.1
1946	12.2
1952	20.0
1956	25.0
1960	28.7
1964	41.9
1966	51.6
1970	66.9

Source: Gerald David Jaynes and Robin M. Williams, Jr., eds., *A Common Destiny: Blacks and American Society,* National Research Council (Washington, D.C.: National Academy Press, 1989), 233.

1960 and 1964 was accompanied by a further shift of blacks toward the Democratic Party. They had leaned strongly Democratic; they now became the party's most die-hard supporters. John F. Kennedy was supported by seven out of ten African Americans in 1960; four years later, Lyndon Johnson won a stunning nineteen out of twenty black votes.[11]

Despite the substantial progress that had been made in the 1940s, 1950s, and early 1960s, in 1964 southern blacks were considerably less likely to be registered than their white neighbors, particularly in the small towns and rural areas of the Deep South. Part of the reason was the variety of legal requirements—poll taxes, literacy tests, and others—that we have already discussed. But more important than the legal barriers was the economic, social, and physical coercion directed against blacks who were so "uppity" as to try to vote. In many southern communities African Americans bold enough to insist on exercising their right to register might find themselves without a job or credit at the store. They might even end up with a bullet in the back, like Medgar Evers.

The fate of three student volunteers working for the Mississippi Summer Project in 1964 brought that appalling truth home to millions of Americans. Mississippi had both the highest proportion of black residents of any state (42 percent) and the lowest percent on the registration rolls (5.3 percent).[12] A coalition of civil rights groups—led by SNCC and CORE—decided to attack the state's closed political system by using college students to run "Freedom Schools" and otherwise assist Mississippi blacks to register to vote. Having learned the importance of media coverage, they wanted mainly students who were white, from Ivy League or other elite schools, and, if possible, from prominent families. The Harvard College contingent, for example, included two sons of the former president of CBS News. Yet another outrage inflicted upon a southern black from an ordinary family without powerful connections might not be national news; violence directed against these children of privilege, SNCC and CORE knew, would create headlines.

Disaster struck while most of the volunteers were still attending a training session in Ohio. Michael Schwerner, Andrew Goodman, and James Chaney—two northern middle-class whites and one black from Mississippi—suddenly disappeared. A few days later the car in which they had been traveling was found abandoned and burned in a swamp. The disappearance attracted enormous national attention, including—not surprisingly—a CBS news special, and it provoked President Johnson to blanket the state with FBI agents. After six weeks their bodies were discovered buried near Philadelphia, Mississippi. The three had been arrested by a deputy sheriff on a trumped-up traffic charge and murdered by the Klan, to whom they had been delivered.[13]

The state was swarming with FBI men and the media, but Mississippi whites were not intimidated. Over the course of the summer, some thirty-seven black churches were burned, thirty houses or other buildings were bombed, and more than one thousand people were arrested.[14] Moreover, by the measure of black enfranchisement, the Mississippi Summer Project was a complete flop. In a state with nearly half a million unregistered, voting-age African Americans, some 800 volunteers working full-time for a summer managed to add a mere 1,600 people to the registration rolls. The black registration rate edged up from 5.3 to 6.7 percent; the rate for Mississippi whites was 62.7 percent.[15]

The real impact of the Mississippi Summer was on national public opinion. Northerners did know that "uppity" blacks in the Deep South got murdered, but most assumed that whites would be treated like whites, with constitutional rights. After the summer of 1964, northern whites knew differently. The road to federal civil rights legislation had been cleared. Arguments stressing the danger posed by a heightened concentration of power in Washington would henceforth fall on deaf northern ears, at least for some time to come.

THE MFDP

The murder of three young, idealistic men in Mississippi created an awkward political problem for the Democratic Party at its 1964 convention in Atlantic City. The SNCC and CORE activists in charge of the project had used the volunteers not only to persuade blacks to fill out voter registration forms but also to sign them up as members of a new organization, the Mississippi Freedom Democratic Party. The MFDP had no legal status in the eyes of the state of Mississippi, but disfranchised African Americans had had no voice in the selection of delegates to the Democratic National Convention, where the candidate most likely to speak for civil rights issues would be chosen. The

MFDP thus picked its own slate of delegates and sent them to Atlantic City, where they campaigned to be seated as the legitimate representatives of the state of Mississippi. One of the party's leaders, Fannie Lou Hamer, in a speech to the party's credentials committee (carried on national television), described how she had been fired from her job, shot at, and beaten so badly she couldn't walk. She had been trying to register African Americans to vote.[16]

Lyndon Johnson refused to grant the MFDP's demands, which would amount to disfranchising Mississippi's white voters as a penalty for their complicity in black disfranchisement. Such an action might provoke another Dixiecrat revolt, as in 1948, or a mass defection of southern whites to Barry Goldwater, whose praise of "states' rights" made him sound much more like a southern Democrat than a traditional Republican. Johnson offered to seat two of the forty-four MFDP delegates as a token, and promised that the selection of delegates for the next convention would be on a nondiscriminatory basis. It wasn't good enough. Dr. King and Roy Wilkins, themselves under pressure, urged the MFDP to accept the plan. But while John Lewis at the March on Washington had agreed to read a bowdlerized speech, this time there would be no compromise. The leaders of the MFDP were too certain of the justice of their cause to engage in sordid political bargaining. They spurned the deal and left the convention.

The walkout was a sign of things to come. The civil rights movement, which had displayed such impressive unity at the March on Washington a year earlier, was splintering. Moreover, tension was rising between whites and blacks within the movement; down the road whites would be thrown out of SNCC and CORE. These were the organizations that had run the MFDP, and they left Atlantic City convinced that white liberals—including LBJ— were no different from white Goldwater conservatives. Liberals put on a good show, singing "We Shall Overcome," but when the chips were down, they went with the system. In fact, the contempt of the MFDP for Democratic Party players extended beyond white liberals to heroes of the movement: Dr. King, Roy Wilkins, and other black leaders who had been in on the Atlantic City deal.[17] The harmony that had won so much was gone.

SELMA AND THE VOTING RIGHTS ACT OF 1965

New rules for the selection of delegates to the Democratic National Convention were not the real solution to the crisis created by the MFDP. The basic problem was black disfranchisement; give southern blacks the ballot, and they would be part of the political process. It was an obvious point that made the president nervous. In 1965 the Great Society program was his top legislative priority; he wanted Medicare, food stamps, and federal aid to education for children in poverty. Although the Democrats had huge margins in both houses of Congress, LBJ was still reluctant to antagonize southern Democrats unnecessarily, as an all-out drive for legislation to ensure Fifteenth Amendment rights would surely do.

Johnson was also skittish about the possible electoral consequences of such legislation. The enfranchisement of blacks would initially swell the ranks of the Democratic Party. But the South would likely be up in arms if the federal government were given an important role in the registration process—left by constitutional tradition to the states and localities. And thus black enfranchisement might drive whites into the Republican camp, more than offsetting the gain. No state had a black majority; blacks alone could not swing an election.[18]

With the president deeply ambivalent, King and the SCLC decided it was time to stage another Birmingham. They picked the city of Selma, Alabama, with Sheriff Jim Clark cast in the key role of Bull Connor. The Justice Department had engaged in four years of litigation attacking black disfranchisement in Dallas County, of which Selma was the seat. Twice a federal court had found widespread Fifteenth Amendment violations, and at first glance it might have seemed that unmistakable progress had resulted: black registration had increased more than twentyfold, from 16 to 383. But there were approximately 15,000 blacks of voting age in that majority-black county.[19] Less than 3 percent of black adults were registered to vote.

King, his prestige enhanced by his recent receipt of the Nobel Prize for Peace, arrived in Selma in January 1965 to launch an SCLC voter registration drive. The aim, he said, was to "dramatize the situation . . . by marching by the thousands to the places of registration" so as to "arouse the federal government."[20] As it turned out, the opportunity to "dramatize" was slow to materialize. For several weeks Sheriff Clark's men hauled protesters off to jail without glaringly obvious brutality—or at least not on camera.

But then the SCLC decided to switch its tactics, in hopes of getting national notice. King called for a march from Selma to the state capitol in Montgomery, which took place on Sunday, 7 March. The governor, George Wallace, ordered that the march be stopped, and stationed several dozen state troopers on a bridge leading out of Selma. Sheriff Clark dispatched dozens of his deputies as well, many of them on horseback. When the six hundred marchers arrived at the Edmund Pettus Bridge, the police on horseback used tear gas, electric cattle prods, nightsticks, and whips, driving them nearly a mile from the bridge before halting the attack. The *New York Times* report described it as something one would expect in "a police state."[21]

Once again, the bloody spectacle was played out in full view of the television cameras and dozens of reporters. Moreover, more blood flowed the following day when a gang of Selma whites beat to death the Reverend James Reeb, a white minister from Boston who had joined the SCLC effort. Two weeks later, another northern white, Viola Liuzzo of Detroit, was shot dead while she was driving to Montgomery to transport marchers.[22] By this time, federal action was inevitable. The president called a special joint session of Congress to plea for a voting rights bill. He wanted the "goddamnedest, toughest voting rights bill" that could be devised.[23]

And, indeed, that's what he got. A simple statistical rule of thumb identified voting rights violations. A state or county that had employed a literacy test in November 1964, and in which less than half the total voting-age population had cast ballots, was assumed to have engaged in electoral discrimination, with the burden on the jurisdiction to prove otherwise. From this inferred presence of Fifteenth Amendment violations, several consequences followed. In "covered" jurisdictions, literacy tests were suspended. Federal registrars ("examiners") and election observers could be dispatched to those areas whenever necessary. Moreover, those states and counties could institute no new voting practice without "preclearance" (approval) by the attorney general or the District Court for the District of Columbia. Southern states could not invent new devices that robbed blacks of their basic right to a ballot.

The act was a mixture of permanent and temporary provisions. Those sections that conferred extraordinary power on federal authorities to override traditional state prerogatives had an expected life of only five years. Nevertheless, members of Congress on both sides of the aisle objected to their unprecedented stringency. Most Republican members of the House Judiciary Committee complained of an "indiscriminate" statistical test that would engulf counties innocent of discrimination in a "tidal wave of Federal control of the election process." Southern Democrats saw the ghost of Reconstruction. The drastic, temporary provisions of the act applied to six southern states in their entirety, a seventh in substantial part, and only scattered counties elsewhere. This was punitive legislation aimed at the South, North Carolina Senator Sam Ervin and others complained. It was a "studied insult" to the region's honorable people.

Such charges, however, were not persuasive. The act was a harsh and blunt instrument, but in 1965 the South was in no position to protest its passage. And in the end the vote was 328 to 74 in the House and 79 to 18 in the Senate. Moreover, the public was firmly behind the act. A Gallup poll shortly after the president's speech in mid-March found that the public favored a law to "make sure that Negroes and whites are given an equal opportunity to register and vote" by almost five to one (76 versus 16 percent). Even southern whites, amazingly, were more favorable than not, by a 49 to 37 percent margin.[24] The political order of the South since Reconstruction had depended on a solid white consensus on the proper role of blacks in politics—namely, no role at all. That consensus had been shattered, perhaps in part because significant numbers of whites saw a difference between depriving blacks of any political voice and running segregated schools. There were (bad) arguments for the latter, but no arguments for the former—or at least none that could be squared with the United States Constitution. With such a high level of popular support in North and South, the bill made its way through Congress easily and was signed into law by President Johnson on 6 August.

Lyndon Johnson regarded the act as his "greatest accomplishment," and Roy Wilkins called it the "most significant" civil rights achievement of the decade.[25] The statute did what it was supposed to do, and very quickly. Five years after its passage the black registration rate had soared in the states covered by the legislation (Table 2). By 1967, Mississippi, taking off from the low point of 6.7 percent, had the highest percentage of black registered voters anywhere in the South. By 1969 southern blacks were nearly as likely to be registered to vote as their white neighbors.

When the political future of Dallas County's sheriff, Jim Clark (responsible for the bloodshed), was decided by 9,800 white voters and 325 black voters, black opinion was a matter of indifference. But by November 1965, Clark already had reason for concern. Almost 8,000 black residents had been added to the voter rolls, and the number was still climbing.[26] The following year, when the sheriff was up for reelection, it was payback time; the county's electorate had become majority-black and Clark was out of office.[27]

Within four years a Supreme Court decision would begin the process by which the Voting Rights Act was reshaped into an instrument for affirmative action in the electoral sphere. But in 1965 the statute had a simple aim: providing ballots for southern blacks. The extraordinary power that the legislation conferred on both courts and the Department of Justice, permitting an unprecedented intrusion of federal authority into local electoral affairs, was meant to deal with an extraordinary problem: continued black disfranchisement ninety-five years after the passage of the Fifteenth Amendment. And its impact was exactly as intended: the most basic right of citizenship had finally been conferred.

Table 2

Percent of Voting-Age Blacks Registered in the Six States Covered by the Voting Rights Act the Year Before and Four Years After Its Passage

	1964	1969
Alabama	23.0	61.3
Georgia	44.0	60.4
Louisiana	32.0	60.8
Mississippi	6.7	66.5
South Carolina	38.7	54.6
Virginia	45.7	59.4

Source: David J. Garrow, *Protest at Selma: Martin Luther King, Jr., and the Voting Rights Act of 1965* (New Haven: Yale University Press, 1978), 18, 200.

The 1964 Civil Rights Act and its companion piece, the Voting Rights Act, were the culmination of a decade-long drive to expand the civil rights of black Americans. As Bayard Rustin noted, with dizzying speed the "legal foundations of racism in America" had been "destroyed." The "elaborate legal structure of segregation and discrimination" had "virtually collapsed."[28]

LONG HOT SUMMERS

The great civil rights statutes of the mid-1960s were an amazing triumph—a revolution whose swift outcome was unimaginable in 1955 when Rosa Parks was told to move from her seat on a bus. In revolutions, however, appetite tends to grow with the eating. Legal equality had been won; social and economic inequality was still rampant. The latter was a problem without an obvious solution. By the end of 1965, King and other civil rights leaders had new mountains to climb and no map to guide them. Indeed, in the difficult terrain ahead, keeping the group together would not be possible, as King himself understood. "There is no more civil rights movement," he observed. "President Johnson signed it out of existence when he signed the voting rights bill."[29]

That a different day had dawned was apparent just five days after the Voting Rights Act became law. On August 11, 1965, a riot broke out in the section of South Central Los Angeles known as Watts. It was the beginning of four "long hot summers," as they came to be called—four summers of civil disorder that tore apart the "Negro-labor-liberal" coalition. The result of this racial earthquake was a resurgence of the Republican Party in national politics and the emergence of racial separatism and black power.

Watts began with a routine traffic arrest. A car driven by a young black man who had had too much to drink was spotted weaving from lane to lane in South Central Los Angeles. When a California Highway Patrol car pulled it over, a crowd quickly gathered. After the driver resisted arrest and was forcibly subdued, a rumor spread that the police had beaten up and arrested a pregnant woman. The rapidly growing mob began to denounce the officers as "motherfuckers" and pelt them with stones and bottles. Although reinforcements from the Los Angeles Police Department soon arrived, the crowd multiplied at a faster pace than the number of officers who could be rushed to the scene. Soon the mob was throwing stones at passing cars, overturning those that were stopped or parked, setting them afire, and attacking whites who happened to be passing through. The following evening matters became even worse. Huge crowds of people broke into stores, stripped the shelves, and often set them ablaze, chanting "Burn, baby, burn."[30]

The arrest of one drunk driver thus sparked five days of immensely destructive chaos, with the television cameras whirring. No more images of peaceful, disciplined black demonstrators praying while whites in uniform attacked them with clubs. Across the nation's television screens flashed the sight of an African-American mob on a rampage, seemingly gleeful while stealing, smashing, and burning.

It required the efforts of 1,000 officers of the LAPD, 700 sheriff's deputies, and 14,000 troops from the National Guard to bring the Watts riot to an end. Temporary military control had to be imposed over an area of more than forty-six square miles. Thirty-four people died in the conflagration, 1,000 were injured badly enough to require medical attention, and 4,000 were arrested. A thousand businesses were looted and destroyed or seriously damaged.[31]

Watts was the first of a series of major riots spread over four summers. Actually, they were not the first disturbances of their kind. A year earlier the police had clashed with residents of black neighborhoods in New York and other northern cities, but these were relatively minor episodes. In Rochester, New York, for instance, a riot resulted in four deaths; in turmoil in Harlem, one person had been killed.[32] An FBI investigation managed to conclude that these episodes were not even "racial"; the author of the report apparently used the term "racial" for uprisings organized for political or ideological ends, not for seemingly unplanned events.[33]

Watts was not so easily dismissed. As one historian has noted, the Los Angeles riots were "so vast, so awesome, so devastating, and so widely reported—for a full week they received front-page coverage nationally and internationally—that henceforth there could be no doubt that a distinct pattern of summer violence was emerging in the black ghettos."[34] The "pattern of summer violence" to which he referred affected almost every northern city of any size in the years 1965 to 1968. (Southern urban centers were largely quiet, a surprising point we shall return to later.) According to one count, 329 "important" riots took place in 257 cities between 1964 and 1968.[35] Close to 300 Americans died in these disorders, at least 8,000 were injured, about 60,000 were arrested, and property losses ran into the hundreds of millions of dollars.[36]

Although the destruction in Los Angeles was shocking, the Detroit riot two years later was even worse. The *Washington Post* called it "the greatest tragedy of all the long succession of Negro ghetto outbursts."[37] Like Watts, the conflict began with an ordinary police action, this time involving not a traffic arrest but a middle-of-the-night crackdown on one of the city's many "blind pigs," unlicensed bars that flouted local liquor and gambling laws. Again, a crowd gathered while the officers were making the arrest; as it grew larger, the crowd began to throw stones and bottles at the officers. Again, a rumor spread, this time to the effect that the police had bayoneted a black man and had left him to bleed to death.

Things spun out of control more rapidly than in Los Angeles, with looting and burning starting almost immediately after the first confrontation with the police. The mayor, Jerome Cavanagh, was a committed liberal with close ties to the local black leadership and ambitions for higher office. The *Washington Post* expressed astonishment that the ghetto explosion had occurred in Detroit, of all places, because it believed that Cavanagh's progressive leadership had made the Motor City "the American model of intelligence and courage applied to the governance of a huge industrial city." The *New York Times* was equally surprised; Detroit, it said, "probably had more going for it than any other major city in the North."[38] In fact, the most important thing Detroit had "going for it," according to the liberal press, was the progress the city had made in race relations. For instance, Cavanagh had chosen a police commissioner determined to change the department's negative image in the black community. The new commissioner ordered the department to follow a "walk soft" policy in dealing with racial conflicts; his men were to be "police officers, not executioners," which meant that they would not use deadly force to prevent a mob of people from getting out of control. The result was disastrous. Forbidden to use their guns or even tear gas to control the crowd, the vastly outnumbered Detroit police could only stand around and watch the looting and burning, while members of the crowd taunted them with comments like "the fuzz is scared; they ain't goin' to do nothin.' "[39]

The mayor should have asked for assistance from the Michigan State Police and the National Guard, but his fear of seeming unduly harsh, even racist, led him to procrastinate. The police commissioner reported feeling "scared stiff" of "slaughter" if outside forces were brought in. In the hours in which Cavanagh dithered, the chaos continued, resulting in further damage to the city and its people.[40] Order was finally restored by state troopers, National Guardsmen, and units from the 82nd and 101st Airborne Divisions of the U.S. Army. By the end, over 7,200 persons had been arrested, twice as many as in Watts. Some 2,500 stores had been looted, burned, or otherwise destroyed, two-and-a-half times as many as in Los Angeles. Detroit ranked first in total deaths as well; 43 citizens were killed, 33 blacks and 10 whites.[41] The swath of destruction the rioters cut through the city was an awesome sight. Even now, three decades later, some parts of Detroit that were ravaged in 1967 resemble what Berlin looked like in 1945.

Although these disorders were commonly referred to as "race riots," it is in fact a misleading label. In the classic American race riots of the World War I era—the one in Chicago in 1919, for example—whites were the aggressors, attacking blacks with the aim of injuring, killing, or driving them from "white" turf. The rioters were white, not black, and they were given a free hand by police who typically stood by, implicitly siding with those on the attack.[42] The uprisings of the 1960s were entirely different, and not only because blacks took the initiative. Whites were not the aggressors, but neither were many of them victims. The sixties riots were not mob attacks on whites comparable to earlier mob attacks on blacks.

The casualty figures establish this beyond any doubt. Well over three hundred—over five hundred by one count—violent racial disturbances occurred in American cities over a span of several years. No reliable estimate of the total number of blacks who participated is available, but we know that about 60,000 African Americans were arrested and that this was probably at best one-fifth of those who took part in the riots.[43] Something on the order of 300,000 people were thus participants. And yet the total number of whites who died in all of these clashes was no more than three dozen.[44] Many of those deaths, furthermore, were not murders committed by black participants but accidental killings caused by gunfire from law enforcement officials.

CAUSES OF THE RIOTS

In Montgomery, Selma, Birmingham, and elsewhere in the South, Dr. King and others at the helm had kept the protests nonviolent. Blacks who took to the streets in Watts and Detroit, however, had no leaders who issued demands or manifestos that represented the collective opinion of the masses.[45] Indeed, it quickly became evident that the established civil rights leadership was both mystified and helpless. These were events beyond their control. Why they occurred and why they ended (as suddenly and unexpectedly as they started) are big questions, not easy to answer. As one recent study has astutely observed, they remain "one of the most enigmatic social phenomena in American history," by now shrouded in mythology.[46]

Enigmatic but much analyzed. In 1964 the FBI had characterized the pre-Watts disorders in New York and elsewhere as "senseless" episodes without "purpose." But in liberal political circles, riots were viewed as protests against white racism in urban America—cries of anguish and rage at poverty, low wages, high unemployment, and other injustices. Bayard Rustin, for example, maintained that Watts had an "express purpose"; not in words, but in deeds, the participants were announcing that they "would no longer quietly submit to the deprivation of slum life."[47] That view was enshrined in the 1968 Kerner report, prepared by a presidential commission that studied the causes of the disorders and recommended solutions. The report portrayed the riots as natural and inevitable protests against "the racial attitudes and behavior of white Americans toward black Americans." An "explosive mixture" had accumulated in the cities "since the end of World War II," and it was not surprising that the powder keg had at last detonated.[48]

The head of CORE, James Farmer, wrote in a similar vein. He deplored the rioting in Watts "unqualifiedly," he said. But "we must remember that the outrage of unemployment and hopelessness that pervades the ghetto remains a prelude to the outrage of . . . the gasoline bomb."[49] Others, younger and more radical, saw nothing to deplore. A CORE field secretary argued that it was inconsistent to "worship our revolt against mother England" and then to turn around and "condemn the revolt of the people in Watts." He saw parallels with the Holocaust as well as the American Revolution: "Watts was saying to white America," he declared, that blacks were refusing to "walk peacefully to the gas chambers."[50] Others with a similar fondness for historical analogies termed the riots "twentieth century slave revolts."[51]

If the riots were in fact protests against "the outrage of unemployment and hopelessness," they should have occurred in those cities in which economic deprivation was the greatest. But Detroit, the city that was hardest hit, did not have the most poverty or the most wretched slums. To the contrary: in 1967, it contained a very large, affluent, and rapidly growing black middle class. Detroit's auto industry was booming, and the black unemployment rate stood at a minuscule 3.4 percent, a figure lower than the national average *for whites* in any year since the end of World War II. The home-ownership rate for the city's blacks was the highest in the country, and the poverty rate was only half that for African Americans in the nation as a whole. Equally striking, the income of the typical black family in Detroit was a mere 6 percent behind the white average, a smaller racial gap than could be found in any other city in the United States at the time.[52] Had they toured Detroit just before the riot broke out, Rustin and Farmer would not have been able to discover much evidence of the "deprivation of slum life" and the "unemployment and hopelessness" of "the ghetto" of which they spoke.

Nor was Watts a particularly horrendous "slum," with appallingly high levels of poverty, unemployment, and hopelessness. It was no Beverly Hills, to be sure. Most of its inhabitants were on the lower rungs of the economic ladder, and it had its share of the problems common to low income neighborhoods. But, for the most part, it was an area of single-family dwellings, not an impoverished neighborhood of teeming tenements and high-rise housing projects. The Los Angeles economy was humming along nicely in 1965, and jobs were generally open to blacks, which had not been the case in the industrializing areas of the South in the 1940s and 1950s.

Just a year before Watts went up in flames, the National Urban League did a study that rated the sixty-eight largest cities in the United States as places to live for black people. After reviewing a wide array of economic and social data, the report ranked Los Angeles number one in the nation.[53] Its attractions had lured tens of thousands of African Americans to the City of Angels over the preceding quarter century, and while many had doubtless been disappointed by what they found, few could have thought that moving to Los Angeles was like walking into "the gas chambers." Neither Detroit nor Los Angeles fit the economic-deprivation theory. In fact, large-scale statistical studies based on comprehensive urban data suggest that "indicators of black disadvantage do not predict either the location of riots or the severity of the violence when it occurs."[54] One study concludes that racial disorders were "most likely to occur when the condition of life for blacks was least oppressive according to objective measures, not most oppressive."[55]

Individual cities, it can legitimately be said, are not islands cut off from one another, places whose inhabitants respond only to local stimuli. An acute sense of deprivation in Newark could be felt by blacks in Los Angeles as well. But if the rioters were really out to challenge the "symbols of white authority," as was so often claimed, why no marches on City Hall, no sit-ins in the mayor's office or the city council chambers?[56]

Those who rioted did challenge the power of one instrument of "white authority"—namely the police. Police actions were usually the precipitating incidents in these disorders, and the police were the initial object of the crowd's rage. But if the ghetto uprisings are interpreted as deliberate and calculated challenges to the authority of law enforcement officials, looting stores and burning them down was a circuitous way of going about it. Why not challenge the police directly, by picketing police stations or even attacking them, storming the local equivalent of the Bastille?

Few of the riot participants had the broad political consciousness that has often been attributed to them. And they were not focused on attacking white authority. Their aim was to appropriate, or destroy, property. And—a crucial point—it was not just white property. It has often been asserted that rioters targeted white businesses and left black ones alone. Signs saying SOUL BROTHER or something similar, it is said, were a deterrent to looters and arsonists, who were out to "get whitey."[57] The claim is unsupported, however, by the evidence. After the smoke had cleared in Detroit, for example, a black merchant observed that if your store had something that the rioters wanted, "you were going to get looted no matter what color you were." The very first store under attack in Detroit did not belong to a white, nor to a proprietor regarded as unusually greedy or unpleasant. It was Hardy's Drug Store, which was both black-owned and known to be generous about filling prescriptions on credit. The best black restaurant in the city went up in flames, and the leading black-owned clothing store was looted. Unaccountably the mob left untouched Azzam's Market, a grocery store owned by an Arab that had been picketed by CORE and other groups two years earlier after the owner's son had shot a black customer to death in a fight. And yet the rioters burned down a black-owned liquor store on the same corner.[58]

Evidence from other cities reveals that the pattern of looting and arson in Detroit was not unusual. A comparative study of ghetto merchants in fifteen large northern cities found that the race of the owner had little to do with how a business would fare during a riot. Black storekeepers were almost as likely to be hit as those who were white.[59] But the fact that rioters made little effort to spare black-owned businesses, becomes less surprising when we look at black public opinion. Racial hostility to whites who did business in black neighborhoods was not nearly as common as often thought. The fifteen-city survey showed that less than a fifth (18 percent) of blacks shared the core black nationalist belief that stores in "a Negro neighborhood should be owned and run by Negroes."[60] Hardly any of those polled believed that white-owned stores overcharged black customers. A small minority (15 percent) saw black shopkeepers as more respectful to them than whites were, but 7 percent thought whites showed greater respect, and the vast majority felt that the race of the owner made no difference at all.[61]

A similar and more surprising finding from the same survey is that urban blacks did not view the police officers with whom they came into contact through a strictly racial lens either. The police forces of most cities in this period were heavily white, which legitimately drew a lot of criticism from the Kerner Commission and others. But the African-American city-dwellers did not seem to believe that they could expect better treatment from a black policeman. Almost three-fourths (73 percent) of the blacks in the fifteen-city study felt that there was no difference in the conduct of white and black police officers. And among those who did think there was a difference, a small majority actually believed that white officers were better behaved than black officers. The same study also showed that only 7 percent of blacks picked out "police brutality" as the "main cause" of the riots, and only 3 percent named "better police treatment" as the "most important thing the city govern-ment . . . could do to keep a disturbance like the one in Detroit from breaking out here."[62] In fact, many white policemen may have been racists; there is no evidence, however, of black anger focused particularly on them.

THE DOG THAT DIDN'T BARK IN THE NIGHT

A little over half of the black population of the United States still lived in the South in the 1960s, but only a few of the riots—and none of the largest and most destructive ones—took place there. Only one of the eight 1967 uprisings the Kerner Commission classified as "major," for example, was in the South, and that one—in Tampa—did not match the scale of those in Detroit and Newark.[63]

Why was rioting either minor or absent in the part of the country with the worst racial history? Here is a case of the Sherlock Holmes dog that did not bark in the night; it is significant yet easily overlooked, since its importance lies in the fact that it didn't happen. Clearly, southern police were not more respectful of the rights of black citizens than those in the North. But the tradition of police brutality in the South—as appalling as it was—may have been a deterrent. One comparative study found that a strong show of force by the police at the first signs of unrest kept the lid on. In every case in which there was a policy of "early use of massive force," it worked; no full-blown riot developed.[64] Thus, when George Wallace's state troopers had not hesitated to use force, the riot that started in Birmingham in the spring of 1963 lasted only one evening. In addition, southern black life was in general more tightly organized, more structured, and more centered on the church. Moreover, the civil rights movement itself channeled racial grievances into action directed against those with the power to provide a remedy.

Northern blacks followed the southern drama closely. Many of them had been born in the South, and still had relatives there. They cheered at movement victories, gave money to the SCLC and SNCC, and voted for candidates with strong civil rights records. But they also felt helpless rage at what they saw. Stokely Carmichael, the head of SNCC, related the riots in northern cities to the fact that each time blacks "saw Martin Luther King get slapped, they became angry; when they saw four little black girls bombed to death, they were angrier; and when nothing happened, they were steaming."[65] Steaming but disorganized. The leadership of the black community in the North was more fragmented than that in the South, the problems were harder to define, and the solutions much more uncertain.

Watching the scenes from Birmingham and Selma, though, had stimulated racial consciousness and fostered discontent. There was a telling incident during the initial confrontation that led to the Watts riot. A woman who was being arrested called one of the officers a "white Southern bastard," although there was nothing the least bit "southern" about him. Another black in the crowd sounded the same note, shouting, "We've got no rights at all—it's just like Selma."[66] The riots were an extension of the southern demonstrations, with the vital difference that the protest in the South had leaders who planned actions with painstaking care and made every effort to ensure that all the violence would be on the other side. Without leaders to define concrete demands and focus the energies of the crowd on peaceful activities, protest in the North took a chaotic, anarchic, and highly destructive form.[67]

BLACK POWER

The mobs gathering in the streets plainly did not consider mainstream civil rights leaders to be *their* leaders. During the 1964 Harlem disorder Bayard Rustin rode through the streets in a sound truck, urging the crowds to cool it; he was called an "Uncle Tom" and ignored. In the early stages of Watts a group of eminent African Americans that included the city's only black congressman, comedian and activist Dick Gregory, as well as representatives from the leading civil rights organizations and black churches, urged the crowd to disperse peacefully. They paid attention only to Gregory; someone noticed his presence sufficiently to put a bullet in his leg.[68] During the Detroit riot black Congressman John Conyers, Jr., was out on the streets telling people to go home. They shouted, "Why should we go home? Tell the cops to go home. This is where we live." Afterward, a shaken Conyers said, "You try to talk to those people and they'll knock you into the middle of next year." His own constituents had become "those people."[69]

Martin Luther King was bewildered, disoriented, and deeply depressed by the violent ghetto eruptions. He wanted to condemn them without seeming to downplay legitimate grievances, and found it hard to strike the right balance. He said that he was trying to be "militant enough to satisfy the militant" and yet "keep enough discipline in the movement to satisfy white supporters and moderate Negroes."[70] The strain of trying to ride two horses that were moving in such different directions was beginning to tell. In July 1967, after the Newark and Detroit riots had set new records for destructiveness, King made the outlandish charge that "Congress has created the atmosphere for these riots." (It had cut funding slightly for the War on Poverty and had refused to endorse King's idea that the federal government should guarantee "a job to every person who needs work.") He confessed to his wife that "people expect me to have answers and I don't have any answers. I don't feel like speaking to people. I have nothing to tell them."[71]

Martin Luther King feeling tongue-tied? It was an amazing turn of events. But if he had nothing to say, there were plenty of cocky young radicals around who had plenty to "tell them." "Black power" was their message. It was a slogan first announced by Stokely Carmichael at a June 1966 protest march in Mississippi. King disliked it for two reasons. It signaled an abandonment of the movement's long tradition of interracial cooperation, the end of "black and white together, we shall not be moved." And it entailed a willingness to acquire power "by any means necessary," a clear rejection of King's commitment to the use of only nonviolent means.[72]

Despite muted criticisms from King and sharper ones from Roy Wilkins, A. Philip Randolph, Bayard Rustin, and Whitney Young of the Urban League, the black power idea caught on. It fit with the new agenda SNCC was developing under Carmichael's leadership, which involved expelling its white members and redirecting its efforts from the rural South to the urban North. CORE moved in the same direction; by 1967 it had even dropped the term "multiracial" from its constitution.[73]

In 1966, Huey Newton and Bobby Seale founded the Black Panther Party, based in Oakland, California. As Hugh Pearson's biography has shown in persuasive detail, Newton was a man who both played at black power politics and led a serious life of crime. He hung around with bank robbers and other low-life types, courted shoot-outs with the police, and was himself addicted to drugs and violence, much of the latter directed against former friends. For a time he lived in Cuba, which he liked, he said, because everyone had a gun.

Newton and his pals not only had a taste for knifings, beatings, rapes, burglaries, and protection rackets, they also marched into the California Assembly, armed with M-1 rifles and 12-gauge shotguns. Enamored of Mao

Tse-Tung's dictum that "power flows from the barrel of a gun," they managed to persuade themselves that the government of the United States could be toppled by an armed revolution, which they would lead.[74] It was heady stuff, which had considerable appeal for these young, impatient urban black men. Whatever "black power" might mean—the term was ambiguous enough to be susceptible to interpretations ranging from the completely banal to the revolutionary—it unquestionably packed a powerful emotional wallop. "We Want Black Power," a 1967 leaflet produced by SNCC's Chicago office announced; "we must fill ourselves with hate for all things white."[75] This was, of course, the sort of sentiment that blacks had long had kept to themselves; it was a mark of changed times that such things could be said.

Antiwhite rage was understandable enough, but it wasn't likely to be greeted with enthusiasm by most whites. On the other hand, uncompromising militancy was certainly an attention-getter and thus strategically wise.[76] For a time, no one was better than Carmichael at playing the publicity game. He had an implicit bargain with the reporters who followed him around: cover me and I'll feed you good (i.e., outrageous) copy. And thus he gave speeches and press conferences sprinkled with references to "offing the pigs" and "killing the honkies." "When you talk about black power, you talk about bringing this country to its knees," he said in a 1966 Cleveland address. "When you talk of black power, you talk of building a movement that will smash everything Western Civilization has created." The speech was denounced on the floor of the U.S. House of Representatives, which undoubtedly pleased Carmichael.[77]

His successor as head of SNCC, H. Rap Brown, was even cruder and less inhibited. "Violence is as American as cherry pie" was the remark that made his name; actually, it was tame stuff for Brown. He liked to refer to President Johnson as "a mad, wild dog" or a "honkie cracker," and said that "if you give me a gun, I might just shoot Lady Bird." Just after the Newark conflagration, he urged blacks to "wage guerrilla war on the honkie white man." While the Detroit riot was raging, he told a rally of blacks in Cambridge, Maryland, that "if America don't come around, we going to burn it down, brother. We are going to burn it down if we don't get our share of it." He urged his listeners to "get you some guns," because "the only thing a honkie respects is force." King had counseled his followers to love their oppressor; they should appeal to the spark of the divine in everyone. Brown replied, "Don't be trying to love that honkie to death. Shoot him to death. Shoot him to death, brother, 'cause that's what he's out to do to you."[78]

The most influential figure behind the black power concept—Malcolm X —was dead before anything that could be called a black power movement had developed. Malcolm had spent his early years as a petty criminal and hustler in Boston and New York. He served six years in a Massachusetts prison for burglary, and became a minister in the tiny black Muslim sect, the Nation of Islam, upon his release in 1952. Malcolm spent a dozen years in the Nation and had become the chief protégé of its head, Elijah Muhammad, before he had a falling out with Elijah in 1964 and was expelled.

At the core of black Muslim doctrine, and hence of Malcolm's thought, was the belief that whites were devils who were doomed to extinction; a gigantic firestorm unleashed by Allah would rage for 310 years, killing only whites. The wait would not be long. After a plane carrying a group of 120 white passengers from Georgia went down near Paris, Malcolm said "a very beautiful thing . . . has happened. . . . We call on our God and He gets rid of 120 of them at one whop." After John F. Kennedy's assassination, Malcolm chortled that it was a case of "the chickens coming home to roost," and that it didn't make him sad, it made him "glad." He referred to the three Kennedy brothers —Jack, Robert, and Ted—as "the K.K.K."[79]

If whites were devils, integration was obviously out of the question. The Nation of Islam supported segregation just as fervently as the KKK. And it celebrated alienation. Africa was the true black home. Accordingly, black Muslims were quiescent: no protests, no political participation of any sort. It is ironic that Malcolm was later often described as "a civil rights leader"; he never led a single civil rights demonstration. He stood aloof from the Montgomery bus boycott, the sit-ins, the demonstrations in Albany and Birmingham, the March on Washington. He had scorn for them all. Why sit-in for the right to have coffee "with a cracker"? he asked. Civil rights workers in the South risked their lives for that right. But Malcolm, Bayard Rustin said scathingly, had to "wait for Allah to reveal to Elijah Muhammad, who will then reveal to him, who will then reveal to us, what their program is to be."[80]

Malcolm defected from the Nation of Islam in the spring of 1964, and a year later was assassinated by two Black Muslims, presumably acting on orders from their superiors. He spent the intervening time groping his way toward new ideas, and established not only his own independent mosque, but a new secular group, the Organization of Afro-American Unity. Despite its grandiose title, the organization attracted only a few dozen members, and failed to forge new bonds of "unity" between Malcolm and any significant element in the black community.[81] What Malcolm did accomplish of enduring importance was to prepare, with the aid of ghostwriter Alex Haley, a remarkable autobiography, which sold an amazing 1.5 million copies within a year of publication.[82]

In that final year of his life, he also distanced himself from the white-devil theory, particularly when speaking to racially mixed audiences. "I have learned that not all white people are racists," he said. "I am speaking against and my fight is against the white *racists*."[83] But the break with his past was far from complete; on numerous occasions he launched incendiary attacks on whites in general and Jews in particular. At a Harlem rally in March 1964, a member of the audience (in a question) referred to Hitler's slaughter of 6 million Jews. Slavery had been much worse than the Holocaust, Malcolm said; he wondered why "everybody's wet-eyed over a handful of Jews who brought it on themselves."[84] This was the kind of red meat Malcolm's audiences had come to expect; high-sounding rhetoric about the brotherhood of man would have alienated many of his most faithful followers. His talent for expressing black rage with icy anger and sardonic humor was the essence of his appeal.

Martin Luther King had led a movement that successfully laid claim to the best in the American tradition, and used that powerful leverage to smash Jim Crow. But Malcolm remained an Elijah Muhammad protégé, seemingly without emotional connection to his native land. "Whenever I refer to America," he said in 1962, "I don't say *we*. I don't say *I* or *our*. I say *you*."[85] Those views did not change. In March 1964 he described blacks as "not Americans." "We're Africans who happen to be in America," he said. "We were kidnapped and brought here against our will from Africa. We didn't land at Plymouth Rock—that rock landed on us."[86] But if African Americans were African, not American, they had no moral claim to that equality which only full citizens enjoyed. It was a problem Malcolm never solved: how to be totally alienated and constructively engaged.

BLACK AND WHITE RESPONSES TO BLACK POWER AND THE RIOTS

"*White* people follow King. *White* people pay King. *White* people subsidize King. *White* people support King. But the masses of black people don't support Martin Luther King . . . ," Malcolm X claimed.[87] In fact, the black nationalists—unlike King—had a very limited following among both blacks and whites. The audience for Stokely Carmichael and H. Rap Brown was composed in the main of black students and members of the cultural elite, both black and white. In retrospect, the infatuation of privileged whites is particularly striking. Huey Newton's admirers and sympathizers included Leonard Bernstein, Norman Mailer, Susan Sontag, Jane Fonda, Candice Bergen, and Yale President Kingman Brewster. The distinguished psychoanalyst Erik Erikson was happy to debate him at Yale. Television talk-show host David Frost interviewed him at length. The University of California at Santa Cruz awarded him a Ph.D.; his contribution to scholarship was a dissertation entitled the "War Against the Panthers: A Study of Repression in America."

The writer Tom Wolfe was later to dub the cultural elite's fascination with the Black Panthers "radical chic."[88] It was not an enthusiasm that most ordinary citizens of either race shared. In a survey of the opinions of black residents of metropolitan areas in the late 1964, 88 percent of respondents rated Martin Luther King as the leader who had "done most to help Negroes." Malcolm X drew a pathetic 1 percent. In the two southern cities in the sample, Atlanta and Birmingham, Malcolm's support was zero, and even in New York

City, his home base, only 5 percent ranked him number one. When asked to name people they didn't like, 48 percent picked Malcolm, while just 1 percent named King. In New York, where Malcolm was best known, his disapproval rating was an even higher 55 percent.[89]

That was a survey taken before Watts and before a self-conscious movement demanding black power had taken shape. But later polls told the same story. The 1968 fifteen-city study focused on the North and thus included no southern blacks, whom one would expect to take a more conservative stance. Even so, 75 percent of black northerners in 1968 approved of the NAACP and only 3 percent disapproved; 72 percent approved of Martin Luther King and just 5 percent disapproved; 50 percent approved of Roy Wilkins and a mere 3 percent disapproved. Compare that with the ratings of the two leaders most associated with black power (now that Malcolm was dead): Stokely Carmichael and Rap Brown. Each got a 14 percent approval rating from blacks. Carmichael's negative rating was 35 percent and Brown's 45 percent, and more than a quarter didn't even know who the two were.[90]

Black nationalists like these were more appealing to members of the white elite than they were to ordinary black people. A summer 1966 survey of blacks found that only 5 percent approved of "Black Nationalism" and 63 percent disapproved. The survey asked, as well, whether blacks "should give up working together with whites and just depend on their own people." Just 11 percent of African Americans said yes, while 81 percent answered no.[91]

The 1968 fifteen-city study was conducted several months after the intense, destructive rioting of 1967. And yet nothing in the report suggested an increased radicalization of northern black city-dwellers. Just 15 percent of those surveyed felt that violence was "the best way for Negroes to gain their rights."[92] Thus, less than one out of six endorsed Malcolm X's slogan that blacks should pursue their goals "by any means necessary." As we noted earlier, a surprisingly low 18 percent shared the black nationalist belief that stores in "a Negro neighborhood should be owned and run by Negroes." An even smaller fraction—14 percent—agreed that "schools with mostly Negro children should have Negro principals," and just 10 percent thought such schools should have "mostly Negro teachers." Although black power advocates of "community control" were then engaged in a bitter struggle to achieve both of these demands in the public schools of the Ocean Hill–Brownsville section of Brooklyn, New York, their views had the backing of only a very small minority of northern urban blacks.[93]

Perhaps most surprising were the answers respondents gave when asked, what was "the most important thing" that public authorities could do to prevent riots in the future? "More black control of institutions" was the logical response for supporters of Malcolm X, SNCC, CORE, and for the Black Panthers; "black control" was the essence of black power. But 0 percent of blacks gave the idea top billing.[94]

Relatively few African Americans endorsed the views of black radicals. But their perceptions were not the same as those of whites either. The fifteen-city study found that "a solid, and at points overwhelming, majority" of blacks saw the disturbances as "largely spontaneous protests against unfair treatment, economic deprivation, or a combination of the two." Some 58 percent of African Americans said that riots were "mainly a protest . . . against unfair conditions," and another 28 percent considered them at least partly a protest action. Naturally, then, blacks inclined toward the view that "the main way" to prevent future riots was to "remove the underlying causes." Better employment opportunities in the ghetto was their top choice as "the most important thing" that could be done to prevent future riots; "end discrimination," "better housing," "other social and economic improvements," and "better police treatment" followed in that order. Hardly any respondents—just 8 percent—believed a police crackdown was the best way to keep riots from recurring.[95]

Most blacks were confident that the rioting was not only justifiable but that it had been beneficial. Less than a quarter of African Americans (23 percent) believed that the disturbances had "hurt the cause of Negro rights"; nearly twice as many thought the riots either had helped or had at least helped and hurt equally. If another similar disorder were to break out, a clear majority (54 percent) said they would feel sympathetic to the rioters, and an additional 8 percent said they would actually join in. Only a quarter declared that they were definitely unsympathetic.[96]

Whites, on the other hand, found very little good to say about the civil disorder. About a quarter (28 percent) had the skeptical view that the riots were not expressions of social protest but "mainly a way of looting." Half of whites thought the disorders were "planned in advance," and another third thought there had been "some planning." Who was doing the planning? "Black Power and other radicals" and "Communists" were the leading choices.[97] Since whites were more inclined to attribute the riots either to the crass desire to rip off the stores or to a radical conspiracy, they were less likely to think that social programs were the best way to ensure social peace. Nearly half (46 percent) believed in "more police control," a "law and order" stance that was taken by six times as many whites as blacks. Almost two-thirds (64 percent) were convinced that the riots had "hurt the cause of the Negro," with 60 percent saying that an increase in antiblack sentiments among whites was the main damage.[98]

AFFIRMATIVE ACTION AND BACKLASH

The Civil Rights Act, with its sweeping antidiscrimination provisions, had been signed into law in July, 1964. The liberal landslide the following November had seemed to invite precisely the sort of innovative social policy that the majority of blacks wanted. But would the two together—vigorous enforce-ment of the act and an expansion of federal programs—in fact work to narrow the vast socioeconomic gap between the races?

In early 1965, Daniel Patrick Moynihan, a young assistant secretary of labor, asked precisely that question in *The Negro Family: The Case for National Action,* a report soon consigned to oblivion, an early casualty of political correctness.[99] Moynihan had warned of the growing number of black female-headed families, a message that his critics called racist. The report, however, was and remains important. The policies it recommended marked an im-portant shift in liberal thinking. The "demand of Negro Americans for full recognition of their civil rights" had been met, Moynihan wrote. But that achievement was no cause for complacency. He foresaw "a new crisis in race relations." Unless equal opportunities meant "roughly equal results," blacks would not long be satisfied. African Americans bore the scars of "three centu-ries of sometimes unimaginable treatment"; they could not compete on equal terms. A new approach was needed.[100]

In June 1965, at Howard University, President Johnson struck these same notes in a speech that had been partly drafted by Moynihan (whose already completed report had not yet hit the media). The speech, which had been cleared by King, Roy Wilkins, and Whitney Young, was a step in the direction of what became affirmative action policies, already under discussion in civil rights circles.[101] "You do not take a person who, for years, has been hobbled by chains and liberate him, bring him up to the starting line in a race and then say, "you are free to compete with all the others," the president argued. It was "not enough just to open the gates of opportunity"; "all our citizens" must have "the ability to walk through those gates." "Equality as a fact and as a result" should be the goal.[102]

The president's speech rested on the arguably demeaning premise that African Americans were severely handicapped. Bringing them up to a starting line after years of exclusion, was not enough; the rules of competition could not be the same for blacks and whites until they were somehow made equally well equipped to compete.[103] In 1965 few detected the racism implicit in the notion that blacks were too crippled to be judged on their individual merit. Johnson's prescription was seen as temporary medicine—a little extra effort to promote short-term catching up. On that basis the Johnson administration began to reshape federal policy to include race-conscious measures at odds with the civil rights statute so recently passed.

Thus, the president's September 1965 Executive Order 11246 directed companies supplying goods and services to the federal government to "take affirmative action to ensure that applicants are employed."[104] At the time, that meant aggressive recruitment—making extra efforts to locate black talent that had been overlooked and to give that talent the chance to develop. But within four years, more color-conscious programs were in place. The administration's

Equal Employment Opportunity Commission likewise rewrote the legal standards by which employment discrimination was to be judged, and laid the groundwork for "disparate impact" cases that invited racial quotas in hiring. This is a story that will be told at greater length in subsequent chapters.

The move toward race-conscious, preferential policies was quiet, gradual, and subtle—not the sort of tale that makes for headline news. Regulatory guidelines and executive orders governing such matters as federal contracting rules are low-visibility items. But if the public had no idea what the EEOC was up to, it did know that cities were burning down, despite the expenditure of federal money on programs to alleviate the poverty that was supposed to have caused the riots. Federal antipoverty funds had been targeted initially at poverty; once the riots began, poor whites increasingly got short shrift, and the money went to cities that had experienced riots or were thought likely to have riots—that is, northern cities with large black populations.[105] To those who believed that civic disorder expressed legitimate grievances, this was only appropriate. After a major riot in Cleveland, a senator from Ohio said that the lesson was simply that the federal government had not done enough. "The housing program is too small. The poverty program is too small. The program for slum schools is too small." [106]

A very sizable fraction of the white population, however, did not believe that the riots expressed legitimate grievances. "Are there no poor whites?" a future Newark city councilman asked. "The Negroes get all the anti-poverty money." [107] The issue was particularly touchy because the seemingly soft-on-rioters policies coincided with the early years of an unprecedented crime wave. The rate of violent crime in the United States rose by 25 percent between 1960 and 1965, enough to produce real public worry. Over the next five years, violent crime jumped by a stunning 82 percent.[108] African Americans—especially young black males—were responsible for far more than their share of the increase (and also were overrepresented among the victims). The rate at which blacks were arrested on homicide charges, for example, tripled in the course of the 1960s, while the white rate climbed only modestly.[109] With most northern cities torn by riots, and with violent crime—and especially crime committed by blacks—soaring, public support for LBJ's costly social programs was eroding. The House Republican leader, Gerald Ford, voiced the concerns of disaffected whites in a September 1966 speech arguing that "law and order—the backbone of any civilization" were being abandoned for "a soft social theory that the man who heaves a brick through your window or tosses a fire bomb into your car is simply the misunderstood and underprivileged product of a broken home." [110]

An era of white backlash was beginning. But the War on Poverty was only one of the reasons. For instance, in 1965 school desegregation became a hot issue in Chicago, provoking a major civil disobedience campaign. The next year Dr. King joined the fray by leading demonstrations demanding both school desegregation and "open housing." He got nowhere. Northern whites who were all for King during the struggles in Birmingham and Selma were now unsympathetic. From their perspective, the Irish, Italians, Poles, and Jews had all lived in their own "ghettos" when they first settled in American cities; it seemed to have done them no harm.

Those who resisted such demands, of course, did not live on Chicago's Gold Coast or in upper-middle-class suburbs; their homes were in working-class neighborhoods like Chicago's "Back of the Yards"—behind the stockyards. The affluent could support King's northern crusade without ambivalence; if the city redrew the lines that determined which children went to what schools, it was no concern to them. Their kids attended private or suburban schools. Nor would "fair housing" laws forbidding racial discrimination in the sale or rental of housing make much of a difference to residents of a community that only a handful of African Americans could afford. The most affluent and highly educated whites favored liberal racial policies not only because they truly believed they were right—which they were in 1965—but because virtue was easy for them.

The wealth and connections of the well-to-do insulated them from other unsettling developments that were deeply disturbing to more ordinary white families. The affluent lived in apartment buildings with doormen or in neighborhoods both far from the ghetto and well policed. Less threatened by crime and riots, they could view civic disorder with more sympathetic understanding, a perspective that had political implications.[111] Liberalism, ironically, was becoming the ideology of African Americans and the best-educated and most prosperous whites, while the average white citizen who was, in theory, a beneficiary of liberal policies was feeling politically abandoned.

Race was only one of several political problems casting a shadow over the Johnson presidency, but it was important. Back in early 1964, when he was twisting arms to secure the passage of the Civil Rights Act, only 28 percent of northern whites thought that the president was pushing for racial integration "too fast," and almost half that many felt that he wasn't pushing "fast enough" (Table 3). A year later, just after the outrages in Selma, the picture was basically unchanged. A few more northern whites felt that things weren't moving quickly enough. But during the thirteen months following the Watts riot in August 1965, the proportion of northern whites saying the drive for integration was proceeding "too fast" almost doubled, and the fraction saying "not fast enough" was cut in half. By September of 1966 those who voted "too fast" outnumbered those who said "not fast enough" by more than six to one.

The Democratic landslide in 1964 was followed in 1966 by another landslide, this one in the opposite direction. Having won an additional thirty-seven seats in the House in 1964, the Democrats lost that entire gain and then some —dropping forty-nine seats in the House and four in the Senate, one of the biggest losses in any election in this century.[112] That still left the Democrats firmly in control of both houses, but only because they were sitting so pretty

Table 3

**Northern White Opinion Concerning Whether the
Johnson Administration Was Pushing Racial Integration
Too Fast or Not Fast Enough**

	Too fast	Not fast enough
February 1964	28	13
April 1965	28	17
August 1965	36	10
July 1966	44	6
September 1966	52	8

Source: James L. Sundquist, *Politics and Policy: The Eisenhower, Kennedy, and Johnson Years* (Washington, D.C.: Brookings Institution, 1968), 499.

before the election. Eight governorships also switched from Democratic to Republican hands. In California, for instance, Ronald Reagan swamped the liberal incumbent governor of California by nearly a million votes. Races for other offices were similarly affected. One of the strongest liberal voices in the Senate, Illinois's Paul H. Douglas, lost his reelection bid when a huge fraction of his white working-class constituency deserted him. Those who left the party would come to be known first as "Nixon Democrats" and then as "Reagan Democrats"; their votes were crucial to Republican victories in five of the seven presidential races between 1968 and 1992.[113]

In the next two years, from 1966 to 1968, there was more bad news for the Democrats. The riots of the summer of 1967 were more numerous and more destructive than those of 1966, which was one reason that Lyndon Johnson's poll ratings sagged to the level of Harry Truman's during the Korean War. In 1968 the uprisings started even before the summer had begun. On 4 April 1968, Martin Luther King was standing on a Memphis motel balcony when he was killed by a rifle shot fired by a racist ex-convict named James Earl Ray. That terrible news triggered an explosion in no fewer than 125 cities, with upheavals in the nation's capital, Baltimore, and Chicago that were severe enough to require federal troops. In the nation as a whole, 46 people died, 2,600 fires were set, 20,000 were arrested.[114]

The killing of Dr. King gave political impetus to the final major piece of civil rights legislation of the decade—the Open Housing Act of 1968, which extended the antidiscrimination principle that underlay the 1964 Civil Rights Act to the sale or rental of residential property. But the new wave of black anger that produced riots across the nation in the wake of King's death provoked plenty of white anger in return. When Chicago mayor Richard J. Daley ordered his police to "shoot to kill" arsonists and "shoot to maim or cripple" looters during the riot, most of the city's whites applauded.[115]

The riots were but one part of a larger, unsettling picture. Nineteen sixty-

eight saw huge demonstrations against the war in Vietnam; President Johnson's forced withdrawal from the presidential race as a consequence of the
war; the assassination of Robert Kennedy in June; and the beating up of
hundreds of demonstrators by Mayor Daley's police during the Democratic
National Convention in Chicago in August. As a perceptive observer of American politics noted, events blurred together, but they seemed to have a common thread. "Ghetto riots, campus riots, street crime, anti-Vietnam marches,
poor people's marches, drugs, pornography, welfarism, rising taxes . . .": add
them up and you had a "breakdown of family and social discipline, of order,
of concepts of duty, of respect for law, of public and private morality."[116] In
September 1968 an astonishing 81 percent of the public felt that "law and
order has broken down in this country." Over half (53 percent) specifically
singled out "racial violence" as something they feared.[117]

No wonder that the Democratic candidate, the quintessential liberal Hubert Humphrey, lost the 1968 presidential race to Richard Nixon, who had
made "law and order" the central theme of his campaign. In fact, Humphrey
lost to Nixon by only half a million votes, a mere 0.7 percent of the total, but
that was deceptive. George Wallace was also in the race, and he drew almost
10 million votes—13.5 percent of the total—on the American Independent
Party ticket.[118] Wallace had recognized that southern-style segregation was a
lost cause, and was now running as a law-and-order populist, pitching his
appeal to working-class and lower-middle-class whites in both North and
South. Wallace was a master at vituperation, and tapped skillfully into public
resentment at rioters, hippies, antiwar protesters, federal bureaucrats, and
"pointy-headed intellectuals."[119] A total of 57 percent of the public thus voted
for either Nixon or Wallace.

The 1968 election returns revealed a flight from the Democratic Party by
white workers. In 1960, John Kennedy had won 61 percent of the ballots cast
by white unskilled or semiskilled manual laborers. In 1968, Humphrey got
fewer than four in ten (38 percent) of such voters. Southern white working
people were the first to leave, alienated by the civil rights policies of the
Kennedy and Johnson administrations. After 1964, when the most intense
racial struggles moved to the North, blue-collar workers in northern cities
defected.[120] Although trade union leaders remained within the Democratic
Party fold, union endorsements were losing their hold on the rank and file.
Only 56 percent of union members voted for Humphrey in 1968, and in 1972
a majority backed the Republican Nixon against George McGovern.[121]

Americans were playing musical chairs. Significant numbers of manual
workers were voting Republican—a real change since the New Deal. The
college-educated, however, had become much more likely to cast their ballots
for Democratic candidates than in the previous three decades. By 1968, white
college-educated voters under the age of 30 were 42 percent more likely to
vote Democratic than their peers who had not been to college.[122] The revised

picture had important implications for race-related policies. Racial liberalism appeared to be the emerging majority view after the election of 1964. By the time of Nixon's election it was becoming a position held by blacks and by elite whites—much less than a majority even when their forces were combined.

IRREVOCABLE CHANGE

Nineteen sixty-eight was a turning point, but the backlash visible that year and in subsequent elections should not be exaggerated. George Wallace did not come close to being elected president. Richard Nixon was not Wallace or even Goldwater. Critics accused him of pursuing a "southern strategy," but his winning message was that of a moderate. Nixon did not call for repeal of the Civil Rights Act or the Voting Rights Act, and indeed endorsed the Open Housing Act, though in a very lukewarm fashion.[123] He seems to have grasped a basic point evident from responses to the fifteen-city study, which tapped opinion in early 1968.

Despite the riots, crime in the streets, and other forms of disorder, most American whites had not concluded that the nation's racial problems would be solved by authorizing the police to shoot to kill. Although whites in 1968 had strongly negative attitudes about riots, their preferred long-term strategy was not punitive. When asked whether "the best thing to do about riots" over the next five to ten years was to "build up tighter police control in the Negro areas" or to "try harder to improve the condition of Negroes," 54 percent of whites wanted measures to make blacks better off, and only a sixth (16 percent) thought that finding another Bull Connor to head up the police force was the answer. Twenty-eight percent favored a combination of both.[124] As the election returns made clear, a majority of whites liked a candidate who stressed "law and order" themes. But nowhere in the voluminous polling evidence available for those years is there any sign that whites were drifting in the direction of the virulent antiblack sentiments so prevalent in the 1940s and 1950s.

There was, in fact, no going back. Backsliding images are a staple of contemporary racial rhetoric—in part a symptom of the continuing sense of vulnerability that African Americans understandably have. They know that racism is not a thing of the past. One-sixth of whites, for instance, still favor laws making interracial marriages illegal.[125] Asked in 1994 whether whites had better jobs, incomes, and housing than blacks because most blacks had "less in-born ability to learn," 13 percent of whites said yes.[126]

Racism exists, but pain distorts perceptions. Real gains are obscured. Until World War II three-quarters of the black population lived in the South, where blacks were largely treated as less than human. Only the lowest occupations were open to blacks, and the pay was abysmal; black women worked dawn till dusk for under $10 a week. Just a small minority of African Americans had incomes above the bare subsistence level. Laws and local ordinances, passed in the 1890s, relegated blacks to separate and inferior public facilities, and the Jim Crow schools that black children attended were, by every measure, simply dreadful. Neither "white" restaurants nor "white" hospitals were open to blacks. The two races could not even share the same burial ground. Indeed, a white did not shake hands with an African American—or use a form of address that smacked of social equality. Blacks had first names only. In most stores whites were served first, and only whites could try on clothes. And of course blacks could not vote, despite the passage of the Fifteenth Amendment in 1870. The most basic rights of citizenship were reserved for whites— including that of physical safety. Southern blacks lived in danger and in terror; they could count neither on the police nor the courts to protect them from violence and other forms of crime.

In the North fear was not omnipresent; casual interracial eye contact was not dangerous, a handshake taboo. There were no WHITE and COLORED signs, or other constant reminders that blacks were considered a lesser breed. And thus those who took the trains to Chicago and other northern cities in two Great Migrations during the two world wars did find both better-paying jobs and much greater freedom. But only by southern standards. Blacks did not have to use the back door in visiting a white home; they were called Mr. and Mrs. And they could vote and elect black candidates to public office. But they might find it difficult or impossible to buy a house in a "white" neighbor-hood or swim at a beach designated as white turf. Many restaurants would not serve black customers, and Topeka, Kansas, was not alone in having segregated schools. Moreover, there was a color line in the labor market, a job ceiling that kept blacks out of many attractive occupations.

World War II brought real change, which has continued to this day. Blacks shared in the prosperity of the war and postwar years, and indeed made economic advances at a rate that has yet to be replicated. A single week's work in a defense plant paid what a southern sharecropper often earned in an entire year; even farm wages went up dramatically. By 1959 black family income in the North had become, on the average, twice that of those who remained in the South. The war brought other changes. Blacks not only left the South in droves, but they headed toward the cities, becoming the urban people we know today. In the urban South they began to become significant players in the political process. And while the military remained a Jim Crow institution through the war, with blacks not only segregated but assigned to lowly tasks such as washing dishes, many acquired the education they had been denied in inferior schools. In addition, soldiers from the South were exposed to northern notions of equality. In fact, both whites and blacks began to see the place of blacks in American society differently—one sign of which was the crumbling of the color line in professional sports.

The war years started the process of change that laid the groundwork for the great civil rights revolution of the 1950s and 1960s. White elected officials did not lead that revolution; to the contrary, the revolution led them. But by 1965, Congress had extended the reach of the federal government to every small restaurant in a rural southern town and to every registrar's office that had been previously closed to blacks. America would never be the same.

In the summer of 1994 a national poll asked, do you think America is "the very best place in the world to live"? Both whites (82 percent) and blacks (74 percent) said it was.[127] But national polls tap into the views of ordinary citizens; those whose views the media reports often have a different voice. Particularly those in positions of leadership. "America is as segregated as it was in 1954," Franklyn G. Jenifer, the president of Howard University, said in 1992.[128] In 1995 a film about Mississippi in the 1960s was being filmed in the town of Canton. As the cameras rolled, John Brown, the president of the local branch of the NAACP asked, "Have times really changed that much?"[129] Others see change but wonder if it has delivered on its promise. "It was better when we were all separate," Yvonne Ewell, a black member of the Dallas, Texas, school board said in June 1996. Segregation had the virtue of black control, she explained.[130] Of course, in fact, it didn't; whites controlled Jim Crow schools in the South. But the nostalgia is telling—and sad.

Denial and doubts have a cost: they widen the racial divide. Alienated blacks and bewildered whites become two quite separate camps—a problem we explore later in this book. The celebration of racial separation is certainly not a new phenomenon in the black community, but even in the 1960s only a minority of blacks joined in. A 1965 poll by Louis Harris just before Malcolm's murder showed that by more than a ten-to-one margin, a cross section of blacks felt that both he and his chief rival, Elijah Muhammad, "had been negative forces in the battle for equal rights." Only 4 percent of the black community rated Malcolm positively. By 1972, however, the D.C. Board of Education had voted to approve an official celebration of his birthday and today black separatism—against which Dr. King fought hard—has become a legitimate part of mainstream black culture.[131]

Black rage of course has never appealed much to ordinary whites. They were deeply alienated by the riots, and by the Nation of Islam, the Black Panthers, and other black power spokesmen. They were disturbed, too, by the rise in black crime, which they did not see as a legitimate expression of black despair. And in 1968, we have argued, white backlash turned back the tide of liberal sentiment. That election year was a turning point in two senses: it was also the beginning of the affirmative action era. Ironically, just at the point at which the majority of white Americans had decided that enough was enough in the way of social engineering on the racial front, the White House, executive agencies, and the Supreme Court banded together to institute more racial engineering of a new and radical sort. Nixon was the first president to endorse affirmative action in its current guise—that is, in the form of racial preferences.

The abandonment of the color-blind standard on which the Civil Rights Act was based, and the pursuit of the goal of proportional representation of the races in schools, jobs, and political office was a shift with momentous consequences.[132] Before examining that shift in public policy, however, we need to look more closely at some of the larger trends that have altered the status of African Americans in recent decades. Part II traces the expansion of the black middle class, the movement of blacks from cities to suburbs, the changing shape of black poverty, rising crime, and the arrival of blacks as major players in national, state, and local politics.

PART TWO

Out of the Sixties: Recent Social, Economic, and Political Trends

CHAPTER SEVEN

The Rise of the Black Middle Class

JACK GREENBERG, THE eminent civil rights attorney, started working for the NAACP Legal Defense Fund in 1949. On the road constantly, he was often in airports and quickly discovered that an African American waiting for a plane was almost always someone he actually knew—an acquaintance or a colleague. It was rare in those days to see blacks with the money to travel by air.[1]

A glance at an airport crowd today reveals a changed America. It's not just that traveling by air is no longer an upper-class privilege. One of the best-kept secrets of American life today is that more than four out of ten African-American citizens consider themselves members of the middle class (as compared with nearly two out of three whites). The number of blacks practicing Greenberg's profession—the law—is eighteen times what it was when he started out. There are nineteen times as many African-American editors and reporters as there were in 1950, and 33 times as many black engineers. In 1949 no sizable city in the entire country had a black mayor, and just two African Americans were members of the U.S. Congress. Today most of our largest cities have—or have had—a black chief executive, and more than forty blacks hold seats in the House of Representatives.

The emergence of a strong black middle class has not received the attention it deserves. "Black" still goes with "poor" in the minds of many. According to this view, blacks live in ghettos, next door to, if not actually in, a high-rise public housing project. The mean streets of their neighborhoods are filled with predatory muggers high on crack. The main source of income for males is crime, and for females, the welfare check.

And in fact these are stereotypes held not only by whites. Blacks are even *more* prone than whites to exaggerate the extent to which African Americans are trapped in inner-city poverty. In a 1991 Gallup poll, about one-fifth of all whites, but almost half of the black respondents, indicated that they believed that at least three out of four African Americans were poor and lived in inner cities. In reality, according to federal poverty statistics, less than one-fifth of the African-American population then consisted of impoverished residents of central cities.[2] As we shall see, blacks who consider themselves to be middle class outnumber those with incomes below the poverty line by a wide margin.

What explains the persisting stereotype of blacks as mostly belonging to the impoverished underclass? In part, of course, the familiar picture reflects the grim reality that disproportionately large numbers of Africans Americans do indeed live in poverty, are unemployed, and dependent upon AFDC (Aid to Families with Dependent Children) and food stamps, have children out of wedlock, and commit violent crimes. But the bad news has been exaggerated, and the good news has been neglected. One reason is that the stereotype serves an important political purpose: it nurtures the mix of black anger and white shame and guilt that sustains the race-based social policies implemented since the late 1960s. To call attention to the rapid growth of a black middle class, defenders of the racial status quo fear, would invite public complacency and undercut support for the affirmative action regime.

Even when the existence of a black middle class is recognized, the timing of its development is often misdated. Upward socioeconomic mobility, it is assumed, began around the end of the 1960s. All significant progress thus came in the affirmative action era, and must be attributable to preferential policies. The African-American middle class becomes proof that preferential policies have worked. Absent preferential policies, advocates insist, the overwhelming majority of blacks would still be poor.

In fact, the growth of the black middle class long predates the adoption of race-conscious social policies. In some ways, indeed, the black middle class was expanding more rapidly before 1970 than after. This does not necessarily prove that affirmative action policies have been a drag on black success. There are important differences between the pre-1970 and post-1970 periods that make comparison difficult—the slower overall rate of economic growth since the early 1970s, most notably. But the historical evidence certainly calls into question the common assumption that preferential policies are a sine qua non for black progress. Many of the advances black Americans have made since the Great Depression occurred before anything that can be termed affirmative action existed. This observation hardly settles this complicated and enormously contentious issue, and we devote most of Part III of this volume to assessing the effects of affirmative action policies in various spheres.

CLIMBING THE OCCUPATIONAL LADDER

Although there are many possible definitions of "middle class," one common indicator is occupation. Corporate executives, business owners, doctors, and electrical and other engineers are usually thought to belong to the "upper middle class"; nurses, teachers, store or bank clerks, and others with routine, salaried "white-collar" or "nonmanual" jobs are "lower middle class." Although we have already said something about the progress blacks made on the job front in the 1940s and 1950s (Chapter 3), going back to 1940 as a baseline is the best way to grasp the full dimensions of change. The 1940 census showed that a trivial 5 percent of black men and just 6 percent of black women were engaged in nonmanual, white-collar work of any kind (Table 1). Only about one in twenty were professionals, owners or managers of businesses, store clerks, salesmen, or secretaries. It is hard to think of an ethnic group in American history whose middle class was at any point less developed than that. Fully six out of ten African-American females were household servants who toiled long hours cleaning, cooking, and watching their employers' children for pathetically low wages. A large majority of black men eked out a bare existence as unskilled laborers, sharecroppers, or domestic servants.

The minuscule white-collar elite in the black community consisted mainly of professionals and the proprietors of small businesses. The largest component of the white middle-class occupational world—clerical and sales workers —was almost completely missing from the black social structure. In the South, where most blacks still lived, white employers would not consider African Americans for such jobs. The only prospects for such work there in 1940

Table 1
Proportion of Blacks in Middle-Class Occupations, 1940–1990

	1940	1970	1990
Men			
Professionals	1.8	7.8	9.4
Proprietors, managers, and officials	1.3	4.7	6.7
Clerical and sales	2.1	9.2	15.9
Total white-collar	5.2	21.7	32.0
Women			
Professionals	4.3	10.8	15.9
Proprietors, managers, and officials	0.7	1.9	7.6
Clerical and sales	1.4	23.4	35.4
Total white-collar	6.4	36.1	58.9

Sources: 1940 Census of the Population, *Subject Reports, Occupational Characteristics* (Washington, D.C.: U.S. Government Printing Office, 1943), table 6; 1970 Census, Subject Reports, *Occupational Characteristics,* PC (2)-7A (Washington, D.C.: U.S. Government Printing Office, 1972), table 2; 1990 Census of the Population, Supplementary Reports, 1990-CP-S-1, *Detailed Occupation and Other Characteristics from the EEO File for the United States* (Washington, D.C.: U.S. Government Printing Office, Washington, D.C., 1992), table 1. The 1990 figure for professionals includes "technicians and related support occupations," and thus is not precisely comparable to the earlier data.

were in black-owned businesses, which were rare and usually quite marginal. Almost all were to be found in the few niches of the economy that were not exposed to competition from white enterprises simply because the white proprietors would have had to enter into unwelcome intimate personal contact with black people. Black operators of funeral homes, barber shops and beauty parlors, restaurants, bars, hotels, and boardinghouses survived because their customers were barred from white establishments. Discrimination created a sheltered market for a modest number of black businesses that could provide such services, but it did not provide a clientele from which to get rich.[3]

The black professional class half a century ago was not only very small, the few African-American professionals tended to be in the most marginal professions, not in the most prestigious and well-paid ones. Black physicians, attorneys, engineers, and college professors, for example, were exceedingly rare. Much the largest black professional group was elementary and secondary school teachers, not an elite group in terms of income. Most of them were women, employed in the Jim Crow schools of the South for approximately half of the meager salaries paid to white teachers.[4]

The largest predominantly male black professional group was the clergy. There were more than three times as many African-American preachers as there were doctors and lawyers, the reverse of the ratio in white society, where doctors and lawyers outnumbered ministers by nearly three to one. The clergy were the core leadership group within the black community, but many black preachers had little education and most earned very little.

In the three decades between 1940 and 1970, the proportion of black people holding white-collar jobs rose dramatically—from 5 to 22 percent of the men and from 6 to 36 percent of the women. The great educational gains made by African Americans in these years meant that there was a growing supply of blacks who had credentials that qualified them for white-collar positions, and the Second Great Migration brought more into communities in which such credentials actually counted for something—communities in which the color bar to employment at jobs above the blue-collar level had disappeared. By 1970 over a fifth of African-American men and over a third of black women were in middle-class occupations, *four times* as many as in 1940 in the case of men and *six times* as many in the case of women. Before World War II, black bank tellers, bookkeepers, cashiers, secretaries, stenographers, telephone operators, or mail carriers were rare. By 1970 they were very common, though far more common in the North than in the South.[5]

In the professions the representation of African Americans also grew very impressively between 1940 and 1970 (Table 2). As other opportunities opened up, the number of black clergymen dropped sharply, both absolutely and as a proportion of all black professionals. By 1970 there were more black college professors and more black engineers than clergymen.

Table 2
Numbers of Blacks and Percent of the Total in Selected Professions, 1940–1990

	1940		1970		1990	
	Number	*Percent*	*Number*	*Percent*	*Number*	*Percent*
Physicians	4,160	2.5	6,044	2.2	20,874	4.5
Attorneys	1,000	0.5	3,703	1.3	27,320	3.5
Clergy	18,400	13.7	13,739	6.2	21,488	6.6
Engineers	300	0.1	14,955	1.2	59,226	3.5
Editors, reporters, and authors	620	1.1	3,835	2.1	20,384	4.1
College teachers	2,680	3.5	16,582	3.4	37,867	4.8
Elementary and secondary teachers	67,580	6.4	227,788	8.2	435,558	9.6
Social workers	2,860	3.9	42,685	15.5	145,894	18.0
Nurses	7,880	2.2	66,400	7.8	165,520	8.9

Sources: 1940 Census, *Occupational Characteristics,* table 6; 1970 Census, *Occupational Characteristics,* table 2; 1990 Census, *Detailed Occupation and Other Characteristics,* table 1.

The biggest gains in the professions in these years, though, were in the less selective, less well paid, and largely female-dominated professions—school-teaching, social work, and nursing. These positions were all in the public or the quasi-public, nonprofit sector of the economy. They did not require long and expensive training in a law school, medical school, or Ph.D. program. Many blacks had feared that the closing down of Jim Crow schools for blacks as a result of court orders would deprive many black teachers of their jobs; white-dominated school boards would get rid of these teachers rather than allow them to instruct white children in integrated schools. A not unreasonable concern, but in fact the number of African-American schoolteachers nearly quadrupled between 1940 and 1970, reaching almost a quarter of a million. The number of social workers and registered nurses rose even more, from under 10,000 to almost 110,000, with much of the expansion preceding the Great Society programs of the late 1960s. By 1970 blacks had a larger share of jobs in social work than in the labor force overall, and were not far below parity in either teaching and nursing.

Thus, there was a substantial black middle class already in existence by the end of the 1960s. In the years since, it has continued to grow, but *not at a more rapid pace* than in the preceding three decades, despite a common impression to the contrary. Great occupational advances were made by African Americans before preferential policies were introduced in the late 1960s.

Whether that progress would have continued without a national commitment to affirmative action is open to debate. But it certainly cannot be assumed that the progress that has been made since then could not possibly have occurred without affirmative action. The data for 1940 and 1970 in Table 1 measure change before affirmative action started, while those for the years since 1970 indicate the extent of change since. The best generalization to make from this evidence is that the trends visible in the first period continued in the second without notable change.

Where we can see an acceleration of the rate of change in the most recent period, possibly due to preferential policies, is in some of the professions listed in Table 2—in law, medicine, college teaching, and engineering in particular—and in government employment. The number of black college and university professors more than doubled between 1970 and 1990. (Detailed figures are unfortunately not available for the years since 1990.)[6] The number of physicians tripled, the number of engineers almost quadrupled, and the number of attorneys has increased more than sixfold. In all of these professions the proportion of blacks is still well below their share of the labor force as a whole, in good part because the pool of black students with the required academic qualifications for graduate work in those fields is so small.

Although the numbers of blacks in these professions grew gradually over the 1940–1970 period, the big post-1970 jump undoubtedly does reflect the fact that the nation's professional schools changed their admissions standards for black applicants, accepting and often providing financial aid to African-American students whose academic records were much weaker than those of many white and Asian-American applicants whom these schools were turning down. Affirmative action "worked" for the beneficiaries of these preferences, in that they were given educational places they would not have won in the absence of a diversity double standard. Whether the benefits of such preferential treatment outweighed the considerable costs this treatment entailed is a question we will have more to say about later on, when we examine affirmative action in higher education in Chapter 14. Suffice it to say here that black practitioners of these professions make up a small fraction of the total black middle class today. Much of its growth would have occurred even if racial preferences at law and medical schools had been outlawed twenty years ago.

On the other hand, various branches of government engaged in affirmative action hiring before preferential policies were extended to cover private employers, with the result that middle-class African Americans have been particularly reliant upon government employment for quite some time.[7] In 1995 more than one out of five blacks in the labor force (22.8 percent) worked for some level of government, as compared with only one in seven whites (14.6 percent).[8] By no means all of them are in middle-class jobs, of course, but a good many are. Half of all black professionals are employed by government, as compared with only about a quarter of white professionals.[9] That is perhaps a source of concern in an era of government cutbacks, but in fact a high proportion of black public employees are public school teachers, social workers, and nurses, whose jobs will not be jeopardized by reductions in federal spending.

The overrepresentation of African Americans in public sector employment is matched by their relatively small numbers among the ranks of the self-employed. Black-owned businesses have been given substantial subsidies in the form of "set asides" in federal, state, and local government contracts for many years now, and other programs subsidize minority enterprise through low-cost loans and in other ways, a subject to which we return in Chapter 15. Despite these efforts, black entrepreneurship remains underdeveloped. In 1995 just 3.7 percent of the blacks in the labor force were self-employed, as compared with 9.5 percent of whites.[10]

GRADUATING FROM HIGH SCHOOL

In the years since World War II education has come to play an increasingly central role in shaping the American class structure and in determining who ends up on which rung of the social ladder. Not only have African Americans obtained much more education than their parents or grandparents, they have made more rapid gains than whites, and have thus narrowed the racial gap in levels of schooling. The upward occupational mobility we have just described could never have taken place without the foundation provided by black educational mobility.

This may seem obvious, but some observers have questioned whether blacks have made any important educational progress at all. Thus, the editor of a recent volume on the African-American experience in school asserts that he feels "hard pressed to identify . . . a hopeful trend somewhere." To him the educational picture for blacks is hopelessly bleak. For example, he claims that in "urban schools nationally," the "African-American dropout rate is close to 50 percent" and is "increasing."[11] The coauthors of a 1993 paper on "Racism and Our Future" contend that the "gap between blacks and whites in educational achievement" is "wide" and "still growing."[12] According to both sources, not only are blacks lagging behind whites in educational achievement; they are falling further behind.

These gloomy judgments are far off the mark. The schooling of African-American youths today leaves much to be desired, certainly, and we will devote ample attention to the problems later on in Chapters 13 and 14. The racial gap in the cognitive skills that young Americans have developed by the time they leave school remains disturbingly large. But a fair-minded assessment of recent social trends must begin with a discussion of how much has changed for the better.

If we look hard enough, we doubtless can find some high schools today in which the black dropout rate is "close to 50 percent" and "increasing." But the evidence on changing rates of high school completion by race reveals that such schools are far from typical of "urban schools nationally." Not so long ago the picture was quite different. As recently as 1960, it was considered an achievement in the United States to have graduated from high school. Hard though it is to believe, in the year John F. Kennedy was elected president only 41 percent of the adults in the United States (people aged twenty-five or older) had completed the twelfth grade. The typical American had attended high school for a year or two, but had left before earning a diploma.[13]

Blacks, not surprisingly, had much less schooling than whites (Table 3). In 1960 six out of ten African Americans still lived in the South, where they had gone to Jim Crow schools. What is more, a majority of those who were living in the North had been born in the South and educated there before they moved northward in the Second Great Migration.[14] In 1960 the typical white adult had completed almost eleven years of school; blacks, on the average, had spent only eight years in the classroom.[15] Only one out of five African Americans had finished high school, a rate less than half of that for whites. And yet most middle-class jobs required at least a high school diploma. Thus, even if there had been no discrimination at all in the labor market, blacks would have fared badly in the competition for jobs.

Table 3
Percent of Population with Four Years of High School or More, by Race, Persons 25 or Older, 1960–1995

	BLACK	WHITE	B/W RATIO
1960	20.1	43.2	47
1970	33.7	57.4	59
1980	51.2	70.5	73
1995	73.8	83.0	89

Sources: The B/W ratio is the black figure as a percentage of the white figure. When there is no racial difference, it will be 100; a ratio of 50 means that the black proportion is half the white proportion, a ratio of 200 that it is twice that for whites. The 1960 figure for blacks comes from the U.S. Bureau of the Census, *Statistical Abstract of the United States: 1984* (Washington, D.C.: U.S. Government Printing Office, 1983), 144; the 1960 figure for whites is from the National Center for Education Statistics, U.S. Department of Education, *Digest of Educational Statistics: 1995* (Washington, D.C.: U.S. Government Printing Office, 1995), 17. All other data come from the U.S. Bureau of the Census, Current Population Survey, PPL-48, *Detailed Tables for Current Population Reports, P-20-489: Educational Attainment in the United States: March 1995* (Washington, D.C.: U.S. Government Printing Office, 1996), table 18. Because of a change in the education question on the Current Population Survey, 1995 data are rates of high school graduation, slightly different from rates of attending for four years.

Since 1960 the overall educational level of the American population has risen dramatically. The proportion of whites with a high school diploma has nearly doubled, rising from 43 to 83 percent. Black progress in these years has been even more striking. The fraction of African Americans with at least four years of high school is now more three-and-a-half times what it was a generation ago. In 1960 the proportion of whites with a high school diploma was more than double the proportion for blacks; by now the white figure is only nine points higher.

Moreover, those nine points disappear when we look not at blacks who had completed their schooling in segregated institutions many decades ago, but rather at the more recent graduates. In 1960, 38 percent of blacks ages twenty-five to twenty-nine (in contrast to 20 percent of the total adult black population) had gone all the way through high school (Table 4). Young blacks were 59 percent as likely as whites to have finished high school. Since then the rate of high school completion has risen so rapidly that by 1995 the difference between the two races was no longer statistically significant.

But what about the alleged 50 percent dropout rates that the media so often reports?[16] Figures in that range may be true of a few highly atypical big-city schools in the worst slums, but generalizing from extreme cases is obviously inappropriate. Moreover, even the extreme cases may not be as described. School officials know how many of their students have disappeared from the class rolls, but not whether the apparent dropouts have simply transferred to another school. Nor do they know whether those who have indeed left school altogether will reenroll at some later point, or qualify for an alternative credential—the General Educational Development certificate.[17] The "dropout" often acquires a degree later.

Schooling is the ticket to economic opportunity, and the rise of a black middle class is in great part a story of more schooling. As Chapter 13 will make clear, however, the closing of the racial gap in high school graduation

Table 4

Percent of Persons 25–29 with Four Years of High School or More, by Race, 1960–1995

	BLACK	WHITE	B/W RATIO
1960	37.7	63.7	59
1970	55.4	77.8	72
1980	76.6	86.9	88
1995	86.5	87.4	99

Sources: Figures for 1960–1980 from *Statistical Abstract of the U.S.: 1984*, 144; 1995 figures from *Detailed Tables for Educational Attainment in the United States: 1995* table 1.

rates has not leveled the educational playing field. There remains a racial gap in the cognitive skills students have acquired by twelfth grade—a gap that must be closed if the black middle class is to continue to expand.

GOING TO COLLEGE

Doors that it took only a high school diploma to enter back in 1960 are now often closed to those who have not attended college. Many of the more attractive middle-class jobs, indeed, require a college degree, and an increasing number demand additional training beyond the bachelor's level. The good news is that black college attendance has risen dramatically since the 1960s. The bad news is that black college graduation rates do not look equally heartening.

In 1960 a mere 7 percent of black adults had ever been to college. By 1980 the figure was triple that (Table 5). The percentage continued to move strongly upward during the next fifteen years, and is now approaching 40 percent. Of course the fraction of the white population going on to college has also risen sharply since 1960. But the rate of black college attendance has grown a good deal more rapidly, and the gap between the races has therefore shrunk. In 1960 blacks were only 41 percent as likely as whites to have gone to college. By 1980 the percentage had risen to 66, and by 1995 blacks were 75 percent as likely as whites to attend college. When we consider that on

Table 5
College Attendance and Completion by Race, Persons 25 or Older, 1960–1995

	BLACK	WHITE	B/W RATIO
	Percent who attended college		
1960	7.2	17.4	41
1970	10.3	22.4	46
1980	21.9	33.1	66
1995	37.5	49.0	76
	Percent with 4 or more years of college		
1960	3.1	8.1	38
1970	4.4	11.3	39
1980	8.4	17.1	49
1995	13.2	24.0	55

Sources: Figures for 1940–1980 from Donald J. Bogue, *The Population of the United States: Historical Trends and Future Projections* (New York: Free Press, 1985), 413; 1995 figures from *Detailed Tables for Educational Attainment in the U.S.: 1995*, tables 1 and 18.

average black students today leave high school with poorer grades than whites and Asian-Americans, and with test scores that put them years behind in their command of reading, writing, mathematics, and science (a point we discuss at length in Chapter 13), the current gap in college attendance is narrower than might be expected.

College completion is another story. In the years since 1980 approximately half of all whites, but only a third of blacks, who started college have made it through four years. And that is not because a much higher proportion of African-American students enroll in junior colleges and are thus not attempting to secure bachelor's degrees. Blacks are only a little more likely than whites to enroll in two-year institutions, and the racial disparity in graduation rates remains sharp even after that is taken into account.[18] We will examine the black college drop-out problem in detail in Chapter 14.

The bad news should not obscure the good, however. The proportion of blacks who have gone through at least four years of college has more than quadrupled since 1960. And the rate of college completion is higher still when we exclude the older age groups who left school before the civil rights revolution. Among African Americans aged thirty-five to forty-four in 1995, for example, one of out six (15.7 percent) had completed four or more years of college.[19] That is just a shade below the overall figure for white adults as recently as 1980.

FROM HOWARD TO HARVARD

Not only has the access of black people to higher education expanded enormously; the younger members of the new black middle class have not been educated in the same kinds of colleges that earlier generations of African Americans attended. The college-educated black elite that Gunnar Myrdal described was not only tiny—just 3.2 percent of blacks in 1940 had ever been to college and a mere 1.3 percent had completed four years or more.[20] It was the product of a small, closed, distinctive educational world—that of the historically black college. There are several dozen of these institutions, virtually all of them in the South, the region in which black students had been uniformly excluded from colleges that enrolled whites. Before World War II nine out of ten black undergraduates attended Howard, Fisk, Spelman, Morehouse, Hampton, Tuskegee, or other black colleges like them.[21] The all-black social world they encountered in those institutions prepared them for living in a Jim Crow society.

After 1940 the Second Great Migration brought a great many young blacks into northern states whose colleges and universities had never followed racially discriminatory policies. By 1950, according to one estimate, the concentration of African-American college students who were enrolled in black colleges had dropped to two-thirds. After the *Brown* decision, traditionally all-white southern institutions of higher learning gradually opened their doors to black students. By the late 1960s the share of black students enrolled in the historically black colleges had fallen to only half.[22] The trend away from these institutions has continued; today the black colleges and universities enroll barely a sixth (16.4 percent) of the African-American students enrolled in institutions of higher education.[23]

The new black college-educated middle class is thus largely and increasingly the product of the same educational institutions that have trained the white college-educated middle class. Five out of six African Americans on campuses today are at schools that have no particular racial identity, and most made their choices without a lot of anguish over whether they were "betraying their race" by attending a racially integrated institution. These students decided on which college to attend, according to a recent survey, for the same basic reasons as white students—its location, its academic reputation, and its cost. Only 5 percent of the African-American undergraduates surveyed reported that the size of the minority population on campus had been "very important" to them in selecting a school.[24]

In one respect, however, the historically black colleges remain more significant than their one-sixth share of total black college enrollments would suggest. Whatever the reason, the students who attend them are more likely to graduate than those who attend predominantly white institutions. In 1992–1993, 28 percent of the bachelor's degrees awarded to African Americans went to the 16 percent of blacks who were attending one of the historically black schools.[25] Despite the dramatic drop over the past three decades in the proportion of black students graduating from these schools, they remain a significant avenue of social mobility for black Americans.

LIVING STANDARDS AND FAMILY STRUCTURE

Half a century ago the number of African Americans with enough income to support what might be described as a middle-class standard of living was tiny. The white-collar class was only 5 to 6 percent of the group, and most of the small businessmen, teachers, and nurses who composed it had to eke out a marginal existence. Black men earned, on the average, little more than 40 percent of what white men earned (Table 6). Employed black women lagged even further behind white female workers, taking in a mere 36 percent of what they earned. The income upon which the typical black family was forced to subsist was likewise little more than a third of that of the typical white family.

These huge disparities in income between the two races have been shrinking since the beginning of World War II. African Americans escaped from

Table 6
**Median Annual Incomes of Blacks as a Percent
of Those of Whites, by Sex, 1939–1995**

	MALES	FEMALES
1940	41	36
1970	59	73
1995	67	89

Sources: The 1940 figures for blacks are for all nonwhites, and give a slightly more favorable picture than would data on blacks alone, because they include the small Asian population; from U.S. Bureau of the Census, *Historical Statistics of the United States: Colonial Times to 1970* (Washington, D.C.: U.S. Government Printing Office, 1975), 303–304. Figures for 1970 and 1995 from U.S. Bureau of the Census, Current Population Reports, P-60-193, *Money Income in the United States: 1995* (Washington, D.C.: U.S. Government Printing Office, 1996), table B-5.

sharecropping, domestic service, and other unskilled jobs that paid dismally low wages, and substantial numbers made their way into middle-class white-collar occupations from which they had always been excluded. By 1970 black men had cut the income gap by about a third, and were earning an average of 59 percent of what white men earned. Black women had made even more impressive advances, upping their incomes from about one-third those of white females to nearly three-quarters as much.

Since 1970 progress in cutting the racial gap in incomes has been much slower than in the preceding three decades. Males have gained just 8 percentage points in the past quarter century, and females 16 points. Of course progress is easier to achieve when you start from a very low base. It is much easier for a group earning only a third of the national median income to double its income than it is for a much more affluent group. In addition, real incomes for both blacks and whites grew much more slowly after 1973 than in the preceding three decades, making the racial gap harder to close.

How many African Americans are earning enough to support a middle-class lifestyle? One arbitrary but useful index of what constitutes a middle-class income would be an amount that is at least double the official poverty line calculated by the federal government. In 1995 an income that was twice the poverty line worked out to be $30,910 for a two-parent family with two children, and $40,728 for a two-parent family with four children.[26] This is not affluence, certainly, but it seems a fair approximation of the income we might expect a middle-class family to have.

Using this definition of a middle-class income, only one out of a hundred black families had enough income to support a middle-class lifestyle at the end of the Depression decade (Table 7). By 1970 the figure was up remarkably, to almost 40 percent. The rate for white families also rose impressively, though

Table 7
**Proportion of Families with Incomes at Least Double
the Poverty Line, by Race, 1940–1995**

	BLACK	WHITE
1940	1	12
1970	39	70
1995	49	75

Sources: Figures for 1940 and 1970 calculated from U.S. Census Public Use Samples by Reynolds Farley and William H. Frey, in "Changes in the Segregation of Whites from Blacks During the 1980s: Small Steps Toward a More Integrated Society," *American Sociological Review* 59 (1994), 30; 1995 figures from U.S. Bureau of the Census, Current Population Reports, P-60-194, *Poverty in the United States: 1995* (Washington, D.C.: U.S. Government Printing Office, 1996), table 2.

not quite so spectacularly. Much less progress has been made since 1970, reflecting the more sluggish rate of economic growth. It is interesting, though, that the fraction of black families with middle class incomes has risen by another 10 points, while the white figure edged up only 5 points.

Black progress on this front would doubtless have been more impressive but for two intersecting changes. First, two-earner families have become the norm, and second, the structure of the black family has altered. Since the 1960s, married women have entered the labor force in record numbers, and women's wages have risen, so that their earnings account for a rising fraction of the income of the average family. More than 80 percent of white families now consist of married couples; in 1995, four out of five families with annual incomes above $50,000 had two or more paychecks coming in.[27] On the other hand, over the past quarter century the proportion of black families consisting of two parents living together has declined steeply (from 68 percent to only 47 percent), and the racial gap in family income has widened as a consequence.[28] Thus, the typical white family earns a lot more today than the average black family because it is so much more likely to collect two paychecks. When we compare black and white family incomes, it is essential that we restrict our gaze to families of the same type. Narrow the focus to married couples—who make up much of the middle class—and the income gap between blacks and whites looks much smaller.

Here's the data: In 1995, the median income of all black "families" was almost $26,000, only 61 percent of the almost $43,000 average for white "families" (Table 8). But almost half the African-American families were headed by female single parents with a dismally low median income of $15,000.[29] Black married-couple families, on the other hand, took in over $41,000, only 13 percent less than that of white married-couple families. Still a gap, but a huge advance. In 1960 such couples had earned 39 percent less

Table 8
Median Income of Families, by Race and Family Type, 1995

	BLACK	WHITE	B/W RATIO
All families	$25,970	$42,646	61
Married couple families	$41,307	$47,539	87
Female-headed family	$15,004	$22,068	68
Female-headed families as a percent of the total	46.8	14.1	332

Source: *Money Income in the U.S.: 1995,* table 4.

than comparable whites, and in 1970 29 percent less.[30] The remaining difference is largely the result of two facts. White families have more education, on the average; nearly twice as many are college graduates, which naturally boosts their incomes. Second, in 1995, 56 percent of blacks (and only 34 percent of whites) lived in the South. Family incomes in the South are 8 percent below the national average—which pulls down the average for black families disproportionately.

In short, while there remains for regional and educational reasons a racial gap in the family incomes of married couples, blacks living in families with a "middle-class" structure generally have middle-class incomes. And while that black middle class has grown impressively in recent decades, the disintegration of the black nuclear family since the 1960s has kept its size down.

WEALTH ACCUMULATION

Information about income—how much money is acquired over a span of time —obviously is important in judging how various groups are faring economically. But another significant measure of a group's welfare is the amount of wealth that it holds—the value of the assets that it has accumulated. Racial differences in wealth today are greater than differences in income—much greater. The median wealth of black households in the United States in 1993 was $4,418; the white median, $45,740.[31] The typical white household had ten times the material assets of the typical black household.

Some of that huge difference has to do with age. Average wealth rises very steeply from one age bracket to another. The median worth of American householders aged 35 to 44 was $29,000 in 1993. For those 45 to 54 it was double that—$58,000. And for those 55 to 64, it was more than half again, some $91,000.[32] This can throw off comparisons between racial groups, because the heads of black households are substantially younger than whites; in 1994, only 22 percent were 55 or more, as compared with 32 percent of white families.[33] If blacks were of the same average age as whites, the racial gap in wealth would be narrower.

Family structure is also responsible for a good bit of the racial gap in the accumulation of wealth. Female-headed households with very low earning capacity are not likely to be able to save as much as two-paycheck families, and many more blacks than whites are in the former category. The 1993 census figures were not broken down by family status, but similar ones for 1988 are, and indicate that the gap narrows considerably when we look only at married couples.[34] In 1988 the median net worth of white households was 10.4 times as much as it was for black households, but white married couples had only 3.5 times as much in the way of assets as black married couples.

A more than threefold difference is still large—much larger than the difference in the median incomes of black and white married couples, currently only 13 percent. This is chiefly because it usually takes a long time to accumulate assets. African Americans are relative newcomers to the process. In fact, only within the past few decades have any but a handful of black people had the opportunity to acquire substantial property; few of their parents and grandparents, living under slavery and then Jim Crow, bequeathed significant estates to their descendants. And it is likely to take a long time for the relatively high earnings of today's new black middle class to generate estates that will approximate in size those of the typical white family.

THE CASE OF QUEENS

Anyone who doubts that a substantial black middle class has emerged in the United States should contemplate recent developments in Queens, one of the five boroughs of New York City. Earlier in this century Queens was a classic way station on the "tenement trail" that European immigrant groups followed in the course of their journey from the ghetto to the suburb. And it now remains, as the *New York Times* puts it, "New York City's quintessential middle-class borough."[35] But one-fifth of the almost 2 million people of Queens are African American; its black community is thus as large as that in Washington, D.C., and not much smaller than those in Baltimore and Los Angeles.

The black people who reside in this "quintessential middle-class" community are not merely marginal members of the middle class. Indeed, the 1990 Census showed that black families in Queens earned slightly *more* on the average than white families. Black married-couple families, for example, had incomes 4 percent above those of white married-couple families. In two predominantly black census tracts that were singled out for analysis, between 1980 and 1990 the proportion of college graduates rose from 30 percent to 52 percent, the poverty rate dropped from 13 percent to 3 percent, and median family income doubled. In Queens as a whole, the income of the typical black household rose 31 percent over the decade, as compared with only a 19 percent gain for white residents.[36]

One major reason that middle-class black families have been flocking into Queens—its black population increased by 50,000 between 1980 and 1990—is that it is possible to buy housing there for a reasonable price. Homeownership has long been a vital ingredient of the American middle-class dream, the most important form of wealth-building for most. That a great many black families have become owners rather than renters is another major indication of their arrival in the middle class. The image of a largely proletarian and impoverished African-American community that is so pervasive in the media leaves us unprepared for the fact that more than four out of ten—42 percent —of all black households in the United States today live in dwellings that they own.[37] This is about a third below the rate for whites (69 percent), but the proportion of black homeowners has doubled since Gunnar Myrdal filed his report. Furthermore, much of the racial gap in this respect is due to the twin effects of age and family structure—black families are younger, and less often have two parents. By the time they reach middle age, black married couples today are far more likely to be homeowners than renters. In 1990, 75 percent of married black couples aged 45 to 54 and 81 percent of those 55 to 64 owned their own homes.[38]

Queens is not a suburb of New York City, but part of the city proper—a very large part of it. (Its scale is indicated by the fact that if it were a legally independent city in its own right, it would rank as the fourth-largest city in the United States, ahead of Houston.)[39] The movement of middle-class blacks into the ranks of homeowners, such a central part of the story in Queens these days, is even more common among those pioneering on the suburban frontier, a topic we will explore in some detail in the next chapter.

CLASS IDENTIFICATION AND THE TRANSMISSION OF STATUS

By almost any objective socioeconomic measure, a very substantial black middle-class stratum has developed in recent decades. But objective changes do not always produce corresponding changes in perception. It would be hard to talk about "the rise of the black middle class" if most of those whom researchers labeled "middle class" did not actually see themselves that way. The earliest national sample survey that assessed how black Americans identified themselves in terms of social class was conducted by the National Opinion Research Center in 1949, and it revealed that only 12 percent of African Americans regarded themselves as middle-class, as compared with a third (34 percent) of whites (Table 9). By the late 1960s the percentage of blacks identifying themelves as middle class was only 15—still just a third of the

Table 9

Proportion of Blacks and Whites Identifying Themselves as "Middle-Class," 1949–1996

	BLACK	WHITE	B/W RATIO
1949	12	34	35
1956–58	14	41	34
1966–68	15	46	33
1976–78	22	50	44
1988–91	30	51	59
1994	44	c. 64	c. 69
1996	41	NA	NA

Sources: Figures for 1949 and 1988–1991 are from National Opinion Research Center surveys, given in "Public Opinion and Demographic Report," *The American Enterprise* 4 (May-June 1993), 83. The figures for 1956–1958, 1966–1968, and 1976–1978 are from American National Elections Studies, recalculated from the data in Philip E. Converse et al., *American Social Attitudes Data Sourcebook, 1947–1978* (Cambridge: Harvard University Press, 1980), 23. Two surveys were combined in each of the three figures given here, to make estimates less vulnerable to chance variation. Figures for 1994 are from a Roper Center poll, as given in "People, Opinions, and Polls," *Public Perspective* 6, no. 3 (April-May 1995), 19. No figure for whites is provided, but a figure for the total population and separate ones for blacks and Hispanics are given, making this rough estimate for whites possible. Figures for 1996 are from Yankelovich Partners Inc., *African-American Study: Topline Report,* prepared for the *New Yorker,* March 1996, 47. The apparent slight drop for blacks between 1994 and 1996 is not significant; the samples are not large enough for this minor fluctuation to be statistically significant.

figure for whites. African Americans were making great strides forward in the 1950s and 1960s, and were narrowing the racial gap in occupations, education, and income (see Tables 1–7), but their own view of their social-class status lagged behind social reality.

The rate at which African Americans labeled themselves as middle class began to climb more rapidly than the white rate in the 1970s, however, and the black/white ratio moved sharply toward equality. One study in the mid-1990s found 41 percent of African Americans rating themselves middle class, and another put the figure at 44 percent, nearly four times what it had been in 1949.

That more than four out of ten black people today consider themselves middle class will likely come as a surprise to many readers. It is not the image of the group that is usually conveyed in the media. The black middle class is now proportionally as large as the white middle class was at the end of Dwight Eisenhower's second term, a time when American society as a whole was usually described as being predominantly middle class.

More than 40 percent of African Americans see themselves as middle class. But are their children likely to have the same social status? In the 1940s, when Gunnar Myrdal wrote, those who belonged to the small black middle class had very little ability to accomplish something their white counterparts considered crucial: to ensure an economically comfortable future for their children. The influence of family background upon the life chances of individuals is a subject American sociologists have long studied, and it's clear that the social class into which one is born leaves its imprint on the future. Movement up and down the class ladder has been very common in American society, but where one starts has had a lot to do with where one ends up.

Until quite recently, blacks—so economically tenuous—have been the great exception. A 1962 survey, for example, showed that neither the occupational levels nor the incomes of African Americans were significantly related to their social-class origins. If you were white, the education and income of your parents mattered quite a bit; not if you were black. Middle-class black parents had no statistically measurable success in passing on their status to their offspring.[40]

Although this survey was conducted in 1962, the patterns it disclosed reflected earlier circumstances. Most members of the sample had been born in the South and had begun work in the 1930s or 1940s. Their socioeconomic status was being compared with that of their parents, whose working lives had begun around World War I or before. The fact that African Americans from middle-class homes were no more successful economically than those of lowly origins largely reflected barriers that confronted black Americans in the pre–World War II era. Only eleven years later, however, a second survey showed striking change.[41] By 1973 "the intergenerational mobility pattern of black men had become only trivially different from that of white men." The typical member of this sample had begun work in the 1950s, and was more likely to have grown up in the North. As had long been the case for whites, disproportionate numbers of the black men who moved into the best jobs during the 1960s and early 1970s came from middle-class homes. This finding was duplicated in another analysis that includes data collected later in the 1970s.[42] And a 1996 survey showed that just 16 percent of blacks who considered themselves lower-class had been downwardly mobile—having grown up in a "middle" or "upper middle/upper"—class home. No less than 44 percent of those who identified as middle-class and 54 percent of those who called themselves "upper middle/upper" started out in middle-class homes.[43] The current social status of African-Americans—like those of middle-class whites —owed much to their advantaged origins.

"THE BLACK COMMUNITY"

We often refer to "the black community"—to its leaders, its problems, its views. And yet we never speak of a "white community." Individual whites are distinctive, individual blacks are fungible—or so the rhetoric suggests. African

Americans are of course a numerically smaller group than whites, and thus potentially more cohesive. And they have something important in common: all have been touched by white racism. Their experience in this sense has been less diverse. Nevertheless, the rise of the black middle class has brought fissures in "the black community." And those fissures have important implications for public policy.

Prince George's County, Maryland, the richest majority-black suburban county in the nation, is next door to Washington, D.C., where many of its residents work. In the town of Perrywood—in 1996 only four years old— houses are expensive and amenities attractive. There's a big, new basketball court, for instance, to which black teenagers from the District started coming. They were not, as it turned out, a welcome presence. The homeowners' association hired off-duty police to ask the ball players whether they "belonged" in the area. The association's newsletter noted the " 'eyesore' at the basketball court every night"—that "eyesore" being the low-income kids from the District.

Was there some reluctance on the part of residents to engage in class warfare? Sure. The pressures for black solidarity are still strong. "We started having problems with the young men, and unfortunately they are our people," said Greta Scott, a Perrywood homeowner. But, she added, "What can you do?" "People who don't live here might not care about things the way we do. Seeing all the new houses going up, largely unprotected, someone might be tempted," another resident remarked.[44]

People who don't "care about things the way we do," "young men" who might be "tempted" by the sight of "unprotected" property: concerns like these are felt throughout urban and suburban America today. Who are the strangers who seek to move into "our" neighborhood, and will they prove that they truly "belong" here after they have arrived? Will they be "eyesores" who drive the crime rate up and real estate values down? For much of this century American urban anxieties about strangers in the neighborhood have focused on race. Before the recent emergence of a substantial black middle class, indeed, race did correlate strongly with social class. But no more. The connection between race and place of residence has changed considerably in recent years, as we shall see in Chapter 8.

CHAPTER EIGHT

Cities and Suburbs

IN TOLEDO, OHIO, in the fall of 1993, William Beals, a white off-duty police officer shot a six-year-old black boy who lived in a nearby public housing project in the leg. The boy had been throwing stones into the Beals's backyard swimming pool. Several days after the shooting the policeman's house was destroyed by arson. The incidents brought together two separate worlds: the residents of Van Buren Avenue (white) and the tenants of the Ravine Park Village (mostly black), divided by a field and a great deal of mutual suspicion. In an effort to heal the wounds, the neighbors—black and white together—held a cleanup, shared a picnic lunch, and planned a Halloween party. "Before the shooting and the fire, we never did anything together," said Leora Robinson, a resident of the Ravine Park housing project. "I was a little apprehensive the first time I went into the village," confessed Lawson Reeder, who also lived in Ravine Park. "But I found out that most of them will talk to me. . . . I also found out listening to some of the younger black people that they're afraid to walk down the street on Van Buren . . ."[1]

Blacks and whites living apart—coming together on the rare occasions when a crisis brings out the best in both worlds. Is that an accurate picture of American society in the 1990s? We will argue that it is not, although there is, of course, a great deal of residential segregation. A simple calculation makes that apparent. Non-Hispanic whites make up 73 percent of the population. African Americans are a little under 13 percent of the total, Hispanics 10 percent, Asian Americans a bit less than 4 percent, and American Indians under 1 percent.[2] If race had no bearing at all upon where people lived—if the residences of members of various racial and ethnic groups were simply assigned to them randomly in some gigantic lottery—then 73 percent of the neighbors of the typical black family would be non-Hispanic whites; only about 13 percent of them would be black.

This is far from the case, obviously. The typical African American today has many black neighbors. Substantial numbers of African Americans, indeed, have no whites at all living close enough to be considered neighbors. The immigrant ghettos that were so common in our big cities earlier in the century have largely vanished by now, but black ghettos have not. Virtually all large American urban centers today have some kind of Black Belt—heavily black neighborhoods that house a substantial fraction of their African-American population. The residential separation of the races is one the most conspicuous features of the typical American metropolis today.

What accounts for it? How much should we worry about it? In the spring of 1994, Housing and Urban Development Secretary Henry Cisneros announced a plan that, among other things, would help public housing tenants relocate in affluent neighborhoods. But, as *U.S. News & World Report* put it, "black urban politicians were . . . cool to the proposal which they saw as a way to disperse black voters."[3] Is the residential clustering of people along racial lines that benefits these politicians inherently damaging to members of minority groups and to the society in general? Is the concentration of racial, religious, and national origin groups in some neighborhoods and not others an inevitable phenomenon in a pluralistic, multiethnic society, or can it be eliminated with the right social policies? Is the residential separation of blacks from whites increasing, decreasing, or remaining more or less constant? What are the prospects for greater residential integration in the foreseeable future?

THE MISGUIDED PROPHECIES OF THE KERNER COMMISSION

In 1968 the issue of residential segregation in American life was raised forcefully by the Kerner Commission, which sought to determine the causes of the wave of riots that came to an abrupt halt shortly after the commission's report was released. The "basic conclusion" of the Kerner report, issued in 1968, was that the United States was "moving toward two societies, one black, one white—separate and unequal." This ominous division, the commission insisted, was rooted in a growing gulf between "white" suburbs and "black" inner cities.[4]

The Kerner report captured headlines but received remarkably little critical scrutiny, then or since. Editorial writers are in the habit of periodically calling for the creation of "a new Kerner Commission." And yet very little of value was accomplished by the original body. Its authors appear to have been so traumatized by the ghetto riots during the long, hot summers of 1965–1968 that they had deluded themselves into thinking that the condition of African Americans in the United States had been deteriorating rather than improving since World War II, and that this supposed deterioration was in good part due to the spatial differentiation between cities and suburbs.

To have argued (as the Kerner report did) that the overall direction of racial change in American society in the civil rights era was toward greater separation and heightened inequality was to ignore a series of enormous changes that had benefited black Americans. The abolition of segregation in the armed forces during the Truman administration, the *Brown* decision, the Montgomery bus boycott, the sit-in movement, the Civil Rights Act of 1964, the Voting Rights Act of 1965, the rising educational level of the black population, the decline of black poverty, the surge in black homeownership rates: these and much else discussed earlier were surely evidence that what the nation was "moving toward" at the time of the Kerner report was expanded rights for black people, greater racial equality, and more racial integration. The commission somehow closed its eyes to all these remarkable and very recent changes and managed to discern only "movement apart" and "deepening racial division."[5]

The Kerner Commission's pessimistic view that race relations were getting worse derived largely from its misinterpretation of what had been happening to the nation's cities. A growing gulf between the races, the commission thought, was starkly visible on the map of the metropolitan area. One of the "two societies" that was emerging was "predominantly white and located in the suburbs, in smaller cities, and in outlying areas." The other one, "largely Negro," was "located in the central cities." Within metropolitan areas, the dominant pattern was one of increasing and "almost complete" residential segregation of blacks from whites. The "accelerating segregation of low-income, disadvantaged Negroes within the ghettos of the largest American cities" was the "most basic" of the "underlying forces" that menaced the nation's future.[6]

The growing cleavage between increasingly black central cities and persistently lily-white suburbs was the chief reason the Kerner Commission advanced for believing that the situation of black Americans had changed for the worse. Unless massive reforms to speed racial integration were carried out, it warned, "our large central cities" were destined to become "mainly Negro." The "continued concentration of Negro population growth in large cities over the next 20 years" was a recipe for "the continuing polarization of the American community and, ultimately, the destruction of American values." An "explosive mixture" of poor blacks had been accumulating "in our cities since the end of World War II." Before long, the report suggested, this "mixture" might well blow the country apart.[7]

These lurid predictions were issued nearly three decades ago. Since then the findings of the Kerner Commission have been invoked repeatedly in discussions of racial issues, but only as an incantation to the effect that "the Kerner report showed that things were terrible, and they're even more terrible now." Those who have referred to the report have shown no interest in assessing how accurately the commission anticipated what has actually happened in American society since it was written. To claim, as many have, that the Kerner report offered a sound diagnosis of the pattern of race relations in the United States has become a mantra for critics who seek to deny or downplay the great progress that has been made on the racial front.[8]

Has residential segregation truly developed along the lines foreseen in the Kerner report? In 1968 the commission reported that the segregation of neighborhoods by race was "almost complete," and at the same time it asserted that segregation was "accelerating"—a bit of a contradiction.[9] If this were true, surely by now, nearly thirty years later, segregation would have reached its maximal limit. The residential separation of the races would have gone from "almost" complete to complete.

Discrimination against blacks in the housing market was a legitimate concern in the 1960s, certainly, and it is not a dead issue today, as we shall see. But we need to assess its extent and causes carefully, and recognize the large changes that have taken place in recent decades. We do not have full-blown, "complete" residential "apartheid" in the United States or anything approaching it. Those who have claimed that the Kerner Commission's dire prediction was "coming true" could do so only by overlooking the concrete analyses upon which it relied. In fact, what is striking, with the benefit of hindsight, is not how prescient the report was, but how far off the mark it has turned out to be. Consider first the claim that the largest American cities were destined to become "mainly black" within the next two decades. Of the twenty largest American cities in 1960, one already had a black majority; Washington, D.C., was then 54 percent black (see Table 1). How many more cities subsequently became "mainly black" in accord with the Kerner Commission's expectation? Just three—Detroit, Baltimore, and New Orleans. Two others—St. Louis and Cleveland—were approaching the 50:50 mark in 1990, with black populations of 48 and 47 percent respectively. Those two might become majority-black before long, but no other cities on the list seem within reach in the foreseeable future.

If we think—quite reasonably—that a "mainly black" city is one that has more than a thin 51:49 black majority, the Kerner Commission prophecy looks even more mistaken. If "mainly black" were to be interpreted to mean a 6:4 black to white ratio, for example, only Detroit, New Orleans, and Washington would qualify, with Baltimore on the verge of doing so and no other city at all close to that ratio.

In several of our largest urban centers, indeed, the black proportion of the population has been growing only very gradually or not at all since the Kerner Commission issued its prophecies. In fact, in four major cities—Los Angeles, Chicago, Washington, and San Francisco—the African-American share of the total has actually declined in recent years. What the Kerner commission saw as an inexorable demographic transformation has actually happened in only a few of the nation's largest cities.[10]

To focus on demographic changes in what were the biggest American cities back in 1960 is of interest, but we should also look at population change in

Table 1

**Blacks as a Percent of the Population of the
Twenty Largest Cities in 1960, 1960–1990**

	1960	1970	1980	1990
1. New York	14	21	25	29
2. Chicago	23	33	40	39
3. Los Angeles	14	18	17	14
4. Philadelphia	26	34	38	40
5. Detroit	29	44	63	76
6. Baltimore	35	46	55	59
7. Houston	23	26	28	28
8. Cleveland	29	38	44	47
9. Washington	54	72	70	66
10. St. Louis	29	41	46	48
11. Milwaukee	8	15	23	31
12. San Francisco	10	13	13	11
13. Boston	9	16	22	26
14. Dallas	19	25	29	30
15. New Orleans	37	45	55	62
16. Pittsburgh	17	20	24	26
17. San Antonio	7	8	7	7
18. San Diego	6	8	9	9
19. Seattle	5	7	10	10
20. Buffalo	13	20	26	31

Sources: Figures for 1960 and 1970 from U.S. Bureau of the Census, *Statistical Abstract of the United States: 1976* (Washington, D.C.: U.S. Government Printing Office, 1976), 22–24; 1980 figures from U.S. Bureau of the Census, *Statistical Abstract of the United States: 1984* (Washington, D.C., U.S. Government Printing Office, 1984), 28–30; 1990 figures from U.S. Bureau of the Census, *Statistical Abstract of the United States: 1996* (Washington, D.C.: U.S. Government Printing Office, 1996), 44–46.

comparable urban centers of *today*—the twenty largest cities in 1990. Although many of the giant urban centers of 1960 were still to be found among the top twenty in 1990, six of them are no longer in the upper tier (Table 2). And even among the repeaters there were many changes in rank order. Just which cities declined and which gained is significantly linked to their differing racial composition.

Those big cities with the proportionally largest black populations have fared badly in the competition for people. Consider what happened to the four major urban centers that had black majorities by 1990. The largest of them, Detroit, lost more than 600,000 of its residents between 1960 and 1990, a plunge of 38 percent. In fact, over *900,000* whites moved out of Detroit in

Table 2

**Blacks, Hispanics, and Asians as a Percent of the Populations
of the Twenty Largest Cities in 1990**

	BLACK	HISPANIC	ASIAN
1. New York	29	24	7
2. Los Angeles	14	40	10
3. Chicago	39	20	4
4. Houston	28	28	4
5. Philadelphia	40	6	3
6. San Diego	9	21	12
7. Detroit	76	3	1
8. Dallas	30	21	2
9. Phoenix	5	20	2
10. San Antonio	7	56	1
11. San Jose	5	27	20
12. Baltimore	59	1	1
13. Indianapolis	23	1	1
14. San Francisco	11	14	29
15. Jacksonville	25	3	2
16. Columbus	23	1	2
17. Milwaukee	31	6	2
18. Memphis	55	1	1
19. Washington	66	5	2
20. Boston	26	11	5

Source: Statistical Abstract of the U.S.: 1996, 44–46.

those years. This stunning 79 percent decline in the white population was the most dramatic example of "white flight" in the nation. The black population of Detroit meanwhile increased by 300,000, offsetting only a third of the loss. By 1990 Detroit had slid from 5th to 7th place on the rank list. Baltimore, Washington, D.C., and New Orleans all lost about a fifth of their populations in these three decades, with much of the decline resulting from white flight, and all three of those cities dropped several places in the rank order.

The two other major Midwestern cities that were close to becoming majority-black in 1990 had demographic patterns much like that of Detroit. Cleveland lost 42 percent of its residents over these thirty years, and fell from 8th to 23rd place. St. Louis lost nearly half (47 percent) of its population in a mere thirty years, and plunged all the way from 10th to 34th place in the rank list.

Conversely, almost all of the cities that grew most rapidly and moved up the rank ladder between 1960 and 1990 had very small black populations, far below the average for the nation's cities as a whole. San Diego climbed from 18th to 6th place, Phoenix from 29th to 9th, San Antonio from 17th to 10th, and San Jose from 57th to 11th. The African-American populations of all of these booming Western cities were only in the 5 to 7 percent range and were either stable or actually declining.

Fixated on the undoubted fact that the mass migration of African Americans into the largest northern cities had been a major source of their growth in the 1940s, 1950s, and early 1960s, the Kerner Commission assumed that this would continue to be the general pattern. A whole chapter of the report was given over to "The Future of the Cities," a discussion that focused exclusively on relations between blacks and whites. The possibility that cities like San Diego and San Antonio might be able to grow into urban giants without attracting significant numbers of black migrants never occurred to the authors. On this point, as on others, the report was far from prophetic.

Why was the Kerner Commission's assumption that our largest cities were destined to become predominantly black so mistaken? One major reason was that the authors of the report were wrong to think that the Second Great Migration would continue, and oblivious to the fact that it was petering out at the very time they were writing. Of the more than 4.4 million African Americans who left the South for northern cities between 1940 and 1970, a mere 5 percent of the total made the journey in the latter half of the 1960s. And after 1970 the net flow of black people between regions was reversed entirely: more African Americans moved from the North to the South than vice versa.[11]

For most of the century the North had been a magnet to southern blacks because it offered them both greater economic opportunity and greater personal freedom. Both of these advantages disappeared after 1970. The labor market was humming in Sunbelt communities in the 1970s and 1980s but sluggish in Rustbelt cities like Detroit, Cleveland, and St. Louis. Economic restructuring brought about a decline in manufacturing jobs in the older industrial urban centers of the Northeast and Midwest. Furthermore, the success of the civil rights revolution meant that African Americans no longer had to leave the South in order to be able to vote and enjoy other basic civil rights.

IMMIGRATION AND THE MULTIRACIAL METROPOLIS

The Kerner Commission's projections of the urban future were mistaken for another reason. The authors failed to grasp the implications of a major but little-noticed change in American public policy that had taken place just three years earlier, a policy shift that provoked no controversy at the time but would have profound consequences for the society. The Immigration Act of 1965 abolished the national origins quota system that had restricted the flow of immigrants into the United States since the 1920s. It is striking that the Kerner report did not even mention this important development. The only references to immigration to be found in the Kerner report were in the past tense; they all had to do with the issue of how the experience of blacks in contemporary America compared with that of immigrants earlier in the century.[12] The immigrant phase of American history, the commission assumed, was long over.

As it turned out, they were wrong. The flood of immigration that resulted from the changes made in the year of the Watts riot drastically altered the composition of the nation's urban population and fundamentally changed racial and ethnic relations in the United States. By the 1980s immigration was averaging over 700,000 a year, triple the average during the 1950s.[13] Most of the newcomers—now chiefly from Asia and Latin America rather than Europe—crowded into the nation's central cities and settled among blacks, giving the urban scene a multiracial complexity the Kerner Commission never dreamed of.

Today a city like Los Angeles appears to be more of a harbinger of the American future than places like Detroit or Cleveland—cities of an older type that the Kerner report assumed would continue to be the norm. Less than a seventh (14 percent) of the population of Los Angeles today is African American, and the proportion has been dropping since 1970. In 1990 there were almost three times as many Hispanics (40 percent) as blacks in Los Angeles, and another tenth of the city's population was Asian.

Los Angeles is a vivid example of an emerging new urban pattern that has attracted little comment and is not widely understood. It is a post–Kerner report metropolis—a major city in which African Americans are not the dominant element of the minority population. Hispanics outnumber African Americans not only in Los Angeles but in five more of the twenty largest cities—in San Diego, Phoenix, San Antonio, San Jose, and San Francisco (Table 2). The two groups are of equal size in a seventh community— Houston. Furthermore, three of these cities—San Diego, San Jose, and San Francisco—also have more Asian than black residents.

In our largest urban center, New York City, there are still more blacks than either Hispanics or Asian Americans, but the two immigrant groups together outnumber African Americans. Since the Hispanic population of the United States is expected to surpass that of blacks within the next dozen years, and the Asian population is also growing far more rapidly than the black population, New York and other big cities seem destined to become more like Los Angeles before long.[14]

Today one can find a few, but only a few, large cities of the type that the Kerner report expected to become dominant throughout the nation—"mainly black" cities that have attracted very few of the new immigrants and thus have not developed a complex population mosaic as a result. Detroit is the most obvious example—76 percent black and merely 3 percent Hispanic and 1 percent Asian. St. Louis (48 percent black, 1 percent Hispanic, and 1 percent Asian) is another example. The stagnating inner cities of these midwestern industrial centers are relics of a phase of urban development that is now past, and do not seem to have a very bright future before them. In the more dynamic corners of urban America, though, the simple two-tone black and white portrait drawn by the Kerner Commission is as outmoded as an old-fashioned black and white movie.

BLACK SUBURBANIZATION

The Kerner Commission made another key assumption that proved to be mistaken. It assumed that virtually all of the growth of the black population in the nation's metropolitan areas in the coming decades would be concentrated in the central cities, and that the suburbs surrounding the inner-city core would remain white. The commission's prediction was a simple extrapolation from trends that were operating then. Tens of millions of white Americans but few blacks left the central cities for the suburbs in the postwar years. Between 1950 and 1970 the number of whites living within metropolitan areas but outside central cities rose by a staggering 33 million. Highly disproportionate numbers of those moving out to the crabgrass frontier were white, so that the fraction of suburban residents who were African American actually declined in the period, dropping from 5.5 percent of the total to 4.8 percent. In 1970 less than a sixth of the total black population lived in suburbia, as compared with four out of ten whites.

Table 3

The Growth of the Black Suburban Population, 1950–1994

	Number (in millions)	Percent of the black population	Percent of the suburban population
1950	2.2	15.0	5.5
1960	2.9	15.2	4.8
1970	3.6	16.1	4.8
1980	5.9	22.3	5.9
1995	10.6	31.9	8.1

Sources: Figures for 1950–1970 from *Statistical Abstract of the U.S.: 1974*, 17; 1980 figures from *Statistical Abstract of the U.S.: 1984*, 18; 1995 figures from U.S. Bureau of the Census, Current Population Reports, PPL-45. *The Black Population in the United States: March 1995* (Washington, D.C.: U.S. Government Printing Office, 1996), table 3.

After that, though, the pattern changed dramatically. A huge demographic shift took place, one even larger than the Second Great Migration. Whites continued to leave the inner cities for suburban territory in the 1970s and 1980s, but proportionally more of the new suburbanites were African Americans. Between 1970 and 1995 the number of black suburban dwellers rose from 3.6 million to 10.6 million. The gain of 7 million considerably exceeded the 4.4-million figure for blacks moving from the South to the North between 1940 and 1970.[15] The proportion of African Americans living in suburban communities nearly doubled as a consequence, rising from less than one in six to nearly one-third.

A few examples will illustrate the magnitude of change. In 1970, 85 percent of the whites in the Atlanta metropolitan area were in suburbia but barely a quarter of the black residents of the metropolis. By 1990 the white figure had moved up a bit, to 94 percent, but the black rate had soared to a striking 64 percent (Table 4). Between 1970 and 1990 alone the black population of Atlanta's suburbs jumped by a remarkable third of a million.[16] Similarly, just a quarter of the blacks in the Washington, D.C., metropolitan area had suburban addresses in 1970, as compared with 90 percent of the whites. Over the next two decades the white concentration in the D.C. suburbs rose by only 3 points while the black figure more than doubled, to 61 percent. In these decades black families were moving out from the nation's capital to suburban communities like those in Prince George's County, Maryland, at an even higher rate than were the city's whites.[17] By 1990 the D.C. suburbs had 620,000 African-American residents, the largest concentration of black suburbanites anywhere in the country.[18] In Cleveland the proportion of black suburbanites climbed from 14 to 34 percent; in Dallas from 13 to 29 percent; in San Diego from 15 to 35 percent; in Seattle from 8 to 36 percent.

There were exceptions, of course. In 1990 the pattern the Kerner Commission had expected to find everywhere was visible in the Detroit metropolitan area, for example, where 93 percent of the whites but only 18 percent of the black population resided in the suburbs. Indianapolis and Milwaukee looked very similar.[19]

Those were atypical cases, though. In the thirty-one metropolitan areas with a population over 1 million in 1980, the average increase in black suburbanization between 1970 and 1990 was dramatic. The proportion of African Americans residing in the suburbs of the largest metropolitan areas nearly doubled, going from 21 to 38 percent, while the figure for whites rose only 10 points, from 62 to 72 percent. In the 1980s alone, the number of blacks residing in suburban America rose by 34 percent, nearly quadruple the rate of growth for whites.[20]

Whites today are more likely to have suburban addresses than blacks, to be sure. But the racial gap in who lives on which side of the central city/suburb divide has narrowed substantially. As Vincent Lane, the African-American head of the Chicago Housing Authority has observed recently, "suburbaniza-

Table 4

**Proportion of Black and White Populations Living in the Suburbs
of the Fifteen Largest Metropolitan Areas in 1990, 1970–1990**

	1970		1990	
	Black	*White*	*Black*	*White*
Atlanta	27	85	64	94
Boston	20	77	30	86
Chicago	10	61	18	69
Cleveland	14	73	34	83
Dallas	13	54	29	71
Detroit	13	77	18	93
Houston	19	43	25	61
Los Angeles	32	58	45	59
Miami	60	76	74	71
New York°	7	24	7	21
Philadelphia	23	67	32	77
San Diego	15	50	35	60
San Francisco	33	69	43	79
Seattle	8	61	36	77
Washington, D.C.	25	90	61	93

Sources: Figures for 1970 from John F. Kain, "Black Suburbanization in the Eighties: A New Beginning or a False Hope?" in John M. Quigley and Daniel L. Rubinfeld, eds., *American Domestic Priorities: An Economic Appraisal* (Berkeley: University of California Press, 1985), 260; 1990 figures calculated from U.S. Bureau of the Census, 1990 Census of Population, *General Population Characteristics: United States,* 1990-CP-1-1 (Washington, D.C.: U.S. Government Printing Office, 1992), tables 266 and 276.
° The New York data available are for the New York, NY PMSA, not for the entire New York–Northern New Jersey–Long Island, NY-NJ-CT CMSA, which explains why the apparent level of suburbanization is so low for both races. Most of the territory within the PMSA so defined is categorized as being within the central city.

tion isn't about race now; it's about class. Nobody wants to be around poor people, because of all the problems that go with poor people: poor schools, unsafe streets, gangs."[21] Middle-class blacks are as eager as their white counterparts to avoid neighborhoods dominated by poor people and the problems that go with them, and in the past quarter century or so great numbers of them have been able to do so.

Is Neighborhood Segregation Declining?

The Kerner report's simple equation of African Americans with the inner city and whites with suburbs is no longer accurate, though many discussions of racial issues today ignore or deliberately obscure this elemental fact.[22] The relationship between race and residence in contemporary America has become far more fluid and complex than it was in the 1960s, at least as judged by the very crude indicator of residence on one side or the other of the central city–suburban boundary.

To establish that a substantial fraction of the black population has become suburbanized, though, does not dispose of the whole issue of residential segregation. The suburbanization of a minority group is not necessarily the same thing as residential integration. Even though the number of black suburbanites has grown enormously, that could have been mainly the result of simple expansion of central-city ghetto neighborhoods into suburban territory. If that is so, as some contend, African Americans who entered suburbia would find themselves living in areas that were about as heavily black as those they left behind in Harlem.[23]

Is this what has happened? To answer the question, we need to look at "indexes of dissimiliarity" computed from census data showing the distribution of racial groups in metropolitan areas. An index of dissimilarity is a simple measure of how similarly two groups are distributed across urban space. The term is a mouthful, but the idea is very simple. Possible scores on this index range from 0 to 100, with 0 meaning complete residential integration and 100 complete residential segregation. When the index is at 0, it means that each census tract (or each city block or each group of city blocks, depending upon the design of the study) has the same racial composition as the city as a whole. An index of 90, on the other hand, means that the community is so segregated that 90 percent of the minority population would have to be transferred into a different census tract in order to eliminate all residential clustering along racial lines and bring the index down to 0.

Table 5 examines recent changes in black-white segregation levels in the fifteen metropolitan areas with the largest black populations in 1990. (Since these fifteen contained almost half of the total African-American population of the United States, the patterns found there tell us a lot.) In 1970 the segregation index was below 80 in only two of these metropolises (Houston and New Orleans), and not much below 80 at that. At least 80 percent of the black residents in the other thirteen metropolitan areas would have had to move to another neighborhood to eliminate residential segregation altogether.

By 1990 the separation of the races had declined in thirteen of the fifteen. New York was the only one in which racial separation had increased, and there the rise was by just a single percentage point. Detroit, very highly segregated in 1970, was completely unchanged two decades later. Chicago and Cleveland—even more strongly segregated than Detroit in 1970—had only very modest declines in their indexes of dissimilarity, drops of just six points. Everywhere else the level of residential segregation of blacks from whites fell sharply—by 24 points in Dallas, 18 in Los Angeles, 15 in Washington, D.C., 14 in Atlanta, and 13 in both Miami and San Francisco. On the

Table 5

**Trends in Residential Segregation Between Blacks
and Non-Hispanic Whites: Indexes of Dissimilarity
by Census Tracts for the Fifteen Metropolitan Areas with the
Largest Black Populations in 1990, 1970–1990**

	1970	1990	CHANGE
Atlanta	82	68	−14
Baltimore	82	71	−9
Chicago	92	86	−6
Cleveland	91	85	−6
Dallas	87	63	−24
Detroit	88	88	0
Houston	78	67	−9
Los Angeles	91	73	−18
Miami	85	72	−13
New Orleans	73	69	−4
New York	81	82	+1
Philadelphia	80	77	−3
San Francisco	80	67	−13
St. Louis	85	77	−8
Washington	81	66	−15
Mean	84	74	−10

Source: Douglas S. Massey and Nancy Denton, *American Apartheid: Segregation and the Making of the Underclass* (Cambridge: Harvard University Press, 1993), 222. The Massey and Denton table is for the thirty metropolitan areas with the largest black populations. Including the additional fifteen makes the segregation index for 1970 a little lower (81) and shows a slightly smaller drop over these twenty years (8 points) than looking at just the largest fifteen.

average, the segregation index for these cities dropped from 84 to 74—not phenomenal, but not negligible either.

The decline in residential segregation was not confined to the very largest metropolitan areas examined in the table. Indeed, the drop was more pronounced in smaller and medium-sized metropolitan centers, where almost four out of ten blacks reside.[24] Between 1970 and 1980 the level of segregation dropped in no less than 208 of the 232 metropolitan areas recognized by the Census Bureau, fully 90 percent of them.[25] In the 1980s, segregation levels dropped again in 84 percent of the nation's metropolitan areas.[26] It can always be argued that segregation is not declining rapidly *enough*, of course, but it is simply wrong to deny that it is decreasing in the vast majority of American communities.

If we measure segregation in another and perhaps more illuminating way, this becomes even clearer. The commonsense meaning of the term "ghetto" is that it is an area that is populated almost exclusively by members of the ghettoized group. A recent study measured ghetto concentrations by determining what proportion of African Americans in major metropolitan centers in 1980 and 1990 lived in clusters of city blocks—what the Census Bureau terms "block groups"—that were at least 90 percent black, which seems a fair operational definition of what the word "ghetto" implies. Judged by this measure, by 1990 a substantial majority of the black residents of these metropolises no longer lived in ghettos (Table 6).

In 1980, Chicago stood out as by far the most segregated metropolis in America, as judged by the fraction of its African-American residents who were living in block groups that were at least 90 percent black. In Chicago four

Table 6

Proportion of African Americans Living in Block Groups That Were at Least 90 Percent Black, Selected Major Metropolises, 1980 and 1990

	1980	1990	CHANGE
Atlanta	49	43	−6
Baltimore	58	53	−5
Chicago	80	71	−9
Cleveland	67	67	0
Dallas	NA	29	NA
Detroit	65	61	−4
Houston	50	30	−20
Indianapolis	45	39	−6
Kansas City	50	44	−6
Memphis	59	58	−1
Miami	41	33	−8
Milwaukee	49	42	−7
Los Angeles	NA	7	NA
New Orleans	50	47	−3
New York	34	31	−3
Philadelphia	53	53	0
Pittsburgh	34	32	−2
St. Louis	57	54	−3
Washington	46	37	−9
Mean	52	44	−8

Source: Analysis of 1990 Census data done for Knight-Ridder Newspapers, as reported in Dan Gillmore and Stephen K. Doig, "Segregation Forever?" *American Demographics*, January 1992, 50.

out of five blacks were ghetto residents. Cleveland and Detroit, with about two-thirds of their African-American populations residing in 90 percent black block groups, were next in line. But only in those three out of the nineteen metropolitan centers included in the study was the proportion above 60 percent, and only in seven of the nineteen was it above half. For this group of communities as a whole, the average black resident was only slightly more likely than not to live in a block group that was 90 percent or more black.

Over the course of the 1980s, segregation by this measure did not increase in a single one of these metropolises, and it dropped in all but two of them (Cleveland and Philadelphia). In 1990 no more than a third of the blacks in six of these urban centers were ghettoized, with Los Angeles taking the prize as the least segregated with a figure of only 7 percent. On the average, the concentration of blacks in overwhelmingly black neighborhoods fell from 52 percent to 44 percent, a pronounced drop in a period as short as ten years. We have no information about the extent to which the decline in such overwhelmingly black neighborhoods involves the movement of Asians and Hispanics into previously black ghettos, but it is clear that racial mixing (white, black, Hispanic, and Asian) at the neighborhood level is much more common than most discussions of this question would allow.

Some of the decline in metropolitan segregation was the result of neighborhood changes within the central cities. The number of racially mixed neighborhoods in the inner city has grown perceptibly, albeit modestly, over the past two decades. The main force bringing increased residential integration, though, has come from the large-scale movement of black people into suburbia since 1970. The shift of a substantial proportion of the African-American population from the central city to the suburban ring was not largely a matter of urban ghettos expanding into adjacent suburban territory. That is, it was not a spurious suburbanization that resulted in no greater residential integration than before. Most black suburbanization brought African Americans into neighborhoods that were much less heavily black than those they left behind, and thus increased integration—and decreased metropolitan segregation.

Perhaps the strongest proof that residential segregation has been declining for a generation comes from a body of evidence rarely mentioned in discussions of the issue. Since the mid-1960s, national surveys have intermittently asked blacks and whites whether members of the other race live in the same neighborhood as they do. The pattern that emerges from this evidence is striking (Table 7). Even in 1964 most neighorhoods were not as rigidly segregated as the Kerner report made it appear. Fully two-thirds of all African Americans at the time said that they had white neighbors. This certainly clashes with the conventional wisdom. So, too, does the fact that the figure was as high as five out of six by 1994. Blacks with no white neighbors at all were in a minority even in the mid-1960s; today they are a tiny minority.

This is an impressive change, but even more impressive is the change for

Table 7

**Percent of Blacks and Whites Reporting That Members
of the Other Race Live in Their Neighborhood**

	BLACK	WHITE
1964	66	20
1976	70	38
1982	69	46
1994	83	61

Source: Figures for 1964–1976 from Philip E. Converse et al., *American Social Attitudes Data Sourcebook, 1947–1978* (Cambridge: Harvard University Press, 1980), 71, 75; other figures were tabulated from the data files of the National Opinion Research Center's General Social Survey, obtained from the Harvard Data Center.

whites. In 1964 only one out of five whites reported having a black neighbor. (One would expect the white figure to be at least somewhat lower than the converse one because the black population is so much smaller. All blacks might have white neighbors at the same time that some whites had no black neighbors; there aren't enough blacks in places like Utah, Iowa, and Maine to provide neighbors for most of the whites who live there.) In the dozen years between 1964 and 1976, as the rate of black suburbanization began to take off, the proportion of whites with black neighbors jumped from one to five to nearly two in five, and by 1994 it was three out of five.

Of course many of the whites who reported having black neighbors and many of the blacks with white neighbors may have had only a few neighbors of the other race, in some cases only one. The apparent salt-and-pepper residential pattern, that is, may involve just a trace of salt in black neighborhoods and a faint sprinkling of pepper in white areas. Data from the 318 metropolitan areas identified in the 1990 Census shed further light on this question, by estimating the racial and ethnic composition of the typical neighborhood inhabited by members of various groups (Table 8).

This is further evidence that African Americans today typically live in neighborhoods that are considerably more mixed than the usual stereotypes would have it. A majority of their neighbors are black, to be sure, but not a large majority. Three out of ten of the people who live nearby are white, fewer are Hispanic, and a small minority are Asian. Whites have many fewer black neighbors—just 5 percent of the people living in their block group, on the average—but, again, that is at least partly due to the fact that whites outnumber blacks by more than six to one, so they would have many more white than black neighbors even if everyone was assigned to residences by means of a random number table. It is unfortunate we have this information only for 1990 and not twenty-five or thirty years before as well. But there can be no

Table 8

**Racial and Ethnic Composition of the Typical Neighborhood
Inhabited by Members of Various Groups in the
318 Metropolitan Areas, 1990**

	PERCENT OF NEIGHBORS WHO ARE			
	Black	*White*	*Hispanic*	*Asian*
Blacks	60	29	9	2
Whites	5	85	7	3

Sources: Neighborhoods here are equated with census block groups. The data are given in a graph in Reynolds Farley, *The New American Reality: Who We Are, How We Got There, Where We Are Going* (New York: Russell Sage Foundation, 1996), 267. The author kindly supplied us with the precise figures. Five of six African Americans and three out of four whites lived in a metropolitan area; U.S. Bureau of the Census, 1990 Census of Population, *General Population Characteristics: United States,* 1990-CP-1-1 (Washington, D.C.: U.S. Government Printing Office, 1992), table 5.

doubt that it would have revealed far less residential mixing. Even then one could doubt that "American apartheid" was a fair description. In any event, it seems very far off the mark now.

WHY DOES NEIGHBORHOOD SEGREGATION PERSIST?

However you measure it, residential segregation has been declining in the United States for the past quarter century. Not as rapidly as some observers would like, obviously, but there can be no doubt about the direction of change. Nevertheless, the pace is slow, and it cannot be denied that residential patterns in the United States today remain closely connected to race. The color of your skin still affects which neighborhood you live in, though much less than before. What explains the persistence of a strong link between race and residence decades after the great victories won by the civil rights movement in the 1960s?

According to conventional wisdom, the answer is very simple—continuing white racism. Although the position of blacks in American society has improved in some ways, the argument goes, most whites still hold strong irrational prejudices against African Americans and panic at the prospect of having them as neighbors. They will do everything possible to exclude blacks from "their" turf, and if exclusionary efforts fail, they will pack their bags and leave. Whites in search of housing will not seriously consider moving into blocks that they perceive as having "too many" black residents. Thus, any vacancies opened up by departing whites are likely to be filled by other blacks. As a result, the neighborhood will eventually "tip" and become all-black or close to it. The whites who fled will relocate far enough from the inner city to be sure of having few if any black neighbors.

Examples of neighborhood change of this sort can still be found today, but this scenario is becoming rare. It was the norm three decades ago, when the rapidly expanding black population of the big cities was pressing against the color line that kept most African Americans confined to ghetto areas. At that time, the entry of the first black newcomers into adjacent, previously all-white neighborhoods was indeed a harbinger that their racial complexions were destined to change completely, and white resistance was often fierce. The violent protests whites staged in opposition to black encroachment on their turf at the Sojourner Truth Homes in Detroit in 1942 were matched by many ugly incidents in Chicago in the postwar years, with the riots at the Airport Homes housing project in 1946, the Trumbull Park Homes project in 1953, and the mob attack on Martin Luther King's marchers in Cicero in 1966 only the tip of the iceberg.

It is heartening that clashes like these have not accompanied the large-scale movement of upwardly mobile middle-class blacks into suburbs across the land since the 1960s. In 1970 twenty-three of Chicago's suburbs had no black residents at all; a decade later the number had dropped to just four. In 1970 another forty-six communities in Chicago's orbit had no more than four black families; in 1980 only eleven of the forty-six still had African-American populations that small. By 1990 almost every suburb in the Chicago area had hundreds of black residents.[27] In Chicago and across the nation the color line between central city and suburb was breached with remarkably little conflict.

These differences in actual behavior confirm what the public opinion polls tell us about changing white attitudes about the issue of race and residence. When the first systematic attempts to measure public opinion on racial issues were made half a century ago, most white Americans were distinctly uneasy about the idea of having any black people at all in their neighborhoods (Table 9). In a 1942 poll, for example, only one out of three (36 percent) whites declared that it would make "no difference" to them if a black person with the same education and income moved into their block. Some fourteen years later, in 1956, the proportion of whites who said that they could tolerate having a black neighbor of the same socioeconomic standing had risen to 53 percent—a majority but only by a hair.

White acceptance of residential integration, as measured by responses to this question, grew rapidly thereafter. Ten years later, in 1966, the figure had reached 71 percent, and by 1972 it had climbed to 85 percent. The number of whites who felt that having a black neighbor of comparable social rank would "make a difference" to them—or at the least the number willing to admit to a pollster that it would make a difference to them—had fallen so much that the question disappeared from surveys. It wasn't an issue anymore.

A slightly different question has appeared on a more recent survey, one

Table 9
**Percent of Whites Saying That It Would Not "make any difference"
to Them if "a Negro with the same income and education"
as Theirs Moved into Their Block**

1942	36
1956	53
1966	71
1972	85

Source: National Opinion Research Center survey data, from Howard Schuman, Charlotte Steen, and Lawrence Bobo, *Racial Attitudes in America: Trends and Interpretations* (Cambridge: Harvard University Press, 1985), 106–107.

asking whether whites say that they would move out if "a black family" (income and education unspecified) moved in next door. In 1990 a mere 5 percent of whites were so dismayed at that prospect that they declared that they would pack up and leave.[28] Prejudice against sharing a neighborhood with African Americans has declined so precipitously that whites today are actually far more nervous about the prospect of having a next-door neighbor who they think is a religious fanatic than they are about having one who is black. A 1989 Gallup poll found that no less than 30 percent of the public objected to the idea of living next door to "a Fundamentalist."[29]

Of course one can always dismiss polling evidence by claiming that respondents are not telling the truth—that in responding to questions about a matter as delicate as race they are just serving up the answers that they think are socially acceptable, answers that may be the opposite of what they really think. Polls certainly do not probe the deepest depths of the soul, and respondents may often shape their answers to conform with what they take to be the conventional wisdom. But the polling data we use here, we are convinced, do reveal real changes in white attitudes about sharing neighborhoods with African Americans.

One reason for our confidence has already been noted—that the liberalization of attitudes disclosed by the polls squares with the changes in behavior relevant to the issue. When whites told pollsters that they opposed having black neighbors, they also made their negative attitudes unmistakably plain by throwing stones through windows, shouting racial epithets, and taking other violent actions to repel those they regarded as "invaders" of their neighborhoods. When they began to express more tolerant opinions to the pollsters, they also began to behave in more tolerant ways.

Another reason for doubting the claim that people say only what they think pollsters want to hear is that answers on a given topic vary considerably in response to the precise question being asked, which we would not expect if they were driven by a desire to sound racially tolerant. The usual survey question about the hypothetical entry of a single African-American family into a neighborhood is only a minimal test of acceptance of residential integration. A more stringent test of changing attitudes is available from surveys that asked whites whether they would move "if black people came to live in great numbers" in their neighborhood. If many respondents do not tell the truth— if they pretend to a tolerance they do not feel because it is fashionable to appear tolerant—then white responses to the question about "great numbers" of blacks should be about as liberal as answers to the question about a single black family. They are not.

When this question was first asked, in 1958, half of all white respondents said that they would definitely move out in the event of such an invasion, and another 30 percent indicated that they might depart (Table 10). Just a fifth said that they would not leave. Over the next nine years responses moved in the liberal direction but not by much. Between 1967 and 1978, though, white tolerance grew substantially. The proportion saying that they would definitely flee dropped from four out of ten to only half that, and the fraction saying that they definitely would not move out in those circumstances rose corres- pondingly, from 27 percent to 45 percent. This is impressive change.

Even in 1978, though—the last time this question was asked—fully one- fifth of all whites declared they would definitely move out rather than accept having "a great many" blacks as neighbors, and another third indicated that they might move to avoid that. But this does not prove that white racism is alive and well today, unless we stretch the concept of "racism" so far that it loses any real meaning. Framed in this way, the question may elicit white objections that derive not from indefensible racial stereotypes but from legiti- mate concerns. An influx of "a great many" blacks could easily mean an influx of a great many impoverished people, an increase in violent crime, and declining property values, imperiling the most costly investment the typical

Table 10

How Whites Said They Would React "if black people came to live in great numbers" in Their Neighborhood

	DEFINITELY WOULD MOVE	WOULD NOT MOVE
1958	50	21
1967	40	27
1978	20	45

Source: Gallup poll data from William G. Mayer, *The Changing American Mind: How and Why American Public Opinion Changed Between 1960 and 1988* (Ann Arbor: University of Michigan Press, 1993), 367.

family ever makes in life. In the years in which Detroit was transformed from a 71 percent white city to a 76 percent black city, its population fell by a staggering 38 percent and the value of the average single-family dwelling in the city was cut in half.[30]

That many whites refuse to move into black lower-class areas and move out of neighborhoods that are experiencing an influx of impoverished African Americans is not proof that they are motivated by racial bias.[31] A study of white residential preferences between 1975 and 1993 found that "white aversion to integration per se declined dramatically," and indeed had disappeared altogether when other variables were controlled. But aversion to living in impoverished, dangerous, deteriorating neighborhoods grew stronger over this period, which meant strong resistance to the entry of blacks of lower social status, whose presence was associated with those ills.[32] Is fear of crime and neighborhood deterioration just a cover for racism? If so, then the many middle-class blacks who are eager to avoid living in poor black neighborhoods are also "racist." Crystal Dozier must have been speaking for many black families when she said in 1994: "I was born in D.C. but I wouldn't live there. Number one is the crime. Number two is quality of life. Third is the investment value of the house. Number four is the schools."[33]

As the last chapter noted, residents of majority-black Prince George's County, Maryland, just east of Washington, D.C., seem no more receptive to the presence of poor blacks than those who live in a typical white middle-class suburb. The county's first African-American county executive campaigned on the charge that housing there was becoming too accessible to low-income District of Columbia families, who would bring crime and other social problems with them. After his victory he used the powers of his office to pressure developers to build larger and more expensive houses that inner-city working-class families could not afford. He also sought release from a court-ordered busing program that brought students from poor neighborhoods on the fringes of the District into the schools in upper-income communities. His stances on both issues were hugely popular with black middle-class as well as white middle-class residents.[34] That should not come as a surprise. An intensive sociological study of eight Chicago neighborhoods found that African Americans were just as likely as whites to believe that crime goes up and property values go down when blacks move in.[35]

The views of middle-class blacks, then, are not basically different from those of whites. But the attitudes of the two groups have different implications. The desire of middle-class whites for middle-class neighbors, combined with the relatively small number of black middle-class families (approximately 40 percent of a group that is only 12 percent of the American population) means that most whites will want to live in a white-majority neighborhood. And that sentiment obviously constrains the amount of residential integration we can expect to find.

WHY NOT MORE MIXING?

Whites who want to live in middle-class neighborhoods will generally want to live in those that are majority-white. And yet, white attitudes would seem to allow for considerably more residential integration than is actually to be found in our cities today. Very few whites object to living in neighborhoods that are as much as 10 to 15 percent black, if the blacks in question are of about the same socioeconomic standing. Why, then, is there not more mixing? Part—a rather small part—of the explanation is economic. Many blacks who might like to reside in the pricier suburban communities cannot afford the cost of housing there. Some scholars have expressed doubt about the importance of economic constraints on the basis of studies showing that income differences account for little of the residential segregation that is currently visible.[36] But wealth, the size of the family's nest egg—a variable ignored in the studies to date—may influence residential patterns more than income does.[37]

Integration is perhaps constrained as well by racial bias in the the real estate market. No one claims that the real estate agents who once refused to sell or rent to blacks still engage in such naked discrimination. For one thing, such conduct has been illegal since the passage of the 1968 Fair Housing Act. But the apparent change in their behavior, some allege, is only skin-deep; the "process of exclusion" has just become "more subtle." African Americans searching for housing now are no longer greeted with a slap in the face; instead, they encounter "a realtor with a smiling face who, through a series of ruses, lies, and deceptions, makes it hard for them to learn about, rent, or purchase homes in white neighborhoods."[38]

The claim that the process of exclusion from housing has become more subtle but no less effective is hard to square with the evidence presented in the preceding pages. By every possible measure—and we have examined several—the residential separation of blacks and whites in the United States has diminished substantially over the past three decades. If many real estate agents have "a smiling face" but a bigoted spirit, they have been doing a mighty poor job of keeping blacks out of white neighborhoods.

Nevertheless, evidence of bias has been found in many "audit studies," investigations in which black and white testers pretend to be seeking a new place to live, and discover whether real estate agents or apartment managers treat them the same way. These experiments find significant differences, though usually not very dramatic ones. Thus, a 1989 study reported that information about all available housing units was withheld from black and Hispanic customers between 5 and 10 percent of the time and that black home buyers and renters were informed about a total of 25 percent fewer housing units than whites.[39] Some racial "steering" was found—customers were encouraged to look at housing units located in areas in which many members of their group already lived. In 6.2 percent of the audits (11.8 percent of those involving property that had not been advertised) black testers were shown housing in neighborhoods that had a significantly higher proportion of black residents than the properties shown the white tester.[40]

These figures do not seem high enough to support the claim that patterns of exclusion are the norm rather than the exception. And they do even less to explain existing patterns of segregation than it might seem. First, white and black testers are matched for income, but the overall populations we want to draw conclusions about are not. Blacks tend to have lower incomes, and that limits their housing choices, a factor the audit studies ignore. Many African Americans, that is, are too poor to be serious candidates for housing in posh neighborhoods where they might encounter discriminatory barriers. Second, testers visit housing units randomly, while people who are actually seeking a different place to live search in particular communities or neighborhoods that seem attractive to them. One of the characteristics that many find attractive is the presence of a "critical mass" of other people of the same race. Such people will not object to "steering" and may steer themselves if the realtor does not. Since they often seek out settings in which many people of the same race already live and avoid those in which they do not, they are far less likely to experience discriminatory rejection than are the testers.[41]

We have already reviewed the evidence that establishes that most whites are unwilling to live in overwhelmingly black neighborhoods. We are about to see that the same holds for blacks—that not many blacks are willing to live in areas that have no more than a handful of black residents. Biases in the real estate market certainly exist, but they appear minor compared to the biases of real estate customers themselves. The "steering" metaphor is misleading in its implication that real estate agents are in the driver's seat, and that they take their clients to destinations they would not have chosen on their own. The agents are more like taxi-drivers; they turn the wheel, control the gas pedal and the brakes, but the customer decides where the vehicle is headed.

BLACK NEIGHBORHOOD PREFERENCES

Something important is missing from most discussions of residential segregation patterns—the neighborhood preferences of African Americans themselves. The statistical tool commonly used to measure residential segregation —the index of dissimilarity—shows how much the actual distribution of a group deviates from the pattern we would expect to find *if* housing were assigned to people by means of a lottery or some other random process. The index seems a neutral device, on the face of it. But employing it invites the implicit assumption that African Americans would prefer to live scattered across the urban landscape in a random fashion; residential clustering along racial lines is deviation from the norm. The higher the index of dissimilarity is for African Americans, according to this logic, the worse off they are. This assumes, of course, that African Americans *want* to live in neighborhoods that are 13 percent black, 10 percent Hispanic, 4 percent Asian, and 73 percent non-Hispanic white, and are disappointed when they do not. But if we reexamine the issue of residential segregation with the proper attention to the residential preferences of both blacks and whites, it appears in a rather different light.

The earliest evidence we have about the residential preferences of black Americans is from the 1960s. It showed that only a very small minority of African Americans at that time wanted to live in neighborhoods that were "mostly white"—just 4 percent in a 1964 study and a mere 1 percent in another conducted four years later. At the same time, only a fifth to a sixth preferred all-black neighborhoods. (Interestingly about twice as many southern as northern blacks wanted to live completely apart from whites.)[42] A 1982 national survey showed little change. Some 15 percent of African Americans expressed a desire to live in an all-black neighborhood, 18 percent preferred to live in a "mostly black" area, and 62 percent desired a 50–50 racial mix. That left a mere 5 percent who wished to live in an area in which whites predominated.[43]

Has anything changed more recently? The fullest evidence comes from surveys in Detroit in 1976 and 1992. It suggests that black attitudes have altered little, and that African Americans there have become less rather than more interested in neighborhood integration (Table 11). Only 5 percent of Detroit's African Americans in 1976 and 4 percent in 1992 gave an all-white neighborhood as their first or second choice. Another group—24 percent in 1976 dropping to 18 percent in 1992—expressed a preference for areas in

Table 11

Black Preferences for Neighborhoods of Varying Racial Compositions, Detroit Metropolitan Area, 1976 and 1992

PERCENT BLACK	PERCENT LISTING AS FIRST OR SECOND CHOICE	
	1976	*1992*
0	5	4
14	24	18
50	82	77
72	68	82
100	17	20

Source: Reynolds Farley et al., "Continued Residential Segregation in Detroit: 'Chocolate City, Vanilla Suburbs' Revisited," *Journal of Housing Research* 4 (1993), 23.

which blacks were only a seventh of the population. These two groups of integration enthusiasts were evidently shrinking a little, making up 29 percent of the black population in 1976 and 22 percent more recently.

The other side of the coin is that the number of African Americans who preferred to live in all-black neighborhoods rose a bit, from 17 to 20 percent, and the number casting a vote in favor of neighborhoods roughly three-quarters black rose steeply, jumping from 68 to 82 percent.[44] No more than a fifth of Detroit's African Americans wanted to live in all-black neighborhoods. Four out of five wanted some kind of "integration." But only a distinct minority—29 percent in 1976, 22 percent in 1992—wanted a form of integration that would put them in a neighborhood in which they would be outnumbered by whites. The "integration" they favored involved a racial balance in which whites were no more than 50 percent, and by 1992, indeed, four out of five Detroit blacks looked favorably on neighborhoods in which they made up 72 percent of the population.

Most Detroit area whites said that they also favored integrated neighborhoods, but this agreement in the abstract concealed a vital practical difference. Whites defined integration in a quite different way than blacks—not as a roughly even balance between the two races but instead as a balance pretty much like that prevailing in American society as a whole. A properly integrated neighborhood to them was one in which the black proportion was something on the order of 12 percent. When asked how they felt about living in a neighborhood that was one-fifth black (not much above the 12 percent level, after all), 42 percent of Detroit whites in 1976 indicated that they would feel uncomfortable, and a quarter of them felt so uncomfortable at the prospect that they said that they would move out (Table 12). When a neighborhood became as much as one-third black, 57 percent of whites said they would become uncomfortable, and four out of ten would depart.

Given these very different preferences in the late 1970s, it was hard to imagine how racially mixed neighborhoods could have developed and persisted for any length of time in the Detroit metropolitan area. Blacks were extremely reluctant to move into neighborhoods that were integrated by the white definition—ones with a very large white majority. Those areas accordingly could be expected to remain all-white or close to it. Whites were even more reluctant to move into neighborhoods that were integrated as blacks defined the term—ones with roughly equal numbers of both racial groups. Six out of seven whites would not consider moving into an area that was 60 percent black. Almost two-thirds of them said that they would depart if the racial balance tipped that much.

Significant changes were apparent from the 1992 Detroit survey, but not changes likely to bring about increased residential integration. Black and white preferences were shifting, but in the opposite direction. By 1992, Detroit's whites had become distinctly more willing to live in racially mixed

Table 12
**White Attitudes About Living in Neighborhoods of Varying Racial
Compositions, Detroit Metropolitan Area, 1976 and 1992**

PERCENT BLACK	WOULD FEEL UNCOMFORTABLE		WOULD MOVE OUT	
	1976	*1992*	*1976*	*1992*
7	24	16	7	4
20	42	30	25	15
33	57	44	41	29
60	72	65	64	53

Source: Farley, "Continued Residential Segregation in Detroit," 26.

neighborhoods. For example, in 1976 half said that they would never move into a neighborhood that was 20 percent black; by 1992 that figure had fallen to less than a third. This change of view would seem conducive to greater neighborhood integration. But, as already noted, black preferences in the matter have been shifting in the opposite direction. In the 1990s, Detroit's blacks were somewhat less willing to move into heavily white neighborhoods than they had been earlier, and considerably more content with (or resigned to) the prospect of living in overwhelmingly black areas.

What explains these preferences? Does the reluctance of African Americans in Detroit to live in predominantly white neighborhoods mainly reflect a sense of racial solidarity, a positive desire to live with fellow members of their group? Or does it stem from a negative feeling that white neighborhoods are likely to be unwelcoming to them and thus should be avoided? The 1976 survey asked black respondents who expressed reservations about living in mainly white areas the basis for their feeling. Nine out of ten said that the reason was that they felt that whites would be unfriendly and make them feel out of place. Some said things like "they would probably blow my house up."[45]

If such fears of being cold-shouldered or worse had been the main deterrent to black movement into largely white neighborhoods, though, blacks in the Detroit metropolitan area should have shown greater willingness to enter white sections after 1976. White receptivity to having black neighbors certainly increased, and African Americans should have been able to discern the change. But in these years Detroit's blacks became less rather than more interested in living in integrated neighborhoods, and distinctly more satisfied with residing in mainly black areas.

Although the richest information on this question is from surveys of the Detroit area, other evidence suggests that Detroit is not atypical in this respect. A 1990 national survey of African Americans found that 60 percent preferred to live in a neighborhood that was half black and half white.[46] A number of local studies, in Omaha, Kansas City, Milwaukee, Cincinnati, and Los Angeles reveal basic similarities of pattern. In each of these communities whites generally approve of the principle of residential integration but strongly prefer to live in neighborhoods that are at least 80 percent white. And in each of them blacks embrace the principle of residential integration, too, but define it as entailing a racial balance that is roughly 50-50. Only a fairly small minority of whites—typically 20 to 25 percent—feel comfortable about dwelling in what blacks define as integrated neighborhoods.[47] Conversely, only a small minority of blacks feel comfortable about living in what whites define as integrated neighborhoods.

The strong preference of blacks for living in neighborhoods that are at least half black constrains how much neighborhood integration can be achieved— to a quite surprising extent. A little thought experiment will make this clear. Imagine a metropolitan area with a population of 1 million, 80 percent white, 20 percent black. (Twenty percent is the mean proportion of black residents in the fifteen metropolitan areas with the largest African-American populations today. We ignore other groups to keep the example simple.) Suppose that everyone in this metropolis has an identical income, and that all of the housing is distributed in accord with the principle that African Americans get first choice; whites must take whatever housing is left over. Suppose further that the 200,000 blacks of the metropolis choose to settle in neighborhoods in a pattern that leaves half of all dwelling units vacant for whites to occupy. Each neighborhood with black residents will then be perfectly "integrated" in the sense in which blacks tend to think of integration. That is, it will have a 50-50 racial balance, as current studies show most blacks today would prefer.

How much segregation would there be in this hypothetical community in which blacks have the sole power to shape the composition of neighborhoods? It seems unlikely that the desire of the 20 percent African-American minority to live in areas that are 50 percent rather than 20 percent black would produce a very high level of residential *segregation*. But a quick calculation shows that it would. If we assume for simplicity's sake that all neighborhoods have equal populations, then the black 20 percent of the population will be spread through 40 percent of the neighborhoods to comprise half the population of each. But there won't be any more blacks left to go around after that, so six out of ten neighborhoods in the metropolis will necessarily be all white. That will produce an index of dissimilarity of 75 between blacks and whites in this imagined community. That is a higher level of segregation than was to be found in 1990 in Washington, D.C. (whose index was 66), Houston (67), San Francisco (67), and six more of the fifteen metropolitan areas with the largest black populations (see Table 5, page 215).[48]

An index of dissimilarity of 75 is a sign of very considerable segregation, and it is illuminating to discover that it could be generated by the mere preference for 50:50 neighborhoods on the part of blacks. This is not to suggest, of course, that black desires for a moderate degree of self-segregation are the main cause of the segregation patterns visible in American cities today. Blacks obviously do not stand at the front of the line in picking housing; most are at the back of the line. But the exercise *does* establish that a considerable amount of residential clustering is likely to continue as long as elements of the population continue to identify as members of racial and ethnic groups and feel some desire to live where other members of the group live. Thus, in Boston in 1970, the index of dissimilarity between people of Irish ancestry and those of Italian ancestry was 51, though both were white Catholic groups that had lived in Boston for many decades. Neither group was close to being randomly distributed across the city's neighborhoods. Even more striking, the index of dissimilarity between Italians and Hungarians was 81, a figure identical to that between blacks and whites in Boston in 1970.[49]

Of course blacks were not separated from whites in Boston in 1970 for the same reason that Italians were separated from Hungarians. It was the crushing force of prejudice that African Americans encountered whenever they tried to break out of the ghetto that led to their marked residential clustering. We have seen, though, that white objections to living near at least moderate numbers of blacks of similar social status have declined to the vanishing point. The question is what that portends for the future shape of our cities. The odds are that the index of dissimilarity will never be 0. The Boston examples serve to make the same general point as our hypothetical metropolitan exercise: hostility from others is not the sole reason that groups sometimes cluster in certain areas.

A Government Fix?

In March 1995, Henry G. Cisneros, the secretary of housing and urban development, scuttled a local test of a housing voucher project, "Moving to Opportunity." The idea was simple. Give the residents of public housing projects, located in what Senator Barbara A. Mikulski has labeled "zip codes of pathology," the financial means to move to better neighborhoods that were at least 65 percent white. As the *New York Times* put it, the hope was "that by scattering one or two poor families in large middle-income areas, they would disappear like salt crystals in a glass of water."[50]

It was a castle of hope built on a foundation of naïveté. There was predictable opposition from some white residents of blue-collar towns fearing an influx of poor blacks whose arrival had been subsidized by federal money. But African-American inner-city families in Maryland and elsewhere were not enthusiastic either. For instance, many former residents of the Logan-Fontenelle public housing project in Omaha (which had been razed), said they wanted to live in their old North Omaha neighborhood. From there they could easily get by public transportion to jobs and downtown stores. As Lori Parks explained, "My friends are here and so's my family." "What these people want," said Eric Whitner, a black lawyer at the Omaha Housing Authority who stayed in North Omaha, "is decent, affordable housing in their own neighborhood." That's the place they call home; it's where the city's lone soul-food restaurant is located, and where standing-room-only crowds gather on Sundays to hear the choir in the local Salem Baptist Church.[51]

The resistance to the we'll-pay-you-to-move program should not have been surprising, and indeed was not unique. As a result of a federal court order, families from largely black and Hispanic southwest Yonkers, New York, were offered subsidized apartments in largely white, middle-class areas of Westchester County. "Many tenants want to stay put," the *New York Times* reported in June 1994. They "cannot bring themselves to leave the familiar faces and folkways and plentiful transportation." Of the 1,400 tenants invited to move, only 12 had accepted apartments as of that date.[52]

"Without an integrated society the country is going to fall apart," Jerrold M. Levy, a Legal Services lawyer involved in the Yonkers suit, warned in the spring of 1994.[53] We agree that a house deeply divided by racial hostility cannot stand. But what are the policy implications? How can government programs work to bring whites and blacks together? Voucher programs, housing specialist Howard Husock has argued, may be the worst way to dispel white jitters about black neighbors. Placing poor tenants—of *any* color—in towns they could not otherwise afford, as Husock has put it, breaks the unspoken rule that you live where you can pay the rent.[54] There's a point to that seemingly harsh rule: it allows poor families to scrimp and save and move one notch up the residential ladder to a neighborhood in which others of similar economic status live. Social class is meaningful. Recall the town in Prince George's County in which middle-class African Americans pulled up the drawbridge against the Washington, D.C., youths who had come to toss a basketball on a brand-new court. "People who don't live here might not care about things the way we do," one black resident noted. Homeowners in Prince George's understood a basic point that apparently eluded Secretary Cisneros: neighborhoods are not arbitrary packages of housing whose occupancy benevolent social engineers can rearrange with predictable and positive consequences. No one should live in a decaying and dangerous environment, but the problems of the urban poor cannot be solved by relocating them to middle-class suburban neighborhoods—black or white—that do not want them. Poverty more than race is the problem that leaves too many African Americans trapped in delapidated neighborhoods.

It is time for a closer look at the poverty issue.

CHAPTER NINE

Poverty

IN THE SOUTHEAST corner of Washington, D.C., a few years ago, African-American kids wore T-shirts with the racially divisive message, "It's a black thing, you wouldn't understand." But in that all-black neighborhood there were no whites who could "understand."[1] Nor is there much interracial contact in the public high schools in our nation's capital. A few hundred white students, two-thirds of whom are concentrated in one school, intermingle with approximately 14,000 blacks. Moreover, the death rate in the city for children aged 1 to 14 is double the national average; the rate of violent crime arrests for those aged 10 to 17 is triple the national average; the birth rate for girls 15 to 17 is 5.3 times the national average; the rate of violent deaths for youths aged 15 to 19 is 5.7 times the national average.[2] In fact, Washington has the nation's highest murder rate, highest percentage of one-parent families and unwed mothers, highest infant mortality rate and highest percentage of adults in prison and adults receiving public assistance.[3]

The District of Columbia is two-thirds African American. And the problems described above are closely associated with black poverty. And yet a majority of blacks are not poor, and a majority of poor Americans are not black. Neither proposition is even close to being true; the black urban underclass does not define black America. According to the most recent figures available (1995), 29 percent of African Americans subsist on incomes that fall below the official poverty line designated by the federal government.[4] We can say that a 29 percent figure is "too high." We can say that it is nearly triple the poverty rate for white Americans (11.2 percent). But we cannot say that 29 percent represents most blacks. The last year in which the black poverty rate exceeded 50 percent was the year of the Civil Rights Act of 1964, when it was just over that mark. By 1968 the proportion of African Americans living in poverty had fallen below 35 percent, and it has never again reached the earlier level.[5]

Nor is it the case that most poor people today are black. In fact, little more than a quarter (27 percent) of Americans living below the poverty line in 1995 were African American; two-thirds of the poor were white. Some of these impoverished "whites" (as counted by the Census) were Puerto Ricans, Mexicans, or other Hispanics, but they were outnumbered by non-Hispanic whites by more than two to one.[6] The black share of the total poverty population has been declining slightly over the past two decades, falling from 31 percent in 1974 to 27 percent in 1995, mainly because of the rise in the number of uneducated and unskilled Hispanic immigrants. Two decades ago Hispanics were only 11 percent of the poverty population; now they are 24 percent of the poor.[7]

TRENDS IN FAMILY POVERTY: PROGRESS AND STAGNATION

A large majority of black people were impoverished to an almost unimaginable degree not so very long ago. In 1940, little more than half a century ago, the poverty rate for black families was a staggering 87 percent, by one estimate, and well over 90 percent by another.[8] By 1940 the worst of the Great Depression was past, but economic deprivation was still the lot of the vast majority of black people. Seven out of eight African-American families (and nearly half of all white ones) still had incomes below the minimum that was later demarcated as the poverty line (Table 1). In the course of the 1940s and 1950s, the level of poverty declined dramatically, with the black poverty rate dropping by 40 points over these two decades. The proportion of black families who had to survive on incomes below the poverty line was thus cut in half. The white poverty rate also fell steeply, by 35 points, and stood at only 13 percent by 1960.

The huge decline in black poverty between 1940 and 1960 occurred well

Table 1

Percent of Families with Incomes Below the Poverty Line, by Race, 1940–1995

	BLACK	WHITE
1940	87	48
1960	47	13
1970	30	8
1980	29	8
1995	26	9

Sources: Figures for 1940–1960 from James P. Smith, "Poverty and the Family," in Gary Sandefur and Marta Tienda, *Divided Opportunities: Minorities, Poverty, and Social Policy* (New York: Plenum Press, 1988), 143–144; figures for 1970–1995 from U.S. Bureau of the Census, Current Population Reports, P-60-194, *Poverty in the United States: 1995* (Washington, D.C.: U.S. Government Printing Office, 1996), table C-3.

before the Civil Rights Act of 1964 outlawed Jim Crow practices in employment, education, and public accommodations. It also was well before the advent of the War on Poverty and various other Great Society programs designed to uplift the poor. The national economy in those years was expanding at a stunning pace. In the great postwar boom period from 1948 to 1973, the gross national product per capita rose by an average of 2.3 percent a year, almost a third higher than the average for the preceding eight decades.[9] Millions of working people, white and black, saw their incomes rise above the poverty line.

The boom times were good for Americans regardless of race, but two other changes in these years benefited black people specifically. One was the striking educational progress of African Americans, which substantially narrowed the gap between blacks and whites. The other was the Second Great Migration— the move of southern blacks from impoverished rural areas into bustling northern cities.

Progress continued during the 1960s. The proportion of black families with incomes below the poverty line continued to fall sharply, dropping from 47 percent to 30 percent over the decade. The forces that were pushing black incomes up and reducing the poverty rate were much the same as before. The overall rate of economic growth remained high; the educational gap between black and white workers continued to shrink. And African Americans were still migrating northward in large numbers. In terms of their immediate economic impact, the passage of the Civil Rights Act of 1964 and various Great Society programs may also have contributed to black progress in the latter part of the 1960s, but governmental action could not have made a very dramatic contribution. Since the pace of economic progress for African Americans after 1964 was no faster than in the preceding two decades, and the causes that produced the gains of the 1940s and 1950s continued to operate, it is hard to see how federal legislation—the one new ingredient in the equation—could have made a very large difference.

Around 1970, though, progress in reducing black poverty came to a virtual halt. In the era of affirmative action (the past quarter century), the proportion of African-American families with incomes below the poverty line has remained almost unchanged, with only slight annual increases or decreases caused by fluctuations in the business cycle. The black family poverty rate was 30 percent in 1970, 29 percent in 1980, and 26 percent in 1995. Its low point in recent years was the 26 percent registered in 1995; the high point was 33 percent, during the recession year of 1982. After three decades of falling very substantially, the figure has been stuck within three or four points of the 30 percent mark for about twenty-five years.

This persistent poverty rate is the single most depressing fact about the state of black America today. Concern that a substantial fraction of African Americans remain below the poverty line drives much of the discussion of affirmative action and other policy issues. Almost everyone agrees it is a problem desperately in need of solution. But it's important to note that the black experience on this count has not been unique. The poverty rate for the American population as a whole has changed very little since 1970; neither among white families nor black families has the incidence of poverty declined. Thus, some 8 percent of white families were poor in 1970, 8 percent in 1980, 10 percent in 1982, and 9 percent in 1995. That black poverty is today a much more serious problem than white poverty is due to the fact that, in 1970, when the wheels of progress ground to a halt, blacks were still so far behind. They had been catching up; when they ceased to gain on whites, more than a quarter were left in poverty.

The poverty rate—for both blacks and whites—has remained steady in recent years for two reasons. First, the national economy has not been expanding at the extraordinary pace at which it grew from the 1940s through the 1960s, the greatest boom period in American history. Since then, the average level of real wages has been flat or close to it.[10] A rising tide lifts all boats, but after 1973, when the great spurt of growth that began with World War II came to an end, the tide rose only sluggishly.

In addition, a sharp increase in the demand for highly educated workers in the 1970s and 1980s brought much higher wages and salaries for those with skills, but few or no gains for workers without advanced education— disproportionate numbers of whom are black. As a result, the distribution of income became less equal, with those on the upper rungs of the economic ladder faring better than those closer to the bottom. Over the course of the 1980s, for example, the real earnings of the average male high school graduate aged twenty-five to thirty-four rose by just 5 percent; those of college graduates increased by 42 percent; those of men with at least a year of graduate study climbed 57 percent.[11] Combine steady but unspectacular overall growth in the national economy with a decline in the share of income going to those on the lower rungs of the economic ladder and you get an overall poverty rate that has been relatively stable for the past quarter of a century.

CHILDREN IN POVERTY

The overall black poverty rate has not fallen since 1970, but that seeming continuity is actually a bit deceptive. The face of black poverty has changed. It used to be that almost all black families were poor; growing up impoverished was the near-universal black experience. Not so today. It is mainly families headed by single mothers who are faring badly economically. And that means that an extraordinary number of black children—the offspring of those unmarried mothers—are born into deprivation.

As recently as 1959, two-thirds of *all* black children under the age of

Table 2
Poverty Rates for Black Children Living in Families, by Family Type, 1959–1995

	1959	1969	1979	1995
All children in families	66	40	41	42
Children in female-headed families	82	68	63	62
Children in intact families	61	25	19	13

Sources: Figures for 1959–1979 from Children's Defense Fund, *Progress and Peril: Black Children in America—A Fact Book and Action Primer* (Washington, D.C.: 1993), 73; 1995 figures from *Poverty in the U.S.: 1995*, table 2. The data for 1959–1979 are unfortunately not tabulated to allow a precise distinction between intact families and female-headed ones. The published census data for those years distinguish children in female-headed families from those in "all other" families. The latter category includes not only intact married-couple families but also those headed by a father with no spouse present. The latter type is relatively rare. In 1960 only 2.3 percent of black families were headed by a man with no wife present. The current figure is not much higher—4 percent in 1994; U.S. Bureau of the Census, *Statistical Abstract of the United States: 1976* (Washington, D.C.: U.S. Government Printing Office, 1976), 42; *Marital Status and Living Arrangements: March 1994* (Washington, D.C.: U.S. Government Printing Office, 1996), table 6. Thus, it is reasonable to treat "all other" families as equivalent to intact, married-couple families, even though the category does include a small number of male-headed households with no wife present.

eighteen lived below the poverty line (Table 2). Three out of five of those who lived with both parents were impoverished. Although both adults in black married-couple families were usually employed, more often than not their two incomes were too low to lift their families out of deprivation. But that picture changed dramatically in the course of the 1960s, when the proportion of black children growing up poor declined from 66 to 40 percent. The gains in the decade went largely to those living in intact families, however. The poverty rate for children living in single-parent families also fell, but not by a lot. The drop was only from 82 to 68 percent, as compared with a plunge all the way from 61 percent down to just 25 percent for those in two-parent families.

For black children living with two parents the poverty rate continued to drop impressively. Since 1969 it has been cut in half, falling from 25 to 13 percent. But the growing number with a female head and no spouse present have come to constitute an underclass trapped in poverty. As Chapter 7 pointed out, today it usually takes two earners to make a middle-class income. There's another side to that coin: single-parent families tend to be poor. In 1994, for example, female-headed black families with children under 18 had a median income of only $9,950, a mere 28 percent of what black married-couple families with children took in.[12] Similarly, 13 percent of African-

American children with two parents at home were impoverished in 1995, as compared with almost two out of three of those with only a mother but no father. Social scientists do not often find such strong and clear correlations.

The increasingly tight connection between family structure and child poverty becomes even clearer from figures showing the proportion of all black children growing up poor who have a mother in the household but no father. That is, Table 2 looks at children in different kinds of families and asks the question: what was their poverty rate? But there is another way of looking at the link between family structure and impoverishment. Instead of asking how many children in female-headed households are poor (the answer being 64 percent in 1994), we can look at *all* black children in poverty and ask what kind of family they live in. In 1995, 85 percent of poor black children resided in fatherless families, as Table 3 indicates. Among the black children who are poor, in other words, six out of seven live in a mother-child household.

Growing up in a black female-headed household is not quite a guarantee that you will grow up poor, but it is pretty close to it. A recent review of the evidence in an article titled "Family Change Among Black Americans" concluded bleakly that "a majority of black children are now virtually assured of growing up in poverty, in large part because of their family status."[13]

THE DECLINE OF THE BLACK TWO-PARENT FAMILY

Thus, it is family structure that largely divides the haves from the have-nots in the black community. The population in poverty is made up overwhelmingly of single mothers. And yet as recently as 1960, two-thirds of all black children lived in intact, two-parent families (Table 4). Two-thirds was well

Table 3

The Concentration of Black Child Poverty in Single-Parent, Mother-Child Families: Percent of All Poor African-American Children in Fatherless Families, 1959–1994

1959	29
1969	58
1979	77
1995	85

Sources: Figures for 1959 and 1969 from *Social and Economic Status of the Black Population,* 52; 1979 figures from U.S. Bureau of the Census, Current Population Reports, P-20-480, *The Black Population in the United States: March 1994 and 1993* (Washington, D.C.: U.S. Government Printing Office, 1995), table O; 1995 figures calculated from *Poverty in the U.S.: 1995,* table 2.

Table 4
**Percent of Children Under 18
Living in Various Family Types, 1960–1995**

	1960	1970	1980	1995
Two parents				
Black	67	59	42	33
White	91	90	83	76
Mother only				
Black	22	30	44	52
White	7	8	14	18
Father only				
Black	NA	2	2	4
White	NA	1	2	3
Neither parent				
Black	NA	10	12	11
White	NA	2	2	3

Sources: Figures for 1960 from U.S. Bureau of the Census, Current Population Reports, P-23-181, *Households, Families, and Children: A 30-Year Perspective* (Washington, D.C.: U.S. Government Printing Office, 1992), 37; the mother-only figures for 1960 are actually for children living with one parent. The vast majority of them would be living with their mothers, though, so this is a fair approximation of the true figure. Figures for 1970 and 1980 from U.S. Bureau of the Census, Current Population Reports, P-20-480, *The Black Population in the United States: March 1994 and 1993*, table G. Figures for 1995 from U.S. Bureau of the Census, *Statistical Abstract of the United States: 1996* (Washington, D.C.: U.S. Government Printing Office, 1996), 65.

below the 91 percent rate for white children in 1960, of course, but the racial difference was small in comparison with what it would soon become. The lower proportion of intact African-American families in 1960 was mainly due to higher rates of divorce or desertion, and to the fact that black women were more often widowed before their children were fully grown.

As early as 1965, Daniel Patrick Moynihan, then an assistant secretary in the Department of Labor, warned of the disintegration of the African-American family, and argued that "national action" of some kind was required to arrest the trend. Civil rights activists and other liberals attacked Moynihan savagely for suggesting that this trend was anything to worry about.[14] But Moynihan was prescient, as Eleanor Holmes Norton, an important civil rights voice, conceded twenty years later.[15] In the past three decades the proportion of intact married-couple families has declined precipitously, even though the fraction of black women aged fifteen to forty-four who were divorced, separated, or widowed also went down. That figure has risen a good deal for white women, from 7 to 13 percent, but not for blacks.[16] It is thus not divorce but the failure to marry that has led to such a momentous change in black family patterns. The marriage rate for African Americans has plummeted in the past third of a century.

In 1960 only a little over a quarter of black women aged fifteen to forty-four were unmarried and had never been married (Table 5). Nearly three-quarters had been married, although a sizable proportion of their marriages had come to an end, as a result of divorce, separation, or the death of their spouse. Black women were only a shade less likely to marry than white women; 72 percent of black females and 76 percent of white females had been married.

The contrast with the present day is stark. Today a clear majority of African-American women aged fifteen to forty-five have never been married, as compared with just a third of their white counterparts. Although American women are currently marrying about four years later than they did back at the height of the Baby Boom in the 1950s, by the time they reach their late twenties (ages twenty-five to twenty-nine), seven out of ten white women today have married. The figure for black females of the same age is only four out of ten.[17] Moreover, this huge racial gap in marriage rates continues to widen.

Many fewer black women are marrying, and yet they continue to have children—which was not the case in an earlier era. The proportion of black children born out of wedlock has mushroomed (Table 6). In 1960 just over a fifth (22 percent) of the births to black women were out of wedlock. At the latest count—1994—the figure stood at a staggering 70 percent. If the trend

Table 5
Marital Status of Women 15–44, by Race, 1960–1994

	1960	1980	1994
Never married			
Black	28	48	56
White	24	33	34
Married, spouse present			
Black	51	31	25
White	69	57	53
Divorced, separated, or widowed			
Black	20	21	18
White	7	10	13

Sources: Figures for 1960 and 1980 from David T. Ellwood and Jonathan Crane, "Family Change Among Black Americans: What Do We Know?" *Journal of Economic Perspectives* 4 (Fall 1990), 67, 69; 1994 figures from U.S. Bureau of the Census, Current Population Reports, P-20-478, *Marital Status and Living Arrangements: March 1994,* table 1.

Table 6
Percent of Births Out of Wedlock, by Race, 1960–1994

	BLACK	WHITE
1960	22	2
1970	38	6
1980	55	11
1994	70	25

Sources: Figures for 1960–1980 from Donald J. Bogue, *The Population of the United States: Historical Trends and Future Projections* (New York: Free Press, 1985), 275; 1994 figures from June 1996 National Center for Health Statistics press release.

continues at anything like the same pace, the proportion of black births that are out of wedlock will hit three out of four births by 1997.

For much of the African-American population, marriage and childbearing have become almost completely dissociated. Since 1987, astoundingly, fertility and marriage have been inversely rather than positively correlated for blacks. In 1987 the birth rate for married black women actually fell *below the birth rate for unmarried black women,* the first time that has ever happened for any ethnic group. It was not a one-time anomaly; the pattern has continued ever since.[18] The disconnect between marriage and childbearing could scarcely become any more complete than that. A great many African Americans appear to be living in what Daniel Patrick Moynihan calls a "post-marital society."

These changes—the huge decline in the proportion of intact, two-parent families, the corresponding surge in the number of single parents, and the explosion of out-of-wedlock births—have not been confined to the African-American population, of course. They are to some extent general trends that have influenced all elements of American society. The number of unmarried white women becoming mothers—"Murphy Browns"—has also increased notably, and white female-headed families have become increasingly common.

If similar changes have been taking place among whites, why point a finger at blacks? some have asked. The political scientist Andrew Hacker has noted that the proportion of female-headed households has been rising just as rapidly among whites in recent decades; the percentage of out-of-wedlock births has increased more rapidly among whites than blacks. The evidence on changing family patterns, then, reveals "not so much racial differences as concurrent adaptations to common cultural trends."[19]

The *percentage increase* in the proportion of births that take place out of wedlock has indeed been higher among whites than blacks in recent decades (see Table 6), and the proportion of single-parent families has multiplied at about the same rate for both races (Table 3). And yet the rate of change is surely not the most important point. A quarter of white children, still a distinct minority, are born out of wedlock. In the case of blacks, it is the vast majority: seven out of ten black children. A black newborn with a married mother is as rare as a white child born to one who is unmarried. A social pattern with devastating economic consequences has become the norm in the black community, while it is still the deviant pattern among whites. To be born out of wedlock is a ticket to an impoverished childhood.[20]

"Single Mother, and Proud," ran the title of a *Washington Post* op-ed article in the summer of 1996. "Working Two Jobs and Raising a Daughter; What's to be Ashamed Of?" was the subtitle.[21] But shame is not the point. Poverty is —as we have already argued. The author (nearly through college) was juggling jobs and school and baby, but the majority of black single mothers are not college-educated and have very limited earning capacity. Child poverty, female-headed families, and out-of-wedlock births are closely connected— especially among blacks. As Table 2 indicated, the poverty rate for African-American children living in single-parent families is nearly *five times* what it is for those living in married-couple families (62 percent versus only 13 percent). Poverty is in fact part of a cluster of closely related problems associated with single-parent families. Recent evidence indicates that children living with mothers but no fathers are two-and-a-half times more likely to repeat a grade in school, more than three times as likely to be suspended or expelled, and twice as likely to end up in juvenile correctional facilities.[22]

It once was common for skeptics to greet such numbers with the argument that they do not show that there is anything wrong with female-headed families per se; these differences all stem from the greater likelihood that such families will have a low income. If you controlled for income, the differences would vanish. There are two flaws in this argument. First, why should we control for income? When the connections between living in a female-headed household and living in poverty are as strong as they are, artificially holding income constant makes no sense. It is possible that a careful study would show that college athletes perform as well in the classroom as nonathletes *if* you control for the number of hours a week they devote to studying. But if most of them don't study nearly as much as other students, their GPA controlled for hours of study is not of great interest. What matters is how well they perform. Likewise, median income in 1995 was only $15,004 for female-headed black families, little more than a third of what it was in black married-couple families. That is not a fact that should be obscured by controlling for other related factors.[23]

Nevertheless, recent studies have done what the critics had asked for; they have held income and a variety of other socioecomomic variables constant. But they reveal that even when you do control for other variables, family structure has an independent effect that is measurable, and that, in important ways, the effect of growing up in a single-parent family is negative.[24]

POVERTY AND EMPLOYMENT

It is not only family structure that determines who will end up poor. Poverty and employment are closely linked.[25] A generation ago, a good many black men and women labored full-time, year-round without being able to earn enough money to keep their families out of poverty, but that is no longer the case. The vast majority of the adults who are poor today—and this includes black adults—are people who do not work for a living or work only part-time.

In fact, whatever your race or gender—whether you're black, white, male or female—your chances of avoiding poverty are excellent if you hold a full-time job that lasts all year. Fewer than 3 percent of black men, white men, and white women who were fully employed had incomes below the poverty line in 1995 (Table 7). There is no racial difference at all in this respect, and no gender difference either among whites. For fully employed African-American women, the poverty rate was 7.5 percent, significantly though not dramatically higher than for whites. Black women are more likely to be impoverished than males of either race because of the lower average wages that females in general earn. And they suffer from more poverty than white females because they are more likely to have children and no spouse to help with their support. Even when their incomes are as high as those of white women, those earnings go to feed more mouths.

Racial differences in poverty rates are sharper for those who worked only part-time or did not work at all. In 1995 only 15 percent of white male part-time workers were impoverished, as compared with 25 percent of black

Table 7
Poverty Rates by Employment Status and Race, 1995

	BLACK	WHITE
Males, 18–64		
Employed		
Year-round, full-time	2.5	2.6
Not year-round, full-time	25.2	14.8
Not employed	38.1	30.6
Females, 18–64		
Employed		
Year-round, full-time	7.5	2.2
Not year-round, full-time	31.6	11.6
Not employed	54.2	25.4

Source: Poverty in the U.S.: 1995, table 3. Year-round work is defined as work for fifty weeks; full-time employment is work for at least thirty-five hours per week.

men; for women it was 12 versus 32 percent. Likewise, blacks who were not employed at all had higher poverty rates than similarly situated whites, with the gap largest among women.

Why this striking racial difference in poverty rates among the underemployed or jobless? A good part of the answer is to be found, again, in the impact of differential marriage rates on family incomes. Less than four decades ago black men were only slightly less likely to be living with a wife than were whites of the same age, as Table 8 shows. But that is no longer the case. Thus, in the twenty-five to twenty-nine age bracket more than half of white men are married, while only a bit more than a quarter of black men have a spouse. And with increasing age the racial gap widens. Marriage influences the family income of employed and unemployed alike. The white men who are not working full-time are more likely to live with someone else (usually a wife) whose income is high enough to support them. A marriage license is, in effect, an insurance policy: a spouse fired from a job will usually have someone else to depend on. That protection has become considerably less available to blacks in recent decades.

In fact, when it comes to staying out of poverty, not only white men, but white women as well have an advantage over African Americans. In other words, the gender inequality so apparent within the black community does not exist among whites. White women and white men with similar employment experiences have similar poverty rates. Again, a notable racial difference. It's tempting to think that white women have higher-paying jobs than black women, but they don't, on the average. Nor does employment status do much

Table 8

Proportion of Men Who Were Married with Spouse Present, by Age and Race, 1960–1994

	BLACK	WHITE
Ages 25–29		
1960	70	78
1994	27	51
Ages 30–34		
1960	79	86
1994	33	65
Ages 35–44		
1960	83	89
1994	47	71

Sources: Bogue, *Population of the U.S.: Historical Trends,* 158; *Marital Status and Living Arrangements: March 1994,* table 1.

Table 9
Work Experience, by Race and Sex, 1995

	BLACK	WHITE
Males, 18–64		
Employed		
Year-round, full-time	52.3	66.9
Not year-round, full-time	23.8	22.9
Not employed	23.9	10.2
Females, 18–64		
Employed		
Year-round, full-time	44.2	42.5
Not year-round, full-time	26.1	33.6
Not employed	29.7	23.8

Source: U.S. Bureau of the Census, Current Population Reports, P-60-193, *Money Income in the United States: 1995* (Washington, D.C.: U.S. Government Printing Office, 1996), table 10.

to explain the greater poverty of black women. An almost identical proportion of black and white females held down full-time jobs for the entire year in 1995, with the black figure actually slightly higher (Table 9). It is true that African-American women were somewhat more likely not to have worked at all than their white counterparts—30 percent did not, as opposed to 24 percent of whites. But these very modest differences are not sufficient to explain why, for example, the poverty rate for black females aged twenty-five to thirty-four was 2.5 times as high as that for white women.[26] The difference is again explained by family structure: many more white women are living in intact families that include other employed adults, and are thus much less often the sole source of support for their children. As a consequence, their earnings alone do not determine whether the family lives in poverty.

Thus, while lack of employment—particularly full-time long-term employment—is the central source of adult poverty for black men, that is not the case for black women. For them the main source of the huge racial gap in poverty rates is the continuing decline of the black two-parent family. The poverty rate for white females is far lower chiefly because a much higher proportion of them reside with a spouse who brings in an income. For adult black women who fall below the poverty line, the problem has more to do with family circumstances than with their position in the labor market—which is essentially the same as that of white women. The single-parent, mother-child families that have proliferated in the black community in recent decades are headed by women who in most cases could hold a job that would give them an income above the poverty line if they had no dependents. But they do have dependent children, and that increases the chances they will live in poverty. The poverty line is obviously higher when there are more mouths to be fed, so more income is needed. And child-care responsibilities interfere with work and reduce the income generated by employment.

BLACK MEN AND THE JOB MARKET

Black men have a much higher poverty rate than whites, we have argued, because fewer are employed full-time throughout the year. Only half (52 percent) of African-American men aged eighteen to sixty-four have full-time, year-round jobs, compared with two-thirds of white males. Nearly a quarter of black men did not work at all in 1995, as compared with only a tenth of white men (Table 9). "You have black men out there who are viable sex partners but not viable husbands," the sociologist Elijah Anderson said in 1992. "They do not have the jobs that will allow them to follow through as husbands . . ."[27] When men can't find work, in other words, they don't marry. It's too simple a view, we will argue later in this chapter; joblessness alone does not explain the flight from marriage. But clearly, there is something to the point.

The most obvious explanation for the difficulties black men have in finding and keeping jobs is racism: employers biased against them. They are the last to be hired, it is said, when other sources of labor have been exhausted, and they are the first to be fired, when the labor scarcity has eased. And yet a glance at how the black unemployment rate has fluctuated over the past half century or so shows that this simple explanation doesn't hold up (Table 10). Before World War II, certainly, sheer racial prejudice—racist employers, closed labor unions, and the hostility of white workers—deprived African Americans of job opportunities. A majority of the nation's African-American population lived in states in which blacks were kept separate and subordinate by law, and most northern whites were deeply prejudiced.

And yet—astonishingly—the black unemployment rate in 1940 was only about a quarter higher than the white rate, and the racial difference in labor-force participation was even less.[28] What is more, the jobless rate for African-American men living in northern states was more than double what it was in the South, exactly the opposite of what we would expect if unemployment had been mainly the result of discrimination.[29] The idea that employers in Mississippi in 1940 treated African Americans more fairly than those in Massachusetts cannot be taken seriously.

The racial gap in unemployment was thus relatively small at a time when societal discrimination against blacks was intense and pervasive, and it was much smaller in the Jim Crow states—where hostility toward blacks was greatest. About 40 percent of southern blacks, it is true, worked for subsis-

Table 10
Racial Differences in Male Unemployment Rates, Ages 25–64, 1940–1995

	BLACK	WHITE	B/W RATIO
1940	9.6	7.6	1.26
1950	6.4	3.4	1.88
1960	7.8	3.7	2.11
1970	4.2	2.6	1.61
1980	9.0	4.4	2.05
1995	7.2	3.8	1.89

Sources: Figures for 1940–1980 from U.S. Commission on Civil Rights, *The Economic Progress of Black Men in America* (Washington, D.C.: Clearinghouse Publication 91, 1986), 44; 1995 figures calculated from U.S. Bureau of the Census, *Statistical Abstract of the U.S.: 1996,* 401.

tence wages on the land, where a lot of partial unemployment was disguised, but that fact does not change the basic point: in subsequent years, during a period of remarkable economic, social, and political progress for African Americans, black joblessness went up. The signs of progress were almost everywhere. White racial attitudes began to change radically right after the first systematic public opinion surveys in the early 1940s.[30] The Jim Crow system crumbled under the assault of civil rights protesters, Congress, and the courts. The Civil Rights Act of 1964 outlawed racial discrimination in employment throughout the land. Within a few years, indeed, employers were under strong pressure to give preferential treatment to minorities in order to meet affirmative action "goals and timetables." The racial gap in incomes, which had been enormous in 1940, shrank dramatically, and large numbers of African Americans moved into middle-class occupations in which they had only a bare foothold before.

In light of these and other signs of racial change, it seems puzzling that racial gaps in unemployment rates and labor-force participation rates grew larger in the 1940s and 1950s, and ever since have remained about as wide as they were in 1960. The black/white unemployment ratios in 1950 and 1995 were virtually identical. Most measures of the relative economic and social status of black and white Americans in recent decades show strong tendencies toward convergence. In terms of educational achievement, occupational attainment, and incomes, for example, blacks and whites resembled each other more in the 1960s than in the 1940s, and still more in the 1990s than in the 1960s. This is not at all the case, though, with respect to unemployment or labor-force participation.

Racial differences in employment are especially sharp today among men in their late teens and early twenties. In the 1950s, though, black youths aged sixteen to nineteen were actually a bit *more* likely to hold a job of some kind than their white peers. Although the unemployment rate for young blacks was also higher than that of whites—just as it was for African-American men in the older age brackets—their higher labor-force participation gave them a slightly higher employment/population ratio.[31] Just over half (52 percent) of black males in their late teens had a job in 1954, a shade higher than the proportion among their white peers (50 percent). Among men aged twenty to twenty-four the racial difference ran the other way, but it was equally slight.

In the year of the *Brown* decision, when the struggle for equal rights for black people was in its earliest stages and when racial prejudice in the United States was clearly much more pervasive and deeply rooted than it would later be, young men of both races were equally likely to have a job. Young white men certainly had much better jobs than young black men, with higher pay, better working conditions, and higher status. But the two groups were equally integrated into the world of work—likely to be holding down a job of some sort.

In the four decades since, the employment/population ratio for white men in their late teens and early twenties has changed remarkably little. In 1994, as in 1954, about half of those aged sixteen to nineteen and three-quarters of those twenty to twenty-four were employed. The proportion of African-American teenage males with a job, however, has fallen dramatically, from a half to only a quarter. The fraction of black youths in their early twenties who are employed has fallen sharply as well, from more than three out of four to six out of ten. Again, the timing of the change here makes it very hard to believe that it was caused by increased discrimination in the labor market. Some other explanation is clearly called for.

THE "SPATIAL MISMATCH" PROBLEM

Paterson, New Jersey, used to be a thriving mill town, but not today. "Everybody out here is struggling," said Raymond Brownfield, an unemployed cook —young and black. "It's hard to survive, to make ends meet," he went on. "This used to be a real city of opportunity—Silk City!—but now there's nothing. Everything used to be here. It's a 'used to be' city. That's all."[32]

The city of Paterson, 36 percent black in 1990, suffers from a familiar problem—a mismatch between the location of people and jobs. African Americans living in one place and looking for work that is actually elsewhere. In fact, the places in which many blacks live are precisely those that have been losing rather than gaining population and jobs in the past two to three decades. The more dynamic urban centers are much more heavily white. In other words, in the cities in which blacks are concentrated, jobs tend to be scarce, and there is a surplus of labor. Where comparatively few blacks reside, on the other hand, the labor market tends to be the tightest, and employers are hungriest for workers. It's what scholars have labeled a "spatial mismatch."[33]

Detroit, with its huge black population and a stagnant economy, typifies the older industrial cities of the Snowbelt or Rustbelt. When tens of thousands of black people moved to Detroit in the 1940s and 1950s, the automobile industry was booming, and work was easy to find, even for people without skills or experience. The unemployment rate for the city's blacks in 1965 was an astonishingly low 3.4 percent.[34] Not long after, though, both the auto industry and the city of Detroit went into an economic tailspin. Domestic car production began to recover in the 1980s, but not in Detroit; most new jobs in the industry appeared elsewhere. The population of Detroit plunged 38 percent between 1960 and 1990, almost entirely due to the departure of whites. By 1990, Detroit stood out as the most heavily black of America's major cities, with its three-quarters of a million African-American residents accounting for 76 percent of its total population. It also ranked among the nation's leaders in unemployment, poverty, and crime.

A substantial proportion of the black population of the nation currently resides in the stagnant and decaying inner-city neighborhoods of places like Detroit, Chicago, Cleveland, and St. Louis.[35] Their concentration in communities like this is one reason for the decline in black labor-force participation rates and high levels of black unemployment. Not many blacks reside in the urban centers whose economies have generated the most new jobs and attracted the most newcomers since the 1960s.

Take San Diego, which now has a larger population than Detroit. San Diego's population nearly doubled in size between 1960 and 1990, while that of Detroit was shrinking by almost 40 percent (Table 11). Less than a tenth of the residents of San Diego are black, and their prospects look a good deal brighter than those of blacks back in the Motor City. The proportion of workers with full-time, year-round jobs was a quarter higher in San Diego than in Detroit, and per capita income was 66 percent higher. In Detroit the poverty rate was higher—67 percent higher. And the unemployment rate was more than triple that in San Diego.

Phoenix, now the nation's eighth-largest city, San Antonio (number 10), and San Jose (number 11) are other urban centers of the San Diego type. They, too, have experienced a tremendous economic and demographic boom within the past generation, but have not attracted a major black migration wave. Unlike any of the major cities of the Northeast or Midwest, they all have black populations that are well below the average for the nation as a whole—a mere 5 percent in Phoenix and San Jose and 7 percent in San Antonio.

"Spatial mismatch" refers not only to the problem of African Americans looking for work in Detroit, while HELP WANTED signs go up in Phoenix. It is

Table 11
Snow Belt versus Sunbelt: Detroit and San Diego Compared, 1990

	DETROIT	SAN DIEGO
Total population (in thousands)	1,028	1,111
Percent change, 1960–1990	−38	+94
Black population in 1990		
Number (in thousands)	778	104
Percent	75.7	9.4
Labor force participation rate,		
persons 16 and up	55	64
Percent of labor force		
Unemployed	20	6
Worked full-time, year-round	49	62
Per capita income	$9,847	$16,401
Poverty rate	32.4	19.4

Sources: Statistical Abstract of the United States: 1974, 24–25; Statistical Abstract of the United States: 1991, 34, 36; 1990 Census of Population and Housing, Summary of Social, Economic, and Housing Characteristics: United States, tables 3 and 5.

also a matter of how people and jobs are distributed between the central cities and the suburbs within metropolitan areas. In nearly all of the country's urban centers, employment opportunities have been drying up in the inner-city core in the past three decades, and have been expanding in suburban locations on the periphery.[36] The trend toward "decentralization" of economic activity in metropolitan areas is the result of technological and social changes that have made it cheaper to do business outside of central cities than within them. Advances in transportation and communication made many firms less dependent upon a central location, and allowed them to move to suburbia, where land has been cheaper, the crime rate lower, and taxes less burdensome. With the black population more centralized than the distribution of jobs, the shift has limited black economic opportunity. Detroit is a good example. The city has lost roughly 40 percent of its population in the past three decades, but the metropolitan area as a whole has not languished. Its population, in fact, has grown by a third—outside the city's boundaries, where few blacks live. Detroit's suburban population has doubled since 1960, which more than offset the 38 percent drop in the city itself.[37]

Of course many Hispanic and Asian immigrants are also strongly concentrated in inner cities today and are thus equally "mismatched" to the job market. But these groups nevertheless have higher labor-force participation rates and experience less unemployment than blacks. Differences in residential distribution, for example, cannot explain why Mexican-American men in

California are much more likely to be in the labor force and less likely to be unemployed than are blacks in the Golden State.[38] Nor do they explain why Mexicans and Puerto Ricans who live in Chicago neighborhoods that are just as blighted as those occupied by blacks are nevertheless considerably more successful at finding stable employment than African Americans.[39] A major new study comparing the economic mobility of African Americans with that of Hispanic and Asian immigrants in New York City reveals identical contrasts.[40]

CRIME, EDUCATION, AND POVERTY

Technological change, advances in communication and transportation, cheaper land and lower taxes: these are some of the reasons why jobs have moved from the inner city. But (as we suggested above), crime has also played a role. It has long been an article of liberal faith that poverty causes crime. We will address that issue in the next chapter. Whatever the merits of that proposition, a strong case can be made for its converse: crime may cause poverty. The absence of employment opportunities and resulting black male joblessness are in part a consequence of black crime.

As we noted in Chapter 6, during the 1960s the United States was hit by the worst crime wave in its history, with crime rates surging most rapidly in the black community. Although crime rates have subsequently fluctuated from year to year, they have never dropped back to anything close to their earlier level, and in fact have continued to rise for young black males. In recent years the estimates of the numbers of black men who are caught in the criminal justice system are staggering. One 1989 study calculated that one-fifth of all black males between the ages of sixteen and thirty-four were either in prison or jail, out on parole, or on probation (with imprisonment a near certainty if they were convicted of another offense). Only a quarter of these men were actually behind bars; another quarter had been locked up but released and were still on parole; the remaining half were on probation under the supervision of a court.[41]

Another study focused on a slightly younger group, African-American males in their twenties, and found that in 1989, 23 percent of them were under some form of control by the criminal justice system. By 1995 the figure had risen to one-third (32.2 percent) of the group. That was 4.5 times the criminal justice control rate for young white men and 2.5 times the rate for Hispanics.[42]

These are national figures, and include residents of suburbs, small towns, and rural areas, where crime rates are lower. In the inner cities of major metropolitan areas, crime is much more common. A 1990 study of Chicago found that 29 percent of black males aged twenty to twenty-nine had spent time in jail or prison. If the number of black youths in Chicago who were on probation was about the same as the number who had been incarcerated (as is the case in the nation as a whole), that would mean that no less than six out of ten of Chicago's young black men had criminal records.[43] A 1991 study of black males aged eighteen to thirty-five in Washington, D.C., found that 42 percent were under criminal justice control. Another study of neighboring Baltimore the same year arrived at a figure of 56 percent.[44]

The appallingly high level of black crime depresses the employment prospects of black men in a number of ways. First, ghetto crime sharply increases the cost of operating businesses in African-American neighborhoods and discourages business activity. Armed robberies of business firms, for example, are four times as frequent in black inner-city neighborhoods as in the suburbs.[45] It costs more to insure your property against loss in such areas, and it sometimes is impossible to get coverage at all. A shopping center in one midwestern inner city had to spend 15 percent more than a comparable suburban shopping complex on security guards and lighting. A recent survey of the business climate in the Boston and Los Angeles areas concluded that crime was "among the most important reasons why companies opening new facilities did not even consider inner-city locations." The study also rated crime as "the second most important reason why existing firms leave, after building costs and space constraints."[46] Both the flight of existing firms from the ghetto to the suburbs and the unwillingness of outside enterprises to move in have the same effect: they reduce the supply of jobs existing near large African-American population concentrations. They aggravate the "spatial mismatch" problem.

Crime diminishes the employment prospects of black men in another important way as well. It makes a substantial proportion of young black men unavailable for gainful employment by putting them behind bars. And having a criminal record damages their employment prospects when they get out. Many employers will not hire someone with a criminal record if they can avoid it. In a national sample of young men whose lives were tracked during the 1980s, black youths who had been imprisoned in 1980 worked 27 percent fewer weeks than those who had stayed out of jail. Having been on probation without doing time also reduced weeks worked—by 7 percent.[47] During the 1980s the proportion of black male high school dropouts with a job dropped sharply. Most of that decline was accounted for by the rise in the proportion who had a criminal record.[48]

In addition, the employment prospects of even those young black men who remain free of any entanglement with the law may suffer as a result of the highly negative image of the whole group that has developed because of the criminal activity of so many. A recent survey of employers in the Chicago area found that they tended to view black men, and especially those who lived in the inner city, as "dishonest," as well as "unstable, uncooperative . . . and uneducated." Thus, they were reluctant to hire African Americans when white or Hispanic job candidates were available.[49] The survey did not include a question tapping employers' attitudes about job applicants with criminal records. But it seems plausible that their skepticism about the honesty of black workers, and perhaps some of their other negative feelings about them as well, had something to do with the high level of black crime in the city. Six out of ten of Chicago's black males aged twenty to twenty-nine had been at some point convicted of a crime, seven times the rate for whites and five times the rate for Hispanics in that age group.[50]

Crime also reduces the number of black males holding legitimate jobs for another reason altogether. A great deal of money passes through the illicit underground economy in the United States, and some people may choose careers in crime because it pays better than the alternatives open to them. It is usually assumed that unemployment leads people to turn to crime in desperation; it is viewed as a "root cause" of crime. Most unemployed black males "have a choice between zero and the drug trade," New York congressman Major Owens asserted in 1989.[51] But, in fact, some young men may find criminal activity a more attractive means of making a living than legitimate employment.

Information about just how well crime pays is, by its very nature, difficult to come by. Those with relatively high incomes from crime try to avoid the census-taker and in any case fail to report their earnings honestly. But one suggestive study found that young blacks with income from crimes were averaging as much $19 per hour, triple what they could expect to earn at McDonald's and, naturally, tax-free.[52] Even in Boston, which had an exceptionally low unemployment rate at the time of the study (the late 1980s), crime was much more lucrative than legitimate work available to young black men without much in the way of educational credentials. A survey of drug dealers in Washington, D.C., found them taking in $30 an hour.

That lucrative pay comes with a price: the years that can be spent in jail, the danger that life will end up being exceedingly short. Nevertheless, dealing drugs remains attractive—particularly to the young. The racial gap in unemployment and labor-force participation rates is now much wider for black males in the age brackets sixteen to nineteen and twenty to twenty-four than it is for older men—a change since 1960.[53] In South Central Los Angeles, writer Joel Kotkin reported in 1989, despite an unemployment rate of nearly 50 percent among younger blacks, few were interested in taking the jobs offered by the small businesses that had replaced the long-gone factories. It was work that (at least initially) paid lower wages and offered less security than the larger plants once had, but Asian and Hispanic immigrants signed up eagerly. "Young blacks today don't want to start at the bottom," George Givens, a black community organizer said. "After the civil rights movement there was a false message that you didn't have to work your way up. If a job didn't pay $15 an hour, you didn't want to do it. In a situation like that, the highest-paying and most popular employer usually ends up being the dope dealer."[54]

Black men today, in sum, are most likely to be living below the poverty line either because they are jobless or work less than full-time throughout the year. Their employment difficulties are partly due to their residential concentration in places with limited opportunity—in inner cities rather than suburbs, in the Detroits rather than the San Diegos. But, in addition, many are involved in crime, which both cuts the supply of jobs and lowers their chance of getting the work that is available.

Black unemployment is also related to educational performance, a complicated subject that we explore at length in Chapter 13. Just a brief word here. As we noted above, in the past two decades economic opportunity in the United States has come to depend increasingly upon education. Highly educated workers have fared extremely well; those with only an average or less than average education have had to make do with flat or declining real wages. This has worked to the disadvantage of blacks, since they still lag behind whites in schooling. And it is a large obstacle in the way of racial equality in the future. A disproportionately large number of black students today are not developing the cognitive skills that are necessary to function effectively in today's workplace.

A 1994 national test of the reading skills of twelfth-graders discovered that only 52 percent of African Americans were able to perform at the "basic" level, as compared with 81 percent of their white classmates. "Basic" in this case was painfully rudimentary, and yet almost half of black youths who were a few months away from entering either college or the job market were not literate at that level.[55] Some 43 percent of whites in their final year of high school were competent enough at reading to be rated "proficient," but just 13 percent of blacks. These glaring differences in levels of literacy, it is reasonable to think, have something to do with the greater difficulty young African Americans experience in the labor market. Although affirmative action requirements limit the ability of employers to take into account the results of tests that would have a "disparate effect" upon blacks (as we discuss in Chapter 15), the decisions employers make about hiring may be influenced by their awareness of these differences.

POVERTY AND FAMILY BREAKUP—WHAT'S CAUSING WHAT?

Some of these obstacles to finding good jobs apply equally well to black women. They live in the same cities and the same neighborhoods, and thus have the same "spatial mismatch" problem. They also lag behind whites (and Asians) in school, though black females are far ahead of their male peers in rates of college attendance and college graduation. In addition, African-American women are not involved in crime to a significant extent, and rarely have records that limit their employability.

Black adult women (and black children) today, we have seen, are most likely to be impoverished because of the structure of the families in which they live—the structure of the families that they chose to form. Since the 1960s, we have seen, the number living in single-parent families with their children but without the father of those children or any other adult male has soared. Why?

The declining rate of marriage and the rise in both female-headed households and out-of-wedlock births is often attributed to the weak economic position of black men. The deteriorating labor-market position of young black males in the 1970s and 1980s sharply reduced the ratio of employed black men to black women of marriage age, Harvard sociologist William Julius Wilson has argued. Men without a paycheck cannot assume family responsibilities. The consequent shrinking of the "male marriageable pool" was the driving force behind the massive change in black family arrangements.[56]

This idea is plausible, but it is far from a full explanation of what has happened to the black family since the 1960s. For one thing, it does not fit well with earlier historical experience. During the Great Depression, marriage rates were higher for blacks than for whites despite the fact that their wages averaged less than half of those of whites.[57] In the 1940s and 1950s, jobless black and white men were equally likely to marry.[58] Why black males who had no job were nonetheless entering into marriages before 1960 but then stopped doing so—why the qualifications for being "marriageable" should have changed—is a puzzle.

The "male marriageable pool" theory has another problem. Black marriage rates have fallen much too sharply to be attributable to any recent change in the labor-market position of black men. The rise in unemployment that took place during the 1970s and 1980s was much too small to explain the dramatic plunge in marriage rates and the surge in out-of-wedlock births. What is more, it is not only poor and unemployed black men who have become less prone to marry. The flight from marriage has affected all segments of the black community, including the most highly educated and most prosperous.[59]

Even if this flight from marriage had been largely confined to men with at best a marginal place in the world of work, as the theory would seem to require, there would remain a chicken-and-egg question to ponder. It is commonly assumed that having a low-paid job or no job at all makes a man both less willing to marry and less appealing to a woman. We know that married men earn substantially more than single men do.[60] Is that because men who command higher wages are better able to support a family and are more attractive to females seeking a mate? Or does the causality perhaps run the other way: Men who are married might feel greater pressure to earn a good living than do single men, and thus might work harder than those without family responsibilities. If so, the employment difficulties that younger black men have experienced since the 1960s have not caused the flight from marriage. Quite the opposite: it is the unwillingness of a growing number of black men to accept family responsibilities that has reduced their incomes.[61] Whatever the merits of one theory against the other, at least one aspect of the male marriageable pool seems clear: a criminal record affects marriage eligibility. A significant fraction of the young black male population lives in a setting that precludes marriage for at least the length of their sentence; they are incarcerated. And a larger fraction have records that both employers and potential spouses may find off-putting.

The black family has changed profoundly within the past third of a century. Social scientists have not been able to establish that this change in family structure is the *result* of poverty, unemployment, low wages, or any other economic variable. The vast majority of African-American families remained intact during the worst economic catastrophe in all of American history, during the 1930s. The rise in illegitimate births and single-parent families has largely taken place since 1960, a period in which black people have made major economic gains and in which the black poverty rate has been either declining or stable. Very little of this transformation can be explained in terms of economic problems afflicting black males. A thoughtful recent review of the literature on the subject in the *Journal of Economic Perspectives* concedes that economic perspectives have been of limited value. "Economic models," the authors conclude regretfully, "have not been very successful in explaining the changes in black or white families."[62]

We do not know precisely why black families have been changing as radically as they have, but it is apparent that much of the answer involves cultural and social factors that are not a matter of economic incentives. It will thus take more than changes in economic conditions to arrest and reverse the trend toward family disintegration.

POVERTY AND THE SINGLE PARENT

East of the Anacostia River in Washington, D.C., lies a land of poverty— almost entirely black. Street corners are crowded with jobless men; public housing projects lie mostly abandoned, unfit for habitation; drug markets thrive in the open; the rate of infant mortality is the highest in the city; storefronts are gutted, and the trash piles up. One day in 1996 a Bible study class had to be canceled when someone was shot to death on a nearby street —hardly an unusual occurrence. In Ward 8, Mayor Marion Barry's political base, even the McDonald's restaurant is closed and boarded up. There is no movie theater, no department store, and only one major supermarket for 72,000 people, although liquor stores are everywhere. In 1989–1990, 84 percent of the children were born out of wedlock and into poverty.[63]

"To say that unwed mothers cause poverty is like saying hungry people cause famine or sick people cause disease," *Nation* magazine writer Katha Pollitt has argued. "It would be closer to the truth to say that poverty causes early and unplanned childbearing." Pollitt evidently believes that pregnancy, like much disease, is an act of God. Unwed mothers are the victims of a plague called poverty.[64] Those are not her views alone, of course. In the single-parent family "both mother and child would be at a distinct disadvantage in life" even if they had a man around, "since so many of them are young, poor, jobless and without much in the way of prospects themselves," the Yale sociologist Kai Erikson has contended. "It is not absent *fathers* that endanger these children, then, but absent *prospects*," he has suggested.[65]

In this chapter we have taken issue with this view. And indeed we not only believe that the absence of fathers, in itself, is a problem, but that "prospects" are not as dim as Pollitt and Erickson assert. There is work available—even in inner-city neighborhoods in places like Chicago. More than 16 million immigrants have entered the United States in the past quarter century, many of them coming with very little education, no capital, and no command of English. And yet this huge influx has not brought about a big jump in the overall unemployment rate. Few of these newcomers have been unable to find jobs, even though they often live on the same block as African Americans who do not seem employable.[66]

In late 1993, the journalist Joe Klein visited Chicago's notorious Cabrini Green housing project and talked with Harriet Dawson, who ran a program called Project Match that linked people and jobs. "The problem isn't jobs," Dawson said. "There are jobs in Chicago. We don't have trouble placing our people. Whether they'll be motivated enough to do those jobs is another matter."[67] "Motivated enough" is in fact a catch-all phrase that includes a lot of other qualities that the ready-for-work possess. Many of Cabrini Green's residents need to learn basic literacy and good diction, and also how to dress appropriately, wake up to an alarm, arrive at work on time, and listen to direction and criticism once there. New York City social workers, the *Wall Street Journal* discovered in 1991, had to teach teens the elementary rules of the working world. "I have a thing about hats," Nilsa Pietri, the head of youth services at Henry Street, said. "I always have to tell the kids to take their hats off."[68] The kids who remove their hats and accept the entry-level jobs for which they are barely prepared will not get rich fast. But those jobs are a start —the start upon which many immigrants build an economic future.

A young man, unemployed and living in a housing project, usually needs to learn some elementary skills if he is ever to hold down a steady job. And if he has a drug or alcohol problem, that, too, needs to be addressed. A teenage mother, living on her own, has an additional burden: coping with one or more children. "Somebody must say that babies making babies is morally wrong," Jesse Jackson has said.[69] It's the way most Americans see the matter. And the point extends to women beyond their teen years. To be born out of wedlock to a jobless mother is a lousy start to life. Among other things, it raises the odds of ending up ensnared in the criminal justice system. As a volume of the respected National Research Council states flatly, "the effect of family disruption on black crime [is] independent of commonly cited alternative explanations (e.g., poverty, region, urbanization, age composition) and [can] not be attributed to unique cultural factors within the black community." [70]

"Something has got to restore family structure," New York Senator Daniel Patrick Moynihan said in 1992. But, he added, "If you expect a government program to change that, you know more about government than I do." [71] Perhaps he's right; perhaps marriage patterns—whatever their origin—have now taken on a life of their own, such that public policy is not likely to have much effect. On the other hand, a recent study demonstrates that the current welfare system discourages pregnant women, especially African-American women, from marrying. A typical black woman who marries loses benefits that amount to a "marriage penalty" of almost $1,900, almost 9 percent of her family income, twice the marriage penalty for whites. [72] In 1996, President Clinton and Congress agreed to a radical decentralization of the entire welfare system. The states will be free to run innovative welfare programs of many different kinds. Critics charge that the revised law is mean-spirited—that it erroneously assumes that "the poor will shape up ... if we can just bring ourselves to take away what little they still have." [73] But the hope of those who advocate experimentation is that changing the structure of incentives for young men and women will lead them to make different marital decisions— the first crucial step down the road to reducing the level of black poverty.

CHAPTER TEN

Crime

IT'S NO ACCIDENT that the question of crime should have been a central theme in Tom Wolfe's riveting portrait of modern urban life, *The Bonfire of the Vanities*. Wall Street bond trader Sherman McCoy may have lived exceedingly well, but, as it turned out, neither his lineage nor his wealth could protect him. The danger was not so much crime itself, as the fear of it—a fear that haunted him even on his own turf, walking his dog just steps from his Park Avenue address. When he strayed accidentally beyond the safe moneyed territory he knew and into the South Bronx, where he encountered two young black men, the Master of the Universe lost his grip. In five minutes the whole elaborate structure of his million-dollar-a-year life came crashing down. A big hot-air balloon of a life, decorated to the hilt was fatally punctured in a moment's confrontation with two project-dwellers on a dark street in an unsavory neighborhood.

In the few moments in which the black youths crossed his path in a foreign land, McCoy became just a big-city dweller, as vulnerable as his poorest neighbor. Most urban residents—whatever their color—have something in common: a fear of crime. But, paradoxically, that shared fear drives blacks and whites apart. Asked in a 1992 interview what kind of world he would like to see his own children born into, filmmaker Spike Lee answered, "A world where they could walk down the street and white women would not have to feel they have to get out of their way and start clutching their pocketbooks." [1]

For Lee—and certainly not for him alone—that clutched purse symbolizes much. The white woman whose body language spells fear turns the object of that fear into a "nigger"—a savage, a sexual predator, a dangerous brute. Or at least that is how many black men view such encounters. Charles S. Johnson, it may be recalled from Chapter 1, found that in the Jim Crow South of the 1940s, resentment at the failure of whites to address African Americans with simple respect seemed more wounding than the fact of segregation itself. More than half a century later, badges of inferiority are still deeply hurtful. "I walk in this building every day in a suit and tie, five days a week, 300-some days a year, and I can still get on the elevator with a white woman, by myself, and she will clutch her purse," a black attorney said on *Nightline* in October 1995. "That should give you an indication of just where black males fit in this society and how they're viewed," he went on.[2]

The allusion is most often to white women, but in fact fear drives a wedge between black and white men as well. "I . . . often find myself in poor Hispanic, Korean, Chinese, Japanese or Vietnamese enclaves," a Los Angeles man wrote the *Wall Street Journal* in 1992. But, he said, "I try to avoid driving through black areas of the city, and wouldn't dream of getting out of my car in them and walking the streets. I would be afraid. . . ."[3] Male taxi-drivers who pick up passengers headed for heavily black neighborhoods express the same fear. "I work everywhere, but sometimes I do get scared. . . . There is not a lot of protection," a cabbie told the *Boston Globe* that same year.[4] No issue so poisons relations between the races as that of black crime.

We speak of "black crime" as a convenient shorthand, hard to avoid. And yet, unlike "black poverty," it is a loaded phrase, implying some sort of innate predisposition to engage in illegal activity. As such, it seems to echo racist assumptions about blacks as a primitive people, gripped by passions, more likely to commit crimes unless controlled by white authorities. In fact, of course, crime is an individual failing, and the statistical generalization that blacks are disproportionately both perpetrators and victims must never obscure the vital fact that most black citizens are law-abiding.

WHITE FEARS, BLACK FEARS

White fear of black crime is not a subject pollsters tend to explore. But in a 1990 national survey, 56 percent of white, Hispanic, and other nonblack respondents agreed that African-Americans were more prone to violence than whites.[5] An October 1993 national survey yielded lower—but still quite high —numbers: 37 percent thought that blacks were more likely than others "to commit crime in our society."[6]

This line of questioning forced people to make generalizations about the character traits of groups defined by skin color—something many (for good reason) would rather not do. And thus more narrowly framed questions are probably more revealing. Is it "common sense" or prejudice when whites avoid driving through black neighborhoods? a 1989 *Washington Post*/ABC News poll asked. Fifty percent of whites said that it was only "common sense."[7] That figure may seem improbably low, but the protection provided by a car obviously makes many people feel relatively safe. No distinction in that survey was made between night and day, but asked in 1987 whether they would "feel afraid to be in an all-black neighborhood during the day,"

66 percent of white respondents said no. When it came to the night, however, 64 percent said that they would be afraid, with another 9 percent unsure.[8]

Whites are afraid—but so are blacks. In a 1991 University of California poll, more blacks than whites (59 percent versus 52 percent) agreed that blacks were "aggressive or violent."[9] A survey of Los Angeles residents in November 1992 posed a related question: "When it comes to the threat of crime, how safe do you feel in your community?" Forty-nine percent of blacks said they felt "unsafe."[10] A 1996 national survey found that 52 percent of African Americans and 31 percent of whites were afraid to walk alone at night in their neighborhoods.[11]

Such fear has political implications. An April 1992 Gallup/*Newsweek* poll found that 91 percent of blacks felt that crime was one of the "more urgent" problems facing their communities. In fact, it topped the "more urgent" list.[12] In May respondents were asked "which issues you think are important for the presidential candidates to discuss and debate?" Ninety-two percent of blacks listed crime as "very important," while only 76 percent of white voters did so.[13] Two years earlier Gallup had explored the "perceived safety of major U.S. cities." In general, whites felt safer than blacks. For example, 72 percent of blacks but 64 percent of whites reported thinking that Chicago was dangerous.[14]

A great many black residents of our central cities would thus seem to lack that basic sense of physical safety upon which a minimally decent life depends.[15] Their constant companion is fear. "I'm just afraid all the time," a black Los Angeles beautician confessed nine months after the L.A. riots.[16] Such fear inevitably shapes the way she lives. As the black police chief in Washington, D.C., put it in 1992, "Fear . . . changes everything." Even the way you look at people. You avert your eyes. "You say, 'I don't want to make eye contact with this sucker because he may break bad on me.' "[17]

Blacks and whites living in fear in poor central-city areas become prisoners in their own homes. Elderly Jewish immigrants in Brooklyn report feeling "locked up like in the ghettos of Europe . . . still . . . not free."[18] Residents of Atlanta's heavily black public housing projects say they are forced to stay in at night to protect themselves.[19] The voices of those who can't trust the streets after dark are regularly heard in the media. "I go home at night and lock the door and don't come out," a resident of a senior-citizens' housing project in a rough New York neighborhood reported in 1992.[20] In San Francisco that same year, a social service provider described nights in the ghetto as "almost like a curfew, dusk to dawn, de facto. The only people who are out are pretty much the cops and robbers."[21]

The daylight hours are safer—but not safe. In Chicago's famed Henry Horner Homes "the one constant," as Alex Kotlowitz has described it, is violence. In the management office of the public housing complex, the sounds of gunfire can be heard throughout the day. The Rivers children, whose life

Kotlowitz chronicled in *There Are No Children Here*, were often forced to crouch against the walls of their apartment to avoid stray bullets.[22] "You'll be in your house and people will be shooting through your damn window," a New York mother said in 1991. "You stick your head out your window, some-body blows your brains out."[23] A Newark mom described much the same scene. "There is always something happening here, always violence, always someone shooting at somebody.[24]

The old-timers in what are now predominantly black neighborhoods plagued by crime say it wasn't always so. They remember front porches used for socializing, windows that were open, and day care centers with swing sets outdoors. Today, razor ribbon adorns roofs, restaurant counters are protected by bulletproof glass, and children play in vandalized yards. "When I came to this country in 1934, you could sleep on the fire escape or in the park and nobody took anything from you. Now you sleep in your own home and any-thing can happen," a retired Puerto Rican landlord in New York told a re-porter.[25] Others make the same point. "At one time, I would sit out on my porch," an elderly resident of heavily black southeast Washington, D.C., re-called nostalgically. Not now. "My home has been broken into. They kicked in my kitchen window. I'm afraid to leave my door open to get air in the middle of the day." In short, "you feel like prisoners in your own house."[26]

TRENDS IN CRIME RATES

Crime is hardly a recent invention. Our opening chapter noted that violence was a major problem within southern black communities in the 1930s, in part because of lax law enforcement. White authorities treated black crimes against whites with the utmost severity, but were not very interested in dealing with black-on-black crime as long as it did not inconvenience white folks. High levels of personal violence could be observed in the small northern African-American communities then and earlier. In Philadelphia in the 1890s the black murder rate was five and a half times the white rate. While immigrant groups like the Irish also had a record of violence, their levels of crime dropped with assimilation. Full assimilation, however, was not an option given blacks in the late nineteenth century.[27]

The level of crime has historically been higher for blacks than whites, but in fact national rates of violent crimes by both blacks and whites have risen and fallen rather mysteriously. The best evidence is for homicides, a crime that has been reported more consistently than others. From the turn of the century to the early 1930s the homicide rate in the United States rose sharply, from 1.2 per 100,000 in 1900 to 8.4 in 1929. And yet in the midst of the Depression, when 37 percent of the nonfarm workforce was unemployed, people began to put away their knives and guns. For the next thirty years the homicide rate slid, dropping by a quarter during the Depression decade to 6.3 per 100,000. The return of prosperity in the 1940s and 1950s did not alter the trend. The murder rate fell off by another quarter, to 4.7 by 1960.[28]

Then in the 1960s not only the homicide rate but the rate for all other violent crimes—rape, robbery, and assault are the chief ones—began to soar. The overall level of violent crime doubled during the 1960s and jumped another 60 percent over the 1970s (Table 1). The trend was reversed for a few years in the early 1980s, but from 1985 to 1993 it resumed its strong upward trend, rising by a third in just eight years. From 1993 to 1995 the rate of violent crime dipped substantially—by 8 percent. But it is too soon to say whether this was just another temporary blip on the screen or the start of a trend that would be sustained. As of the last report, in 1995, the violent-crime rate was more than four times as high as it had been only three decades before.

It is possible that the change was less dramatic than these numbers make it appear, at least in the past two decades. The evidence in Table 1 comes from the FBI's annual *Uniform Crime Reports,* a compilation of information voluntarily supplied by city, county, and state law enforcement agencies. Some of the huge increase in crime that it shows may reflect changes in the accuracy of the reporting by the many thousands of cooperating agencies. Information collected not from police but from random samples of ordinary people—the annual "victimization surveys," to which we will return—suggest a less alarming picture. Nevertheless, there is no doubt that the level of crime in

Table 1
Rates of Violent Crime per 100,000 Population, 1960–1995

	VIOLENT CRIME TOTAL	MURDER	FORCIBLE RAPE	ROBBERY	AGGRAVATED ASSAULT
1960	161	5.1	9.6	60	86
1965	200	5.1	12.1	72	111
1970	364	7.9	18.7	172	165
1976	468	8.8	26.6	199	233
1980	597	10.2	36.8	251	299
1985	557	7.9	37.1	209	303
1990	732	9.4	41.2	257	424
1993	747	9.5	41.1	256	440
1995	685	8.2	37.1	221	418

Sources: Figures for 1960–1970 from U.S. Bureau of the Census, *Statistical Abstract of the United States: 1976* (Washington, D.C.: U.S. Government Printing Office, 1976), 153; 1976–1995 figures from U.S. Department of Justice, Federal Bureau of Investigation, *Crime in the United States—1995: Uniform Crime Reports* (Washington, D.C.: U.S. Government Printing Office, 1996), 58.

the United States has been far higher since the 1960s than it was before then.[29] Crime on a scale unknown to previous generations is a continuing legacy of the 1960s.

The explosion of crime in the closing decades of the twentieth century was not confined to the United States. Most of the industrialized nations in the world seem to have followed our lead in this respect, for reasons which are not well understood. Despite the common impression that American society is far more crime-ridden than European countries, by 1984, France, Britain, and Sweden all had higher rates of auto theft; burglary rates in the Netherlands were double those in the United States and were substantially higher in Britain and Germany as well. The level of serious violent crime was as high in Australia as in the United States at the end of the 1980s, and it was not much below that in Canada.[30] The United States stood out, though, both in having a much higher homicide rate than any other advanced country—a difference that is centuries old—and in having exceptionally high levels of youth violence, especially on the part of an alienated nonwhite, underclass population concentrated in big cities.

The crime wave of the past three decades has worried and angered many whites, but it has done the greatest damage in the African-American community. Black men today, for example, are murdered at twice the rate they were in 1960, and at more than seven times the rate white men are. The murder rate for black women is much lower than it is for males, but it has risen by a quarter since 1960, and is nearly five times as high as the rate for white females. Half of all the murder victims in the United States in 1995 were African Americans, though they comprised just one-eighth of the population.[31]

Blacks also experience more than their share of other forms of violent crime. In 1995 they were the victims of violent crimes other than murder at a rate one-third higher than that for whites.[32] What is more, the rate of African-American victimization for such violent crimes has risen much more over the past two decades than it has for whites.[33] "There is nothing more painful to me at this stage in my life than to walk down the street and hear footsteps and start thinking about robbery—then look around and see somebody white and feel relieved," Jesse Jackson said in late 1993.[34] As Jackson himself had implicitly acknowledged, the vast majority of the offenses committed against black people are the acts of criminals who are themselves black.

Table 2 shows the racial composition of those arrested for various crimes in 1995. Not only were about half of all the murder victims in the United States black; more than half (56 percent) of all those who were arrested for murder were also black. The two figures are closely related, because more than nine out of ten (93 percent) of the blacks who were murdered were killed by a fellow African American, and 85 percent of the murders committed by blacks were of black people.[35]

Blacks also comprised 60 percent of those apprehended for robbery, 42

Table 2

Proportion of Black Persons Arrested and Arrest Index
for Selected Crimes, 1995

	BLACK	ARREST INDEX
Murder and nonnegligent manslaughter	54.4	4.3
Forcible rape	42.4	3.4
Robbery	59.5	4.7
Aggravated assault	38.4	3.0
Burglary	31.0	2.5
Motor vehicle theft	38.3	3.0
Fraud	34.7	2.8
Receiving stolen property	39.4	3.1
Weapons violations	38.8	3.1
Drug violations	36.9	2.9

Source: Crime in the United States—1995, 226. Arrest index equals the proportion of black arrests divided by the black proportion of the U.S. population in 1995, 12.6 percent.

percent of those arrested for rape, and almost 40 percent of those arrested for aggravated assault. As the arrest index given in Table 2 shows, African Americans were not arrested in proportions less than their 12.6 percent share of the total population in 1995 for any of the crimes listed; in no case, that is, was their arrest index less than 1.0. They consistently had more than double —in most cases more than triple—their share of the arrests. Although African Americans were particularly conspicuous among those arrested for violent crimes like murder, rape, robbery, and assault, they also were far more likely than whites to be arrested for property crimes such as fraud and handling stolen property. Contrary to what many allege, these figures do not show that blacks are particularly singled out for violations of the drug laws. They were more heavily represented among those arrested for most other crimes.

Perhaps this huge disproportion in arrest rates only means that the police sometimes round up blacks without sufficient cause. In that case, though, one might expect—certainly one would hope—that the disproportion would vanish or at least shrink drastically when their cases actually came to trial, unless juries and judges are equally racist. That is, the falsely arrested would not be convicted at the same rate as other defendants charged on the basis of more substantial evidence. In fact, not only are African Americans represented far out of proportion to their numbers in the ranks of those arrested for crimes; they are equally overrepresented among those convicted, and among those who end up behind bars. In 1993, 44.2 percent of all the prisoners confined to U.S. jails and 48.2 percent of all those serving terms in state or federal penitentiaries were black.[36]

THE LEADING KILLER OF YOUNG BLACK MALES

Some of the most disturbing changes in black crime involve the young—often the very young. An appalling number of young black boys are growing up criminal fast. "The leading killer of young black males is young black males," Dr. Louis W. Sullivan, the secretary of health and human services under President Bush, said in 1991. A government study had just found that nearly half of black male Americans from fifteen to nineteen years old who died in 1988 were killed by guns.[37] The rate at which black boys aged fourteen to seventeen become homicide victims has tripled since 1976, and is now eight times what it is for their white peers (Table 3). For black men in their late teens and early twenties, the homicide victimization rate is up 75 percent, and has gone from being 8.5 times the white rate to 10.5 times the white rate.

That's the picture for the victims of homicide. If we look at who is killing these children, the racial disproportion is even more pronounced. For boys fourteen to seventeen, the black/white ratio for homicide offenders has risen from 6.49 to well over 10; for men eighteen to twenty-four, the jump has been from 8.14 to over 10 again. Among both victims and offenders in both age

Table 3
**Murder Rate per 100,000 for Young Black and White Males,
1976–1993**

	VICTIMS					
	AGES 14–17			AGES 18–24		
	Black	White	B/W ratio	Black	White	B/W ratio
1976	24.8	3.9	6.36	104.7	12.4	8.44
1980	28.0	5.2	5.38	116.7	17.6	6.63
1986	27.1	4.1	6.61	109.0	14.5	7.52
1993	77.3	9.2	7.93	184.1	17.4	10.58
	OFFENDERS					
1976	50.0	7.7	6.49	136.8	16.8	8.14
1980	49.0	9.0	5.44	146.1	20.8	7.02
1986	50.6	9.1	5.56	116.6	18.5	6.30
1993	147.3	14.0	10.52	210.2	20.7	10.15

Source: U.S. Department of Justice, Bureau of Justice Statistics, *Sourcebook of Criminal Justice Statistics: 1994* (Washington, D.C.: U.S. Government Printing Office, 1995), 340.

groups, almost all of this dramatic change for the worse happened in the late 1980s and early 1990s, when the crack cocaine epidemic hit the cities. In the turf wars that selling crack provoked, a gun was an indispensable tool of the trade. Between 1984 and 1990, the firearm death rate for white males aged fifteen to nineteen rose by about 50 percent; for black males it tripled.[38] The number of arrests of white juveniles for gun violations rose by 90 percent between 1985 and 1995; for black juveniles the figure was up 160 percent.[39] One more stunning statistic sums up the sad story; black males aged fourteen to twenty-four make up 1 percent of the population but 17 percent of all the homicide victims and 30 percent of all the homicide offenders. Only a decade ago they were 9 percent of the victims and 17 percent of the perpetrators.[40]

Murder to gain and maintain control over the lucrative sale of drugs has at least a modicum of criminal rationality about it. But much youth violence today seems senseless; kids murder kids over a pair of earrings, a radio, a pair of sneakers.[41] Thus, in 1992 a fifteen-year-old was shot to death after exchanging a few words with another boy in a crowded New York subway train.[42] Three days later, in that same city, a sixteen-year-old girl got into an argument with a boy she hardly knew; annoyed by the way she looked at him, he pulled out a gun, threatened to kill her, and then did so when she sounded more skeptical than afraid.[43] "Two guys were going with one girl, so after one found out then he just pulled out his gun and shot him," another high school student told several *New York Times* reporters that same month.[44] The reporters had gathered together a group of students from Thomas Jefferson High School in East New York; almost all spoke of the casual violence that had become routine. "I had a boyfriend that recently died," one girl said. He had refused to fight and "so they just decided just to come up and kill him." "People got shot over basketball. . . . Got shot dead. Two times in the head," another boy reported. "Now, it's like I could look at you wrong," said another.[45] In May 1994 a fifteen-year old black boy in New York shot someone to death in a holdup because his Nikes "was messed up" after three months of wear, and he needed the money for a new pair. "I'd walk down the block and the people who know me would start laughing," he said.[46]

Violence has become more casual, and perpetrators seem less remorseful. On Halloween night, 1990, several members of a street gang in Boston set out to look for a party but ended up beating, raping, and stabbing a woman 132 times. The motive, a fifteen-year-old assailant told the police, was boredom. "There was nothing to do and so I guess we had the impression of going out . . . [to] kill somebody," he said.[47] In Washington, D.C., in November 1991 a nineteen-year-old rolled down his car window and shot a woman dead as she and her husband were driving home. Why? "I feel like bustin' somebody," he had announced beforehand.[48]

Kids often sound like hardened criminals, oblivious to the value of life, indifferent to notions of right and wrong.[49] Interviewed in 1991 by a *New*

York Times reporter, Bronx teenager Mike R. admitted that, yes, he had shot a lot of people and fatally hit some of them. But although the slayings had been at close range, the victims had not left much of an impression. "They were just people," he said. "Just people."[50] The next year, in Cambridge, Massachusetts, a high school student charged with murder bragged that the knife "had gone clear through [the victim's] body." His classmates wondered "what the big deal was. People die every day."[51]

The violence is partly for thrills—as it undoubtedly has always been. But the forthright admission of kicks does seem new. The more than 120 muggings he had pulled off by the time he was fourteen were "fun," a young man told a reporter. It was "getting away with something . . . a high. . . ." Did he understand it was wrong? "Not really," he said. He "didn't think much about it."[52]

Growing up in Harlem in the 1940s and 1950s, writer Claude Brown also got a certain thrill from being bad. "It was a whole lotta fun," he subsequently wrote.[53] But "it" meant little more than playing hookey, cursing, hitching bus rides, sneaking into movies, stealing from stores, and throwing bottles from rooftops. By age sixteen, it is true, he was dealing in pot, but he was ahead of the curve, on the cutting edge of street culture. Lots of guys—many of whom came from "righteous doing" households—weren't "going the crime way."[54]

In part, most youth were more law-abiding because the "righteous doing" households kept a keen eye on the deviants. Claude Brown has described that watch. So has Johnnetta B. Cole, who became the president of Spelman College. "On that block [where I lived]," she has recalled, "I couldn't cut up because older folk would get after me."[55] Today, Cole noted in 1993, "these older folks are behind closed doors scared to death an angry youth will come and beat on them."[56]

Claude Brown in Harlem did plenty of fighting—but he used his fists. Only the real "bad niggers" had guns, and although he had a "rep" for being truly "bad," in the end he chose (and could choose) to do without anything more than a symbolic knife—one that he knew he would never use.[57] In the 1990s, in neighborhoods like the one in which he lived, deadly weapons have become commonplace. "Just beating someone doesn't get it any more," a sixteen-year-old reported.[58] Unarmed, kids feel unprotected.

A serious weapon is not necessarily a gun. Knives are commonplace: box-cutters, razors, screwdrivers, and the like. Of the 399 weapons confiscated in the Boston schools in 1992–1993, for instance, almost all (380) were knives or razors.[59] Unlike guns, in Massachusetts these weapons were not illegal; they could be carried without fear of arrest. And they could be easily hidden in clothes or a fancy hairdo. Moreover, if left to rust in water, soaked in bleach, taped together, or in other ways modified, such weapons ensure the permanent disfigurement of anyone against whom they are used.[60]

Blacks are more frequently armed, as the arrest rates reported above suggest. In a national survey of weapon-carrying among high school students in 1993, the Centers for Disease Control and Prevention found that 21 percent of black male high school students had carried a gun at least once during the thirty preceding days—though not necessarily into a school building. The figure for whites was little more than half that—12 percent. Furthermore, in 1994 four out of ten black students—male and female together—reported that they had either been injured with a weapon or threatened with a weapon in the past twelve months, exactly double the proportion among whites.[61]

Weapons carried for a purpose acquire symbolic importance. "Guns are becoming like a badge of honor with young people," the New York police commissioner noted in 1991.[62] Teenage youth often choose weapons on the basis of style. For a time, the 9-millimeter semiautomatic pistol, often featured in violent TV shows, was the fashion rage.[63] Youths jam such pistols into the waistband of their jeans, and know they "got the power."[64] In fact, some feel naked without their guns. "I put on my shoes, my pants, my shirt, my hat and my gun," one young man explained.[65]

Given these dismal facts, it is no wonder that a 1994 New York Times/CBS poll found that 54 percent of black teenagers worried "a lot or some of the time" about being the victim of a crime, versus 36 percent of white teenagers. No less than 27 percent of young African Americans worried about being shot, more than five times the proportion among whites. A remarkable 70 percent said that they knew someone who had been shot in the past five years, more than double the white figure.[66]

CHARGES OF RACIAL BIAS IN THE CRIMINAL JUSTICE SYSTEM

Disproportionately large numbers of African Americans are accused of crimes, convicted of crimes, and punished for crimes, many of which are perpetrated against other blacks. Perhaps, however, the problem is a system of criminal justice tainted with racial bias. That assertion is certainly frequently made. In 1994, Harvard law professor Charles Ogletree asserted that "ninety-nine percent of black people don't commit crimes."[67] Obviously this was not meant to be taken as a literal claim that a mere 1 percent of blacks commit criminal acts. But Ogletree was certainly implying that many, perhaps most, of the one-third of all black males aged twenty to twenty-nine who are currently under control of the criminal justice system are innocents caught in the snares of a racist system.[68]

The O. J. Simpson verdict in October 1995 made black distrust of white justice national news, and the trial itself created a potent new symbol of the racist police officer allegedly out to frame an innocent black. It's a perspective that has long had advocates both within the black and white liberal communities. Blacks accused of crimes are victims of a white society that wears (in effect) a white sheet; the black crime rate has been grossly exaggerated; the number of blacks incarcerated is a reflection of persistent white racism; the courts cannot be trusted; nor can the police.

This was the view that Willie Brown—then the Speaker of the California Assembly, before becoming mayor of San Francisco—expressed in 1992 after police officers charged with beating a black man were acquitted in what became known as the "Rodney King" trial—named for the victim rather than the accused. The Simi Valley jury's not-guilty decision, he said, was "a confirmation of years and years and years of racism within the criminal justice system." Violence against white victims gets prosecuted; black victims are a different matter.[69] Black lives are expendable.

This is also the voice that the media tend to record. "If the homicide rate were the same among white males in suburbia you better believe there would be something done," a doctor told a *New York Times* reporter in 1990.[70] In other words, racist indifference explains the high number of violent black deaths. On the other hand, racism is also said to explain the high number of black arrests. Whites have been simultaneously closing their eyes to black homicides and too zealously rounding up black suspects. "If you're white and you hit someone, you can get off. If you're black and you hit someone, you pay," a black city councilwoman from Compton, California, thus argued. "If our clients were white, this wouldn't be happening," the attorney for the L.A. Four, accused of beating truck driver Reginald Denny during the 1992 Los Angeles riots, stated.[71]

Such charges are a medley of overlapping points, the most important of which is double standards, on the beat and in the courtroom. "It doesn't matter if the cop is white or black. It's a racist system," a member of the audience at a 1992 community meeting in Boston said.[72] The point was echoed that same year by a Detroit city councilman. The problem, he said, is not black versus white, but police "blue versus everybody else."[73] At its 1991 annual convention the NAACP announced it would conduct a series of national hearings on the subject of police conduct; the result was a report that spoke of "race, police, and violence" as "inseparable in this country."[74]

"Racism," the report found, "informs every aspect of policing. . . ." Indeed, the point of the police is "to protect [whites] from violent black men." Whites view blacks "as the enemy . . . not quite . . . like other people."[75] From the NAACP—and other civil rights groups—this had become pretty standard fare. The black leadership regularly charges the cops with racially selective brutality.[76] The 1991 police beating of motorist Rodney King in Los Angeles thus confirmed a story they believed they knew. The Los Angeles Police Department, one local black organizer said, is "here to prosecute and abuse."[77]

Racism shapes sentencing decisions as well, civil rights advocates often assert. For instance, the Sentencing Project, a liberal advocacy group, aims to reduce the level of incarceration in general, but its literature contains a strong message condemning racial bias in the criminal justice system. Blacks, it contends, end up with stiffer sentences than do whites.[78] Charges of racial bias in sentencing have been a media staple. "We always end up in jail; we do a little something and we go to jail for a long time." Whites "just railroad the black people for some crazy reason, like we are animals or something," a young black man told a Los Angeles reporter in May 1992.[79] A white guy is sentenced for "obstructing justice, doing insurance fraud—oh God, let that be a black man and you'd see what he'd get," the *Boston Globe* reported a resident saying that same year.[80]

The racial bias argument actually takes two quite different forms, although often packaged as one. Prosecutors, juries, and judges treating blacks and whites differently is the first. The second implies that disparate treatment is actually just. Blacks should be given a break. "The social and economic decline of our inner cities and diminished opportunities for young people; [and] the continuing failure of our schools, health care systems, and other institutional supports," the Sentencing Project has suggested, are mitigating circumstances.[81] A 1990 report by two private nonprofit organizations in New York made that argument explicitly. "It is no accident," it said, "that our correctional facilities are filled with African-American and Latino youths out of all proportion to their numbers in the general population. Prisons are now the last stop along a continuum of injustice for these youths . . . no prenatal care, poor health care, substandard housing, dirty streets, failing schools, drugs, joblessness, discriminatory deployment of police, and prison."[82] A 1992 *New York Times* editorial also expressed that view. "Quickly, glibly," young black men are "classified as criminals. And yet . . . many . . . have sunk into the criminal justice system . . . [because] the safety nets have disappeared."[83]

Take that argument one small step further and it becomes a full-blown conspiracy theory in which black crime is not simply the consequence of white racism but part of a racist plot. "They're getting rid of us, man . . . making us kill each other," one of the black men whom sociologist Bob Blauner interviewed for his book *Black Lives, White Lives* said.[84] In *Boyz N the Hood,* a much-praised movie about life in South Central Los Angeles, a central figure says much the same thing. "How do you think crack comes here?" he asks his neighbors. "We don't own any ships. We don't own no planes! . . . Why is it that there's a gun shop on every corner. . . . I'll tell you why: because they want us to kill each other off. What they couldn't do in slavery, they are making us do ourselves."[85]

As the film's creator, John Singleton knew, it's a view that has found expression not only in neighborhoods with much crime and few explanations, but on black talk radio and among the middle class as well. "Our sons are at risk—to suicide, murder, jail and hopelessness. Really it's genocide. . . ." a Detroit community organizer told journalist Ze'ev Chafets in the late 1980s.[86] Students with whom the mayor of New York and members of his administration met in the wake of the Rodney King verdict reserved their most sustained applause for the young man who asked: "Is there a conspiracy to allow and condone the destruction of black people?"[87] In 1992 California state senator Diane Watson, whose district includes much of the area hit by the Los Angeles riots, argued that Police Chief Daryl F. Gates may have purposely delayed taking action to control the violence in order to let blacks "show their violent nature."[88] These aren't sentiments expressed by blacks alone. In his best-selling book *Two Nations,* political scientist Andrew Hacker has written: "Despite constitutional safeguards, police and prosecutors and judges still find it relatively easy to ensure that one out of every five black men will spend some part of his life behind bars."[89] Whites, in other words, are deliberately locking black men up; it's a plot easily carried off.

ASSESSING THE EVIDENCE OF BIAS

That these charges have been repeated so often and so vehemently does not make them true. The issue is complicated. Statistical disparities between groups in matters like arrests or incarcerations are not conclusive evidence of discrimination. Take, for example, the fact that a mere 5.8 percent of the inmates in state and federal prisons in 1993 were female, even though women comprised 51.2 percent of the population.[90] It is also the case that just 5.7 percent of the convicted felons who began serving a prison sentence in 1992 were aged forty-five or more, even though that age group made up one-third (32.4 percent) of the population.[91] Obviously, the criminal justice system is not biased against men or the relatively young. Women commit many fewer crimes than men, and people over forty-five commit many fewer crimes than people under forty-five. On the other hand, we cannot assume that the same holds for the racial disparities we have observed. The history of racism in the United States lends special plausibility to the charge of racial bias.

Nevertheless, a great deal of evidence about who commits crimes comes not from law enforcement officials (alleged to be biased), but from ordinary, anonymous victims of crime, via an annual national household survey conducted by the Bureau of the Census since 1973. The most recently published results of the National Crime Victimization Survey are for 1993, and they support the assertion that the crime rate for blacks is indeed disproportionately high. African Americans who said that they had been victims of violence within the past year identified four out of five (79.7 percent) of the perpetrators as black. In the case of robberies it was 87 percent; of aggravated assaults, 88 percent. The survey reported a total of 1.3 million victimizations of black people by lawbreakers who were themselves black.[92]

These figures ignore the crimes black criminals committed against whites. It is often said that crime is segregated—that most violence is within rather than between racial groups. It is only a partial truth. Most victims of violent crime do report having been attacked by someone of their same race; in 1993, 68 percent of victimized whites and 81 percent of their black counterparts named someone of their own race as the perpetrator. But it is also true that a majority—54 percent—of all the victims of blacks who committed violent crimes were white. White criminal violence directed at blacks is fairly rare, but black-on-white crime is not. The 1993 victim survey reported 1.7 million interracial crimes, crimes involving either a white victim and a black offender or vice versa; 89 percent of these cases of interracial crime involved black perpetrators and white victims.[93] With the differences in the size of the white and black populations taken into account, blacks were fifty times more likely to commit violent crimes against whites than whites are against blacks.[94] There is no reason to assume that black criminals are going out of their way to prey on whites in particular. If African Americans are seven times as likely to commit violent crimes as whites, and there are seven times as many whites as blacks available as victims, one would expect a disproportion of this order of magnitude.

Victim surveys can also be utilized to verify the accuracy of the arrest data. If blacks are arrested in disproportionately large numbers because the police are out to get them, the victimization surveys should make that clear. Those surveys would show blacks to be a much smaller proportion of the offender population than the police records at the time of arrest indicate. The two sets of data are not fully comparable in a number of respects, but a careful analysis does not suggest substantially different results. The most recent review of the literature, by Michael Tonry, an author with unimpeachable liberal credentials, concludes that "black incarceration rates are substantially higher than those for whites . . . [because] black crime rates for imprisonable crimes are substantially higher than those for whites."[95]

An altogether different route leads to the same conclusion. One can look at what has happened to crime in the many cities in which African Americans have become politically dominant since the 1960s. To varying degrees, for varying lengths of time, African Americans have controlled and do control local politics in Atlanta, Baltimore, Birmingham, Detroit, Memphis, Newark, New Orleans, Washington, D.C., and a good many smaller cities. Black mayors and black majorities on city councils set law enforcement policies, and black police commissioners and police chiefs are responsible for executing them. In overwhelmingly black Washington, D.C., the police force is slightly more heavily black than the total population.[96]

These cities provide us with a laboratory in which to observe the relationship between black crime and control of the criminal justice system. The extent of black political power in a community should make a big difference in the black crime rate if the huge racial disproportions to be found in the statistics for arrests, convictions, and sentencing are mainly—or even substantially—due to bias in the criminal justice system. So far, at least, no one has produced any evidence suggesting that the arrest rates of African Americans in black-controlled Detroit or Atlanta are any different from what they are in San Diego or San Antonio, where blacks make up less than a tenth of the population and have little influence on public policy.

Further evidence pointing to the same conclusion is available in a major survey completed by the Justice Department's Bureau of Justice Statistics in 1993.[97] This study tracked the experience of over 10,000 adult felony defendants arrested in 1990 in the nation's seventy-five largest counties (which included 59 percent of the black population of the United States). It found that after charges were filed, 66 percent of the accused blacks were actually prosecuted, versus 69 percent of those who were white. No greater zeal to punish African Americans was evident at this stage. Among those who were prosecuted, 75 percent of blacks and 78 percent of the whites were convicted. Again the only hint of racial disparity was to the advantage, not the disadvantage, of blacks accused of crimes.

A 1996 analysis of 55,512 felony cases filed in state courts for the seventy-five largest counties in the nation in 1992 provides a more detailed picture of how race affects rates of conviction for particular offenses (Table 4). In the fourteen major categories of crime, accused blacks were more likely than

Table 4

Percent of Prosecutions That End in Dismissals of Charges or Acquittals, by Type of Crime and Race, 1992

	BLACK	WHITE
Murder	24	23
Rape	51	25
Robbery	38	35
Assault	49	43
Burglary	25	21
Felony theft	27	25
Drug dealing	24	14
Other drug offenses	32	23
Other crimes against persons	48	28
Other property offenses	27	26
Public order offenses	32	31
Weapons charges	32	22
Felony traffic offense	4	10
Other felonies	14	22

Source: Robert Lerner, "Acquittal Rates by Race for State Felonies," in Gerald A. Reynolds, ed., *Race and the Criminal Justice System* (Washington, D.C.: Center for Equal Opportunity, 1996), 92.

whites to be acquitted or to have the charges dismissed. Only in the categories of felony traffic offenses and "other felonies," which together totaled 1.1 percent of all cases, were African Americans more likely to be convicted than their white counterparts.

The 1993 Department of Justice study found a racial disparity in the other direction at the sentencing stage: 51 percent of blacks who were convicted but 38 percent of whites were sent off to prison.[98] However, it turned out that the seeming racial difference was entirely attributable to legitimate, nonracial considerations. Convicted blacks had committed more serious crimes, had worse prior records of crime, and happened to live in counties that tended to be tougher on criminals in general, whatever their race.

Professor Randall Kennedy of the Harvard Law School reads the evidence as we do, and sums it up well with the observation that "the most lethal danger facing African-Americans in their daily lives is not white, racist officials of the state, but private, violent criminals, typically black, who attack those most vulnerable to them without regard for racial identity."[99]

IS THE DEATH PENALTY RACIST?

The issue of the death penalty arouses particularly strong emotions, and allegations that it is meted out in a racially disproportionate manner figure large in complaints about bias in the criminal justice system. The death penalty, critics say, "is a first cousin to lynching."[100] It *was* in the South in Jim Crow days, as our first chapter noted, but it is questionable that this is still the case. One can doubt the wisdom of capital punishment on a number of grounds, but the evidence does not seem to support the charge that it is administered in a racially biased manner.

Blacks are 12.5 percent of the population but a much higher proportion of the prisoners on Death Row—40.4 percent at the most recent count.[101] In other words, 3.2 times as many African Americans are on Death Row as in the population as a whole. But, as we have seen, statistical disparities may be suggestive but are not definitive. They are the start of an inquiry, not the end. People who receive death sentences, after all, are not representative of the population in many respects. Only 1.3 percent of them are female, for example; middle-aged people and senior citizens are also grossly underrepresented among those the courts order executed. Blacks are substantially overrepresented on Death Row, but distinctly underrepresented by another, more meaningful standard: 58 percent of those currently serving sentences for murder are African Americans. That 40 percent of the seats on Death Row are occupied by blacks is thus not a surprisingly high but a surprisingly low figure—about a third lower than it would be if all convicted murderers were equally likely to get a death sentence.[102]

Assuming that the relevant population is that of convicted murderers, black offenders over the past generation have not been sentenced to death at a higher rate than white offenders. No careful scholarly study in recent years has demonstrated that the race of the defendant has played a significant role in the outcome of murder trials. There is still some argument about the issue, though, because it is difficult to control all the nonracial variables that could quite properly influence who is sentenced to die and who is not.

A closer look at the most careful statistical study of the problem, concerning almost 2,500 murder cases in Georgia between 1973 and 1979, will help to clarify this hotly contested issue. The study was commissioned by the NAACP's Legal Defense Fund, and its sponsorship by an advocacy group looking for evidence of racial bias could have slanted the results in subtle ways. Some experts have found fault with the authors' use of evidence.[103] Nonetheless, the results of the study are illuminating, as Table 5 suggests.

The first finding to emerge from this project has almost never been mentioned in subsequent discussions of the research. White defendants who were convicted of murder, it turned out, were 80 percent more likely to be sentenced to die than black defendants (7.4 percent versus 4.1 percent). Opponents of the death penalty who call it "a first cousin to lynching" should find this hard to explain. A Deep South state that was once near the top of the list in the number of African Americans it lynched was by the 1970s apparently a lot tougher on white killers than on black killers.

Table 5

The Death Penalty by Race of Victim and Offender, Georgia, 1973–1979: Percent of Murder Cases in Which Convicted Defendant Was Sentenced to Death

By race of defendant	
White	7.4
Black	4.1
By race of victim	
White	11.0
Black	1.3
By race of both	
Black defendant/white victim	21.4
White defendant/white victim	7.8
Black defendant/black victim	1.2
White defendant/black victim	3.3

Source: David Baldus, George Woodworty, and Charles A. Pulaski, Jr., *Equal Justice and the Death Penalty: A Legal and Empirical Analysis* (Boston: Northeastern University Press, 1990), 150.

This finding and others, elsewhere, have forced sophisticated opponents of the death penalty to shift the grounds of their attack. The old argument that the death penalty is biased against black defendants has been dropped, although that claim is sometimes still heard in popular discussions of the issue. Opponents generally charge, instead, that the bias in the system is a matter not of the race of the defendant but of the victim. The Georgia findings seem to support this complaint, showing that 11 percent of the killers of white people but only 1.3 percent of the killers of black people were sentenced to death.[104] The death penalty "symbolizes whom we fear and don't fear, whom we care about and whose lives are not valid," the evidence is said to suggest.[105] We care about the death of whites, but not that of blacks.[106]

In fact, the disparity that is so troubling to these critics—the racial disparity between those victims whose killers do or do not get the death penalty—is problematic only if we assume that all murder is the same thing, that it admits of no gradations. But death sentences, we must recall, are not handed down in the typical murder case. Only 128 of them were awarded in the 2,484 cases included in the Georgia study—just 5 percent. The penalty is reserved for particularly heinous crimes—for the roughly 5 percent of killings that society judges to be exceptionally reprehensible.[107] Shooting a policeman is one way to get on Death Row; killing a bank guard or store-owner in the course of an armed robbery is another; raping and murdering a child is a third. If there are racial disproportionalities among the victims of these special crimes, what looks like bias in sentencing may not be that at all. It happens to be the case, for example, that 85 percent of the police officers who are killed in the United States are white.[108] If a substantial fraction of the small numbers of death sentences that are imposed are for the killing of police officers, that will raise the number of white victims whose killing provokes the death penalty, even though it is not their race but their occupation that determines the decision.

The contention that those who murder blacks—almost all of them other blacks—are less often sentenced to death because society values black life less highly ignores the context in which interracial and intraracial killings characteristically take place. Why do more white perpetrators than black ones receive the death penalty? Why do more killers of whites than killers of blacks receive the death penalty? Why do blacks who murder whites get death far more frequently than those who murder blacks? The answer to all three questions is the same: the types of murders are of a different character. For example, 67 percent of all the black-on-white murders involved armed robberies, but just 7 percent of the black-on-black murders did. Almost three-quarters (73 percent) of the black-on-black killings occurred during a dispute or fight, for example, in the kitchen, the local bar, or the neighborhood.[109] They were hot-blooded killings, not murders of the more cold-blooded and brutal sort that society penalizes most severely. White defendants whose victims were white got the death penalty at a lower rate than black defendants who killed whites (7.8 versus 21.4) because more of the white-on-white kill-ings were hot-blooded offenses in which the parties knew each other. The nature of the crime, not the race of either the defendant or the victim, was the main source of the difference in outcomes.

Whether this is the full explanation for the harsher treatment the killers of white people received in Georgia in the years 1973 to 1979 is open to debate. Those who conducted the study don't think so; they maintain that there was racial bias—not bias against black defendants but bias in the less harsh treat-ment given to killers of African Americans. But only 128 of their cases in-volved a death sentence. When these are broken down by race and by the character of the crime, the numbers are so small that the patterns may be the result of chance variations. It is certainly not implausible that white prosecu-tors, judges, and jurors in Georgia found it easier to identify with white victims than with African Americans, and viewed crimes with African-American vic-tims differently from crimes whose victims were their fellow whites. The capacity to feel empathy across racial lines is in short supply today, it seems to us, and it would not be surprising if there had been even less of it among Georgia whites in the 1970s.[110]

It is nonetheless very striking that whatever bias prejudice may have intro-duced, it did not result in the imposition of a disproportionate number of death penalty sentences upon African Americans convicted of murder. Quite the opposite. That was always the chief complaint against the death penalty on racial grounds, and it by now is at least a quarter century out of date. It could be that other findings of the Georgia study are also out of date. The final year for which data were collected—1979—is almost two decades in the past. Whatever tendency there may have been for Georgia authorities to treat the (usually black) killers of blacks differently from those who killed whites, the black population of the state had much less political and economic clout than it has now, and American society as a whole has changed. Whether or not a similar pattern still holds true awaits further study.

IS THE WAR ON DRUGS RACIST?

Critics say that the war on drugs, begun in the mid-1980s, was "racially biased on all fronts." It "made young black men its enemy and the entire African American community its victim."[111] The drug crackdown sharply increased the prison population, and since African Americans are disproportionately involved in the drug trade, it increased the proportion of blacks behind bars. A California judge has gone so far as to charge that the racial bias involved in the effort to combat illegal drugs is "at least as serious as the Jim Crow conduct was 30 or 40 years ago."[112] A paper in the scholarly journal *Crimin-ology* contends that "the iron fist of the war on drugs" is filling our prisons with "minority drug offenders . . . who in essence are being punished for the 'crime' of not accepting poverty or of being addicted to cocaine."[113] This would seem to translate into the remarkable assertion that it's quite all right to peddle drugs as an alternative to "accepting poverty" or as a means of generating the income to feed your drug habit. One wonders whether the author of this statement would excuse mugging a stranger in the park or robbing the corner grocery as just another way of "not accepting poverty."

We offer no brief for or against the war on drugs here. We do, though, have a few quick observations about how the drug war relates to the topic of this chapter—race and crime.

The war on drugs has been pictured as the exclusive invention of racist, right-wing Republicans. A report from the Sentencing Project implies that the main intent of the drug war was just to lock up more blacks, though conceding that "whether or not these policies were consciously or unconsciously designed to incarcerate more minorities is a question that may be debated."[114] But Representative Charles Rangel, a liberal black Democrat from Harlem, remains a vigorous supporter of federal antidrug efforts. Critics of the war on drugs have focused much of their fire on a 1986 law that made the penalties for the possession or sale of crack cocaine much harsher than those for powder cocaine. This, they allege, is blatantly racist, because crack tends to be used by blacks and powder cocaine by whites.[115] If so, it is certainly peculiar that the Congressional Black Caucus backed the law, and that some of its members proposed even tougher penalties on crack.[116] They knew that crack was much more common in black neighborhoods than in white ones, and that more blacks than whites were likely to be incarcerated as a result of the change. And in fact, that was precisely their reason for supporting the legislative change: a conviction that it might reduce the havoc on the streets where their constituents lived.

In 1991 the Minnesota Supreme Court sided with the critics by ruling that a state law penalizing crack more severely than powder cocaine was racially discriminatory, in violation of the Fourteenth Amendment. But as Harvard law professor Randall Kennedy has pointed out, the heavier penalty for crack burdened only a subset of the black population—the subset of drug-sellers and drug-users—while offering important benefits to the "great mass of law-abiding people" in black neighborhoods.[117] The claim that the War on Drugs made "young black men its enemy and the entire African-American community its victim" blurs that vital distinction. Whether the benefits have outweighed the costs is the subject of legitimate debate, but constructive debate is impossible when this crucial point is ignored.

In addition, critics who depict the War on Drugs as "an unmitigated disaster for young blacks" typically exaggerate its impact on black incarceration rates.[118] As Table 2 demonstrated, African Americans are a bit *less* likely to be arrested for drug offenses than they are for most other crimes. What is more, in 1980, before the antidrug crackdown, African Americans were 34.4 percent of the inmates in federal prisons, and 46.6 percent of those in state penitentiaries. By 1994, their share of the federal prison population had risen only slightly, to 35.4 percent. Among state prisoners, the black proportion rose three points between 1980 and 1993 to 49.7 percent.[119] (No 1994 state figures are available as yet.) The increase among state prisoners was not completely trivial, but it was hardly "an unmitigated disaster."

The black prison population would be smaller, but not much smaller, if the drug laws were different—if, for example, crack and powder cocaine were treated identically. But a calculation made on data for prisoners newly admitted to penitentiaries in thirty-eight states in 1992 indicates that if the percentage of black men serving drug sentences had been reduced to the figure for white men, the black proportion of the total would have fallen from 50 percent to 46 percent. Again, not a trivial difference, but hardly a monumental one.[120] A similar calculation done for prisoners in federal facilities yields even less of a difference; we could have made the proportion of black males sent to federal prisons for drug offenses in 1994 identical to the proportion among white males by setting free just 855 African-American men, a mere 3 percent of those sent to a federal penitentiary that year.[121]

THE CAUSES OF CRIME

How can we explain the great rise of crime in general and black crime specifically since the 1960s? One standard explanation locates the "root causes" of criminal behavior in socioeconomic deprivation. "Warring on poverty, inadequate housing, and unemployment is warring on crime," said Lyndon Johnson's President's Crime Commission in 1967. "A civil rights law is a law against crime. Money for schools is money against crime."[122]

It was classic expression of the liberal view. Crime—most crime, at least—results from the failure of society to provide a suitable environment in which all can lead satisfying lives. Growing up in a household with an income below the poverty line inclines young people toward criminal activity. Living in a dilapidated tenement or public housing project in a neighborhood dominated by such housing promotes crime. The inability to find a job leads people to seek income from illegal activities. If "money for schools is money against crime," insufficient funds for public education will likewise foster crime.

As an explanation for overall trends in crime in twentieth-century America, this line of reasoning doesn't get us very far. As noted earlier, homicide rates actually declined during the Great Depression of the 1930s, even though the deprivation model would lead us to expect the opposite. Murder rates continued to decline slowly until the 1960s. But thereafter, not only homicide but all other forms of violent crime rose spectacularly, despite the fact that the economy was surging ahead and the federal government was devoting unprecedented resources to alleviating poverty, expanding educational opportunity, and protecting civil rights. Numerous benefits may have come from these social reforms, but as ways of "warring on crime" they were utterly ineffectual.

If one turns to the narrower question of the fluctuating rate of crime committed by African Americans, changes in social and economic conditions again don't have much explanatory power. Black crime exploded in the 1960s, a decade in which black incomes rose rapidly and black poverty rates dropped rapidly. If "a civil rights law is a law against crime," the landmark civil rights and voting rights acts of 1964 and 1965 certainly should have sent the crime rate plunging. Furthermore, blacks received a disproportionate share of the benefits from the social programs of the Great Society because they were a disproportionate share of the poverty population, but that did not stop the wave of black crime. Since the 1960s, African Americans have continued to make progress on most economic and social measures; that progress has done nothing to drive their crime rate down to lower levels.

It can be argued, however, that those who have been committing most of the crime have not experienced the progress apparent from the average figures. As we saw in the previous chapter, the overall poverty rate for African Americans today is little different from what it was in 1970; approximately 30 percent of blacks still fall below the poverty line. With such a substantial fraction of the black community impoverished, why should the crime rate have gone down? The question neglects the progress of the 1960s: that 30 percent represents a substantial drop from what the poverty rate had been. And less poverty should have meant less crime. That is the conundrum for those who depict crime as a function of economic deprivation. In the 1950s, the black poverty rate was roughly double what it has been since the early 1970s. But while poverty went down, crime soared; in fact, in the 1950s, the incidence of crime committed by blacks was less than half its current level.

An explanation of an altogether different kind has been offered by critics of the jurisprudential revolution that also began in the 1960s. A series of innovative decisions by the Warren Court expanded the procedural rights of those accused of crimes and limited the freedom of law enforcement officials in several ways.[123] *Miranda v. Arizona* (1966), for example, set forth rules that made it considerably more difficult to obtain confessions from offenders, and other decisions prevented the use of evidence that had not been gathered in accordance with strict procedures governing search and seizure. Those who believe that crime is deterred by swift and severe punishment will be inclined to believe that these new restraints upon law enforcement contributed to the explosion of crime by making it harder to prosecute and convict lawbreakers. On the other hand, the most generous estimate that has been made of the number of criminal cases lost as a result of *Miranda*-style legal loopholes is 3.8 percent, so it is doubtful that these developments had a major impact.[124]

We have argued that less poverty has not meant less crime; economic progress has been accompanied by rising crime rates. And yet we do not deny a connection between the socioeconomic environment in which people live and their propensity to break the law. We know that a teenager from the affluent suburb of Lake Forest is a lot less likely to mug someone than a teenager who lives in public housing in Chicago.[125] There is no contradiction here. Poor people are more likely to break the law, but lawbreaking is not a monopoly of the poor, so that a decline in the number of poor would not necessarily bring about a decline in the amount of crime. In fact, the connection between breaking the law and poverty was never very close and has been getting weaker.

THE COSTS OF VIOLENCE

Violent crime is a much bigger problem in the United States today than it was a generation ago. And it is a problem that is inextricably bound up with race. Disproportionately, blacks are perpetrators and victims. Nothing has been more harmful to the black community, and nothing has done more to poison race relations, than the explosion of black violent crime since the 1960s. The decade that saw the greatest leap forward for African Americans since Emancipation also marked the beginning of a social trend that has had calamitous consequences.

Consider first the cost to individuals. In 1993 black criminals were responsible for nearly 3 million violent acts, according to the testimony of their victims (Table 6). A majority of these crimes—54 percent—were directed against whites, but the 1.3 million crimes committed against the much smaller black population meant that blacks were victimized by their fellow blacks at a much higher rate than whites. Millions of African Americans suffered bodily harm and economic and psychological damage from the predatory actions of black criminals.

The costs to individual victims are not the only ones that must be weighed. Where there's violent crime, there's also disorder—vandalism, graffiti, litter, stripped and abandoned cars, boarded-up buildings, public drinking, the sale and use of drugs, loitering youths, prostitution, and panhandling.[126] The civic order breaks down on several fronts at once. And that breakdown leaves little in a community untouched. The impact is evident in the absence of stores, jobs, well-functioning schools, and middle-class residents in many predominantly black sections of our cities. The kid with a knife, the drunk on the corner, and the burned-out car have a domino effect that destroys the quality of the life around them.

Social and physical disorder—the bands of roaming youths and the piles of accumulated trash—signal danger. People who live in fear lead different

Table 6
Crimes by Blacks as Reported by Victims, 1993

		BLACK VICTIMS	
	Total	Number	Percent
All violent victimizations	2,832,740	1,295,331	46
Robberies	514,541	273,310	53
Aggravated assaults	514,193	199,450	39
Rapes	74,782	38,097	51
Murders	6,299	5,393	86

Sources: Totals for all violent crimes and for robberies include multiple-offender as well as single-offender incidents. Other figures are for single-offender victimizations only, since multiple-offender information was not broken down in sufficient detail; U.S. Department of Justice, *Criminal Victimization in the U.S. 1993*, 45, 49. The murder figures come not from murder victims, obviously, but are for offenders charged with the crime. They are from U.S. Department of Justice, *Crime in the United States—1993* (Washington, D.C.: U.S. Government Printing Office, 1994), 17.

lives. They stay at home, abandon their porches, and cease to monitor their neighbors' kids. The parks meant for play become off-limits. Out on the street they watch their surroundings warily. In fact, if they have a car, they never walk or use mass transit.[127] Life becomes as constricted, in some ways, as it was under Jim Crow. Only now the worry is not that you will get into trouble by seeming too "uppity" to a white, but that some fellow African American will take your wallet, your purse, or possibly your life.

No one knows how many jobs have been lost as a direct result of crime and disorder, though we mentioned in the previous chapter some estimates of how much crime increases the costs of doing business in the ghetto. No one knows how many former residents have fled in search of safer ground. Inner-city neighborhoods have too many liquor stores, too few banks and supermarkets, too few factories, and too many poor people for a variety of reasons. But logic and anecdotal evidence suggest fear of violence plays a part in shaping their economic and demographic landscape. More than a dozen years ago Thomas Atkins, then general counsel of the NAACP, observed that crime "destroys our businesses and hinders our ability to organize politically because people won't come out at night. It drives down the value of property in our communities and undercuts the possibility of economic development."[128] It destroys as well—he could have added—much of inner-city cultural life; the summer festival, for instance, that once graced the Watts ghetto in Los Angeles has now been moved to greener—that is, safer—pastures.[129]

The testimony of those who have fled to safer suburbs is unequivocal. Los Angeles resident Terry Nunley decided to leave the city after being held up at an automated teller machine. He moved his family to a town almost two hours away from where he worked. To Angelenos, his was a familiar story;

community leaders in the heavily black areas of the city such as Compton find themselves regularly urging local residents to stay. Without much success.[130] "I honestly haven't noticed anyone talking about moving back to the inner cities once they've left," the black editor of *Emerge* magazine has confessed. "When you think about what you're going to do with the money you worked so damned hard for, your first priority is to make sure that the people you care about are safe," she went on.[131] In the 1980s nearly 50,000 African Americans moved out of Washington, D.C., a net decline of about 11 percent in the city's black population. Francis and Constance Taylor moved out of the District to nearby Prince George's County in 1983. "I didn't feel I needed to be patriotic towards Washington," Mrs. Taylor told the *New York Times* in 1996. "I felt I needed to look out for what any family needed to prosper and grow." Those are sentiments echoed often in the majority-black county. "Everybody out here understands that there but for the grace of God go I," said Lucenia Dunn, who left Washington behind when she bought a house in one of Prince George's County's gated communities boasting private security and a golf course.[132]

Crime is *the* urban problem. It is a principal reason that so many people are fleeing from our largest cities. There remain upscale sections in almost every metropolis; apartment dwellers in the Upper East Side of Manhattan generally like where they live, and where they live is relatively safe. But it is literally the case that the revitalization of our central cities awaits a solution to the problem of crime. Urban advocates can demand federal dollars for enterprise zones and other such projects, but until the streets are safe, no store, factory, or theater is likely to flourish.

Crime is not only *the* urban problem; it is inextricably related to the other great urban problem, education. We will look in some detail at the impact of violence and disorder upon the public schools at a later point (see Chapter 13). For now, we need only say that schools in which children don't feel safe do not provide good education.

Urban violence not only eats away at the lives of those whom it affects directly; it also poisons relations between the races. As we noted at the outset, a shared problem divides whites from blacks. A tragedy in the black community is made even worse by the reinforcement of an old racial stereotype. Gunnar Myrdal reported in 1944 that "whites *believe* the Negro to be innately addicted to crime."[133] Most whites today would shy away from words like "innately" and "addicted," but in large numbers (as we've seen) they say that blacks are more "prone" to violence. That a majority of African Americans agree does not solve the basic problem: as long as the arrival of lower-class blacks in a neighborhood is associated with a jump in crime, residential areas will remain segregated. The link between blacks and crime—strong in reality and even stronger in the popular mind—is the greatest single source of resistance to the racial integration of residential neighborhoods.

Black violence stigmatizes young black males of every social class. In the mid-1980s, jewelry shops in Washington, D.C., adopted the practice of letting customers in only by a buzzer; by this means they could screen out young black males. In 1990, Boston Celtics player Dee Brown was treated roughly by Wellesley, Massachusetts, police who mistook him for a man who had robbed a bank the week before; Brown had stopped at the post office in the upscale, suburban town in which he had planned to buy a house.[134] In the spring of 1995, police in New York's Grand Central Terminal stopped and questioned Earl Graves, Jr., the senior vice president of advertising and marketing for the magazine *Black Enterprise*. They were acting on an anonymous tip about an armed man aboard the commuter train that he had been riding into New York, but the man described by the informant was five feet ten, with a mustache, while Graves was six feet four and clean-shaven. "These white police officers only see black," Graves charged, adding that he was "humiliated and embarrassed . . . [as well as] angry because the incident is part of an overriding problem in the city between white officers and African-American males."[135]

The Dee Brown and Earl Graves incidents are not unusual. Young black men, particularly, regularly complain that they are treated like social pariahs. When he was a graduate student at the University of Chicago in the 1970s, *New York Times* editorial writer Brent Staples liked to walk to the lakefront at night. One evening, in late fall, he was headed home.

> I turned out of Blackstone Avenue and headed west on 57th Street, and there she was, a few yards ahead of me, dressed in business clothes and carrying a briefcase. She looked back at me once, then again, and picked up her pace. She looked back again and started to run. I stopped where I was and looked up at the surrounding windows. What did this look like to people peeking out through their blinds? I was out walking. But what if someone . . . called the police. . . . I'd been a fool. I'd been walking the streets grinning good evening at people who were frightened to death of me. I did violence to them by just being. . . . I became expert in the language of fear.

For the first time, it occurred to Staples that he was big—over six feet tall. He tried to be innocuous but didn't know how. He tried to avoid people, letting them clear the lobbies of buildings before he entered, and out of nervousness, began to whistle—popular tunes from the Beatles and Vivaldi's *Four Seasons*. But then, he writes, he changed, without knowing why. He began to play a game that he called "Scatter the Pigeons"—terrifying whites by walking aggressively right in their path. It worked every time.

Those who encountered Staples on the streets of Chicago's Hyde Park neighborhood had, as he acknowledges, every reason to be scared. "Hyde Park was an island of prosperity in a sea of squalor," he notes. Earl Graves claimed that New York police looked at him and only saw black, but as Staples explains, the whites he encountered saw not black, but a friend and neighbor the minute he began to whistle his soothing tunes. "The tension drained from people's bodies when they heard me. A few even smiled as they passed me in the dark," he reports.[136] It took so little, although he found it too much. But Staples's experience suggests a larger truth: If the African-American crime rate suddenly dropped to the current level of the white crime rate, we would eliminate a major force that is driving blacks and whites apart and is destroying the fabric of black urban life.

CHAPTER ELEVEN

Politics

IN TWO CITIES in Maine—Augusta and Lewiston—blacks have captured the mayor's seat. Maine! Blacks are barely a presence in the state. "No one gives a squat" about skin color, says the mayor of Lewiston, John Jenkins, who won a runoff in 1993 against an incumbent councilman by a three-to-one margin in a city that is over 99 percent white. In Augusta, William Burney was first elected mayor in 1988 and has been reelected twice since then. He was a "hometown hero" (in the words of his predecessor)—a basketball star in high school and a graduate of the University of Maine Law School. Evidently, "no one gives a squat" about race there, either.[1]

"As Maine goes, so goes the nation," ran an old political saying. And, while there are plenty of places where color still does matter, perhaps those black electoral victories in a state 0.4 percent black do tell us something.[2] When it comes to politics, the importance of color may finally be fading. Black mayors are popping up all over. The conventional wisdom has it that most are elected in majority-black cities. True—and misleading. That count includes victories in many tiny municipalities in the South. Eliminate those small dots on the urban map, and the picture looks quite different. Between 1967 and 1993, African Americans won the mayor's seat in eighty-seven cities with a population of 50,000 or more. A remarkable two-thirds of those mayors were elected in cities in which blacks were a minority of the population. Half of them, in fact, were in municipalities less than 40 percent black, and over a third in cities in which no more than three out of ten residents were African-American.[3]

Thus, in 1967, when Carl Stokes first became the mayor of Cleveland, the city was only 38.3 percent black. He picked up about 20 percent of the white vote. In subsequent years African Americans were elected mayor in a string of cities, big and small, that were minority-black when they first ran. For example: James Howell McGee in Dayton, Theodore Berry in Cincinnati, Lyman Parks in Grand Rapids, Wallace Holland in Pontiac, Penfield Tate in

Boulder, Coleman Young in Detroit, Noel Taylor in Roanoke, Charles Bussey in Little Rock, Wilson Goode in Philadelphia, Carrie Perry in Hartford, David Dinkins in New York, and Ron Kirk in Dallas—to name just a few. The city of Los Angeles was never more than 18 percent black in the twenty years Tom Bradley was mayor. In fact, when he was first elected in 1973, he didn't even need his black support; with white votes alone, he would have won.

Lani Guinier has described blacks as "still the pariah group: systematic losers in the political marketplace."[4] That certainly was true once, but it is no longer the case. "People in political life are reluctant to say how much progress has been made . . . ," the black journalist Juan Williams has noted. "In fact . . . ," he went on, "segregationist politics is out; race-baiting is gone. Yes, there is racially-tainted politics, but nothing like it was."[5] His point, of course, was primarily about the South. And indeed a political revolution swept the South in the wake of the passage of the 1965 Voting Rights Act. In 1962, George Wallace won the Alabama gubernatorial race by "out-segging" his opponent; in 1970, he was still warning white voters, "If I don't win, them niggers are going to control this state."[6] But by 1974 he had begun to solicit black votes, and by 1982 he was asking black Alabamians to forgive his past. Four years later, in a survey of Alabama black opinion, Wallace came off as the best governor in the history of the state. One year after that, Jesse Jackson, running for president, made time to pay his political respects to a man he once loathed.[7]

Wallace was not alone in seeing the political light. Early in his phenomenally long political career, Strom Thurmond had been the presidential candidate of the Dixiecrat party, vowing last-ditch resistance to any change in the racial status quo; in 1970, as a U.S. senator from South Carolina, he became the first among his southern colleagues to put an African American on his staff and later sponsored the South's first black federal judge. He began, as well, to court the black vote with constituent services and federal funds.[8]

These are not singular stories. White supremacists always knew that fundamental change would follow once blacks acquired the right to vote. And it did —in part by forcing those politicians to change their tune or retire from politics. Demography made the South a good place for blacks to run and win. In each of the five Deep South states—South Carolina, Georgia, Alabama, Mississippi, and Louisiana—blacks are more than a quarter of the population. In four more states—Virginia, North Carolina, Maryland, and Delaware— the black population is in the 16- to 25-percent range. No northern state has concentrations of African-American residents that large.[9]

In 1968 in the entire South there were 3 black mayors; by 1973 the number had risen to only 38, and in 1996 it stood at 290.[10] As late as 1970, no African Americans held elective office in state government in Alabama, Arkansas, or South Carolina, while Florida, Louisiana, Mississippi, and North Carolina each had a single black member of the state legislature. The total for the eleven ex-Confederate states was just 32. By 1993 those states had almost ten times that many black state legislators—a total of 312—and 16 African Americans represented them in Congress.[11] In fact, 69 percent of all black elected officials in the nation in 1993 were southerners, with the largest numbers in Alabama and Mississippi, the most hard-core of the segregationist states not so long ago.[12]

A NATIONAL STORY

Of course the South is not the only region in which blacks roam the corridors of political power. The simplest and clearest evidence of the remarkable change in the national political picture may be seen in the statistics assembled in Table 1, which charts the numbers of black candidates who have been elected to national, state, and local offices in recent decades. The information available on black elected officials is quite scanty before 1970, but their numbers were very small. Just 4 African Americans were members of the U.S. House of Representatives in 1960; in 1964, there were 5. Detailed data are not available, but we know that when the historic Civil Rights Act was passed, a black population of 20 million people could claim no more than 103 elected officials at any level of government—national, state, or local.

The picture changed suddenly and dramatically thereafter. By 1975, 18 African Americans were in Congress; nearly 300 were sitting in a state legislature; 135 occupied the mayor's office in a city; close to 400 were judges, sheriffs, or other elected local officials, In the two decades since, the pace of change has not slowed. The number of blacks in Congress has more than doubled; the number in state legislatures has almost doubled; and the number serving as mayors has tripled. Thus, the U.S. House of Representatives, after the 1994 elections, had 40 black members, 9.2 percent of the total—a figure actually a bit higher than the group's 8.5 percent share of the ballots cast in 1994.[13] (The number was reduced by one as a result of the November 1996 elections.)[14] Furthermore, in several state legislatures today, African Americans hold a higher proportion of seats than their share of the voting-age population. As of 1993, this was true in nine states, including California, Florida, Ohio, and Wisconsin.[15]

Although the number of blacks holding elected office has grown impressively, overall black officeholding still falls far short of proportionality. Some take this as proof that the electoral system is not racially fair. Blacks are 11.3 percent of the voting-age population, and yet the nearly 8,000 elected offices African Americans held in 1993 were only 1.6 percent of the total.[16] In fact, that number is quite misleading. Black candidates are almost invariably Democrats—usually liberal Democrats. They're very weak competitors in places where Republicans generally win. Thus, the real question is: What

Table 1
Black Elected Officials, 1960–1995

	U.S. CONG.	STATE LEG.	MAYOR	OTHER CITY OR COUNTY	JUDICIAL AND LAW ENFORCEMENT	TOTAL
1960	4	36	NA	NA	NA	NA
1964	5	94	NA	NA	NA	103
1970	10	169	48	667	213	1,469
1975	18	281	135	1,743	387	3,503
1980	17	309	182	2,650	526	4,607
1985	20	387	286	3,231	661	6,016
1990	24	412	313	4,172	769	7,335
1993	39	561	356	4,463	922	7,984
1994	41	NA	NA	NA	NA	8,406
1995	41	NA	367	NA	NA	NA
1996	41	NA	405	NA	NA	NA

Sources: U.S. Bureau of the Census, Current Population Reports, Special Studies, P-23-80, *The Social and Economic Status of the Black Population in the United States: An Historical View, 1790–1978* (Washington, D.C.: U.S. Government Printing Office, 1979), 156–157; Sar A. Levitan, William B. Johnston, and Robert Taggart, *Still a Dream: The Changing Status of Blacks Since 1960* (Cambridge: Harvard University Press, 1975), 178; Harold W. Stanley and Richard G. Niemi, *Vital Statistics on American Politics,* 4th ed. (Washington, D.C.: Congressional Quarterly Press, 1994), 399; U.S. Bureau of the Census, *Statistical Abstract of the United States: 1996* (Washington, D.C.: U.S. Government Printing Office, 1996), 284; Joint Center for Political and Economic Studies, *Black Elected Officials: A National Roster, 1993* (Washington, D.C.: 1994), 247–248; Joint Center for Political and Economic Studies, *African Americans Today: A Demographic Profile* (Washington, D.C.: 1996), table 4; Joyce Jones, "Mayors to Meet in Memphis, but their Attention will be Focused on Washington," *Black Enterprise,* May 1995, 24; National Conference of Black Mayors, *Program of 22nd Annual Convention* (Atlanta, 1996), unpaginated. City or county officials include aldermen and city or county council members; judicial and law enforcement officials include judges, sheriffs, constables, and justices of the peace.

proportion of those offices held by Democrats (or more specifically, liberal Democrats) do blacks occupy? And for how many of those offices have they made a run?

To the first question, we do have a partial answer. In 1992, blacks made up 14 percent of the voters in Democratic Party primaries. After the 1992 general election, African Americans held 14.4 percent of the seats occupied by Democrats in the U.S. House of Representatives. The 1994 congressional elections resulted in a loss of seats by the Democrats, which increased the black percentage of the party's total strength to 18.[17] It declined slightly as a result of the 1996 elections, which returned a few more Democrats but the same number of black Democrats to the House. If one focuses on the party to which almost all blacks belong, in other words, their representation in the lower house of Congress has been strong.

At the state level, black success is less impressive but still notable. Nationwide in 1992, blacks averaged 10 percent of the Democratic presence in the lower state legislative chambers and had 8.1 percent of the seats in the state senates.[18] But these figures include, of course, a great many states in which blacks are a tiny fraction of the population. In 1992, in the states with sizable black populations, the percentage of black Democratic state legislators was proportionate to the black voting-age population.[19]

African Americans are residentially concentrated—in certain cities as well as certain states—and that, too, has affected the likelihood of their winning office. The 1990 Census showed that over four out of ten (41 percent) of all blacks in the United States lived in the central cities of metropolitan areas of 1 million or more, as compared with only 15 percent of the white population.[20] There are forty such metropolitan areas, and blacks hold the mayor's seat in the central cities of sixteen of them. But the total number of black faces in office may be disproportionately low in part precisely because African Americans are such an urban people. In big cities the ratio of population to the number of elected offices tends to be lower than in smaller communities and rural areas. For instance, the school committee in Lexington, Massachusetts, a town of 29,000 with only a small black population, is roughly the same size as that serving all of Boston.[21]

Furthermore, blacks still disproportionately reside in the South; over half the black population is southern, while the figure for whites is just under one-third.[22] Historically, the southern political system has had fewer elective offices than other regions of the nation.[23] Outside the South there is nothing equivalent to the Charlotte-Mecklenburg School District, which spans 542 square miles; in Illinois an area that size would contain a multitude of independent school systems, each with an elected governing body. Atlanta is 67 percent black, but it has fewer elected offices than an older, multilayered, big public-sector city of a similar size—Pittsburgh, for example, which is only 26 percent African-American. In short, where the white population is concentrated, there are more elective offices to fill. Even if African Americans in every town and city held public office in proportion to their numbers, the national picture would still seem suspiciously white. Blacks would appear, in the aggregate, underrepresented in political office.

The national data on black officeholding, in short, paint a deceptively dreary picture. Blacks have become major players in the American political process, and in the years since the 1960s have advanced more impressively in politics than in any other arena. In Alabama in 1956 the State Senate unanimously passed a resolution asking Congress for the funds to move the entire black population out of the state.[24] Today that Senate is 11 percent black, and in Birmingham, Montgomery, Selma, and elsewhere, memorials celebrate the civil rights revolution that Governor Wallace and others once so brutally opposed.

THE POWER OF THE BLACK VOTE

Those memorials are testimony to the power of the black vote—its impact on white as well as black officeholding. Blacks are the nation's most solidly Democratic voting bloc. Few Americans realize it, but the Democratic Party would have lost every presidential election from 1968 to the present if only whites had been allowed to vote. Jimmy Carter carried only 47 percent of the white vote in 1976, but was elected because his 83 percent support from blacks more than made up the deficit. Bill Clinton did even worse among white voters, getting only 39 percent of their vote in 1992 and 43 percent in 1996. But Clinton, too, got five out of six black votes, and that was enough to give him wins over George Bush in 1992 and Bob Dole in 1996.[25]

That white senators know how to count black ballots was evident in the 1991 vote on the appointment of Judge Clarence Thomas to the U.S. Supreme Court. Despite the opposition of many civil rights groups, polls demonstrated that a majority of blacks supported Thomas. Crucial votes for his confirmation came from three southern Democrats who had been supported by only a minority of white voters in 1986—Democrats who were up for reelection in 1992, and who needed every African-American vote they could get.[26] Even a small drop in black support might have made a difference in those Senate contests.[27]

Blacks are becoming more powerful politically both because their numbers are growing and because they have become politically mobilized. In the three decades following the passage of the Voting Rights Act of 1965, the total black population of the United States increased by 56 percent, double the rate of increase for whites, raising the black share of the total population from 10.8 percent to 12.5 percent. In those same decades, the number of African Americans registered to vote increased even more rapidly. The number of blacks on the voting rolls rose 7 million—from under 6 million in 1964 to nearly 13 million in 1994, 2.4 times the white rate of increase.[28]

Despite these advances, however, African Americans are still somewhat less likely to be registered than whites. In 1968, the percentage-point gap was 9 points—75 percent of whites as compared with 66 percent of blacks had signed up to vote. The gap narrowed a little in the mid-1980s, to 4 points in 1984 and just 1 point in 1986, but then it gradually widened again, and was 6 points in both 1992 and 1994.[29] In the South, however—where 55 percent of the black population currently lives—the clear trend has been toward greater equality. In 1968, the black-white gap in the southern states was 9.2 percentage points; by 1992 it had fallen to 3.8 points.[30] That was the year that the

Voter Education Project—once at the forefront of the civil rights struggle—died a natural death. Its job was done.

Not only are African-American registration rates a few points lower than those for whites, the rate at which blacks who are registered actually turn up at a polling place is also lower.[31] In 1980, for example, 61 percent of whites on the voting lists cast a ballot on election day; for African Americans the figure was 51 percent. In 1984 the turnout gap dropped to 5 points, and to 4 points in 1986, but then it widened again. In both 1992 and 1994 the turnout difference was 10 points.[32] In the South, however, the trend was once again clearly toward equality. In 1968 blacks who were registered (most of them first-time voters) were 20.3 points behind whites in their actual voting rate; by 1992 the gap was down to just 6.5 points.[33] When racial differences in registration and turnout are controlled for income, education, and the like, they shrink further or even vanish.[34]

Local and state registration and turnout rates often don't match those reported in national surveys; averages conceal many variations. Thus, in a number of mayoral contests, proportionally more blacks than whites have cast ballots. In the New York 1989 mayoral race almost 66 percent of the registered voters in the predominantly black neighborhoods showed up at the polls —2.5 points above the average for the city as a whole.[35] In several black congressional districts in Georgia and Alabama, turnout in the 1984 Democratic presidential primary (with Jesse Jackson in the race) was 15 to 25 percentage points higher than the statewide average.[36] In 1992, black registration rates actually exceeded those of whites in three states (Tennessee, Louisiana, and California).[37]

Black political participation will rise and fall in response to particular candidates. When voters care, they reach for a ballot. When white supremacist David Duke ran for governor of Louisiana in 1991, the black turnout reached a record 80 percent, exceeding that for whites.[38] The high level of participation of blacks in the 1989 mayoral election in New York was affected by the fact that David Dinkins was the first serious black candidate to run for the post. In the New Orleans mayoral race in 1994, a heavy black turnout was attributed in good part to the circulation of anonymous antiblack campaign fliers linked to the white candidate.[39] In Chicago prior to the state and congressional elections of 1982, before Harold Washington had decided to enter the mayoral fray, black antagonism toward both President Reagan and Mayor Jane Byrne seems to have been one element in a wildly successful black registration drive that helped convince Washington to run.[40]

In turn, Harold Washington himself—like other well-organized strong black candidates—pulled in still more voters. His own campaign conducted a massive and effective voter registration drive, involving over two hundred grassroots groups.[41] In one black church the minister admonished his parish that it was a "sin" not to register to vote.[42] The combined result: black registration went from being 10 points lower than white registration to being almost

6 points higher.[43] Black turnout also rose—to an impressive 73 percent of those who were eligible, 6 points higher than the white figure, an increase of 25 percent over 1979.[44]

The point extends to a variety of races. In the 1989 Virginia gubernatorial race, L. Douglas Wilder used the black churches to reach the black electorate. He also earmarked $750,000 for a "get out the vote" drive that targeted 190,000 households.[45] Voter registration drives also accompanied Jesse Jackson's two presidential bids, and seem to have been particularly effective in 1984. In that year, in the seven states for which we have reliable data, black turnout in the Democratic primaries in which Jackson ran almost doubled.[46]

Harold Washington, Douglas Wilder, and Jesse Jackson all ran groundbreaking campaigns, and the fact that they were "firsts" almost certainly inspired black participation. In 1967, when Carl Stokes was first elected mayor of Cleveland, turnout in the predominantly black wards reached almost 82 percent.[47] As the political scientist Katherine Tate has noted, "Black officeseeking, particularly in elections involving Blacks as political newcomers, seems to be associated with astoundingly high Black turnouts." The reasons are obvious: group loyalty, racial pride, and the assiduous courting of black voters.[48] As one observer has remarked, "To black Chicagoans, Washington embodied the hopes and dreams of centuries of struggle." Across the black economic spectrum, from Hyde Park to the Cabrini Green housing project, "it was not uncommon to see the red, black, and green flag of black unity flying high with Washington's name displayed in bold print."[49] On the other hand, when the novelty wears off or voters' expectations are not met, black turnout for a black incumbent can drop. Katie Hall was elected to Congress from Indiana's majority-white first district in 1982 with an impressive 57 percent of the vote; two years later she went down to defeat when many black constituents failed to show up at the polls.[50]

The power of black ballots has, to some extent, been deliberately enhanced since the early 1970s by electoral arrangements designed to promote black officeholding. Those arrangements are part of the story of the 1965 Voting Rights Act—or rather of its enforcement by courts and the U.S. Department of Justice. It is a tale we tell in Chapter 16. Suffice it to say here that, pressured by federal authorities, states in the South and elsewhere took to drawing race-conscious legislative districts—to creating the maximum possible number of majority-black constituencies. Such districts served to protect black candidates from white competition; they were safely black. Whites do not bother to run in them. And thus they have been a swift and sure way of ensuring more black officeholding—and in this sense of making sure that black votes "count." On the other hand, guaranteed officeholding has arguably meant fewer seats for representatives particularly sensitive to black interests, and the racial gerrymandering of legislative districts raises serious normative and constitutional questions. But these are arguments we address later.

The power of the black vote has changed American politics—and will bring

more change if the remaining still significant racial gap in political participation can be closed. In 1994 blacks were 11.5 of the voting-age population but
only 8.5 percent of those who voted.[51] They were riding down the political
road with only three out of their four cylinders operating. Black electoral
power was about a quarter less than it would have been if their registration
and turnout rates had matched those of whites. It is estimated that in the
1996 elections the proportion of the total vote coming from African Americans
rose to one-tenth.[52] If this finding is not the result of mere sampling error, it
hints at advances in black political mobilization.

Winning in Majority-Black Communities

Black enfranchisement in the South after 1965 changed the political identity
of towns, cities, and counties throughout the region. Majority-black settings
governed by whites became places in which blacks lived, worked—and, for
the first time, voted. And where blacks voted, black candidates sought public
office. In 1976 there were 150 black mayors nationwide; 50 were in southern
towns of less than 1,000 inhabitants. Over half (84 out of 152) were in southern towns of less than 15,000.[53] By 1993 the number of black mayors had
risen to 356, with 253 in the South. In Mississippi alone that year, 32 towns
had black mayors, and, again, almost all were majority-black and very small.[54]
In May 1996 the membership of the National Conference of Black Mayors
stood at 405, with 65 percent from southern states.[55]

For the most part, these are places that blacks came to govern because
black residents, long a majority, could finally vote. But other cities—in North
and South—are now majority-black for a different reason. Their demography
has changed. The urban landscape is blacker, which means more blacks are
likely to run and win. In 1940 no large American city had a black majority. By
now the list of majority-black cities includes Detroit, Baltimore, Memphis,
Washington, D.C., New Orleans, Atlanta, Newark, and Birmingham.[56]

The results have been predictable: black mayors elected where black residents are a majority. And mayors aren't the only story. Black cities elect blacks
to Congress, state legislatures, county offices, and the judiciary. That stands
to reason. Generally only a very small percentage of blacks fail to vote for
black candidates (perhaps a consequence of the relative novelty of their political power), and in majority-black settings, there are always blacks in a race.[57]
"In Birmingham, I mean if you're not black, then you're [politically] nobody,"
one resident said in 1993.[58] It has become true in politics (at least with respect
to the mayor's seat) in a variety of places: Washington, D.C., Atlanta, Detroit,
and Newark, among others.

In such cities black politics are the only true game in town. "White candidates are no longer taken seriously in Detroit," the journalist Ze'ev Chafets

wrote in 1989.[59] White politics went out when Coleman Young came in. That was in 1973, the same year that Atlanta got rid of its last white mayor. It's not that whites have lost all potential power in such cities; with a divided black electorate, whites become the swing vote. But the mayor's office and a majority of the city council seats are safely black.

WHEN WHITES VOTE FOR BLACKS

There's a final reason for the increase in black officeholding in recent decades —one to which we have already alluded. Whites are voting for blacks. In increasing numbers. To a degree that was unimaginable thirty years ago. And not just in places (like Detroit) where only blacks run. In a contest that pits a black against a white, blacks will generally vote for one of their own, but whites won't necessarily support the candidate who is white. That is, while black candidates can usually count on almost every black vote, whites who run in a racially diverse setting have no such advantage.

In the New York 1989 mayoral race, for instance, Rudolph Giuliani lost an estimated 25 to 30 percent of the white vote to his black opponent, David Dinkins. At least 38 percent of whites deserted John Derus in Minneapolis in 1993, and cast their ballots for Sharon Sayles Belton, the black president of the city council.[60] That same year, 31 percent of St. Louis's white electorate voted for Freeman Bosley, Jr., although three white candidates were in the field.[61] Belton and Bosley were making their first try; incumbents generally do even better.[62] The 1991 Memphis mayoral contest was extremely racially polarized and Willie Herenton, an African American, won by only 142 votes, but a year later the mayor had a 60 percent approval rating among the city's whites.[63] Dallas is only 30 percent black, but in 1995 Ron Kirk won the mayor's race with nearly two-thirds of the vote.[64]

In 1996, 67 of the nation's cities with populations of 25,000 or more had black mayors. Many of those cities are majority-black, but most are not. Almost six out of ten (58 percent) of the black mayors of these urban centers were elected in places in which whites outnumbered African Americans.[65] And if we look only at cities outside of the South—two-thirds of the total— 70 percent of those with black mayors do not have black population majorities. African-American candidates needed significant white support to win—and they got it.

It is not only in mayoral races that white voters often choose black candidates over those who are white. L. Douglas Wilder, in his successful gubernatorial run in 1989, got an estimated 40 to 43 percent of the vote of Virginia whites. Skeptics will say that that figure still represents less than half of the white electorate, but Charles Robb, the Democratic governor who preceded Wilder, did only a shade better—45 percent.[66]

When Virginians size up a candidate, a euphoric Douglas Wilder said right after his victory, they "don't care what that person looks like, what that person's religion would be or what that person's gender is."[67] It was the politic thing to say, and perhaps, in the flush of an historic victory, he even meant it. The truth is more complicated. Of course race determines how some whites vote some of the time. In the 1991 Memphis mayoral contest, 97 percent of the whites voted for the white candidate, 99 percent of the blacks for the black one. In the March 1994 New Orleans mayoral election, the black candidate won an estimated 90 percent of the black vote, while 91 percent of whites supported his white opponent. Despite the fact that the white had worked for years to build a biracial political coalition and had kicked off his campaign in a black church, there was very little crossover voting.[68] But the mayoral race that year was unusually dirty; anonymous campaign fliers with antiblack and anti-Semitic slogans were widely circulated.[69] That's not an everyday occurrence. It now makes news; it has become the unexpected—even in New Orleans where black mayoral candidates in earlier races had picked up more than 20 percent of the white vote.

Voting rights experts frequently argue that almost all elections in which blacks run are "polarized"; black and white voters form, in effect, opposing teams. But that conclusion rests on a definition of polarization very much open to argument—one that depicts whites and blacks as separate and hostile in any election in which black voters support black candidates in proportionally greater numbers than do white voters.[70] By this dubious logic the Douglas Wilder election in Virginia was racially "polarized" even though at least 40 percent of whites voted for him; his black support was greater. In fact, blacks and whites had come together in Virginia to elect a governor.

Race cuts both ways. Although it is rarely acknowledged, in some races and with some white voters, it's actually a political asset to be black. To begin with, as journalist Michael Barone has pointed out, political newcomers need to get noticed and black candidates are clearly visible.[71] More important, a portion of the white electorate is often eager to vote for an African American. In 1989 in New York, race-conscious voting, particularly by whites on the Upper West Side of Manhattan, undoubtedly put David Dinkins over the top.[72] "One reason Mr. Dinkins did so well among whites was wishful thinking," the New York Times noted. White voters hoped "he would be able to say and do things . . . that a white mayor would not say or do"—on the subject of black crime, for instance.[73] In addition, New York had just been torn apart by a racially motivated killing, and Dinkins, with his soothing low-key style, promised to heal the wounds.[74] In 1992, Carol Moseley-Braun, too, was certainly helped by the color of her skin when she won the Illinois Senate race by ten points over her white GOP opponent. As the Economist observed at the time, "Ms Braun's supporters [were] less enamored of her than of what she represent[ed]"—a racial first.[75]

Moseley-Braun ran a campaign well-financed by whites. Much of the early money—in fact, toward the end of the primary season, about $2,500 a day— came from Emily's List, a national organization formed to support female, pro-choice candidates. Some of her subsequent funding, too, came from out of state—from fund-raisers hosted by New York Governor Mario Cuomo, for instance.[76] Hers is not a unique story; whites have been both casting ballots and writing checks in support of black candidates. Harvey Gantt, who made unsuccessful bids to unseat North Carolina senator Jesse Helms in 1990 and 1996, held fund-raisers in New York and Los Angeles, among other cities, and raised the bulk of his large war chest from contributors out- side the state, with much of the money undoubtedly coming from whites.[77] Two blacks made the runoff in the 1991 Denver mayoral election; the white business community picked its candidate and helped raise $1.5 million for his unsuccessful campaign.[78] In May 1995, Ron Kirk was elected mayor of Dallas; a lawyer and former Texas secretary of state, he was able to raise $700,000, twice the amount collected by either of his two major opponents. The business establishment in the city had endorsed Kirk and filled his cof- fers.[79]

The change in white attitudes extends to the highest office in the land. In 1957 a national sample of whites was asked whether they would vote for a well-qualified black candidate for president if he were nominated by their party; 63 percent said no. In 1994 just 10 percent of whites held to that view.[80] Growing white receptivity to a black presidential candidate opened the door to General Colin Powell, though he has not yet chosen to walk through it. In the 1995 presidential primary season Powell was the nation's most wanted political candidate; in an October 1995 *Time*/CNN poll, he beat Clinton 51 to 34 percent.[81] Moreover, exit polls conducted on election day in November 1996 suggest that he would have defeated President Clinton by 11 points. Another poll shortly after had Powell smashing Vice President Gore by 28 points in the presidential contest in 2000.[82]

"Blacks," Governor Wilder once said, "cannot wait until there is a majority in a district or region to dream of running for office. [They] cannot isolate [themselves] in enclaves and retreat, leaving vast areas totally untapped and unchallenged."[83] Had Powell run for the presidency, he would of course have tested Wilder's implicit confidence in the potential for white support. Successful black candidates in statewide races and other majority-white set- tings have, it is true, been few in number. But African Americans cannot win contests they do not enter. And scholars who attempt to assess white willing- ness to support black candidacies cannot settle the question on the basis of elections in which no black candidate has been in the race.[84] Or on the basis of contests in which the political views of African-American candidates have been at odds with the majority of voters in their districts—a subject to which we will return.

THE NEW BLACK MAYORS

A deep divide separates those black politicians who (like Wilder) make an effort to appeal to white voters and those who don't. The difference is often generational. In Prince George's County, Maryland, a new crop of leaders arrived on the political scene in 1994. They're young, they're black and "their favorite color is green," a local lawyer and mentor said. "They want to see prosperity."[85]

The description fits a number of black mayors as well. In Cleveland in 1989 two black candidates made it into a nonpartisan runoff. One was fifty-eight-year-old George L. Forbes, who, by his own admission, found soliciting votes in white neighborhoods "very painful." "My generation came out of a strong black civil rights movement," he explained, "and we always went back to black issues." His opponent, twenty years younger, was Michael White, who knew, he said, that "you don't make progress standing outside throwing bricks." He was the first black elected student body president at Ohio State, and described himself as never having "been a radical in my entire life about anything." He won.[86]

Other black mayors, too, have been stressing clean streets, reduced crime, a balanced budget, and even the cost to blacks of court-ordered busing.[87] Take Detroit. For twenty years Coleman Young dominated that city's politics. He did "more than broaden access to the pork barrel," writer Ze'ev Chafets noted. "Under him, Detroit [became] not merely an American city that happen[ed] to have a black majority, but a black metropolis, the first major Third World city in the United States. The trappings [were] all there—showcase projects, black-fisted symbols, an external enemy and the cult of personality."[88]

Dennis Archer, elected in 1993, was a definite change. As one columnist put it, " 'Our turn' platforms with the symbolic rhetoric of racial justice [took] a back seat to the more practical demands of governing."[89] Throughout the campaign Archer had intimated that the business of Detroit was business, and as mayor-elect, he spent his first morning with the Republican governor of the state.[90] In Atlanta, too, in 1993 there was a changing of the guard; Bill Campbell rode to victory promising more police, efficient government, economic growth, and no new taxes. He was the first black mayor of that majority-black city without close ties to the city's illustrious civil rights community.[91]

Old-style black politicians are still around. Marion Barry, mayor of Washington, D.C., is a man cast in the Coleman Young mold. In small cities and towns —the places that only the locals know and scholars and media ignore—there could be others. Nor do all black mayors fit one mold or the other. The urban political scene is full of variety. Politicians are idiosyncratic, and consequently often hard to classify.

THE CONGRESSIONAL BLACK CAUCUS

If some mayors have dropped the rhetoric of racial empowerment and veered from the straight and narrow liberal path, that rhetoric and those programs have remained very much alive among the members of the Congressional Black Caucus—the CBC. For many black representatives in Congress time has stood still; they remain old-school civil rights warriors, whose power base is typically so heavily African-American that they need display little concern for white sensibilities. Coleman Young no longer occupies City Hall in Detroit, but Congressman John Conyers, Jr., is cut from the same cloth. First elected in 1964, he has been a militant voice for racial justice who demands that the United States pay reparations to all descendants of slaves.[92] The *Congressional Quarterly*'s 1996 *Politics in America* described him as "sarcastic and abrasive," seemingly "less interested in becoming a power broker than in being a liberal voice of protest."[93]

Not all members of the CBC have Conyers's views or style, but they have tended to be markedly more ideological and racially militant than the typical black mayor. Part of the explanation may lie in the composition of the electorate that puts them in office. In early 1996, 82 percent of the African-American members of Congress—in contrast to 42 percent of the black mayors of cities of 25,000 or more—were elected by constituencies in which African Americans were a majority. The average congressional district that elected an African American was 56 percent black; the average city that voted a black mayor into office was only 42 percent black.[94] A fourteen-point difference, in other words, the result of which is that the many black candidates who seek the mayor's seat in majority-white cities are forced to fight for the white vote. And those who survive have the desire and ability to put together biracial or multiethnic coalitions—to reach across racial and ethnic lines. If it took a 56 percent black population concentration (the congressional district average) to elect an African-American mayor, the number presently occupying City Hall in cities of 25,000 or more would not be sixty-seven; it would be just twenty-one. In other words, the impressive black showing at the mayoral level has been possible only because black candidates have reached out to white voters.

Had black mayoral candidates been unwilling or unable to gather white support, there would have been many fewer African Americans elected, and in all likelihood, a much higher proportion with the ideological profile of most members of the CBC. For the majority-white settings that encourage biracial coalitions also encourage—as part of the same political package—a less racially strident style. By the same token, the constituency that is heavily black is likely to promote candidates whose main appeal is the stress they place on racial identity.[95]

Most of the districts sending blacks to Congress have, in fact, been heavily black—although Supreme Court decisions that declared unconstitutional some of those most obviously racially gerrymandered have altered the picture somewhat. Those decisions brought about a steep drop in the proportion of African-American members of Congress who came from majority-black districts in the 1996 elections, a fall from 82 percent to 62 percent.[96] But the typical black member of the House still had a considerably blacker constituency than the typical African-American mayor. Moreover, in the majority-black districts the real election has been the Democratic primary. And particularly in the South, where the GOP has attracted much of the white electorate, that's often an election in which relatively few whites participate.[97]

In the general election, too, it's black votes that count in the majority-black congressional districts. When the field has been reduced to, at most, two candidates, the competition for black ballots disappears and whites are marginalized. Nonpartisan mayoral runoffs will often pit two black candidates against one another, making whites the swing vote. But in partisan congressional races one Democrat runs either without opposition or against one (usually white) Republican, and in majority-black districts that means one black Democrat owns the seat. Incumbents are hard to beat, and in the safe black districts black incumbents are rarely challenged. In short, the electoral context matters. Most blacks in Congress—unlike mayors—have been secure; they've been elected largely by blacks; and have thus been free to pursue policies with a racially militant edge.

But if recent judicial decisions forcing less race-conscious districting turn many districts that were once majority-black into biracial playing fields, most of the candidates who run in them will likely become more centrist. (The exceptions will be those—like California Representative Ronald Dellums—whose constituency is majority-white but very liberal.) As Representative Charles Rangel, Democrat from New York, has suggested, it generally takes "a different kind of black politician to win in a majority or largely white district than in a majority black district."[98]

The racial composition of the average CBC district may not be the only reason its members have generally been politically left and racially militant. The job of a member of Congress is more ideological than that of a mayor; move a Michael White to Congress and he might sound different. Mayors are managers; they need to get the trash off the streets, and will be held accountable if they don't. They can't so easily afford the luxury of advocating policies that depress economic growth and send the middle class (black and white) scurrying to the suburbs. Their greater need for white support is thus only one part of the story. Voters who might go for a left-leaning African-American candidate for Congress may not be equally receptive to the standard liberal fare at the municipal level. Thus, in Detroit's 1993 mayoral election Dennis Archer, a business-oriented coalition-builder, did well among both whites and educated, employed blacks. Representative John Conyers, Jr., ran against him and got just 3 percent of the vote.[99] The man the city's voters were still willing to send to Congress was not even seriously considered when he went for the mayor's seat.

This is not to say that members of the Congressional Black Caucus are politically indistinguishable. Not only the racial composition of their districts, but the region makes a difference. It used to be that African Americans in Congress were mostly from the urban North. The southern membership of the CBC stood at six before the 1992 elections; by 1993, the number had risen to nineteen. The racially gerrymandered districts created after the 1990 census, in other words, had a dramatic impact; the caucus grew by almost 50 percent, with every one of the additional members from the South. Those southerners "have agricultural and rural interests that frequently put them on a collision course with assumed positions of the caucus," Representative Conyers has said. "We never had a problem with taking away tobacco subsidies before."[100]

Regional differences aside, it nevertheless remains the case that, as *Newsweek* reporter Howard Fineman noted in 1993, the Congressional Black Caucus "may be the only place on Capitol Hill where entitlements are still spoken of with reverence."[101]

POLITICAL DISSENT

The only deviations from the monolithically liberal stance of African Americans in Congress have been on the part of two Republicans, Gary Franks of Connecticut and J. C. Watts of Oklahoma. Franks was first elected in 1990, from a district less than 5 percent black, but was defeated in 1996; Watts arrived in 1994, elected by a district only 7 percent black. Their maverick politics put both at odds with the CBC, which Watts declined to join ("I didn't come to Congress to be a black leader or a white leader, but a leader," he said).[102] Franks became a member, but in the fall of 1993 was briefly barred from the weekly luncheon meetings—or rather told he could eat but not meet. He was allowed to participate in the group's deliberations only after a flurry of negative publicity threatened to turn a political nonconformist into a full-fledged martyr.[103]

The expectation of ideological conformity within the CBC—a conformity that the majority-black districts helped create—was revealed in a July 1993 "Open Letter" to Congressman Franks from Missouri representative William Clay. The letter charged that Franks had shown a "callous disregard for the basic rights and freedoms of thirty-five (35) million black Americans." His greatest crime, was his support for the appointment of Judge Clarence Thomas to the Supreme Court, which exposed "millions of individuals, mostly black and poor, . . . [to] the ravishes [*sic*] of now Supreme Court Justice Clarence Thomas's indecent, cynical, distorted vision of equal justice under law." [104]

In the aftermath of Franks's defeat in the November 1996 elections, Clay produced another open letter to Franks. This time he labeled him "a Negro Dr. Kevorkian" whose goal was "to maim and kill other blacks for the gratification and entertainment of . . . ultraconservative white racists." [105] Representative Clay's diatribes were unusually incoherent, illogical, and vicious, but his assumption that no member of the GOP could properly represent African Americans was shared by most members of the CBC. Their extraordinarily scarce numbers make black Republicans elected to office particularly vulnerable to the charge of being racially incorrect. As of 1996, according to data compiled by the Joint Center for Political and Economic Studies, only about 60 of the more than 8,000 black elected officials in the nation identified themselves as Republican. The only black Republicans holding statewide office were J. Kenneth Blackwell, the state treasurer in Ohio, and Victoria Buckley, secretary of state in Colorado. Out of the 550 black state legislators in the country, a mere 11 were Republican. [106]

Black Republican officeholders are not alone in being labeled, in effect, "white." It's an old smear tactic that has been used on many occasions. In 1964 members of the Congress for Racial Equality in Berkeley, California, attacked the local U.S. district attorney as a man who "used to be Negro." [107] Such invective seeped into campaigns for public office when blacks began to run in significant numbers and against one another. Thus in 1987, in the fight for the leadership of Chicago's black community following the death of Mayor Washington, a number of politically prominent African Americans branded Eugene Sawyer, chosen as acting mayor, an "Uncle Tom." [108] In Cleveland, Michael White's troubles didn't end when he won the mayoral election in 1989; critics dubbed him "White Mike." [109] In a 1993 race in Miami, the black candidate was known for his annual "Nigger of the Year" awards to those with whom he disagreed. [110] In the black-on-black mayoral race in Detroit the same year, Dennis Archer became the surrogate white in the contest for black votes; white suburbanites were "getting ready to take the city back" and had their candidate, his opponent warned. [111]

Such blacker-than-thou, not-one-of-us rhetoric works—or works in the right setting. As did whiter-than-thou charges in the Jim Crow South, where white racial moderates often found themselves labeled "Nigger-lovers." And for the same reasons. Rallying 'round the racial flag feeds on racial distrust—of which there is always plenty, a subject to which we will return in Chapter 17.

THE POLITICS OF BLACK VOTERS

Black allegiance to the Democratic Party—across social classes—has been extremely stable since 1964. In presidential elections, at least five out of six African-American voters have cast their ballots for the Democratic candidate.[112] Furthermore, fewer than 10 percent of blacks identify themselves as Republican.[113]

Nevertheless, Democratic candidates cannot take black support absolutely for granted. Black support for GOP presidential candidates has been quite unwaveringly low, but that is not the case when it comes to congressional races. Thus, in 1990, 21 percent of black voters (a record high) cast their ballots for Republicans running for House seats. That's an average; some individual GOP candidates have done better. For instance, Senator John Danforth got 27 percent of the black vote in Missouri in 1988, while Senator Richard Lugar picked up 25 percent of the black vote in Indiana that same year. In 1990, 24 percent of African Americans in Texas supported Phil Gramm, and in 1992, 30 percent cast their ballots for Arlen Specter in Pennsylvania.[114]

Black defectors from the Democratic Party have helped white Republicans running for state or local offices as well. New Jersey's governor Thomas Kean was reelected in 1985 with an extraordinary 62 percent of the black vote.[115] In 1993 in that same state 25 percent of the black electorate went for Christine Todd Whitman in the gubernatorial race, and one year later George Voinovich was elected governor of Ohio with 42 percent of the state's black vote.[116] The Democratic National Committee brought the Reverend Jesse Jackson to Jersey City to help defeat mayoral candidate Bret Schundler in 1993. But 40 percent of the black vote, nonetheless, went to the Republican.[117]

When black voters cast their ballots for a Thomas Kean or a John Danforth, it makes news. And yet it has long been a bit of a puzzle why more African Americans are not attracted to the GOP. The Joint Center's January 1996 survey found that 31 percent of blacks identified themselves as liberals, 32 percent as moderates, and 30 percent as conservatives (most of the latter "Christian" conservatives). A year earlier Gallup had asked blacks whether they thought the political views of the Republican Party too conservative, too liberal, or just about right. Only 53 percent said "too conservative."[118] Those findings are not surprising: polling data indicate that on a number of issues, substantial numbers of blacks favor "Republican" policies. For instance, in the 1996 Joint Center poll, 76 percent of black respondents favored a constitutional amendment allowing prayer in public schools; 49 percent wanted no benefit increases for single mothers on welfare who had additional children; 48 percent supported school vouchers; and a whopping 73 percent were enthusiastic about "three strikes and you're out" laws that sentence to life imprisonment violent criminals convicted of a third offense.[119]

Conservatism on significant social issues, however, does not translate into political support for conservative candidates. Part of the reason is surely the fact that on other questions, blacks live up to their reputation as liberal Democrats. For instance, asked in the fall of 1995 whether they thought "that the federal government can do something to help those African Americans with severe problems," 70 percent of blacks said yes, whereas only 38 percent of whites agreed. In 1994, on the issue of government assistance to blacks, 74 percent of African Americans but only 16 percent of whites said too little was being spent. There is also a marked racial divide on questions such as: Would you rather have the federal government provide more services, even if it means more in taxes? Is it the responsibility of government to reduce the differences in income between people? And, do you agree that the government has an obligation to help people when they're in trouble?[120] The affirmative action issue likewise splits blacks and whites—to different degrees, depending on how the question is asked.[121]

A high degree of commitment to an expansive, protective federal government clearly separates blacks from whites. The historic sense of vulnerability continues to affect black political attitudes. Even the middle class views its hard-won status as fragile, with the consequence that individual blacks see their own fate as tied to that of the race, the political scientist Michael Dawson has persuasively argued. In believing that the fate of the race depends on the helping hand of government—that only its forceful presence keeps the enemies of racial justice at bay—most blacks remain in the Democratic camp. Whites are all over the political map; blacks disagree among themselves, but generally vote left. "The perceived economic domination of blacks by whites became intertwined with a sense of political domination as well," Dawson has suggested.[122]

Perhaps it is the status anxiety of African Americans and their unshakable commitment to big government and the Democratic Party that frees black elected officials (to an unusual degree) from concern about the views of their constituents. In the jockeying over the 1994 crime bill, when the CBC was working hard to soften hard-line provisions like mandatory minimum sentences, at least one member admitted that his "soft on crime" approach wasn't necessarily that of his constituents. On the other hand, he said, "I would no more go to my constituents and ask how I would wage a war on crime than I would ask how I should wage a war internationally."[123]

It was a refreshingly candid admission. White liberals who need black votes assiduously court them; black liberals need to worry less about taking stands their constituents agree with. In the summer of 1994, the CBC (with the exception of Ronald Dellums and Gary Franks) pushed hard for an invasion of Haiti, although their own constituents weren't with them. In a survey taken in July only 21 percent of the black respondents said they supported sending in troops.[124] The black leadership was eager for action, but clearly had no mandate for military action from its own constituents. Apparently that didn't matter; they could count on incumbency and racial solidarity to provide political cover.

The strong allegiance of African-American voters to the Democratic Party does not mean that black Democrats always stick together. In the 1991 Chicago mayoral race, for instance, the white incumbent, Richard M. Daley, carried 26 percent of the black vote, even though his opponent was an African American running on the Harold Washington party line. That same year, Edward Rendell (white) became mayor of Philadelphia after he took 20 percent of the black vote in a Democratic primary in which there were three black candidates.[125] Seven years earlier New Orleans voters casting their ballots in a congressional district that was 55 percent black, had chosen Representative Lindy Boggs over a serious black candidate; black turnout was higher than white, but Boggs was a trusted incumbent, endorsed by a wide variety of black organizations.[126]

Boggs had found her black support both in housing projects (where her staff held office hours) and in upscale black neighborhoods in New Orleans. In 1990, Donald Mintz, a white mayoral candidate in that same majority-black city, was not a popular incumbent and managed to win only 14 percent of the total African-American vote. But in the more affluent black precincts, his black support went as high as 39 percent.[127] Social class, in other words, can send black Democratic voters heading in quite different political directions. That's particularly apparent in all-black contests. Again, New Orleans (with its long history of sharp color stratification within the black community) illustrates the point. In the city's 1986 mayoral race, state senator William Jefferson was said to have been the choice of low-income and dark-skinned blacks, while Sidney Barthelemy, himself very light, attracted middle-class Creoles.[128] Likewise, in the 1981 Atlanta mayoral race Andrew Young appealed to the solid black middle class, while Reginald Eaves, also African American, was the candidate of the less economically secure.[129] In the summer of 1994, Marion Barry, the former mayor of Washington, D.C., was back out on the hustings with a carefully scripted ("Son of a Sharecropper") appeal to class. He won, despite his lack of support from the well-heeled, black and white.[130]

It's not class alone that splits the black vote. In ethnically complex cities like New York, whites have never been one group. Working-class Catholics in Queens have little in common with Manhattan's Upper West Side Jews, and those Jews don't share much with their ultra-Orthodox brethren in Brooklyn. By now the black "community" is also ethnically fragmented. Racial incidents will still unite black voters—behind the candidacy of Mayor Dinkins in 1993, for instance. But even in that election, significant differences simmered beneath the surface consensus. "West Indian blacks in Flatbush and Crown

Heights," a reporter noted at the time, ". . . consider themselves politically and culturally distinct from American-born blacks one neighborhood over in Bedford-Stuyvesant." New York politics have become "post black-white."[131] Even among the American-born, all is not politically harmonious. Admirers of the demagogic style of an Al Sharpton are not likely to lick envelopes for conventional black politicians running for the city council.[132] In New York and elsewhere, if Louis Farrakhan and other black Muslims enter the electoral arena, they are likely to further divide the African-American vote.

WHEN BLACK CANDIDATES LOSE

Differences among black voters can spell trouble for black candidates; competition can sink them all. For example, in the 1989 Chicago mayoral race two African-American candidates split the black vote and turned that black-run city over to a white, Richard M. Daley, "Son of Boss" (Daley), as the reporters had dubbed him five years earlier.[133] But most often when black candidates don't win, the reason is whites voting for whites. Needed white votes aren't there. And when that happens, the explanation most commonly given is white racism.

Which means what? The answer is not obvious. Take the 1982 California gubernatorial race between Tom Bradley and George Deukmejian. Bradley, the black mayor of Los Angeles lost—by a whisker. (The margin for Deukmejian was 93,000 votes out of 7.8 million cast.) Some called it "racism as usual."[134] Voters who swung to Deukmejian at the last minute, California Assembly speaker Willie Brown said, were driven by a "great fear of anything that is different from what is considered WASP."[135]

In fact, Bradley did stunningly well, polling 48 percent of the vote in a state that was only 7 percent black, and winning nearly 3 million white votes. But neither blacks nor whites saw Bradley as a black candidate, polling data suggested, and low black turnout cost him the election.[136] His race, per se, had not generated the enthusiastic black turnout that he needed. In addition, he had a problem with white voters: he was viewed as a liberal Democrat, which was not to his advantage.[137] Four years earlier California voters had passed a cap on property tax in the state, and a year after that they had voted to amend the state constitution to stop all busing for purposes of school integration. In 1982 they didn't go either for Bradley or for Jerry Brown (running for the U.S. Senate). Nor did they back handgun control, also on the ballot, favored by Bradley, and important in drawing conservatives to the polls.

More than 20 percent of white Democratic voters did defect from their party, but that was not a particularly telling number. In his two successful gubernatorial runs Jerry Brown's Democratic support had been similarly weak. Moreover, Pat Brown had lost considerably more Democratic votes when he was defeated by Ronald Reagan in the 1966 gubernatorial race.

Political convictions that defeat a black candidate are not necessarily racist.[138] The failure to distinguish the one from the other marred much of the discussion not only of the Bradley race but of New York's 1993 mayoral election as well. Even before 3 November the contest between David Dinkins and Rudolph Giuliani had been declared race-driven. In campaigning for Dinkins in September, President Clinton had charged that many New Yorkers are "still too unwilling to vote for people who are different than we are." [139] Dinkins's loss was indeed noteworthy; he was alone among black mayors of big cities in having been tossed out of office after only one term. But the president's view was both a rush to judgment and a warped view of the electorate.

As it turned out, most whites did cast their ballots against Dinkins. But was that fact alone "a stark reminder" of the importance of race, as a *New York Times* reporter, among others, argued? [140] "Race prevailed over reason . . . party and . . . voter tradition," Jesse Jackson alleged.[141] His was one important voice in a large chorus. "Unfortunately, the numbers are quite clear," the principal of a Brooklyn public high school remarked. "This has been a referendum on race." [142] And yet, while color had clearly been the first consideration among African-American voters, roughly one out of four whites had stuck with the mayor, and those who did not had plenty of reasons other than race for choosing Giuliani. Dinkins had been tried and found wanting, survey data suggested. In a *New York Times*/WCBS-TV poll taken just before the November election, 59 percent of New Yorkers said life in the city had gotten worse on the mayor's watch, and only 8 percent thought it had improved.[143] The city was on the economic skids; its streets, subways, and parks were not safe; a sense of civil disorder was pervasive, and the old formulas, to which Dinkins was wedded, no longer worked. In addition—and perhaps most important—the mayor had managed, as columnist Jim Sleeper wrote, "to deepen racial and other differences in the name of respecting them . . ." [144]

Some argued that Dinkins had been held to an unfairly high standard.[145] Jesse Jackson was sure that Dinkins "did everything required of a candidate seeking re-election." [146] But what was "required"? By what objective measures are politicians legitimately judged? Did Marion Barry, who could hardly be called a model mayor, "deserve" his reelection after a stint in jail?

Race undoubtedly played some part in the outcome in New York; in a variety of ways, Dinkins himself made color an issue. But where race still plays a role, it is usually but one element in a subtle, complicated picture, and its impact is hard to judge. That has become true even of races in the Deep South. For instance, in the 1990 gubernatorial race in Georgia, the lieutenant governor, Zell Miller, trounced Andrew Young in the Democratic primary. That was no picture-perfect, racially polarized contest, however. In a crowded primary field Miller won roughly 20 percent of the black vote in Atlanta (although Young had been the city's mayor), and was endorsed by three black Georgia state senators. In other respects as well, Young was at a political disadvantage. He failed to get the support of U.S. Representative John Lewis, black and highly respected; his reputation as a mayor had been tarnished by an explosion of crime and Miller had proposed a state lottery, a popular idea.[147]

WHERE RACE MATTERS

In New York, California, and even Georgia, skin color seems to have taken a backseat to other issues in these elections. But obviously there are contests in which race does figure prominently. Some voters turn to race as a "cue" when black and white candidates are either equally appealing or equally unknown.[148] Race is also clearly a factor in those now very rare elections in which explicit racial appeals are made. David Duke's campaigns for the U.S. Senate in 1990 and in 1991 for the Louisiana governor's seat are the obvious examples. A one-time Klan leader, a Nazi sympathizer, and the founder of the National Association for the Advancement of White People, Duke ran (in effect) against black citizens and the white Democrats for whom they voted.

There are no other David Dukes in the 1990s, however. In the 1983 Chicago mayoral race, Bernard Epton ran unsuccessfully against Harold Washington with a racially charged slogan: "Epton for Mayor. Before It's Too Late." His followers sang "Bye Bye Blackbird" at rallies and sported buttons featuring a crossed-out watermelon. He thus had a reprehensible slogan and a racist following. Nevertheless, Epton was no former Nazi. Yet, like Duke's, his campaign made news precisely because that sort of racism had become so unusual. Moreover, it was the last mayoral race of its kind in the city; by 1989 the leading white candidate, Richard M. Daley, was working hard to attract black votes.

Racist campaigns have almost entirely disappeared because they cost votes. In Chicago, Epton's loss was followed five years later by that of the white Republican candidate for the recorder of deeds in Cook County (Chicago). He had asked reporters to "just run a picture" of his black opponent, Carol Moseley-Braun—a request to which voters did not respond kindly.[149] Likewise, in the New Orleans mayoral race in 1994, the white candidate, Donald Mintz, used (but probably did not create) anti-black and anti-Semitic fliers. In the waning days of the campaign, those fliers galvanized black votes that tipped the balance against him.[150]

Explicitly racist campaigns—blatant appeals to antiblack prejudice—are out. But what about references to controversial public policies that involve race? In North Carolina in 1990 the former mayor of Charlotte, Harvey Gantt, made a bid for the U.S. Senate seat held for eighteen years by Jesse Helms.

Helms had been behind in the polls until mid-October, when he began to run racially charged advertisements that raised his ratings. One of the ads showed a pair of white hands crumpling a job notice while an off screen voice said, "They had to give your job to a minority." Another charged that Gantt had used "his office and minority status" to make a $450,000 profit on a $679 investment in a television station license that was then sold to a white corporation. It was the last that seems to have been the real killer. Labeled "racist" by Helm's opponents, it was in fact accurate.

The television spot that linked the Democratic candidate to affirmative action employment preferences got a great deal of national attention, and was indeed questionable. On the other hand, whether it made a difference to the outcome is doubtful. Gantt was an unabashed liberal in a relatively conservative state. He refused to come out against an increase in the tax on cigarettes, a North Carolina staple; he opposed the death penalty, was pro-choice, and hedged on the question of tough sentencing for drug dealers and other criminal offenders.[151] In addition, Helms was a tough man to beat. In 1984 his white Democratic opponent had done a mere 1 percent better than Gantt did in 1990, even though he was a former governor who had won his gubernatorial races with huge margins.

More often the subject of race is raised more subtly, as Cleveland mayor Michael R. White observed in 1992. "You hear code words like welfare, crime, drugs, and unwed mothers in the inner city. . . ."[152] In other words, "crime" (surely an issue worthy of debate) is a "code word" for blacks—and as such, out of bounds. In Mayor White's view, a great many important topics are off-limits. To discuss them is to appeal to prejudice at a time when explicit racism is off-limits.[153]

Code words are thus said to be "rhetorical winks" that have allowed a variety of candidates—for instance, Barry Goldwater, with his talk of states' rights—to play on white racial resentment. A willingness to exploit racial resentment, it is charged, was also central to the 1988 campaign of George Bush for president. Bush won the backing of racially conservative whites through coded appeals—most notably, the two "Willie Horton" ads attacking Michael Dukakis as soft on crime. One showed convicts moving through a revolving door, but with a picture sufficiently grainy as to make the men racially unidentifiable. The other—not produced by the Bush campaign itself, but by an independent Republican activist named Floyd Brown—had a mug shot of Horton, who was black.[154]

Horton was a Massachusetts prison inmate, convicted of murder and sentenced to life in prison, who was nevertheless granted a weekend furlough in 1986. On that weekend out, he broke into a house, pistol-whipped a man at home, sliced him twenty times with a knife, and tied him up in the basement. When the victim's fiancée arrived at the house, Horton tied her up and raped her twice. Dukakis was governor at the time, and had vetoed a bill that would have ended the furlough program. After this appalling incident, he had refused to meet with Horton's victims. The Bush campaign did not pull the story out of a bag of dirty tricks, as frequently alleged; the Lawrence, Massachusetts, newspaper had run it right after Horton was captured in Maryland. Although Democrats denounced it as racist when employed by Republicans, the name of Willie Horton was actually first used as a club against Michael Dukakis by none other than Senator Al Gore, running in New York as a Democratic contender in the 1988 primaries.

The Willie Horton ads were thus factually sound, and they raised a serious policy issue: the risks to the public that furlough programs entail. Nevertheless, the racial identification of Horton in the Floyd Brown ad improperly played on deep popular fears linking blacks with crime, and thus reinforced a stereotype that had no place in political discourse. Democrats, of course, said precisely that—at ever possible opportunity. In fact, the ads were still an issue in the 1996 presidential season, often referred to in the media. The Willie Horton story is so often cited as an example of the indelible racism of white America, and yet clearly Democrats have calculated that they gain more than they lose by reminding the public of the sort of racially inflammatory ad that a GOP activist was willing to run in 1988. Apparently they believe that white revulsion against negative racial stereotypes is greater than white fears of black crime. It is one more sign of heartening racial change.

VISIBLE MEN AND WOMEN

"An invisible man" is what Ralph Ellison called himself. Whites who stared in his direction saw "surroundings, themselves, or figments of their imagination —indeed, everything and anything except me," he wrote in his 1952 classic. The problem was the "peculiar disposition of the eyes . . . their *inner* eyes . . ."[155]

What the *inner* eyes of whites see today is of course open to debate. But we have tried in the preceding chapters—in Part II of this book—to draw a picture both more nuanced and more accurate than is usually found in the media and in the literature on race. We opened Part II with "the rise of the black middle class" and we close with, in effect, "the rise of the black political class." Too often, blacks are viewed as down and out—impoverished, uneducated, caught in central cities, where life is short and mean. On the outskirts of American society—economically and politically. It's much too crude a picture.

Blacks participate—often decisively—in elections; had Colin Powell chosen to run, we might well have inaugurated our first African-American president in January 1997. The black underclass often seems to define black America, but less than one-fifth of African-Americans are actually poverty-stricken residents of central cities, and (contrary to conventional wisdom) almost all get a high school diploma. Median family income for black married couples is now only 13 percent below that of white couples; half of all black families have incomes that are at least double the poverty line. Almost no adult black men with full-time jobs are destitute, and the substantial black middle class that has emerged since 1940 is passing on its status to the next generation. Moreover, the dire prediction of the Kerner Commission report —a growing gulf between white suburbs and black inner cities—was off the mark. Not only has residential segregation declined in most big cities; 30 percent of the black population lived in suburbs by 1994. Both in cities and suburbs there remains a great deal of racial clustering, but not primarily for the reason that so long separated whites and blacks: simple racial bias.

There is, of course, bad news as well as good, as Chapters 9 and 10 should have made clear. Most blacks are not poor, and most of America's poor are not black. Nevertheless, nearly a third of African Americans are still impoverished, a consequence in large measure of the number of single-parent black families. A social pattern with devastating economic consequences has become the norm in the black community; in 1995, 85 percent of black children in poverty lived in households with no father present. In addition, since the 1960s, crime rates have been surging in the black community, particularly among young black males. In fact, no issue so poisons relations between the races as that of black crime. But the real victims of black crime are blacks, not whites—often black youth. The leading killer of young black males is young black males.

Some whites do still turn blacks into "figments of their imagination"— thinking "crime" when they see a well-dressed young black male, for instance. And they imagine African Americans as a looming presence in their midst. Asked in 1990 "what percent of the American population today would you say is black?" the median response was 32 percent.[156] But in part, that rather amazing answer is surely a result of the racial consciousness that has come from unprecedented concern about the status of black Americans. In the past few decades a sustained and deliberate effort has been made to pull blacks into the cultural, economic, and political mainstream—to erase the historic distinction between visible whites and invisible blacks. Beautiful black women now routinely grace upscale Bloomingdale's ads in the *New York Times;* MIT and other universities have special programs for minority entrepreneurs; a 1994 national survey of firms with at least one hundred workers found that 56 percent provided "diversity" training; and President Clinton in his first term, having vowed to have a cabinet that "looked like America," appointed blacks to head the Departments of Commerce, Agriculture, Energy, and Veterans' Affairs.[157]

Paradoxically, such heightened visibility helps to make African Americans invisible—but in quite a different sense than Ralph Ellison had in mind four and a half decades ago. Ronald H. Brown was secretary of commerce in the Clinton administration until he was killed when his plane went down in Bosnia. Accompanying him on that fateful trip in April 1996 were twelve American industrial leaders; on trips to Japan, Brazil, Africa, and elsewhere, a seat on Ron Brown's plane had become "one of the most coveted perks of the Clinton Administration," *Time* reported.[158] However he saw himself, clearly in the view of those who jockeyed for a place by his side, Ron Brown was a man of power and charm—not a *black* man who (incidentally) had those qualities.[159] Likewise, had General Powell entered the presidential fray, it seems unlikely that most white voters would have looked at him and seen "black."

And yet if some African Americans are now perceived as individuals—Ralph Ellison's wish come true—consciousness of blacks as a distinctive group still runs very high on both sides of the racial divide. In Part III we will argue that that has been one of the regrettable results of public policies that stress racial identity. In pre–civil rights days, in the South particularly, ugly racial rhetoric was rampant; the rhetoric has changed, white racial attitudes have changed, but there is still too much ugliness in the way both blacks and whites think about racial issues. Policies grounded in a great deal of goodwill, we believe, have not generated further goodwill. Indeed, some polling evidence suggests quite the opposite. "It is unfortunately . . . true that a number of whites dislike the idea of affirmative action so much and perceive it to be so unfair that they have come to dislike blacks as a consequence," Paul M. Sniderman and Thomas Piazza found in an analysis of public opinion surveys. "Hence the special irony of the contemporary politics of race. In the very effort to make things better, we have made some things worse. . . . Wishing to close the racial divide in America, we have widened it," they concluded.[160]

If Sniderman and Piazza are right, if the affirmative action policies that are in place today have in fact further polarized the races, we must ask what exactly they have accomplished. Much progress in the status of blacks occurred in the years from 1940 to 1970, in the pre–affirmative action era. There has been no progress since then in reducing black poverty, for instance. By other measures, life for African Americans has continued to improve, but can we credit that ongoing change to race-conscious programs? That is the central question that runs through our discussion of public policy in Part III.

PART THREE

Equality and Preferences: The Changing Racial Climate

CHAPTER TWELVE

With All Deliberate Speed

IT WAS IN 1968 that Sam Fulwood—then in sixth grade and attending an all-black elementary school in Charlotte, North Carolina—was told that he had been picked by the principal to integrate the town's white junior high school. It wasn't welcome news. He realized something was wrong, he wrote many years later when he had become a Washington, D.C. correspondent for the *Los Angeles Times*. "It was more serious than having to stay after school for running down the halls. . . . Mrs. Cunningham was redirecting my life, suggesting I go to a WHITE junior high school. I had been looking forward to going to Northwest Junior High, where some of my friends were already in seventh grade. . . . I wanted to be with my friends. This was no honor. . . . It was a disaster."

Fulwood's life, he realized, was no longer entirely his own. Mrs. Cunningham "was conscripting me on behalf of all colored people."[1] Fourteen years after the decision in *Brown v. Board of Education*, it was time to end the segregation of Charlotte's schoolchildren, and Fulwood was an unwilling conscript in the fight for racial justice. Nineteen sixty-eight was in fact a watershed year, and not just in Charlotte. On the United States Supreme Court as well, it had become time to act decisively. Patience with southern white racism had finally worn thin. Fourteen years after *Brown*, the Court that had once believed in "all deliberate speed"—the gradual and cautious enforcement of a fundamental constitutional right—had grown weary of the resistance that it had, itself, partly invited. The Court's pent-up frustration did lead to significant changes in the law, and the consequence was much more interracial contact in the schools. But there was a cost. Fulwood had been tapped by the principal in his own school—but with his parents' approval. In subsequent years, however, thousands of other children—both black and white—would find themselves assigned by federal courts to schools neither they nor their families had chosen.

A 1995 survey of 103 urban school districts found that 45 percent were under court order to maintain racially balanced schools; for the large districts the figure was 69 percent. And many more had voluntarily adopted some sort of desegregation program.[2] The results have been decidedly mixed. In many cities outside the South, the schools are as "segregated" as they ever were, although not of course by law—an important distinction too often ignored. In many communities, in fact, racial balancing efforts provoked huge numbers of middle-class parents (both black and white) either to move to the suburbs or to transfer their children to private and parochial schools, sending the urban school systems they left behind into a spiral of decline.

DESEGREGATION AT A SNAIL'S PACE

At a press conference after the *Brown* decision, Thurgood Marshall, the head of the NAACP's Legal Defense Fund, was asked how long he thought it would take to eliminate segregation in the public schools. "Up to five years," he replied, "for the entire country."[3]

In 1959, five years after *Brown*, the battle over school desegregation had barely begun. The southern states that required separate schools for black and white students proved to be far more stubborn than Marshall anticipated. And, in dealing with that resistance, the Supreme Court turned out to be much more cautious than he had expected. Fearful of getting too far ahead of white opinion and losing the moral authority upon which public acceptance of its decisions depended, the Court was careful not to press for too much change too soon. When the Court had spelled out its plan to implement the *Brown* decision—in *Brown II* a year later—it had called for "all deliberate speed," but had left the concrete interpretation of that formula to judges in federal district courts who owed their appointments to their political connections in the Jim Crow South.

In practice, "all deliberate speed" entailed endless deliberation and no speed at all. In 1962, eight full years after the initial ruling, not a single black pupil attended a white public school anywhere in Mississippi, Alabama, or South Carolina. By then, black children who had been mere fourth-graders at the time of *Brown* had gone all the way through high school without ever having had any white classmates![4]

Deep South states like Alabama and Mississippi were certainly recalcitrant, but so too was Virginia, the one southern state that actually closed down its public schools for a time to prevent desegregation from proceeding, re-opening them only when compelled to do so by a federal court order. In the eleven ex-Confederate states as a whole, a mere *1.2 percent* of black public school students attended schools that had any white pupils at all during the 1963–1964 school year.[5] Considerable progress toward desegregation was made in the Border states, where the decision did not provoke as much passionate resentment. But in what had been Confederate territory a century earlier, *Brown* seemed never to have happened. Since the black birth rate was high enough to more than offset the slight decline in segregation, the number of southern black children who were attending Jim Crow schools was actually greater in 1964 than it had been in 1954.[6] Desegregation, said one observer, was proceeding with "the pace of an extraordinarily arthritic snail."[7]

If southern school authorities had wanted to comply with *Brown*, the obvious solution would have been simply to adopt a system of geographic zoning —to assign all pupils in the district to the school nearest them regardless of race. Since black and white residences were not strictly segregated from each other in the typical southern community, that rule would have produced racially mixed student bodies in most schools. Not racially balanced student bodies, though. Few neighborhoods were evenly balanced between the two races, and few schools would therefore have been racially balanced. There would, in other words, have been much de facto "segregation."

Such neighborhood assignments, leaving many schools racially imbalanced as a consequence of residential patterns, would have been acceptable to the courts and the NAACP at the time of *Brown* and for many years after. In his oral argument in the case Thurgood Marshall had said that plaintiffs sought an order barring schools from assigning pupils to schools on the basis of race; school authorities could draw district lines on what he referred to as "a natural basis"—by which he meant along neighborhood lines.[8] In spelling out what it expected in its 1955 implementation decision, the Supreme Court called for "a revision of school districts and attendance areas into compact areas to achieve a system of determining admission to the public schools on a nonracial basis."[9] A few years later one of Thurgood Marshall's chief legal aides, Jack Greenberg, declared that if there were "complete freedom of choice, or geographical zoning, or any other nonracial standard, and all the Negroes still ended up in separate schools, there would seem to be no constitutional objection."[10]

By the late 1960s, however, that was water under the constitutional bridge. Few southern school authorities had chosen to comply with the law. Instead of abolishing their dual school systems and assigning pupils to the nearest schools, they typically made only the most minimal and grudging gestures toward desegregation, inviting much more aggressive judicial intervention than otherwise would likely have been the case. For example, they adopted pupil placement laws that theoretically assigned children to particular schools on the basis of such vague, nonracial factors as "the suitability of established curricula," the "adequacy of the pupil's preparation," and the possibility that the assignment would result in "breaches of the peace or ill will" within the community.[11] (The latter criterion meant that if any whites strongly objected to having blacks in a school, it was necessary to abide by their wishes rather than incur their "ill will.") When all these "factors" had been weighed, school authorities (not surprisingly) almost invariably ended up sending children to the same single-race schools they had attended before.

After such evasive tactics were thrown out by lower federal courts in the early 1960s, many southern jurisdictions adopted "freedom of choice" plans, another "desegregation" scheme that in most instances changed little. In theory, these plans allowed parents to choose their children's school, but in fact almost no whites selected a "black school," and perhaps more surprising, only a handful of black parents picked a "white school." The typical southern school therefore remained as racially identifiable under "freedom of choice" as it had been in the days of Jim Crow.

Why did so many black parents opt to keep their children racially isolated when they were formally free to choose others? The NAACP did not speak for all black parents on this issue—or even for all members of the black cultural and political elite. The distinguished African-American writer Zora Neale Hurston refused to cheer for "a court order for somebody to associate with me who does not wish me near them." Hurston rejected as false and demeaning what she took to be the premise underlying Brown—that black children required the presence of white people in order to learn—and saw the decision as "insulting rather than honoring" her race.[12] Public opinion polls show that only about half—53 percent—of all southern blacks approved of the Court's action.[13]

The 47 percent of southern blacks who disapproved presumably preferred the all-black schools where the students were protected from virulent white racism. And among the 53 percent who backed the Court's decision, many must have been reluctant to offer their children as guinea pigs in the new racial order. Sam Fulwood's parents, in other words, were not necessarily typical even in the late 1960s. There was also the fact that in the years just preceding Brown, school authorities in the South had begun to pour money into black schools in hopes of keeping the Supreme Court at bay. Between 1940 and 1954, per-pupil expenditures on southern black schools nearly tripled (in constant dollars), ten times the rate of increase in spending for white schools.[14] The huge disparities between white and black schools in class size, teacher pay, and school facilities had been largely eliminated by the mid-1950s. Furthermore, in most states all the teachers in those schools were African-American. Given white racial attitudes, it was reasonable to fear that those teachers would lose out in the competition for jobs in integrated schools.[15]

School integration thus proceeded at a glacial pace. White resistance, a Supreme Court seldom willing to speak, the power of southern judges on federal district courts, the ambivalence of many black parents: it was a combination that made for a decade of inaction. A few events did force the High Court to take a stand—most notably the crisis in Little Rock, Arkansas, in the fall of 1957. But the first truly important post-Brown decision did not come until 1964. *Griffin v. County School Board* involved Prince Edward County, Virginia, whose white citizens had gone to the extraordinary lengths of voting to close down all public schools rather than keep them open on a nonracial basis.[16] Their children did not stay home, however; they attended "segregation academies," which were at once private and yet largely publicly funded. Local black families, on the other hand, were left to fend for themselves, and their children received essentially no formal education for the five long years in which the case meandered down the judicial road.[17] But in 1964 the High Court finally put its foot down. "There has been entirely too much deliberation and not enough speed," it said—an overdue statement that had obvious implications far beyond the immediate locality.[18] It ordered the county to open desegregated public schools.

The story in Prince Edward County had become a national outrage by the time the Court heard the case, and that helped to explain its willingness to act so decisively. What is more, by 1964 the Court was not waging a lonely battle against Jim Crow. The civil rights struggle had moved to center stage, and both Congress and the White House were deeply involved. With powerful new allies in both of the other branches of the federal government, the Court could act with much greater vigor and dispatch.

FROM DESEGREGATION TO INTEGRATION

Congressional action against segregated schools and other Jim Crow institutions had been out of the question in 1954; the Court had been quite alone. But ten years later Congress passed the first of two monumental civil rights statutes, and two provisions of the 1964 Civil Rights Act particularly affected education. Title IV empowered the Department of Health, Education, and Welfare to assist school districts in devising and implementing desegregation plans. Recalcitrant districts that were not making progress on the desegregation front could be sued by the Department of Justice.[19] The NAACP had limited resources; after 1964 the deep pockets of the federal government financed complaints against school authorities. Many more cases could be fought and won.

In addition, Title VI of the Civil Rights Act made school districts and other institutions that engaged in racial discrimination ineligible for federal funds. This seemed a peripheral provision, because in 1964 the federal government still put little money into education. But the 1965 Elementary and Secondary Education Act changed the picture radically. Under the ESEA, for example, Mississippi qualified for more federal education dollars than the *total* the state had spent to operate all of its schools in 1963. For the South as a whole, annual federal educational expenditures quintupled between the 1963–1964 and 1971–1972 school years, rising from $2.7 billion to $14.7 billion.[20] Control of billions of dollars a year in new federal funds gave Washington officials powerful new leverage to use in pressing for desegregation; districts that practiced discrimination got no money.

But which districts were discriminating? In the administrative guidelines that the Department of Health, Education, and Welfare issued in 1965, the definition of discrimination was the traditional one: it meant assigning pupils on the basis of race. That definition squared with the language of Title IV, whose section 401(b) defined desegregation as "the assignment of students to public schools and within such schools without regard to their race, color, religion, or national origin." The law explicitly stated that desgegregation did not require pupil placements designed to "overcome racial imbalance."

Nevertheless, a second set of guidelines issued only a year later ignored the clear injunction against equating racial imbalance with segregation. HEW now insisted that districts would be ineligible for federal funds absent evidence of "substantial" desegregation—as measured by the percentage of minority students who were attending majority-white schools.[21] The agency had the authority to implement the 1964 statute, but the new guidelines it set forth assumed that desegregation might actually require something that the statutory language had expressly prohibited: the assignment of students to schools on the basis of their race.

The distinction between desegregation and racial integration was thus obliterated. The test of whether the schools were "open to children of all races" became whether they were actually attended by children of all races in roughly equal proportions. A simple body count could thus reveal which districts were in compliance with the mandate to desegregate and which were not. It was not a minor change. The HEW guidelines served not only to pressure local communities seeking access to federal educational funds, but had an impact as well on federal courts, which treated administrative regulations as equivalent to legislative acts and thus embraced HEW's unauthorized redefinition of desegregation.[22]

The Supreme Court ratified this radically new understanding in two key decisions in 1968 and 1971. *Green v. School Board of New Kent County* (1968) struck down a freedom-of-choice pupil assignment plan that was in use in a tiny rural county in Virginia. New Kent had barely 1,300 students and only two schools. Traditionally one had been for whites, the other for blacks, but in 1965 the county had removed the racial labels and formally opened both schools to any applicant, prompted largely by the desire for the new federal money that was contingent upon a desegregation plan.

New Kent, like many rural counties in the South, was residentially integrated; black-owned farms were interspersed with those held by whites. The population was about half black, and had the county simply drawn attendance zones around each of the two schools, both would have ended up racially mixed. The freedom-of-choice plan, however, left integration up to the decision of individual parents, and not a single white pupil chose to attend the formerly black school. A substantial minority of blacks did enroll in the formerly white school, making it 83 percent white, but 85 percent of the county's black students remained in the same all-black school they had once been forced to attend.[23] Moreover, that was where all the black teachers—and none who were white—taught.

Had New Kent County made enough progress toward desegregation to satisfy the Constitution? And was the chosen means of dismantling the dual school system—that previously imposed by law—adequate? By the standard of *Brown* the answer to both questions was probably yes. Although one school was still 100 percent black, it was not because local law required it to be. On the other hand, fourteen years had gone by since the original desegregation mandate, and the South had dragged its feet so long resisting even the mildest of school desegregation measures that the small step forward in New Kent County seemed too little, too late.

It is not coincidental that the Supreme Court handed down the *Green* opinion, the most important school decision since *Brown,* in the spring of 1968, in the midst of what seemed an unprecedented racial crisis. Less than two months earlier the Reverend Martin Luther King, Jr., had been assassinated, triggering another massive wave of riots in the nation's cities. Only a few days before King died, the Kerner Commission had issued its scorching report, which denounced "white racism" and predicted that the United States would have to endure many more long, hot, and bloody summers unless much greater efforts were made to integrate black Americans into the life of the nation.

The Court's unanimous opinion in *Green* seemed to bear the stamp of these events. The time for "mere 'deliberate speed' " had "run out," the Court said. It was not enough for the county authorities to throw open "the doors of the former 'white' school to Negro children and of the 'Negro' school to white children," and then let families make whatever educational choices they wished. The *Brown II* decision, which specified how *Brown* was to be implemented, had placed upon local authorities "an affirmative duty to take whatever steps might be necessary to convert to a unitary system in which racial discrimination would be eliminated root and branch."[24]

Two crucial concepts in the *Green* opinion—"affirmative duty" and "unitary system"—had in fact appeared nowhere in either *Brown* opinion, the source from which the Court claimed to have derived them. These notions revealed that the Court's thinking about the problem of school segregation had entered a new phase. Fourteen years after *Brown,* merely stopping discrimination no longer seemed sufficient. It was necessary to take "affirmative" steps that would "so far as possible eliminate the discriminatory effects of the past"—to create schools as they would have been had there been no history of enforced segregation.[25] The parties responsible had a duty to "make whole" the victims whose status had been diminished by discriminatory practices.

The *Green* Court was right in thinking that in New Kent County, with one

school still all-black and the other 83 percent white, there was much continuity with Jim Crow arrangements of the past. And it had run out of patience
for good reason. Justice Clarence Thomas is no friend of judicial activism, but
looking back at *Green*, seventeen years later, he saw it as "understandable."
"Resistance to *Brown I* [had] produced little desegregation by the time we
decided *Green* . . . ," he wrote. "Our impatience with the pace of desegregation and with the lack of a good-faith effort on the part of school boards led
us to approve . . . extraordinary remedial measures."[26]

But the Court's decision in *Green* represented a major doctrinal shift that
had large and worrisome implications, particularly because it mirrored a
change in employment and voting rights policy, as later chapters will make
clear. Had the Court assumed broad equitable powers to remedy past wrongs
only temporarily and only "to overcome the widespread resistance to the
dictates of the Constitution," Justice Thomas subsequently argued, it would
have been a different story. But, as things worked out, *Green* was but the first
step down a road that would eventually lead to measuring racial fairness in
North and South with a statistical yardstick. The race of students would
become the determining factor in school assignment decisions; to achieve
a "nonracial" system, pupils would be treated as if race were their only
characteristic. Schools that were predominantly black—even in states that
never had de jure segregation and in which "resistance" to *Brown* was not
an issue—would be considered educationally inferior and constitutionally
suspect.

THE ORIGINS OF BUSING FOR RACIAL BALANCE

The busing story begins with *Swann v. Charlotte-Mecklenburg Board of Education* (1971).[27] Like *Brown* and *Green*, *Swann* was a unanimous decision, the
last unanimous major school desegregation opinion that the Supreme Court
would be able to produce. The case involved a North Carolina metropolitan
area with a population of over half a million. The simple and relatively painless
remedies for racially segregated schools that had been available to the authorities in *Green* would not work in the Charlotte-Mecklenburg megadistrict,
which covered 542 square miles. In fact, given the residential patterns in the
county, nothing short of transporting many thousands of children to distant
schools would suffice.

The huge school district that included the city of Charlotte, North Carolina,
and its suburbs in surrounding Mecklenburg County contained nearly 85,000
students, 29 percent of them black. In 1965 the Charlotte-Mecklenburg
County school board had adopted a desegregation plan that assigned pupils
to neighborhood schools. But after *Green* a district court threw out that plan
(which had left almost 60 percent of black students in schools that were

all-black or nearly so), and instituted a new one that involved a substantial amount of busing.

With a long history of de jure segregation in the entire state of North Carolina, the only question was the permissible scope of the remedy. The "objective today," the Supreme Court said, "remains to eliminate from the public schools all vestiges of state-imposed segregation." It was a tall order. But "once a right and a violation have been shown, the scope of a district court's equitable powers to remedy past wrongs is broad . . . ," the Court went on.[28] And while there was no constitutional requirement that "every school in every community must always reflect the racial composition of the school system as a whole," looking at the numbers was a legitimate starting point in shaping that broad remedy.[29] The district court had established a strict racial quota (71 percent white, 29 percent black) for each school throughout the district, matching the overall racial makeup of the system. That quota would not be perfectly met, the High Court noted, but "the very limited use made of mathematical ratios was within the equitable remedial discretion of the District Court."[30]

The revised remedy, involving busing, was still for wrongs rooted in the Jim Crow South—for the intentional segregation of students even ten years after *Brown*. And the district court in the case did make an unconvincing argument that the racial identity of many of the schools was due to residential patterns that were partly caused by governmental action. Decisions of public authorities, in other words, were said to account, in some measure, for the prevalence of neighborhood schools that were overwhelmingly one-race. This ignored the crucial fact that whites across the nation had been fleeing the cities for suburban neighborhoods in enormous numbers since World War II. The inner-city homes they left behind were filled largely by black migrants from smaller towns and rural areas, who could not afford to live in a suburb and would not have been welcome there in any case. Some 88 percent of the black children in the Charlotte-Mecklenburg School District were living in the city of Charlotte, while most of the white population was out in suburbia. If students attended neighborhood schools, these schools would inevitably be racially imbalanced.

The racially identifiable schools in Charlotte-Mecklenburg were thus the result of a combination of intentionally segregative action by the state and residential patterns that were common throughout urban America. The unsavory history of de jure segregation in North Carolina allowed the Court to emphasize the former and ignore the latter. Down the road, when the battle shifted to the North, that would become much harder. Intentional, discriminatory state action would become more difficult to find, and drastic remedies to remedy less obvious constitutional wrongs would raise more questions.

THE PROGRESS OF SCHOOL DESEGREGATION IN THE SOUTH

The Civil Rights Act of 1964, the HEW school desegregation guidelines, and a series of federal court decisions made it unmistakably plain to southerners that further delay of school desegregation would not be tolerated. As a result, the walls of the Jim Crow school system suddenly came tumbling down. In the 1963–1964 school year, barely 1 percent of southern black children attended a school that had any whites enrolled in it. By the time of the *Green* decision, in 1968, the figure was up to 32 percent. That was an impressive jump, obviously, but it still meant that two out of three black pupils in the South had no white classmates at all. *Green* and *Swann* turned up the heat so that by the 1972–1973 school year no fewer than 91 percent of southern black students were attending school with whites.[31] By this minimal measure, at least, integration was nearly complete.

Some of these black children in integrated schools, of course, had only a few white classmates, and one may wonder if such token integration was meaningful. But more refined figures, showing the proportion of black students attending schools with various racial mixes, are available for the years 1968 and 1980, and they demonstrate that enormous and rapid change took place in the southern states. In the year of the *Green* decision, four years after the passage of the Civil Rights Act and the first major HEW efforts to speed the pace of desegregation, nearly three out of four southern black students were attending schools 95 percent or more black. Less than a quarter of them went to a school in which white enrollment was as high as 25 percent. A dozen years later the picture was dramatically different. By 1980 only a fifth of all black pupils were in schools that were 95 percent or more black. A large majority of them—almost two-thirds—were in schools with a student body that was at least 25 percent white. Indeed, by that year levels of racial segregation in the schools of the ex-Confederate states had dropped well *below* that which could be found in other parts of the United States. For example, fewer than half of the black students living in the Northeast and the Midwest were in schools with a white enrollment of 25 percent or more in 1980, as compared with 65 percent of those in the South. More than four out of ten black students in the Northeast and Midwest attended schools with a white enrollment of 5 percent or less in 1980, compared to only a fifth of their southern counterparts.[32]

The integration of the public schools of the South in these years was accomplished with surprisingly little conflict, considering all the kicking and screaming that *Brown* had provoked and the temporary popularity of diehard politicians like George Wallace, Orval Faubus, and Ross Barnett. As we have seen, southern white attitudes on racial issues had been gradually shifting in a more liberal direction since World War II, as a result of rising educational

Table 1
**Southern Black Public School Students by Percent
of Classmates Who Were White**

PERCENT WHITE	1968	1980
0–5	73.6	20.9
6–25	2.7	13.7
Over 25	23.7	65.4

Source: Finis Welch and Audrey Light, *New Evidence on School Desegregation* (Washington, D.C.: U.S. Commission on Civil Rights Clearinghouse Publication 92, 1987), table 10.

levels, urbanization, and economic development.[33] After "massive resistance" to integration became identified with the likes of Bull Connor, and Congress passed the Civil Rights Act and the Voting Rights Act despite near-unanimous southern opposition, most southern whites saw that the game was up and the Second Reconstruction was here to stay. In 1961 two-thirds of southern whites declared themselves in favor of "strict segregation." By 1968 that proportion was down to 30 percent, and by 1976 just 20 percent. Most still were not in favor of "desegregation"; in 1976, 55 percent of the total favored "something in-between." But those who said they wanted a return to the racial patterns of the days before *Brown* were a dwindling minority.[34]

PURSUING RACIAL BALANCE IN THE NORTH

Until the 1970s, litigation challenging school segregation in the United States was largely confined to the South. All the cases the Supreme Court heard were from states that had mandated (or allowed local communities to mandate) segregated public education.[35] The *Green* and *Swann* decisions, though, had implications that transcended region. Both cases originated in states that required segregated schools, and that context was important. Indeed, it probably accounted for the unanimity of the Court's decisions. But the stress on enrollment statistics, on the overconcentration of black pupils in certain schools and their corresponding scarcity in others, invited a hard look at the North as well. Racial imbalance was not peculiar to the South. It was common throughout the land, wherever black and white residents were segregated residentially—which is to say, in virtually every city in the United States. A neighborhood school system plus residential segregation was a formula that added up to schools that were racially imbalanced, and thus segregated de facto.

The separation of the races in schools that resulted from neighborhood segregation in the North was never as strict as it had been in the Jim Crow South, of course. The lines separating black from white neighborhoods shifted frequently, and there were always some racially mixed areas. Nevertheless, a look at the composition of the schools attended by African-American children in Detroit and Chicago in 1963 reveals very considerable clustering along racial lines (Table 2). A huge majority of elementary school pupils in both cities were in overwhelmingly black schools, and most of the rest were in black-majority schools.

Kenneth Clark, the black psychologist whose research on the harmful effects of segregation had been cited in a footnote in the *Brown* opinion, thought the segregated schools in northern cities like Detroit and Chicago were clearly harmful to black children. Not long after *Brown* he argued that the decision did not "apply only to the Southern states that have laws which require segregation." The Supreme Court had not limited itself to "the statement that only legal segregation is detrimental to the human personality. It was explicit . . . in stating that various forms of racial segregation are damaging to the human spirit."[36]

Brown was generally understood to have held that black children were damaged by the stigma imposed on them by the state when it confined them to separate schools for their race. But Clark altered the argument. "Racial isolation"—even when not caused by deliberate actions by public authorities —was innately stigmatizing, he asserted.[37] He did not entirely persuade the

Table 2

**Patterns of De Facto School Segregation in
Two Northern Cities in 1963**

	DETROIT	CHICAGO
Percent of black pupils attending schools that were		
90 percent or more black		
Elementary	73	86
High school	47	60
50–89 percent black		
Elementary	18	10
High school	25	26
Majority-white		
Elementary	9	4
High school	28	14

Source: Horace Mann Bond, *The Education of the Negro in the American Social Order* (Englewood Cliffs, N.J.: Prentice-Hall, 1934; rev. ed., Chicago: Octagon Books, 1966), 487.

Supreme Court, which never discarded altogether the de jure/de facto distinction. But in the cases involving school desegregation in northern cities in the 1970s, the Court came close to abandoning that important distinction by expanding its definition of de jure segregative practices to include any action by a public authority that might have contributed to racial imbalance in the schools. Moreover, while the Supreme Court stepped with some care, finding a constitutional violation only where there seemed to be some evidence of intentional discrimination, the lower courts often did not. Even in *Swann* the district court, for all intents and purposes, had embraced the notion that neighborhood schools in the context of residential segregation were in and of themselves discriminatory.[38]

The first northern case to reach the Supreme Court was *Keyes v. School District No. 1,* decided in 1973.[39] Racially imbalanced schools in Denver were the issue. No state law had ever separated the races in Colorado, and the school board had argued that residential segregation in the city explained the racial makeup of the schools. But the lower court had found intentional segregation in the subtle steps taken to confine black students living in one section of the city to predominantly black schools. These subtly segregative actions were said to have encouraged and reinforced the residential patterns that separated whites and blacks. School board policies that created racially imbalanced schools were thus a cause of neighborhood segregation, rather than the other way around. (The Court offered no evidence to demonstrate this novel proposition about the link between school board policies and the residential choices of Denver residents, and indeed could not have found any in the social science literature.)

The alleged segregative actions of the school board seemed to involve only a few of Denver's 119 schools. But intentional segregation in one neighborhood tainted the whole system, the Supreme Court held, and a system-wide remedy was hence justified. "A finding of intentionally segregative board actions in a meaningful portion of the school system . . . creates a presumption that other segregated schooling within the system is not adventitious."[40] The proper remedy—upon such a finding—was a desegregation plan that embraced the entire school district. And that meant extensive involuntary busing.

The Court depicted a seamless web between *Brown* and *Keyes.* The operation of a "dual system" was the issue in both. Intentional state action separated black and white pupils in both cases and was a similar constitutional violation, the Court stated.[41] A more candid concurring opinion from Justice Powell admitted that *Green* and *Swann* had profoundly altered the law—that there was no straight and narrow path between the 1954 decision and *Keyes. Brown* had demanded only "state neutrality" toward pupils of different races, while those two recent decisions (Powell argued) required nothing less than "affirmative state action to desegregate school systems." Minority students had acquired a constitutional right that had not been specified in *Brown.* They had a right to attend racially integrated schools—schools in which educational decisions were made "with a view toward enhancing integrated school opportunities." In Powell's view it was a waste of time to argue about whether the racial imbalances to be found in the schools of cities like Denver were attributable to de jure action by local officials; to do so was "perpetuating a legalism rooted in history rather than present reality." If the Court dispensed with the "legalisms," it would be plain that "the evil of operating separate schools" was "no less in Denver than in Atlanta."[42]

Justice Powell was right to acknowledge the distance traveled since 1954. But it seems no accident that Justice Brennan's majority opinion refrained from making the blunt assertion that minority students had a constitutional right to attend integrated schools. Had the Court embraced such an entitlement, judges would have been assigning (and busing) pupils to schools in every city in the country. Not even Justice Brennan thought such a rule could be enforced. A large majority of Americans were deeply attached to neighborhood schools. To uproot children from the school just down the street and bus them into unknown territory was under the best of circumstances strong and bitter medicine. It was medicine much of the nation, including the White House and both houses of Congress, thought appropriate when administered in the South. But there was little chance it would be willingly swallowed in cities in which no evidence suggested that school authorities had engaged in intentional discrimination. The Court did sense the limits of its own power.

WHY THE SCHOOL BUS STOPS AT THE CITY LIMITS

That understanding perhaps explains the Court's decision in *Milliken v. Bradley,* decided just a year later—in 1974.[43] The issue was the racial makeup of public schools in Detroit, where merely busing children of different races was not going to eliminate segregation. In the Denver case the Court had defined a "segregated" school as one in which blacks and/or Hispanics were a majority and non-Hispanic whites were a minority.[44] But whites comprised only 30 percent of the public school pupils in Detroit, and the proportion was falling every year. (By the 1993–1994 academic year, non-Hispanic white enrollment in the Detroit public schools was down to just 6.6 percent.)[45] With the most inventive of transportation plans, every school would still end up "segregated" by the *Keyes* definition.

The district court judge who dealt with the original complaint in *Milliken* arrived at a bold solution. After finding the Detroit Board of Education guilty of delaying and obstructing racial integration (and thus of intentional discrimination), he ordered a merger of the city's school district with fifty-three suburbs. The result would have been one immense superdistrict with four white students for every black pupil, a demographic balance that would have made it possible to eliminate altogether schools that were majority-minority. Moreover, it would have curbed the problem of "white flight" to the suburbs that had been created elsewhere by court decisions. Moving to Grosse Pointe or Royal Oak would have been useless; children living there might still be assigned to an urban school.

The plan, however, would have required the busing of a staggering number of students—more than 300,000—from suburb to city and city to suburb. While four members of the Supreme Court voted to uphold the lower court's remedy for the entire metropolitan area, five came down on the other side, making *Milliken* the first desegregation case in which the Court acted to limit rather than expand the scope of the remedy ordered. It also marked the emergence of a clear liberal-conservative split on desegregation cases, with liberals quicker to find segregative intent and more receptive to far-reaching remedies.[46]

Thus, although the Court in *Keyes* had held that a violation in one corner of the Denver school system justified a system-wide remedy, the majority in the *Milliken* case would not take what some saw as the next logical step and rule that the entire city of Detroit was equivalent to a Denver neighborhood. It was not willing to treat the existing city boundaries as arbitrary and irrelevant, and to force, in effect, a merger—eliminating the independence of dozens of other school systems. As the majority opinion noted, the trial record had not demonstrated that the suburban communities were themselves guilty of segregative practices, or that any actions taken by the suburbs were responsible for the racial mix in the Detroit schools. It was a well-established legal principle that the scope of remedies had to match that of wrongs.[47] Only an interdistrict violation could justify an interdistrict remedial plan. Since the suburbs had not caused school segregation in Detroit, they could not be forced to cure it.[48] What about the harm that black children attending overwhelmingly black schools would suffer? The Court had never accepted the argument that the potential damage, standing alone, constituted a constitutional violation, and its reluctance to do so served it well in *Milliken.*

To have required a metropolitan solution in the Detroit case would have had profound political reverberations across the land. In many of the nation's largest urban public school systems minority students were either already a majority or becoming so. Suburban dwellers zealously guarded the boundaries that separated them from the big city nearby, and they typically took particular pride in their schools. For the courts to put suburban schools under the thumb of a gigantic educational bureaucracy centered in the inner city and to require that suburban children be shipped into schools in neighborhoods their parents regarded as dangerous would have created a political firestorm.

In theory, the Supreme Court is oblivious to political considerations; in fact, the justices live in the same world as the rest of us. "The burden on a school board today is to come forward with a plan that promises realistically to work, and promises realistically to work *now*," a unanimous Court had said in *Green*.[49] That urgent language was characteristic of much public discourse in 1968, the year of the Kerner report and the assassination of Martin Luther King. But by 1974 the country was in the sixth year of the Nixon administration, and there was less crusading zeal abroad in the land. Perhaps, too, there was greater realism on the Court about what could be changed by judicial fiat. By then Nixon had appointed four of the justices, and it was their votes and one other that formed the majority that came down against involuntary busing across city lines.

THE BATTLE OVER BUSING

The Detroit decision was the death knell for metropolitan desegregation plans, although interdistrict busing schemes were subsequently imposed in a few places (Wilmington, Delaware; Louisville; and Indianapolis), after lower courts found evidence of violations in suburban communities. These metropolitan areas were arguably not that different from Detroit, but the Supreme Court refused to review the decisions and so they stood.[50]

In a few other cases the High Court also sounded a note of caution, and indicated limits to available remedies. In an important 1975 decision involving Pasadena, California, for example, the Supreme Court ruled that once local authorities had achieved a reasonable degree of racial balance in school systems that had once been intentionally segregated, they were not required to revise pupil assignments each year to preserve that balance in the face of continuing local demographic changes.[51]

In general, however, federal courts pressed ahead in the direction mapped out in *Keyes*. Boston, San Diego, San Francisco, Omaha, Minneapolis, Cleveland, Columbus, Dayton, and dozens of other urban centers were found guilty of operating deliberately segregated schools, and were ordered to restructure their educational systems to maximize racial balance. Others, like St. Louis, were able to avert a court order only by signing consent decrees that committed them to swallowing the same medicine. In these cities neighborhood schools were largely phased out, and a large fraction of pupils in the system were bused off to whatever school needed more students of their particular race to get the racial mix right. It was an immense social experiment, with many unanticipated results.

Court-ordered busing was wildly unpopular everywhere. In a 1972 poll just 13 percent of whites backed busing for desegregation purposes; in 1977 it was 12 percent; in 1983, 21 percent. If those numbers at least suggested some softening of the opposition, a question worded slightly differently found 9 percent of whites in favor in 1972, 10 percent in 1976, and 9 percent in

1980.[52] It is hard to think of another long-running major social policy in the United States that has been more profoundly unpopular with the general public. Although proponents of busing painted those who objected as racists, opposing mandatory busing was not at all the same thing as objecting to racial integration of the schools. Since busing was favored by no more than a slight majority of blacks—56 percent in 1972, 53 percent in 1978, 52 percent in 1982—it is obviously wrong to see opposition to it as unmistakable proof of racism.[53]

Why was busing disliked so intensely? Parents—not just white, but black as well, as we'll discuss further on—wanted their kids, especially the youngest ones, in schools close by. Families who had scrimped and saved to buy housing in what seemed to them orderly, clean, safe neighborhoods naturally looked with great dismay at the prospect of having their children bused to schools on the other side of town in neighborhoods that not even their own residents celebrated. And then, too, parents took for granted that they had choices about their children's education. They were accustomed to dealing with a school system that was democratically governed, one in which their opinions mattered. As a result of desegregation suits, basic decisions about how the schools operated were removed from officials responsive to majority opinion and put in the hands of just one person, a federal judge who was politically protected by lifetime tenure and had no educational expertise. "I want my freedom back," said one Boston parent after court-ordered busing began there. "They took my freedom, They tell me where my kids have to go to school. This is like living in Russia. Next they'll tell you where to shop."[54]

Nowhere was the battle over busing fiercer than in Boston. The chief stronghold of the abolitionist movement before the Civil War, Boston won national notoriety as the center of the antibusing movement a century later. In June 1974 federal judge Arthur W. Garrity, Jr., who had concluded that the Boston School Committee had been guilty of concentrating minority pupils in certain schools and steering them away from others, issued a sweeping desegregation order, to take effect that fall.[55]

It was hard to disagree with the judge in his criticism of the conduct of Boston school authorities, but the plan he ordered as a solution was remarkable in the zeal it showed for maximizing racial mixing without regard for the sensitivities of the families affected. Most white Bostonians liked their schools just as they were. It's tempting to think that all parents want schools that teach their children the skills they need to "better" themselves. But the white working-class families of South Boston, Charlestown, and East Boston did not see education as an avenue for social mobility. Quite the opposite: the high schools, especially, were viewed not as stepping-stones to the larger world, but as centers of local pride—places where South Boston kids became South Boston adults. Busing opened the doors of cherished community institutions to, in effect, foreigners.

Moreover, if white opposition to the court's busing decree was inevitable, it got an extra boost from the judge himself. The plan that Garrity imposed upon the city was punitive in the extreme. Indeed, the judge's advisors and the state board of education believed that those against whom it was directed —in their eyes, localist, uneducated, and bigoted—deserved to be punished. The plan thus paired Roxbury High, in the heart of the ghetto, with South Boston High, in the toughest, most insular, working-class section of the city. Blacks bused in from Roxbury would make up half of the sophomore class at South Boston High, while the whole junior class from "Southie" would be shipped off to Roxbury High.[56] Both neighborhoods already had much more than their share of housing projects, gangs, and street violence. Adding racial friction to the mix did not seem likely to promote more tranquil race relations and a better atmosphere for learning.

The busing plan provoked a huge boycott of the schools by white parents and pupils. Furious mobs shouted vicious racial epithets and threw stones at buses transporting black children into predominantly white schools. Things were so out of control at South Boston High School that it had to be closed for a month, and required a detachment of state troopers to keep order for the next three years. Elsewhere in the city marches, boycotts, and fights between black and white students regularly disturbed the peace. School and police officials and the Boston press did their best to downplay the extent of the disruption, so as not to encourage further resistance, but little learning could take place in so inflamed an atmosphere.[57]

To affluent liberals in the Boston area, including most of the reporters who covered the issue in the local media, the protests confirmed the assumption of the judge and his experts: opponents were racist boors. With their own children safely ensconced in suburban or private schools that were unaffected by the busing orders, these observers found it easy to advise others about the need to sacrifice their cherished neighborhood schools for the sake of racial justice. Protesters certainly did display appalling racism during the conflict, but the antibusing movement was not the equivalent of the Ku Klux Klan. Indeed, an aspiring young demagogue named David Duke, who then called himself the Imperial Wizard of the KKK, arrived in South Boston with the dream of signing up thousands of recruits, but found almost no takers. The American Nazi Party met with even less success; its effort to open a headquarters in South Boston provoked enough picketing to shut it down.[58]

Very few of the Boston whites who resented becoming the objects of liberal social engineering were embittered enough to seek solace in the arms of the Ku Klux Klan or the American Nazi Party. But the experience certainly destroyed their traditional loyalty to the Democratic Party, whose national leadership by the 1970s was identified with the likes of Judge Garrity and the black plaintiffs who brought the suit that led to the busing order. The political transformation of South Boston illustrates the point vividly. South Boston was a classic New Deal stronghold, heavily working-class and Catholic, where

Republicans were once not much more common than Buddhists. LBJ defeated Barry Goldwater there in 1964 by a hearty nine to one margin. Even George McGovern, whose antiwar views and counter-cultural associations were repugnant to most South Bostonians, had carried the community by almost two to one in 1972. Then came busing. In the next presidential election —in 1976—South Boston actually went Republican.[59] "Reagan Democrats" had become a majority there even before Ronald Reagan was on the ticket. A variety of other issues contributed to the shift of urban working-class, often Catholic, voters from the Democratic to the Republican parties during the 1970s, but busing was a major factor, and not just in Boston.

Most opponents of busing did not object to racially integrated schools; they objected to having their children used in a social experiment dreamed up by suburban liberals living in white communities where the racial mix was not even an issue. The polling evidence reveals that white support for the principle of school integration did not decline in the least after busing began in the 1970s; it continued to increase. And that support did not mean mere grudging acceptance of schools with a token black pupil or two. Direct evidence from Boston is lacking, but surveys of parental attitudes in several cities between 1977 and 1991 revealed that an average of no more than 13 percent of whites objected to sending their child to a school with a student body that was fully half black, so long as it was a neighborhood school.[60] In 1959, 35 percent of northern whites had said they would be unhappy about sending their children to a school whose student body was half black; the drop to 13 percent was thus an impressive change. The 13 percent who did object only slightly outnumbered the 8 percent of black parents who objected to sending their child to a school that had as many white as black pupils.

Judge Garrity had the formal authority to tell Boston's schoolchildren what public school they must attend. But that was not enough to engineer the precise racial balance that he felt was constitutionally required. Citizens who objected to the desegregation plan had alternatives that the judge was unable to foreclose. And in fact, over time, almost all who could escape the city's system—by moving to a suburb, faking an address, boarding children with relatives, or switching to a parochial school—did so. The suburban move was the most striking. Even before Judge Garrity took over the city schools, Bostonians had been moving out of the city in search of better schools, a more responsive local government, and a safer, greener environment. The busing order sharply increased white flight.

THE FAILURE OF BUSING

White flight had devastating consequences for the desegregation effort in Boston. Enrollment in the Boston public schools dropped, and white enrollment plunged. In 1970, 62,000 white children attended Boston public schools,

64 percent of the total. In 1994 there were but 11,000 white pupils, a mere 18 percent of total enrollment, even though 58 percent of the city's population was white.[61] If Judge Garrity was correct in his belief that attending minority-majority schools denied black students equal educational opportunities, his remedy was a dismal failure. A study that calculated an "interracial exposure index" for children in the Boston public schools shows that clearly. The index indicates the proportion of the enrollment that is white in the school attended by the average minority child. In 1973, when the court found racial imbalance in Boston's schools intolerably high, the average minority child attended a school that was 24 percent white. In 1974 the Garrity decision forced the abandonment of the neighborhood schools, and race was made the chief criterion for deciding which pupil went to which school. For a brief time the desegregation plan brought a rise in the interracial exposure index, but it was temporary. After 1975 it steadily declined. In 1993, after immense, disruptive effort and enormous expenditures to reduce racial imbalance, the average black child attended a Boston public school that was only 17 percent white, substantially more racially isolated than had been the case before the busing experiment began.[62] Busing did not remedy segregation; it actually aggravated it.

With white pupils becoming an endangered species in the Boston public schools, one might think that by the mid-1990s the school authorities would have stopped worrying about engineering racial balance. But the busing program had become institutionalized, and the administrators who had risen within the system over the past two decades had made their peace with it, while the parents who were most critical had simply left. Thus, although Boston largely extricated itself from court oversight in 1987, since 1989 a "controlled choice" plan for assigning students to schools has been in place. The plan is another desegregation strategy—long on control and short on choice, aimed at preventing what its defenders call the "resegregation" of the system.[63]

To maintain this charade, it has been necessary to revise the definition of "segregation" rather drastically. By the 1990s it no longer made sense to call a school with a majority of black or Hispanic pupils "segregated," since those two groups made up 72 percent of total enrollment. Boston school officials thus changed the definition. Hard though it is to believe, a school is today "segregated" if its minority enrollment is above the 91 percent mark. If minority pupils make up 91 percent or less of the student body, the school is "desegregated."[64] An elementary school with a total enrollment of 350 is segregated if 28 of the students are white; add a 29th white child and the problem is fixed. Moreover, although the supply of white pupils has shrunk to the vanishing point, in 1994 Boston was still spending no less than $30 million a year to bus pupils around in order to avert "resegregation" of its schools.[65] This sum amounted to nearly $500 a year for each pupil, in a system in which there are chronic complaints of shortages in books and writing material.

The story has been much the same in other cities in which large-scale mandatory busing schemes went into effect. The racial balance that the judges made strenuous efforts to create rarely materialized, because so many of the parents of the children being used in the game of balancing the races refused to play. They took their children out of the school system, and often out of the city altogether.[66] Thus, in Denver, for example, two-thirds of the pupils in the public schools were non-Hispanic whites in 1973, the year the busing began. Two decades later the proportions were reversed, with two-thirds of all the students black or Hispanic and just one-third non-Hispanic white. Total enrollment in the system was down by 38 percent; enrollment for non-Hispanic whites was down by 71 percent. During those twenty years or so, a continuing, informal, popular referendum on the busing plan was held, and many thousands of Denver parents voted no with their feet. In 1995, Denver's schools were more segregated than they had been before the busing experiment began, just as they were in Boston. In Denver, in 1995, a federal judge ruled that a continuation of busing was futile and authorized a return to neighborhood schools, an offer that local authorities were happy to accept.[67]

PARENTS AGAINST BUSING

"White flight" is the familiar term for the shift of students from urban school systems to suburban or private schools in response to court-ordered busing schemes. The label is somewhat misleading in two respects. First, not all whites were able to flee from cities like Boston. It was middle-class whites, for the most part, who abandoned inner-city public schools; their less affluent neighbors were stuck unless they could game the system in some way with something like a false suburban address.

Second, as we suggested before, it was not just middle-class whites who left Boston, Denver, and other cities hit by busing. The black middle class has expanded dramatically since the 1960s, and many of its members have been as repelled by the deteriorating condition of the big-city public schools as their white counterparts. Although it was middle-class black leaders of the Boston chapter of the NAACP who brought the suit that led to busing, few of them, ironically, actually patronized the Boston public schools. According to the most careful history of the busing controversy, the children of "most black civil rights leaders" did not attend public schools in Boston, but were instead among the 2,500 African-American pupils who were bused out to nearby suburban schools in the METCO program, with all the costs paid for by the state.[68] METCO had been created in 1966 to give black inner-city students better educational opportunities than they could find in Boston's public schools. Although its rationale might seem to have disappeared once the Boston schools came under Judge Garrity's protective power in 1974, it survived. The program was a vehicle for "black flight" from a public school system disrupted by busing, and one fully subsidized by Massachusetts taxpayers.

The desegregation order was supposed to benefit black children, but it was not the middle class alone that had its doubts. In 1971, when an attempt was made to redraw attendance zones to promote school integration, impoverished black families were furious; the new lines barred their children from an excellent neighborhood school. In fact, in 1974, on the eve of the judge's order, black politicians were pushing for black control of black neighborhood schools—not busing.[69]

Boston parents had no monopoly on such sentiments. In other cities as well minority parents have made their desire for neighborhood schools clear. In fact, even busing that is instituted not for purposes of integration but simply to deal with the problem of overcrowding will often meet with parental resistance. In 1993 a Brooklyn district decided to fill empty seats in its East New York school with some of the overflow from Cypress Hills, just fifteen minutes away. But the mostly Hispanic parents who thought of Cypress Hills as their neighborhood school did not want their children bused even that short distance to a mostly black neighborhood. They thought of the East New York school, across the street from a housing project, as dangerous, and they complained that the distance meant they could neither drop in on classes nor deliver something a child left at home. They worried that the ethnic mix could become combustible—that the usual hallway shoving and pushing could turn ugly. School officials agreed that parents became less involved with their children's education when they could not walk down the street to meet with a teacher or guidance counselor, and that the students themselves did not stay for extracurricular activities when they lived a bus ride away. "Neighborhoods are psychological and physical barriers," the superintendent of the district acknowledged. "Kids have to cross a line that is regarded as a community line."[70]

THE DEMOGRAPHY OF URBAN PUBLIC SCHOOLS TODAY

The battle over busing was particularly intense in Boston, and it would not be surprising if we found that the number of white (and black) parents who abandoned that city's public schools was higher than elsewhere. In fact, it was not notably higher. The school systems of most of our largest cities have lost most of their middle-class students, with unfortunate consequences for the quality of the education they are able to offer.

Busing has not been the only reason, obviously. Similar changes in the public school population, though usually less dramatic, occurred in most cities, whether or not they underwent court-ordered busing. The explosive growth of the suburban population after World War II sharpened socioeconomic differences between central cities and suburban areas, with the result that a growing share of students in urban schools today come from families that are minority, low-income, or both.

The quest for racial balance in urban schools, however, and consequent departures from the old neighborhood school pattern, contributed to this transformation. A study of 125 large urban school districts found that all but 14 percent of them implemented desegregation plans in the years 1961–1985.[71] How many of them limited parental choice to such a degree that it provoked flight from the system is unclear, but at a minimum these efforts at preventing racial imbalance took energies and resources that might otherwise have gone toward academic improvements that middle-class parents tend to care about—programs that would increase their child's chances of getting into a desirable college, for example. Nearly one in every twelve school dollars spent in Boston in 1991 paid for transportation, in part because of routes created to pick up only two children.[72] In 1993 the State of Missouri spent $25 million on interdistrict busing—over and above the $34 million spent on other desegregation programs.[73]

Whatever the cause, the dramatically altered demography of the urban public schools today makes the task of figuring out what "segregation" looks like, and what (if anything) should be done far more difficult than it was before. Table 3 sums up the relevant information for seventeen of the nation's twenty largest cities. Boston, for example, has a population that is 58 percent non-Hispanic white, but white pupils make up less than a fifth of total enrollment in the public schools. As the index indicates, that means that there are only a third as many white children in the public schools as their share of the population would lead us to expect.[74] Judged by the proportion of whites in the public school population, Boston is typical of big cities; eleven of the other sixteen have an even lower white enrollment. Not one of these cities has a white majority among public school students.

The paucity of whites in the big-city public school population is not a sign that they all have moved to the suburbs. In every one of these cities, non-Hispanic whites are a larger share—usually a much larger share—of the total population than they are of the public school population. Boston, with its index of 33, is pretty close to the average for the group as a whole. Only in San Diego, San Jose, and Columbus, Ohio, is non-Hispanic white representation in the public schools as much as half the expected share, and in all three it is far below parity.

"Desegregation" in the sense in which the term was used in the 1970s—breaking up large clusters of minority students and dispersing them into majority-white schools—is thus an obsolete and irrelevant concept. No big city in the country has a non-Hispanic white majority left in its public school system. Officials often still give high priority to racial balance, and warn of the dangers of "resegregation," but the "resegregation" they have in mind bears

Table 3

Percentage of Non-Hispanic Whites in the Public Schools and Total Populations in Seventeen of the Twenty Largest Cities, 1993–1994 School Year

	STUDENTS	POPULATION	INDEX
Washington, D.C.	4.0	26.8	15
San Antonio	5.9	35.9	16
Detroit	6.6	20.3	33
Chicago	11.4	37.3	31
Los Angeles	12.1	35.8	34
Houston	12.4	39.9	31
Dallas	13.7	46.9	29
San Francisco	13.8	45.6	30
Baltimore	15.8	38.4	41
New York	17.5	39.5	44
Memphis	17.6	43.5	40
Boston	19.3	58.0	33
Philadelphia	21.7	51.6	42
Milwaukee	27.0	60.4	45
San Diego	32.2	57.5	56
San Jose	35.0	48.5	72
Columbus	46.1	73.7	63

Sources: Enrollment data from U.S. Department of Education, *Digest of Educational Statistics: 1995* (Washington, D.C.: U.S. Government Printing Office, 1995), table 91. Population data are from 1990 Census, as given in U.S. Bureau of the Census, *Statistical Abstract of the United States: 1992* (Washington, D.C.: U.S. Government Printing Office, 1992), 35–37. The index is the percent of non-Hispanic whites enrolled in the public schools divided by the percent of non-Hispanic whites in the city's population. If whites use the public schools at the same rate as other groups, the index will be 100. Phoenix, Indianapolis, and Jacksonville were the other 3 cities in the top 20 as of 1990. They were excluded here because their school districts include their suburbs, and they are not comparable to the others for that reason.

no resemblance to the patently unequal, oppressive dual system that *Brown* struck down. The "resegregated" junior high school in Boston is one that has slipped from 9 or more percent white to 8 or less percent white. If minority children truly cannot obtain a decent education except in the company of a majority of white pupils, as liberals insisted twenty years ago, Table 3 reveals that their situation in virtually all of our large cities today is hopeless.

Looking at recent demographic data alerts us to another important complication. The major desegregation cases from *Brown* through *Keyes* and *Milliken* were conceived in simple black and white terms. Segregation was a problem for blacks, the result of decisions made by hostile whites. "Minority" and "majority" were pretty much synonymous with "black" and "white." It took an effort to fit the facts from the Denver case into this Procrustean bed, but the Court managed to do so. The plaintiffs who filed the suit were African Americans, but Hispanics actually outnumbered blacks (20 percent versus 14 percent) in the public schools. Were these Hispanic students just blacks with a Mexican accent, or should they have been recognized as a distinct group in assessing segregation in the Denver schools? The Court was content to lump them in with African Americans as part of an undifferentiated "minority"; a school whose student body was one-third white, one-third black, and one-third Hispanic thus was deemed segregated because its enrollment was two-thirds "minority." It had to be majority-white to be desegregated.[75]

The resumption of mass immigration in the past three decades has made this two-race, black-white model of society outmoded, a point already discussed in Chapter 8. Since 1970 public school enrollments of Hispanic, Asian and Pacific Islander, and American Indian children have grown at a much faster rate than those for either non-Hispanic whites or African Americans (Table 4). As recently as 1970 all but 6 percent of American students fitted into either the white or black racial categories; by 1993 the proportion of minorities other than black was triple that figure.[76] In California today Hispanics, Asians, and American Indians are half of the school population, in Texas 38 percent, in Arizona 36 percent, and in New Mexico 57 percent.[77] And of course in our biggest cities, particularly in the Sunbelt, the concentration of Hispanic and Asian students is even greater than the statewide figures suggest.

In thinking about what constitutes a "segregated" school, can these groups properly be lumped together as "disadvantaged racial minorities"? Different groups pose different questions. For obvious historical reasons a school in

Table 4

**Race and Ethnicity of Public School Students
in the United States, 1970–1993**

	BLACK	NON-HISPANIC WHITE	ASIAN	HISPANIC	AMERICAN INDIAN
1970	14.9	79.1	0.5	5.1	0.4
1993	16.6	66.0	3.6	12.7	1.1

Sources: Figures for 1970 except Asian, from U.S. Bureau of the Census, *Statistical Abstract of the United States: 1976* (Washington, D.C.: U.S. Government Printing Office, 1976), 131–132; the Asian 1970 figure was estimated from the total Asian-American population in 1970 and the ratio of Asian school enrollments to the total population of Asians in 1993; figures for 1993 from U.S. Department of Education, National Center for Education Statistics, *Digest of Educational Statistics: 1995* (Washington, D.C.: U.S. Government Printing Office, 1995), 60.

which all the students are black suggests the possibility of discriminatory state action. But it's not clear why a predominantly Asian school should raise eyebrows any more than one that is mainly Jewish. Nor is the necessity for a racial mix in each school that reflects the makeup of the overall population evident. If that's what we want, why stop with such crude categories as "Asian-American" or "Hispanic," umbrella labels that subsume many national origin groups with quite different characteristics? In other words, why should not each school be required to have its proper share of Koreans, Chinese, Filipinos, and Vietnamese? The principle would extend as well to Mexicans, Cubans, Puerto Ricans, Costa Ricans, Chileans, and other Central or South Americans.[78] Neither the "Asian" nor the "Hispanic" groups are comprised of identical, interchangeable parts. The more we recognize the highly complex, multiethnic character of American society in the closing years of the twentieth century, the harder it is to imagine engineering just the right mix in each school, and the wiser it seems to abandon the whole effort.

HOW MUCH DESEGREGATION WAS ACHIEVED?

The assault upon de jure school segregation in the South was victorious. It was a battle that had to be won. The Jim Crow schools were an essential part of an elaborate system of racial oppression, and the Supreme Court's attack upon them was the opening wedge for a broader assault upon the entire caste system. By the end of the 1970s, as we noted above, enrollment patterns in the public schools of the southern states looked much like those elsewhere; indeed, they were actually somewhat less segregated than in other regions of the United States.

The Supreme Court's logic in the crucial *Green* and *Swann* decisions, though, started it down an unfortunate path. Infuriated by the never-ending foot-dragging by southern officials, in 1968 an impatient Court declared that all school districts that had previously been intentionally segregated had an "affirmative duty" to eliminate all "racial discrimination . . . root and branch." Three years later, in districts with a history of segregation and racially imbalanced schools, the burden was placed on the authorities to prove the absence of discriminatory practices. Proving a negative is always difficult, and was made doubly so by subsequent decisions that defined intentionally segregative action very broadly. In the Denver and Boston cases, among others, federal judges equated decisions that influenced the racial composition of a school (for instance, the selection of a school construction site) with the complete separation of black and white students in the Jim Crow South. A "dual" system was one in which an attendance zone or two somewhere in the city had been found to have been racially gerrymandered. At that point the distinction between de jure and de facto segregation had been all but erased. And yet the difference was in fact important. Because no Jim Crow laws had created the racial clustering found in northern urban schools, the alleged "segregation" proved to be much less amenable to alteration by judicial fiat.

How much the judicial decisions aimed at creating "integrated" schools actually accomplished may be seen from Table 5. We have already observed (Table 1) that the public schools of the South desegregated very rapidly between 1968 (the year of the *Green* decision and the Kerner report) and 1980. What about the rest of the nation? In 1968, 43 percent of the African Americans attending public school in the Northeast were in schools that had a minority enrollment of 90 percent or more.[79] In 1980, despite victories by minority plaintiffs in desegregation suits in dozens of cities, in the New England and Middle Atlantic states school segregation had not declined by this measure. Indeed, the percentage of black students attending schools with a 90 percent or higher minority enrollment had increased a bit, to 49 percent. It has not fallen since then. More progress was made in the Midwest and the West, but only until 1980. Thus, there was a very steep decline in segregation during the 1970s, dominated by changes in the South; since 1980, however, the overall national pattern has remained essentially unchanged.

More progress is apparent if we look at a different measure—if we turn the question around and ask what proportion of white students attend schools that are at least 90 percent non-Hispanic white. The segregation of *whites* in the schools dropped steeply between 1968 and 1980, and it has continued to drop since. Furthermore, it has fallen steadily in every geographic region. Over three-quarters of whites were in nearly all-white schools back in 1968; a dozen years later the figure had dropped to six out of ten. By 1992 fewer than half of whites went to "white" schools. The exposure of black students to

Table 5

Measures of Desegregation, 1968–1992

	U.S.	SOUTH	NORTHEAST	MIDWEST	WEST
Percent of black students in schools more than 90 percent minority					
1968	62.9	77.5	42.7	58.0	50.9
1980	34.8	24.6	48.7	43.6	33.9
1992	34.1	26.5	49.9	39.4	26.6
Percent of white students in schools 90 percent white					
1968	77.8	68.8	82.5	89.4	61.4
1980	60.9	32.2	79.5	81.0	40.0
1992	48.9	26.0	66.7	71.9	26.7

Source: J. Michael Ross, "Trends in Black Student Racial Isolation, 1968–1992," unpublished manuscript, Office of Educational Research and Improvement, U.S. Department of Education, 1995.

whites has not increased nationally since 1980 or so, but the exposure of white students to "minority" students (in some places mainly blacks but in others Hispanics and/or Asians) has risen very considerably. In great part this is because the population of nonwhite students has greatly increased since the late 1960s; nevertheless, it is noteworthy that a good many of these minority students have moved into schools that once had no minority enrollment.

Since engineering and preserving racial balance over the long run has proven to be so difficult, it is fortunate that there is no compelling evidence to support the belief that black students cannot learn, or cannot learn as well, when they attend schools with few white classmates. Actually there is no compelling evidence one way or another; it is not a question that social scientists can conclusively answer. But what we do know is this: when all is said and done, there remains a difference between de jure and de facto segregation. And we know, too, that remedies that are arguably appropriate to the one circumstance (intentional segregation) are surely not equally so to the other (racial clustering).

Perhaps it will be recalled from Chapter 4 that Chief Justice Warren's main contention in Brown was not that racial classifications in the law were in themselves pernicious, but that school segregation was psychologically harmful to black children. It was an argument that was bound to raise doubts about predominantly black schools, wherever they were found. And yet the Court has never embraced the notion that a concentration of black students in a particular school, in itself, violates the Fourteenth Amendment. It has understood the point that Harvard law professor Randall Kennedy has made well. Where the state demands that the races be kept separate in public schooling, Kennedy has written, it has (in effect) hurled a racial insult directed at all blacks. But that is not the case when the school is all-black because no whites live in the neighborhood.[80] The former creates a caste system with all blacks as second-class citizens; the latter does not.

This vital distinction between the messages delivered by de jure and de facto systems makes the heightened concern about racial isolation in the one circumstance quite different from the other. Thus, it has been essential for the Court to maintain the fiction that the imposition of a remedy depends on finding a "dual" system—a commitment that has led to the adoption of an increasingly strained definition of "dual." That strained definition is not the only problem that cases beginning with Swann and Keyes have posed. If Denver was classifying its students along lines of race (engaging in de jure segregation), the remedy for that classification—race-conscious school assignments—was more of the same. After Green, the courts took to fighting fire with fire. And yet if racial classifications are dangerous, if they hurl racial insults, arguably they are dangerous in whatever form they take. And if so, the "benign" sorting that school assignments based on race involves is not so benign after all.

Enough, Already

"Not so benign" is precisely how four Philadelphia families—two white, two black—had come to see the matter by September 1995. They sought an injunction in federal district court to stop the implementation of the city's desegregation plan that prevented their children from transferring into schools of their choice. The grandparents of one of the children, Kharisma McIlwaine, had been plaintiffs in one of the cases that had been combined in the *Brown* decision. Four decades later Kharisma was dismayed that Philadelphia was telling students which schools they could attend, and which they could not, on the basis of the color of their skin. When she had tried to switch from her neighborhood elementary school, where more than 75 percent of the students performed below average on standardized tests, to one that had a high achievement record, the city said no. Too many black children were already enrolled in the school she wanted to attend; there was a cap of 65 percent African-American pupils at any one school. There were empty seats at the school, but they were reserved in hopes of persuading some white students to enroll. The white plaintiffs in that 1995 suit complained of the same thing: schools to which they wanted to transfer were holding places open for blacks, in case some applied.

Racially imbalanced schools are still blamed on white racism. But in Philadelphia neither whites nor blacks were choosing schools in which their race was a minority, although the school authorities thought that was the only legitimate choice. Had they been doing so, of course, there would not have been empty seats being held for children of the "right" color. Obviously, the Philadelphia school board's policies were not equivalent to those in Topeka, Kansas, in 1954, but there was a dismaying degree of overlap. "In essence, the school district has turned *Brown v. Board of Education,* the Bill of Rights of the United States Constitution, and the federal Civil Rights Act upside down by precluding white and minority children from attending the schools of their choice in order to impose arbitrary and illegal racial quotas," the lawsuit contended.[81]

There was nothing unusual about the school assignment rules in Philadelphia—or about the consequent parental frustration. By 1995 many black parents in Prince George's County, Maryland, had likewise come to resent the system of reserved classroom seats for members of racial and ethnic groups. In the name of desegregation, over 4,000 black children were on a waiting list for magnet programs that had already filled their African-American quotas. Those programs had at least 500 openings for nonblack students, but no takers. Eza Gartrell, age fourteen, who finished eighth grade in June 1996, had applied to a creative and performing arts magnet program, but was put on the waiting list simply because she was black. "There are a lot of people like me who really want to [be in the program], and for them to say no just because of your race is disgusting," she said.[82] The Prince George's story had a happy ending for students like Eza Gartrell; a federal judge suspended the racial quotas—although only for one school year, pending further review.

Across the country, desegregation plans that deny students educational opportunity—in the name of expanded opportunity—are in some trouble. Just how much has yet to be seen. In recent years the Supreme Court has changed its stance considerably. Thus, in 1991 it allowed Oklahoma City, despite its history of de jure segregation, to return to neighborhood schools. The duty of school authorities was only to act in good faith to eliminate all vestiges of past intentional segregation to the extent "practicable."[83] Desegregation decrees were "not intended to operate in perpetuity." They were temporary measures. "Local control over the education of children allows citizens to participate in decision making, and allows innovation so that school programs can fit local needs." The trial court had noted that residential segregation was not the consequence of intentionally discriminatory acts, but of "private decision making and economics," and the Court did not challenge that finding.[84] A year later the Court paved the way for a return to local control over school assignments in DeKalb County, Georgia, just outside Atlanta. "Returning schools to the control of local authorities at the earliest practicable date is essential to restore their true accountability," Justice Anthony Kennedy wrote for an 8-to-0 majority.[85]

Citizen participation in the formation of school assignment policies, local control to allow local innovation and ensure accountability—these had traditionally been fighting words in the civil rights community. But the illusion that better schools, better kids, and a racially harmonious society could be created by judicial fiat had been shattered. For one thing, in many school systems there were not enough white children to engineer the racial balance that remedies had traditionally called for. The desegregation plan for Prince George's County went into effect in the mid-1980s; "we knew even back then the day would come when we were going to run out of white kids to get that kind of racial balance," the former superintendent said in June 1996.[86] There was also the growing disaffection of black political and educational leaders. "Apartness has never been unconstitutional," one of Prince George's black school board members correctly noted in October 1995.[87] The county executive, also black, had already signaled support for a return to neighborhood schools.[88]

The racial and political climate was changing, and with just a smidgen of encouragement from the Supreme Court, school boards and districts courts in scattered cities were concluding that enough was enough. Thus, in Cleveland in 1993, the school board largely dumped (with court approval) its cross-city busing and substituted a plan to improve neighborhood schools, which—district authorities admitted—was likely to result in some one-race schools.[89]

A year later Dallas school officials were in court arguing that desegregation was a moot issue; the district was only 15 percent white.[90] In 1995 in Minneapolis the city's first black mayor called for neighborhood schools, and in Denver as well, to the applause of the black mayor, a federal judge released the city from the busing plan mandated in *Keyes*, followed soon by cities from Buffalo to Little Rock.

Denver's long-running experiment in busing from which the judge had released the city was an unmitigated disaster, as we have indicated. The return to neighborhood assignments quickly brought at least some change for the better. "Enrollments are up, parental involvement is up," one school official said. "Having neighborhood schools back [will help] us to rebuild the neighborhoods," the mayor predicted.[91]

In Denver the families who chose to leave the public schools placed themselves safely out of judicial reach. But in a number of other cities the *Milliken* decision (which barred cross-district busing remedies without a cross-district wrong) did not entirely discourage federal judges bent on single-handedly changing the racial composition of the schools and the allegedly related educational performance of minority children. If the Supreme Court had understood the limits of judicial power in the Detroit and other decisions, a number of lower court (and state court) judges did not.

The prime example is surely Judge Russell Clark of Kansas City, Missouri, who had extraordinary faith that a court, exercising its remedial authority, could fashion urban schools that suburban white families would find irresistible. Prior to 1954, the state had mandated segregated learning; thirty years later, Judge Clark found, there were still "vestiges" of that dual system. But "to accomplish desegregation within the boundary lines of a school district whose enrollment remains 68.3% black is a difficult task," he admitted. Additional mandatory student assignments would only "increase the instability" of the Kansas City, Missouri, School District—code language for more white flight. The judge thus approved instead a comprehensive magnet school and capital improvements plan that, he believed, would be "so attractive that it would draw non-minority students from the private schools who have abandoned or avoided the [city's public schools] and draw in additional non-minority students from the suburbs."

The order was naïve—to say the least. Clark thought he could buy indispensable white students by offering them lavishly equipped schools. He doubled the local property tax, and ordered the state as well to pay up; the money financed a Central High School with one computer for every three pupils, a $5 million swimming pool, a six-lane indoor track, a weight-training room, and fencing courses taught by an eminent coach. Other amenities in the system included air-conditioned classrooms, movie-editing and -screening rooms, a 2,000-square-foot planetarium, greenhouses and vivariums, a twenty-five-acre farm, a model United Nations wired for language translation, radio and television studios, huge elementary school animal rooms for use in zoo projects. By 1995 the cost of the enterprise had reached $1.3 billion over and above the normal school budget—which amounted to an extra $36,111 for each of the system's 36,000 students.[92]

Judge Clark said he had "allowed the District planners to dream" and "provided the mechanism for [those] dreams to be realized."[93] From beginning to end, the dream was a fantasy. Five-million-dollar swimming pools and planetariums did not alter the racial balance in the schools. White enrollment did not increase over the 1985–1995 decade; it fell further.[94] Nor did the academic performance of African-American students improve.[95] All these frills did nothing to raise the test scores of students who needed help learning basic skills.

In another desegregation case, in Rockford, Illinois, in 1996, a federal judge mandated that the gap in standardized test scores between whites and Asians, on the one hand, and blacks and Hispanics, on the other, must be narrowed by at least 50 percent within five years. The precision with which he stated the target was novel, but the means of reaching it were familiar ones that had not had that effect anywhere else—racial quotas for every classroom, and even on the cheerleading squad.[96] Two years earlier a state judge in Pennsylvania had made the same demand: balance the schools and classrooms in order to reduce the racial disparities in academic achievement.[97] But what was the logical connection between black students' scores and the presence of whites? Judge Clark had assumed such a link—hence his all-out, desperate strategy to lure whites. In their absence, he apparently believed, black pupils would sink educationally.

While the Supreme Court in the Kansas City case had expressed doubt about the validity of that assumption, it was in fact a conviction with a long pedigree, reaching back to 1954. The emphasis in *Brown* on the psychological harm inflicted on black children in segregated settings, as we earlier noted, contained the seeds of future doubt about every predominantly black school. Kenneth Clark, the sociologist upon whom the *Brown* Court had so heavily relied, had later argued that racial isolation was in itself stigmatizing. At the heart of busing and other desegregation strategies aimed at creating racially balanced schools was an assumption about the educational benefits of whites in attendance. Clark and other judges took that implicit assumption and ran with it.

"It never ceases to amaze me that the courts are so willing to assume that anything that is predominantly black must be inferior," Justice Thomas wrote in a concurring opinion in the Supreme Court's 1995 decision in *Missouri v. Jenkins*.[98] This view is gaining currency. Even in Kansas City, where the court-imposed state spending has meant luxurious schools for a mostly black student population, doubts about the desegregation order are now openly expressed. Edward Newsome was a well-known black opponent of Judge

Clark's plan before he was elected to the school board in 1994. "There is no inherent academic benefit in black kids mixing with white kids," he has said.[99] Newsome now has considerable company among black elected officials across the country—in Denver, Prince George's County, Minneapolis, St. Louis, and elsewhere. "I don't think there is anything wrong with the schools being populated by one ethnic group if that ethnic group lives in that community and wants their schools to facilitate their cultural or linguistic interests," a black member of the board of education in Philadelphia remarked in 1993.[100] Even within the NAACP, a few local officials are questioning the traditional pro-busing views of the civil rights community.[101]

"The key issue today," Denver mayor Wellington Webb said in 1995, "is to assure that kids receive the best education, regardless of what neighborhood they are in."[102] Webb and other disaffected proponents of busing no longer worry—as they once did legitimately—that heavily black schools will not be properly funded. But they want higher levels of academic achievement for black students. Their primary concern, in other words, has become the racial gap in learning—a gap that desegregation strategies have not closed. What the gap looks like, why it hasn't closed, and what might be done are questions explored in the next chapter.

CHAPTER THIRTEEN

Skills, Tests, and Diversity

IN 1995, WELLINGTON WEBB, Denver's first black mayor, called for the "best education" for the city's students—"regardless of what neighborhood they are in." Good public schools for everyone—schools that will prepare them for a world in which only the skilled get good jobs. Not such a tall order. And yet it seems to be a demand that is astonishingly hard to meet. Somewhere in our educational travels over the last decades, we lost our way. And the confusion seems particularly marked when it comes to schooling for disadvantaged students, many of whom are African-American.

We ask too little of the students and too little of their teachers, and even minimal demands are often stymied by what Shelby Steele has called the deep and painful sense of "racial vulnerability" that whites and blacks share. The vulnerability of whites is to the charge of racism, that of blacks is to the claim of inferiority. In different ways both are racked by powerful doubts about their own self-worth. And both have found a means of escape—through what Steele calls recomposed narratives of who they are. Some blacks dispel the myth of inferiority by reducing themselves to victims of white racism, too crippled to compete—a myth in which some whites have continued to be complicit. Racially well-meaning whites, terrified of the label racist, remake themselves as angels of mercy, embracing policies built on deference to black victimization through which they can display their racial virtue. These recomposed narratives—psychologically soothing tales—are an educational disaster. They are the morass in which rigorous academic standards sink.[1]

High academic standards, Steele argues, ask black students to risk failure —and thus risk confirming the legend that blacks just can't make it. And for whites, too, there is danger: that in seeming to set blacks up to fail they will reaffirm their reputation for racism. Whites and blacks, both in flight from stereotypes: that is the context in which affirmative action and other policies that ask less of blacks are born. In telling the story of the drive to replace merit and the pursuit of academic excellence with such safe and protective strategies—the theme that runs through this chapter—we start with the CBEST controversy.

CAN THEY TEACH WHAT THEY DON'T KNOW?

CBEST stands for the California Basic Educational Skills Tests that the state has required its teachers to pass since 1983. California is not alone in making such a demand; as of 1995, 26 states were insisting that those who wanted to teach demonstrate "minimum competency."[2]

"Minimum competency" is certainly what these tests demand of teachers; they require at most a tenth-grade command of reading, writing, and math. In California, as of 1996, in the thirteen years the test had been given, almost nine out of ten prospective teachers had managed to pass it, although not necessarily on the first try. They are asked such questions as: "Amy drinks 1½ cups of milk three times a day. At this rate, how many cups of milk will she drink in one week?"[3] Five possible answers are provided. The reading section consists of short paragraphs, and again, multiple-choice questions. Aspiring teachers must also demonstrate an ability to write brief essays on topics of a personal nature that require no knowledge of an academic subject.[4]

Eighty percent of whites have been passing CBEST the first time they take the test, but only 35 percent of African Americans. Those results, allegedly racially biased, were the basis of the largest employment discrimination suit ever filed in federal court.[5] CBEST may be simple "from a Euro-centric point of view," the president of the Oakland Alliance of Black Educators has argued, but "when you are a person who has difficulty with the English language, it's going to take you a little longer to figure it out. It's a matter of processing."[6]

It is difficult to see why African Americans born in the United States should have any particular difficulty in "processing" material in their native language.[7] Nevertheless, in 1993 the California Teachers Association, a branch of the powerful National Education Association, filed a brief in support of the plaintiffs arguing that the test was a "major impediment" to achieving ethnic and racial diversity in the schools.[8] The president of the San Francisco Board of Education, Steve Phillips, declared that the stated concern about educational quality behind the testing of teachers was just "political rhetoric"—that there was "nowhere near a basic skills crisis in our schools on this order of magnitude."[9] And yet other evidence has suggested precisely such a crisis; in 1995, 60 percent of all freshmen in the California State University system, which draws from the top third of high school graduates, required remedial instruction in reading, math, or both.[10]

Phillips did not appear to be worried about what students are learning—or not learning. The racial identity of the teaching staff was his sole concern. CBEST, he alleged, "excludes thousands of accomplished educators of color from public schools every year." But, as Albert Shanker, the head of the American Federation of Teachers, noted, no "accomplished educator" can find such an excruciatingly elementary test unfair.[11] "Ask the parents in the Asian or Hispanic or African-American communities," he wrote, "whether they want role models for their children who can't read and write English at a high school level. Ask them where their children will be in 20 years if they have not learned those skills because their teachers didn't have them."[12]

The 50,000 minority plaintiffs in the class action suit not only sought to dumb down or abolish the CBEST altogether; they also wanted back pay for all prospective teachers who flunked the test and were not hired. Not just back pay: additional monetary damages to compensate for psychological trauma. One teacher (who did eventually pass on her fifth try) said she "felt horrible. I didn't know what I was going to do if I didn't pass this test, because I had spent my life thinking I was going to be a teacher."[13]

Committed teachers—those for whom it's a lifelong dream come true—are certainly greatly to be desired. But as Judge William Orrick, Jr., wrote in ruling for the State of California in the fall of 1996, "schoolteachers who use improper grammar or spelling, or who make mistakes in simple calculations, model that behavior for their students—much to the detriment of their education."[14] In plain language: teachers can't teach what they don't know.

How could the "right" of teachers to fail such a simple test have become a civil rights cause? As will be clear from data presented below, black children (on average) desperately need better schooling; they are falling through the very wide cracks in the American educational system. The plaintiffs in the CBEST case labeled as discriminatory traditional methods of selecting teachers and saw an inevitable conflict between equity and rigorous academic standards—between racial justice and testing. Eliminating CBEST would not have helped children in educational need. The racially caring policy for which the plaintiffs argued was, in reality, cruel to students.

The unmistakable fear that ran through the plaintiffs' case was that the performance of black teachers on CBEST was a terrible judgment on the innate capacity of African Americans. The results contained no such judgment. But in resisting minimum competency testing, the plaintiffs were defending the low educational standards that had served miserably those who ended up unable to pass CBEST. Surely the solution was not more of the same.

EQUALIZING EDUCATIONAL OPPORTUNITY

Students deserve better schools, which means schools that are better funded, it is often said. Fix the money problem and you fix the school. Alas, it has not proved so simple. The schools to which black children go are not generally financially starved. Between 1965 and 1994, school expenditures per pupil (in constant 1994 dollars) rose by 122 percent, a gain one-third higher than the overall rise in per capita personal income in the period. As a result, the pupil/teacher ratio in the public schools dropped by a third, from an average of over twenty-five students per teacher down to just seventeen per teacher.[15]

A good deal of the increase in spending was channeled into programs aimed specifically at assisting schools with high enrollments of economically disadvantaged children, in which African Americans are, of course, well represented. The two largest federal efforts were Head Start, for preschoolers, and Title I of the Elementary and Secondary Education Act of 1965 (for a time known as Chapter 1), the funds for which were targeted at pupils from low-income families. Both were Great Society programs that have continued to grow. Title I spending in 1995 exceeded $7 billion, about a quarter of the total budget of the U.S. Department of Education. Head Start, which is run by the Department of Health and Human Services, cost another $3.5 billion.[16]

This drive to level funding for children of different racial and class backgrounds has been strikingly successful. Social critics can still be heard claiming that suburban white schools are wallowing in money, while big-city schools attended mainly by minority students are starved for funds.[17] This is doubtless true in isolated instances, but as a generalization it is just plain wrong. As a consequence both of programs like those alluded to above and of court decisions demanding greater equity in school financing, racial, class, and suburban-city variations in school spending have pretty much disappeared in recent years.

It can be argued that mere equality in expenditures is not enough, because minority children living in central cities have greater needs. The homes and neighborhoods they come from are not conducive to learning, and the schools must do more for them to compensate for those disadvantages. We are sympathetic to this argument, but it is very different from the customary claim that big-city schools are not nearly as well funded as their suburban counterparts. That common charge is false.

The best evidence comes from the National Center for Education Statistics' comprehensive analysis of variations in per-pupil expenditures for the academic year 1989–1990. It found that the higher the percentage of minority students in a school district, the *higher* the level of spending, even after differences in costs of living and other variables were held constant. Districts with a "minority majority" were not "starved" compared to overwhelmingly white districts; they actually spent 15 percent more, on the average, than districts in which minority enrollment was less than 5 percent. What is more, contrary to widespread popular belief, average expenditures per pupil in the central cities of metropolitan areas were identical to average spending in the suburbs around them.[18]

For example, in the 1992–1993 academic year the Atlanta public schools spent 20 percent more than suburban DeKalb County. The Hartford public schools, 94 percent minority, spent $8,817, far more than the Hartford suburbs. Washington, D.C.'s public schools, with a 96 percent minority enrollment, spent $8,382 per student, 55 percent higher than the amount for the prosperous suburban Prince George's County. And that's a low estimate, since in fact the city seems to have been reporting inflated enrollment figures.[19]

THE SHRINKING RACIAL GAP IN COGNITIVE SKILLS

The shift toward greater equality in educational expenditures may have helped to narrow the racial gap in academic performance in at least one respect. In 1965 just over half of all black men and women aged twenty-five to twenty-nine had completed four or more years of high school, as compared with 73 percent of whites.[20] By 1995, as we noted in Chapter 7, 86.5 percent of all young blacks in this age bracket were high school graduates, a figure so close to the one for whites that the difference between them was not statistically significant. That seems a striking and heartening advance to have made in three decades.

Before we celebrate this achievement, though, we must consider whether having completed high school today means what it meant in 1965. African Americans have caught up with whites in the rate at which they complete one stage of the educational process, but is that proof that the typical black student at the end of secondary school has acquired as much actual "education" as the typical white student? Some critics have argued that high school graduation has become almost universal because the schools have been so dumbed down that possession of a high school diploma has become virtually meaningless. If the racial gap in high school completion has been overcome mainly through school policies giving "social promotions" to pupils who have done little more than warm a seat, then it isn't much of an achievement.[21]

Thus, it is important to ask how much students of different races have actually been learning—what cognitive skills they can demonstrate. We need to go beyond what has been called "the incarceration theory of education"— the assumption that what matters is keeping the students inside the school's four walls, because "it is only the quantity, not the quality of the educational experience that counts."[22] On the question of what has been learned, the best evidence comes from the National Assessment of Educational Progress (NAEP), a federally sponsored series of national tests sometimes called "the nation's report card." For the past quarter century, the National Assessment has regularly tested representative samples of American elementary and secondary school pupils in reading, mathematics, science, and other subjects at the ages of nine, thirteen, and seventeen (or sometimes in grades four, eight, and either eleven or twelve). The NAEP examinations measure the cognitive skills that pupils have developed at key points in their school careers, and indicate how well prepared they are to move up to the next level of the educational system or to take jobs that require some literacy and numeracy. And with respect to black children the NAEP news—as we will discuss below —has not been good.

Not everyone takes as seriously as we do the NAEP and other scores; the emphasis on cognitive skills and the testing of those skills have both been widely attacked in recent years. Thus, Theodore R. Sizer, chairman of the Coalition of Essential Schools and a former dean of the Graduate School of Education at Harvard, urges that students be "assessed with tools based on student performance of real tasks," with the final diploma awarded on the basis of an "exhibition" demonstrating that the students "can do important things"—whatever that means.[23] The National Education Association, the nation's largest teachers' union, is on record as opposing all testing that is "mandated by local, state, or national authority," whether of students or of teachers.[24] For the NEA it is of course in good part a jobs issue; even the testing of students can threaten employment security if parents blame teachers for the low scores of their kids. But the trade union is also motivated by broader ideological concerns. It fervently opposes any strategy that sorts out students hierarchically. "Most progressive educators regard standardized tests as a backward, even discriminatory tool for assessing performance and push for methods like 'portfolios,' compilations of students' classwork that are graded individually without reference to national standards or norms," a *New York Times Magazine* staff writer reported in 1996.[25]

The 1994 publication of *The Bell Curve: Intelligence and Class Structure in American Life* by Richard J. Herrnstein and Charles Murray sparked a controversy that may have unjustly reinforced the bad name that standardized tests had already acquired in mainstream educational circles.[26] The fact that African-American children, on the average, have been performing poorly on such tests does not suggest they are deficient in innate intellectual ability. We strongly differ from Herrnstein and Murray on this point. The NAEP and other tests cited in this chapter are not assessments of "pure intelligence," if there is such a thing, and we do not find IQ—understood as a fixed and largely hereditary trait—a useful concept.

Our genetic inheritance may set some limits on our likely proficiency, quite independent of the social environment in which we grow up. Whether or not that is the case, we are convinced, however, that those limits do not much matter for purposes of educational policy. Almost all young people are capable of learning more than schools demand of them today. The National Assessment of Educational Progress tells us how well young people are able to read a prose passage, write a paragraph, grasp a scientific concept, or solve a mathematical problem. NAEP does not measure the innate, immutable abilities of students; it measures the level of cognitive skill they have attained by a certain age. And that level of achievement is what matters. If young people are to be prepared for the increasingly sophisticated demands of a postindustrial economy, they need precisely those cognitive skills that tests measure and that too few young Americans—particularly black Americans—possess.[27]

The magnitude of that skills deficit is made plain in Table 1, which contains the basic evidence showing how well black and white students in selected years over the past quarter century were able to read and to do math and science problems at the age of seventeen, when they were on the verge of entering either college or the labor market. The results of the earliest of these tests—for science in 1970, reading in 1971, and mathematics in 1973—were dismaying. They revealed an immense racial gulf in cognitive skills. Since the tests at each level included some of the same questions, and they were graded on a single scale, it is possible to calculate how many years African-American 17-year-olds were behind whites. In 1971, for example, their reading score of 239 was far below the 261 achieved by white 13-year-olds. It fell almost exactly halfway between the score for whites who were 13 and those who were only 9 (214). Black students were thus (on the average) reading at the level of the typical white aged 11.1 years; they were 5.9 years behind white 17-year-olds. The gaps in science and mathematics in 1971 were somewhat smaller, yet still shockingly large. African Americans lagged 4.3 years behind whites in mathematics, and 4.7 years behind them in science.

It is easy for the eye to pass over the phrase "six years behind whites in reading" without its meaning quite registering. African Americans in their final year of high school in 1971 were as adept at handling the printed word as whites in their last year of elementary school—that is, in the sixth grade. In 1971 only the top 10 percent of African-American teenagers could read with as much facility as the *average* white student of the same age. Conversely only the bottom tenth of white students were as poor at reading as the average black student. A twelfth-grade English teacher dealing with a racially mixed class of average students could have felt confident that most of the whites in the class were capable of struggling through *Julius Caesar* or *Silas Marner.* But most of the black students would have found such a reading assignment completely overwhelming, as the typical white sixth-grader surely would have.

A score of 300 on a NAEP reading test means that a student aged seventeen is "proficient" at reading, defined as being able to "find, understand, summarize, and explain relatively complicated literary and informational material."[28] That sounds like a fair description of the level of competence in reading that we might expect of an entering freshman at most colleges and universities. If you can't read that well, it seems reasonable to assume, you need remedial instruction before attempting to do college work. In 1971, fewer than 8 percent of African-American seventeen-year-olds scored 300 or more in reading. More than five times as many whites—43 percent—were proficient readers.[29] Since about 30 percent of young blacks were going on to college in

Table 1

Mean Scores of 17-Year-Olds by Race, and the Racial Gap Between Blacks and Whites in Years, National Assessment of Educational Progress, 1970–1994

	BLACK	WHITE	GAP IN YEARS
Reading			
1971	239	291	5.9
1980	243	293	6.0
1988	274	295	2.5
1990	267	297	3.4
1994	266	296	3.9
Mathematics			
1973	270	310	4.3
1982	272	304	4.1
1986	279	308	3.4
1990	289	310	2.5
1994	286	312	3.4
Science			
1970	258	312	4.7
1982	235	293	7.1
1986	253	298	4.4
1990	253	301	5.7
1994	257	306	5.4
Writing			
1984	270	297	3.1
1988	275	296	2.1
1990	268	293	2.3
1994	267	291	3.3

Sources: 1970–1973 and 1994 scores from National Center for Educational Statistics, *NAEP 1994 Trends in Academic Progress: Report in Brief* (Washington, D.C.: U.S. Government Printing Office, 1996), 7; all others from National Center for Education Statistics, *Digest of Educational Statistics: 1994* (Washington, D.C.: U.S. Government Printing Office, 1995), 113, 118, 121, 126. Writing scores are for 11th-graders rather than 17-year-olds, a close enough approximation for our purposes.

The racial gap in years was computed by taking the mean scores of whites at ages 9, 13, and 17 (or at grades 4, 8, and 11 in the case of writing), interpolating white scores for the intervening ages, and calibrating black scores against them. This method is a slight variant of that employed by John Bishop in *The Economics of Employment Testing*, Working Paper No. 88-14 (Ithaca, N.Y.: Center for Advanced Human Resources Studies, Cornell University, 1989), 58. Bishop's interpretations were more upbeat than ours, because the last NAEP scores available to him were for 1988. Since 1988, regrettably, the picture has become much gloomier.

1971, roughly three out of four must not have been able to read well enough to understand the relatively complicated reading that college students are expected to master—or should be expected to master.[30]

How much has changed since the early 1970s? The latest NAEP figures available for comparative analysis are from 1994. The first thing to notice is that in the two decades or so since the first NAEP tests, white 17-year-olds have not made any educational gains to speak of. They picked up 5 points in reading between 1971 and 1994, and 2 points in math between 1973 and 1994; they lost 6 points in science from 1970 to 1994, and dropped 6 points in writing from 1984 to 1994. The losses were as big as the gains. This evidence does not show that the overall quality of American public education has deteriorated drastically within the past generation, as some pessimists have argued. On the other hand, there is no sign that things are getting any better. And that is a great disappointment, given the increased resources that have been devoted to schools in the hope of improving student performance, as well as the higher educational requirements for good jobs in today's economy.[31]

That is the picture for white students. What about African Americans? Black students have made great strides forward, and have narrowed the racial gap. In the 1970s, African Americans who were in high school made little educational progress, but scores rose perceptibly for students in the younger age groups—nine-year-olds and thirteen-year-olds (not given in the table).[32] A solid foundation for progress at the high school level was thus being laid in grade school and junior high during the 1970s. The scores of white students in the younger age brackets were level or declining a bit, while those of black students were rising. As these better-prepared black students reached high school in the 1980s, the racial gap began to narrow there as well.

Thus, the racial gap in reading competence shrank dramatically between 1980 and 1988, falling from 6 years to just 2.5 years—a truly remarkable, but, alas, short-lived, change. In 1980 only 7 percent of black youths could read at the proficient level; by 1988 the figure had jumped to 25 percent (as compared with 45 percent for whites). In mathematics a gap of 4.1 years in 1982 narrowed to 2.5 years in 1990. In science the gap fell from an appalling 7.1 years in 1982 to 4.4 years in 1986. The first assessment of student ability to write the English language was not attempted until 1984, but between 1984 and 1988 the gap narrowed from 3.1 years to 2.1 years.

Not only were black students in general performing much better in these years; the gain was especially pronounced for those at the bottom. Between 1971 and 1988 the score for a black seventeen-year-old who was reading at the 5th percentile leaped 50 points, for a student at the 25th percentile, it went up 40 points. On the other hand, African-American students in the 95th percentile gained only 23 points. The same pattern shows up in the math results for the years 1978–1990.[33]

Had the rate of progress from 1980 to 1988 continued, black-white differences in reading skill would have been wiped out entirely by 1994. If the pace of change in science between 1982 and 1986 had been maintained, the racial gap would also have vanished by 1994. Attaining equality in math and writing would have taken somewhat longer, but the goal seemed definitely within reach.

THE RACIAL GAP WIDENS AGAIN

Such were the grounds for optimism several years ago. But since the late 1980s, alas, the positive trends have been reversed, with the result that much of the earlier progress has been lost. In math the racial gap of 2.5 years in 1990 grew to 3.4 years by 1994. At last report, the average African-American high school senior had math skills precisely on a par with those of the typical white in the middle of the ninth grade—an improvement over the gap of four years or more that existed in the 1970s and early 1980s but still a huge handicap in a world in which numeracy is becoming at least as important as literacy.

In the other test areas things look even worse. Although the racial gap in reading dropped by a remarkable 3.5 years between 1980 and 1988, it then widened by nearly a year and a half from 1988 to 1994, erasing close to half of the previous gain. As a result, in 1994 blacks aged seventeen could read as well on the average as the typical white child who was a month past his or her *thirteenth* birthday. In 1992 just 18 percent of black students were rated "proficient" in reading, as compared with 47 percent of whites. In 1994 it was 13 percent of blacks and 43 percent of whites.[34]

Similar regression occurred in both science and writing, with the science gap widening by a year after 1986 and the writing gap increasing by 1.2 years between 1988 and 1994. Blacks in the twelfth grade could deal with scientific problems at the level of whites in the sixth grade and write about as well as whites in the eighth grade. If we project these gloomy trends into the future, it won't be all that long before the racial gap is as wide as it was when the first NAEP tests were introduced. (Of course the projection may be no more predictive than the optimistic projections of a decade earlier; let us hope so.) Although much has changed for the better since the early 1970s, much has also changed since the mid-1980s, and it is all for the worse.[35]

Why this alarming turnaround? What brought about the earlier gains that have now been reversed? These important questions have not attracted the attention of many researchers. (The issue has just come to national attention as a result of the December 1996 publication of *Education Watch: The 1996 Education Trust State and National Data Book.*[36] Neither this report nor the sympathetic stories it generated in the national press, though, shed any light on the causes at work.)[37] Were the desegregation efforts of the seventies and eighties the chief reason for the gains during that period? It is plausible to think that they helped significantly, but a recent analysis suggests not. Those black students who have remained in predominantly African-American schools have improved their scores as much or more than those attending integrated schools.[38] Even if desegregation could be shown to have contributed to the initial black achievement gains in the 1970s and much of the 1980s, what would explain the backsliding since the end of that decade? The level of desegregation has not gone down—as the evidence discussed in the previous chapter suggests. Patterns of de facto school segregation seem to have been stable since 1980, and a variable that does not vary cannot explain a change in academic performance.

Neither the gains nor the losses are explained by changes in black family income or other measures of socioeconomic status either. In his 1992 essay "Why Is Black Educational Achievement Rising?" sociologist David Armor argued that the expansion of the black middle class was the source of improving NAEP scores.[39] But Armor failed to notice that black educational achievement had already begun to decline by the time he posed the problem. The racial gap in reading widened for all three age groups between 1988 and 1990, for all three age groups in science between 1986 and 1990, and for the two younger age groups in math between 1986 and 1990.[40] That turnaround occurred despite the fact that the black middle class had not suddenly begun to shrink, and was indeed prospering by most measures.

On the other hand, poverty among blacks remained high. Is there some simple relation between poverty rates and educational achievement? The major reductions in poverty for black children occurred between World War II and the end of the 1960s, well before the gains revealed in NAEP tests in the 1970s and early 1980s.[41] The educational advances after 1970 came at a time when the poverty rate was not changing significantly.[42] Thus, poverty was not going down steeply when the racial gap in educational achievement was narrowing; nor was it going up dramatically when that gap began to widen once again.

Nor would the huge rise in out-of-wedlock births and a steep and steady decline in the proportion of black children growing up with two parents seem to explain adequately the educational performance of African-American children. It is well established that children raised in single-parent families do less well in school than others, even when all other variables, including income, are controlled.[43] But the disintegration of the black nuclear family—noted by Daniel Patrick Moynihan as early as 1965—was occurring rapidly in the period in which black scores were rising.

Perhaps the post-1965 educational advances of blacks were the result of the growth of such federal compensatory-education programs as Head Start and Chapter 1.[44] But these programs do not seem to have had much positive effect on the black children exposed to them. The first major longitudinal study of the effects of Chapter 1 yielded "little or no evidence to suggest any differential gain in achievement between students receiving compensatory services and those not receiving such support."[45] In any event, the Chapter 1/ Head Start theory would not explain what happened in the late 1980s. Funding for these programs was not cut off or even reduced. Quite the opposite: the number of students in compensatory programs and the dollars spent on them kept going up.

What about changes in the curriculum and patterns of course selection by students? The educational reform movement did succeed in pushing students into a "New Basics" core curriculum that included more English, science, math, and social studies courses. The proportion of black high school graduates who had fulfilled the "New Basics" requirements rose from 12 percent in 1982 to 42 percent in 1990, one point ahead of whites. The proportion of black high school graduates who had taken geometry, for example, rose from 29 percent in 1982 to 58 percent in 1994.[46] There is good reason to believe that taking more in the way of tough courses did contribute to the impressive rise in black test scores in the 1970s and early 1980s; tightening requirements further and raising standards seems essential to future progress.[47]

But this is another one of those explanations that nicely fits the facts for the period before the late 1980s but not the very different picture thereafter. The number of black students going through "New Basics" courses did not decline a decade or so ago, pulling down their NAEP scores; it was still on the rise as of 1994. It may be that courses that were called "geometry," say, became more and more diluted as schools required or pressured their students to take them, so that what appeared from the label to be tough basic instruction was in fact a soft, watered-down version of the real thing. As we will argue in the conclusion to this chapter, course-taking patterns at Catholic schools suggest that tougher academic demands do bring about higher levels of educational achievement. But the hypothesis that the additional courses taken in the core subjects were watered down around a decade ago is one that we cannot properly test with existing data.[48]

LOW EXPECTATIONS, LOW PERFORMANCE

We're thus stumped. We don't have a simple answer to the question of why black scores—having shown encouraging gains—should have declined since 1988. We can, though, suggest some elements of an explanation. First, the increased violence and disorder of inner-city lives that came with the introduction of crack cocaine and the drug-related gang wars in the mid-1980s likely had something to do with the reversal of black educational progress. A climate of violence, as we will suggest later, is not conducive to learning, and too many of the schools attended by African Americans are in dangerous environments. Second, we would argue that American education is not in general in good shape, and that fact may be having a disparate impact on black children. Although that has long been true, strategies designed in recent years specifically to address the educational needs of African-American students have been, in our view, counterproductive more often than not. Whether we can blame the increasing racial gap upon these strategies is not clear, but they surely are not helping to close it.

When we say that American education in general is in trouble, we have in mind the degree to which American students lag behind their peers in other countries—which we see as the result of a misguided educational culture. That culture stresses acquiring the tools to learn rather than covering specific subject material, allowing children to explore what interests them rather than using teachers to convey knowledge. It celebrates the uniqueness of individual children and the ethnic or racial group to which they belong, such that common academic standards, standardized tests, and grades are disdained as part of a culturally biased and judgmental package.[49] As educational critic E. D. Hirsch, Jr., has pointed out, the "deep aversion to and contempt for factual knowledge that pervade the thinking of American educators" means that students fail to build the "intellectual capital" that is the foundation of all further learning. That will be particularly true of those students who come to school most academically disadvantaged—those whose homes are not, in effect, an additional school.[50] The deficiencies of American education hit hardest those most in need of that education.

There is, we believe, an additional reason why black children, specifically, are (on the average) faring badly academically. The drive for racial equality has had the opposite of its intended effect. Behind much suspicion of standardized tests and demanding academic expectations, we argued at the outset, lies a heightened racial consciousness. It is Shelby Steele's point: standards are lowered, tests attacked because both whites and blacks—for different reasons—fear black failure. However well intentioned such concern, it has been a recipe for academic disaster. Educational policies instituted in the name of equality have in fact increased inequality.

The point is a perfectly commonsense one. Ask little of children in the way of academic achievement and little is what you tend to get—unless they come from homes in which the educational expectations are such as to outweigh an undemanding school. If the bar is raised, children work harder, and hard work is the road to success. It matters much more than innate ability. It seems like a perfectly obvious point; it is not one that the educational establishment, for the most part, accepts. In fact, in an alarming number of instances, the expected disparate racial impact of high standards has forced advocates to back off.

Thus, in 1990, the Boston School Committee voted to require that high school seniors demonstrate eighth-grade reading competence in order to graduate. The committee beat a hasty retreat from this pathetically modest demand, however, when the school superintendent said that 40 percent of the city's seniors (a class from which there had already been a high dropout rate) were not up to the task—they could be expected to fail an achievement test designed for the average thirteen-year-old. If Boston's three elite examination schools were eliminated from the test-taking pool, the projected failure rate jumped to 52 percent. Moreover, 84 percent of white students, but only 53 percent of those who were black—including those who attended the selective examination schools—were expected to make the grade.[51] Authorities in Boston might have admitted that the schools were failing to do their job, and failing their African-American pupils most of all. They took the painless route instead: the test was canceled. They killed the messenger even before the message could be delivered.

Chicago outdid Boston, in a way, in 1996. Without even the excuse of having a new graduation requirement that some students might flunk, the Chicago public school system decided to stop giving its students the Iowa Tests of Basic Skills, which it had been doing for thirty years. The reason? Chicago public school pupils—nearly nine out of ten of them black or Hispanic—were so far behind educationally that the Iowa tests had ceased to be a useful yardstick. The city's schools decided instead to devise new tests to "more accurately gauge what their students are being taught." The problem with the Iowa tests, used in most school districts in the United States, is that they revealed with brutal clarity what Chicago students were *not* being taught —or at least were not learning.[52]

The same issue arose in Florida and Ohio, with different and happier outcomes. In 1979 a federal court granted a preliminary injunction forbidding Florida from enforcing a new requirement that students pass a basic skills test in order to receive their high school diplomas. Initially the judge was impressed with the argument that the test would have a disparate impact and would thus be discriminatory—since the black failure rate would be higher than that for whites.[53] After prolonged litigation, however, the court grasped the vital point that such tests could, in fact, be essential tools for overcoming past discrimination. By setting clear, attainable goals, they could spur minority pupils to work harder to develop their cognitive skills, skills they especially needed if racial bias continued to affect their employment prospects.

A 1994 challenge to an Ohio law that required students to pass a ninth-grade-level exam in order to graduate from high school was likewise defeated. The Cleveland branch of the NAACP filed a suit claiming that the requirement was discriminatory, and sought the backing of the Office of Civil Rights in the U.S. Department of Education. The state, however, was able to demonstrate that its funding of predominantly black schools was equitable, and that the apparent racial differences in rates of passing were almost entirely due to

differences in patterns of school attendance. The students who failed, whatever their color, were mainly those who were often truant—those who had
not understood the link between work and achievement. The Office of Civil
Rights refused to back the complaint and the suit was dismissed. After new
efforts were made to raise levels of school attendance, pass rates across the
state soon exceeded 95 percent.[54]

Those who are concerned about racial justice often charge that white teachers have low expectations for black students. But too often civil rights advocates and much of the educational establishment have said, in effect, that *all*
teachers—black and white—should lower their sights. By hanging tough in
the face of civil rights suits, Florida and Ohio had in fact gone to bat for
African-American students—the view of the NAACP to the contrary notwithstanding. Legislators in those states had faith in the capacity of black children
to learn. More faith than did those who thought junior high school tests for
high school seniors were just "too hard"—and more than that of the Boston
School Committee, whose racial sensitivity in 1990 had allowed students who
had difficulty reading a comic book to continue to collect their high school
diplomas.

BLAMING THE TESTS

One might think that the poor performance, on the average, of black students
on standardized tests would suggest the need for new educational strategies
—strategies that would more effectively teach the skills that these students
lack. But too often the disproportionately low scores are viewed as an indictment of the tests themselves, and those who devise and use them.

Civil rights advocates did not always take this view. In 1955, at a Supreme
Court hearing to debate methods of implementing *Brown,* Thurgood Marshall
responded to the segregationist argument that racially separate schools were
necessary because the average black child was so far behind the average white
child academically. Marshall said that the solution was "simple." "They give
tests to grade children. . . . Put the dumb colored children in with the dumb
white children, and put the smart colored children in with the smart white
children—that is no problem."[55] Test them all, in other words, and sort them
out accordingly.

It is inconceivable that the chief counsel for the NAACP Legal Defense
and Education Fund would today blithely advocate such a strategy. In fact, by
the mid-1960s the civil rights community no longer shared Thurgood Marshall's earlier willingness to rely upon objective tests as a basis for decisions
about black students—or, for that matter, prospective black employees. As
early as 1964, ten years after *Brown,* a hearing examiner for the Illinois Fair
Employment Practice Commission was dismissing employment tests as unfair

to "culturally deprived and disadvantaged groups" because they did not take into account "inequalities and differences in environment."[56] And by 1971— a story we tell in Chapter 15—the Supreme Court had signaled its agreement: tests and other screening devices neutral on their face could not be maintained if they had a disparate racial impact and were not an obvious "business necessity."[57]

Tests given to assess the educational progress of students were inevitably seen in the same light. "When standard aptitude tests are given to low income Negro children . . . test scores become practically meaningless," federal district judge Skelly Wright concluded in a 1967 Washington, D.C., desegregation decision. "Because of the impoverished circumstances that characterize the disadvantaged child, it is virtually impossible to tell whether the test score reflects lack of ability—or simply lack of opportunity."[58] Judge Wright's views have remained conventional wisdom in civil rights and mainstream educational circles. Thirteen years later the NAACP, the NEA, and the National PTA, among others, signed on to a "Statement to Urge a Ban on Standardized Testing of Young Children."[59]

Testing critics often argue that black students' scores are actually meaningless. It's not only that socioeconomic disadvantage has handicapped these test-takers, the students have been asked the wrong questions. The exams are racially and culturally biased. They measure nothing appropriate to blacks. That was the view that informed the decision in the 1979 California case, *Larry P. v. Riles,* which banned the use of IQ tests in the public schools— although (amazingly) only for blacks. Whites, Asians, and Hispanics were unaffected. California had used the tests (along with other indicators) in determining placement in an "educable mentally retarded" (EMR) track. "Black children's intelligence may be manifested in ways that the tests do not show . . . ," Judge Robert F. Peckham ruled.[60] He depended upon the testimony of Georgia State professor of education, Dr. Asa Hilliard, best known for his subsequent advocacy of an Afrocentric curriculum for black children. (We will consider this misguided movement in some detail shortly.) Hilliard claimed that blacks had "a cultural heritage that represent[ed] an experience pool" unacknowledged by standardized tests.[61] It's been an oft-repeated argument. In 1989 the Committee on Policy for Racial Justice, a group of black educators, charged that customary tests failed to assess "student acquisition of an independently determined knowledge base."[62] A year later Harvard University education professor Charles V. Willie, an influential spokesman in civil rights and education circles, argued that standardized testing is flawed because it fails "to recognize that in social organization there always are at least two norms, the norm of the dominant people of power and the norm of the subdominant people of power."[63]

The "norm of the subdominant people" has been said to include nonstandard English—a fact that tests routinely ignore, Hilliard complained in his testimony in the *Larry P.* case. "Vocabulary is not standard," he said, "even when people use the same word."[64] Syntax is not standard. Nor are cultural references—to Shakespearean plays, historical events, or even recreational scenes—Judge Peckham noted.[65] The black child "uses language requiring a wide use of many coined interjections (sometimes profanity)," according to the *African-American Baseline Essays,* teaching material for an "Afrocentric curriculum" published in 1987 by the largely white Portland, Oregon, school system, and subsequently adopted as a teaching guide in Atlanta, Detroit, Fort Lauderdale and other cities.[66] Carol Chomsky of the Harvard Graduate School of Education has argued that to label as "mistakes" such constructions as "He didn't want to ride in no cars" is an objectionable value judgment.[67] A widely cited 1988 article in *Phi Delta Kappan,* a leading magazine for professional educators, referred to the "elaborated, stylized English commonly used in standardized tests [that] prevents such tests from accurately measuring the achievement, ability, or skills of students who speak nonstandard (e.g., African American . . .) dialects."[68] This view was carried to its logical conclusion by school authorities in Oakland, California, when they announced in December 1996 that most of their black students were not native speakers of English at all; their mother tongue was "Ebonics." Although Oakland's announcement provoked national controversy, the public schools of San Diego all had Ebonics programs for several years, and, as of 1996, the Los Angeles Unified School District was spending $3 million a year on an Ebonics program for 25,000 students.[69]

The argument that black children speak the distinct language of a separate culture has been given an even more radical twist by some. It's not simply that black children do not know and have no need to know who Columbus was; blacks actually think differently than whites. Standardized academic tests are inescapably biased because they involve "linear thinking" alien to black culture. Educator Janice Hale-Benson has complained that "Western social science overly emphasizes linguistic and logicomathematical skills in assessing intelligence." Citing the examples of Michael Jordan and Michael Jackson, she suggested that "athletic . . . and musical skills" should be "nurtured" by the schools in order to "support the self-esteem and achievement of Black children," instead of being "virtually ignored."[70] "African-American students and European-American students have very different learning styles," according to educational consultant Jawanza Kunjufu.[71] Likewise, a 1987 New York State Board of Regents booklet—an official state document—stated that "children's racial, ethnic and emotional backgrounds and cultures influence the manner in which they learn concepts and process information." It enumerated a number of "qualities noted in African-Americans": a "preference for inferential reasoning rather than deductive or inductive reasoning" and a "tendency to approximate space, number and time instead of aiming for complete accuracy," among others.[72] The *Phi Delta Kappan* article mentioned above also spoke of the "different ways of knowing and problem solving that . . . are often related to race or ethnicity." [73]

If black children learn differently, they must be tested for different skills. And indeed in 1990 Nancy Amuleru-Marshall, a researcher for the Atlanta public schools, contended that "any tests that emphasize logical, analytical methods of problem solving will be biased against minorities." [74] Under her direction Atlanta sought to develop tests to identify gifted and talented pupils based on their "athletic ability, 'street smarts,' and interpersonal skills." [75] In the same vein, Thelma Mumford-Glover, director of Atlanta's gifted and talented program, contended that "multicriteria are essential to the identification of gifted and talented African-American children." [76] Her office discouraged all use of IQ and achievement tests.

Different learning styles is perhaps what Judge Peckham had in mind in stating that the problem of test bias would not be solved by eliminating certain items and substituting others. [77] FairTest, an important anti-testing group, has called such questions as "What do you call a baby cow?" unfair to inner-city children. [78] Peckham had other examples. But removing the offensive items would not rid a test of its pervasive cultural bias, critics have agreed. As one public interest advocate has put it, "The danger is giving people the impression that the problem with the test is specific questions and if you weed out those questions, it'll be OK." [79]

For these critics, the problem with the tests, at bottom, is their disparate racial and ethnic impact. "The consequences of testing . . . constitute the most damning evidence against the fairness of tests. Poor and minority students consistently score lower than do whites," UCLA education professor Jeannie Oakes has written in a widely quoted book on tracking. [80] In 1991, civil rights groups fought a Bush administration education proposal that entailed national testing of students on the ground that a disproportionate number of black (and other minority) students were likely to score low. By implication, tests were legitimate only when the distribution of black and white scores was identical. [81]

The reason is clear: such a disparate racial impact is viewed as inexplicable except as a consequence of discrimination. It was a point that Judge Peckham had made explicitly in an earlier ruling in the same *Larry P.* case. He had called the concentration of black children tracked into "educable mentally retarded" classes an "unmistakable sign of invidious discrimination," and had gone on to argue that academic potential—or the lack thereof—is surely distributed randomly across racial and ethnic groups. [82] Peckham's 1979 decision made the same claim. [83]

Of course, in thinking about the validity of standardized tests, the question is whether they accurately measure not "the ability to learn" but academic performance. The two are too frequently confused; "student performance on time-restricted, multiple-choice, standardized tests does not show innate

aptitude," the Committee on Policy for Racial Justice said in its 1989 statement.[84] We agree. Twenty-six percent of the Asian-American students taking
the SATs in 1995 scored 650 or better in math, while only 13 percent of
whites and 2 percent of blacks did so.[85] These glaring disparities do not
suggest to us that Asian students have twice the brain power of whites and
thirteen times as much as blacks. They do mean that (for whatever reason)
many more Asians than whites have developed an excellent grasp of math by
the time they reach age seventeen or so, and that African Americans in turn
lag far behind whites.

"If children have not had equitable educational opportunities, then the
equity of the assessment becomes questionable," a 1995 volume on equity
and testing argued.[86] But whatever the level of educational opportunity, at the
end of the day students will not function well in our advanced, knowledge-
based industrial economy if they have not learned to read sophisticated material or solve equations. And thus it remains vital to assess those skills. Only
those who do not care how black children perform can legitimately be charged
with racist indifference. Moreover, the whole line of argument that black
children cannot learn "logical, analytical methods of problem solving" is uncomfortably reminiscent of the racist generalizations about the intellectual
capacities of black people that were widely held by white southerners in the
days of Jim Crow. Many passages in Howard Odum's 1910 segregationist
classic, *Social and Mental Traits of the Negro*, for example, bear an uncanny
resemblance to what Janice Hale-Benson has to say on the same subject,
except that Odum believed the alleged tendency of African Americans to
think in what today is called a "nonlinear" way was a great handicap, while
some current writers claim to find it a positive asset.[87]

Tracking

If standardized tests are unfair to blacks—or more broadly to students from
other than middle-class homes—it follows that using them to assign students
to particular courses or academic tracks is unjust and indefensible. In recent
years civil rights activists and educational progressives in general have demanded the elimination of what has been variously called "tracking," "ability"
grouping, or "performance" or "competency" grouping. FairTest maintains
that, although children are "different," none have academic "deficits."[88] The
Massachusetts Advocacy Center declares that schools should promote "a
sense of community and social justice, not privilege or definitions of 'deserving' and 'undeserving.' "[89]

It is impossible to tell how much actual practice in the schools has been
changed as a result of such attacks, but criticisms of this sort dominate the
professional educational literature. The very process of sorting and grouping

students is said to be a self-fulfilling prophecy; students labeled as less competent quickly become so. It is a well-founded concern when long-term judgments about likely academic performance are made on the basis of tests at an early age. It is also legitimate to object to every form of dumbed-down schooling. Almost every student can meet academic standards higher than those generally in place in the United States.

Critics of tracking charge that identifying students as academically deficient has a special impact on black children; minority status (in and of itself) lowers teachers' expectations, with the result that students learn less.[90] That was an argument that Judge Skelly Wright made in the D.C. desegregation case, which was in turn cited approvingly by Judge Peckham in his first *Larry P.* decision.[91] Judge Wright referred to teachers' "misjudgments" about the ability of black students. Other tracking critics are not so kind. They make the very serious charge that racism—not poor judgment—determines who ends up in what level classes. In a September 1990 newscast an ABC News reporter stated flatly that "throughout the nation schools are sorting students into high- and low-ability groups, often with racial bias regardless of their test scores." The program went on to quote UCLA's Jeannie Oakes. "Often you'll see high-scoring kids in low tracks, low-scoring kids in high tracks and often that relates to ethnicity and social class," she said.[92] It's a perception that, on occasion, has triggered organized parent protest. This was the case in early 1990 in Selma, Alabama, when parents took to the streets in part over the tracking issue. "We have black children who are high achievers, who have high test scores, who have not been allowed to take algebra," an attorney and activist with a high school daughter complained.[93] A year later, parents in the Richardson, Texas, school district charged that black children were put in special-education classes not only because they spoke, dressed, and acted differently, but also because whites didn't want any academic competition from blacks.[94]

No qualified child should be "not allowed" to take algebra; indeed, schools should expect almost all children to take geometry and trigonometry as well. And there is no doubt that in tracked public schools, black (and Hispanic) students cluster disproportionately in the less demanding courses. But while racial bias may be a small element in some settings, there is no evidence that it is the main factor. Schools that sort students on the basis of performance are undoubtedly relying on test scores—and it is the lower average scores of minority pupils (which are not peculiar to schools that track) that are the basic problem. Instituting policies that ignore differences in educational achievement in the name of racial and ethnic equality does not address the real issue.

Tracking takes a variety of forms. A number of public schools—the Bronx High School of Science and Stuyvesant High in New York, Lowell High in San Francisco, and the Boston Latin School, among others—only admit those students who meet high academic standards. These are "top-track" schools, which admit students mainly on the basis of their performance on an entrance examination or some form of standardized test. The result is substantial over-representation of whites and Asians, and a corresponding underrepresentation of blacks and Hispanics—raising, at least in some cities, the familiar questions about racial bias.

Boston is one of those cities. Admission to the Boston Latin School and the city's two other "examination" high schools was purely a matter of academic achievement—test scores and grades—until 1974, when the school commit-tee was found guilty of segregating black students. A 35 percent racial quota for black and Hispanic students at Boston Latin was included in the citywide desegregation plan that Judge Arthur Garrity ordered that year; the traditional admissions criteria had resulted in a disproportionately white school. After the court surrendered control of the Boston school system in 1987, the quota was maintained voluntarily. But to meet its target for black and Hispanic enrollment at Boston Latin, each year the school turned down hundreds of white and Asian applicants with higher grades and test scores than those admitted to fill the set-aside.[95]

To meet the quota in filling its entering class of 440 students, in 1995, Boston Latin took in minority students ranked as low as number 848.[96] ("Mi-nority"—the shorthand term used by proponents of the set-aside—is actually a misnomer, since Asians are obviously members of an ethnic minority, but they don't count as minorities under the quota.) Julia McLaughlin, a white girl who was turned down by Boston Latin even though her scores and grades were higher than those of 149 students who were accepted, took the issue to court, arguing that the policy amounted to an unconstitutional racial classifi-cation that denied her equal protection of the law.[97] Judge Garrity was com-pelled to order her admission to Boston Latin, and Boston school authorities decided to replace the 35 percent quota with a more complex system that would keep black and Hispanic numbers up without being so vulnerable to constitutional challenge.[98]

The quota at Boston Latin was a logical response to the claim that standard-ized tests misjudge blacks' ability—that scores should be substantially ignored in making decisions with respect to admissions and grouping for instructional purposes. And that arrangements that seem judgmental and hierarchical should in general be modified or eliminated. In the interest of racial justice, "meritocratic" standards (as traditionally defined) and differences in educa-tional achievement should be ignored.

But different arguments have different implications. Those that suggest that black children think and learn differently call for something more. In addition to "culturally appropriate," racially fair assessment processes, they suggest the need for both different curricular materials and more black teachers.

AFROCENTRIC DELUSIONS

One of the salutary effects of the civil rights revolution was to force changes in the public school curriculum, which had traditionally paid too little attention to the role of African Americans in American history and culture. Textbooks since the 1970s have gotten better; they tell a racially and ethnically more inclusive story. Cultural pluralism is celebrated; children now learn, as the educational historian Diane Ravitch has noted, that "variety is the spice of life . . . that differences among groups are a national resource."[99]

But, alas, as Ravitch goes on to say, "these painstaking efforts to expand the understanding of American culture into a richer and more varied tapestry have taken a new turn, and not for the better." What she calls "pluralist multiculturalism" has come to vie with "particularist multiculturalism"—a belief not in a richer common culture, but in the importance of the allegedly distinctive cultural DNA that children inherit.[100] And that has meant, for black children, the importance of their African ancestry, and of an "Afrocentric" educational curriculum built around its significance. Thus, in the early 1990s a variety of urban school systems—Atlanta, Detroit, Washington, D.C., Baltimore, Indianapolis, Milwaukee, Pittsburgh, Richmond, and Philadelphia, among others—began to offer instruction that put Africa at the center of the student's educational universe. This entailed the use of curricular materials that depicted Egypt as the black cradle of civilization, and attributed most of the great philosophical, cultural, and even scientific advances in world history to black Africans. Children in kindergarten began learning how to count in Swahili.[101] In Detroit, for example, twenty-one of the city's schools were "fully African-centered" by the spring of 1996, and the system was three years into the process of "incorporating a new Afrocentric curriculum in all 261 schools."[102]

The basic myths of Afrocentricism are not new. They first appeared in the writings of a few nineteenth-century black nationalist theorists and were picked up by Marcus Garvey, Elijah Muhammad, Malcolm X, and others.[103] What is entirely novel is their endorsement by those responsible for the instruction of hundreds of thousands of pupils in tax-supported public schools. It is in fact difficult to know exactly how much a typical "Afrocentric" classroom differs from what it replaced. There doubtless is much variation, and some of what passes for Afrocentrism may be a mild form of harmless ethnic cheerleading. Nevertheless, the movement has a number of exceedingly worrisome aspects.

First, some of the supposed "experts" responsible for designing the curriculum can only be described as charlatans. Afrocentrism is not a recognized field of knowledge with established scholarly traditions, and it has more than its share of hustlers who have talked their way into positions of responsibility for which they have no qualifications. School systems that would not dream of hiring an astrologist as a consultant have fallen for the equivalent. Thus, in 1993 the Washington, D.C., public school system, which certainly was not short on funds to commission sophisticated expert advice, paid a woman named Abena Walker $164,739 to create an Afrocentric program and run a training program in "African-centered methodology" for D.C. teachers. The training was conducted at something called the Pan-African University, a grandiose name for an unaccredited and unlicensed school whose founder was none other than Mrs. Walker. Mrs. Walker's academic credentials? She had a master's degree—a master's from her own Pan-African University, which she had generously awarded to herself to make her curriculum vitae look more impressive.

It turned out to be the only degree that the newly invented "university" had ever awarded anyone.[104] Even after the scandal became public, the school superintendent kept her on, saying that the controversy over her qualifications was "unfair," and announcing that Afrocentric instruction would be expanded. Teachers who took courses from Mrs. Walker were given recertification credit for doing so, even though Pan-African University was a one-woman school that had never been evaluated by any accrediting body. Supporters of Mrs. Walker attacked the *Washington Post* for the "white supremacy and white chauvinism" it had supposedly shown in raising questions about Mrs. Walker's qualifications.[105]

A volume produced by the Portland, Oregon, public school system, *African-American Baseline Essays,* is the only textbook produced by the Afrocentric movement so far. It is the primary source, for example, of the Afrocentric instruction given from kindergarten through the twelfth grade to 60,000 students in the Atlanta public schools, a system in which 92 percent of the students and 93 percent of the teachers are black.[106] Although the superintendent of the Portland public schools assured the reader that each of the six "baseline essays" were the work of "an individual who was both knowledgeable about the specific discipline and recognized as an expert on African and African-American history," and that each one was reviewed by a long list of committees and consultants, this was not true. The essay on science, for instance, was written by someone with no college education at all.[107] The only scientific credentials of the author, one Hunter Adams, were a high school diploma and work experience as a lab technician.[108]

Adams's lack of credentials might have been excusable if his work had been better, but it was scandalously bad. His contribution to the Portland teacher's guide was a defense of the proposition that "African people are the wellspring of creativity on which the foundation of all science, technology, and engineering rests"—that, for instance, the ancient Egyptians had understood the "pervasive *transmaterial*" causes beyond "the material cause-and-effect relationships of modern science," and had anticipated "many of the philosophical aspects of quantum theory" as used in modern physics.[109]

At the heart of Adams's essay is the claim that "for the ancient Egyptians as well as contemporary Africans worldwide, there is no distinction and thus no separation between science and religion."[110] Note the curious reference to "contemporary Africans worldwide," which clearly is intended to include black students in the United States today. Such students are being told that in *their* culture—which is totally distinct from the culture of the United States, the Portland essays insist—science and religion are regarded as one. It would seem to follow that they would be untrue to their racial heritage if they learned to think about the question from the perspective of modern science, which insists upon precisely that separation. The school superintendent in Washington, D.C., has claimed that "learning about Africa and its role in science will help motivate black males into going into science."[111] (Why he ignored females altogether is not clear.) Alas, if black youths come out of secondary school with a conception of science learned from such teaching materials, they will be hopelessly unqualified to pursue one of the many careers for which scientific and technical skills are now a requirement.

Although the rest of the Portland essays are not as atrocious as the science essay, they are not much better. The mathematics essay, according to one knowledgeable critic, is similarly "riddled with pseudoscience and pseudohistory."[112] The others are crude and chauvinistic efforts which attempt to support Professor Leonard Jeffries's claim that "Africans are at the head of the human family."[113] They bear a strong resemblance to pre–World War I racist theories that saw the whole historical record as proof of the genius of "the white race" in general or of the "Anglo-Saxon," "Nordic," or "Teutonic" races specifically.

Molefi Kete Asante, chair of the Department of African-American Studies at Temple University, has been described by the *Chronicle of Higher Education* as "the major proponent of 'Afrocentricity'" and as a leader in building "a theoretical base" for the Afrocentric idea. Since Temple is presently the only university in the United States that has awarded doctoral degrees in African-American studies, and Asante heads the program, it is particularly disheartening to read his work. His 1988 volume, *Afrocentricity*, begins with a preface by one Kariumu Welsh, which declares that the book is "historically without precedent" because the author "has fused a scientific notion (the bicameral mind) with the spirit (godforce) with the historical (Africa) and the present (technicultural, African-American) to formulate a philosophy that allows for questions and analysis and provides answers and actualizations."[114] Asante then offers many more pages of similar gobbledygook. The author believes in "African *personalism,* energizing every aspect of nature. Where the West is said to favor materialism, and the East . . . is said to favor spiritualism, Africa combines the material and spiritual." The reader is urged, when flying in a plane, to examine "the design of the cabins, think how you would design it Afrocentrically." And when in a restaurant, the "Afrocentrist" will react to the waiter's question "What kind of salad dressing do you prefer?" by refusing to be "inundated by a symbolic reality which denies her existence." The culturally sensitive eating establishment will apparently offer the Afrocentrist not the insulting choice of French, Russian, or Italian dressing but of Nigerian, Ethiopian, or Tanzanian.[115]

Pseudo-science, historical inaccuracies, warped logic, and racial resentment are all part of the Afrocentric picture. Some of the leading figures in the movement also embrace poisonous racist ideas.[116] A theory that distinguishes the biologically superior, melanin-endowed "sun people" from the inferior, melanin-deprived "ice people," is the main contribution to scholarship made by Professor Leonard Jeffries, who was appointed chief consultant to a state curriculum task force by New York State Commissioner of Education Thomas Sobol in 1989.[117] Others talk of cleansing black education—innoculating the black community against white influence.[118] It is a core premise of many Afrocentrist programs that, as Kwame Kenyatta, a member of the Detroit school board, has put it, "For over 400 years, African Americans and other people of color have been seen through the eyes of Eurocentric education and have been mis-educated."[119] "African people for 500 years have lived on the intellectual terms of Europeans," Molefi Asante has argued.[120] African blacks had a glorious culture, stolen by whites who plucked the best things out and claimed them as their own. In a remark that struck to the heart of the matter, Kenyatta declared that children "of African descent shouldn't be infused with a different culture."[121] That "different culture" is of course American culture, of which blacks have been such an integral part.

Have we painted a far too lurid picture on the basis of a few scattered statements by extremists? It is unclear precisely how many children are regularly exposed to such teachings. *Education Week* attempted to answer the question in October 1996, and concluded that

> amid all the debate, no one knows for sure how many explicitly Afrocentric schools exist or how many teachers across the nation have, on their own, introduced elements of the philosophy into their teaching. More important, no one knows how much of this controversial curriculum is actually filtering down to students or what effect it might have on their lives.

Since controversy had erupted over the movement, *Education Week* reported, some proponents of Afrocentrism had gone underground and were refusing to talk to reporters.[122] But there is no doubt that such ideas have been built into the curriculum of the public schools of many of our largest cities. "I'm learning that mathematics didn't just come out of anywhere. My people originated this. America's number system is not the original one," a high school student in Atlanta told a reporter in 1993.[123]

"My people": compare this constricted vision with that of Ralph Ellison, looking back on his college years at segregated Tuskegee College. "In Macon County, Alabama," Ellison wrote,

> I read Marx, Freud, T. S Eliot, Pound, Gertrude Stein and Hemingway. Books which seldom, if ever, mentioned Negroes were to release me from whatever "segregated" idea I might have had of my human possibilities. I was freed not . . . by the example of [the black novelist Richard] Wright but by composers, novelists and poets who spoke to me of more interesting and freer ways of life. . . . It requires real poverty of imagination to think that this can come to a Negro only through the example of other Negroes.[124]

As the historian C. Vann Woodward has noted, "American blacks are not the first racial group with wounded pride to seek comfort in myths of a glorious past." But the desperate effort to instill pride and self-esteem in black children, he has rightly said, will not work. It is an abuse of history, and a misuse of education.[125] Black children do not need therapeutic strategies. They need cognitive skills—skills that won't be taught as long as teachers believe that black children think and learn differently, that both the standard curricular materials and widely used assessments are culturally inappropriate, and that schools as currently organized "reinforce the racial and social hierarchy in our society."[126] Afrocentrism is the natural flowering of that deep distrust of American society that pervades much of the literature on education.

BLACK TEACHERS FOR BLACK CHILDREN

The *Brown* decision assumed that black and white schoolchildren learned the same way, and could thus receive precisely the same instruction. Had the Court taken seriously the view that students needed to have teachers of the same race either because whites don't understand blacks or because African-American children need "role models," it would logically have voted to uphold the Jim Crow arrangements that guaranteed black teachers for black children. Two decades later the Boston School Committee did attempt to persuade Judge Garrity that the great majority of Boston's black teachers were assigned to predominantly black schools because "black teachers serve as adult role models and inspirational examples to black pupils." But the judge would have none of it, and demanded a racially balanced staff in every school.[127]

Although rejected as a defense against charges of de facto school segregation, the role-model argument was revived by the diversity movement, but in a curiously asymmetrical form. No one today would dare suggest that white students require white teachers as role models; such a proposal would be denounced as racist. White pupils, it is assumed, will inevitably benefit from having teachers "of color" to prepare them for living in an increasingly diverse, multicultural society. Strangely, though, the converse does not hold for students "of color." Being taught by a white, many appear to believe, does not prepare black students for living in a diverse society. "I want minority children to know that they can become school teachers, not just custodians," declared the vice-chairman of the Massachusetts Unity Coalition for Equality in Education.[128] Without more minority teachers, "children would have little contact with people of color they could look up to," and "teachers would write their lessons in one voice."[129] By a nice bit of legerdemain, we are led to the conclusion that all students, whatever their race, would be better off with African-American teachers.

The logic here leaves much to be desired. Surely the Supreme Court was not wildly misguided in thinking that exposing black pupils to white teachers rather than black ones would not do them irreparable harm. We know of no empirical research demonstrating the superiority of black teachers for students of either race. Indeed, what helps students to perform well is not the race of their teachers but their intellectual competence. The most effective teachers, the evidence indicates, tend to be those who scored highest on their SATs and ACTs (American College Tests) when they were in high school.[130]

Nevertheless, two theories, intertwined, have become articles of educational faith. Black children need black teachers as role models; and black teachers have a different "voice," as the vice-chairman of the Massachusetts Unity Coalition has suggested. For many years now, school districts have accordingly been engaged in a successful search for more black teachers and principals. In the 1993–1994 academic year, the date of the most recent figures, 7.4 percent of the teachers in the nation's public schools were African American. That was well below the proportion of elementary and secondary school students who were black—16.6 percent—but that is not the proper basis for comparison. The relevant standard is the black share of college graduates in the age bracket (ages forty to forty-four) of the average teacher today. In 1993, African Americans constituted 6.2 percent of those with a bachelor's degree or more, so they were actually slightly overrepresented as classroom teachers.[131] Moreover, they were more than a little overrepresented in the ranks of school principals. In 1993, 10.1 percent of all public school principals in the United States were African American, a figure one-third larger than the 7.4 percent share of teaching posts that they held.[132] Since principals are drawn from the ranks of teachers, this substantial disparity suggests that school authorities in a great many American communities in recent years have given fairly strong preferences to black candidates seeking to pursue administrative careers.

Black teachers and principals thus have an edge in the competition. "When you go to teacher fairs," one Minnesota official remarked in 1991, "you'll see some of the best-qualified teachers of color walking around with five and six contracts in their pocket, just ready to choose." Those contracts often included college loan forgiveness and other such enticements.[133] In 1995 an administrator from a Connecticut suburb had "files and files of qualified Caucasians" who had applied to teach in his district, but he was determined to recruit more "teachers of color."[134] A year later the supervisor of instructional personnel in Hillsborough County, Florida, said they "were doing everything we can to hire qualified black teachers."[135] That same year, 1996, a report of a study by the Council of the Great City Schools claimed to have found a "dire need" to get "more minorities to work in the classroom" in thirty-nine of the nation's largest cities.[136] The only proof of need that was offered was simply that the student body was becoming "ever more racially and ethnically diverse," and the authors of the study assumed that nonwhite students naturally required teachers of the same skin color.

The executive director of the American Association of Colleges for Teacher Education was so eager a few years ago to have more minority teachers that he endorsed an open double standard in teacher salaries—higher pay for African Americans and members of other minority groups. He conceded that an overt racial differential in pay would "cause some tensions" in the profession. (It would also have caused some lawsuits in the profession, since it would seem a naked violation of the 1964 Civil Rights Act.) Nonetheless, he argued that it was essential. Blacks were not going into teaching in sufficient numbers, he argued, because they had especially large college loans to pay off, because they were more often the sole support of their family, and because testing requirements "present[ed] a greater challenge to them." Since the reward of being a positive role model was "inadequate for most," to attract more into the profession would require better pay than that given to other teachers with the same education and seniority.[137]

The skeptic will notice that the reference to "the greater challenge" that meeting the certification requirements poses to minority teachers is a delicate euphemism for saying that their academic qualifications might be subpar. And it seems somewhat bizarre to argue that people with weaker academic qualifications for a job should be paid more because they had to work hard to pass the test for it. One hopes that we don't pick airplane pilots or heart surgeons that way. But such objections only have force if you doubt the initial premise that a black teacher's race is his or her most important job qualification—a premise the educational establishment generally accepts.

A similar mentality is exhibited by the authors of an article on the supply of minority teachers in Florida in an education journal.[138] As we noted earlier, in 1977 Florida raised standards and imposed new tests for high school graduation, provoking a legal challenge that was defeated. Florida went a good deal further down this road, by also raising standards for admission to the state-run University of Florida, for entry into teacher-education programs, for advancement from the sophomore to the junior class, for college graduation, and for teacher certification. Anyone who believes that students should be able to demonstrate a higher level of intellectual competence as they proceed through school would think this a sign of progress. To the authors, though, it was all deplorable, because at each stage African-American students were less likely to succeed than whites; fewer blacks qualified to be teachers than would have been the case without the new requirements.

But what if that meant fewer but more highly skilled black teachers, until the higher standards produced a larger crop of qualified minority teachers? The authors do not linger over that plausible possibility. They claim that there was "evidence that pencil-and-paper tests do not predict abilities to teach," without citing any that was persuasive. Might not a teacher's inability to perform adequately on mere "pencil-and-paper tests" be a bit of a handicap when it comes to preparing their students to take such tests? Or is it that it doesn't matter how their students do on "pencil-and-paper tests" either, because tests by definition have a white, middle-class bias? If you accept that assumption, then you can preserve your faith that black teachers by definition have superior "abilities to teach" African-American students. And here we're back to the view upon which support for an Afrocentric curriculum in good part rests. Asked at the Atlanta conference about the likelihood that black students who were learning about Egyptian hieroglyphs and cleansing rituals would get a good job down the road, Wade Nobles, a black educator from Oakland, replied, "When we educate a black man, we're not educating him for a job, we're educating him for eternity." [139] Skills and the jobs that demand them, it seems, are "white." Such views certainly encourage just such an educational outcome: whites at an educational and occupational advantage.

SCHOOL VIOLENCE AND DISORDER

The rise in violent crime over the past generation, Chapter 10 demonstrated, has taken much more of a toll upon African Americans than upon whites. Blacks are considerably more likely to be the victims of crime. And since blacks are also greatly overrepresented among those committing crimes, more are either behind bars or walking around with criminal records that limit their chances of getting a decent job. These depressing facts have an important bearing upon the educational opportunities available to African-American children, and may in fact (as we earlier suggested) in part explain the drop in NAEP scores in the past decade. Traversing a war zone to get to and from school is a distracting and draining experience, and the violence and disorder out in the streets affects life within the school itself.

A 1993 survey revealed that 7.1 percent of all black high school students in the United States "felt too unsafe to go to school," more than double the rate for whites (3 percent). If at first glance 7 percent doesn't seem such a lot, recall that those who were willing to say flatly that they felt too unsafe to go school were probably only a fraction of those who were sometimes concerned about their safety in school but were reluctant to admit it. In 1993, for example, some 15 percent of black students reported that they had carried a weapon on school property for personal protection at least once in the preceding thirty days, a rate 38 percent higher than that for whites. Furthermore, one out nine African-American students had been threatened or injured with a weapon on school property, nearly twice the rate for whites.[140] Many of our big city schools now use metal detectors. If anyone thirty years ago had predicted that we would come to need metal detectors and armed guards to keep guns and switchblades out of our schools, he would have been dismissed as absurdly pessimistic.

Teachers as well as students in inner-city schools feel unsafe. Surveys confirm the commonsense impression that threats and actual attacks against teachers are most common in schools "located in areas characterized by poverty, unemployment, and a high proportion of female-headed families," and all of these characteristics are present in high concentrations in black inner-city neighborhoods.[141] The data often do not distinguish between "cities" and "central cities," blurring the picture. Nevertheless, the contrast in the teacher-victimization rates between "city" and other schools (including those in the "suburban/urban fringe") is striking. In a 1991 survey, for instance, 15 percent of "city" teachers reported being "threatened with injury in the last 12 months," while the figure for the "suburban/urban fringe" was 6 percent. In 1989, a fifth of black students aged twelve to nineteen reported that they had seen teachers attacked or threatened with attack.[142]

Figures on the order of 15 to 20 percent must look awfully good to teachers in some cities. A 1992 survey of teachers in the Washington, D.C., public schools found that 40 percent had been threatened by students.[143] Teachers in junior high schools are particularly vulnerable; in the upper grades many of the worst troublemakers will be gone. In the mid-1970s, an important government study found, 36 percent of inner-city junior high school teachers had had a student threaten to hurt them. Among big-city teachers in general, 28 percent reported hesitating to confront misbehaving students for fear of their own safety. (The suburban figure was only 11 percent, and the rural one 7 percent.)[144] To a dismaying degree the authority that school administrators and teachers are expected to have over their students appears to have collapsed. More than a quarter of teachers were afraid of retaliation if they stopped students engaged in unacceptable behavior.

The problem is not altogether new. It has been with us since roughly the end of the 1960s, when teachers and principals began to lose their grip on schools. Jackson Toby, the country's leading authority on school crime, locates the major change in that era.[145] His picture squares with those drawn by

Gerald Grant in *The World We Created at Hamilton High* and Robert Sam Anson in *Best Intentions: The Education and Killing of Edmund Perry*. In the late-1970s and early-1980s, Anson reports, fights in the Harlem junior high school that Perry attended were "frequent and vicious." In fact, one board of education study found that even in those years the best New York teachers spent 75 percent of their time simply maintaining order.[146]

Anson was describing fights among students, and indeed most victims of in-school violence (then and now) are the students themselves. Here again the data suggest a dismaying correlation with the presence of blacks in or around the school. For instance, a survey of twenty-six big-city schools during the academic year 1974–1975 found that 75 percent of the perpetrators of violent offenses were black, even though blacks constituted only 29 percent of the population of those cities.[147] In that same school year more than three-fifths of the robberies in which a student was attacked by an outside intruder (trespassing on school property) involved white victims and black perpetrators. Likewise, in about half of the cases in which students were robbed by other students, the victims were white and the perpetrators black. On the other hand, whites almost never robbed blacks. The picture was much the same for the crimes of aggravated assault, simple assault, and larcenies.[148]

The figures above are only for crime; disorder is harder to measure. Although the evidence is spotty, it is undeniable that keeping reasonable order in school has become far more difficult that it was a generation ago. In fact, things seem to have gotten worse even within the past few years. National surveys asking teachers what they perceived to be "serious problems" in their schools show a rise from 7.4 percent in 1987–1988 to 9.9 percent in 1993–1994 in the proportion identifying "verbal abuse of teachers," and a jump in the fraction naming "student disrespect for teachers" from 11.8 percent to 16.6 percent between 1990–1991 and 1993–1994.[149] Only the figures for 1993–1994 are broken down by type of school, but they reveal the expected pattern. Verbal abuse of teachers was 73 percent above the national average in central-city public schools, and higher still in schools with a minority enrollment of 20 percent or more. Likewise with student disrespect for teachers. Fully 36 percent of public secondary schoolteachers in 1990–1991 felt that the "level of student misbehavior" in their school interfered with their teaching.

Still more disturbing is the fact that the proportion of secondary school teachers reporting that physical conflicts between students was either a "serious" or at least a "moderate" problem at their school rose from 26 percent in 1987–1988 to 40 percent in 1993–1994, while the percent who said that student possession of weapons was a problem jumped from 10 percent to 20 percent. In secondary schools with more than 750 students, most common in the cities, 47 percent of teachers complained of physical conflicts between students and 27 percent of weapons possession.[150]

Anecdotal evidence supports and supplements the statistical picture; dismaying tales of disorder, crime, and fear in central-city schools abound. Thus, in 1992 one New York teacher told a reporter she had learned to keep a careful watch on the stairways, to stick to the middle of hallways, and to stand behind doors she is opening to protect herself from hurled objects.[151] Students regularly report feeling "anything can happen at any moment."[152] The potential for violence exists "in any school in the District of Columbia and in any school in an urban environment," a principal in the nation's capital noted in 1993.[153] "We teach with one foot in the doorway so that we can keep one eye on what's going on outside in the hall," William Kaupert, a teacher at a Washington, D.C., high school said in 1994. The job of "teaching" in the District includes an hour a day of hall patrol—breaking up fights.[154]

One reporter who moved from the newsroom to the classroom has provided a particularly compelling picture. In the academic year 1989–1990, *New York Newsday*'s education reporter, Emily Sachar, took a job teaching eighth-grade mathematics at the Walt Whitman Intermediate School in Brooklyn, New York, where 89 percent of the students were black. Many kids, she discovered, had never been taught how to sit still, how to control what they said, how to behave.[155] Her students called her "cuntface," told her "to fuck off," spat in her face, played radios during class, and threw chairs at one another. Even if a majority wanted to learn, a small group of troublemakers could turn the room upside down in minutes.[156]

Or in seconds if they brandished a weapon. At a "Getting Started" workshop designed to help new teachers, Sachar was warned: "Be careful: the year before, a teacher was assaulted after opening his classroom door to a student passing by. Close and lock the doors always."[157] But locked doors provide no sure protection against those students for whom violence is a way of life. Even a relatively small number of angry, defiant students who come to school irregularly and have no interest in learning can make serious trouble.[158] "Hallwalkers," teachers call them—youngsters who frequent the halls but not the classrooms. As one teacher put it: "Their friends are here, the heat is here, the meals are here." That's why they come. But "they just want to cause problems for others."[159]

The problem of unruly, disobedient, disruptive students besets all schools, whatever their racial composition. But it is a worse problem in big-city schools, where disproportionate numbers of black youths are among the troublemakers. Thus, in 1978, African Americans made up 16 percent of enrollments in public elementary and secondary schools but accounted for 29 percent of disciplinary suspensions, 27 percent of expulsions, and 29 percent of those given corporal punishment.[160] This squares with a fall 1996 survey that found that 41 percent of black high school students, as compared with 27 percent of whites, felt that disruptive students were a "very serious" problem at their school.[161]

The disproportion is not surprising, given the number of black children who grow up in impoverished, female-headed families in high-crime neighborhoods. And yet many educators, children's advocates, and civil rights spokesmen have long seen the racial disparity as evidence of racism. Teachers and administrators out to persecute black pupils is the explanation for the disproportionate number of black students in disciplinary trouble. Thus, Marian Wright Edelman, director of the Children's Defense Fund, told a committee of the U.S. Senate in 1975 that "higher suspension rates for black children" did not "simply reflect greater misbehavior on the part of black students."[162] They revealed "racial discrimination and insensitivity in the use of disciplinary sanctions." The solution thus lay not in more suspensions but in fewer. "We believe," Edelman said, "that the substantive grounds for suspension must be drastically pruned. . . ."

At the same hearing a representative of the American Civil Liberties Union chimed in with the remarkable claim that "substantial violence and disruption" would not be found in schools in which there was "meaningful education."[163] So when a student won't turn off his blaring boom box in class, tells a teacher to "fuck off," and throws a chair at another student, it's the school's fault for not having provided him with "meaningful education." In Chapter 10 we argued at length that racism in the criminal justice system does not explain the high number of African Americans arrested, prosecuted, convicted, and sentenced to prison. We recognize that racism does exist and that stereotypes about black males may have an effect on the disciplinary decisions of some school authorities; nevertheless, we are equally skeptical of the charge that racial bias accounts for the disproportionate number of black students whom teachers view as disruptive or violent.

The views of the Children's Defense Fund and the ACLU expressed in 1975 still have plenty of defenders. Two decades later, a dispute arose between Albert Shanker, the president of the American Federation of Teachers, and the leaders of the Council of the Great City Schools, the members of which are big-city school superintendents.[164] In a speech to the council, Shanker had argued that lack of discipline and order was a serious problem in the public schools, and he recommended that students "whose violence or chronic disruptions prevent other students from learning" be removed from regular classes and placed in "alternative settings." Shanker had made the point on numerous other occasions; just a month before, he had noted that "parents want their children in schools where they can be safe and where there's not so much disorder that kids can't learn." Disruption is tolerated, he had gone on to say; those who make classrooms unmanageable need to be placed in a separate track.[165] Low-level common sense, it would seem, but heretical in the eyes of the Council of the Great City Schools.

The council's self-described mission was to "help level the playing field for the poor, the disabled, the limited English proficient, and racial minorities," and it responded to Shanker's comments with two letters that illuminate why our big-city schools today are in such dismal shape. Shanker had launched "a campaign of exclusion," "exploiting public stereotypes," "pandering to a nation afraid of its own children," and "blaming the victim," the executive director, Michael Casserly, charged. By "the victim," Mr. Casserly did not mean either the teachers or the students deprived of the orderly environment essential to learning; "as leaders of the nation's urban schools, we believe our responsibilities include educating all children—not just those who sit still all day," he declared. Racism was the thinly veiled insinuation; the reference to "those who sit still all day" was obviously to whites—by implication, the sole concern of the AFT president who trafficked in "exclusion" and "stereotypes." Others have echoed Casserly's suggestion that "quietness" is part of a package of norms reflecting "the dominant cultural establishment." Donna V. Ford, an educational psychologist at the University of Virginia has maintained that "black students have difficulty staying in their seats," and that the demand that they do so is racially insensitive, culturally inappropriate.[166]

Not disorder in the schools, but "misleading rhetoric" by critics like Shanker was the heart of the problem, Casserly argued. After all, a 1993 poll of urban teachers had shown that 76 percent did "not find it hard to keep order in their classrooms." But if so, a quarter of all urban teachers did find that merely keeping order was "hard," a fact that would seem less than reassuring. And the term "urban" is so broad that it includes places like Fargo, North Dakota; Palm Springs, California; and Ogden, Utah, which do not have large, impoverished minority populations like the cities whose school systems belonged to the council.

The ACLU spokesman had been right to say that there would not be "substantial violence and disruption" in schools in which "there [was] meaningful education," but right for the wrong reason. He had the causal sequence backward. As Shanker had pointed out, poor education is a consequence—not the cause—of disruption. It's a vicious circle. Violence and disorder inside the schools and on surrounding streets drive away those families whom the urban schools can least afford to lose. And their departure aggravates the problem. That's no secret; most black families know it, polls suggest.[167] "When you go into any public school, a lot of things are just out of order," one black mother participating in a privately funded voucher experiment noted. "There wasn't any security there . . . ," she added.[168] Shanker himself has attributed the high interest in choice, charter schools, and vouchers precisely to the desire for discipline in the classroom.[169]

We have suggested that mounting levels of school violence and disorder could in part account for the reversal of black educational progress in the past decade. We lack sufficient evidence to test the notion, but it's a hypothesis worthy of further research. Is it just a coincidence that the crack cocaine epidemic, the spectacular rise in the homicide rate for young black males, and the reversal of black progress in educational achievement all began in the latter half of the 1980s? Even if it is a coincidence, it still seems safe to say that children can't learn in chaotic and dangerous school environments. In the fall of 1996 a New York State appellate court tossed out the conviction of a fifteen-year-old who had come to school with a loaded handgun; the security guard who noted a suspicious bulge in the young man's jacket had violated his Fourth Amendment rights in searching him, the judge said. The executive director of the New York Civil Liberties Union applauded the decision, as did the *New York Times*. The court's ruling was "not unreasonable, given the need to deter abusive practices by school guards," the *Times* editorialized.[170] It is unlikely that such editorial writers have children in schools in which youngsters roam the halls with deadly weapons; if they did, perhaps they would understand that kids who go to school afraid inevitably learn less.

Beyond the Classroom

Some kids who are afraid just don't come to school. Or come erratically. At least that is one of the reasons given for the fact that on a typical day at a school like New York's Brandeis High School more than a quarter of the students are absent, with the problem particularly severe among young black males.[171] Their truancy makes a larger point. How much children learn is often beyond the control of the teachers and administrators. An enthusiastic and dedicated teacher won't make much headway with the youngster who hangs out at a laundromat playing video games all day.

Kids not only have to show up; they have to study. Recent research has lent new support to the old-fashioned view that students who do more homework learn more. A 1996 study shows that students who put in an additional half an hour per day on math homework through junior and senior high school perform an average of two years above their grade level by the time they graduate.[172] This elementary point might be the main reason why American students in general lag behind so many countries in international competitions; they spend a lot more time playing with friends, watching TV, or in after-school jobs than their peers elsewhere. The typical American high school student spends four hours per week doing homework; in other industrialized countries, the figure is about four hours a day.[173]

Systematic evidence about how much time American students of different racial and ethnic backgrounds devote to homework is not readily available, but we have a few scraps of data that point to a tentative conclusion. We know that black children watch a great deal more television than white children. According to a 1996 survey, 69 percent of African-American fourth-graders were glued to the tube for at least four hours a day, as compared with 37 percent of whites. Nearly half of these black children watched TV for at least six hours a day, more than triple the proportion among whites.[174] As for older students, in 1992, 21 percent of black twelfth-graders watched five or more hours of television on a typical weekday, more than triple the rate for whites. And 20 percent of African Americans said that they spent an hour or more each day playing video games, nearly double the percentage for whites.[175]

The more hours spent watching television, the fewer (presumably) devoted to homework. An intriguing 1996 book, Laurence Steinberg's *Beyond the Classroom,* reported on a ten-year study of more than 20,000 high school students in nine schools in California and Wisconsin. It revealed that ethnicity made more of a difference in student performance than social class. The gap in grades between the Asian students, who were at the top, and the black students, who were at the bottom, was almost twice as large as that between those from the richest and the poorest homes. But Asian students spent twice as much time doing homework as the average student, cut classes less often, paid more attention to the teacher, and were more eager to get good grades. Blacks, by contrast, cut classes more, paid less attention, and did less homework. Whites were in the middle in all these respects.[176]

It is not easy to say what accounts for these differences in student attitudes and behavior. But *Beyond the Classroom* contained some suggestive clues. Contrary to conventional wisdom, the author claimed, Asian parents did not "appear to be doing anything particularly special" that would account for their children's success, nor were black parents "doing anything noteworthy that would explain their children's relatively weaker performance."[177] However, Steinberg's conclusion seems to neglect one of his own crucial findings: Asian students were "more likely than other students to believe that not doing well in school would have negative consequences for their future," while black students didn't "really believe that doing poorly in school [would] hurt their chances for future success." Asian students also were much more likely than others to believe that their success or failure at school depended upon how hard they worked, and less inclined to "see success or failure as resulting from things outside their personal control, such as luck or favoritism of teachers."[178] The study did not explore where these beliefs came from, but it is difficult to believe they had nothing to do with the socialization Asian children received at home.

Another crucial factor, emphasized by the author, lay in contrasting peer groups. Asians had mostly close friends who valued academic success highly, while blacks did not. Blacks viewed doing well in school as "acting white" and thus betraying one's race.[179] Black students with high academic potential were thus forced to choose between academic and social success. The price of popularity was to embrace the values celebrated in rap music, and that was not conducive to high grades and good SAT scores. For more young blacks to develop their full academic potential, this cultural barrier to achievement must be overcome.

A DISCIPLINED, TOUGH EDUCATION

In 1996, Boston school authorities jettisoned the system of admissions for the Boston Latin School that reserved 35 percent of the seats for black and Hispanic students. But instead of replacing the racial set-aside with a race-blind reliance on grades and test-scores, it adopted a complicated formula that "recognize[d] the hard work of students and also ensure[d] diversity." In the interest of "diversity," black students whose academic record left something to be desired would continue to be admitted, although high scores and grades would still be demanded of all whites and Asians.[180]

How whites in Boston and elsewhere came to have so little confidence in black academic talent—and managed to get blacks themselves to go along with educational policies built upon that doubt—is a bit of a mystery. Educators worry a great deal about the self-esteem of students, particularly that of minority students. But it is their message that, if taken seriously, undermines a sense of self-worth on the part of black youngsters.

Why is the racial gap in cognitive skills once again widening? we asked early in this chapter. When black youngsters were for a time making real progress, what happened that their performance on the National Assessment of Education Progress should have gotten worse after 1988? In the fall of 1995 the *Journal of Blacks in Higher Education* asked that same question, although in response to falling SAT scores, and it came up with a long list of "possible explanations." That list included:

- The fact that "in recent years it has become increasingly 'uncool' in black inner-city schools to tackle serious academic pursuits."
- "The steady disappearance of the two-parent family."
- The contrast between "parents and teachers in white suburban schools [who] are now strengthening back-to-basics core courses in reading, mathematics, and science . . . [and what is] happening in predominantly black urban schools."
- "School reform movements—particularly in the inner cities—[that] are increasingly teaching black students to feel good about themselves instead of concentrating on teaching them reading and mathematics."
- The lack of "safe and orderly schools with high academic standards that pay attention to core academic subjects."
- And the "increasing emphasis on Afrocentric studies in predominantly black schools [which] has reduced study in core math and reading programs."[181]

In other words, social disorder coupled with self-esteem strategies and Afrocentric fantasies that entail low academic standards and insufficient attention to core subjects. Condescending policies masquerading as racially sensitive ones that have made a bad situation worse. Blacks and whites, working together, have conspired to rob black children of a fundamental civil right—access to quality education.

It is not hard to teach well. There is no great mystery about how to get better academic results. The Catholic schools, for one, seem to know the formula—especially (as Diane Ravitch has noted) for the poorest kids.[182] They are safe, orderly communities with a shared educational outlook and an extraordinary commitment to the students. That is, their clear, uncomplicated missions are defined by a staff truly in charge. Moreover, they tend to have a few-frills demanding curriculum. Thus (Ravitch reports), 76 percent of their students are enrolled in a college-preparatory curriculum, compared to only 45 percent of public school students. That means that in public high schools, Algebra II is studied by 65 percent of students whose parents have a college degree, but only 43 percent of those without one. But in the Catholic schools the picture is quite different: 62 percent of students with college-educated parents and 65 percent of those lacking that higher degree take Algebra II. The picture is much the same with geometry and trigonometry: little difference in the Catholic schools between the course-taking of those who come from educationally advantaged homes and those who do not. A marked contrast with what one finds in the public schools.

Not surprisingly, the different course-taking patterns result in different levels of academic achievement. On the reading and math NAEP assessments, black high school seniors who live in "disadvantaged urban" communities but attend Catholic schools do significantly better than their peers in the public system. Moreover, a much higher percentage than in the public schools take the SAT tests and go on to college.[183]

Self-appointed advocates for black children attack the "meritocratic ideology" that pervades schools, and the standardized tests used to assess both students and teachers that are in fact "designed to measure the values generally espoused by [the] White middle-class."[184] They associate educational policies that recognize differences in levels of educational achievement with racial injustice. And they urge black teachers—and sometimes a "black" (or Afrocentric) curriculum—for black kids. In the meantime, the Catholic schools do what the public schools are supposed to do: they equalize educational opportunity. They greatly narrow the gap in performance between the haves and have-nots by offering the same solid education for all children in a safe and orderly environment. In too many of today's public schools, that's a revolutionary idea whose time has yet to come.

CHAPTER FOURTEEN

The Higher Learning

In 1995, STANFORD University's new president, Gerhard Casper, announced a number of measures to raise academic standards, including a reinstatement of the grades of D and F and an end to the privilege of dropping courses on the eve of the final exam without paying an academic penalty. But President Casper's effort to control grade inflation and to encourage students in other ways to take seriously the courses in which they were enrolled was apparently viewed by many black students as a direct attack on them. Or at least so the *Journal of Blacks in Higher Education* reported.[1]

It was, alas, a believable report. Stanford had for some time been a sea of racial troubles. The school had certainly tried to make blacks feel welcome. Indeed, it had gone to extraordinary lengths to do so. But the effort itself became part of a cluster of problems, of which the protest directed at President Casper was but one sign. The university not only instituted an aggressive affirmative action admissions policy; it trained students in racial sensitivity, created dorms with an ethnic "theme," and drastically altered the curriculum to meet minority demands. The result was more minorities on campus; a curriculum that included courses on such subjects as black hair; frustrated, bewildered white students; and blacks who felt more alienated, more culturally black, and perhaps more hostile to whites than when they arrived.

The university had wanted to make minority students feel at home. But with the dramatic increase in minority numbers and with the creation of ethnic theme houses, the level of minority student discomfort actually rose. With more minority students in this environment came more interracial tension—especially tension between whites and blacks. When blacks first demanded their own dorms, they hoped to live entirely separate from white Stanford. The college insisted, however, on a quota of 50 percent white. As it turned out, it wasn't quite the "comfortable" arrangement that the university wanted.

A widely reported incident in September 1988 made that abundantly clear.

In the wake of an argument over black lineage, two intoxicated white students defaced a Beethoven poster in such a way as to make the composer look black. The action took place in Ujamaa, the African-American residential house, and subsequently provoked a number of racially ugly meetings and a flyer on which the word "niggers" was scrawled by unknown actors. The scrawl was unfairly attributed to the students who had altered the Beethoven drawing, and thus they quickly became victims themselves—blamed for acts they didn't commit. Antiwhite leaflets began to appear, most of them urging an all-black dorm, and pins were jammed into the photographed faces of white students on a picture board.

How could the situation have become so ugly so quickly? Stanford had almost no students who did not think of themselves as liberals. Only 15 percent of seniors surveyed identified themselves as even somewhat conservative. These were students, then, painfully self-conscious about having enlighted racial attitudes. But the Stanford campus—like so many others—was a racial tinder box, ready to explode. In the 1960s few had doubted that more interracial contact would bring understanding and friendship: a family of man. Less than three decades later, things looked a lot more complicated.

As a series of interviews conducted in 1988 and 1989 by John H. Bunzel, a political scientist at the Hoover Institution, made clear, by then blacks and whites were not even talking the same language.[2] Most important, they couldn't agree on the meaning of racism. White students talked of prejudice, stereotyping, and overtly racist acts, and believed evidence of such personal hostility was exceedingly hard to find. Black students, on the other hand, viewed racism as something akin to a pervasive vapor—invisible but lethal. Only 30 percent of blacks in a student survey reported direct experience with prejudice, and the majority of those described that experience as "subtle" and "hard to explain." Nevertheless, "covert," "elusive" discrimination deeply affected their daily life, they said. Racism, as they described it, was institutional or structural. The greater "power" (undefined) of whites had racist consequences: too many white tenured faculty and too few black students had been receiving academic honors, for instance.

Almost half the blacks Bunzel interviewed said their views on racism had hardened while they were students at the university. Not suprisingly, whites (as one of the seniors interviewed put it) found it "hard to know how to react to charges of racism when there [were] no specific incidents or examples." In fact, their experience at Stanford made white students more skeptical of black charges of racism and less likely to reach out. It was not rhetoric alone that alienated white students. Whites were bewildered and angered by black separatism. In the interviews black students were quick to say they kept largely to themselves, celebrating their distinctiveness. Blacks were expected, they reported, to talk black, dress black, think black, and certainly date black. In so doing, they did create safe psychological havens, but whites experienced such separatism as hostile. What had they done to provoke or deserve the enmity? they asked.

Relations between the races had thus become, in Bunzel's words, "reserved, and circumspect, restrained by apathy, fears, and a certain amount of peer pressure." In a senior survey 70 percent of the students agreed that racial tension had increased in the years they had been on campus. And thus, thirty-two years after the first lunch counter sit-ins, privileged blacks on the most enlightened of college campuses were insisting on eating apart. At Stanford and other institutions of higher education, the integrationist dream of Martin Luther King, Jr., had been shattered.

What a mess. How did it come about? Does a greater black presence on campus inevitably mean greater racial tension? Of course not. Not if black students arrive as equals and are treated as such. At Stanford neither was true. As of 1994, black undergraduates were entering Stanford with an average combined SAT score of 1,164—a very good score by national standards, putting them in the top sixth of all test-takers in the country. But their white classmates had been admitted with a 1,335 average, placing them in the top 3 percent of all students nationally.[3] As Shelby Steele has argued, black students pay a heavy price for their letters of acceptance on the basis of lower academic standards. To begin with, the affirmative action programs call attention to racial differences—they heighten racial consciousness. And then, too, they reinforce that myth of black inferiority upon which we touched in the last chapter. Almost all students start competitive colleges like Stanford feeling insecure, but for African-American students "the anxiety is not only personal but racial."[4] Hence the reaction when President Casper raised academic expectations—the sense of insecurity instantly revealed.

High anxiety—the deep-seated fear that black inferiority may not be, after all, a myth—is just one source of what Steele has called a campus "politics of difference," in which groups assert rights and vie for power based on their racial identity. The charge of (invisible) white racism becomes the solution to the pain of self-doubt, and that charge not only transfers the problem to others but legitimizes a politics of 1960s-style racial protest. Add to the mix the ideology of black power (which sanctions demands made on the basis of color) and college administrators who make a virtue of appeasement and reward those demands, and the result is precisely that resegregation of campus life so clearly and appallingly on display at Stanford—but certainly not confined to that school.

Without an admissions system involving racial preferences, the picture would be quite different.

THE SURGE IN COLLEGE ENROLLMENTS

In 1960, the year that black students at North Carolina Agricultural and Technical College sat down at the Woolworth's lunch counter in Greensboro and insisted upon their right to be served a cup of coffee, fewer than 150,000 African Americans were enrolled in colleges or universities in the United States, just 4 percent of the total student body (Table 1). There are almost ten times that many black college students today.

Blacks were even less visible on the typical campus, and even further behind in the educational competition, than the 4 percent figure would suggest. Most of the black student population—two-thirds of it, in fact—was concentrated in segregated southern colleges like North Carolina A&T. The education these schools offered, with few exceptions, was distinctly inferior to that provided in the typical predominantly white institution of the day. In their penetrating 1968 survey of American higher education, *The Academic*

Table 1

Black Enrollments in College, 1960–1994

	Number (in thousands)	Percent of Enrollments	
		Total	In other than black colleges
1960	146	4.1	1.8
1970	522	7.0	4.2
1980	1,007	9.9	8.2
1994	1,317	10.7	9.0

Sources: Enrollment data for 1960 from Sar A. Levitan, William B. Johnston, and Robert Taggart, *Still a Dream: The Changing Status of Blacks Since 1960* (Cambridge: Harvard University Press, 1975), 84; 1970–1980 figures from U.S. Bureau of the Census, Current Population Reports, P-20-479, *School Enrollment-Social and Economic Characteristics of Students: October 1993* (Washington, D.C.: U.S. Government Printing Office, 1994), tables A-1, A-5, and A-6; 1994 data from American Council on Education, *Minorities in Higher Education, 1995–96: Fourteenth Annual Status Report* (Washington, D.C.: 1996), tables 1 and 5. Figures on the proportion of black students on campuses other than those of the historically black colleges include graduate students, since they are not separated out in the data on attendance at historically black colleges. Estimated from data in Frank Bowles and Frank A. DeCosta, *Between Two Worlds: A Profile of Negro Higher Education* (New York: McGraw-Hill, 1971), 199; Sar A. Levitan, William B. Johnston, and Robert Taggart, *Still a Dream: The Changing Status of Blacks Since 1960* (Cambridge: Harvard University Press, 1975), 84, 102; National Center for Education Statistics, *Historically Black Colleges and Universities, 1976–1990*, NCES 92-640 (Washington, D.C.: U.S. Government Printing Office, 1992), table 5; National Center for Education Statistics, *Digest of Educational Statistics, 1995* (Washington, D.C.: U.S. Government Printing Office, 1995), 208, 225. Nineteen ninety-four figures are for the 1993–1994 academic year.

Revolution, Christopher Jencks and David Riesman concluded that the approximately one hundred historically black colleges ranked "near the end of the academic procession in terms of student aptitudes, faculty competence, and intellectual ferment." The typical freshman at such schools, judging from average SAT scores, was "semiliterate" and performed at about the ninth-grade level.[5] Well into the 1960s such Jim Crow colleges were the only option available in most southern states to black students who wanted a higher education, unless they had the money to go to school in the North and the confidence that they could survive the competition despite having attended segregated elementary and secondary schools. Significant numbers of African Americans from the North attended one of the historically black colleges as well.

In 1960 only about 50,000 black students attended predominantly white colleges and universities in the North, accounting for less than 2 percent of enrollments. The more prestigious, selective, and expensive the school, the smaller the proportion of African-American students there. Very few were to be found in Ivy League schools or similar institutions with intensely competitive admissions. They were less often enrolled in the flagship campuses of the state university system, more often found in the state colleges than the state university campuses, and still more often in community colleges and junior colleges.[6]

As the civil rights movement reached a climax and the issue of race moved to center stage in the 1960s, black college enrollments took off like a rocket. The economy was booming, higher education was expanding to accommodate the children of the Baby Boom, the incomes of black families were rising, and it was widely believed that increased education was the route to racial equality. In addition, institutions of higher learning actively sought to increase their black enrollments. The number of blacks in college more than tripled over the decade, and then doubled in the 1970s. College attendance rates for all groups were rising, but they were rising far more rapidly for blacks than for others; the black share of total enrollments jumped from 4 percent to almost 10 percent between 1960 and 1980. What is more, the share of the African-American college population attending the historically black colleges plunged, dropping from two-thirds in 1960 to about half in 1968, and just 17 percent by 1980, where it remains today.[7] The proportion of African-American students enrolled in predominantly white schools quadrupled between 1960 and 1980, rising from 1.8 percent to 7.7 percent. These are striking gains to have been achieved in a relatively brief span of years.

Since 1980 blacks have made further impressive gains in higher education. The number attending college has risen by another 30 percent, lifting the black share of the total by almost a full percentage point.[8] The most illuminating figures to consider in assessing the changing landscape are presented in Table 2. Here we see rates both of college attendance and of college comple-

Table 2
**College Attendance and Completion Rates for Persons
25–29 Years of Age, by Race, 1965–1995**

	BLACK	WHITE	B/W RATIO	BLACK	WHITE	B/W RATIO
	Percent who had attended college			*Percent who had completed 4 or more years*		
1965	15.2	26.2	58	6.8	13.0	52
1970	17.2	32.8	52	7.3	17.3	42
1975	27.6	42.8	64	10.7	22.8	47
1980	32.8	46.2	71	11.7	23.7	49
1985	34.4	44.5	77	11.5	23.2	50
1990	36.0	45.3	79	13.4	24.2	55
1995	44.9	55.4	81	15.3	26.0	59

Source: U.S. Department of Education, *Youth Indicators 1996: Trends in the Well-Being of American Youth,* NCES 96-027 (Washington, D.C.: U.S. Government Printing Office, 1996), 70.

tion for young people (aged 25 to 29) at six different points over the past three decades.

As the table makes evident, in each successive cohort between 1965 and 1995, the fraction of blacks who have been to college has risen. Advances were more rapid at some times than at others, but the gains of the first half of the 1970s were nearly matched by those in the first half of the 1990s. Over these three decades, the African-American rate of college attendance has jumped 195 percent, while the rate for whites has risen only 114 percent. Three decades ago blacks were only about half as likely as whites to attend college; in 1995 it was just over 80 percent of the white rate.

THE LAG IN GRADUATION RATES

That's the good news. The racial gap in rates of college attendance has declined very sharply over the past three decades. The bad news is that the striking increase in the number of African Americans enrolled in higher education has not produced an equally noteworthy gain in the number who who have completed college and obtained their degrees.[9] The problem of black youths dropping out of high school has been pretty much solved; high school graduation has become virtually universal in the United States, and the racial difference has disappeared. The real dropout problem for African Americans is at the college level. Although almost half (45 percent) of African Americans in the twenty-five-to-twenty-nine age bracket today have been enrolled in college, barely one out of seven holds a bachelor's degree. The drop-off here—45 percent at the starting gate but only 15 percent reaching the finishing line—is disturbing. In 1965, blacks were only about half as likely as whites to go to college, and those who did go were only about half as likely to graduate. In 1995, African Americans were only about 20 percent less likely to attend college, but those who did go were still not much more than half as likely to graduate.

Of course not everyone who enters college needs to stick it out for four years to derive some benefit. But when greatly disproportionate numbers of one group fall by the wayside long before commencement, we need to ask why. Finishing college is important. In 1995 men who had some college but not a degree had median incomes that were just one-fifth higher than those who were only high school graduates; for women the advantage was 29 percent. Males with a bachelor's degree, though, had incomes 82 percent above those of high school graduates and 55 percent above those who had attended college but dropped out. A college diploma paid off even more for women; the incomes of graduates were 220 percent of those with only a high school education, and 170 percent of those with some college but no degree.[10] Furthermore, a college diploma is a necessary passport for entry into graduate school, with its promise of even greater returns.[11]

After reviewing the graduation rates of black students at some three hundred major colleges and universities, the *Journal of Blacks in Higher Education* declared in 1994 that the black college dropout rate was nothing short of "disastrous." Among the full-time students who enrolled in degree programs as freshmen between 1984 and 1987, 57 percent of whites earned a degree within six years, and 43 percent dropped out.[12] Only 34 percent of African Americans, by contrast, completed a degree; 66 percent dropped out. The black dropout rate exceeded the white rate by more than 50 percent. More recent evidence, for freshmen who began college in the 1989–1990 academic year, shows only a slight improvement. The black six-year graduation rate had risen to 40 percent as compared with 59 percent for whites.[13] That left the black dropout rate at 60 percent, almost 50 percent higher than the 41 percent dropout rate for whites.

Why have large numbers of black students been able to make it *to* college but not to make it *through* college? It is natural to look for an economic explanation. Black students are less likely to come from affluent households than are their white classmates, and thus they receive less financial help from home. Indeed, their families may turn to them for aid in hard times, forcing some to abandon school and take a job. But while economic status does have a lot to do with who goes to college and who completes college, it doesn't help much with the problem at hand. A high proportion of these students come from the greatly expanded black middle class. In addition, over the last three decades financial aid programs have greatly expanded. The Economic Opportunity Act of 1964 channeled federal funds to needy college students through the work-study program. The Higher Education Acts of 1965 and 1972 vastly increased the federal commitment to aiding college students and institutions by providing both direct grants and federally guaranteed student loans. By 1995 the federal government was spending over $18 billion a year to subsidize college students, and most states were also devoting sizable sums to grants and loans for students in higher education, on top of the subsidy involved in operating state university systems.[14] Coming from homes with lower average incomes, black students were more often the recipients of such aid. According to the most recent figures available, 54 percent of black undergraduates were receiving some form of financial aid, as compared with 39 percent of whites. Almost four out of ten African Americans had federal grants to defray college costs, double the proportion among whites.[15]

In the coming pages we offer an alternative explanation for the low graduation rates for black college students. Affirmative action admissions policies, we will suggest, did work to increase enrollments, but if the larger aim was to increase the number of African Americans who would succcessfully complete college, preferential policies had disappointing, even counterproductive, results.

DOUBLE STANDARDS IN ADMISSIONS

It is not surprising that few black students were enrolled in the most selective institutions of higher education in the early 1960s. Most of them did not have families who could afford to pay the bill, and, as a consequence of the inferior schooling they had received, very few had the academic preparation to qualify for admission. James Coleman's monumental 1966 survey demonstrated that even in the North, black twelfth-graders were more than three years behind their white peers in reading comprehension, on the average, and about five years behind in math. Southern blacks (from Jim Crow schools) lagged even further behind.[16] The first NAEP tests a few years later disclosed similarly glaring racial gaps.

The small numbers of black students to be found on white campuses, especially elite white campuses, suddenly became an issue when the civil rights revolution erupted in the national consciousness. The civil rights cause had broader and deeper support in higher education than in any other American institution, and the question of what those who lived in the ivory tower could do for the cause of racial justice seemed increasingly urgent. Enrolling many more African-American students was the obvious step. A college education would open doors to large numbers of young people whose prospects had been blighted by racism. It would mean better-educated leaders in the black community in the next generation, and would prepare white students for life in a society that would be more diverse culturally.

In time, institutions of higher education would search for both more black students and more black faculty and administrators. But the two stories are quite separate. The commitment to hiring more blacks to fill teaching and other positions was due in great part to federal pressure. In the early 1970s, grants to twenty leading universities that amounted to more than $28 million were held up because these schools had not filed with the federal government satisfactory plans to obtain more African-American employees, as they were obligated to do under an executive order.[17] The obligatory affirmative action plans had met with resistance; academic departments generally believed in appointing scholars and teachers on the basis of their academic merit— conventionally defined. The large-scale affirmative action programs governing student admissions and financial aid, however, were freely adopted as the right thing to do.

"Affirmative action" in the selection of students initially meant greater outreach, making a bigger effort to seek out talent in places that the recruiters had never visited before. For example, admissions officers from elite schools began to visit predominantly black inner-city high schools and to solicit applications from the top students there. This was commendable, but the unfortunate fact was that, given the poor education most black students had received, the most imaginative and intensive searches turned up very few diamonds in the rough. It soon became apparent that the most highly selective and competitive schools could not enroll a significant concentration of African-American students without admitting most of them under a different and lower academic standard.

Race thus became a qualification for admission, and a very important one. Letters of acceptance and scholarship offers went to students whose applications would have been turned down in a flash had their skins been white. There was a certain irony here. Until the mid-1960s, liberals had demanded that colleges remove questions about race on their application forms, and cease to require photographs of applicants. To eliminate racial discrimination, they believed, the admissions process should be made strictly color-blind. Massachusetts actually passed a law forbidding race questions on college applications in 1949.[18] When the focus of liberal concern shifted from preventing discrimination to overcoming the effects of past discrimination, and the idea of color-blind solutions was abandoned in favor of preferential treatment for the victims of historic discrimination, the law was ignored.

Fred Abernathy, who finished high school in the spring of 1995, was a beneficiary of that shift, and his is a familiar story. Abernathy got 19 on the ACT—a score that put him in the bottom half of all test-takers. Nevertheless, he was flooded with college invitations, including one from the College of Engineering at the University of Illinois, where he chose to go. The school is highly selective; most white students were scoring in the 98th or 99th percentile. They came, in other words, well prepared to meet tough academic standards, and that meant that close to 90 percent were graduating. The black record, on the other hand, was quite different: almost half the black students were leaving.[19]

To give someone a coveted place in the freshman class at a competitive university is not like handing the recipient a winning ticket in the state lottery. The curriculum at elite institutions assumes that students arrive with highly developed academic skills—that they are capable of reading and assimilating a great many pages of complicated material each week, writing essays that are coherent and grammatical, and grasping problems expressed in mathematical language. President Johnson's rationale for affirmative action in his 1965 Howard University speech, let us recall, was that it was unfair to take someone who has long been "hobbled by chains" and put him at the starting line in a race and say "you are free to compete with all the others."[20] And yet affirmative action in admission to elite colleges amounted to precisely that. It put ill-prepared African-American students at the starting line and told them that they were free to compete with students who entered with calculus, several Advanced Placement credits and combined College Board scores often above 1400.

With the aid of wishful thinking about the irrelevance of scores on standardized tests, well-meaning educators glossed over the difficulty. A classic example was a 1967 report of a committee of the Southern Regional Education Board. The committee asserted that "there is considerable evidence that the scores do not accurately reflect the potential of disadvantaged youths for college training," but did not specify what "evidence" it had in mind.[21] It warned that recruiting "exceptionally talented Negro students" who met regular admissions standards was not nearly enough. Institutions also had an "obligation to participate in the education of students whose disadvantage ha[d] been more severe." Although the committee referred to "exceptionally talented" students, it was unwilling to speak of any as less talented or not very talented at all. The least adept were merely those whose "disadvantage" had been "more severe," which seemed to suggest that the more dismal a student's academic record was, the more the student deserved admission to college. All colleges and universities therefore had a moral duty to "adopt 'high risk' quotas which commit them to admitting disadvantaged students" who were "not ready for college work and [to] place them in compensatory or remedial programs."

However benevolent the motives of such progressive thinkers, their muddled thinking has had unfortunate consequences, as we saw with the University of Illinois example. The risk in taking in a "high risk" student like Fred Abernathy is that of academic failure. When it does not work out, the loser is not the institution but the individual student, who suffers a crushing, humiliating personal defeat that may have lasting results. That should be of special concern when the student (who might be fine at a less competitive school) has already been scarred by encounters with racial prejudice. The proponents of affirmative action at elite schools gave little thought to the problem of those who might fall by the wayside. But, if their high-risk students did not make it, the schools had little to lose and much to gain—namely, applause for their benevolence. No one could say that they hadn't made special efforts to do their bit for the cause of racial justice.

The real difficulties involved in dealing with students who did not meet traditional standards was evaded with rhetoric about the "remedial" and "compensatory" efforts that institutions would supposedly make to close the gap. But remediation was easy to talk about and hard to accomplish. Twelve years of dismal education take a heavy toll. Schools did not know how to take a group of eighteen-year-olds whose reading, writing, math, and science skills were four or five grade levels below those of their average student and bring them up to par in a semester or two—or even a year or two. Such remediation was certainly not a job that the typical professor at an elite school had any talent for. The more distinguished the university, the less adept its faculty was likely to be at this task. Thomas Sowell, the most penetrating critic of affirmative action in higher education, has noted the illogic of the core idea of putting black students into fast-paced colleges for which they were so ill prepared that they required special slower-paced courses.[22]

Filled with idealistic zeal and convinced that academic deficiencies that had developed over twelve years of schooling could be quickly overcome by instructors whose hearts were in the right place, the nation's colleges and universities rushed to adopt preferential admissions policies. Such measures were assumed to be temporary, a way of giving a jump start to the process of social change. No one anticipated that these efforts would harden into a regime of racial preferences that would last into the twenty-first century. But three decades later that seems to be what has happened. A 1993 survey of fifty-nine randomly selected colleges and universities found that every one of them claimed to have taken specific steps aimed at increasing minority enrollment. That could mean only a general interest in aggressive recruiting, but in fact, three out of four of these schools either aimed for a student body with a racial mix matching that of the population of the state or had other specific numerical goals for minority enrollment.[23]

The pervasiveness of the affirmative action mentality was strikingly illustrated in a 1995 announcement by administrators at the University of New Hampshire, located in a conservative and practically all-white state with a minority population of only 2.6 percent (0.6 percent black). University officials complained that minorities were "only" 3.2 percent of its student body and "only" 5.8 percent of its faculty, and that something had to be done about this disturbing imbalance, even though minorities were overrepresented at the university in both categories relative to their numbers in the state.[24] The university committed itself to the goal of making both the student body and the faculty 7.5 percent minority by 2005. The plan provoked no criticism.

Even in New Hampshire the idea that society had a special duty to be sure that racial minorities were well represented—indeed overrepresented—in higher education was apparently so widely accepted that the proposal attracted no critical notice.

To grasp why affirmative action, originally a temporary expedient, is so firmly entrenched some three decades later, we need to look closely at evidence about the academic performance of African-American youths since the 1960s. The information from the National Assessment of Educational Progress (NAEP) analyzed in the previous chapter provided a useful starting point, but here we look more closely at the segment of the population that might be college material. The best data come from the most widely used instrument employed by admissions officers in selective colleges and universities—the SATs.

THE RACIAL GAP IN SAT SCORES

Each year the College Entrance Examination Board administers tests to approximately 1 million high school students who aspire to admission to one of the nation's more selective colleges or universities.[25] Unlike the NAEP tests, SATs are not administered to a random sample of the entire student population. Although some school systems require it, in most cases students elect to take it. Changes over time in the SAT scores of particular racial groups thus may not be evidence of changes in the academic skills of the group as a whole; the membership of the group taking the test differs from year to year.[26] Nevertheless, the SAT is a vital gatekeeper that strongly influences who is admitted to which college.

How well have black students performed on the SATs? Racial breakdowns of SAT scores are only available since 1976. In the two decades that have elapsed since then, the performance of African-American college-bound seniors has risen substantially, reflecting the progress also evident from the NAEP tests. The mean verbal scores of black youths rose 24 points between the mid-1970s and 1995, while white scores actually dropped a little—by 3 points (Table 3).[27] The racial gap thus narrowed by 27 points, a drop of about a quarter, a shift of the same magnitude as that displayed in the NEAP reading results. Progress in closing the racial gap, though, came to a halt in 1991. Since then white scores have actually risen a little more than those of blacks. The verbal SATs show only a tiny hint of the sharp regression evident in the NAEP results, but it is troubling that virtually all of the progress came in the late 1970s and early 1980s, and that something has gone awry since then.

The mathematics results look quite similar. Black scores rose by 34 points, while those of whites increased just 5 points. The gap shrank by 29 points, again about a quarter, and again a drop of approximately the magnitude as

Table 3

**Mean College Board Scores of College-Bound Seniors
by Race, 1976–1995**

	VERBAL			MATHEMATICAL			
	Black	White	Gap	Black	White	Gap	Total gap
1976	332	451	119	354	493	139	258
1981	332	442	110	362	483	121	231
1984	342	445	103	373	487	114	217
1987	351	447	96	377	489	112	208
1991	351	441	90	385	489	104	194
1995	356	448	92	388	498	110	202

Source: National Center for Education Statistics, *The Condition of Education, 1996* (Washington, D.C.: U.S. Department of Education, 1996), 240.

that found in the NAEP results. But the SAT math scores show more than a hint of the regression revealed by the NAEP tests. The racial gap has widened by 6 points since 1991, not a huge reversal but not a trivial one either.

These figures are averages. A somewhat different—and distinctly less encouraging—picture is revealed when we look at how many blacks have SAT scores that would make them strong prospects for admission into the nation's top colleges and universities if they were judged exactly as any other applicant, on a color-blind basis. Consider the universities that *U.S. News & World Report* rates as the nation's top twenty-five, where the average combined SAT score for entering freshmen is approximately 1300.[28] To be in the running for admission at such a school, the ordinary white applicant needs to score a minimum of 600 on the verbal portion of the test (7 percent of all test-takers in 1981 and 8 percent in 1995) and at least 650 on the mathematics section (8 percent of the total examined in 1981 and 7 percent in 1995).

How many black students have SAT scores that would qualify them for admission to top colleges and universities when judged by the same standards as white applicants? In 1981 fewer than 1,000 (1.2 percent) of the more than 70,000 black students taking the SATs scored as high as 600 on the verbals. (See Table 4.) Almost 58,000 whites, 8 percent of the total, had verbal scores that high; they outnumbered blacks in the verbal elite by a ratio of 61 to 1. Asian Americans also ranked well ahead of African Americans; the proportion scoring 600 or more was six times the black rate.

If we look at the very top scorers—those with 700 or more on their verbals—the disparity is even sharper. Only 70 African Americans in the entire country were on the top rung of the verbal ladder, and well over 8,000 whites. There were 118 whites for every black among the highest scorers, and even the tiny Asian-American group had more than five times as many students with verbal scores of 700 or better.

Table 4

Number and Percent of Black, White, and Asian Students with High SAT Scores, 1981 and 1995

	1981			1995		
	Black	*White*	*Asian*	*Black*	*White*	*Asian*
Verbal						
700–800	70	8,239	366	184	8,978	1,476
650–699	221	16,216	655	465	19,272	2,513
600–649	596	33,231	1,119	1,115	36,700	4,201
Total >600	950	57,685	2,140	1,764	64,950	8,190
Percent >600	1.2	8.0	7.2	1.7	9.6	10.0
Mathematics						
750–800	24	5,077	633	107	9,519	3,827
700–749	132	16,257	1,514	509	29,774	7,758
650–699	393	35,353	2,488	1,437	51,306	9,454
Total >650	549	56,687	4,635	2,053	90,599	21,039
Percent >650	0.7	7.9	15.6	2.0	13.4	25.8
Number examined	75,434	719,383	29,753	103,872	674,343	81,514

Sources: College Entrance Examination Board, *Profiles, College-Bound Seniors, 1981* (New York: College Board, 1982), 41, 60, 79; College Entrance Examination Board, *1995 National Ethnic/Sex Data* (New York: College Board, 1995), unpaginated.

Racial differences on the 1981 math test were even larger than on the verbal test. Only 549 blacks out of the 75,000 taking the test had scores of 650 or higher, 0.7 percent of the total. Whites outnumbered them by 103 to 1. Indeed, more than eight times as many Asians as blacks did that well, though there were many more black test-takers. In the very top group, with scores of 750 and up, the white to black ratio was 212 to 1. It is especially striking that the 30,000 Asian test-takers produced 26 times as many 700-plus scorers as the 75,000 blacks.

In 1995 the number of blacks taking the SAT was up by more than a third, and the number scoring in the upper reaches had expanded by considerably more than that. The proportion with verbals of 600 or more rose from 1.2 percent to 1.7 percent, and the fraction with math scores of 650 and up went from 0.7 percent to 2.0 percent. The racial gap, though, remained huge. In the 700 and up bracket of the verbals, the ratio of whites to blacks was 49 to 1; in the 750-plus category in math it was 89 to 1.

The contrast with the Asians is also marked. Just 3.5 percent of the population in 1995, Asians were 13 percent of all students scoring 700 or more on the verbals and a stunning 27 percent of those with 750 and up in math. If we look at a still more rarefied level of achievement—at the 734 superstar students named Advanced Placement Scholars by the College Board in 1995 because they had high grades on eight different AP tests—the picture is still more dramatic. An amazing 29.7 percent of all the winners were Asians, and 53.1 percent were non-Hispanic whites. Just 2 out of the 734—less than 0.3 percent—were African-American.[29]

The spectacular academic achievements of the Asian students—records that have made these students impossible for colleges to turn down—account for the surge in their enrollments in elite colleges and universities over the past decade and a half. Less than 4 percent of the population, they account for 24 percent of undergraduate enrollment at Stanford and Columbia, 19 percent at Harvard, 17 percent at Cornell, and 16 percent at Yale.[30] The striking differences between Asian and black students clarify the difficulties involved in engineering racial balance in highly competitive institutions. The number of Asian students at places like Harvard has soared, but not because of admissions policies designed to recruit more of them for "diversity" purposes. By now, indeed, Asian Americans are so overrepresented at many elite schools that their presence actually reduces diversity, if it is defined as some approximation of proportional representation for all groups.[31]

Defenders of affirmative action often claim that race is used only as a tie-breaker when two candidates have otherwise identical qualifications. Instead of tossing a coin, admissions officers give the nod to the student from a disadvantaged and underrepresented racial minority—a category that does not include Asians. Few Americans today would complain much if that's how the process worked. Even those who believe that race-conscious policies are profoundly pernicious in principle might condone putting a thumb on an otherwise evenly balanced scale as a temporary expedient.

These metaphors—breaking a tie, tipping the scales a bit—are appealing but irrelevant to the actual issues in higher education today, as the data above should have made clear. If race were being used only to break ties between equally qualified students, unfortunately we would expect the leading schools to have student bodies in which the percentage of blacks was very small. In fact, the California Institute of Technology, which had a 1.1 percent black enrollment in 1994, seems to be the only example of a nationally known institution in which racial identity merits (at most) a thumb on the scale. Cal Tech is known to be—or at least thought to be—a school that students with less than 750 on the math SATs needn't bother applying to. Since only 0.8 percent of the nation's students who score that high in math are black, Cal Tech might have needed to give some preference to black applicants to get even as many as 1.1 percent. If so, the preference given is modest.

MIT, which also expects entering students to have advanced mathematics skills, takes in more than four times as many black students as it would if it only picked top scorers on the math SATs, and three times the number who would qualify on the basis of both verbal and math scores. Bowdoin College, located in Maine, which has barely 5,000 black residents, has a student body

Table 5

Black Percentage of the Student Body at Selected High-Ranking Colleges and Universities, 1994

University of Virginia	8.9	Brown University	5.6
University of North Carolina	8.9	Princeton University	5.4
Wesleyan University	8.3	Swarthmore College	5.4
Amherst College	8.1	Stanford University	5.3
University of Michigan	7.9	UC-Berkeley	5.3
Duke University	7.5	Dartmouth College	5.1
Wellesley College	7.1	Rice University	4.2
Harvard University	6.9	University of Chicago	3.7
Yale University	6.9	Cornell University	3.7
Columbia University	6.6	MIT	3.6
Williams College	6.6	Bowdoin College	2.1
Johns Hopkins University	6.3	Cal Tech	1.1

Sources: "Long-Term Black Student Enrollment Trends at the Nation's Highest-Ranked Colleges and Universities," *Journal of Blacks in Higher Education* 12 (Summer 1996), 10–14, and "The Status of Black Faculty at the Flagship State Universities" in the same issue, 14–16.

that is 2.1 percent black, and nearby Bates and Colby achieve something similar (with 2.6 and 1.8 percent respectively).

The editor of the *Journal of Blacks in Higher Education* has made a similar calculation of the distribution of SAT scores by race, using 1994 data, and applying it to the twenty-five highest-ranked national universities. African-American students held 3,000 of the 48,000 places in the freshmen classes at those institutions, or 6.3 percent. If test scores alone had been used in making admissions decisions, he estimates, only about one-quarter as many blacks— 720—would have been accepted, reducing their share of the class from 6.3 to 1.5 percent.[32] The author takes this as a powerful demonstration of the need for affirmative action; we see it as evidence that our universities have gone too far in bending their admissions standards in pursuit of greater racial balance.

MORE BAD NEWS

The gulf in test scores is immense. But should we care about mere tests? Many educators profess to believe that performance on such standardized examinations as the SATs is irrelevant. In 1996, for example, the president of Amherst College charged that it was "simple-minded, incorrect, and even racist" to believe "the ridiculous notion that 'qualifications' and test scores are synonymous." (His denunciation of tests was so unqualified that it was difficult to understand why Amherst College continued to require applicants to take the SATs at all.) The president of Williams College also dismissed the salience of SAT scores, claiming that "the best measures" of "academic potential" are "rank in class and the degree to which applicants have taken the strongest academic program offered at their schools." On those counts—supposedly much more predictive of college performance than the SATs—he went on to claim, "Williams students of color closely resemble the student body as a whole." [33]

It may be true of Williams, but it cannot be true of our most selective institutions of higher education in general. When they heap scorn on "mere tests," defenders of affirmative action pick an easy target, and deflect attention away from a wealth of evidence demonstrating that the racial gap in other measures of academic achievement and preparation is just as large as the gap in SAT scores.

Information about the class rank, grade averages, and courses taken by the 1 million–plus students who took the SATs in 1995 is summarized in Table 6. If rank in class is what should matter to admissions officers, twice as many white as black students ranked in the top tenth of their class. Furthermore, only 8 percent of African Americans but 21 percent of whites had grade averages of 93 or better. Whites were far ahead of African Americans in the average number of courses taken in core academic subjects, and in the proportion taking honors-level courses. In almost every case, Asian students were well ahead of both whites and blacks. When it came to taking honors courses in math and science, indeed, they were as far ahead of whites as whites were ahead of blacks. If one ignored SAT scores altogether and admitted students

Table 6
Academic Preparation and Achievement of College-Bound Black, White, and Asian Seniors, 1995

	BLACK	WHITE	ASIAN
Percent in top tenth of their class	12	23	28
Percent with A average (93 or higher)	8	21	27
No. of year-long courses in 6 academic subjects	27	44	44
Honors course taken in			
English	27	39	40
social science	19	29	35
natural science	18	29	38
mathematics	18	29	42

Source: College Entrance Examination Board, *1995 National Ethnic/Sex Data,* unpaginated.

on the basis of measures like these, the results would not differ significantly from the pattern produced by using SAT scores alone. As the editor of the *Journal of Blacks in Higher Education* points out, "Data from The College Board clearly demonstrate a direct and strong correlation between grade point average and SAT scores."[34]

These criteria all relate to academic performance. A college may wish to reward students who have been outstanding in music, drama, athletics, or some other extracurricular activity. Would taking extra-academic excellence into account greatly change the racial and ethnic profile? A study by the National Center for Education Statistics assessed qualifications for admissions to top-ranked schools more broadly, considering not only SAT scores, GPAs, and academic coursework but also extracurricular participation and recommendations by teachers. Assessing 1992 data in terms of these five criteria, the NCES estimated that just 0.4 percent of African-American seniors met the standards for admission at the top schools, as compared with 6.5 percent of non-Hispanic whites and 8.8 percent of Asians. If elite colleges and universities had abided by this formula in making all their admissions decisions, white students would have outnumbered blacks by a ratio of 65 to 1, an even bigger gap than using test scores alone would have produced.[35]

Taking these other factors into account did somewhat reduce the edge that Asians have over whites, probably because the typical Asian student devotes less time to extracurricular activities. But broadening the criteria in this fashion does nothing whatever to reduce the gap between blacks and whites. It is possible that the president of Williams College is correct in his claim that black freshmen there are just as likely as their white and Asian classmates to have ranked at the top of their class, and to have taken the most rigorous and demanding academic classes available to them. But if so, Williams must have had exceptionally good luck in its recruitment efforts, because African Americans lag badly in these respects, too. So far, at least, critics of tests have been unable to demonstrate that any other measure of academic preparation and achievement yields a significantly different result.

NOT RACE BUT SOCIAL CLASS?

However we measure the academic preparation and achievements of students at the age at which they are applying to college, we find large and disheartening racial differences. Such disparities in academic performance were only to be expected three decades ago, when the dual school system was still largely intact in the South and the black middle class was much less developed than it is today. It is surprising and disturbing that they still loom so large today. The reasons are undoubtedly complex and not entirely known but here we look just at one possibility: the impact of the remaining social-class differences between African Americans and whites. Children from low-income families, we know, do less well on tests and in school in general than those from middle-class homes. The children of highly educated parents do better than those from families with less education.

A crude but illuminating test of the hypothesis that social-class differences are the main cause of the racial gap in SAT scores may be obtained from data available from the College Board (Table 7). The results are very disturbing. In 1981 black students coming from families in the top income bracket—those earning $50,000 or more—had a mean verbal score of 414 and a mathematics score of 433. That was 47 and 76 points below what white students from the same income bracket scored in the verbals and in math respectively. The scores were approximately those of white students from families in the *lowest* income category—under $6,000 a year. The poorest whites were only 10 points behind affluent black children on the verbal test and actually a shade ahead of them in mathematics.

Low-income Asians performed much less well than well-to-do blacks on the verbal SATs, which doubtless had much to do with the fact that many were recent immigrants with a limited command of English. In math, though, the poorest Asians outscored the most prosperous blacks by more than 50 points. Poverty doubtless depressed overall black scores, but white and Asian children from families that also lived in poverty were not nearly as handicapped by it.

The other social-class variable that should have an impact on the educational performance of children is the education of their parents. Black children perform much less well than whites on the SATs partly because black parents have less education, on the average. But that explanation doesn't take us very far. In 1981 white students whose parents had only a grade school education had higher scores than blacks whose parents had acquired a graduate degree, and Asian children of similarly uneducated parents lagged on the verbals, as seen previously, but they performed nearly 100 points better in math than black youths from the highest parental education bracket.

Fourteen years later, in 1995, the patterns looked about the same. Black students from families in the top income bracket—now $70,000 and up—were a shade behind whites in the lowest income bracket on the verbal test, and significantly behind them in math. They were well ahead of the poorest Asian children in the verbals, but also well behind them in math. The only hint of progress was that blacks from families in the top educational category did better than in 1981, while whites in the lowest one—this time those without a high school diploma—did a little worse. But African-American children from families in which at least one parent had a graduate degree still were not performing as well as white youths whose parents had no education beyond high school, and in math they fell behind the offspring of Asian high school dropouts. In short, the rising educational level of the black population and the continued expansion of the black middle class since the 1960s has not yielded the expected gains in educational achievement by the younger

Table 7
**SAT Scores by Family Income, Parental Education,
and Race, 1981–1995**

	VERBAL	MATHEMATICAL
1981 median scores		
Family income		
Blacks, $50,000 or more	414	432
Whites, under $6,000	411	436
Asians, under $6,000	299	485
Parental education		
Blacks, graduate degree	388	406
Whites, grade school only	395	429
Asians, grade school only	333	501
1995 mean scores		
Family income		
Blacks, $70,000 or more	407	442
Whites, under $10,000	409	460
Asians, under $10,000	343	482
Parental education		
Blacks, graduate degree	406	438
Whites, no high school diploma	374	418
Asians, no high school diploma	338	478
Whites, high school graduates	414	459
Asians, high school graduates	382	502

Sources: College Entrance Examination Board, *Profiles, College-Bound Seniors, 1981,* 36–37, 54–55, 73–74; *1995 National Ethnic/Sex Data,* unpaginated. It is unfortunate that the College Board tabulated medians for the 1981 data and means in 1995. For data of this kind, however, the difference between the two summary statistics is not significant. The 1981 data on parental education gives separate figures for the education of mothers and of fathers; scores for the two have been averaged here. The 1995 parental education figures are for the highest level of education attained by either parent.

generation, the kind of payoff that Asian students are receiving today. Why that should be so undoubtedly has much to do with the weakness of the elementary and secondary education that many are receiving—a topic we addressed in the previous chapter and one to which we will return.

PREFERENTIAL ADMISSIONS AND DROPPING OUT

We have seen that since the 1960s black enrollments in college have increased much more dramatically than the rate of black graduation. The college dropout rate for black students is at least 50 percent higher than it is for whites. We suggested earlier that misguided affirmative action policies may have done a lot to create the problem. Here we examine that argument more fully. The point is simple. When students are given a preference in admissions because of their race or some other extraneous characteristic, it means that they are jumping into a competition for which their academic achievements do not qualify them, and many find it hard to keep up.

Affirmative action policies in higher education rest upon the optimistic assumption that a student's past record has little predictive value. Exposure to the college environment, it is assumed, will have a transforming effect upon minority students and stimulate them to perform at a much higher level than before. "We are interested in applicants' academic potential rather than past performance," the president of Williams declares.[36] Just how Williams admissions officers discern the "potential" of applicants except by considering their past performance is unclear. Whatever divining rod they use, it is one that somehow detects more untapped potential in minority students than in others.

Until recently it has been impossible to obtain evidence about the magnitude of the preferences involved in affirmative action admissions or about the performance of students who have been its beneficiaries.[37] And the picture is still incomplete, but we do have bits and scraps of important information. We now know, for instance, that at the University of California at Berkeley, the evidence of "past performance" that the president of Williams thought of doubtful value proved to be highly predictive of academic success in college. In July 1995 the regents of the UC system voted to abolish racial and ethnic preferences in admissions and to admit students on a color-blind basis in the future.[38] The controversy that led to that decision forced the release of illuminating data. Table 8 shows the connection between the SAT scores of freshmen who entered Berkeley in 1988 and their graduation rate. Only 58 percent of students who entered the school with a combined score in the 700s made it through to a degree; among those who scored in the 800s, 62 percent finished. Students with scores in the 1200s, by contrast, had an 86 percent graduation rate, and those in the 1300s an 88 percent rate. (The pattern reverses somewhat for those scoring in the 1400s and 1500s, but the change may not be statistically significant because of the relatively small numbers at that level. It is also possible that some of these seeming dropouts merely transferred from Berkeley to other elite schools—for instance, Cal Tech, Stanford, or Harvard).

Such figures are not available broken down by race, regrettably, but we have enough additional information to draw some conclusions. First, black freshmen in that class had combined SATs that averaged under 1,000, fully 304 points below the white average and 326 points below the Asian average. They also had high school grade averages of only B+, while their white and Asian classmates had GPAs close to straight-A.[39] The black students with the

Table 8

Proportion of 1988 Freshmen Who Had Graduated by 1994, by SAT Scores, University of California at Berkeley

700–799	58
800–899	62
900–999	72
1000–1099	78
1100–1199	83
1200–1299	86
1300–1399	88
1400–1499	84
1500–1599	79

Source: "Affirmative Action Under Attack on Campus Where It Worked," *New York Times,* 4 June 1995, A22.

strongest credentials—with verbal and math scores in the top quartile for African-American freshmen—ranked in the bottom quarter of all students at the school.[40] Second, we know that the black graduation rate was only 59 percent, as compared with the white rate of 84 percent and the Asian rate of 88 percent. It is very difficult to believe that there is no connection between these two sets of facts. The very high black dropout rate would seem logically the result of the inadequate academic skills with which African-American students arrived as a result of preferential admissions. They were put in this predicament by the unfortunate combination of poor preparation and preferential admissions.

The 41 percent dropout rate for African Americans entering Berkeley in 1988 was not exceptionally high by national standards. As we saw earlier, about six out of ten blacks who begin college fail to complete it, an attrition rate about 50 percent higher than that of whites. The picture looks somewhat different, however, if we focus on the very top colleges and universities, most of which have much lower dropout rates than Berkeley. Since some observers have interpreted the record of such schools as proof that affirmative action is a great success, a closer look at these elite schools should be useful (Table 9). At Harvard, all but 5 percent of entering African Americans graduate within six years, not dramatically different from the 3 percent figure for whites. Those figures are important because Harvard's admissions policies are often cited as the model. In the landmark 1978 case *Regents of the University of California v. Bakke,* for instance, Justice Lewis Powell made much of the fact that racial considerations entered into Harvard's admissions decisions as one of many factors. We will return to the *Bakke* case later. For now, we note that Table 9 suggests that Harvard is a very dubious model, since it attracts much better prepared black applicants than any other school, and obtains a substantial black enrollment—close to 7 percent—with nothing more than a light thumb on the scale. With a 1,305 mean SAT score for African Americans entering the freshman class in 1992, it is the only school in the country where the racial gap in SAT scores is not in the triple digits.

In any event, Harvard is a very special case. The mean SAT score of its African-American students was 133 points higher than that of black students admitted to Princeton, the closest contender. Their score was actually higher

Table 9

SAT Scores of Black Freshmen, 1992, the Racial Gap in Scores, and Dropout Rates in Selected Elite Universities

	SAT RACIAL GAP	MEAN BLACK SAT	BLACK	WHITE
			Percent dropping out	
Harvard	− 95	1,305	5	3
Princeton	− 150	1,172	9	5
Brown	− 150	1,160	13	6
Pennsylvania	− 150	1,135	28	10
Cornell	− 162	1,118	23	8
Stanford	− 171	1,164	17	6
Northwestern	− 180	1,075	21	10
Columbia	− 182	1,128	25	12
Duke	− 184	1,126	16	5
Dartmouth	− 218	1,112	16	4
Virginia	− 241	979	16	7
Rice	− 271	1,093	26	11
UC-Berkeley	− 288	947	42	16

Sources: SAT scores of students starting college in the 1992–1993 academic year from Theodore Cross, "What if There Was No Affirmative Action in College Admissions? A Further Refinement of Our Earlier Calculations," *Journal of Blacks in Higher Education,* 5 (Autumn 1994), 55. The dropout rate is the proportion of the students entering those schools in the four classes from 1986–1987 to 1989–1990 who failed to graduate within six years of entry, as given in National Collegiate Athletic Association, *1996 NCAA Division I Graduation-Rates Report* (Overland Park, Kans.: 1996). The dropout rates are not for the same entering classes; such figures for students starting college in 1992 obviously will not be available until 1998. The data available are for earlier entrants, so the gap in scores documented here cannot have directly caused these dropout patterns. The fragmentary data available, though, suggests that the average scores of students at a particular school and the proportion dropping out do not fluctuate much from year to year. At UC-Berkeley, about which the evidence is richest, the SAT gap and the gap in dropout rates changed very little between 1984 and 1994; see "Affirmative Action Under Attack," *New York Times,* 4 June 1995, A22.

than the average score *for whites* at such distinguished schools as the University of Chicago, Cornell, and Penn. It was 50 points above the score of whites at Northwestern, 70 points above those at Berkeley, and 80 points above those at Virginia. What is more, a score of 1,305 was so close to the top of the scale that it is questionable whether the 95 points separating the average black freshman from the average white freshman at Harvard was even statistically meaningful, since the SAT was not designed to make fine distinctions among students at the very top of the distribution.

In none of the elite schools in Table 9 is dropping out a huge problem. The vast majority of all students graduate. It is extremely difficult to get accepted in the first place, but also hard to flunk out. On the other hand, none of them can boast no racial gap in graduation rates. At all but Harvard and Princeton, which top the list, African-American students are at least twice as likely to fall by the wayside and fail to take a degree. These are very able students, and it is dismaying that a fifth to a quarter or more of them are dropping out in many cases. It is difficult to doubt that there is a connection between the academic double standards in the admissions procedures of these schools and the differences in academic outcomes.

THE ECONOMIC COSTS OF DROPPING OUT

Elite schools are by definition atypical. At less selective institutions the overall dropout rate is higher and the black-white gap is correspondingly larger (Table 10). Economists Linda Datcher Loury and David Garman analyzed a representative national sample of young males from the time of their high school graduation in 1972 down to 1986, when they were in their early thirties, and found that graduating from selective colleges—with selectivity defined by average SAT scores—paid off in the labor market. Giving African Americans a better chance at the best-paid jobs might seem a good reason for affirmative action. Loury and Garman discovered, however, that many of the blacks who attended the more selective schools never graduated to reap the rewards; indeed, their chances of graduation were powerfully affected by how their SAT scores compared with the average at the schools they attended. The greater the gap, the lower their chances of making it through.

Some white students, it is often said, are also admitted preferentially—although on the basis of such nonacademic factors as being the child of an alumnus or having special athletic or musical talents. But these considerations are given much less weight than race in the admissions decisions of most schools, with the result that whites typically attend schools in which their academic credentials are about the same as those of their classmates.[41] Thus, the average white student in the Loury and Garman study had an SAT score of 1,011, and had gone to a college at which the median score was almost

Table 10

How Graduation Rates of Black Students Vary with Their SAT Scores and the Median SAT Score at Their College, 1972 High School Graduates

	COLLEGES WITH MEDIAN SATs OF	
Percent graduating of students with SATs of	900	1,000
700 or less	38	26
701–850	56	39
851–1,000	77	51
over 1,000	77	51

Source: Linda Datcher Loury and David Garman, "College Selectivity and Earnings," *Journal of Labor Economics* 13, no. 2 (1995), 304. The failure of the pattern evident in the three lower SAT groups to show up for those with scores over 1,000 may reflect the fact that the number of blacks in this category was very small.

precisely that—1,019. Whites were well matched to the colleges they attended, and could survive academically simply by doing the same amount of schoolwork as their fellow students.

But those African Americans in the study who had been to college had experienced a less comfortable and more threatening environment. The typical black student in the sample had a combined SAT of 768—unexceptional at many institutions of higher learning. But African Americans with scores in this range did not attend schools in which the average SAT was in the high 700s. The blacks in the study had instead been enrolled in colleges in which the average student scored 936, making the typical African-American freshman 168 SAT points behind the typical white freshman. And equally far behind, of course, in all the other academic measures correlated with SAT scores—in grade point averages, number of years of coursework in academic subjects, and number of honors courses taken. Naturally they faced an uphill struggle getting through.

Did they not benefit from attending "better" schools than they would have enrolled in without affirmative action, however? Proponents of preferential policies assume that it is an unmixed blessing to give minority students access to the most prestigious and demanding colleges. If it forces the beneficiaries of preferences to stretch themselves more than their white peers who enter with stronger credentials, fine. In some cases the pressure is undoubtedly beneficial, but many students break under the strain.

The Berkeley story contained in Table 8, in other words, applies to black students nationally. When a student and a college are mismatched, the lower the SAT score, the less likely that student is to graduate, the Loury and Garman evidence showed. Blacks with SATs in the 701-to-850 range, for example, had a 56 percent chance of graduating from a college where the median score was 900. If they were given a bigger affirmative action boost and admitted to a school where the median SAT score was 1,000 and the racial gap was 100 points larger, their chances of making it through to a degree dropped sharply, to just 39 percent. Likewise, African-American students with scores from 851 to 1,000 had a three-to-one chance of graduating from a school in which their scores were average or even a little above average. On the other hand, the odds of their succeeding fell to 50-50 if they were generally below the college SAT average. The point, of course, squares with common sense.

The Loury and Garman study also looked at what happens to students after college, answering those who argue for giving black students a crack at places like Berkeley even if their chances of graduating are not good. Failure carries a painful price. In 1986, fourteen years after leaving high school, black college dropouts were earning one-quarter less than their counterparts who went to less selective schools in the first place but managed to graduate. When colleges attempt to display their social commitment by admitting "high-risk" students from minority groups, in other words, it is the students who suffer when the risks don't pan out. The schools may feel better, having demonstrated their racial virtue, but many of the beneficiaries end up worse off.

THE OLE MISS MODEL

The black-white gap in graduation rates is trivial at Harvard and a few other elite institutions like it. It is surprising and intriguing, though, that the gap is still smaller at another university of an entirely different sort. Difficult though it is to believe, the university that comes closest to racial equality in graduation rates is none other than the University of Mississippi, the "Ole Miss" that was the object of such a bitter, ugly fight over integration in the early years of the Kennedy administration. Of the freshmen entering the school from 1984 through 1987, 49 percent of the whites graduated; for black students it was a nearly identical 48 percent.[42]

What is more, a similar pattern prevailed at other southern schools that are not generally seen as bastions of racial liberalism. At the University of Alabama, 55 percent of whites and 49 percent of blacks graduated. At the University of South Carolina it was 62 and 56 percent, and at the University of Georgia, 60 and 48 percent. These Deep South institutions, among the very last in the nation to accept black students, had smaller racial gaps in graduation rates than most of the elite, mainly private, schools listed in Table 9.

What explains this rather startling pattern? It is not that these schools have become more committed to giving special assistance to black students than northern colleges with a strong liberal tradition. Not at all. The answer given by the *Journal of Blacks in Higher Education* is that Ole Miss and its sister schools in neighboring Deep South states require students of both races to achieve a minimum SAT score that is set high enough to bar students likely to experience severe academic difficulties. Although these southern institutions claim to have affirmative action programs, they nevertheless impose admissions requirements that screen out the high-risk students who would be accepted at comparable schools that employ a double standard in evaluating black applicants.

The *Journal,* a fervent advocate of affirmative action, expressed unhappiness that "only the most highly qualified black students" in these states "are admitted to the predominantly white institutions." It complained that African Americans were severely underrepresented at Ole Miss, making up 9.4 of the student body but 35.6 percent of the population of the state.[43] If the racial disparity in SAT scores and grades that is the main source of that underrepresentation is attributable to deficiencies in the state's public schools, something should obviously be done to address the problem at that level. Racial double standards in college admissions allow elementary and secondary schools to continue to serve students poorly, offering a quick fix that in fact is no remedy.

LEGAL CHALLENGES TO PREFERENTIAL ADMISSIONS

Giving spaces in competitive educational programs to minority students with academic records notably weaker than those of whites who were turned away has inevitably provoked controversy. The practice has been hard to square with the moral code of the civil rights movement—that of judging people on the basis of their individual merits rather than group characteristics. And thus it has been hard to square with the crowning achievement of that movement: the Civil Rights Act of 1964, which barred discrimination on the basis of race, religion, or national origin. In addition, racial preferences seemed to violate the equal-protection promise of the Fourteenth Amendment.

As a legal matter, the issue first surfaced in suits challenging preferential admissions policies not in colleges but in professional schools at state universities. They were the most logical points of attack because their announced admissions policies gave more weight to strictly academic qualifications than did most selective colleges, which generally looked at such extracurricular activities as drama clubs and the like. Professional schools thus found it harder than colleges to claim that race was just one of a great many nonacademic factors they took into account in making admissions decisions. They also had specialized tests like the Law School Aptitude Test (LSAT), the Medical College Aptitude Test (MCAT), and the Graduate Records Examination (GRE), which predicted performance in graduate programs more reliably than the SATs predicted college grades. Not all professional schools, however, were equally vulnerable to suits challenging their affirmative action programs.

The Fourteenth Amendment, the obvious starting point for plaintiffs, could only be used against state institutions, since it did not bar discriminatory action in the private sector.

The first case challenging such racial preferences in higher education was heard by the Supreme Court in 1974. Marco DeFunis had sued the University of Washington Law School for having turned him down while accepting thirty-six minority students, all but one of whom had lower college grades and poorer scores on the LSATs than he did.[44] But he had been admitted when he won the first round in the battle, and by the time his case wended its way through Washington state courts and arrived at the Supreme Court, he was beginning his final term at the law school. The High Court thus declared the matter moot. Four years later, however, a white plaintiff was back before the Supreme Court, asking much the same set of questions: Was it legitimate to attempt to promote the advance of members of a racial group that had long suffered from prejudice by making special allowances for their prior racial disadvantage? Was it morally offensive to dispense benefits on the basis of group membership only when majorities employed racial categories to harm minority interests, as had been the case for much of our history? The Fourteenth Amendment had been passed to guarantee African Americans the basic citizenship rights they had long been denied. Did the Constitution nevertheless set limits on what could be done to overcome the effects of centuries of discrimination against black people?

The plaintiff in 1978 was Allan Bakke, who had graduated from the University of Minnesota in 1962, and stayed on briefly for graduate work. He had gone on to serve in the Marine Corps in Vietnam, work as a research engineer in California, and earn a master's degree in mechanical engineering from Stanford. By the time he applied to the medical school at the University of California at Davis in 1973, he was in his early thirties, and his age was a serious handicap. (Professional schools in the days before the Age Discrimination Act of 1975 seldom trained students who had been out of college for more than a few years.) On the other hand, Bakke's credentials were excellent. His grade record was stronger than that of most regular admittees, and his MCAT scores were much better. He was in the 97th percentile in the science section of the test and just a shade below that on the verbal and quantitative sections. But he was rejected for the 1973–1974 entering class, and rejected again the next year.[45]

Although his age may have been Bakke's biggest handicap, the school's two-track admissions procedure, prompting his legal complaint, also limited his chances. Sixteen of the hundred places in the first-year class at the Davis medical school were set aside for (in theory) "economically and/or educationally disadvantaged" applicants. In fact, since no white ever got one of the sixteen places, it was really a special minority admissions program. Not only were the slots reserved for blacks, Hispanics, and an occasional American

Indian (no Asians), they were filled by an entirely separate committee that accepted and rejected candidates without comparing them to students in the regular applicant pool.

The academic records of the minority admittees were dismal compared to that of Allan Bakke. In 1974 they had C+ grade averages as undergraduates, compared with Bakke's A−; their MCAT scores put them at the top of the bottom third of all test-takers, while Bakke was well up in the top 10 percent. In terms of traditional academic qualifications, there was no comparison. The MCAT averages for the minority students fell below the 50th percentile in every category and averaged around the 33rd, while the lowest percentile average for the regular admittees in any MCAT was the 67th. A school that had refused admittance to a black student with Bakke's record while admitting whites who were as academically weak as those of the minorities accepted for special admissions would surely have been successfully sued for racial discrimination.

Allan Bakke's case was first heard in a state court, which ruled that the special admissions program was indeed an unconstitutional racial quota, and that the admissions preferences given to minority applicants violated Bakke's right to the equal protection of the laws.[46] The university took its argument to the California Supreme Court. Although that court had a strongly liberal reputation, it upheld Bakke by a 6-to-1 vote and declared the racial set-aside a clear violation of the Fourteenth Amendment.[47] UC-Davis appealed once again and the case—by then a cause célèbre—went to the U.S. Supreme Court. A record fifty-seven "friend of the court" (amicus curiae) briefs were filed in the case. About three-quarters of them, from leading universities, civil rights groups, and minority organizations, sided with the University of California. Seven Jewish organizations, a smattering of other ethnic, conservative, and business groups backed Bakke.[48]

The Supreme Court's decision in *Regents of the University of California v. Bakke* was a personal victory for Allan Bakke—he got to go to medical school —but not for the color-blind principle at the heart of his case. Racial preferences were left standing, thanks to Justice Powell, who, although largely writing on his own, essentially gave the Court's opinion. Shuttling between two camps in a 4–1–4 decision, Powell voted with one group of four to strike down Davis's quotas, but used the votes of four liberals to allow the school to consider race as one factor in admissions. Although there was no single majority opinion, he thus cast a decisive fifth vote for the liberals on one issue, and a decisive fifth for the conservatives on another.

The *Bakke* decision is perhaps best known for Justice Harry Blackmun's famous dictum that "in order to get beyond racism, we must first take account of race. There is no other way. And in order to treat some persons equally, we must treat them differently. We cannot—we dare not—let the Equal Protection clause perpetuate racial supremacy."[49] It was not clear why racial quotas and racial supremacy were the only two alternatives. But the vaguely Orwellian notion that it was necessary to treat some persons "differently" in order to treat them "equally" had already, by 1978, become civil rights orthodoxy.

Justice Blackmun was the phrase-maker, but Justice William Brennan's was the most important voice supporting the university. His opinion dismissed the classic liberal insistence that "[o]ur Constitution is color-blind" as an interpretation that had "never been adopted by this Court as the proper meaning of the Equal Protection Clause."[50] That was true enough, but it did not answer the question of whether it wasn't time for the Court to say precisely that. Brennan's view, however, was clearly that Justice John Marshall Harlan (dissenting in *Plessy* in 1896) had been wrong and remained wrong. Racial discrimination that stigmatized a group was wrong, but not that which was "benign." "Government may take race into account when it acts not to demean or insult any racial group, but to remedy disadvantages cast on minorities by past racial prejudice, at least when appropriate findings have been made by judicial, legislative, or administrative bodies with competence to act in this area." Those "disadvantages cast on minorities by past racial prejudice," Brennan argued, were behind "the failure of minorities to qualify for admission at Davis under regular procedures." But for "pervasive discrimination," Bakke (it is reasonable to conclude) "would have failed to qualify for admission even in the absence of Davis's special admissions program."[51]

It was an imaginative rewriting of history, and it was rejected by Powell. All previous racial preferences had been remedies, Powell emphasized, usually for the constitutional violation of school segregation or the statutory violation of employment discrimination. "We have never approved a classification that aids persons perceived as members of relatively victimized groups at the expense of other innocent individuals in the absence of judicial, legislative, or administrative findings of constitutional or statutory violations." So far, so good, but Powell's next step was to open the back door to quotas. It was legitimate, he said, for a school to make admissions decisions aimed at producing a "diverse student body"; race could thus be taken into account. Invoking both academic freedom and the First Amendment as protecting a university's interest in selecting "those students who will contribute the most to the 'robust exchange of ideas,' " he accepted with a wink the notion that UC-Davis thought of this concern when it created its quotas. The whole argument, of course, rested on the very stereotyping that the Fourteenth Amendment was supposed to bar—the notion that racial differences were a proxy for differences in "points of view, backgrounds, and experiences."[52]

Powell's "diversity" edifice had all sorts of cracks in its foundation. With the exception of "geographical origin," all the characteristics that he mentioned (musical or athletic talent, for instance) were individual; to list racial identity as a desirable characteristic is to engage in racial stereotyping on the basis of group membership. Most important, however, was his embrace of one sort of "diversity" program—that which Harvard College had adopted—while rejecting that in place at UC-Davis, when in fact it was a distinction with no important difference.

Harvard College, Powell said, had no numerical quotas for "the number of blacks, or of musicians, football players, physicists or Californians to be admitted in any given year," but nonetheless allowed such factors to be a "plus" when an applicant was compared with others.[53] Race had to be "simply one element—to be weighed fairly against other elements—in the selection process." Harvard College, he thought, used it that way; the medical school at the University of California at Davis did not. There was much wrong with Powell's use of the Harvard model. The college wasn't a professional school, and thus did look for nonacademic talents. Moreover, it drew an incredibly talented pool of applicants (as we noted before). And what did it mean in practice to say that race could be a "plus" but not a decisive factor? When did the "plus" become decisive? Justice Powell wanted race to be "weighed fairly," but provided no illumination as to just how much weight could "fairly" be given to it. Enough to make up for having a GPA or a MCAT score just a bit below that of the typical white student accepted? Or enough to compensate for grades or scores in the bottom 30 percent when the average student enrolled at the school was in the 90th percentile? And if it was only the former, then not only UC-Davis but almost every other institution of higher education with an affirmative action program violated both the Constitution and Title VI of the 1964 Civil Rights Act, which barred discrimination in institutions receiving federal funds. (All medical schools are recipients of federal grants.)

Institutions of higher education, with the arguable exception of Harvard College, all violated the *Bakke* standard because, given the academic performance of most applicants, race could not be simply a "plus" factor. Indeed, though Justice Powell probably did not know it, in the mid-1970s the Harvard Medical School was reserving 20 percent of the places in each entering class for minorities, a larger proportion than at Davis.[54] And it was Justice Brennan who made clear just how useless Powell's distinction between good and bad discrimination was. Any admissions program, he said, that "accords special consideration to disadvantaged racial minorities" must determine how much preference to give them. But any amount of preference will to some extent exclude whites, so as a constitutional matter "there [was] no difference" between Davis's and Harvard's approaches. The amount of preference, or weight, or "plus," a minority applicant receives could only depend on how many minorities the school wished to admit:

There is no sensible, and certainly no constitutional, distinction between, for example, adding a set number of points to the admissions rating of disadvantaged minority applicants . . . with the expectation that this will result in the admission of an approximately determined number of qualified minority applicants and setting a fixed number of places for such applicants as was done here.

Harvard itself, in a part of the plan that Powell relegated to an appendix, as much as admitted this.[55] Harvard's approach merely allowed it to be less frank than Davis, Brennan explained. While this may have had public relations advantages, it had no constitutional relevance.

Justice Powell conceded that programs like those at Harvard might be viewed as "simply a subtle and more sophisticated—but no less effective— means of according racial preference than the Davis program." He insisted, however, that a "facial intent to discriminate" could be seen in the Davis plan but not in the Harvard program. As long as a school professed to "employ a facially nondiscriminatory admissions policy," he said, no court would assume that it would "operate it as a cover for the functional equivalent of a quota system."[56] Professed intent was thus the key.

Justice Thurgood Marshall, the Court's only black member, viewed the Davis program as an effort to "remedy the effects of . . . centuries of unequal treatment," although Davis had crafted a preference program with no authority or effort to identify victims of discrimination and without identifying either itself or anyone else as guilty of discrimination. Both he and Brennan defended quotas as reparations—compensating applicants who (in Brennan's words) were "fully qualified to study medicine."[57] Marshall's bitter opinion conjured up the specter of another great reversal in the nation's treatment of African Americans, a rhetorical strategy that, in subsequent years, has been employed increasingly by civil rights advocates. With the retreat from Reconstruction at the close of the nineteenth century, Marshall wrote, the Supreme Court had "destroyed the movement toward complete equality" by sanctioning segregation under the separate-but-equal doctrine. Now the Court was "again stepping in, this time to stop programs of the type used by the University of California."[58]

The final opinion was that of Justice John Paul Stevens. Title VI was the issue, he said. The university received federal funds; it excluded Bakke because of his race; therefore, by "the plain language of the statute," it violated the law and, as the California Supreme Court ordered, must admit him. Only if the facially color-blind statute "misstate[d] the actual intent of the Congress that enacted the statute" could the Court justify another conclusion. It didn't. The Civil Rights Act protected individuals, of whatever race, and protected them all equally. Neither the statute nor the legislative history left any room for allowing discrimination that lacked "racial stigma." "As succinctly phrased during the Senate debate, under Title VI it [was] not 'permissible to say "yes" to one person; but to say "no" to another person, only because of the color of his skin.' "[59] That settled the matter for Justices Stewart, Rehnquist, and Burger, as well as Stevens. They needed one more vote, however, to make theirs the majority opinion. And had they had it the subsequent history of affirmative action in higher-education admissions policies—and indeed perhaps of preferential policies altogether—would have been entirely different.

As it was, Justice Marshall's lurid estimate of the impact of the *Bakke* decision on the admissions policies of the nation's colleges and universities proved to be far off the mark. *Bakke*—thanks to Powell—did little to curb affirmative action. The decision gave Allan Bakke his chance to become an M.D., but other disappointed applicants who felt that they had been denied educational opportunities because of their race had little to cheer about. Schools were to look at individuals, judging them on a "case-by-case basis," and not as members of groups, Powell had said.[60] It was an exercise in pure wishful thinking. In the immediate wake of the Court's decision, another branch of the UC system—Boalt Hall, the law school at Berkeley—adopted an affirmative action admissions procedure in which applicants who were members of one racial group were judged only against other members of that group; blacks competed only against blacks, in other words. In addition, the school maintained racially separate waiting lists, such that students received notices that ran something like "You are number 10 on the black waiting list."[61]

Fourteen years later the (Republican-controlled) U.S. Department of Justice finally said, no, Boalt Hall could not maintain almost precisely the same sort of program that the Court had struck down in 1978. "After *Bakke*, Berkeley decided it was safest to use subtlety and deception to accomplish the important goal of a racially diverse student body," Ruben Navarrette, Jr., the editor of *Hispanic Student USA*, wrote in the *Los Angeles Times*. "For 14 years," he went on, "Berkeley and its UC sisters . . . pretended not to violate *Bakke*. . . . Did Boalt violate *Bakke?* Of course." As a high school senior seven years earlier, Navarrette had obtained a copy of what he called "the University of California's not-so-subtle five-year affirmative-action plan." Had it set a "goal" or a "quota" for each minority group? "Same difference," he answers. "I was accepted to Berkeley under a quota that the Supreme Court had ruled illegal; I was accepted to Harvard under a goal that had the court's blessing."[62]

Berkeley agreed to go to a single admissions committee and had already (in 1989) given up on its ethnically sorted waiting lists—although from the beginning of the process to the end, applicants were still racially identified. As the executive director of the Association of American Law Schools stated, these were certainly "minor adjustments." And while the president of a similar organization (the Association of Colleges and Universities) said he had "no reason to think [Boalt Hall's] practices were unique or even unusual," no other school—at least publicly—took any significant steps to mend its affirmative action ways.[63]

Thus, eighteen years after *Bakke* the Fifth Circuit Court of Appeals took a hard look at admissions procedures at the University of Texas Law School and found a system that could not, by any stretch of the imagination, meet the already pathetically weak legal standards set out in the High Court's landmark 1978 decision. Justice Powell had written an opinion that required a small shift in rhetoric (race as a "plus" factor, "diversity" as the goal), but which, by and large, schools simply ignored.

HOPWOOD

If judicial decisions contained subtitles, the majority opinion in *Hopwood v. Texas* might have read, "the road to hell, paved with the best intentions." The University of Texas (UT) Law School had ("with the best of intentions," Judge Jerry E. Smith acknowledged) adopted a policy of preferential admissions that confirmed the worst fears of those opposed to quotas. Blacks and Hispanics were admitted by a segregated evaluation process (conducted by a minority committee of three whose word was final) and were held to much lower academic standards than whites and Asians. For the latter two groups, the school was extremely difficult to enter; the median LSAT score of whites in the 1992 class was in the 91st percentile. But the story was quite different for African Americans (not blacks from abroad) and Hispanics (citizens or aliens) —the preferred "minorities." The black median score that year was in the 78th percentile. The grade point averages of the two groups were similarly different. Cheryl Hopwood, white but disadvantaged by any normal measure, along with three other students filed a Fourteenth Amendment suit after they had applied unsuccessfully for admission to the 1992 entering class. According to the plaintiffs, six-to-seven hundred higher-scoring white Texas residents had been passed over before the first blacks were denied admission.[64]

As Judge Smith, writing the court's opinion put it, "race was always an overt part of the review of any applicant's file."[65] The school said it lowered standards to meet a goal of 10 percent Mexican Americans and 5 percent blacks —a target set to overcome the effects of past discrimination and to ensure "diversity." One is tempted to ask, how did UT think it could get away with such obviously vulnerable arguments for admissions procedures that were so wrong from so many angles?

What exactly, for instance, were the lingering effects of past state-sponsored discrimination that the program addressed? Most of the black students at the law school came from out of state; were those who grew up in New York victims of Texas policies such that a Texas state institution was obligated to provide a remedy? And if not, surely it was insufficient to point in the vague direction of harms from "societal discrimination"—a bottomless pit that could be used to justify any and all racial preferences. The "diversity" rationale had been used by Justice Powell—and only Powell—in *Bakke*, and it had cropped up in one other, overruled decision. What did "diversity" mean? The concept was simply "too amorphous" and "too insubstantial" (as Justice Sandra Day O'Connor had once noted) to justify sorting out citizens on the basis of race —which was highly suspect under the best of circumstances.

The whole admissions process, in fact, reeked of discrimination—precisely the discrimination that the Constitution forbids. The point of the Fourteenth Amendment had been to end all racially motivated state action; the UT law school was a state institution that was using race to decide who was entitled to a seat in its classrooms. Segregated admissions policies; segregated waiting lists; blatant racial double standards: the whole system was uncomfortably close to a Jim Crow nightmare, ostensibly for benign ends. As a professional school, the admissions office did not look at nonacademic talent. But it did look at race, which was certainly not a "plus" factor; for most black and Hispanic students it was decisive. The Fifth Circuit said simply, call it quits: "The law school may not use race as a factor in deciding which applicants to admit."[66] *Bakke*-like facts had produced a very un-*Bakke*-like holding—eighteen years later. The Supreme Court did not take the case, but had it done so, would it have signed on to Judge Smith's sweeping rejection of race-based state action? The question, of course, cannot be answered, but, as the next chapter will make clear, in 1996 there was certainly less sympathy on the High Court for race-driven policy than there had been in the 1970s, when Justice Powell danced—or stumbled—around the issue.

CAN WE DO WITHOUT?

The reaction to the *Hopwood* decision on the part of higher-education spokesmen was borderline hysteria. Justice Marshall in 1978 had warned that the extremely mild—indeed, utterly innocuous—curbs upon racial preferences contained in the *Bakke* decision might have led America to "come full circle"—that the nation seemed once again back at the end to Reconstruction.[67] Eighteen years later, when *Bakke* was in effect relitigated, the same cry of impending disaster went up. If the Supreme Court did not overturn the decision, the law school would become a "passive participant in a system of racial exclusion," the U.S. Department of Justice said.[68] Not just that law school, the Justice Department—and others—clearly believed. University of Miami law professor Donald Jones envisioned "lily-white universities across the United States." University of Texas president Robert M. Berdahl predicted that the decision, if upheld, would lead to "the virtual resegregation of higher education."[69]

Given the credentials of the minority applicant pool to the UT law school, there is no doubt that even reducing race to the "plus" factor that *Bakke* allowed (but the Fifth Circuit did not) would greatly diminish the black and Hispanic presence at that particular law school—one would hope, only in the short run. Unless, that is, the school came up with some sort of subterfuge— a different means to the same end. By one calculation, if Texas had based its 1992 admissions on a strictly color-blind standard, the entering class of five hundred students would have included, at most, nine who were black, all of whom would have been courted by the most prestigious law schools in the country.[70] But would the total number of black students at law and other professional schools and attending college be similarly reduced? Yes and no.

The black students enrolled at the UT law school would have all gone to other schools; they all had the academic credentials to get into a less competitive institution—fair and square, without playing the race card. But there are no professional schools that are not selective, and those black students with the weakest grades and scores in the nation would probably be left having to choose another profession. On the other hand, the undergraduate picture would be very different. Some of the black students now at Michigan would instead find themselves at Western Michigan or Wayne State. But would any now enrolled have been left out altogether? A large majority of the more than three thousand colleges and universities in the United States essentially have open admissions. Sign up and you can go. And if you do well, even at virtually unknown places, the doors to jobs and further education will have been opened. Ward Connerly, a highly successful black businessman who was appointed to the University of California Board of Regents in 1993, started out at a community college. "That's not depriving kids of education," he has rightly said.[71]

TRUE EQUALITY

"The contest between white suburban students and minority inner-city youths is inherently unfair," the chancellor of the University of California at Berkeley, Chang-Lin Tien, said in the summer of 1995.[72] It was not a very persuasive argument for the racial double standards he was defending. If inner-city youngsters are educationally deprived, surely the real solution—indeed the only effective and just solution—has to be one that attacks the problem of K–12 education directly. But in any case, most of the beneficiaries were not the inner-city youths upon whom Tien chose to focus; 30 percent of the black students in the 1994-1995 freshmen class came from families with annual incomes over $70,000. In fact, the Berkeley admissions office, studying the question, found that preferences reserved only for students from low-income families would have reduced the black enrollment by two-thirds.[73] Relatively privileged students—by the measure of economic well-being—had acquired privileges on the basis of the color of their skin.

Affirmative action is class-blind. Students who fall into the category of protected minority will benefit whatever the occupation and income of their parents. As the *Boston Globe* has put it, "officials at even the most selective schools recruit minority scholars with the zeal of a Big 10 football coach." The overwhelming majority of four-year institutions buy expensive lists of minority students and their scores from the Educational Testing Service. Admissions counselors and a network of thousands of alumni comb the country, visiting schools and the special preparatory programs that Phillips Academy in Andover and other private high schools run. Some universities, like Tufts, start the recruitment process in the elementary school years; others, like Boston College, have been known to bring minority students, all expenses paid, for a visit, complete with a chauffeured tour of the area.[74] And if that student can already afford the air fare and more? That's not relevant. Until 1996, when the policy was changed, the African-American student whom the Harvard Graduate School wanted automatically qualified for a Minority Prize Fellowship—even if that student was the son or daughter of a black millionaire.[75]

It's not a process likely to encourage its beneficiaries to work hard in high school. The message is clear: color is the equivalent of good grades. If you don't have the latter, the former will often do. When the University of California regents decided in July 1995 to abolish racial and ethnic preferences in admissions, the executive director of a YWCA college-awareness program told students that the UC vote meant that their "application would be sent in with everybody else's—people who are on college tracks and are prepared." One of the minority students at the session, Jesley Zambrano, reacted at first with anger: "The schools are mostly run by white people. If they don't help us get in, how are we going to get in?" she asked. But then she answered the question herself: "I guess I have to work harder," she said.[76]

That was exactly the point Martin Luther King had made in a speech Shelby Steele heard as a young student in Chicago. "When you are behind in a footrace," King had said, "the only way to get ahead is to run faster than the man in front of you. So when your white roommate says he's tired and goes to sleep, you stay up and burn the midnight oil."[77] As Steele went on to say, "academic parity with all other groups should be the overriding mission of black students. . . . Blacks can only *know* they are as good as others when they are, in fact, as good. . . . Nothing under the sun will substitute for this."[78] And nothing under the sun except hard work will bring about that parity, as King had said. Challenge the students academically rather than capitulate to their demands for dorms with an ethnic theme, Steele has urged universities. And dismantle the machinery of separation, break the link between difference and power. For as long as black students see themselves as *black* students—a group apart, defined by race—they are likely to choose power over parity.

CHAPTER FIFTEEN

Jobs and Contracts

IN 1994, UNDER pressure from the federal government, the University of California at San Diego agreed to pay $600,000 to twenty-seven men and women who had applied for jobs they didn't get. The school denied doing anything wrong; indeed, the assistant vice-chancellor for human resources, an African American, claimed not to have known the applicants' racial or ethnic identity. Color wasn't the issue, he said; the jobs required skills these applicants lacked.

That same year in that same city the Marriott Hotel promised to pay back wages totaling $627,000 to thirty-four black women, unsuccessful applicants for jobs. As part of the settlement with federal investigators, Marriott offered jobs to the women, established on-the-job training, and gave them credit for the vacation time and sick leave they might have had. It created a training program for managers and agreed to regular meetings with department heads to "review, update and reaffirm" Marriott's affirmative action policies. In addition, the hotel promised to keep careful track of its hiring record, so that members of staff assigned to interviewing prospective employees would know if members of designated minority groups were underrepresented in the relevant positions; in fact, managers were expected to justify the hiring of a white whenever the number of minorities in the position was disproportionately low.[1]

Why plead guilty if in fact the school and hotel were (as they claimed) innocent? Investigations into possible employment discrimination by those who do business with the federal government—most often undertaken in the absence of a single complaint against the suspect institution—are lengthy and, for those whom the government targets, arduous and expensive. Refusing to settle is costly, with part of the cost being the loss of lucrative contracts. On the other side of the ledger is the necessity not only to pay salaries and benefits that were not earned, but to engage in diversity training and race-based hiring—costs, indisputably, but most often viewed as less pricey than a fight.

These are not exceptional stories, and they are but one corner of a much larger picture. Affirmative action considerations now affect almost all federal and many state government contracts, as well as much employment, both public and private. Has the heavy hand of the government become too intrusive? Or is vigorous enforcement of racial equity in employment and government contracts essential to keep discrimination in check? Those who support preferential policies view them as vital to the economic well-being of blacks. They are seen as an essential life raft—the means by which many blacks stay economically afloat, the antipoverty program that really works, the only real guarantee against a resurgence of racism that will wipe out the economic progress made by African Americans.

Critics of preferential policies, of course, have a different view. Aside from philosophical opposition to programs in which skin color determines the beneficiaries and to inferring inequality of opportunity from statistical disparities, they note abuses—large and small. For instance, a September 1994 audit of fifty of the larger minority-owned firms that had been the beneficiaries of a federal set-aside for "small disadvantaged businesses" uncovered a startling fact. Thirty-five of the fifty owners had a net worth in excess of $1 million; five of them had personal residences valued at between $800,000 and $1.4 million.[2] Other levels of government have set-aside policies that are plagued by similar problems. In 1993 a controversy erupted over a minority business enterprise program that reserved 35 percent of Atlanta's contract work for blacks. The program, instituted by a black mayor in 1975, was supposed to help black entrepreneurs; instead, it became the means by which a handful of mostly white businessmen got rich through a system of kickbacks and bribery.[3]

Whatever the merits of these opposing arguments, one thing is clear: we have come a long way since the Civil Rights Act of 1964, which focused on stopping acts of intentional discrimination in the workforce. How we got from here to there: that is the main question this chapter addresses. We concentrate on the federal story, although we touch on affirmative action policies in state and local government and in the private sector as well.

TITLE VII AND THE REDEFINITION OF DISCRIMINATION

The story begins with Congress, and a key provision of the 1964 Civil Rights Act: Title VII. Its initial aim was straightforward: to ensure fair employment by outlawing discrimination in a variety of settings—private employers with at least twenty-five employees, labor unions, and employment agencies of any size. The political opposition to covering employment in the 1964 act was considerable, and, in fact, nearly blocked passage of the entire bill. The final compromise transformed the President's Committee on Equal Employment Opportunity, a body created by a Kennedy administration executive order, into a permanent enforcement agency that was still largely toothless. It established a five-member Equal Employment Opportunity Commission (EEOC), which could receive and process individual complaints of discrimination, negotiate settlements, hold hearings, conduct studies, issue reports, and make recommendations. But the EEOC could not go to court; actual suits against private employers were up to the Justice Department.

On the question of race-based preferences, the intent of Congress in 1964 was very clear. The act explicitly prohibited quotas, and the legislative history left no room for doubt on that point. If anyone can find "any language which provides that an employer will have to hire on the basis of percentage or quota related to color, race, religion, or national origin," the chief sponsor of the act, Senator Hubert H. Humphrey said, "I will start eating the pages one after another, because it is not in there."[4] Almost immediately after the passage of the 1964 act, the EEOC began to rewrite the legal standards by which employment discrimination was to be judged. Title VII was initially conceived to protect individuals against intentional discrimination—what was called "disparate treatment." In other words, plain old-fashioned bias. But from the outset the EEOC's first compliance chief, Alfred W. Blumrosen, scorned that protection as inadequate and much too slow. Blumrosen was in a position to determine policy almost single-handedly. The first chairman of the EEOC, Franklin Delano Roosevelt, Jr., spent most of his time off on his yacht, and while he didn't last long, neither did those who succeeded him; Blumrosen thus became the steady hand in a choppy administrative sea.

"Creative administration," Blumrosen later wrote, "converted a powerless agency operating under an apparently weak statute into a major force for the elimination of employment discrimination."[5] He wanted the provisions of the Civil Rights Act to be construed "liberally" rather than literally—to be read "as charters of equality. . . ." Enforcement procedures should be "shaped to the needs of the minorities for whom the statute had been adopted."[6] African Americans needed more and better jobs, and the EEOC would move full steam ahead to see that they got them. A statute designed to prevent acts of discrimination against members of minority groups was thus transformed into an instrument to maximize the hiring of members of the group.

Though the commission lacked authority to make substantive rules, Blumrosen crafted guidelines for validating employment tests, which were designed to discourage their use altogether. He later admitted that the EEOC's power to issue such guidelines did not "flow from any clear congressional grant of authority."[7] He nevertheless used them to decide whether there was "reasonable cause" for a finding of discrimination, with the result that employers were pressured to recruit a racially balanced workforce.[8] If they chose to sort prospective employees out through the use of a traditional test, and if that test had a disparate racial impact, they risked being charged with racial bias.

Title VII had also prohibited the agency from requiring employers to submit racial statistics on their workforce in any states that had Fair Employment Practices Commissions, which almost all outside the South did. But here again, the statute was easily circumvented. This provision, Blumrosen decided, was simply an effort on the part of Congress to prevent duplication; the EEOC could require statistics from businesses unless a FEPC had already done so—which (conveniently) none had. Blumrosen admitted a problem with this interpretation, namely that it "required a reading of the statute contrary to the plain meaning." But no one in Congress objected. Thus, a national reporting system was born. Companies with a hundred or more employees were forced to report on the racial (and gender) composition of their workforce at each occupational level, a rule that today affects close to 100 million American workers.[9]

These were changes that the EEOC made in the first months after the Civil Rights Act took effect. Much more was to come. The EEOC radically refined the concept of discrimination. The disparate treatment standard, which required evidence of intent to discriminate, was replaced by a disparate impact or results standard, in which discrimination could be inferred from statistical patterns. It might not be deliberate; it might not even be "conscious," but it was still "institutional discrimination" if it left African Americans with less than their equal share of jobs at every level.

"The traditional definition of discrimination," Blumrosen wrote in 1972, "permitted the employer to translate the unfair treatment of minorities in other segments of society into a limitation on employment opportunities." For example, more blacks than whites had arrest records; employers who used those records to deny employment to black applicants were insulating their hiring practices "from the social and economic problems that [are] . . . a consequence of the pervasive pattern of discrimination." Hiring practices that took note of a criminal history were penalizing blacks for white racism.[10] In Blumrosen's view this was an interpretation that made the 1964 act "viable"—which the law that Congress had passed was not.

These were not Blumrosen's views alone. They had become common in civil rights circles by the mid-1960s. As late as 1959, Jack Greenberg of the NAACP had declared that "civil rights groups do not aim to perpetuate their group interest since the group interest itself is to eliminate the socially enforced group identity."[11] That was precisely the idea behind the 1964 Civil Rights Act: to ensure the right of blacks to be treated as individuals rather than in terms of their "socially enforced group identity." But by 1964—when Congress seemed finally to have made an unequivocal commitment to color-blind law—more color-conscious ideas were already on the scene and gaining ground. The initial commitment to "the right of blacks to be treated as individuals" was fading, replaced by an interest in policies that civil rights activists thought more in the "group interest" of African Americans.

As early as 1960, the historian Hugh Davis Graham has noted, "phrases like 'positive effort' and 'affirmative program' had become common currency in the lexicon of civil rights . . . especially among liberal Democrats."[12] A full three years before the 1964 Civil Rights Act, a National Urban League official told a congressional committee that "being color-blind for an official of government is no longer a virtue. What we need to be is positively color conscious. . . ."[13] A year later CORE began pressuring businesses to give preferences to blacks, arguing that blacks would be proportionally employed in each job category but for historic discrimination. Urban League head Whitney Young charged that "our present concept of equal opportunity [was] not sufficient," and called for "a decade of discrimination in favor of Negro youth" to help close the gap left by "300 years of deprivation."[14] Even Roy Wilkins of the NAACP was beginning to suggest that blacks should be placed in jobs until the racial imbalance caused by their exclusion had been corrected.[15]

In 1963 President Kennedy remarked, "I think we ought not to begin the quota system."[16] At the same time, however, his President's Committee on Equal Employment Opportunity, chaired by Vice President Lyndon Johnson, was hard at work persuading corporations to survey the racial makeup of their workforce and take affirmative steps toward righting an imbalance.[17] And soon after the passage of the 1964 act, a number of participants at a major White House conference asserted that discrimination under Title VII included institutional, as well as intentional, racism.[18] Disparate impact theory and other tools used by the courts and the executive branch to institute preferences had begun to be fashioned even before the 1964 act became law. As the historian Herman Belz has noted, disparate-impact theory and affirmative action policies arose so quickly after the act took effect that it cannot be argued that color-blind policies had failed; they had not been tried.[19]

By 1970, advocates for racial preferences were on a roll. They had become a lobby both outside and within the government, but it was their unprecedented status as insiders that was particularly important. As Hugh Davis Graham has written, "the arcane, technical nature of the modern administrative state yielded enormous advantages to the new social regulators." The public is unlikely to get exercised over a regulation buried in the *Federal Register* implementing an executive order or statutory provision. "Yet students of public policy and public administration are increasingly aware that out of such bureaucratic boilerplate . . . can come fundamental shifts in public policy."[20]

RACIAL PREFERENCES IN EMPLOYMENT BY FEDERAL CONTRACTORS

Order No. 4, an obscure implementing directive to Executive Order 11246 issued in 1970, marked one such fundamental shift in public policy. Its key sentence specified what kind of racial mix employers who had contracts with the federal government should have in their labor force: "The rate of minority applicants recruited should approximate or equal the ratio of minorities to the applicant population in each location."

The Fourteenth Amendment and Title VII protect against race-based employment discrimination in the private and public sector. Employees of a firm with fifteen or more people on its payroll are covered, as are those who work for any level of government. Over the years, the EEOC has used the threat of a class-action suit as a powerful incentive to develop affirmative action plans. But neither the Constitution nor Title VII authorizes the government to order race-based hiring directly, except at the remedial stage. Only when a violation of federal law has been established can racial preferences can be explicitly mandated.

Executive Order 11246, which governs federal contracts, is quite different. While it does not, on its face, embrace quotas, it does forthrightly demand affirmative action as a condition of supplying goods and services to the federal government. Signed by President Johnson in 1965, 11246 lifted language verbatim from a 1961 order issued by President Kennedy: "The contractor will take affirmative action to ensure that applicants are employed, and that employees are treated during employment, without regard to their race . . ."[21] The president directed "each executive department and agency [to] establish and maintain a positive program of equal employment opportunity."

In 1965, however, that "positive program" meant aggressive recruitment to find or to train qualified minority applicants, a form of affirmative action consistent with the 1964 act. That definition changed in 1969, at the beginning of the Nixon administration. Concerned about the continuing high level of racial tension, and eager to improve the image of the party of Abraham Lincoln (damaged by Nixon's courting of the South in the 1968 campaign), the Department of Labor launched the "Philadelphia Plan."[22] It first interpreted 11246 as requiring strict numerical quotas for each of the skilled trades in the construction industry, which had very few African-American workers and a history of exclusionary practices, and then, in 1970, it issued Order No. 4, wich extended the demand for racially proportionate hiring to all federal contractors, not just those involved in construction. Employers who "underutilized" minority workers were required to set and meet "significant, measurable, and attainable" hiring goals.[23]

Today, 11246 (with its hundred-plus pages of implementing regulations) dictates the conditions for doing business with the federal government for all firms and institutions of higher education that have fifty or more employees or that seek a federal contract exceeding $50,000. Companies like Raytheon, the maker of the Patriot Missile defense system, are expected to assess the availability of black employees and file with the Department of Labor's Office of Contract Compliance Programs (OFCCP) a written affirmative action plan that includes minority hiring goals and a timetable. They must show "good faith" efforts to meet those goals and timetables. If the effort seems insufficient, OFCCP has the power to cancel federal contracts and permanently keep a business or educational institution off the list of those eligible to submit bids for government work. It can also recommend that the EEOC take further legal action.

Roughly a quarter of the total American workforce is employed by firms from which the federal government buys goods and services. For these many millions of jobs the executive order accomplished what Title VII did not—at least not at first. It brought about hiring by the numbers. The executive order was directly coercive. The imposition of affirmative action policies did not require a judicial finding of unlawful employment practices, nor did the definition of what constituted appropriate affirmative action depend upon a court. ("Affirmative action is anything that you have to do to get results," Edward C. Sylvester, the first director of the OFCC had said.)[24] Of course, employers could escape the coercive nature of 11246 by avoiding government contracts altogether, but that was too steep a price to pay for many. For many companies, in fact, the federal government is their best—or only—buyer.[25]

GRIGGS AND THE CONCEPT OF "DISPARATE IMPACT"

Thus, almost immediately following the passage of the Civil Rights Act, Title VII began to be reshaped into the instrument that many in the civil rights community had wanted all along, although they dared not come before Congress to say so. In its new guise, the law protected not only individuals, but groups as well—opening the door to group-based statistical measures of racial fairness and thus to group-based remedies (the road to quotas). And it came to protect blacks not simply against formal barriers or malicious intent, but also against "systemic" or "institutional" racism—that is, discriminatory patterns of employment that are woven into the fabric of society and maintain white dominance in the absence of any specific intent to discriminate. Finally the measure of those discriminatory patterns became their effect; the element of intent disappeared. The emphasis on rules and processes that enabled individuals to demonstrate their personal worth, whatever the color of their skin, was thus replaced by a stress on racially just outcomes—racially proportionate results. The protection *against* race-conscious hiring that had been the heart of Title VII in 1964 became an *insistence* on race-conscious hiring, although of an allegedly benign, not invidious, sort.

What the EEOC had done with employers covered by Title VII was paralleled quite precisely by what the Labor Department was doing with the federal contractors whose practices were governed by 11246. And while the U.S. Supreme Court might have blocked these bold new departures in antidiscrimination law, instead it gave a go-ahead. The first case was *Griggs v. Duke*

Power Company (decided in 1971) and the question was whether an employer, consistent with Title VII, could make a high school degree or a satisfactory score on a standardized test a requirement for initial employment or promotion. Prior to 1965, the North Carolina company had clearly discriminated against African Americans, and had hired them in only one of its departments. But there was no evidence of discriminatory intent behind the adoption of diploma and test requirements in 1955 and 1965. Moreover, Title VII explicitly authorized employers to use "any professionally developed ability test," so long as it was not intentionally discriminatory.[26]

Nevertheless, the Supreme Court found Duke Power guilty of discrimination and thus in violation of Title VII. Disproportionate numbers of black workers both lacked a high school diploma and failed the tests; whites continued to have an advantage. Practices, procedures, or tests neutral on their face cannot be maintained "if they operate to 'freeze' the status quo of prior discriminatory employment practices," Chief Justice Warren Burger wrote for a unanimous Court.[27] He called the test in question a "headwind" that slowed the progress of black advancement because blacks had attended segregated and inferior schools. That is, the tests penalized African Americans for an inadequacy imposed by the state. The company had been attempting to administer a test of merit against a backdrop of unequal educational opportunity. Fair enough, but the Court's argument was much more sweeping than it need have been. Segregated and inferior schools were the product of a particular time and place, and yet there was no hint that the Court's concern was the immediate legacy of the Jim Crow South—no suggestion that the same requirements with the same racially disparate impact in a state like Illinois would have been okay.

In 1964 Congress had been concerned about "the *consequences* of employment practices, not simply the motivation," Justice Burger claimed. It was an audacious rewriting of the statutory history that simply ignored Section 703(h) and other provisions. The Civil Rights Act had maintained the traditional distinction between employment practices that were intentionally racist and those that were normal to the world of business and thus legitimate. Yet *Griggs* branded all aptitude tests and other sorting mechanisms—whatever the intent behind them and however fairly they were administered—as discriminatory devices if they were not indisputably job-related and if proportionately more blacks than whites failed them. "Business necessity" (a phrase nowhere to be found in the actual law) became the "touchstone."[28]

Burger's means of ignoring the text and evading the intent of the law became a model for future courts. By stating the legislative purpose as generally as possible, he could gloss over the actual compromises and concerns of Congress as well as the explicit language of the statute. Abstractions, glaring omissions, and distortions of the statutory language greased the slide to measuring discrimination by the standard of racially proportionate outcomes.[29]

The Court had put its own creative stamp on the EEOC's ingenuity in refashioning a law in accord with the wishes of the civil rights community. It had said explicitly, in fact, that "the administrative interpretation of the Act by the enforcing agency is entitled to great deference," giving a green light to "creative administration."[30] Employers had to be prepared to prove the indispensability of any method they used to sift job applicants if more blacks than whites were adversely affected.

The meaning of disparate impact was clear enough, although that of "business necessity" was not. Nevertheless, it was evident that the employers had a tough job on their hands if they chose to assess the merits of applicants by means of a standardized test or its educational equivalent—unless blacks and whites were proportionally represented among those whom they hired. And thus while Title VII did not refer to affirmative action except as an available remedy for proven wrongs, with *Griggs* the Court took a significant step toward encouraging employers to rely on race in deciding whom to hire. If a firm's workforce was racially balanced—if the numbers were "right"—the expense of hiring experts to justify particular employment criteria as matters of "business necessity" could be spared. This was also the obvious way to keep litigators at bay. For those who wished to avoid an expensive, time-consuming, and image-damaging battle in the courts, the best defense was a good offense: anticipatory race-conscious hiring.

THE "MAKE-WHOLE" THEORY OF RELIEF

Griggs was the opening chapter in a dreary story of judicial creativity and confusion involving not only Title VII but the Fourteenth Amendment as well. Anyone who looks for doctrinal consistency in the Supreme Court's decisions on employment discrimination will be severely disappointed. In fact, the Court did not even manage to articulate clearly competing principles; its decisions, for want of a better term, can best be described as a mess.

Title VII was considerably strengthened in 1972. The Equal Employment Opportunity Act extended Title VII to state and local governments (even though they were already covered by the Fourteenth Amendment), educational institutions, and employers of fifteen or more (rather than the original floor of twenty-five), and added a section prohibiting discrimination against employees of federal agencies. In addition, the power given to the EEOC to enforce Title VII was greatly enhanced. The agency was authorized to sue employers directly. And while the original provision had empowered courts to "enjoin" an employer from continuing an unlawful employment practice, and to "order . . . affirmative action . . . , [including] reinstatement or hiring of employees with or without back pay," new phrases greatly augmented the remedial power that Title VII conferred.[31] Courts could order any equitable relief "deem[ed] appropriate"—including, by implication, racial quotas. Perhaps the most important thing about the legislative history of the 1972 amendments is that Congress seems to have endorsed the EEOC's "creative administration," which had so stretched the original meaning of Title VII.

The post-*Griggs* story opens with *McDonnell Douglas Corp. v. Green*, a 1973 decision that was not notable except for the fact that it fell into the "disparate treatment"—not "disparate impact" category.[32] It was a rare bird: just the sort of case that the 1964 statute had contemplated. It was a Title VII suit in which the plaintiff did not point to a statistical imbalance suggesting a pattern of discriminatory hiring but simply charged the employer with prejudice against blacks, especially blacks who had engaged in civil rights protests. Perhaps the conventional nature of the case accounts for the Court's generally sensible approach. The question, Justice Powell said, was whether the employer could "articulate some legitimate, nondiscriminatory reason for the employee's rejection" that was not—upon closer examination—a pretext for racism. The employment statistics at the company were not irrelevant, but they were only "helpful."[33] By implication, proportionally more whites than blacks working at a firm might often have a nonracial explanation.

"Legitimate" reasons for rejection were of course very different from the "business necessity" that *Griggs* had demanded. Ironically, the more amorphous the charge (invisible racism that nevertheless had a "disparate impact"), the easier it was for a plaintiff to prove discrimination.[34] Charged with intentional discrimination—true racism—an employer who could point to "legitimate" reasons was in relatively good shape. No showing of "business necessity" was necessary. Since the Justice Department and the EEOC were more interested in bringing disparate-impact rather than old-fashioned, individual disparate-treatment cases, that wasn't much of a consolation to employers.

McDonnell Douglas was followed by a series of cases in which the Court again picked up the threads of *Griggs*. For instance, Title VII had given courts broad discretion in crafting remedies for unlawful discrimination, although section 706(g) had explicitly conditioned such remedies on a finding "that the respondent has intentionally engaged in or is intentionally engaging in an unlawful employment practice." The Supreme Court, however, both limited the trial court's discretion and declared intent irrelevant. In *Albermarle Paper Co. v. Moody* (1975), the Court said that back pay was not a discretionary item—plaintiffs were entitled to it in disparate-impact as well as disparate-teatment cases. The racial imbalance in a company may have been due to inferior schools or other circumstances beyond the employer's control, predating the 1964 act. Although the act was obviously not retroactive, plaintiffs were nevertheless owed a remedy that would "mak[e] persons whole for injuries suffered through past discrimination," whatever its source.[35]

The Supreme Court's embrace of an aggressive "make-whole" theory of relief in the employment discrimination context was a big win for the plaintiffs' bar. The power of a court to give black workers the jobs and benefits they might have had—had the society been racially more equitable—reinforced the incentives to engage in preemptive race-based policies created by *Griggs.* Once plaintiffs had established employment discrimination (by the standard of disparate impact), they became entitled to extensive monetary and other relief, the nature of which was determined by a court's reading of history as it might have been. Judges had entered the business of reconstructing an imaginary once and future world—the world that true racial equality might have created. If the jobs and benefits of that lost world would be declared an entitlement in court, it was in the clear interest of employers to skip the litigation and simply provide them.

In addition, in *Albermarle* the Supreme Court embraced the EEOC's exceedingly difficult-to-meet standards for assessing the racial neutrality of employment tests, leading Justice Blackmun to "fear that a too-rigid application of the EEOC Guidelines will leave the employer little choice, save an impossibly expensive and complex validation study, but to engage in a subjective quota system of employment selection."[36] Blackmun was the first member of the Court to see where the disparate-impact concept was taking the Court and the country, but his momentary insight had no long-run impact.

By 1975 an employee did not need to show discriminatory intent in order to make a prima facie case of discrimination; nor could an employer point to evidence of good faith in defense. Good intent was irrelevant if the results were bad. Moreover, once a prima facie case, for which the standard was hazy, had been established, the employer bore the Herculean burden of justifying a test or other hiring or promotion process as a "business necessity" under the EEOC's guidelines. The very tests that Section 703(h) of Title VII had been designed to protect—customary vocational tests of the sort that were routinely used in 1965—had ceased to be presumptively valid. Even if the employer could demonstrate a close and direct link between his test and performance in a particular job, he could still lose his shirt (given the "make-whole" rule) if a plaintiff managed to unearth a similar test with less of a racial "impact."[37] Again, the obvious means of self-defense was race-based hiring.

DIVORCING "SPIRIT" FROM SUBSTANCE

The Court's interpretation of Title VII had certainly encouraged employers to adopt race-based hiring and promotion quotas. Were such quotas legal, however? Yes, when "voluntarily" adopted in the private sector, a majority of five on the Court said in *United Steelworkers v. Weber,* decided in 1979.[38] In 1974 the United Steelworkers of America and the Kaiser Aluminum & Chemical Corporation negotiated an agreement that included an affirmative action plan.

Almost all of the skilled craftworkers at the plant in Gramercy, Louisiana, were white. Kaiser agreed to establish an in-house training program, selecting candidates on the basis of seniority, but giving at least half of the places to blacks. Brian Weber, who was white and had been rejected for the training program, brought a class action suit alleging discrimination under Title VII when blacks were chosen over more senior whites. The Civil Rights Act, Weber assumed, protected not only blacks but also whites against race-based preferences—i.e., discrimination.

The Supreme Court, in a five-to-four decision, said that Weber was wrong. Title VII, a majority of five on the Court agreed, did not forbid private employers and unions from adopting an affirmative action plan that involved explicit preferences for blacks. Brian Weber's argument, Justice Brennan wrote, "rests on a literal interpretation" of the statute, and as such is "misplaced." Applying the same technique as Chief Justice Burger in *Griggs,* he explained that it was necessary to distinguish between "the letter of the statute" and its "spirit." How could a program that helped African Americans possibly conflict with that "spirit"? "It would be ironic indeed if a law triggered by a Nation's concern over centuries of racial injustice . . . constituted the first legislative prohibition on all voluntary, private, race-conscious efforts to abolish traditional patterns of racial segregation and hierarchy." [39]

Stirring rhetoric, but, as Justice Rehnquist made clear in a furious dissent, there was nothing "voluntary" about the affirmative action plan at issue. Kaiser had adopted it both to protect itself from a suit based on the racial imbalance of its skilled workforce and to keep its eligibility for lucrative government contracts that only went to firms that pursued such affirmative action policies. [40]

Even if the 50 percent racial set-aside had been truly uncoerced, Rehnquist insisted that it flunked Title VII. "Taken in its normal meaning, and as understood by all Members of Congress . . . [Title VII] prohibits a covered employer from considering race when making an employment decision, whether the race be black or white," he wrote. What, he inquired, was "ironic" about a law that was inspired by a history of racism but forbade discrimination of every sort? "The evil inherent in discrimination against Negroes is that it is based on an immutable characteristic, utterly irrelevant to employment decisions. The characteristic becomes no less . . . evil, simply because the person excluded is a member of one race rather than another." [41]

Brennan had invoked the "spirit" that animated the act, ignoring its actual language and history. Rehnquist instead chose to walk step-by-step through the actual legislative record. He found that the chairman of the House Judiciary Committee, among numerous others, directly addressed the question of preferences instituted to rectify a racial imbalance in an employer's workforce. "With virtual clairvoyance," Rehnquist concluded, "the Senate's leading supporters of Title VII anticipated precisely the circumstances of this case. . . ." [42]

Debate in the Senate had lasted an unprecedented eighty-three days. "Not once," Rehnquist notes, "did a speaker . . . suggest that the bill would allow employers *voluntarily* to prefer racial minorities over white persons." Given the language of the statute, "such a contention would have been, in any case, too preposterous to warrant response."[43]

Similar issues were fought out in *Fullilove v. Klutznick* (1980).[44] Although not an employment discrimination case but one involving contracting, *Fullilove* again addressed the legitimacy of benign racial quotas in distributing jobs. The issue was the constitutional permissibility of Congress's mandatory 10 percent set-aside in federal construction grants for minority business enterprises (MBEs)—which meant, in practice, that primary contractors had to ensure that 10 percent of the subcontracts went to black and other minority-owned firms.

The racial preferences contained in the 1977 Public Works Employment Act were constitutional, six members of the Court agreed. Although Congress had not commissioned research that demonstrated the need for such a set-aside, it was owed judicial deference when it exercised its constitutional power to "provide for the . . . general Welfare" (Article I, Section 8) by spending money, Chief Justice Burger argued. Quotas did raise obvious equal protection questions, but this one (though based on no specific findings of discrimination in the construction industry) was "strictly remedial." And while the set-aside burdened white-owned firms competing for those same contracts, that burden was light, especially in light of the racial skeletons undoubtedly in their closet and the benefits of privilege they had presumably reaped in the past.[45]

Fullilove was the first decision since the Japanese internment cases to uphold the use of racial classifications in an act of Congress, and by 1980 most students of American law believed that the Court had erred in allowing Japanese-Americans to be rounded up and incarcerated not because they had committed acts of disloyalty but because of their race. Thus, one would have thought that the Court might have felt a special obligation to give close and skeptical scrutiny to a set-aside program that dispensed benefits on the basis of blood, and would have spelled out persuasively the distinction between benign and invidious racial classifications. The *Fullilove* opinion did not live up to that expectation. Nor did any of the Court's other decisions in this area over the next several years, most of which upheld programs that gave racial and gender preferences.[46]

The case of *Johnson v. Transportation Agency, Santa Clara County, Calif.* (1987) involved gender, not race, an unimportant distinction in this instance.[47] Although there were five separate opinions, a majority of five did agree to uphold the affirmative action program of a public employer with absolutely no evidence of past discrimination and thus nothing to remedy, rejecting the claims of a white man denied a promotion. It thus allowed employers, even public agencies subject to Fourteenth Amendment constraints, "voluntarily" to enact affirmative action programs any time there was (for whatever reason) a "conspicuous" racial or gender imbalance in the company's workforce. The Court maintained that it was not sanctioning preferences that entailed the hiring of "unqualified" workers; nor was it agreeing to a permanent program.[48] But what about the *less* (as opposed to the more) qualified candidate? Paul Johnson, the plaintiff, was easily the top applicant for the road dispatcher's job at issue. (Precisely the same issue is raised by preferential admissions in colleges and universities, where the question is never "qualified," but less or more so.)

In *Griggs*, Chief Justice Burger had acknowledged that the whole point of Title VII was to make an employee's race or sex irrelevant, forcing an employer to focus instead on "qualifications."[49] By 1987 race and sex had themselves become qualifications. As Justice Scalia put it in one of his dissents: "Ever so subtly . . . we effectively replace the goal of a discrimination-free society with the quite incompatible goal of proportionate representation by race and by sex in the workplace."[50] In Scalia's view it required a "willing suspension of disbelief" to accept the Court's tortured reading of Title VII and the assumptions behind that reading.

SETTING LIMITS ON RACIAL PREFERENCES

In a series of decisions beginning in 1989, the Supreme Court at last began to take such objections seriously. It had become increasingly difficult to suspend disbelief in a racial context that was so different from that in which *Griggs* was decided eighteen years before. The first important step away from preferences involved a minority set-aside in contracts awarded by the city of Richmond, Virginia, a program of the sort typical in states and cities across the nation.[51]

In 1983, Richmond was a majority-black city with an African-American majority on the city council and a black mayor. The council passed an ordinance requiring that all construction firms engaged in municipal work (all of them white-owned at the time) subcontract at least 30 percent of the dollar amount of the prime contract to minority business enterprises. Minority-owned firms far and near were eligible to bid for the work; they did not have to be located in Richmond or even in Virginia; nor had direct evidence of discrimination by these firms been presented to justify this action. Moreover, less than 5 percent of all American construction firms were minority-owned in 1983, and nearly half of those were in California, New York, Illinois, Florida, and Hawaii, making it unlikely that they would bid on jobs in Virginia. Before this set-aside, in the years 1978–1983, MBEs had won less than 1 percent of Richmond's "prime construction contracts."[52]

The J. A. Croson Company was the sole bidder on a contract to install plumbing fixtures at the city jail; 30 percent of the work, however, had to go to an MBE. After a frustrating search, Croson finally found a minority-owned company, Continental Metal Hose, but using that firm would have significantly increased its costs—and thus the city's. When the city decided to put the whole project up for a new round of bids, Croson challenged the ordinance itself as an unconstitutional racial classification.

Fullilove had settled the question, the lower court assumed; not so, held Justice O'Connor for a majority of six on the Supreme Court. The deference the Court had paid to an act of Congress was not similarly owed to a municipal ordinance.[53] "The framers of the Fourteenth Amendment . . . desired to place clear limits on the States' use of race as a criterion for legislative action . . ."[54] Classifications based on race were deeply suspect. They carried "a danger of stigmatic harm. Unless they are strictly reserved for remedial settings, they may in fact promote notions of racial inferiority and lead to a politics of racial hostility."[55]

"Strictly reserved for remedial settings": if that was the test, the set-aside failed miserably. Plaintiffs' counsel, sounding a familiar theme, had argued that, absent discrimination, minority firms could be expected to get a proportionate share of contracts. The Court responded that it was "sheer speculation how many minority firms there would be in Richmond absent past societal discrimination."[56] Moreover,

> to accept Richmond's claim that past societal discrimination alone can serve as the basis for rigid racial preferences would be to open the door to competing claims for 'remedial relief' for every disadvantaged group. The dream of a Nation of equal citizens in a society where race is irrelevant to personal opportunity and achievement would be lost in a mosaic of shifting preferences based on inherently unmeasurable claims of past wrongs.[57]

It was a clear turning point. Justice O'Connor had grasped where the Court had been leading the country in embracing race-based policies, and was putting the brakes on.

Nineteen eighty-nine was a year of second thoughts, and not just about the Fourteenth Amendment questions that were raised by *Richmond v. J. A. Croson*. The Court began as well to try to clean up the debris-littered landscape surrounding Title VII. In *Wards Cove Packing Company v. Atonio*, in fact, Justice Byron White, writing for a majority of five, produced the first opinion to revise *Griggs*'s disparate-impact test for discrimination. It was a turnabout for White, who had joined the unanimous opinion in *Griggs*.

The Wards Cove Packing Company was certainly no model of racial democracy. Located in Alaska, it packed salmon in the summer months, and thus hired almost entirely on a seasonal basis. The unskilled "cannery" jobs were filled mostly by local Alaskan Natives and Filipinos; the "noncannery" (skilled) positions, on the other hand, were generally held by whites hired through the company's offices in the Northwest. The predominantly white noncannery workers lived in dormitories separate from their unskilled colleagues and ate in separate mess halls. A suspicious set of facts, but the plaintiffs chose a disparate-impact argument—the impact of the company's hiring practices on the racial composition of the two groups of workers.

Looking at the raw numbers—simply counting minority and nonminority heads—won't tell you much, Justice White argued; how many Alaskan Natives and Filipinos had the education and skills needed for the noncannery jobs? And among those who did, how many actually applied? To ignore those questions would be to make every employer with a racially imbalanced segment of his workforce vulnerable to expensive and time-consuming litigation. "The only practicable option for many employers [would] be to adopt racial quotas," which Title VII "expressly rejected," he said.[58]

Here the Court was at last rethinking *Griggs* and *Weber,* and significantly altering the Title VII law that the Court (with considerable help from the EEOC) had so creatively concocted. *Wards Cove* restricted the use of crude statistical comparisons. Plaintiffs had to pinpoint the "specific employment practices" causing the racial disproportion, the Court held. And while *Griggs* had made "business necessity" the test of an applicant screening process, the majority in *Wards Cove* spoke instead of "the legitimate employment goals of the employer," borrowing from the intentional discrimination test in *McDonnell Douglas.*[59] "Necessity" had been a very tough standard to meet—especially when the burden of proof rested on the employer—and thus, in this crucial sense, the decision broke with prior case law. The ultimate burden of discrediting hiring practices remained with the employee throughout the course of litigation, White said, ignoring many precedents to the contrary.[60] If you came into court charging racial bias, you had to have the evidence to prove it.

"One wonders," Justice Blackmun said in dissent, "whether the majority still believes that race discrimination . . . is a problem in our society, or even remembers that it ever was."[61] The majority had displayed "an icy indifference . . . to the hopes of discrimination victims," the *New York Times* editorialized.[62] What the critics considered icy indifference might better have been described as a sobering realization that the disparate-impact test, unconnected to direct evidence of discrimination, resulted in the racial preferences that had been explicitly outlawed by the statute. Racial preferences were encouraged as well, the Court had recognized, by the heavy burden placed on employers to prove a negative—the absence of discrimination, despite a racially imbalanced workforce. But those who dissented believed that returning to the original focus on intentional discrimination was mere indifference.

The *Wards Cove* decision was condemned by most leaders of the Democratic Party, which then controlled both houses of Congress. It was the main impetus behind the passage of the Civil Rights Restoration Act of 1991, which President George Bush threatened to veto but finally signed into law. The act allowed damages and compensation, including nontaxable backpay, for intentional discrimination, which increased the exposure of employers' and thus gave them more of an incentive to hire by quota.[63] The 1991 act also overturned parts of *Wards Cove* by explicitly reinstating the burden on employers to prove the business necessity of aptitude tests and other hiring practices whenever those practices had a disparate racial impact—whenever fewer blacks than whites passed.[64] *Griggs* was largely restored.

There was one small bit of arguably good news in the 1991 act. Section 106 outlawed race-norming—the adjustment of employment test scores to eliminate the overall racial differences in their distribution. In a race-normed exam, if blacks on the average did worse than whites, then black scores would be adjusted to be identical to much higher white scores. A white's score and a black's score fifty points lower would be reported as being in the 99th percentile.[65] Candidates were ranked within their separate racial groups (with Asian Americans treated as white). Blacks were compared only to blacks, and were thus protected from white (and Asian) competition.

Such protection is at the heart of almost every affirmative action program; separate admissions standards to a medical school mean that identical scores between whites and blacks are treated differently. But the admissions officers at, say, Stanford Medical School are at least privy to precisely how the system works and believe it to be just. This was not the case with the General Aptitude Test Battery (GATB). Designed by the Labor Department, it was widely used in the 1980s by state employment services to screen people looking for mostly blue-collar work in the private sector. Unbeknownst to many prospective employers, however, the states routinely engaged in "within-group score conversion." That is, they race-normed the raw scores of the job applicants, with the consequence that an employer who interviewed two candidates for a secretarial position, one white and one black, both appearing to have identical GATB scores, would not know that they did not. The employer had been given only the race-adjusted percentiles and, even if forewarned, had no means of converting them back to the raw data.

In the mid-1980s Reagan administration officials began to raise questions about the practice. But it was only during the debates on the 1991 Civil Rights Act that it became a public issue. At that point, cooking the books, as Illinois Republican congressman Henry J. Hyde put it, became difficult to defend, and Democrats had to agree to including a ban on such race-based group norming in order get the legislation passed.[66]

Whether the prohibition made much of a difference is questionable. In its wake "many employers dropped their aptitude tests altogether, or set the cut-off points for all candidates at the lowest possible levels," Jeffrey Rosen wrote in the *New Republic* in 1994. "The desire to 'look like America' . . .

[had] become too much a part of our social fabric to be suppressed by a legal rule."[67] And courts still had the power to interpret what Section 106 meant. *Griggs* remained good law, and the 1991 statute had reinforced the already strong incentives for employers to adopt racial preferences.

RACIAL SET-ASIDES IN FEDERAL CONTRACTS

Executive Order 11246 regulates the racial composition of a firm's employees when the federal government is footing the bill; it says nothing about the race of the employers doing business with the federal government. But numerous statutory provisions are like the one at issue in *Fullilove;* they dictate which businesses will provide the goods and services that the federal government buys—specifically, how many federal dollars go to firms owned or controlled by minorities (and women).

All federal agencies are required by statute to establish set-asides to benefit "small disadvantaged businesses." The law is generally known by the statute's most important section, 8(a), which authorizes the Small Business Administration (SBA), an independent agency, to act as the contractor for the federal government in awarding subcontracts to deserving firms. Those firms have been certified by the SBA as disadvantaged; absent a government stamp of approval, a small company is ineligible for special treatment from the federal government. The federal government is of course the nation's largest consumer, spending money in the private sector to construct public buildings for civilian and military use, as well as to purchase almost everything from pencil sharpeners and toilet paper to fighter planes. In 1995 the 8(a) program steered roughly $5.8 billion in federal procurement funds into "disadvantaged" enterprises—meaning those that had been certified as 51 percent owned or controlled by members of minority groups. By definition, white-owned firms are not disadvantaged.[68]

Certified (officially "disadvantaged" and hence privileged) businesses are most often awarded contracts without even having to engage in competitive bidding. The U.S. Navy, for instance, will decide to solicit bids to construct a flight simulator to train pilots to operate an attack helicopter.[69] The Department of Defense, like all federal agencies, must meet (or try to meet) its quota, and in order to do so, has signed an agreement allowing the SBA to act as an intermediary between it and minority-owned companies. The Small Business Administration then, not the Navy, awards the subcontract to one of the firms approved under the 8(a) program—the only firms eligible for the award. In doing so, with some restrictions, the SBA could choose to select a "small disadvantaged business" (SDB) on what is called a "sole source" or "sheltered" (from competition) basis. That is, it could skip the process of competitive bidding and give the contract to a company of its choice. In

1996 more than 90 percent of SBA contracts were being awarded without competition.[70]

Similar preferences appear in appropriation or authorization acts governing the conduct of federal business in a wide variety of areas—agriculture, communications, defense, education, public works, transportation, foreign relations, energy and water development, banking, scientific research, and space exploration, among others. For instance, the Omnibus Diplomatic Security and Antiterrorism Act contains a minority set-aside in the allocation of funds appropriated for diplomatic security projects.

Set-asides for minority businesses are but one of several ways in which federal statutes insist that agencies consider race and ethnicity when spending the taxpayers' money. Other programs channel federal funds into minority neighborhoods, minority-owned banks, historically black institutions of higher education, and organizations providing technical assistance designed to improve social services available to minorities. Thus, 10 percent of the Eisenhower Exchange Fellowship Program funds are "available only for participation by individuals who are representative of United States minority populations." The Secretary of Education has been authorized to make grants for teacher training and placement, giving special consideration to schools that have "enrollments of at least 50 percent minority students in their teacher education programs."[71]

These are all programs of which the American public is barely aware. Indeed, they were often adopted surreptitiously. Take the Energy Policy Act of 1992, which contains a 10 percent minority set-aside.[72] The statute is programmatic, not agency-specific. It affects a wide variety of energy policies in a number of executive departments—policies involving such issues as nuclear power, questions of climatic change, offshore oil drilling, and our need for natural gas. The original bill was shaped by an extensive legislative debate and, as it emerged from House and Senate committees, contained no set-aside provision. That omission, however, was soon rectified; the final bill included a 10 percent set-aside for "disadvantaged" firms, as defined by the SBA. Clearly the set-aside was an important addition to the Energy Policy Act, and yet it was never debated on the floor of the House or Senate. Moreover, the provision could not be called remedial. No legislative findings suggested that African Americans and other protected minorities had suffered discrimination in competing for federal procurement contracts in the energy industry. But Michigan Democratic representative John Conyers was a set-aside advocate who, at the very last minute, inserted the provision in the final bill voted by the House. In the House-Senate conference committee, the addition was briefly discussed; no voice was raised against the racial classification, however, and the provision became law.

The earmarking of 10 percent of certain federal contracts for minorities might seem a relatively trivial commitment. It is not, as a lawsuit involving a

$15 million road construction project at a military base in New Mexico made clear. The federal government sets annual minority procurement goals, but those goals ignore the question of what sorts of minority firms are available to do what jobs and where. To make up for a shortfall in other areas, a federal agency may be forced to meet its quota by turning all of its construction dollars over to minority firms, since there are in fact a considerable number of minority-owned construction businesses. As a July 1995 report to the president on affirmative action admitted, more than 35 percent of the Department of Defense (DOD) construction awards went to minority companies, two-thirds of whom were not required to submit competitive bids. DOD was filling its across-the-board quota by using a disproportionately high number of minorities in those occupations in which they could most readily be found. Thus, contracts for landscaping and janitorial services would be set aside for minority firms, on "the presumption" that this is the work the 8(a) firm . . . can handle."[73]

Minority firms tend to be geographically concentrated as well, and thus in ten states "small disadvantaged businesses" got more than 40 percent of all construction contracts awarded to small firms, the 1995 report to the president stated. "In rare instances," it went on, "virtually all small business contracting is with SDBs."[74] New Mexico's White Sands Missile Range was one such site; white firms were virtually excluded from bidding on contracts to build its roads.[75] Again, DOD was filling a national quota by a heavy use of minority firms in those regions in which they could best be found.

Set-asides mandated by state law tend to exhibit the same problems. In April 1996, a lawsuit forced Ohio State University to scrap its practice of funneling literally all of its painting contracts to minority-owned companies. The school had never formally decided to create a 100 percent set-aside, but that is precisely what it ended up with in implementing a 1980 state law that directed public agencies like Ohio State to reserve 15 percent of their contracts for minority-owned businesses. The reason: contracting services other than painting did not attract many minority companies; the school thus had to "overcompensate" in the area that did attract minority bidders. Whites were simply shut out; minority firms had a lock on certain jobs.[76]

"DISADVANTAGED" BLACK MILLIONAIRES

The 8(a) program requires participants to be both socially and economically disadvantaged. Nevertheless, some participants are exceedingly well off, an SBA audit discovered. "Owners who receive high annual compensations should be found ineligible for continued participation." But continuing participation was not the primary issue; how did anyone living in a million-dollar house qualify in the first place? As of early 1995, the list of 8(a) eligible firms included thirty-two of the top hundred black businesses in the country, and $440 million in federal dollars had gone to a single company.[77] Moreover, 1 percent of the 5,155 participants in the 8(a) program had received more than 25 percent of the $4.4 billion in contract dollars awarded in 1994.[78]

The problem of wealthy black businessmen benefiting from other sorts of set-asides became national news in the spring of 1995, when the Republican-controlled Congress repealed a Federal Communications Commission (FCC) program that allowed companies to defer paying taxes on profits from the sale of broadcast properties purchased by firms that were at least partially minority-owned. Frank Washington had designed the policy in 1978 when he was at the FCC as assistant to the chairman. In 1995 he headed up a partnership planning to purchase (for $2.3 billion) a cable television system owned by one of the world's largest entertainment-media conglomerates, Viacom. Had Congress not intervened, it would have been a fabulously lucrative deal for the California multimillionaire who—as an African American—qualified for the break he had invented; the tax deferral was worth about $600 million to Viacom, whose savings Washington and his partners would have shared by buying at a below-market price.[79] The long list of other prominent and prosperous African Americans who profited handsomely from the preferential treatment the FCC accorded members of minority groups included General Colin Powell, O. J. Simpson, Patrick Ewing, Bill Cosby, and Vernon Jordan.[80]

Other problems have plagued set-aside programs, many of them involving the difficulty in determining when the minorities involved in a particular business are only there as a front for others. The bribes and kickbacks that enriched white businessmen in Atlanta (mentioned at the opening of this chapter) were not an isolated instance. In May 1995 two brothers identified as Mafia members were arrested in New York, charged with creating companies in which minorities were serving as a front in order to obtain contracts that were off-limits to whites. Having been certified by the state as minority business enterprises, those sham minority-owned companies had obtained about $5 million in city and state contracts for work in schools, hospitals, and the subway system, even though their bids were not the lowest submitted. The problems were not new; eleven years earlier a state investigation had labeled the entire set-aside program a failure.[81]

ASSESSING THE EVIDENCE OF BIAS IN EMPLOYMENT AND CONTRACTING

Whatever the problems, the civil rights community and the Democratic Party continue to argue, race-conscious employment and contracting programs remain essential. "There are those who say, my fellow Americans, that even good affirmative action programs are no longer needed," President Clinton said on 19 July 1995. But "let us consider" that "the unemployment rate for African Americans remains about twice that of whites. . . . In the nation's largest companies only six-tenths of 1 percent of senior management positions are held by Africans Americans. . . . Black home loan applicants are more than twice as likely to be denied credit as whites with the same qualifications. . . ."[82]

The issue the president raised is obviously serious and complicated, and those who have studied the evidence do not agree on either the level of discrimination in the economy or on the remedy for that which persists. If blacks are still unemployed at twice the white rate, affirmative action has not been putting people back to work, critics argue. If three decades of medicine hasn't cured the disease, why continue? they ask. Supporters, on the other hand, believe that traditional antidiscrimination policies, with their focus on invidious intent and their insistence on race-neutral hiring, will not do the trick. The problems are too systemic and too subtle; they require a certain measure of race consciousness. "Set-asides" in government contracts and specific hiring "goals and timetables" in both the private and public sector are at least a hedge against calamity.

How much discrimination? is obviously the first question. We start with the figures for annual income by race and sex for 1994, the most recent data currently available in sufficient detail for our purposes. In 1994 the incomes of black men averaged only 64 percent of those of non-Hispanic white men, while black women took in 90 percent as much as white women (Table 1).

These numbers alone, however, are insufficient to conclude that discrimination depresses the incomes of black males by 36 percent and the incomes of black females by 10 percent. We know, for instance, that earning power depends on education. Even if the labor market were perfectly fair, racial differences in educational qualifications would lead to differences in income. Although African Americans have made very impressive educational gains since World War II, in 1994, 27 percent of blacks aged twenty-five or over had no high school diploma, as compared with only 15 percent of whites. And nearly twice as many whites as blacks (24 percent versus 13 percent) were college graduates.[83] Since high school dropouts, whether white or black, typically earn a lot less than college graduates, the racial gap in education inevitably results in some racial gap in income as well.

Table 1 controls for this factor by looking at racial differences in income for people with roughly similar amounts of education. It shows that black women are pretty much on a par with white women who have had roughly equivalent schooling. Black women who never completed high school have lower incomes, but those with a high school diploma earned 3 percent more than similarly educated white women, and college-educated African-American women had a slightly bigger advantage. This does not prove that employers are discriminating against white women; the small difference could be the

Table 1

**Black Incomes as a Percent of Non-Hispanic White Incomes,
by Sex and Education, Persons 25 or Older, 1994**

	MEN	WOMEN
All	64	90
Less than 9 yrs. of school	71	87
9–12 yrs. but no high school diploma	69	90
High school graduate	69	103
Some college	77	106
College graduate	77	107

Source: U.S. Bureau of the Census, Current Population Reports, PPL-45. *The Black Population in the United States: March 1995* (Washington, D.C.: U.S. Government Printing Office, 1996), table 9. Note that the comparison here is between blacks and non-Hispanic whites, not all whites, the usual comparison made elsewhere in this book. Differences between blacks and non-Hispanic whites will be sharper than those between blacks and all whites, because many Hispanics are recent immigrants or the children of immigrants and pull down average incomes for whites as a whole. Since the Census Bureau has only recently tabulated the data in this form, analyses of trends over time will have to be done in terms of the simple white-black comparison. The necessary data to do that for 1994 have not been published. A few tabulations for whites are provided in *Black Population in the U.S.: 1995,* table 16, but no breakdown of incomes by education.

result of their working slightly shorter hours, of being a bit more concentrated in rural areas where wage levels are lower, or any one of a dozen other factors.

Racial differences in incomes for men are considerably larger, and controlling for education does less to eliminate them. Black male high school dropouts had incomes that were 69 percent of those of non-Hispanic whites with similar educations; for black men who had graduated from college, the percentage was not much higher—77 percent. In every educational category the income of black men was further behind that of white men than was the case for women.

Before concluding that discrimination against black men in the job market is still severe, however, we need to ask whether racial differences in educational achievement have been adequately measured. The educational categories are broad and crude, and thus they conceal differences that are relevant to earning power. The highest educational class listed is college graduates, but we know that people who go on to attain advanced degrees in law, medicine, or computer science are likely to earn more than those with no more than a bachelor's degree. Since whites pursue graduate study at a higher rate than blacks, we can expect white "college graduates" (a group that includes those who have still higher degrees) to earn more than black "college graduates"; they are more likely to have the credentials necessary for certain occupations that are paid extremely well.

Moreover, knowing only that someone is a high school dropout or a high school graduate or a college graduate does not tell us very much about the skills he possesses. Measuring how well educated that person is by counting the number of years he spent in a classroom is like judging how well someone plays the violin by counting up the hours he has spent practicing. The hours may have been wasted, and, likewise, in judging the education of workers, it makes sense to look not at years in school, but at the level of cognitive skill they are able to display on standardized tests. The question, then, is not whether blacks and whites with exactly eleven years of education, say, have the same incomes. Instead, we should ask whether blacks and whites who read, write, and do math at the eighth-grade level or the twelfth-grade level have the same incomes—ignoring how many years of school it took for them to obtain that level of skill.

As we saw in Chapter 13, the National Assessment of Educational Progress (NAEP) and College Board tests show that African-American students, on the average, are alarmingly far behind whites in basic cognitive skills. A number of economists and sociologists investigating discrimination in the labor market have recently concluded that this is the principal reason why they don't have average incomes that are as high as those of whites. What looks like discrimination, this body of research suggests, is better described as rewarding workers with stronger cognitive skills. Thus a study of men twenty-six to thirty-three years old who held full-time jobs in 1991 found that when education was measured in the traditional way (years of school completed), blacks earned 19 percent less than comparably educated whites. But when the yardstick was how well they performed on basic tests of word knowledge, paragraph comprehension, arithmetical reasoning, and mathematical knowledge, the results were reversed. Black men earned 9 percent *more* than white men with the same education—as defined by skill.[84]

Other research suggests much the same thing.[85] For instance, *Teaching the New Basic Skills* by economists Richard J. Murnane and Frank Levy, has demonstrated the increasing importance of cognitive skills in our changing economy. Employers in firms like Honda now require employees who can read and do math problems at the ninth-grade level at a minimum. Their entry-level positions involve tasks that cannot be adequately performed without that foundation of elementary skills.[86] And yet the 1992 NAEP tests show that barely two out of five students at the end of their high school years could read that well; only three out of five had the requisite skills in math. Looking at the incomes six years after graduation of two national samples of high school seniors from 1972 and 1980, the authors found that their performance on reading and math tests in high school greatly affected their later earnings; moreover, the connection was even stronger for the class of 1980. The difference between the annual earnings of a man with no more than a high school education and weak basic math skills and those of a male employee with the same amount of schooling but strong math skills was striking. Those who had been seniors in 1972 and knew more math earned (six years later) $1,200 more; the more skilled group that had been in the twelfth grade in 1980 took in an additional $2,700. For young women the difference was even greater; in the 1980 group those who were stronger in math earned $3,400 a year (23 percent) more than women with a poor grasp of numbers.[87]

The implications of this analysis for the subject of our book are obvious. Basic shifts in our economy have been placing an increased premium on cognitive skills, and scores on the best national tests given demonstrate that groups that perform better earn more. That is why racial differences in scores on tests of cognitive skill go a long way toward explaining racial differences in earnings. The 1992 NAEP math tests, for example, revealed that only 22 percent of African-American high school seniors but 58 percent of their white classmates were numerate enough for firms like Honda to consider hiring them. And in reading, 47 percent of whites in 1992 but just 18 percent of African Americans could handle the printed word well enough to be employable in a modern automobile plant. (By 1994, depressingly, the proportion of whites with this rather low level of reading skill had fallen by 4 points, and the figure for blacks had fallen even more—by 5 points, to just 13 percent.)[88] With racial differences of this magnitude in the cognitive skills many employers are increasingly demanding, one can only wonder why the racial gap in income is not larger than it is.

This body of evidence, based upon large, representative national samples of the workforce, obviously does not prove that employers never discriminate against African Americans. Nor does it prove that employers would not discriminate against blacks a good deal more in the absence of vigilant governmental oversight. It does, though, show that inferring racial bias from differences in incomes or earnings is too simple. It is necessary to control for education, and to control for education measured by a better yardstick than years spent in the classroom.

One other body of evidence relevant to this issue merits brief mention. In 1990 researchers from the Urban Institute, a Washington, D.C., research center, attempted to assess employment discrimination in Washington and Chicago by having matched pairs of testers, male college students who (in theory) had identical qualifications but were of different races, apply for advertised jobs. A similar study was conducted in Denver in 1991. When a position was offered to the white rather than the black member of the pair, it was taken to be evidence of discrimination. Since some observers—including justices of the U.S. Supreme Court—have taken the results as powerful evidence of continuing bias in the labor market, those findings require some critical comment here.[89]

In Chicago black and white testers were treated the same way by employers 86 percent of the time—either both were offered the job or neither was.

Whites were favored over blacks 10 percent of the time, and blacks were favored over whites in almost 5 percent of the tests. In light of the small sample size (197 cases) and other methodological flaws, it is hard to take that small differential seriously. If it is attributable to discrimination at all, rather than chance variation, it is discrimination at a level that can barely be detected.

In Washington, D.C., the white member of a testing pair was favored over his black partner almost a fifth of the time, while the African American was preferred only one out of twenty times. This seems a sizable, though not a huge, difference. What to make of it, however, is complicated by the fact that Washington, D.C., is quite atypical of large American cities in one crucial respect: it is a company town, with the federal government by far the most important local employer. Despite that, the Urban Institute chose to focus its attention solely on private businesses in the area; none of its testers applied for federal jobs to see if they would be treated on a color-neutral basis. Since the federal government is very strongly committed to affirmative action hiring, an investigation of the District of Columbia labor market that did not exclude its dominant employer would very likely have yielded different results. Since the largest employer in town probably would have offered white testers fewer jobs than black testers, the overall results might have shown a pattern opposite to the one reported—with employers favoring blacks over whites by a margin of 15 points or even more. We cannot know this for sure, but the failure to include the federal government among the D.C. employers severely limits the generalizations that can be drawn from this study.[90]

Other important methodological questions can be raised about the Urban Institute's audit studies.[91] The most significant involves the motivations of the testers. Employers may place a very high premium on finding job applicants

Table 2

Racial Preferences Shown by Employers to Matched Pairs of Testers in Three Cities, 1990 and 1991

	PERCENT OF CASES SHOWING		
	No racial difference	White preferred	Black preferred
Chicago, 1990	85.8	9.6	4.5
Washington, 1990	75.1	19.1	5.8
Denver, 1991	77.9	11.7	10.3

Source: Data as summarized in tables 5.1 and 5.3 of James J. Heckman and Peter Siegelman, "The Urban Institute Audit Studies: Their Methods and Findings," in Michael Fix and Raymond J. Struyk, eds., Clear and Convincing Evidence: Measurement of Discrimination in America (Washington, D.C.: Urban Institute Press, 1993).

who truly want to work for them. An effective tester thus would have to be one who successfully deceived his interviewers. Did all testers try equally hard to do so? College student testers who devoted a summer to working on studies like these might have had political and ideological beliefs that influenced what they *hoped* to find. Given the study design, the real finding was perhaps a self-fulfilling prophecy. The white testers may have been trying very hard to elicit job offers, while black testers could have been conveying in subtle, even unconscious, ways that they weren't really all that keen on getting it. The training given to the testers may have exacerbated this problem. As economists Heckman and Siegelman have observed, "an explicit part of the training" was instruction about "the pervasive problem of discrimination in the United States," with the result that "they may have inadvertently been motivated to find it."[92]

The results of the 1991 Denver study have received far less publicity than the others, perhaps because of its unexpected findings—namely, that black and white testers had met with the same reception 78 percent of the time. The African American was favored over the white in 10 percent of the cases; the white was favored in 12 percent, yielding no statistically significant discrimination against blacks at all. The study also found that more employers discriminated in favor of Hispanics over whites than vice versa.

In short, the "audit studies" of hiring decisions that have been done thus far cannot bear the heavy burden that proponents of preferential policies have placed upon them. Two of the three major studies show hardly any discrimination or none whatever, and the third—in Washington—is problematic on a number of counts. We are left with the conclusion suggested by the several studies examining racial differences in income controlled for cognitive skill: that the racial differences that remain today are primarily the result of differences in what the economists call "pre-market factors"—differences in what was learned in school (and home and community) before the first job was sought.

DOES AFFIRMATIVE ACTION WORK?

"There's one simple reason to support affirmative action," an op-ed writer in the *New York Times* argued in 1995. "It works. The black middle class has grown only when a strong economy has been complemented by affirmative action programs. . . ."[93] It is an oft-made claim. Preferential policies have led to "the creation of a thriving black middle class in Atlanta," the *Economist* contended in April 1995.[94] "Everybody who is a person of color in this country has benefited from affirmative action," Atlanta's mayor asserted in June 1996. "There's not been anybody who's gotten a job on their own, no one who's prospered as a businessman or businesswoman on their own. . . . Without our affirmative-action programs, our minority businesses would wither."[95] Atlanta is 67 percent black. Does the mayor really believe that, in the absence of minority set-asides, no one (inside or outside government) would buy goods or services from businesses owned by blacks? And that indeed, no employer (presumably all of them white) would hire blacks?

The effects of the elaborate set of affirmative action policies pursued by government, private employers, and many other institutions over more than a quarter century are very difficult to assess. A few things, though, can be said. First, it is manifestly absurd to claim that black progress would not have occurred without preferential treatment. As readers of this book know, African Americans in the United States were making enormous economic progress before affirmative action came into being around the end of the 1960s. The black middle class, Chapter 7 demonstrated, did not suddenly appear from nowhere in 1970; it had been developing gradually since the 1940s.

Second, the effects of affirmative action policies that scholars think they have identified were limited both temporally and regionally. Two leading scholars, John J. Donahue III and James Heckman, concluded their review of this issue with the judgment that the greatest gains for African Americans were in the years 1965 to 1975 and occurred mainly in the South.[96] Furthermore, it is striking that Donahue and Heckman found "virtually no improvement" in wages of black men relative to those of white men outside of the South over the entire period from 1963 to 1987.[97] If they are correct, a policy that in 1996 was still being pursued and strenuously defended as absolutely necessary for further black progress only "worked" in the South, and ceased to be effective more than twenty years ago. In his book *Antidiscrimination Law and Minority Employment*, economist Farrell Bloch was even more skeptical. Even in the years in which preferential policies did have an impact, Bloch contended, they mainly served to redistribute blacks from smaller firms to larger ones, doing nothing to improve the overall level of black employment.[98]

How well have racial set-asides in government contracting achieved their ends? The State of Maryland decided in 1994 that at least 10 percent of the contracts it awarded would go to minority- and female-owned firms. It more than met its goal. Did the program therefore "work"? Yes, if the goal were merely the narrow one of dispensing cash to a particular group. When the government sets aside a pool of money and declares that only black businessmen can receive it, it will have no trouble finding willing takers. But advocates of such programs claim that they accomplish far more than that. The larger aim is to expand the number of minority businesses that are capable of flourishing in the much larger private market, where they are no longer sheltered from the competition. How often does that happen? How frequently do minority firms leave the comfortable nest that set-asides give them and fly on their own? That is the crucial question, to which we have no definitive answer. One study found, however, that the larger the share of government work done by a minority business enterprise, the less likely it was to survive for more than a brief period.[99]

In addition, set-asides carry a price. Atlanta's first black mayor, Maynard Jackson, introduced affirmative action programs in 1974; at the time, the city was approximately half black and yet only 0.5 percent of city contracts went to black contractors. When Jackson left office after three terms, more than a third of those contracts were signed by firms owned by African Americans. But that record looked better than it was. Some of those contracts involved race-based graft—awards to high-bidders with the right political connections. Others were fraudulent. White contractors had offered deals: a signature in exchange for 15 percent of the contract, with no obligation to do any of the work. That 15 percent was added to the total price. (In 1995 one contractor reckoned that a building job costing $60,000 in a nearby county where the lowest bidder got the job carried a price of $100,000 in Atlanta.) Moreover, white-owned firms doing city construction at several sites simultaneously were known to move black laborers from one to another, keeping one step ahead of the compliance officer.[100]

Set-asides have been a magnet for corruption—for cozy arrangements between black and white firms in which the white firms get the actual business. Affirmative action hiring mandates are also easily circumvented. The Philadelphia Plan has been running for more than a quarter of a century, with meager long-term gains, the *New York Times* found after taking a close look at the Philadelphia construction industry in 1995. A tour of building sites revealed very few members of minority groups working at skilled jobs. In part, the problem may have been a paucity of black workers either already trained to do the work or willing to receive such training on an unpaid basis. But the *Times* concluded that there was also continuing and successful resistance to change on the part of white-dominated unions—white foremen hiring white friends.[101] If so—if not even the Philadelphia Plan can boast results more than twenty-five years down the road—perhaps affirmative action advocates should be having second thoughts.

Politicians who have created or operated affirmative action programs naturally would like to convince their black constituents that none of them could possibly have "gotten a job on their own" or "prospered as a businessman or businesswoman on their own." A great many elected officials—from the mayor of Atlanta to the president of the United States—benefit from the gratitude of African-American voters. But if the message is politically powerful, it's also condescending and wrong. Although there is room for debate over interpretation of the evidence, it cannot seriously be argued that racial preferences are essential to keep black workers from plunging into joblessness and poverty.

BIG BUSINESS BACKS AFFIRMATIVE ACTION

Whatever its actual impact, affirmative action has become an established part of the way big business operates. Small employers may be resistant (they find it tougher to absorb the costs), but large companies frequently profess actual enthusiasm. A poll of CEOs conducted in the spring of 1995 found that 73 percent, mainly from companies with more than 10,000 employees, said they would continue their affirmative action programs even if contracts with the federal government no longer required them. A majority said their race-conscious hiring had helped their marketing.[102] "We feel diversity is critical. CEOs think it's the right thing to do and it only makes sense," Johanna Schneider, a spokeswoman for the Washington office of the Business Round-table, a group of large-company executives said in 1995.[103] "I have never felt a burden from affirmative action, because it is a business imperative for us," the chairman of Mobil remarked that same year. "That's not a maverick view," the *Washington Post* reported; "at many of the nation's large corporations, affirmative action is woven into the fabric of the companies."[104]

Such enthusiasm suggests that much of what's in place is here to stay. Part of the reason is that large corporations need to protect themselves against lawsuits. But that does not explain why many companies (some federal contractors, others not) go well beyond what the law requires. For instance, in the early 1980s, Du Pont decided to make half of its new hires for professional and management positions women or minorities.[105] In the mid-1980s, Gannett, the country's largest newspaper chain, began providing financial bonuses for managers who helped meet its "equal-opportunity" goals.[106] At about the same time, the chairman of Corning Glass Works, James R. Houghton, warned male executives that their own promotions would depend in part on how frequently they promoted women and minorities under their supervision.[107] In the spring of 1995, Chrysler, Aetna Life & Casualty, and General Motors, among others, told a gathering of Washington lawyers that they should hire more minorities; we will use those firms who do so, American Airlines announced.[108]

A diverse workforce is of course much to be desired, but racial double-standards driven by financial and other forms of coercion raise precisely the question posed in *Croson:* could the "the dream of a Nation of equal citizens in a society where race is irrelevant" survive such race-conscious policies? The problem in fact has been exacerbated. The "diversity" rationale for race-conscious hiring has turned affirmative action—once seen as a temporary remedy for the lingering effects of past discrimination—into a permanent fixture of American corporate life. And racial stereotyping has been encouraged by the training that companies often institute in an effort to raise the general level of racial and cultural sensitivity. Employees are taught to "value differences"—that is, not individual differences, but those attached to race and ethnicity. Thus, they are told, for instance, that "people-oriented" African Americans should not be expected to fit into "white male culture," which is "very goal-oriented, future-oriented, very competitive, intensely individualistic, work-centered, oriented to objective goals and measurements, affectively neutral, competitive, and [assumes] that the best man wins."[109]

Not all race-conscious policies reinforce stereotypes and threaten to widen the racial divide. A number of large corporations offer aid to minority-owned businesses. General Motors Corporation works closely with minority suppliers to make sure their businesses thrive, the *Wall Street Journal* reported in the fall of 1995. GM, AT&T, and J. C. Penney Co. all provide capital for the Business Consortium Fund, a corporate lending program serving minority firms. Chrysler and Ford sign long-term purchasing contracts with minority vendors who can then obtain financing from otherwise skittish banks. Sears banks with minority-owned financial institutions, which in turn lend to minority businesses. And one of New York's largest insurance brokers provides computer training, access to its database, and other administrative help to minorities in the insurance industry.[110]

All of this is just good business, these companies say. And good public relations. It is a sign of a profoundly changed racial climate that in the arena of public opinion there is nothing to lose and everything to gain from a strong commitment to helping African Americans and other minorities get ahead. In addition, that commitment keeps civil rights organizations quiet, not a minor consideration. The power of those organizations was evident when a scheduled "Mickey Is a Rat" protest outside Walt Disney World in March 1994 forced the company to sign on to a package that included a contribution of $1 million toward the start-up costs of new minority construction firms, a 10 percent set-aside for such firms, and a promise to help local governments in central Florida improve the region's minority business climate.[111] If American society has changed as little as many profoundly pessimistic black voices insist, one wonders why most businesses regard being tarred with the brush of racial insensitivity as a kiss of death.

ADARAND'S CHALLENGE TO PREFERENTIAL POLICIES

The Xerox Corp should probably be taken at its word when it says that affirmative action is "a corporate value, a management priority and a formal business objective." Whatever happens in Congress, in the states, or in the courts, that picture is not likely to change. But racial preferences in the public sector are increasingly vulnerable to legislative and judicial attack.

The 1989 decision in *Croson*—which applied only to state and local governments—was a first sign of things to come. Six years later, in *Adarand Con-*

structors v. Pena, the Supreme Court extended to all federal programs the requirement that race-based action meet the demanding test of "strict scrutiny"—narrow tailoring to serve a compelling state interest.[112] Adarand Constructors, Inc., had challenged the substantial financial bonus that the Department of Transportation awarded to prime contractors to induce them to hire minority subcontractors. In 1989 the Mountain Gravel & Construction Company had hired a subcontactor officially certified as "disadvantaged" to build a highway guardrail in Colorado, even though the subcontractor was not the lowest bidder. That choice cost the taxpayers money, but paid Mountain Gravel handsomely. The federal government owed the company a bonus worth 10 percent of the subcontract (although the amount paid could not exceed 1.5 percent of the total award in the prime contract).

The Small Business Act had labeled blacks and other minorities presumptively disadvantaged; the white-owned company contended that this presumption resulted in racial discrimination against it. And in a five–four decision, the Supreme Court agreed that a regulation that singled out racial and ethnic minority groups for distinctive treatment was inherently suspect. (Whether this program actually did so, and if so, whether it could nevertheless survive the demanding test of strict constitutional scrutiny, were questions returned to the lower court for determination.)

Adarand was the bad news that the civil rights community had feared since *Croson.* It threatened every race-based federal policy, as the Clinton Justice Department immediately recognized. "As we read *Adarand,"* said the associate attorney general John R. Schmidt, "its holding is not confined to contracting, but extends to all federal affirmative action programs that use racial and ethnic criteria as a basis for decision making."[113]

The doubts about race-based decision making that were expressed by the majority of the Court in *Adarand* were in tune with a changing political climate. In the November 1994 elections the Republicans had captured both houses of Congress for the first time in forty years. Republican complaints that the Civil Rights Restoration Act of 1991 had endorsed quotas were easily ignored as long as the Democrats controlled Congress, but it was a different ballgame after the elections. In February 1995 the Congressional Research Service responded to a request from Senate Majority Leader Robert J. Dole, and released a list of no less than 160 federal programs that used racial and ethnic criteria in awarding benefits. Although majorities of Republicans, including Dole himself, had voted for most of these programs, this new evidence that racial preferences were written into the rules that governed the operations of virtually every federal agency was disturbing to all but the most committed proponents of affirmative action. Republicans in Congress mounted a campaign to end the lucrative FCC tax breaks that had lined the pockets of rich and well-connected blacks and other minorities.

The ground was shifting. One of the most remarkable facts about the preferential policies that have been pursued since the late 1960s is that it took so long for them to become the subject of political debate. Most whites felt that African Americans were entitled to some remediation to make up for past mistreatment, and were content to have only the vaguest knowledge of the policies being pursued in the name of that objective.[114] Only within the past few years has opposition to preferential forms of affirmative action become politically salient. The "white hands" ad Senator Jesse Helms used against Harvey Gantt in the 1990 North Carolina senatorial race was the first significant example.

The seismic shift in the political landscape, though, began four years later in California, the nation's most populous and ethnically most diverse state. In 1994 two obscure academics, old-fashioned liberals committed to the color-blind policies the civil rights movement had once stood for, launched a campaign to amend the California constitution so as to ban all racial and gender preferences by state and local governments. Although the California Civil Rights Initiative (CCRI) got no backing from the leading interest groups in the state and was opposed by most of them, it nevertheless caught fire with ordinary voters and became the rallying point for a grassroots mass movement. Led by an African-American businessman and member of the University of California Board of Regents, Ward Connerly, CCRI garnered enough signatures to appear on the November 1996 ballot as Proposition 209, and it passed by a solid margin. In addition, in July 1995, the regents of the University of California followed the lead of Connerly and Governor Pete Wilson and voted to end all racial preferences on the nine campuses of the University of California, the leading state university system in the nation.

The significance of these political developments was not lost on the Democratic Party leadership. Five days after the release of the Congressional Research Service's long list of federal preferences, ending the secrecy in which these programs had long been cloaked, the president had a closed-door meeting with House Democrats. "We have to outsmart the Republicans," the president declared, according to one participant. "We cannot walk away from this fight," he added, ordering an "intense, urgent review" of federal affirmative action policy.[115] At a news conference a few days later he said it was "time to look at all these programs . . . and ask ourselves, do they work; are they fair; do they achieve the desired objectives?"[116]

The questions were good ones, but the answers to them were preordained. As a senior administration official acknowledged, if the administration took a truly hard look, "our base would go nuts."[117] That consideration was decisive. A vital part of the party's "base" had already sounded a loud and clear warning. "I want to make sure review does not mean retreat," Jesse Jackson had announced—hinting at serious political trouble to come if the review questioned the need for the affirmative action programs uncovered by the Dole request.[118] Jimmy Carter had alienated the left wing of the Democratic Party and his bid for reelection in 1980 was dealt a damaging blow by Ted Kennedy's challenge from the left. A similar challenge to Bill Clinton by Jesse Jackson might have been equally damaging.

CIRCUMVENTING *ADARAND*

By the time the *Adarand* decision came down in June 1995, the affirmative action issue was already politically hot, and threatening to become more so. Among the ominous signs: the momentum gathering behind the CCRI; a 1 June executive order by Governor Wilson ending those preferences that the California governor had direct power over; indications that the regents of the University of California were ready to junk racial preferences; and news that congressional Republicans would be filing an "Equal Opportunity Act" aimed at federal affirmative action programs.

The Clinton administration quickly launched an all-out defense of its preferential policies. The first step was a 28 June Justice Department memo, written by Assistant Attorney General Walter Dellinger and intended to provide "preliminary legal guidance" to the general counsels of the executive agencies. The Dellinger memo was followed three weeks later by the White House review that the president had ordered in February; written by Christopher Edley, Jr. (special counsel to the president) and George Stephanopoulos (senior advisor), it promised "a candid and balanced description" of federal affirmative action programs, as well as a set of policy recommendations. Two further memos outlining administration views about the implications of *Adarand* came from Associate Attorney General John R. Schmidt in February and May of 1996.

Only in retrospect was the Dellinger memo, written two weeks after *Adarand,* a hint of things to come. At the time, it read like a legitimate attempt to put the best face possible on the decision, emphasizing its limits and urging no precipitous action in its wake. Many programs, Dellinger assumed, could survive strict constitutional scrutiny.[119] But Dellinger's quick-read of the decision was the administration's last careful and lawyerly analysis. The Edley and Stephanopoulos report, less than a month later, basically ignored the Supreme Court's holding after a perfunctory nod in its direction. A brief on behalf of every federal affirmative action program (the authors did not recommend dropping a single one), it put the administration squarely on record as intending to carry bravely on, whatever the High Court had said. As Edley and Stephanopoulos described them, those federal programs were above legal, political, or ethical reproach; the Court's concerns in *Croson,* *Adarand,* and related decisions (on voting rights, for instance) were thus woefully off-base. In *Croson* the Court had warned that racial set-asides ran the danger of "stigmatic harm" and heightened racial hostility."[120] Edley and

Stephanopoulos spoke blandly of policies that simply offered "every American a fair chance to achieve success," a necessary tool "to move us away from a world of lingering biases . . . toward one in which opportunity is equal."

The voice of these White House aides was of course precisely that of the president. "Affirmative action has been good for America," he said at the National Archives speech that same day. "When . . . done right, it is flexible, it is fair, and it works."[121] Clinton tossed a small bone in the direction of affirmative action critics: "Don't end it," he said, but do "mend it." Along with the caveat "when . . . done right," it was one of his meaningless conciliatory phrases meant to soothe the opposition. In fact, the president had caved in in the face of relentless pressure (reported regularly in the press) from civil rights spokesmen and black politicians.[122] He identified nothing at all to "mend"; every preferential program on the books was evidently being "done right."

That was the message conveyed in the two key memos from Associate Attorney General John R. Schmidt who concluded that "nothing in *Adarand* requires a retreat."[123] What the decision demanded was "a demonstrable factual predicate" for an agency's race-conscious actions. Those actions could be justified by statistical evidence indicating minority underutilization (a "lingering effect" of historic discrimination) or perhaps by "an agency's operational need for a diverse workforce." Of course more neutral means of increasing minority participation in the workforce should be considered, but if found inadequate (as would certainly be the case), reliance on race and ethnicity became legitimate. In 1994 Congress had enacted the Federal Acquisition Streamlining Act (FASA), a bipartisan effort to streamline federal procurement—the purchase of goods and services (ranging from construction to paper clips) from private companies. Included in the streamlining effort was a government-wide extension of two tools that had previously been available only to the Defense Department: the so-called "rule of two" and a bidding preference. The "rule of two" allowed the Pentagon to remove a contract from competitive bidding anytime there were at least two minority businesses eager to do the work, while the bidding-preference proviso allowed the DOD to award a contract to a minority-owned company as long as the cost was no more than 10 percent above that of the lowest-bidder.

In extending these tools to other agencies, FASA was not in theory instituting a new program; it was making procurement rules uniform. But the statute could not take effect until final implementing regulations were issued—a process that, as it turned out, took more than a year as a consequence of the clear constraints *Adarand* imposed on such blatant racial preferences. In fact, in the interim the Pentagon itself decided to abandon its "rule of two" in the face of a constitutional challenge, thus killing any possibility of its wider use. There was thus the question of how the implementing regulations should look, and Schmidt's second memo provided an answer. It offered a "model" for amending the race-conscious procurement provisions of FASA—a model that had no legal standing, however. The proposal was, in essence, an exploratory advocacy essay.[124]

The memo made clear the Clinton administration's continued commitment to the entire creaky edifice of federal race-conscious programs. The title promised "Proposed Reforms." Yet Schmidt himself said his starting "premise" was "a need for affirmative action in procurement," and White House senior advisor George Stephanopoulos agreed that "we want to do everything we can to promote minority contracting."[125] Moreover, the memo's stated aim was to create "a structure for race-conscious procurement . . . in a manner that will survive constitutional scrutiny." The reference to "reform" was thus not serious. Abandoning the "rule of two" was all the administration was willing to change. Even that concession was close to meaningless, since the same ends could be achieved by other means, most notably, via the sole-source bidding allowed by 8(a).[126]

The entire report, in fact, was an exercise in rationalization, denial, and deception. The government had an indisputably compelling interest in "affirmative remedial efforts," the memo claimed at the outset, lifting it over the first hurdle of "strict scrutiny" by bureaucratic decree. Discrimination was assumed as a given, and remedies were thus a necessity—remedies that were "affirmative." These were not racially exclusive set-asides; nor were they social engineering. They were beneficial and therefore harmless.

The only issue (as Schmidt described it) was whether such programs were sufficiently "narrowly tailored" to meet the constitutional standard, and so that question was the memo's focus. To that end, Schmidt proposed several alleged "reforms." For instance, it should be made slightly easier for white firms to prove their eligibility as small disadvantaged businesses (SDBs). To concede that at least a few whites might be "disadvantaged" seemed a good idea; a month earlier, however, the assistant attorney general for civil rights had (with refreshing candor) admitted he was "not convinced that means anything in practical terms."[127]

Likewise, the memo suggested that the usual goals and timetables should be replaced by "benchmarks" that would establish the appropriate level of minority contracting in each industry. No fixed, permanent 10 percent goal for highway construction, in other words. But the benchmarks would be set by determining "the level of minority contracting that one would reasonably expect to find in a market absent discrimination or its effects." In other words, by figuring out how many minority businesses would get what sort of contracts had history been different—had discrimination never been a problem. The assumptions behind Order No. 4, the Philadelphia Plan, and the *Albermarle* decision were alive and well.

Such allegedly exact calculations of what might have been were the stuff of pseudoscientific dreams. The notion that a paucity of minority firms in a particular sector of the economy always indicated discrimination or its "lingering effects" was naïve and simplistic. Evidence reveals particularly strong cultural differences among racial and ethnic groups in the realm of entrepreneurship; some group cultures seem highly conducive to business success and some do not. Jews, Armenians, Chinese, Japanese, and Koreans, among others, have had notably higher rates of self-employment in the United States than the Anglo majority. Over a fifth of the Korean-American men who were employed in 1990, for example, were self-employed, almost triple the average for the population as a whole.[128] The success of such groups obviously cannot be attributed to any discrimination in their favor. Quite the contrary; they succeeded despite considerable prejudice against them.[129] Thus, the fact that blacks were long the objects of discrimination may not be the major reasons for their disappointing track record when it comes to running a business.

The Schmidt memo meant that SBA administrators and other procurement officers would continue to set goals (in effect, quotas) that seemed "fair." And to meet those goals, as the memo acknowledged, the government could continue to use not only the 8(a) program but such race-conscious mechanisms as bidding credits (giving the contract to the minority company whose bid was not more than 10 percent above that of the lower bidder) and bonus points for prime contractors who used SDBs for part of the work, both very similar to the program struck down by *Adarand.* The bidding preference alone fatally stacked the deck against small white firms, who could not lower their price by 10 percent to compete with privileged minority firms. *Adarand,* as the Department of Justice read it, had been a waste of the Supreme Court's breath.

THE UNCERTAIN FUTURE OF RACIAL PREFERENCES

By 1996, then, a remarkable state of affairs had emerged: the Supreme Court and the U.S. Department of Justice were at war. In the early 1950s and immediate post–*Brown v. Board* years, southern states played endless games in an effort to evade the law. Southern politicians and often southern judges were adept at keeping one step ahead of the Justice Department; federal victories were repeatedly circumvented by southern ingenuity. By the mid-1990s, however, it was the Justice Department that had become the skilled evader of the law that had been laid down by the highest Court in the land. The actors had changed, but the scene was much the same: rebellious government officials determined to take matters into their own hands.

From one perspective, however, the High Court was tasting a bit of its own medicine. In the 1960s and early 1970s, administrative agencies had refashioned the 1964 Civil Rights Act, and the Supreme Court had signed on, with the consequence that the statute (with judicial blessing) was altered beyond recognition. By the mid-1990s, after the Court had redone the careful work of Congress, the White House and the Department of Justice took to rewriting the work of the Court.

Unless the Supreme Court turns against its own Fourteenth Amendment decisions, however, it's not a strategy with a future. As *New Republic* writer Jeffrey Rosen argued ten months after *Adarand,* the whole resistance effort seems doomed.[130] Not even the 8(a) program could survive the Court's strict scrutiny; like the "rule of two," 8(a) set-asides shelter certain groups from competition, groups selected on the basis of their racial identity. Only a record of ongoing federal discrimination against minority firms can possibly justify such preferential treatment; evidence of exclusion two decades earlier will not do. As the Court has acknowledged, if the past is forever present, then racial preferences will never end.[131] In addition, as a percentage of small businesses (whose owners can be racially identified, unlike those of a publicly traded company such as Lockheed), minority firms are in fact overrepresented in federal procurement. The administration's starting premise was thus wrong. Finally, as suggested earlier, it is not possible to divine how many black-owned businesses would be getting what sorts of contracts in a "fair" world.

Schmidt was not the only member of the Clinton administation to advance shoddy arguments on behalf of hard-to-defend race-conscious programs. The Edley-Stephanopoulos report, for instance, slipped effortlessly from the question of discrimination to that of disadvantage, which may have many nondiscriminatory sources and is not a basis on which to sustain constitutionally questionable programs. In insisting that beneficiaries of preferences were all qualified, and ignoring the issue of whether some applicants are more qualified than others, it glossed over the serious problem of a conflict between racial preferences and merit, as the Court had done earlier in the *Bakke* case and in *Johnson v. Santa Clara.* And it promised the moon: the eradication of all discrimination and its lingering effects—the "inclusion of everyone in the opportunities America promises us all."[132] "Inclusion" was clearly a code word for proportionate ethnic and racial representation on the job and in government procurement, a standard the Supreme Court had explicitly rejected.

The testimony of the assistant attorney general for civil rights, Deval Patrick, before Congress in December 1995 was in much the same vein. Affirmative action was rechristened "affirmative consideration," which presumably sounded kinder and gentler. Goals and timetables were not quotas; on the other hand, statistical measures of progress (which result in quotas) were "essential." The lack of sufficient racial progress was evident in the refusal of cabdrivers to pick up black males; never mind that no affirmative action program would cure that problem.[133]

These spokesmen for the Clinton administration—and by extension, for the civil rights groups—have had two aims. They have wanted both to nullify

Supreme Court rulings and to keep the public on board. These would seem to be incompatible goals. In the 1950s and 1960s, civil rights leaders were often branded as "extremists," and yet, outside the South, the principles they articulated were widely accepted.[134] From the courage and determination they displayed in those years, they accumulated a great deal of moral capital in the political bank. But in using that moral capital to pursue race-based policies, the civil rights leadership squandered its deep and wide support. In perhaps no area was that truer and more obvious to the ordinary American than in the realm of employment and government contracting.

CHAPTER SIXTEEN

Voting Rights

"BEFORE WE HAD the right to vote, politicians publicly called us niggers," ran a 1981 political advertisement aimed at black voters in Mobile, Alabama. "After we received the right to vote, but our numbers were few, they called us Nigras. When we reached 5,000, they called us colored. 10,000, they called us black people. Now that we have reached 50,000, they call us Commissioner Wicks, Judge Cain Kennedy, Representative Yvonne Kennedy, and Senator Figures. If you don't want to go back to square one, vote for Mims and Greenough."[1]

The 1965 Voting Rights Act transformed southern politics. The story captured in that radio spot in Mobile was replicated in cities, towns, and rural counties in every corner of the South. At the time of its passage, the act was universally acknowledged to be, as black congresswoman Barbara Jordan later put it, "very, very strong medicine."[2] Critics and supporters alike agreed that it was "radical"—"a substantial departure from ordinary concepts of our federal system."[3] A 1972 report calling for more rigorous voting rights enforcement described the act's provisions as "harsh," but necessarily so.[4] Its remedies were characterized as "stringent" by the Supreme Court, and the assistant attorney general for civil rights readily acknowledged in 1975 that it was "unusual" legislation.[5] But while the South had cried foul, in fact the "usual" legislation had failed to break the usual pattern of black disfranchisement.

Change was very quick to come; the act was extraordinarily effective. For more than a decade the South had played evasive games with school desegregation. But voting rights were different. There was no escaping the federal registrars ("examiners") that could be dispatched if necessary. And there remained no possibility of manipulating literacy tests for racist ends. Those tests had been wiped from the books in what were called "covered" jurisdictions—that is, those states and counties in which total turnout had been below 50 percent in the 1964 election. A state or county that had employed a literacy test in November 1964, and in which less than half the voting-age population (both black and white) had cast ballots, was assumed to have deliberately depressed the political participation of its black residents, with the burden on public authorities to prove otherwise. A simple statistical rule of thumb thus replaced the extended and complex judicial process traditionally used to establish voting rights violations. In addition, any "covered" state that tried some fancy new footwork to compromise Fifteenth Amendment rights (something equivalent to the long-gone white primary, for example) would be stopped in its tracks by the necessity to "preclear" any change in electoral law with either the D.C. district court or the U.S. Department of Justice.

The enfranchisement of southern blacks changed both black and white politics in the South, as we showed in Chapter 11. Segregationists disappeared or changed their stripes. South Carolina's Senator Strom Thurmond led the Dixiecrat rebellion from the Democratic Party in 1948 and filibustered the 1957 civil rights bill for a record twenty-four hours and eighteen minutes. But by the 1970s he was securing federal funds for South Carolina's black mayors and black colleges, and extending his famed constituent services to black voters. In 1982, when the Voting Rights Act was amended and extended, Thurmond was chairman of the Judiciary Committee, but he made no effort to block the legislation.

Those 1982 amendments were actually the third occasion on which the Voting Rights Act had been revised. The statute was permanent legislation, but the tough provisions that made it so effective were temporary. It permanently protected all citizens from procedures denying the right to vote on account of race or color—finally enforcing the Fifteenth Amendment ninety-five years after its passage. Those sections that banned literacy tests, made available federal examiners, and froze existing electoral procedures pending federal approval of any proposed changes, on the other hand, were enacted as short-term "emergency" measures. Assuming powers traditionally left in local hands, they had an expected life of only five years.

In 1970 the emergency provisions of the act were extended for another five years; in 1975, for seven years; and in 1982, for twenty-five years. On each occasion the process of renewal became an occasion for amendment. In fact, the history of the act is paradoxical. The legislation quickly solved the problem of black citizens unable to vote. Yet with black enfranchisement came new congressional effort to protect against disfranchisement. As the emergency subsided, the emergency powers expanded.

Thus, in 1970, with blacks throughout the South registering and voting in unprecedented numbers, Congress not only renewed the special provisions for five years; it imposed a five-year, nationwide ban on literacy tests, and extended the preclearance and other emergency provisions to a wide variety of nonsouthern states and counties in which voter turnout had dropped below 50 percent in 1968. Many of these states and counties had no history of electoral discrimination remotely comparable to that of the South in 1965.

For example, under the revised act three counties in New York City came under coverage, but not because there was new evidence of electoral discrimination against blacks. Turnout for the 1968 presidential election had been low across the nation, and participation in New York, reflecting the national trend, had dropped slightly to just under the determining 50 percent mark. Once the city was "covered," however, every change in electoral procedure—even the relocation of a polling place—had to be approved (precleared) by either the Justice Department or the D.C. district court.

The amendments of 1970 both greatly strengthened the act and paved the way for more radical changes in subsequent years. Moreover, once minorities in places like New York (where blacks had long been voting) qualified for the extraordinary protection provided by the statute, there was no logical place to stop. The new use of preclearance both increased the usefulness of the act to blacks in already covered jurisdictions and alerted other groups in other states to its benefits. As a consequence, the amendments of 1975 brought under coverage four additional groups: Hispanics, Asian Americans, American Indians, and Alaskan Natives. And the geographic scope of the legislation was once again extended, further decreasing the likelihood that the preclearance and other temporary provisions would soon be allowed to expire. In 1982 the statute was altered anew, this time to give minority voters more leverage in challenging districting plans and other electoral arrangements all across the nation—not just in the "covered" jurisdictions that in 1965 had included only those with an egregious history of Fifteenth Amendment violations. That change allowed plaintiffs to file suits in any state against any practice, whose "results" were discriminatory.

In neither 1975 nor 1982 was there any serious, sustained congressional opposition to the proposed amendments, in part because civil rights lobbyists skillfully downplayed the revolution in southern black politics and painted a picture of ever more subtle disfranchisement. They described a record of spectacular success as one of near-dismal failure by equating racist registrars and violence at the polls with electoral procedures (citywide voting, for instance) that allowed a majority of whites to outvote blacks.[6] Opening the Senate hearings, Democrat Birch Bayh of Indiana referred to gains as "more apparent than real."[7] Progress as initially conceived might be unmistakable, but redefined to ensure black officeholding, it disappeared.

The conflation of opportunity (access to the polls) and sure results (black officeholding) meant that members of Congress tempted to question the necessity for more protection were forced to defend themselves against charges of insufficient commitment to racial equality. Given the glare of lights under which all business was conducted and the power of the highly organized, well-funded civil rights community, few were willing to take that political risk. In fact, in 1982, Republicans in the House thought it politically unwise even to call witnesses to testify at the hearings. Only Orrin Hatch in the Senate, who was from Utah, a conservative state with few minority residents, conducted an open fight.

THE REWRITING OF SECTION 5

In 1965 the Voting Rights Act had a simple aim: to provide ballots for southern blacks. Attorney General Nicholas Katzenbach made that goal very clear on the opening days of the congressional hearings held prior to the passage of the legislation. "Our concern today is to enlarge representative government," he said. "It is to increase the number of citizens who can vote."[8] The point was reiterated throughout his testimony: "The whole bill is really aimed at getting people registered," he explained.[9] Other witnesses did not even mention the purpose of the bill, viewing it as obvious and beyond discussion. Instead, they described the continuing obstacles to rudimentary electoral participation. Every advocate had the same thing in mind—realizing the promise of the Fifteenth Amendment almost one hundred years after its passage.

In 1965, access to the local restaurant, the local hospital, and the polling booth was the aim that informed the whole civil rights movement. But the shift in focus from the right to vote to the number of blacks holding office—so evident in the 1975 congressional hearings—had actually begun within four years of the passage of the act. The point of Section 5, the preclearance provision, had been to stop states from devising clever new ways to keep blacks from the polls; in the "covered" jurisdictions (almost all in the South) no change in voting procedure could be made without federal approval.[10] In 1969, however, the provision acquired an unexpected purpose. Public officials in Mississippi and elsewhere had made all too plain their readiness to alter the electoral environment by instituting, for instance, countywide voting, eliminating the single-member districts from which some blacks were likely to get elected. They switched from a system of single-member districts (some of them majority-black) to a method of election that forced black candidates to seek white support, robbing black citizens of legislative seats that would otherwise have been theirs. The Supreme Court, in response, sanctioned federal objections not simply to discriminatory innovations involving registration and the mechanics of voting, but to the introduction of at-large voting and methods of election that reduced the likelihood of black officeholding.[11]

Southern resistance to black political power thus began a process by which the Voting Rights Act was radically transformed. Preclearance became an instrument that protected blacks not only against obvious disfranchising devices, but also against those which in more subtle ways "diluted" the impact of their vote. The Court had turned a minor provision of the act—Section 5 —into a major tool with which to combat white resistance to black power.

Clearly the Court could not stand by while southern whites in covered states—states with dirty hands on questions of race—altered electoral rules to buttress white hegemony. Yet a right to protection from action intended to minimize black power, once established, could not be easily contained. By acting to avert such rearguard measures, by prohibiting the adoption of countywide voting and other electoral procedures that threatened to rob black ballots of their expected worth, the Court had implicitly enlarged the definition of enfranchisement. Now there were "meaningful" and "meaningless" votes—votes that "counted" and those that did not. And once that distinction had been made, a meaningful vote was almost bound to become an entitlement. It was a subtle but important change: the shift from black ballots safe from deliberate efforts to dilute their impact on the one hand, to a right to a vote that fully counted on the other.

A provision initially inserted to guard against the manipulation of an electoral system for racist ends thus evolved as a means to ensure that black votes had value—had the power, that is, to elect blacks. For that was the meaning of ballots that carried their proper weight. The initial protection against white resistance to simple black enfranchisement became a means to stop the use of electoral rules that lessened the likelihood that blacks would gain the legislative seats to which they appeared entitled. When a city chose for economic reasons to expand its municipal boundaries (adding more white voters to the population mix), when demographic change forced a political jurisdiction to draw new district lines, when a county abandoned the gubernatorial appointment of county commissioners in favor of at-large elections, black candidates acquired a level of protection that politics as usual would not have provided. Moreover, as noted above, statutory amendments in 1982 gave blacks dramatic new power to challenge methods of election on grounds of their discriminatory result.

By 1975 those who enforced the Voting Rights Act had arrived at a point no one envisioned in 1965. The right to vote no longer meant simply the right to enter a polling booth and pull the lever. Yet the issue retained a simple Fifteenth Amendment aura—one that was pure camouflage. An alleged voting rights violation had become a districting plan that contained nine majority-black districts when a tenth could be drawn.[12] The question became: to how much special protection from white competition were black candidates entitled? For instance, when a different districting plan might have given another legislative seat to a black, should the (usually legitimate) interests of white incumbents give way to the goal of minority officeholding?

The temptation to provide maximum protection (a maximum number of seats) was strong and only intermittently resisted. The Court, in determining that annexations and redistricting were "voting" matters covered by Section 5, imposed upon federal authorities the task of fashioning acceptable electoral arrangements. Neither districting lines nor the territorial expansion of a city were boundary alterations that could simply be reversed. If an annexation (usually undertaken for sound economic reasons) reduced the black proportion of the population and thus its voting strength, a remedy short of de-annexation had to be found. And if districting plans were torn up following a decennial census, there was no going back: revised lines that met the one-person, one-vote standard had to be drawn. There was thus the need to devise new plans, to determine when black ballots "fully counted." The phrase itself invited a definition that gave those ballots maximum weight, defined as officeholding; anything less suggested a compromised right. Yet maximum weight implied an entitlement to proportional racial representation—a concept that proved no less controversial with respect to legislative bodies than with reference to schools and places of employment.

THE PROPORTIONAL REPRESENTATION STANDARD

An entitlement to proportional racial representation: that was certainly how the Department of Justice and the D.C. district court (the only court that could hear Section 5 suits) quickly came to interpret the preclearance provision. The right to vote included the right to representation; minority representation could be measured by the number of minority officeholders; justice demanded a national commitment to protecting black candidates from white competition; and black ballots were meaningless in the absence of black electoral success. Proportional representation was thus implicitly the standard by which to judge the racial fairness of districting and other electoral arrangements.

The wording of the provision partially invited such an interpretation. Only those electoral practices and procedures that were not discriminatory in either "purpose" or "effect" could be precleared. In 1965 the reference to discriminatory effect was innocuous and thus unnoticed. The framers and sponsors of the act hoped to eliminate every device whose impact was to keep southern blacks from the polls—whatever its stated purpose. And, in the context, "effect" and "purpose" were close to interchangeable terms; the former was simply circumstantial evidence of the latter. In a jurisdiction known to have had a long history of Fifteenth Amendment violations, any alteration in voting procedure was viewed as a signal of improper motive when that change affected newly enfranchised blacks.

Once changes such as annexations and redistrictings were covered by the preclearance provision, however, "effect" was released from its intimate connection with "purpose." When a municipality annexed a suburb, it might have added more white voters than black to the city's voting rolls, but such an effect would not be a sure clue to its purpose. In 1969 the Court had suddenly applied the prohibition of Section 5 to all changes that might have a disparate racial impact, whether intended or not. A districting plan that was racially neutral in intent could nevertheless be found discriminatory in effect.

Disparate impact as the standard by which to judge discrimination implicitly creates an entitlement to proportional representation. Only where African Americans are proportionally represented (on the job, in schools, in legislative seats) can it be said with total confidence that racism has had no effect. Nevertheless, at least in its decisions involving districting, specifically, the Supreme Court never interpreted the law as containing such an entitlement. The judicial record is very thin; in very few instances have jurisdictions actually chosen the option (built into the law) of going to the D.C. district court and then on to the Supreme Court. The simpler, faster, less expensive alternative of administrative preclearance (Justice Department review) has been the norm.[13] Moreover, the High Court's few Section 5 decisions are not easy to decipher, and the incoherence of its rulings released both the Department of Justice and the D.C. court from the confines of principled decision making. The annexation cases, particularly, left the lower court and the DOJ free to pick and choose among disparate elements in muddled majority opinions.[14] However, one clear and enduring message did come through: in drawing a districting map, a city, county, or other jurisdiction was not obligated to create a maximum number of safe black legislative seats.

The leading case was *Beer v. United States,* decided in 1976, all but ignored by both the Justice Department and the D.C. district court, but never abandoned by the High Court itself.[15] The case involved ward lines drawn for elections to the New Orleans City Council. None of the old wards had had black majorities; in the new plan submitted for preclearance, there were two majority-black districts. The Justice Department and the D.C. court had found the plan wanting; more safe black wards could be drawn. But the Supreme Court came down on the city's side. How could a new districting plan that improved the political position of African Americans be called discriminatory? Justice Potter Stewart asked. The purpose of section 5 had been to bar alterations that would result in a "retrogression in the position of racial minorities with respect to their effective exercise of the electoral franchise."[16] Since the change at issue had actually increased the likelihood of a victorious black candidate, it could hardly be termed "retrogressive."

A method of voting had an unlawful "effect" (the Section 5 term) only if its impact would leave black voters worse off, the Court said. Districting lines that actually increased minority electoral power could not be discriminatory. It was an interpretation that squared with the initial structure of the act. Section 5 was intended to protect against purposeful discrimination and, beyond that, only against backsliding—attempts to undermine the effectiveness of the enfranchisement that other sections in the act ensured. Those who drafted the act assumed that, faced with the new and unwelcome prospect of blacks going to the polls, white racists in states that had denied basic constitutional rights might try to prevent blacks from actually gaining legislative seats. The provision provided a means to stop such action.

One of the remarkable aspects of the voting rights story, however, was that the D.C. court and the Justice Department remained deaf to the voice of the Supreme Court. Except with respect to annexations, the lower court paid minimal heed to the High Court, and the Department of Justice none at all. Such disdain for the Supreme Court's interpretation of the law might have been harder to pull off had its decisions been consistent. But its ruling in *Beer* was buffeted by winds the Court itself generated. The annexation cases were most clearly at odds with the New Orleans decision.[17] Annexations were frequent in the economically vibrant, expanding cities of the South and Southwest, many of which had at-large electoral systems. When a city altered its external boundary lines and added more whites than blacks to the voter rolls, blacks became entitled to single-member districts drawn to promote black officeholding, the Court held.[18] And yet when New Orleans adjusted its internal boundary lines—those delineating the wards from which the city council was elected—there was no need to do more than guarantee the number of safe black seats that the previous plan had contained.

The Court embraced a double standard, bound to cause trouble. The result was serious tension within the structure of the Voting Rights Act. Justice Byron White, who had written one of the important annexation decisions, could discern no rationale for the implied distinction between annexation and redistricting cases, and, as a result, dissented in *Beer*.[19] His view won out. Justice Department objections to changes in electoral procedure submitted for preclearance routinely began to demand that redistricting plans "fairly reflect" minority voting strength. Without explanation, the annexation standard was lifted out of context and applied to redistricting submissions.

DISTRICTING IN GEORGIA

Just how far the Justice Department carried its insistence that districting plans "fairly reflect" minority voting strength—that they guarantee (to the extent possible) proportional black officeholding—finally came to light in an important 1995 decision, *Miller v. Johnson*.[20] The story of the DOJ's intrusive preclearance processes and its adherence to a standard of proportional representation was well known to those who followed closely the work of its voting section in the civil rights division. But others had been kept in the dark until *Miller*, a constitutional case that involved a challenge to Georgia's eleventh congressional district, redrawn after the 1990 census.

The contours of Georgia's eleventh district had been determined by "a far-flung search for black voters," as the trial court put it.[21] Its population was drawn from "four discrete, widely spaced urban centers that [had] absolutely nothing to do with each other, and stretch[ed] the district hundreds of miles across rural counties and narrow swamp corridors."[22] But the decision to create such a wild-looking creature was not one that Georgia legislators would have made on their own. The Department of Justice, to which the state must submit for preclearance all districting plans, was an important player in the redistricting process.

In fact, the Justice Department intervened in the redistricting process even before it had begun. It had announced to all the covered states of the South that they must draw as many majority-black districts as possible.[23] As it happened, an American Civil Liberties Union attorney, in her capacity as advocate for the Black Caucus of the Georgia General Assembly, had been working on a map that provided three majority-black districts, which later acquired the name "the max-black plan." The race-driven bug-splat districts scooped up every black population concentration in the state.

Kathleen Wilde, the ACLU attorney, submitted her "max-black plan" to Justice several times during the redistricting process; in fact, she was in constant touch with the DOJ attorneys overseeing preclearance. The trial court that heard the subsequent constitutional challenge to the racially determined district later reported "countless communications, including notes, maps, and charts, by phone, mail and facsimile, between Wilde and DOJ." It was obvious "that Ms. Wilde's relationship with the DOJ Voting Section was informal and familiar; the dynamics were that of peers working together, not of an advocate submitting proposals to higher authorities." In fact, "DOJ was more accessible—and amenable—to the opinions of the ACLU than to those of the Attorney General of the State of Georgia," the court noted. "Ms. Wilde's triumph of demographic manipulation became DOJ's guiding light."[24]

It was "disingenuous" of Justice Department lawyers to argue that "DOJ's objections were anything less than implicit commands," the district court found. What the ACLU and the black caucus demanded, Justice commanded. And what Justice commanded, the state did. The eventually precleared plan included three majority-black districts whose contours both the district court and the U.S. Supreme Court found unacceptably race-driven, violating the Fourteenth Amendment's guarantee of equal protection. "The concept of government allocations on the basis of race, coupled with drawing lines tracing concentrations of black citizens, smacks of government-enforced ghettoization," the lower court concluded. "If efforts to *require* proportional representation of minorities in democratic institutions are not stopped with clarity and force, they will divide this country into a patchwork of racial provinces, and ensure that elected officials represent races before they represent citizens." It wasn't what the framers of the Voting Rights Act had in mind: "the devolution of voting rights into racial bargaining chips to be bickered over by special interests."[25]

The Supreme Court had sent mixed signals, suggesting one thing with respect to districting and quite another in the annexation decisions. Nevertheless, the contempt with which the Justice Department viewed the Court's interpretation of the law was startling. From the beginning the "retrogression" test by which to judge the discriminatory "effect" of districting plans was opposed by civil rights groups and the Justice Department. If three majority-black districts could be drawn, then only a plan that contained all three should be considered racially "fair," civil rights groups argued. Their view prevailed. *Beer* was simply ignored. The New Orleans districting map that met Supreme Court approval in 1978 would not in subsequent years have withstood administrative review.

Needless to say, this was not how things were supposed to work. We are a "surrogate of the [D.C.] district court," a 1982 letter from the attorney general to Port Arthur, Texas, stated.[26] In theory, federal attorneys wore the robes of impartial judges. In fact, the voting section had the aura of a law office, its files suggesting attorneys at work constructing a case for clients. In the Georgia case its clients were the advocacy groups; it even sent an objection letter (rejecting the second of the state's proposed districting maps) first to the ACLU, then to the Black Caucus, and last to the office to which it was properly addressed—that of the attorney general of Georgia—by which time the Black Caucus had already been discussing the matter with the press.[27]

Not only with respect to voting rights, but in other areas of the law, civil rights activists had all along been skeptical that opportunity alone—in the case of voting, black ballots—would shake the pillars of the racist status quo. And their concern about the disproportionately low number of southern blacks holding public office was legitimate. Against a backdrop of historic disfranchisement, access to the polling booth alone did not everywhere open the doors to black political opportunity. But as the lower court in *Miller* and the Supreme Court (in that and other cases) came eventually to understand, the drive to secure "racially fair" results carried a high price. Cleansing the nation's political system of discrimination, Justice Anthony M. Kennedy wrote in affirming the lower court's decision in *Miller,* is a goal "neither assured nor well served . . . by carving electorates into racial blocs . . . It takes a shortsighted and unauthorized view of the Voting Rights Act to invoke that statute . . . to demand the very racial stereotyping the Fourteenth Amendment forbids."[28]

THE ELUSIVE SECTION 2

After 1982, Section 5 was not the only provision in the Voting Rights Act used to carve electorates into racial blocs. Section 2 was amended that year to give plaintiffs in voting rights suits a powerful new weapon. In 1965 the provision had been a seemingly insignificant preamble to the act, restating the core of the Fifteenth Amendment: states could not deny the right of citizens to vote on account of race or color. Once amended, however, it became the centerpiece of the act, dwarfing all other provisions in importance, in part because the Justice Department came to judge submissions of electoral changes for preclearance by both Section 5 and Section 2 legal standards.

Preclearance applied only to changes in electoral procedure in "covered" jurisdictions, and prior to 1982, suits that challenged methods of election that Section 5 did not reach had to rest on the Fourteenth and Fifteenth Amendments. But two years earlier, in *City of Mobile v. Bolden,* the Supreme Court had held that a successful constitutional attack on an at-large or other method of voting would have to show that invidious *intent* infected the challenged electoral procedure.[29] Ballots cast in an electoral system uncontaminated by racial purpose carried their full, constitutionally guaranteed weight.

The ruling sent a ripple of alarm through the civil rights community; the Court had demanded, spokesmen said, the display of a still-smoking gun: overt racist statements by often long-dead public officials.[30] It was a rhetorically powerful argument of questionable validity; plaintiffs in successful school desegregation suits did not need to find such directly incriminating evidence, although they were also obliged to prove purposeful discrimination. Nevertheless, civil rights attorneys went to work immediately on an amendment to Section 2 that would allow plaintiffs to circumvent the need to show discriminatory intent. The fruit of their labor was a radical revision of the statute that obviated the need to demonstrate invidious purpose when attacking a method of voting outside the limited range of Section 5. Section 2 was rephrased to contain a "results" test, allowing plaintiffs to challenge at-large elections, district lines, or other voting-related arrangements as discriminatory in their "result." The change left the constitutional test standing but idle—henceforth irrelevant. Suits once brought under the Fourteenth Amendment, where intent was a vital factor, could now rest on the statute, with discrimination much easier to prove.

The new language of Section 2 was not made up out of whole cloth. Those who drafted the revised provision wanted simply (they said) a return to the constitutional standards of the pre-*Mobile* years; thus, they lifted language from a series of earlier rulings. Those decisions had guaranteed precisely what Section 2 now explicitly offered: an equal opportunity "to participate in the political process and to elect representatives of [one's] choice." Plaintiffs would henceforth prevail in Section 2 suits if they could show that a method of voting had the "result" of denying that equality of opportunity.

But what did that mean? Where political processes were less open to blacks than whites, the black vote was "diluted," the Court had said in its pre-1982 constitutional decisions. But when did minority and white voters stand on "equal" electoral footing, such that a districting scheme, for instance, was "fair"? In the two most important of those decisions, *Whitcomb v. Chavis* (in 1971) and *White v. Regester* (two years later) the high Court had directed trial courts to assess the electoral environment—the setting in which the voting took place.[31] Judges had thus been asked to distinguish the failure of minority voters to elect candidates of their choice for reasons of race from normal electoral defeat—that to which every group, however defined, was vulnerable. It had been, however, a very tall order. What criteria distinguished the one setting from the other?

It wasn't clear and it couldn't be. Unequal electoral opportunity was an elusive concept. Did black and white Democratic Party voters stand on the same electoral footing when the candidates of their choice were regularly defeated in a particular county? Or were blacks distinctively entitled to some degree of representation? As Justice Felix Frankfurter had pointed out in 1962 (dissenting in *Baker v. Carr*), we can only know if voters are adequately represented if we know who counts as a representative.[32] In other words, we need a theoretical framework. Without settled standards, how could judges weigh such competing considerations as the value of an experienced incumbent and the need to respect traditional political boundaries, for instance? His question still resonated twenty years later.

In an important 1994 Supreme Court decision, *Johnson v. De Grandy*, Justice David Souter, writing for the majority, noted that "one may suspect vote dilution from political famine, but one is not entitled to suspect (much less infer) dilution from mere failure to guarantee a political feast."[33] A "feast" was obviously a plan that ensured minority officeholding in excess of proportional representation: an occasional treat, not an absolute right. But what constituted a famine? That was the question the Court didn't and couldn't answer.

De Grandy involved a redistricting plan for the Florida state legislature that ensured proportional racial and ethnic representation. It was thus easy to turn down the plaintiffs' extraordinary demand for more. But what about a districting scheme in which only 20 percent of the seats are safe for black candidates, when the state is 30 percent African-American? Or suppose that a Republican-dominated, white-majority town elects its governing council at large, and that African American candidates (all Democrats) generally lose.[34] Are the town's black residents, a small numerical minority, politically famished, and thus entitled to relief? White Democrats lose elections because they're Democrats; does race—and race alone—defeat those who are black?

The Court in *De Grandy* answered neither these nor other equally important questions, for reasons it made plain in another 1994 voting rights decision: *Holder v. Hall*.[35] *Holder* involved a rural Georgia county that had been governed by a single commissioner since 1912. No African American had ever occupied the office, raising the question of whether such a concentration of power in one office denied black voters their proper opportunity to elect the candidates of their choice. The Court held that a challenge to the size of a governing body could not be brought under the Voting Rights Act. How could a judge assess the legitimacy of a sole-commissioner form of government without knowing how many commissioners there should be? They would need a standard against which to measure the adequacy of the representation. And yet "there has been no principled reason why one size should be picked over another," the Court said.[36] Fair enough. But, as Justice Clarence Thomas pointed out in a long and eloquent concurring opinion, there is no principled benchmark in redistricting cases either.[37] On a five-member city council in a municipality that is 40 percent black, what is the right number of safe black districts? If the answer is two, why?

A PARTIAL ANSWER

Section 2 asked courts to measure an inadequately defined phenomenon—electoral inequality. Nevertheless, some guidance was provided. For instance, in adopting the legal standard contained in *Whitcomb* and *White,* Congress clearly rejected a head count of African Americans holding public office as the measure of discrimination. Black voters were guaranteed not their "fair share" of political offices, but only a "fair shake"—a chance to play the electoral game by fair rules. That is, the provision unequivocally rejected the notion that black voters were entitled to legislative seats reserved for black officeholders. The language "representatives of their choice" plainly suggested a definition of representation broader than that which would have been conveyed had the wording been *"minority* representatives of their choice."

In addition, the concern was clearly with elections held in racist settings. Blacks, Congress concluded, lacked an equal chance to elect representatives of their choice where race had left them politically isolated—without potential allies in electoral contests. That focus was spelled out both in the 1982 hearings and in the Senate Judiciary Committee Report of that same year.

The report thus listed "factors" to which courts were instructed to refer in judging the merits of a vote dilution suit. The point of the list was clear: to help judges identify those situations in which either a history of discrimination or ongoing racism had left minority voters at a distinctive disadvantage in the electoral process. Not only the list, but other language in the report signaled the importance of past and present racism. The Senate Subcommittee on the Constitution had expressed concern that all races lost by black candidates would be seen as racially tainted.[38] Not so, retorted the full committee's own report. In *"most"* jurisdictions white voters give substantial support to black candidates. But "unfortunately," the report noted, ". . . there still are some communities . . . where racial politics do dominate the electoral process."[39]

Others made the same argument, Armand Derfner, a leading civil rights attorney and key witness at the 1982 hearings, testified that single-member districts had no "precisely correct racial mix." The entitlement was not to districts that were, say, two-thirds black, one-third white—districts designed to protect minority candidates from white competition. Section 2 only promised an electoral process that was fluid—open to racial change—not "frozen." Would minority voters have "some influence"? courts were expected to ask. Claims of dilution would rest, Derfner said, on "evidence that voters of a racial minority [were] isolated within a political system . . . 'shut out,' i.e., denied access . . . [without] the opportunity to participate in the electoral process."[40]

When were minorities "frozen" out? Neither Derfner nor any other witness offered a definition of that total electoral exclusion against which the act protected, except to say that the test had been met when a group had "really been unfairly throttled."[41] "Unfairly throttled" by racism, the Senate report— and the entire history of the act—had made clear. The point of the statute, after all, had been effective enforcement of Fifteenth Amendment rights, and in 1982 those who wanted Section 2 revised did not object to the Supreme Court's focus on racism, but only to its alleged insistence on hard evidence of racist motive.

In revising Section 2, Congress thus unequivocally and properly rejected the notion of group entitlement to even one legislative seat—however concentrated or dispersed black residential patterns were found to be.[42] Group membership would be significant only where blacks could prove themselves distinctively excluded from the electoral process. An increase in the number of majority-black single-member districts was viewed as a remedy, not a right. A remedy for that total exclusion against which Section 2 was seen to protect.

This is a history upon which both courts and the Justice Department turned their backs. Section 2 quickly became a means to insist on methods of election likely to maximize black officeholding wherever possible—nationwide.[43] It was a predictable revision of the statute—and indeed was predicted in 1982. To judge electoral systems by their "results" was implicitly to measure electoral equity by the standard of proportional racial representation. By what other measure would "you evaluate the totality of circumstances, as the statute would demand?" Senator Orrin Hatch asked at the congressional hearings on the proposed amendment. "How [would] you weigh all the factors?"[44] Or as James F. Blumstein, professor of law at Vanderbilt University, testified, courts would be asked to judge deviation from the norm of electoral equality, but "what [could] the norm possibly be except racially based entitlements?" The "trend towards using an easy standard, the numbers standard" would be "inexorable," he predicted.[45]

He was right. In part, however, because the civil rights groups believed the standard was correct, and their view became that of many federal judges: in a racially fair society blacks would hold public office in proportion to the black population. Discrimination was evident from the numbers. Only blacks could represent blacks.

THE NEW SECTION 2

"We have not yet secured . . . the right of every American . . . to wield that awesome power to which every American citizen is entitled"—namely, the right to vote, the assistant attorney general for civil rights in the Clinton administration said in 1994.[46] But while Deval Patrick depicted the current struggle for civil rights as indistinguishable from that in the mid-1960s, in fact neither the aims of that earlier era nor the means of attaining them bear any resemblance to those of today.[47] In 1965 blacks and whites risked their lives marching from Selma to Montgomery to secure basic Fifteenth Amendment rights; thirty years later "voting rights" has become a cause that has lost its earlier moral clarity.[48] Plaintiffs in voting rights cases come to seek not a basic constitutional right, but districting plans drawn to provide maximum protection from white competition for minority candidates. They want affirmative action arrangements that will remove minority candidates from the rough-and-tumble world of normal politics, ensuring (to the degree possible) minority officeholding at least in proportion to the minority population.[49]

Often that demand is made in settings in which there is already considerable black electoral success. Take *Barnett v. City of Chicago,* a voting rights suit brought in a jurisdiction in which minorities were already, by ordinary standards, political insiders—important partners in the politics of the city.[50] The case involved Chicago's fifty aldermanic (city council) districts. Plaintiffs argued that the existing map distributed the city's legislative seats unfairly; additional majority-black (and majority-Hispanic) wards could be drawn. The city contained roughly equal numbers of whites and blacks, and yet blacks were a smaller presence on the city council. On the other hand, there were considerably more voting-age whites than blacks and proportional officeholding was not an entitlement under the Voting Rights Act. In addition, counting whites and minorities on the council was only one way of looking at the picture. The city contained one majority-black ward that had elected a white. And in a quarter of the wards from which white aldermen had been elected, black and Hispanics were the numerical majority. Were those white aldermen, elected by minority voters, unable adequately to represent their nonwhite constituents? They certainly could not afford to ignore them; indeed two were plaintiffs in the case.

Barnett thus posed the question that would not go away: Was this a setting in which minority voters lacked an "equal opportunity to elect the candidates of their choice," as plaintiffs alleged? And if so, what was the standard against which "inequality" was to be judged? If the definition of electoral equality had been a problem from the outset, it had gotten worse over time. Chicago was a northern city with a long history of black political participation, a record of black success in two mayoral contests, and solid black representation on the city council. Not only were blacks well-represented in the city; by 1995, when the suit was filed, Chicago had already engaged in a great deal of race-conscious line-drawing. And the result was a very high level of protection for minority candidates—nearly as many safe minority seats, wards in which whites were not even tempted to run, as could possibly be provided. In cases like *Barnett*, the question of equal "opportunity"—that which the Section 2 poses—has become: When is enough truly enough in the way of race-conscious legislative districting?

The Florida redistricting plan that was challenged in *De Grandy* fell just short of containing every last possible majority-minority state legislative district. Were states compelled, under the Voting Rights Act, to draw districts in which "keep-out" signs, directed at white candidates, were posted at all possible spots? Not quite, the Court said. The proportional racial and ethnic representation that the plan provided, along with other "relevant facts," indicated that minority voters had adequate opportunity to participate in the political process and elect the candidates of their choice.

Had the Florida plan provided less than proportional representation for its black (and Hispanic) residents, plaintiffs would likely have won, as they did in the district court.[51] By 1994, when *De Grandy* reached the Supreme Court, the protection provided by Section 2 bore almost no relation to that which had been proposed in 1982. The provision was advertised as an unwieldy tool to be used in exceptional circumstances—a tool no different from the Fourteenth Amendment before the decision in *Mobile*. As it turned out, however, Section 2 suits became neither infrequent nor difficult to win.[52] They became so easy, in fact, that jurisdictions whose electoral methods had been challenged seldom went to court. *Barnett* was the exceptional full-scale trial; the city, county, or other unit of government whose method of electing commissioners was challenged most often simply gave up and met the plaintiffs' demands. It was cheaper, faster, and in a biracial setting politically safer. A spokesman for a Texas municipality that had shifted from citywide voting to single-member districts put the point simply: "Because of recent changes in the law," he said, his city "felt a voluntary move to single-member districts to be more efficient from an economic and political standpoint."[53]

CONSTITUTIONAL SECOND THOUGHTS

By the early 1990s, as one scholar has put it, the combination of Sections 2 and 5 had made the Voting Rights Act a "brooding omnipresence." Fear of voting rights litigation along with the greater black presence in legislative halls had prompted the creation of an unprecedented number of majority-black districts, especially in the South.[54] In jurisdictions with significant minority populations, at-large voting (the object of countless threatened Section 2 suits) was heading toward extinction, and wherever redistricting maps failed to maximize the potential for black officeholding, jurisdictions found themselves in court battling plaintiffs who had a "better" plan. But quite suddenly an unexpected roadblock appeared, bringing to a halt what had been such an unimpeded, successful drive for race-based districting.

The line of Fourteenth Amendment cases that struggled to define electoral equality in the years 1965 to 1980 came to an abrupt stop with the congressional revision of Section 2 in 1982, which allowed plaintiffs to pose the old constitutional question of electoral equality in a new and more receptive statutory context. And to this day, vote "dilution"—black votes without their proper weight—remains a question that arises only in Section 2 cases. But in 1993, in *Shaw v. Reno,* Fourteenth Amendment voting rights suits made a surprising comeback—although in very different form. The constitutional question reemerged, radically changed. The issue now was not equal electoral opportunity, but instead the limits imposed by the Fourteenth Amendment on precisely that race-conscious districting that was the remedy of choice in constitutional and (after 1982) Section 2 suits, and on which the Justice Department so freely insisted in its Section 5 enforcement. How race-conscious could districting be, given the limits imposed by the equal-protection clause on policies that deliberately divided whites from blacks? That was the central issue posed in *Miller v. Johnson,* the Georgia case.

Until 1993 black plaintiffs in Section 2 cases had gone to court to assert their right to have their race explicitly acknowledged. That is, they demanded highly race-conscious electoral arrangements, most often race-based single-member districts that ensured minority officeholding. But *Shaw* raised a new question: was not the racial sorting of citizens constitutionally suspect? Race-based districting, the Court held in *Shaw,* is actually no different from other forms of discriminatory state action. "A plaintiff challenging a reapportionment statute under the Equal Protection Clause may state a claim by alleging that the legislation, though race-neutral on its face, rationally cannot be understood as anything other than an attempt to separate voters into different districts on the basis of race, and that the separation lacks sufficient justification."[55] Districts that constitute race-based classifications, in short, are not distinctive; they, too, are subject to strict judicial scrutiny.[56]

"In order to get beyond racism, we must first take account of race," Justice Blackmun had said in *Bakke* (1978), as we noted in Chapter 14.[57] It was that highly dubious notion that had informed the first line of Fourteenth Amendment decisions sanctioning race-based districting. And it was that idea that *Shaw* implicitly challenged. Taking race into account—drawing race-conscious legislative districting lines—may not get us beyond race at all,

Justice Sandra Day O'Connor suggested, writing for the majority. In fact, race-consciousness may widen the racial divide, heightening our sense of racial identity. It was a point reiterated in 1995 by Justice Kennedy in *Miller v. Johnson,* who quoted at length from *Shaw.*[58]

If the very remedy for electoral discrimination so frequently ordered by courts and the Justice Department was now under close scrutiny, the switch had to be seen as a sign of changed times. The country had come a long way. With the tremendous number of blacks holding office, in the 1990s, racial *exclusion* from the political arena may no longer be the main problem, the Court implied in *Shaw.* Racial and ethnic fragmentation, driven in part by racial districting and other public policies, was perhaps the greater danger.

CLASSIFYING VOTERS BY RACE

Race-based districting raised constitutional questions, the Court held in *Shaw.* But when was a state sorting voters along lines of race in such a way as to violate the equal protection clause? Justice O'Connor's answer in 1993 was neither altogether reassuring nor entirely clear. "This Court never has held that race-conscious redistricting is impermissible in *all* circumstances," she wrote.[59] Sometimes it was okay, in other words—just your everyday, garden-variety "reasonable" racial classification. But problems clearly arose when a district was "so extremely irregular on its face that it rationally [could] be viewed only as an effort to segregate the races for purposes of voting, without regard for traditional districting principles and without sufficiently compelling justification."[60] "Bizarre" districts, "unexplainable on grounds other than race," were thus the source of concern. Districts that looked bad *were* bad. Highly irregular contours obviously drawn with race in mind suggested racial stereotyping, reinforcing "the perception that members of the same racial group . . . think alike."[61]

And yet surely contours less "highly irregular" could also be drawn "with race in mind." Shape, as Justice Kennedy acknowledged in *Miller,* could not be the only test. In 1994 a lower court had decided a case involving a challenge to Louisiana's fourth congressional district, and in both *Hays v. Louisiana* and *Miller,* the "looks bad" test was supplemented by essentially uncontroverted direct trial evidence that clearly established the overriding importance of race.[62] In *Hays,* the contours of the fourth district could "only be explained credibly as the product of race-conscious decisionmaking," the trial court had concluded; twelve of the fifteen parishes the district contained had been split, as had four of the top seven cities in the state.[63] In the Georgia case, too, the contours of the eleventh district, as we noted above, were determined by "a far-flung search for black voters."[64]

That "far-flung search" had been greatly aided by extraordinarily detailed census information and highly sophisticated computer technology made avail-able in the post-1990 round of redistricting. As the trial court in its 1994 decision in a Texas case put it, the state drew its map "with nearly exact knowledge of the racial makeup of every inhabited block of land in the state. This insight, worthy of Orwell's Big Brother, was attainable because computer technology . . . superimposed at a touch of the keyboard block-by-block racial census statistics upon the detailed local maps vital to the redistricting pro-cess." The software that was used meant that racial and ethnic data were displayed on the computer screen at all times; "racial data were an omnipres-ent ingredient in the redistricting process."[65] The resulting districts had bor-ders that switched from one side of a street to the other, and that traversed as well bodies of water and commercially developed areas "in seemingly arbitrary fashion until one realiz[ed] that those corridors connect[ed] minority popula-tions."[66]

"If these [Texas] districts—tortuously constructed block-by-block . . . to sat-isfy the desired racial goal, are constitutional, then the State could more easily hand each voter a racial identification card and allow him to participate in racially separate elections," the district court concluded.[67] And yet the Con-gressional Black Caucus persistently described all such districts as "among the *least* segregated . . . in the Nation."[68] In Louisiana, Georgia, Texas, and elsewhere, these majority-black constituencies did of course contain signifi-cant numbers of white voters. But they were politically 100 percent black; the whites within their boundaries were included so as not to waste black ballots, as two proponents of race-based districting have acknowledged with re-freshing candor.[69] A 65 percent black district is a sure seat for an African-American candidate; additional black voters are superfluous.

That is, these are districts in which only black ballots are meant to count. They have been designed to become safe black seats.[70] In fact, whites who have been tempted to run in a majority-black constituency have often been informed that the color of their skin disqualified them—that they were tread-ing where they did not belong. In 1992 several members of the U.S. House of Representatives chose to retire or move to other districts under pressure from black leaders to let blacks run in Democratic primaries free from white competition in those districts that had been designed for them.[71]

Thus, as the Court made clear in *Miller,* Georgia's eleventh and other majority-black districts constituted racial classifications not because they looked bizarre (the emphasis in *Shaw*), but because the classification of voters by race was precisely their point.[72] When the DOJ drew a map for South Carolina's House districts in the post-1990 reapportionment round, a voting section attorney actually went so far as to label districts either "B" or "W," although at the trial on the constitutionality of such racial sorting, she could not "speculate as to why [she] wrote that on the map."[73] In Georgia, too, districts were clearly "B" and "W"—race, not community, having so obviously determined their tortured contours. Race was "the predominant factor motivating the legislature's decision to place a significant number of voters within or without a particular district."[74] Indeed, those districts were intentionally race-based for a goal their proponents believed in: maximizing black officeholding.

Until the Court's 1993 decision in *Shaw v. Reno,* minority voting rights was perhaps the most debatable, yet least debated, of all affirmative action issues. The enforcement of the 1965 act was controversial policy that stirred no controversy. It was scarcely an exaggeration to say that race-conscious action in the electoral sphere had only adherents. The opposition to busing was loud and clear; behind closed doors, affirmative action in employment was certainly discussed. But protest against racial gerrymandering to increase minority officeholding was confined to the odd academic. Who else was likely to object? Black and white parents cared where their children went to school, but few voters paid attention to the rules by which their county governing board was elected.

The constitutional decisions turned an obscure issue into headline news. Race-conscious strategies are often hard to discuss because the basic facts are so successfully kept under wraps. Districting is different. That is, affirmative action programs at colleges, for instance, also amount to protective racial sorting; by setting racially separate admissions standards, they pit African-American applicants primarily (sometimes only) against other members of the racial group. But almost no school will publicly describe how its affirmative action policy works. With race-conscious districting, on the other hand, a quick glance at the map makes the racial sorting perfectly obvious.

Take the North Carolina map at issue in *Shaw.* When the Justice Department forced the state to create a second safe black congressional seat, the result was a long, exceedingly thin district that stretched approximately 160 miles along an interstate highway. As Justice O'Connor wrote in *Shaw,* the district wound "in snake-like fashion through tobacco country, financial centers, and manufacturing areas 'until it gobble[d] in enough enclaves of black neighborhoods.' "[75] "If you drove down the interstate with both car doors open," one state legislator quipped, "you'd kill most of the people in the district."[76] This seemingly ridiculous situation actually raised serious issues, deeply troubling to a number of commentators generally sympathetic to affirmative action. Stuart Taylor, Jr., a widely respected writer on legal affairs, was among them. The redistricting process has been transformed into a "race-driven spoils system more likely to aggravate than to heal [racial] divisions," Taylor wrote not long after the decision in *Shaw.*[77]

That was not how the civil rights community saw the decisions. The Supreme Court had suddenly threatened black gains. Race-conscious districting had substantially increased the size of the Congressional Black Caucus (and added black members to state legislatures and other governing bodies as well).

The number of African Americans in Congress increased from twenty-six in 1990 to thirty-nine in 1993, with almost half (seventeen) elected from the South. What would happen now?

IN THE BACK OF A TAXICAB

The answer was perfectly clear, in the view of Theodore Shaw of the NAACP Legal Defense and Education Fund. If plaintiffs won in these constitutional cases, he had predicted, the minority members of Congress "could meet in the back seat of a taxicab."[78] It became an oft-repeated image. Laughlin McDonald, an Atlanta-based voting rights specialist for the ACLU, described a Supreme Court "determined to dismantle the structure of civil rights in this country," the result of which would be "a return to the days of all-white government."[79] "Ethnic cleansing," Jesse Jackson called the decisions.[80] The Supreme Court's constitutional rulings "really torch the fundamental right of African-Americans, Hispanics and others to be included as participatory citizens in this democracy," Elaine Jones, director of the NAACP Legal Defense and Education Fund, said.[81] Voting rights scholar Pamela Karlan worried that with decisions like *Shaw,* "the Voting Rights Act may be finished."[82]

Civil rights pessimism—the belief that racism remained pervasive and undiminished—had blinded voting rights advocates to a changed America. In the wake of the 1996 congressional elections, it will take a mighty big back seat of a taxicab to hold the Congressional Black Caucus; in fact, its members would fill a bus. The 104th Congress, elected in 1994, had thirty-eight black members in the House; the 105th has thirty-seven. Louisiana representative Cleo Fields decided not to run after his district was redrawn (following the Court's decision in *Hays*), and Connecticut representative Gary Franks, a Republican, was defeated. But in Indiana, Julia Carson ran in the 69 percent white tenth district and won with 53 percent of the vote.[83]

In short, every member of the Congressional Black Caucus whose constituency had become majority-white in the postlitigation round of districting and who nevertheless chose to run was reelected. In Georgia, Cynthia McKinney whose very liberal politics might have been expected to disqualify her in the South, won with 58 percent of the vote in a district only 35 percent black, although two years earlier she had said that black officeholders faced "the same level of extinction" as they did during Reconstruction.[84] Her Georgia colleague Sanford Bishop also had a constituency only 35 percent black and was elected with 54 percent of the vote. In Florida, Representative Corinne Brown won with 61 percent of the vote in a newly drawn district only 42 percent African-American. The story in Texas was much the same, although the districts were Hispanic as well as white and (minority) black.[85] These victorious candidates—African-American members of Congress who won where they couldn't possibly win—attributed their success to the power of incumbency.[86] But prior to the election, none had mentioned incumbency as an advantage, and indeed they were not incumbents in the redrawn districts in which they were forced to run. The constituencies that sent them back to the House were those that had been (allegedly) "ethnically cleansed."

With the Republican ascendancy in 1994, no group in Congress was more politically marginalized than the Congressional Black Caucus, whose members tend to hover at the left end of the political spectrum. In Chapter 11 we suggested that congressional districts that were deliberately drawn to be overwhelmingly black invited the sort of ideological militance that became the model for the black legislative candidate. In contrast to the more heavily white cities in which blacks have been elected mayors, these districts beckoned candidates with racially strident voices.[87] If true, then settings in which candidates are forced to forge biracial coalitions will send representatives to Congress who are more centrist—and thus less politically marginalized.

There is a related point. With fewer majority-black districts and a greater number in which African Americans are the swing vote, the likelihood is *more* black representation—defined, that is, as Democrats (black and white) closely allied with the civil rights community. Race-driven districting, especially in the South, benefited the Republican Party. The concentration of black voters in black districts further "whitened" those that were already majority-white, and overwhelmingly white districts were just what Republican candidates liked. The point has frequently been made with respect to the roughly fifteen seats the GOP picked up in Congress as a consequence of the racial redistricting after 1990; the process was apparent at the local and state level well before that.[88] Thus, in Jefferson County, Alabama, an out-of-court settlement in 1985 replaced an at-large system (under which only whites had been elected) with five single-member districts. Two safe black seats were created, leaving three that were equally safely white—and Republican. Unless unopposed, Democrats could not win in districts drained of black voters, and in 1986 two Democratic incumbents lost.[89]

The civil rights community wanted an absolute guarantee of black officeholding, and politicians, whatever their color, like safe districts in which to run. But the price black voters paid for the race-driven districting (to which the NAACP and the GOP were equally committed) has arguably been high. And thus the Supreme Court's constitutional decisions, reducing the number of majority-black districts, may well have been a political gift to black voters —as some black legislators have acknowledged. "As an African-American," Georgia state representative Calvin Smyre said in 1995, "I want as much black representation in the U.S Congress as possible. But at the same time, what have we gained? We gained a large Congressional Black Caucus, but we lost all the chairmanships and the subcommittee chairmanships, where the power really lies."[90]

Reluctant Swimmers in the Biracial Waters

The 1996 congressional elections did not return those chairmanships to black Democrats (Republicans still controlled both houses), but they did send back to the House every black Democratic incumbent who ran. How could civil rights spokesmen have been so mistaken in their dire preelection predictions? In part, they had their eyes glued to the wrong history. Reviewing the debate over white willingness to vote for black candidates, Steven A. Holmes of the *New York Times* noted the skepticism of "traditional civil rights advocates and others on the left." In the early 1970s, they said, 2 percent of majority-white legislative districts in the eleven states of the old Confederacy were represented by black lawmakers; in the 1980s, the figure dropped to 1 percent.[91] But to judge the potential in 1996 by the record in the 1970s and 1980s is to miss the story of enormous change in white racial attitudes, one result of which has been the rise of a black political class many of whose members owe their positions to white support. As Chapter 11 noted, between 1967 and 1993 blacks won the mayor's seat in eighty-seven cities with a population of 50,000 or more. In two-thirds of those cities blacks were a minority of the population.[92]

The mayor's office may be more accessible than a congressional seat. Congressional campaigns are hard to launch. The districts are not only large; unlike cities, which usually have only one major newspaper, they contain within them several media markets and many of their residents are often widely dispersed.[93] Get-out-the-vote efforts are thus usually more difficult than in cities even such as New York, whose black poor (prone to low voter turnout) are residentially concentrated. In addition, the distance between city council seat and mayor's office is shorter than from, say, state legislature to Congress. City councils are usually small, and name recognition—an essential ingredient in a successful campaign—is easily achieved. On the other hand, the state representative who has been elected from a constituency of, say, 25,000, is hardly known in a congressional district more than twenty times as large. Are congressional contests, then, exactly like a mayor's race? No. But is the record of black mayoral success relevant? Yes—as the 1996 House returns confirmed.

Successful black candidates for Congress who run in majority-white constituencies must run the centrist campaigns that characterize most municipal elections, however. As Chapter 11 suggested, most black contenders cannot hope to win if their platform is significantly to the left of the white voters whose support they need. It's a race-blind rule: white candidates also lose if their views are out of sync with those of the voters. David Bositis, a senior fellow at the Joint Center for Political and Economic Studies, and others have nevertheless complained that the burden on blacks is especially heavy. "Why is it there are white leaders who can represent extreme positions within the white community and that's O.K?" he has asked. "Why is it that black officials have to move to the center?"[94]

The answer should be obvious: they wouldn't have to *move* to the center if that is where they started out. The center is where the majority of voters are —most of whom are white. And the center is also where the majority of white candidates feel at home, which means they need do no political traveling. To say that the doors of political opportunity are generally open is not to argue that they are open to black candidates with any and all political convictions. Colin Powell can win the presidency, the polling data suggest; Jesse Jackson cannot.

The number of black legislators in Congress and elsewhere will remain limited if African-American candidates are not willing to wade into the biracial waters—to run in majority-white constituencies and put together biracial coalitions. In 1996 a number of black incumbents ran in majority-white districts newly drawn as a consequence of Supreme Court decisions, but prior to that election, few black candidates were ready to do so. Representatives Julia Carson (D-Ind.), Gary Franks (R-Conn.), J. C. Watts (R-Okla.), Ron Dellums (D-Calif.): they have been part of a very small group of African Americans elected to Congress in majority-white settings.

Black candidates cannot win elections in which they do not run. And social scientists who calculate the odds of winning in a majority-white constituency cannot assess contests in which there has been no black candidate in the race. The scholarly literature on voting rights is littered with such statements as "The state's history demonstrates no evidence for the election of African Americans to the state legislature or the U.S. House of Representatives other than in majority-minority districts."[95] But the authors of such statements (often quoted by the civil rights community) are reviewing a history in which potential black candidates, even in recent years, have stayed on the political sidelines.

In fact, had Cynthia McKinney read the scholarly literature and listened to the voices of civil rights activists, she would have known she could not possibly win in a 65 percent majority-white district in Georgia. It's an oddly discouraging line for civil rights advocates to peddle. They have been telling potential candidates, in effect, don't bother to run; it's hopeless. And to black voters they say: don't bother to vote unless you can cast your ballots in a majority-black setting; where whites are a majority, you waste your time.

Even after the successes of the 1996 elections, the drumbeat of self-defeating pessimism persisted. On December 9, 1996 black voters from Georgia, represented by the ACLU and Department of Justice, returned to the Supreme Court where they urged a restoration of one of the two discarded majority-black districts.[96] In winning handily in majority-white constituencies in that Deep South state, Cynthia McKinney and Sanford Bishop had made history; in insisting that they were still in need of electoral arrangements that protected black candidates from white competition, McKinney and Bishop were (in effect) asking the Court to ignore those significant victories. They had remained reluctant swimmers in the biracial waters that just a month earlier had proven so hospitable to them.

BUT WHAT ABOUT SECTION 5?

The year 1993 was a turning point. *Shaw* and its progeny significantly altered the rules of the districting game. Just how significantly was unclear, however. A central question had not been answered: What did the Voting Rights Act itself demand? Had the Court's concern with the racial sorting of citizens set the Constitution and the Voting Rights Act on a collision course, as a number of scholars subsequently argued?[97] Did not the Voting Rights Act itself explicitly demand race-conscious districting? If so, what the Fourteenth Amendment forbade, the act required.

The issue had been touched upon in several of the constitutional decisions. In *Shaw* the Court had referred to the possibility that the State of North Carolina, in drawing a second majority-black district, "went beyond what was reasonably necessary to avoid retrogression"—the discriminatory effect against which Section 5 protected.[98] Much the same point was made in *Bush v. Vera*, a case involving the constitutionality of race-conscious districting in Texas.[99] But it was not the state that was out of bounds in these cases; the source of the problem, as the Georgia decision noted, was the Justice Department which, in insisting on "max-black" and other such plans, had "expanded its authority under the statute beyond what Congress intended and [the Court had] upheld."[100]

A new districting plan that improved the political position of blacks could not be called discriminatory, the Supreme Court had said in *Beer*. But the Department of Justice had long played fast and loose with the definition of "retrogression"—the Court's term for backsliding. In the 1980s, for instance, voting section attorneys often argued that since existing districting plans inevitably became malapportioned with the passage of time, any newly drawn plan should be compared not to an existing map, but to a hypothetical, racially "fair" alternative. A plan that was not "fairly drawn" was thus "retrogressive." As the voting section staff explained in a 1981 memo to William Bradford Reynolds, the assistant attorney general for civil rights, calculating what was "fair" was simple; the standard was proportional black officeholding.[101] The argument had a small problem: retrogression was a comparative test, but to ask whether a districting plan is "fairly drawn" was to measure discriminatory effect by some absolute standard of racial fairness. Nevertheless such calculations became a routine part of the preclearance process.

Under Section 5, discriminatory "effect" was one question, discriminatory "purpose" another. But the two gradually became indistinguishable. And thus by 1991 John R. Dunne, the top civil rights enforcement officer in the Bush administration, was openly warning that "discriminatory purpose means a design or desire to restrict a minority group's voting strength . . . below the level which that minority group might have enjoyed under a fairly drawn plan." [102] At the trial on the constitutional issues raised by race-conscious districting Louisiana and Georgia, the Department of Justice readily acknowledged that the first plans submitted had no retrogressive effect. Nevertheless, it refused to clear them. Allegedly better ones could be drawn, and the failure to do so was a sin of omission that betrayed discriminatory intent, the department concluded. [103]

As a number of lower courts had recognized, the revised definition of purpose was an indefensible distortion of the law—and common sense. [104] If the question of discriminatory intent could be answered by counting the number of safe black districts, then that of discriminatory effect—to which the provision separately refers—became superfluous. Every electoral plan with an allegedly insufficient number of safe black districts was presumed to be infected with racist intent. [105] In addition, the Department's position turned the enforcement of a federal law over to the civil rights groups. It gave every organization with a "preferable" districting scheme—one that seems to ensure more black officeholding—the power to veto a proposed districting plan. Of course, that was precisely what happened in the case of Georgia: federal attorneys allowed the American Civil Liberties Union to assume the government's job.

Was the Court's interpretation of the Fourteenth Amendment—its finding that a number of majority-black districts constituted impermissible racial classifications—on a collision course with Section 5, as proponents of such districting alleged? Not unless one accepts the Justice Department's erroneous interpretation of the law.

THE QUESTION OF SECTION 2

Where did the Court's decisions leave Section 2, however? Were the constitutional considerations raised in *Shaw* and subsequent cases heading for conflict with the demands of the 1982 provision? "The state drew Districts 18, 29, and 30 in order to comply with Section 2 of the Voting Rights Act," the Justice Department brief in *Bush v. Vera*, the Texas case, stated. A court would most likely have required the same number of majority-minority districts, the Democratic National Committee declared. [106] But what a court would have demanded had plaintiffs prevailed in an actual Section 2 suit was irrelevant. The provision was standard remedial legislation; black voters had to prove in court a violation of their statutory right to equal electoral opportunity before they were entitled to even one deliberately drawn safe black district. [107]

In part, Texas and other states had drawn the challenged districts not because they felt legally obligated to do so, but in order to forestall the possibility of future Section 2 suits. Litigation is costly and disruptive. Redistricting is a politically complex and laborious process, and to design a plan that is not litigation-proof may be a waste of extensive political effort. That Texas wanted to play it safe was understandable, but it was not a consideration so compelling as to override the deep and proper suspicion of all racial classifications built into the law.

Section 2 has come to play another role in districting and other voting rights cases: as an element in the Section 5 preclearance process. Plans that jurisdictions present for federal approval are reviewed not only for the obvious elements in Section 5—discriminatory purpose and effect—but also for their possible violation of the Section 2 "results" test. In January 1993, Bossier Parish (County), Louisiana, submitted its proposed map for school board elections to the U.S. Attorney General. The parish was 20 percent black and the plan contained no majority-black districts; it was identical, however, to a police jury map—one drawn for the local legislative body—that had already been precleared. Nevertheless, on the basis of "new information"—namely, the existence of a proposed alternative plan that promised two safe black seats —the Justice Department objected. Among its arguments: while the school board was not required to "adopt any particular plan, it is not free to adopt a plan that unnecessarily limits the opportunity for minority voters to elect candidates of choice"—which was, of course, the language of Section 2. And indeed, when the case went to court, the Justice Department stated explicitly that it could not preclear a plan that ran afoul of Section 2.[108]

A three-judge panel of the D.C. district court flatly rejected the federal government's "latest—and by now rather shopworn—effort to squeeze Section 2 into Section 5."[109] As the court recognized, in 1982, when Section 2 was transformed from an inconsequential preamble into a powerful instrument for ridding the nation of methods of election with a discriminatory "result," there was literally no discussion of a consequent change in Section 5.[110] In fact, during the debates of 1981 and 1982, civil rights spokesmen directly and indirectly assured members of Congress that the amendment of Section 2 would not alter the preclearance provision.[111]

Those assurances fell on deaf administrative ears. In January 1987 the Justice Department "incorporated" Section 2 into Section 5, changing the legal standards by which submitted maps and other changes in the method of voting were assessed. An objection would henceforth be lodged if the proposed change was arguably discriminatory in purpose or effect (the Section 5 questions)—or "result" (Section 2), with the burden on the submitting jurisdiction to prove the racial neutrality of its proposed action. The Department of Justice thus unilaterally and drastically rewrote Section 5—on the assumption, evidently, that Congress had implicitly done so, acting without debate.[112] And yet, in justifying such a radical overhaul of a key provision—one whose limits were clearly understood—the department could point only to one foot-note, buried in the 1982 Senate Judiciary Committee Report and unsupported by the text to which it was appended.[113]

The change in Section 5 had no basis in legislative history, and the Justice Department had assumed an inappropriate role. Federal administrators, re-mote from the scene, became plaintiff, defendant, and judge all rolled into one, with no reliable way of gathering information on race and politics in the local jurisdiction remotely comparable to that which opposing attorneys present at a trial. Retrogression is a manageable before-and-after test, but cases resting on Section 2 involve complex questions of electoral opportunity; courts are asked to judge whether the "totality of circumstances," for instance, in the city of Chicago suggest electoral inequality between minority and white citizens. Adjudicating competing claims about racial fairness requires, as the Supreme Court noted in 1973, an "intensely local appraisal"—the specific detailed knowledge that only a court can obtain.[114] It was for that reason precisely that Section 2 (as written and understood at the time) did not offer—as Section 5 did—the option of administrative preclearance as an alternative to a full-scale court proceeding in which evidence and rebuttal evidence is presented.[115] Administrative procedures are no substitute for a trial.

To allow a process of federal administrative review to settle the broad and subtle question of equal electoral opportunity is to permit excessive intrusion upon constitutionally sanctioned local prerogatives.[116] Section 5, by all ac-counts, was a drastic provision. Districting and other voting-related changes became subject to federal veto if discrimination was even suspected. The provision placed the burden on the jurisdiction to prove the racial neutrality of its actions beyond any doubt. Section 5 thus entailed a radical shift in federal-state relations, originally sanctioned on an emergency basis and as-sumed to be of limited scope.

That limited scope remained critical. The point of preclearance was not to ensure optimal electoral arrangements for minority candidates, but to stop an already suspect jurisdiction from taking steps to minimize the impact of the enfranchisement guaranteed by other provisions in the act. By dictating the rules of election procedure, Section 5 objections override decisions arrived at democratically. To do so on the basis of suspected continuing inequality—with that suspicion resting on some unarticulated theory involving good gov-ernment and racial justice—would seem to strain the bounds of constitution-ality. Certainly the intrusiveness of such power strains the bounds of wisdom.

THE REAL ISSUES

In voting rights cases the argument between plaintiffs and defendants occurs on two levels, the second often largely hidden from sight. In plain view are disputes over such legal matters as the meaning of "retrogression," the relationship between preclearance and Section 2, and the demands of "strict scrutiny," as well as a medley of technical and normative questions. For instance: the proper benchmark by which to judge the level of black representation; whether white officeholders elected with black support qualify as black "representatives"; how to discern when minority voters have cohesive group interests different than those of whites; whether white support for black mayoral candidates is telling when the case involves city council elections.

Beneath the surface of the fancy legal and social science footwork, however, are the real questions that courts are implicitly asked to address in these minority voting rights cases—questions that go to the heart of how we see ourselves as a multiracial, multiethnic nation. At issue between the opposing sides in these cases are quite different views of American society, the place of blacks in it, its openness to change, and the costs of race-conscious policies. These are, of course, the central questions that run through all debates on affirmative action; in voting rights cases, they are but variations on a common theme.

The assumptions that inform opposing positions are thus familiar and predictable. In the Chicago case, for instance, the plaintiffs' experts looked only at the racially contested elections for the city council, a decision challenged by attorneys for the city who argued that blacks were electing a candidate of their choice when they cast their ballots for the winner in a white-on-white contest. Plaintiffs assumed that whites were never the true "choice" of blacks; race was the characteristic that counted.[117] White politicians were just as culturally at odds with black voters as white teachers were with black students. It was the two-nations view that permeates much civil rights writing—a view with which the city disagreed.

The belief that blacks and whites are different, that whites are not to be trusted on racial matters, and that historic discrimination continues to affect the status of blacks are the assumptions that run through almost all briefs for affirmative action. Those of voting rights advocates are no exception. What might appear to be strong evidence of white racial tolerance under particular circumstances (white support for Virginia gubernatorial candidate Douglas Wilder, for instance) is thus described as aberrational—nothing blacks can ever count on.[118] Moreover, in those exceptional races in which blacks do win in majority-white settings (the argument runs), those elected officeholders are not truly "black." As one scholar has put it, "black leadership of white majorities is not properly speaking to be regarded as black politics."[119]

In the Chicago case black voters lacked a "realistic opportunity" to elect the candidates of their choice in those wards in which there was not a "sufficient" black population—i.e., where blacks were not a substantial majority and thus protected from (racist) whites.[120] That was particularly the case because "the depressed socio-economic status of African Americans in Chicago" hindered their ability "to participate equally in the political process."[121] Hence the plaintiffs' demand that the city be carved into wards giving blacks a maximum number of safe city council seats; anything less, it was assumed, would diminish the representation of a group for whom members of no other groups could speak. Again, these were convictions fundamentally at odds with the view of the city's lawyers. Plaintiffs had referred obliquely to the "depressed socio-economic status" of blacks as "related to the effects of past discrimination," while the city saw poverty, crime, and single-parent households as problems with multiple and complex causes.[122] In addition, the defendants believed not only that many whites had shown themselves ready to vote for Mayor Harold Washington and other black candidates, but that (most importantly) individuals, not racial groups, had distinctive voices. Blacks could thus represent whites—and whites blacks.

This last point raised another basic issue. Plaintiffs in *Barnett* argued that blacks on Chicago's south and west sides shared "communities of interest."[123] And, by implication, "communities" did not contain both whites and blacks. But the city's blacks seemed to have a more complicated view. Thus, in the fall of 1995, black middle-class residents on the south side were openly hostile to planned low-rise public housing in the area—to an influx of residents with the same skin color but different incomes.[124] A few years earlier, middle-class blacks and whites had been allied in an effort to keep poor blacks out of their school attendance zone, and thus out of the neighborhood school.[125] In fact, one of the plaintiffs' experts, arguing that race could be used as a proxy for socioeconomic interests, ignored his own scholarship indicating that class, not race, defined a "community."[126]

Whether blacks across socioeconomic lines have distinctive interests and views, whether individuals are defined by the racial groups to which they belong, and whether white racism remains as virulent as ever: these are issues that usually hover between the lines in briefs and judicial decisions. But they did make an explicit appearance in *Shaw* and the subsequent constitutional cases in which the legitimacy of classifying citizens by race was the central question. "Racial classifications of any sort pose the risk of lasting harm to our society," Justice O'Connor said (writing for the Court) in *Shaw v. Reno*. "They reinforce the belief, held by too many for too much of our history, that individuals should be judged by the color of their skin." Race-conscious districts, she argued, carry a special risk. They "may balkanize us into competing racial factions . . . [and thus] carry us further from the goal of a political system in which race no long matters.[127]

That was the central message that ran from *Shaw* through *Bush* and *Miller*. "All citizens are stigmatized by the notion that their 'interests' can be defined by race or will be represented adequately only if a member of their racial 'group' holds a particular office," the district court in the Louisiana districting case concluded.[128] It was, of course, true as well of the segregated institutions of the Jim Crow South. Blacks and whites were both harmed when drinking fountains carried WHITE and COLORED signs.

Racial classifications deliver the message that skin color matters—profoundly. They suggest that whites and blacks are not the same, that race and ethnicity are the qualities that really matter. They imply that individuals are defined by blood—not by character, social class, religious sentiments, age, or education. But categories appropriate to a caste system are a poor basis on which to build that community of equal citizens upon which democratic government depends. Equal citizens are free to define themselves, and do so differently in different contexts. A voter whose choice of a candidate in a presidential primary is shaped by racial considerations might react to the issues in a school board contest as parents of other races do. It is precisely that fluidity of individual political identity that prevents the formation of castes, which are rigid and hierarchical by nature.

By no demographic or other measures are African Americans truly a people apart, we have argued at great length in this book. And yet if both they and whites believe they are, it may well become true. This is especially the case if that perception informs the law. Separate admissions procedures for whites and minorities, separate hiring processes, separate legislative districts: when given a stamp of approval by Congress and the courts, they paint an official, influential, and ultimately dangerous portrait of American society.

CHAPTER SEVENTEEN

The Racial Climate

IN JANUARY 1996, *Nightline* host Ted Koppel gathered a group of blacks and whites together to discuss the issue of race. He divided the assembled participants into two groups—one black, the other overwhelmingly white. Segregated into separate studios, the groups took turns talking and (via a monitor) listening. Koppel, who went first to the "black" room, began by asking the participants to tell personal and family stories—for instance, stories of lynchings, he suggested. And with that rather bizarre request, the curtain went up on a drama. Almost everyone had a tale: of grandparents, fathers and mothers, and of their own painful experiences. Not of actual lynchings, but of past and present wrongs, many serious. "Metaphorical lynchings," one woman called the degrading treatment that in 1996 was still, she said, woven into her life.

"We're as racist a society today as we were in the days of slavery," she went on to say. "White America does not understand the pain and degradation that blacks experience," another member of the group remarked. Other comments were in the same vein. Thus, one participant charged that "white people had not dealt with their own anti-Africanism," while another noted that even in 1996 "all blacks [drink] from the bitter cup of white supremacy." [1]

A "dialogue" on race, Ted Koppel had said he wanted to have. But he had evidently thought blacks and whites could not converse together—not in the same room, at least. Did blacks need the special protection that segregated settings provide? And if so, in order to . . . what? Talk honestly? Feel at ease? Rhetorical inhibition among highly educated, nationally prominent African Americans would not seem to be a problem. And in this instance, as in so many other settings, a "racially sensitive" white in charge had not only provided a forum, but had encouraged a collective antiwhite rant. Most of the whites, on the other hand, in their separate quarters, clearly felt less comfortable speaking their mind. And thus, while one racially identifiable camp was rhetorically armed, the other carried a white flag. It was a deceptive surrender, however, for the whites had conceded nothing important and the blacks had gained nothing tangible.

Americans sorted out by race into separate rooms, unable to look directly at each other, talking through closed doors; a conversation ostensibly orchestrated by a white, but in fact led by blacks whose racial hostility was a source of intimidating power; whites at the listening end for the most part eager to prove themselves sympathetic and thus morally okay.

Was the scene in the *Nightline* studios a metaphor for race relations in 1996? If so, we have come a long, sad way since the days of high hope in the mid-1960s. But in fact the picture is both more complicated and harder to discern than the *Nightline* metaphor would suggest. For while the status of blacks is statistically measurable (X percentage of black families above the poverty line, for example), the state of race relations is not. And thus this chapter is a collage created out of bits and scraps of information—polling data, news events, anecdotes.

BLACK ANGER, WHITE SURRENDER

While the racial climate is composed of a wide variety of diverse, sometimes contradictory, elements, the *Nightline* voices—those of black anger and white surrender—are a staple of modern racial discourse. Moreover, both the notion that whites and blacks are more divided than ever and that white racism remains pervasive are the conventional wisdom in academic and media circles.

Thus, the historian Roger Wilkins (a frequent television presence) has charged that racism is still "as virulent and as obvious as weeds in a garden."[2] In fact, racism is "worse today than it was in the '60s," the Reverend Benjamin Chavis, the former executive director of the NAACP, has argued.[3] That is a gross understatement, according to Carl Rowan, who asserted in 1996 that "racism has not been as virulent throughout America since the Civil War, with short fuses burning on a thousand powder kegs."[4] Other voices, both black and white, speak of continuing racial subjugation, and even ongoing "slavery." Lani Guinier has called the "abusive" relationship between whites and blacks hard for whites to relinquish.[5] Popular culture is infused with "racial signs and symbols that have no meaning other than pressing African Americans to the lowest level of the racial hierarchy," Toni Morrison has said.[6] Political scientist Andrew Hacker has referred to "the new slavery," by which he means the demand, for instance, that "black women who have children and don't have a husband in the house . . . go work, even if it's domestic service, even if it's shelling shrimp at a minimum wage."[7]

These are not views confined to the academy. In December 1995, in Tenafly, New Jersey, white families expressed their opposition to a proposed regional busing plan by tying orange ribbons to trees. The ribbons (in the local high school color), some black residents said, were much the same as cross burnings.[8] Democratic congressman Charles Rangel of New York, on the eve of the November 1994 elections, likened the "black suits and red ties" of conservative politicians to the sheets and hoods of the Ku Klux Klan. In 1992 the Speaker of the California assembly, Willie Brown, saw the ghost of the Klan-supported poll tax lurking behind the movement for term limits. Both, he said, "were designed to limit choices. One wore a sheet and the other didn't."[9]

It's tempting to dismiss such rhetoric as the stuff of political theater. But to what end? In Chapter 1 we described a small black protest that rocked the Library of Congress in late 1995. The library had hung an exhibit of photographs depicting life on southern plantations from the slave point of view. The photographs and the narratives of former slaves contained an uplifting message: the resilience of the African-American spirit. But the minute it went up, about twenty black employees objected; the pictures of white overseers on a plantation reminded them, they said, of the white "overseers" at the library.[10] What can explain such a bewildering distortion of the present to dramatize historic wrongs? For many blacks, Lani Guinier has said, slavery and Reconstruction are not ancient history. "They . . . feel the legacy of slavery in their daily lives."[11] Perhaps. Or perhaps seemingly intractable current inner-city problems—problems that define black America in the media—make the preoccupation with the morally simple wrongs of the past a source of comfort.

In addition, such protests work, further dispelling the terrible sense of helplessness. The Library of Congress exhibit was dismantled within hours of its opening. The balance of power in racial confrontations has shifted. When blacks raise their voice, whites most often retreat—as they did in that *Nightline* studio. Intimidation is part of the story. But retreat is also a signal of racial sympathy—and thus a means by which whites attempt to reassure themselves. *Others* are racist; not me.

When conversations about race begin, it's confession time, the writer Joe Klein said in 1991. The message becomes, "It's our fault, we're racists."[12] In November 1994, *Newsweek* published a conversation between its art critic, Peter Plagens (white), and Ellis Cose (black and a member of the magazine's staff) about a Whitney Museum of American Art exhibit entitled "Black Male: Representations of Masculinity in Contemporary American Art." "When a show such as 'Black Male' comes along, the title alone causes spasms of defensiveness in the art world," Plagens noted. " 'I'm not prejudiced,' I, for example, think, 'I had a black brother-in-law, I'm sometimes the only white guy in pickup basketball games, and my daughter goes to a rainbow public school and loves it.' " But all the effort is pretty much for naught, Plagens is forced to admit. The truth is evident: he's "hollow, fearful and whiny."[13]

Others try still harder, embracing—indeed, celebrating—black anger as the ultimate test of racial compassion, and conflating (as the journalist Jim

Sleeper has put it) "the noisiest, most aggressive black leadership with the entire black community."[14] That anger is seen as authentically black, which enables whites to distance themselves while simultaneously experiencing a certain fascination with the seemingly exotic and thrillingly dangerous stranger in their midst. A belief in the "authenticity" of the always dangerous and usually down-and-out African American is of course not a new story. Norman Mailer's 1957 essay "The White Negro" celebrated African Americans as primitive, sensual, violent creatures who showed "courage" when they robbed a candy store and murdered the owner. In the late 1960s and early 1970s, white liberals were infatuated with the Black Panthers—an infatuation wonderfully described by Tom Wolfe in his essay "Radical Chic."[15]

The Panthers are gone, but the celebration of "real" blacks has continued. In his autobiography, *Parallel Time, New York Times* editorial writer Brent Staples recalled the white editor who checked him out for his "racial bona fides"—his credentials as the legitimate voice of black oppression. "He wanted to know if I was a Faux, Chevy Chase, Maryland, Negro or an authentic nigger who grew up poor in the ghetto besieged by crime and violence."[16]

Not only that white editor, but the American reading public, it seems, is titillated by racially hostile black anger. Hence the best-seller status of such books as Derrick Bell's *Faces at the Bottom of the Well*. Bell's thesis was that almost all whites are born evil (he allowed a few exceptions). And almost all blacks (not the likes of Justice Clarence Thomas) are born good. Melanin is destiny. Only an irredeemably depraved race could have ever owned slaves; the once-enslaved, however, have been permanently morally elevated by their subordinate status. They are a communal, cooperative people, with "warm, rich voices," a "tenacity for life," and a remarkable ability to experience freedom even under the most oppressive conditions.[17]

Packaged in allegorical tales and fables, Bell offered an ugly, hostile message that whites eagerly bought. One tale involved "White Citizens for Black Survival," a group that aimed to build a national network of secret shelters to house and feed black people "in the event of a black holocaust or some other all-out attack on America's historic scapegoats." It was a possibility that Bell took very seriously. "Such an attack," he suggested, was "not only possible, but probable."[18]

A holocaust or its equivalent was a theme that ran through many of Bell's fictional stories. Sometimes, as in "A Law Professor's Protest," only a relatively small number of African Americans were liquidated—in that case all 196 black professors and administrators at Harvard University.[19] In "The Space Traders," however, every American black was turned over to an armada from outer space that offered riches in exchange. The trade was the culmination of a long tradition of sacrificing black rights to further white interests; black outrage had "as usual" no credibility. Whites only wanted to hear their own racist views—"almost ad nauseam."[20]

It's an odd inversion of an obvious truth. In the real world, only the lunatic fringe buys racist tracts written by whites, while black racism apparently sells. Bell's is a black voice that many whites, as well as blacks, seem to like to hear. Nathan McCall's autobiography, *Makes Me Wanna Holler,* a work in much the same vein, was also a best-seller. Its purpose was clear: telling whites, in no uncertain terms, just how despicable they were. McCall, born in 1955, started hating whites early. In fact, in the opening scene of the book he tells how very good "fucking up white boys" made him and his buddies feel. A hapless youngster had come pedaling on his bike through their neighborhood. "Every time I drove my foot into his balls, I felt better," McCall writes. Some of the kicks were for specific racial slights; others were for "G.P.—General Principle —just 'cause you white." [21]

It was the right opening; stomping on whites as a means of emotional release was what *Makes Me Wanna Holler* was all about. Rage was the organizing principle in McCall's life. He said simply, "We all hated white people. . . . After we reached the ninth grade . . . we fucked up white boys more than we went to class." When the Black Panthers came to town, McCall and his friends "didn't give a shit about all that political stuff," but they "hated white folks" and "felt so much better striking out at them in the name of a lofty cause." After he fired into the living room of a white family's house with a sawed-off shotgun, he "told the fellas . . . 'We fucked up some white folks . . .' " He "felt proud." [22]

Eventually, McCall wound up in jail for three years, "half burned out on drugs, depressed . . . , hopelessly lost," and convicted of armed robbery. It was an educational experience; he learned something about the dignity of work, the virtues of patience, and the power of words, but he also acquired new knowledge of "the white man's evil ways." He came to understand that "white men are the most lying creatures on the face of the earth," that whites "had oppressed people of color whenever they encountered them," and that "black people had been systematically brainwashed." [23]

Released from prison, he went to a school of journalism at a black college, where he learned that whites "place a premium on conquering people and developing objects." [24] Upon graduation he landed a job first with a Virginia paper and then with the *Atlanta Journal-Constitution,* before going to the *Washington Post.* A happy end to a sad story? No. His racial hatred remained undiminished.

White infatuation with such writers (there were no critics of these works outside of conservative circles), and in general a willingness to honor black anger (and often black racism) means that those who see the KKK lurking everywhere are combatants in a bizarre war in which both camps are on the same side. "The dumbest thing a black person can do is trust a white man," Nathan McCall has written. [25] Whites in the media, in the universities, in the institutions whose voices are most clearly heard, generally seem often to agree.

The war has a point, however. The relentless pretense that almost all whites are an enemy, that white racism remains a constant, serves a purpose. It invites whites who are nervous about their racial rectitude to remain supplicants. The result is an unending game (black anger, white guilt) in which the white score is always zero, and the illusion of power is bestowed upon a group whose members seem to live in constant fear that their hard-earned status is not quite real—that they remain the "invisible" men and women they once so clearly were.

CHANGING RACIAL ATTITUDES

It is impossible to think of another group whose hostility to outsiders is greeted with such enthusiasm by those against whom the anger is directed. And if that anger confers power, then of course every opportunity to exercise it will be seized. The invitation is irresistible. Hence the absurd references to ongoing slavery and the careless charges of racism.

Such careless charges are a staple of civil rights discourse. In 1994 an NAACP spokesman said that a proposal to raise the age of eligibility for Medicare and Social Security from sixty-five to seventy "could exacerbate racial divisions," because black life expectancy was shorter than that of whites.[26] In October 1995 a coalition of groups filed a civil rights lawsuit against the New York Metropolitan Transportation Authority charging that an upcoming fare hike discriminated against the 61 percent of bus and subway riders who were members of minority groups.[27]

If some claims seem far-fetched, others are patently fraudulent. In 1987 Tawana Brawley, a sixteen-year-old black girl from a small New York town, disappeared from home for four days and then showed up with a wild tale of having been kidnapped and raped by half a dozen members of the KKK, some of them policemen. Her story was riddled with inconsistencies, and the physical evidence provided no support for it. But the Reverend Al Sharpton and other black nationalist demagogues cited the Brawley case as proof of the nation's incorrigible racism.[28]

Equally fraudulent was the charge of a student at the Amherst, Massachusetts, Regional Junior High School who in 1994 alleged that she found two threatening notes in her locker. The next day more notes appeared, reportedly signed "KKK" and including hate words. Others charges followed. But the police, after seizing the backpack in which the notes were alleged to have been found, discovered a notebook from which the pages containing the ugly messages had clearly been taken.

The Amherst incident had been a hoax, but it gave the NAACP a platform from which to air a variety of demands with respect to the local public schools: more black teachers, a multicultural curriculum, and so forth.[29] And many in Amherst evidently reacted to the incident by suggesting that the value of raising the issues outweighed any harm that might result from a hoax. "This is just a blip on the screen," said Reynolds Winslow, president of the Amherst chapter of the NAACP. "It's unfortunate if it's not true . . . but if nothing more, the fact that there's a dialogue going on is very positive."[30] Such spokesmen overlook the fact that such stories work to cast doubt upon all charges of racism, encouraging public indifference, as *Washington Post* columnist Colman McCarthy has argued. "The reckless manner in which charges of racism are hurled around is befogging the air, decreasing visibility when bigotry really is happening," he has rightly noted.[31]

The racial views of most whites, as we hope the opening chapters of this book made clear, were once abhorrent. In fact, Gunnar Myrdal painted too rosy a picture in *An American Dilemma;* in 1944 most Americans felt less guilty about matters of race than he supposed. But the myth of a nation with a heart of gold (beneath the trappings of bigotry) was put to excellent use, and it soon became a self-fulfilling prophecy—a story that took on a life of its own, a tale that inspired a moral crusade that helped change the nation's racial landscape. By 1995, Coretta Scott King was able to say that the ideals for which Martin Luther King died had become "mainstream"—"deeply embedded in the very fabric of America."[32] A year earlier a young northern black who had decided to travel south to see where his grandparents grew up found a very different picture than he had expected. "Everywhere I went," he said, "people were far more open and congenial than in the North, even in the most casual interactions. And everywhere, in cities and small towns, I saw blacks and whites working together, walking down the street together, talking together. . . . [One morning,] eating in a restaurant, I heard the waitress, a redhead with pale skin and a sweet Southern voice that made me think of clear mornings and cool mountains, tell the black man at the counter beside me that she'd be over later because she wanted to hear the new record he'd bought."[33]

In the years before the civil rights revolution, hard-core white racism was ubiquitous; in the 1990s, it is largely a thing of the past. In the early years, Myrdal and others misleadingly portrayed whites as ambivalent on racial issues; today much of the civil rights community depicts them as barely reconstructed racists. Misplaced optimism in the past; excessive pessimism in the present: in both periods the rhetoric has been out of sync with the actual racial landscape. How much that landscape has changed in the intervening years is clearly evident in polling data on racial attitudes today.

It is important to recall the depth of racial prejudice that public opinion surveys in Myrdal's day revealed. In the year *An American Dilemma* was published, only 45 percent of whites thought that African Americans should "have as good a chance as white people to get any kind of job." Most whites assumed that they deserved to be at the head of the line, and that blacks should be content with the leftover jobs whites didn't want. Less than half of whites believed that blacks were "as intelligent as white people." Only a third felt that black and white children should attend the same schools, and roughly the same percentage were willing to live on the same block as an African American with a similar education and income.[34]

These views were transformed within a generation. By 1972, for example, 97 percent of whites said they believed blacks should have equal opportunities to get a job, a figure so high that the question was thereafter dropped. Likewise, by the early 1970s, 80 percent of whites believed that African Americans were of equal intelligence; 84 percent favored racially integrated schools; and 85 percent had no objection to having a black neighbor of the same social class.[35] The only further change since then has been in the same direction. These questions as well are likely headed for the wastebasket, since the responses are too close to unanimous to be illuminating.[36]

These enormous shifts in what people profess to believe about racial issues cannot be dismissed as meaningless—as signifying only that it is no longer fashionable to express publicly hostile racial sentiments that are still obstinately held in private. Polls are not infallible guides to the depths of the human psyche, but the mountain of evidence we reviewed in researching this book indicates that white racial attitudes have truly altered. Whites with a pathological hatred of African Americans can still be found, of course. But the haters have become a tiny remnant with no influence in any important sphere of American life. The view that "nothing has changed" can only be held by those who believe that social science evidence is worthless.

In fact, not only have racial attitudes been transformed; the question of race has lost the moral simplicity it once had. This is the main point made by political scientists Paul Sniderman and Thomas Piazza in their important book *The Scar of Race*. At least when it comes to questions of public policy, few whites are now racists. Whites may oppose particular items on the standard civil rights agenda (busing and racial preferences, most obviously), but that does not mean they are bigots. Contemporary discussions of race too often fail to distinguish between "what white Americans think about blacks" and "what they think about public policies dealing with blacks."[37]

What they think about public policies dealing with blacks depends, in fact, on the precise issue, Sniderman and Piazza have shown. "There is no longer *one* issue of race, but a number of distinct issues, and the politics of these issues differ in telling ways." That is, disagreements over affirmative action, fair housing, and other racial questions are primarily political; the positions adversaries take are not determined by gut feelings toward African Americans but by ideological bent. For instance, conservatives (the authors found) tend to reject the idea that an undependable black worker deserves a lot of help in finding a new job. But, of course. "Being conservative, they are naturally inclined to oppose government help of this kind, whoever will get it. They do not single blacks out." In fact (and here's the surprise) they are even *more* opposed to giving help to a white—however dependable he or she may be.

Sniderman and Piazza's findings, resting on five public opinion surveys, thus paint not one picture but many. "A large number of racial issues stand substantially on their own," the authors concluded. In other words, claims for government assistance are one question; busing is another. Only those who insist on an all-purpose racial litmus test (are you for or against blacks?) remain blind to the diversity of the racial scene.[38]

Or perhaps not blind, but simply politically astute. For clearly it's in the interest of the civil rights lobby to maintain the illusion of moral simplicity. As long as race remains a problem of the heart, they own the high moral ground. Admit that "the politics of affirmative action," as *The Scar of Race* has put it, "has remarkably little to do with whites' feelings towards blacks" and much to do with conflicting notions of rudimentary justice, and the monopoly on virtue that civil rights advocates have so long enjoyed instantly vanishes.[39]

But the effort to depict racial preferences as integral to an ongoing, basically unchanged fight for racial justice has entailed a substantial cost, Sniderman and Piazza have made clear. As we noted in Chapter 11, that cost has been especially clear when it comes to affirmative action, which (they found) "is so intensely disliked that it has led some whites to dislike blacks—an ironic example of a policy meant to put the divide of race behind us in fact further widening it."[40]

The message that race-related issues are morally simple and racism ubiquitous divides blacks and whites for another reason. It suggests that all the social ills particularly prevalent in the black community can be blamed entirely on whites. The charge is a conversation-stopper on subjects such as crime and out-of-wedlock births that many black politicians and other civil rights spokesmen would rather not discuss. And it is a sure means of stoking the fires of white resentment. "If I were something like the Pope of black America and had the moral authority to make such suggestions, I would propose that no African American use the terms racism or racist," Lance Morrow wrote in *Time* magazine in late 1994. "The words," he went on, "are a feckless indulgence,

> corrosive to blacks and whites alike and to relations between them. Such rhetoric has given blacks a leadership that has built its career upon mere race-grievance agitation, and is therefore profoundly, almost unconsciously committed to its perpetuation. As in a hateful Strindberg marriage, each party somehow requires the abuse of the other. It is a catastrophic pattern. The lingering ghost of the plantation haunts it. The word racism has degenerated to being a mere ritual term of abuse and self-pity, part of the Kabuki of manipulation.[41]

OUTSIDE THE NORMS

In arguing that white racial attitudes have come a long way, we do not claim that racism has entirely disappeared. It is obviously not the case, as a number of well-publicized incidents in recent years make clear. For instance, in 1993 the editors of an AT&T employee magazine commissioned a cartoon showing people on various continents making phone calls; the caller from Africa was depicted as a gorilla. The company apologized.[42] That same year two white laborers in Tampa, Florida, were convicted in the burning of a black tourist who had been taunted with racial slurs, doused with gasoline and set ablaze.[43] In 1995, five white Greenwich, Connecticut, high school seniors were suspended from school for slipping a racist message into their yearbook.[44] A year earlier a number of restaurants in the Denny's chain had been quickly closing when blacks showed up; those not turned away were often harassed in a variety of ways.[45]

Other incidents described as racist are often less clear-cut. In late 1989, a Boston-area suburban couple, expecting their first child, were robbed and shot in the city on their way home from a prenatal clinic. The mother and baby died; the father was gravely wounded but lived. The couple—Charles and Carol Stuart—were white; their alleged assailant was black. A black man in a jogging suit had forced his way into their car and made them drive to an abandoned spot in a crime-ridden neighborhood, Charles had reported. But the handsome man for whom the city wept was the murderer himself, his brother told the police ten weeks later, after the police had engaged in a massive manhunt, routinely searching young black men.[46] Blacks in the city charged the mayor and police with racism, but the gullibility of those in authority was at least partially understandable. There was not only the high homicide rate in the predominantly black neighborhood in which the shooting took place; the message of much rap music and of books like *Makes Me Wanna Holler* is precisely that young black males are filled with justifiable, murderous rage.

Five years later, in South Carolina, Susan Smith tried to pull the same stunt. Having drowned her two children in a lake, she fabricated a story of black violence, although this time the police were suspicious from the outset. "This case demonstrates once again the stereotypical view of black men in America, that they are Other, that they are dangerous, that they should be imprisoned," Aldon Morris, chair of the sociology department at Northwestern University, said. "It was the same view that guided lynch mobs during the days of segregation in the South," he went on. The voice of Morris was joined by others. The *New York Times* reported that Harvard University physician Dr. Alvin Poussaint, among others, believed "the lies the 23-year-old mother told to cover her trail fit a long history of scapegoating black men for the ills of the nation"; Poussaint had depicted Susan Smith as "in tune with the racism in society."[47] The real point is just the opposite. Smith clearly was out of tune with the racial tolerance of American society. The public was appalled by Susan Smith's lie, as it has been by other nationally reported incidents of racism. In the fall of 1995 secretly taped conversations revealed that a white Dallas school board member repeatedly used racial slurs. In the most in-

flammatory section of the tapes, he referred to Dallas schoolchildren as "ignorant goddamned little niggers." That sort of language could not, of course,
survive the light of day; he was forced to resign and issued a three-page
statement expressing his remorse and apology.[48]

There were no consequences attached to the use of the *N* word in the Jim
Crow South. And prior to passage of the 1964 Civil Rights Act, southern
restaurants where whites dined did not keep black customers waiting, as
Denny's had; they did not serve them at all. At a news conference on the
settlement in the Denny's case, the assistant attorney general for civil rights,
Deval Patrick, remarked that these were "stories repeated again and again."
In fact, the six black Secret Service officers who were plaintiffs in the suit
confessed bewilderment that such attitudes still existed. Evidently, they had
not previously experienced such discrimination.[49] That should not have been
surprising; the sort of raw racism that was on display in the Denny's case has
become rare. And when it happens, it makes news—bad news for Denny's.
The company found itself labeled racist in every major newspaper, and was
forced to pay dearly for the contemptible behavior of some of its personnel:
the parent company coughed up $54.4 million to settle the litigation.[50]

As Everett Carll Ladd, director of the Roper Center for Public Opinion
Research, noted in 1989, in every society there "are haters, people who are
going to stand outside the norms, people who can and will do horrendous
things." But, he added, the public now reacts negatively to obvious incidents
of racism and racial violence.[51] Arizona's refusal (later reversed by 61 percent
of the voters) to make Martin Luther King's birthday a holiday, cost the state
the 1993 Super Bowl and an estimated $300 million in lost tourism and
convention spending.[52] Even in the small-town South, racists stand "outside
the norms." In Thomasville, Georgia, a Baptist church had allowed the burial
of a mixed-race baby, not knowing that the father was black. But three days
after the funeral, the board of deacons asked the relatives of the child to
exhume her tiny body because they wanted to keep their graveyard exclusively
white. Members of their own congregation condemned them; an official with
the Southern Baptist Convention called it an embarrassment to the gospel of
Christ. "I can't go to town now without someone coming up to hug me and
tell me how sorry they are that this all happened." the baby's grandmother
said. The deacons apologized.[53]

The charge of racism has powerful consequences, as Texaco learned at
great expense. In November 1996 the *New York Times* broke the story that a
Texaco executive had taped a meeting at which high officials had referred to
African American employees as "niggers" and "black jelly beans," and had
plotted the destruction of documents pertinent to an employment discrimination suit the company was fighting. This provoked a flurry of headlines like
"Hate on Tape at Texaco" and "Surreptitious Tapes Betray Texaco's Outrageous Racism" in the national press.[54]

Expert analysis of the tapes quickly revealed that no one had in fact employed the *N* word. Furthermore, the idea of referring to African-American employees as "black jelly beans" was not a racist invention; the phrase had entered the corporate vocabulary after it had been recommended in a speech to Texaco executives by a leading African American diversity consultant, R. Roosevelt Thomas, Jr., the former president of the American Institute for Managing Diversity.[55] The taped comment that "you can't just have we and them. You can't just have black jelly beans and other jelly beans. It just doesn't work" was a criticism of the divisive results of the diversity training the company had been doing for years. Pigeonholing employees in many separate racial and gender boxes did not produce greater harmony; instead, accentuating differences was a recipe for lawsuits like the one at hand. This argument may be right or wrong, but it is not unquestionably racist. A crack about "the black jelly beans" being "glued to the bottom of the bag" was undoubtedly objectionable.[56] But it was on about the same level of insensitivity as referring to New York City as "Hymietown," as Texaco's chief critic, Jesse Jackson, had been in the habit of doing until a reporter made it public during his 1984 presidential campaign and he was forced to apologize.[57]

The taped evidence suggesting that documents relevant to legal proceedings were being destroyed was certainly disturbing, but that charge got far less play than one that was simply false and another that gave an incomplete and distorted picture of the incident. The media feeding frenzy, however, was enough to bring the nation's fourth largest corporation to its knees. It quickly agreed to a $176 million settlement of the suit that had been brought by six African American employees. As part of that settlement, it also: gave black employees a 10 percent raise; set a 29 percent "goal" for minority employment; and stated its intention to use executive search firms with good "diversity" (i.e., affirmative action) records, to finance internship and scholarship programs earmarked for minorities, and to introduce executive mentoring programs. It agreed to make their record of advancing minorities and women who served under them an important part of the performance evaluations of its managers, providing a strong personal incentive to meet racial quotas and thus to treat employees not as a diverse mix of individuals, but first and foremost as members of groups defined by race and gender.[58]

The company also promised to institute diversity training for all employees, thus further inviting that jelly bean counting that had been found so objectionable. It agreed to buy $1 billion worth of goods from businesses owned by nonwhites and women; to use banks, money managers, and insurance companies owned by minorities and women; and to dispatch senior executives to every major Texaco workplace in the United States in order to meet with employees and (in the words of the chairman) "apologize . . . for the embarrassment and humiliation this has created." Finally, it suspended two officials and cut the retirement benefits of two others.[59] All in all, it was quite a package, delivered as a mega–public relations gesture. The company's harsh treatment of its own executives, *Washington Post* columnist Richard Cohen argued, was an example of "racial McCarthyism." Cohen noted that "the accusation of racism—unproved though it may be—has become the functional equivalent of what communism used to be. It can cost you your job, your benefits and what used to be called your good name."[60]

The press and a substantial segment of the American public—including a president of the United States—have proven themselves extraordinarily quick to believe any and all charges of racism on other occasions as well. In June 1996, President Clinton described the burning of African-American churches in the South over the previous eighteen months as driven by the same sort of "racial hostility" that had led to the bombing of a Birmingham church and the death of four black children in 1963. We are witnessing an "epidemic of terror," Clinton's top civil rights official charged. Clinton and members of his administration were not alone in evoking such horrors of the past. The fires "speak of racial divisions out of the Old South," the *New York Times* reported in July.[61] The black churches stand for something disenchanted whites "cannot abide: they were the birthplace of the civil rights movement, and for some that's unforgivable," a novelist invited to write in *Newsweek* argued. "The flaming old churches are like signal fires from one disgruntled band of whites to another."[62]

Words to stir the conscience of a nation. But they bore little relation to the truth. Nearly as many white churches as black had burned; the number of fires had not been on the increase; some were accidental; some were the work of mentally unstable people; others were deliberately started for a variety of reasons, racism being among them. But most important, as Michael Kelly argued in the *New Yorker,* the story was "a large fiction spun out of smaller truths. The acts of a relatively few misfits and miscreants in the night cannot be equated with the vast and purposeful campaign of terror directed against black citizens in the South during the civil-rights struggle." To create a myth of conspiracy and institutional oppression, to say that nothing has changed, Kelly concluded, "is a disservice to history, to the generations of whites who have labored to rid themselves of racism, and, above all, to the thousands of brave people who risked their lives fighting, and defeating, the real thing."[63]

"Still after all these years, I worry that I am a racist," *Washington Post* reporter Henry Allen said in 1994. "So do a lot of white guys my age, I think," he went on. "The best minds of my generation have worried and worried about it. Worrying about it proved we were hip, we were righteous." At the private high school in New Haven that he once attended, "what you thought counted the way what you wore counted—especially what you thought about racism." His classmates invited him to join "the club of those who were not racists. It was clearly the right club to be in, right up there with the Lawn Club."[64]

The "right club to be in" when Allen was in the rarefied political atmosphere of a Connecticut day school is now almost everywhere the "right club." It's a story of remarkable—and insufficiently celebrated—change.

PAIN AND PESSIMISM

"There is so much pain in black America," Jesse Jackson has said.[65] As Harvard sociologist Orlando Patterson has noted, despite all the good news, the pain completely dominates the gain in much of the current discourse on race.[66] The problem is not confined to the rhetoric of a Derrick Bell or a Nathan McCall; at least some polling data also suggest a dismaying level of black pessimism about the state of race relations.

In a 1989 ABC/*Washington Post* survey, 26 percent of blacks agreed that most whites shared the racist views of the Ku Klux Klan; another 25 percent of blacks believed that at least a quarter of *all* whites were in the KKK camp. Between 1983 and 1994, the proportion of African Americans who believed that "most white people" wanted to see them "get a better break" dropped from 33 to 25 percent; the fraction who thought that most whites either wanted to "keep blacks down" or didn't care either way rose from half to two thirds.[67]

A 1992 poll conducted for the Anti-Defamation League found that 81 percent of blacks and 76 percent of whites thought that race relations were "not so good" or "poor." Most blacks (68 percent) and whites (73 percent) agreed that "about half" of whites in America were "basically prejudiced."[68] Asked a year later whether they thought "relations between blacks and whites [would] always be a problem" or that "a solution [would] eventually be worked out," only 44 percent of blacks were optimistic that "a solution" would be worked out, a dismaying drop of 26 percentage points since 1963—a year before the 1964 Civil Rights Act was passed![69] Nor has that figure risen subsequently, it appears; an October 1995 *Time*/CNN poll found again that just 44 percent of blacks thought race relations would eventually improve.[70] A Harris poll the same month found that 59 percent of African Americans believed that the country was on "the wrong track" in race relations. According to a *Washington Post*/Kaiser Foundation survey a month earlier, 68 percent of African Americans believed that racism remained "a big problem" in American society, and 71 percent felt that blacks had "less opportunity" than whites to "live a middle class life."[71] (By comparison, only 38 percent of whites were impressed with persistent racism, with 31 percent believing that blacks had less opportunity.)

Whether you think these figures are evidence of excessive black pessimism or only realism depends, of course, upon your assessment of how much progress has actually been made in rooting out the racism that long infected American society. We are impressed by the gains, obviously, and see the overwhelming pessimism as something of a puzzle. Orlando Patterson has offered at least a partial explanation. The level of white prejudice is way down, but, with blacks only 12 percent of the American population, there are still (by his calculation) roughly two white racists for every African American. But this estimate of the size of the white racist hard core is arguably much too high. When Sniderman and Piazza measured the level of white racism by examining responses to five negative stereotypes about African Americans, they found that only 2 percent of the whites in a national sample endorsed all five. Furthermore, each one of these stereotpyes about African Americans, they discovered, was more widely held by blacks than whites, suggesting that measurements of white racism may be tapping into widespread tendencies to stereotype groups—even one's own.[72]

There is another part to the Patterson argument: the whites with whom blacks come into contact are exactly the wrong ones. As Patterson has put it:

> the vast majority of blacks will rarely come in contact with the 75 percent of whites who are tolerant, for simply socioeconomic reasons. More educated, more prosperous and more suburban, the tolerant three-quarters tend to live exactly where blacks are least likely to be found: in the expensive suburbs. On the other hand, it is the least educated and most prejudiced of whites who tend to be in close proximity to blacks.
>
> Further, the behavior of the tolerant three quarters of whites, and their attempts to improve the condition of blacks, tends to intensify racist feelings among whites most likely to come into contact with blacks. The cost of racial change is disproportionately borne by those whites who have traditionally been most hostile to blacks. . . .[73]

Whatever the explanation, pessimism has become the public voice of black America. The work of writers like Nathan McCall sets the tone of the discussion of racial issues throughout the media. Blacks who work for the major networks, magazines, and newspapers have a near-monopoly on black topics, and from the bleak tone of their message there is little dissent.

McCall, for instance, described "two distinct worlds": one for blacks, "dark and limited," and one for whites, full of promise. When a white teacher reached out to him, he wondered how he could possibly " 'make something' of [himself] in the fucking white man's world?" It's damn hard, Ellis Cose answered in *The Rage of a Privileged Class*. He and McCall agreed: blacks can have fancy jobs and all the accoutrements; they're still "niggers" in "the fucking white man's world."[74]

Cose rested his case mainly on other peoples' stories—and interviews with "experts" who "explain" those stories. Neither the plot line nor the spin ever varied. Talented black with superior education met grudging white institution, worked like hell, did everything he was supposed to do, only to discover it was never enough. "Blacks with fast-track credentials" were not allowed on the track, "certainly in nothing approaching the proportions of their white peers." They were "stymied"—stopped from rising by a ceiling "made of cement and steel." Whites with fancy degrees prospered "with such seeming ease"; for blacks, success came "harder" and "later," and "at a lower level than for comparably credentialed whites."[75]

About whom was Cose talking? Mostly his friends, and the friends of his friends, it seems. There was no pretense at scientific sampling (research by Rolodex seems to be the method), and every tale was accepted at face value. Thus, when the Harvard Law School did not offer a permanent position to a visiting black female law professor, it was a clear case of racial bias. ("Including black women in higher education arouses inherent suspicion.") Why prejudice did not stop the school from appointing several distinguished black male professors was unclear. In *The Rage* Cose was an odd sort of journalist— totally credulous. He believed what he heard so long as blacks were the source.

In a racist society, tales of racism are ipso facto true, Cose implied. And the normal rules of evidence did not apply. The lawyer who "sensed" that "he was not really seen as a litigator but as a *black* litigator" was justifiably aggrieved. As was the business executive who got the top job in his firm but "sensed resistance." "Many whites have great difficulty differentiating a black go-getter from a black bum," Cose concluded. In fact, black employees were often denied promotions because customers would be "disturbed to see a black person in a job where only whites are normally seen."[76] How did Cose know? He knew what he *felt*. It's what columnist Robert J. Samuelson has called (in a different context) "the triumph of the psycho-fact." The alleged "facts" aren't true, "but we feel they are and, therefore, they become so."[77]

The point applies more broadly. Psycho-facts have come to govern the way racial matters are talked about in civil rights circles, in the academy, and in most of the mainstream media. "The American dream . . . is white at its heart," Cose asserted.[78] WHITES ONLY remains the sign on most of the doors through which blacks want to walk. The point is utter nonsense, as we hope earlier chapters have shown. But it may be widely believed.

The perception of relentless white racism, of doors closed to African Americans, of America "white at its heart," won't stop the course of racial change, but it will influence the shape of that change. Increasing numbers of blacks are likely to enter the middle class, whatever the media have to say on the subject of persistent white racism. But books matter, and the perception of closed doors feeds anger and alienation, which together make for racial isolation. Moreover, while the bleak and hate-filled message of *Makes Me Wanna Holler* clearly appealed to those white readers who made it a best-seller, if the majority of Americans come to see McCall's views as representative of black opinion, they may conclude that all the good civil rights work of the past thirty years has been in vain. And—most ominously—that future effort is likely to be equally futile.

TALES FROM NEW YORK

Crime is the setting in which black distrust of white America is most apparent —as we noted in Chapter 10. Guns and drugs planted by whites, police, and judges out to get blacks: such conspiratorial notions make for criminal trials in which the police and courts seem overwhelmed by the politics of racial grievance, with the result that the law is politicized and the races polarized. A series of cases in New York City tell the story. These cases are best known by the locale of the crime: Howard Beach, Bensonhurst, Crown Heights, the Central Park Jogger, and the Subway Vigilante. And that fact is in itself important. These were trials in which individual guilt or innocence was not the only—and perhaps not the central—question. The city itself was on the line: the integrity of those with legal and political power, the moral fiber of its people, the safety of its subways, parks, and streets.

Howard Beach is a predominantly white neighborhood in the borough of Queens, New York. In December 1986 three black men whose car had broken down were set upon by a group of white youths (who had been partying and drinking) outside a pizzeria. Chased by the pack of whites, Michael Griffith tried to run across a highway and was struck and killed by a car; one of his two friends was badly beaten. Bensonhurst is the Italian neighborhood in Brooklyn, New York, where, in August 1989 a young black man was shot to death. The victim, Yusef Hawkins, had intended to meet with a man selling a used car; the perpetrators were on the lookout (weapons ready) for a group of blacks who had been invited to a local party.

Crown Heights is also in Brooklyn: a black and Hasidic Jewish community in which racial tensions had long been simmering. In August 1991 a car driven by a Hasid ran a red light, hit the sidewalk, and killed a black seven-year-old child. Violence erupted immediately, and in the ensuing melee a visiting Australian Jew was fatally stabbed by attackers shouting "Kill the Jew." In Howard Beach and Bensonhurst, in short, the victims were blacks, the perpetrators white. In Crown Heights, the black child died in the course of an accident; the victim of deliberate violence was white.

The victim in the 1989 Central Park Jogger case was also white—a young investment banker at Salomon Brothers. Running at night in the park, she was raped, viciously beaten with a lead pipe, rocks, and bricks, and left to die. The accused black and Hispanic youths said they were "wilding," admitted looking "for trouble," and described the attack as "fun."[79] In the 1984 case of the "subway vigilante," however, the four youths who were shot (but survived) were black, while their assailant, Bernhard Goetz, was white. Goetz had been mugged on several previous occasions; surrounded by youths asking for money in a subway car, he had reached for his gun and fired.

These cases had much in common. All had the makings of standard courtroom drama. But for much of the black audience and some of the participants, they became something more: skirmishes between whites and blacks in an ongoing racial war. From this perspective, in each case black innocence was pitted against white guilt; white perpetrators, but also whites with prosecutorial, judicial, or political power. In fact, the assumption of guilt encompassed white victims of black crime as well.

Of course, in Howard Beach and Bensonhurst, the individual whites who were charged were indeed guilty of serious crimes—a conclusion that said nothing, however, about white guilt in general. But in the Central Park Jogger case, the victim was white. Nevertheless, the defendants' lawyers and some members of the black media argued that the jogger's own boyfriend had not only raped her but smashed her skull with such brutality as to leave her unrecognizable even to a close friend. Onlookers at the trial called her "a prostitute . . . a whore." One labeled the whole matter a "white hoax," a lynching.[80] The publisher of an important black newspaper stated flatly that "there is just no evidence of a rape, none," while a prominent black minister dismissed the prosecutor's case as just good old-fashioned American racism. "The first thing you do in the United States when a white woman is raped is to round up a bunch of black youths," he said. "I think that's what happened here."[81]

The black youths, not the Central Park Jogger, were thus depicted as the innocent ones. Moreover, interracial incidents in which blacks suffered were not seen as individual tragedies. Thus, the death of seven-year old Gavin Cato in Crown Heights, on its surface a tragic accident, became an evil deed—indeed a "murder."[82] In the words of the Reverend Al Sharpton (a man with a substantial black following in the city), it was but the latest in a series of racial assassinations that included not only the young black men in Howard Beach and Bensonhurst, but Malcolm X and the four children killed in a Birmingham church in 1963.[83] Sharpton and others thus called for the arrest of the Hasidic driver who had swerved and crushed the child. And they called the failure to file criminal charges part of a state cover-up that included rigging the results of a Breathalyzer test.[84]

Likewise in Howard Beach, although the young men who chased Michael Griffith to his death on a high-speed highway were clearly guilty, the driver of the car that actually hit Griffith was not. He was an innocent motorist on his way home. But in view of those who practice the politics of racial grievance, no white is an innocent and every public official is suspect. The driver, said an attorney for one of the surviving black victims, "murdered Michael Griffith by coming up on to the highway and running him down."[85] Others described the violence that started outside a pizzeria as an indictment of every pizza parlor employer, employee, and patron, and called for a citywide boycott.

White violence, in short, indicted every white—and even some blacks (those who were part of the "establishment"). Black activists leading the charge for "justice" in the Howard Beach case thus described the city's black chief of police as a "puppet" of the white "power structure."[86] The mayor, the police department, the district attorney's office, and some members of the "Negro leadership," they said, were a "lynch mob . . . running loose in New York City."[87] In the course of the Bensonhurst trial, too, a prominent black lawyer labeled the black mayor, David Dinkins, "a traitor . . . a lover of white people and the system," a man who "ain't got no African left in him."[88]

How many of the city's black (or white) residents subscribed to such a picture, drawn mainly by a handful of prominent black provocateurs? Sam Roberts, a *New York Times* reporter, called the Reverend Al Sharpton (often at center stage in these racially charged cases) "a creature of the white media" —his political power a gift from the press. But as Roberts acknowledged, Sharpton clearly "struck a responsive chord among many blacks."[89] On a moment's notice, Sharpton and his friends could organize well-attended marches in Bensonhurst and elsewhere—marches that sent shivers down New York's political spine.

New York writer Jim Sleeper makes another point. The message of Sharpton and other demagogues acts like drops of dye in water; the color quickly spreads. The views of their black listeners alter—especially because the will to believe is already there—the sense that the "system" is alien and "the powers that be" can't be trusted. Many of those affected won't take to the streets, and they won't show up in a courtroom to harass victims like the Central Park Jogger. But their heightened sense of collective embattlement will reinforce an already dangerous culture of disbelief.[90]

A politics of racial grievance is understandable, given the long history of black victimization by white power. The legacy of fear remains—the suspicion that nothing fundamental had changed. But the culture of disbelief carries a cost. Prosecutors are forced to wage war on two fronts: against the lawyers for the defendants (white or black) and against a sizable segment of the black public for whom the just resolution of the legal case is secondary—even when the victims are black. Thus, in Bensonhurst "Black Power!" was one of the slogans that marchers chanted.[91] In Howard Beach, the willingness of the state to honor an irrational demand became the test of respect for blacks in general. Attorneys for the surviving black victims insisted on the appointment of a special prosecutor—an appointment that (for complicated reasons) would have been a gift to the white defendants. In Crown Heights the death of the black child, as journalist Joe Klein put it, "was immediately transformed from a tragic accident into grist for the black-nationalist 'struggle.' "[92] And the subsequent, astonishing acquittal of Lemrick Nelson, Jr., the black youth charged in the stabbing death of the Australian Jew, was declared a triumph of good over evil—that is, black over white.

Black anger can be legitimate, and in Bensonhurst, particularly, the heckling of black marchers by some whites did reveal raw racism. But these were deeply polarizing events, poisoning the racial climate in the city. Both in Bensonhurst and in Howard Beach many residents saw their communities as unfairly, infuriatingly stigmatized. And while the *New York Times* op-ed page might be receptive to the views of a black pastor who linked the violence of a few white teenage thugs to that of "Western civilization" in general, and described the murder of Yusef Hawkins as an expression of widespread "contempt for . . . African humanity," such talk just made most whites mad.[93]

Equally important, the picture drawn of white guilt and black innocence in these and other cases denied the reality that many whites experienced. Accidents happen—to both whites and blacks. True racist conspiracies are rare. And villains and victims come in all colors. But not in equal numbers, everyone knew. The disproportionately high rate of black crime—and especially of that of young black males—was no secret to New York residents. Bernhard Goetz was an outlaw. His actions were indefensible, but menacing black youth on the subway got no sympathy in a city with shattered nerves. Police hot lines were flooded with support for Goetz. GOD BLESS YOU, BERNIE signs popped up almost everywhere.[94] And when he was acquitted of almost every charge, 83 percent of whites approved.[95]

FROM SCOTTSBORO TO SIMPSON

The New York cases were followed mainly by New Yorkers. The trial of O. J. Simpson—winner of the Heisman Trophy, National Football League star, and nationally known actor, sportscaster, and commercial spokesman—was another matter. From the opening scene on a Friday evening in June 1994 (when the double-murder suspect was on a run from the law in a white Bronco with the police in tow and seven media helicopters hovering overhead), it was a tale like no other. Along the route taken by Simpson and a longtime friend, spontaneous crowds formed with black spectators chanting "Free the Juice." Only at his Brentwood home was he finally taken into custody by members of the LAPD, which had long indulged his wife-beating.[96] The charge: first-degree murder. His ex-wife, Nicole Brown Simpson, and Ronald L. Goldman, a waiter at a neighborhood restaurant, had been found dead in the blood-spattered courtyard of Nicole's condominium. Both had been stabbed repeatedly; Nicole's throat had been slashed through the spinal bone.[97]

In extraordinary numbers both blacks and whites followed every detail of the nationally televised trial, transfixed by the racially charged and deeply divisive show. The drama was heightened by its setting. Los Angeles had a racial history that became a powerful weapon in the defense team's arsenal. The sixties riots had started there, in Watts, triggered by the arrest of a drunken black motorist. Despite the fact that the city had an African-

American mayor, Tom Bradley, from 1973 to 1993, relations between the Los Angeles Police Department and the black community were even more strained than in most big cities. (The mayor had little influence over the LAPD, which was governed by an independent commission.) An episode on 3 March 1991 made things notably worse. Rodney King, a paroled convict, led the police on an eight-mile, eighty-mile-per-hour chase through the city streets while driving with a blood-alcohol level double the legal limit. King resisted arrest when he was finally stopped and was viciously beaten after being wrestled to the ground, while an onlooker with a camcorder got the scene on tape. Images of King writhing under the blows were a staple on national television for months to come. Most Americans reacted with the same horror they felt at seeing Bull Connor's fire hoses and police dogs.[98]

Four of the officers were prosecuted for excessive use of force, but were aquitted by a suburban, nearly all-white, jury on 29 April 1992. That news was a spark that ignited a huge riot in South Central Los Angeles. The toll was more than 50 deaths, 2,300 injuries, and $1 billion in property damage, dwarfing the worst of the sixties riots in destructiveness. This time, though, it was not the first of many but an isolated, local clash; it was not reenacted in other cities within the next few years. It was more organized than the sixties disorders, but the organization was the work of Bloods, Crips, and other criminal gangs. The conflict was not a simple black-white affair, but rather a confused melee that involved not only African Americans and Anglo whites but Koreans, Mexicans, and other Asian and Latino groups. Hispanic and Asian merchants, not whites, owned most of the businesses that were hit; more Hispanics than blacks were arrested during the turmoil, with many of them very recent immigrants.[99] Despite these complexities, the riot inflamed long-standing hostilities between African Americans and the LAPD—hostilities that deeply affected the Simpson trial and the public's response to it.

There had never been anything like the long-running show that began with the chase and eventual arrest of O. J. Simpson on 17 June 1994. Literally the talk of the nation, it was part soap opera, part sporting event, with an array of television pundits keeping score. On the day of the verdict an estimated 100 million television viewers watched—an audience larger than that for the first night of the Gulf War, the resignation of Richard Nixon, or the Apollo 11 moon walk.[100] But while the level of national interest made it unique, many of the basic elements had been apparent in one New York case or another: deep suspicion of the police and the D.A.'s office as (in effect) a lynch mob; charges of conspiracy; a black prosecutor attacked as not truly black; in the name of racial justice, a flagrant disregard of the facts, and thus of the overwhelming evidence of guilt; in fact, an assumption of guilt encompassing even a white victim; the racial decency of every white on trial; the case viewed as one more skirmish in an ongoing racial war. It was, in short, another instance in which a court was overwhelmed by the politics of racial grievance.

Simpson as a black martyr in the cause of racial justice: it was a role for which he was a most unlikely candidate. One juror, after the verdict was announced, raised his fist in a black power salute, but Simpson had never for a moment been a Stokely Carmichael.[101] He had worn his racial identity lightly. He had black friends, but his life was not notable for involvement in black issues or causes. He lived in a largely white neighborhood, and his murdered ex-wife was white, as was his current girlfriend. The model and former Los Angeles Raiders cheerleader who testified that he phoned early in the evening of the murders to say he was "finally . . . totally unattached" was also white.[102] Before the jurors came for a site visit, Johnnie L. Cochran, Jr.—the lead trial counsel on the legal "Dream Team"—felt he had to redecorate Simpson's home. Down went the photos of white girlfriends (bound to turn off the many black women on the jury), and up went pictures of African Americans—enlarged at Kinko's and framed to look nice. It was, as a journalist later put it, pure "stagecraft."[103] As Simpson himself once said, "I'm not black. I'm O.J."[104] Jesse Jackson had described him as "a kind of de-ethnicized Negro."[105] For good reason, for a number of years the black media had largely ignored Simpson's activities. Apart from a bit part in the television miniseries *Roots* almost two decades earlier, it was hard to think of any connection between him and anything race-related. Booked for murder, however, he became a racial cause.

In most criminal cases the prosecutors have the upper hand. But celebrity status shifts the balance of power. In O.J.'s case, every move—from arrest to trial—was watched by the black public with deep suspicion. And while in an earlier era authorities could have ignored the deeply felt emotions stirred by such cases, in 1995—especially in Los Angeles, the city of Rodney King —they could not. Thus, despite the brutality of the crime, the apparent overwhelming evidence of Simpson's guilt, his flight from arrest, and a sordid history of domestic abuse and violence, the prosecutors chose not to seek the death penalty. Rather than try the case in the largely white locality where Mr. Simpson lived and the crime had been committed, the Los Angeles district attorney selected a downtown venue. A conviction by a mostly white jury drawn from affluent West Los Angeles would "lack credibility," he privately explained. Racial fairness, he concluded, demanded a heavily black jury.[106]

And that was what the D.A., Gil Garcetti, got. The original jury consisted of six black women, two black men, two Hispanics, one white woman, and one juror who identified himself as half white and half Native American. (No white males were selected as either jurors or alternates.) Alternates replaced many of those initially selected, without any significant shift in the overall racial and gender mix, with the result that the final count was one black man, eight black women, two white women, and one Hispanic man.

The panel was thus three-quarters black. Even for downtown Los Angeles, this was unusual. The makeup of recent juries had been, on the average, 25 percent black; the pool of 900 from which the O.J. jurors were drawn was 28 percent black.[107] How then did the final panel become 75 percent African-American? The defense team kept firmly in mind what its jury consultants had discovered: blacks were ready to acquit before the trial started. Prosecutors stubbornly ignored the same information and focused instead on picking women in the belief that they would listen with particular sympathy to the domestic violence evidence—an assumption that could not have been more wrong with respect to black women.[108] The gamble worked out badly. Cochran didn't just play the race card; he "dealt it from the bottom of the deck," as defense attorney Robert Shapiro later told ABC News.[109] "You will do the right thing," Cochran said in his closing words, suggesting none too subtly that the jury should ignore the O.J. evidence in the interest of racial justice.[110] His appeal to racial solidarity, in fact, had an eerie resemblance to the white defense attorney's final argument on behalf of the two white men accused of the brutal murder of the fourteen-year-old black youth Emmett Till, after he "wolf-whistled" at a white woman in 1955: "I am sure that every last Anglo-Saxon one of you has the courage to acquit these men."[111]

Cochran's final words got the most press, but in fact he had built his whole case—and indeed his whole career as a lawyer—on a foundation of racial resentment, especially against the LAPD. As *New Yorker* writer Jeffrey Toobin said in his book on the case, he "had been waiting his whole life for this case, and this case had been waiting for Johnnie Cochran." Cochran, as Toobin put it, "knew that a black defendant could scarcely go wrong crying racism in the downtown Criminal Courts Building," and thus O.J. became one more black man framed by a racist police department whose massive (and literally incredible) cover-up Cochran exposed.[112] How could such an unbelievable conspiratorial tale (Simpson's blood planted on the rear gate of Nicole's house, Nicole's blood on the sock found in Simpson's bedroom, just for starters) be expected to have a shred of credibility with the jurors? Alas, Cochran knew his audience, inside and outside the courtroom. Conspiracy theories were rife in the black community, as we noted in Chapter 10. And belief in them cut across the lines of social class; indeed, the problem became worse in the upper rungs of the educational ladder.

Asked in 1990 whether "the government deliberately makes sure that drugs are easily available in poor black neighborhoods in order to harm black people," an astonishing 29 percent of college-educated blacks said, "true," while another 38 percent said "might be true." That is, 67 percent were prepared to entertain the idea seriously. These figures were significantly higher than those for blacks with only a high school education, only 18 percent of whom answered "true," with 24 percent thinking it might be so. When black respondents were asked whether "the virus which causes AIDS was deliberately created in a laboratory in order to infect black people," roughly the same percentages of high school graduates and college-educated respondents answered "true" (9 and 10 percent respectively). But among those who thought it "might be true," the percentage for college-educated was strikingly larger (31 percent versus 8 percent for high school graduates). The more educated, the more credulous, in other words. Moreover, merge the two categories of respondents, and 39 percent thought AIDS was a racist plot. When the question became not drugs or AIDS but the deliberate persecution of black elected officials by the government, the numbers were even higher, with the same tendency of those with more education to think in more conspiratorial terms. Among blacks with a college degree, 84 percent thought the government either definitely guilty or perhaps guilty of such racist action.[113]

Only two of the actual jurors in the Simpson case were college graduates, but given the general readiness-to-believe, the beating of motorist Rodney King by white police in 1991, and the revelation that Mark Fuhrman was indeed a true racist cop on the scene, the notion of a police conspiracy against O.J. was certainly an easy sell to those in the jury box as well as to the black public. That Cochran's arguments would fall on receptive ears was evident early. After the preliminary hearing about 60 percent of whites in a national sample said they believed Simpson did it, and the same was true in March 1995, two months into the trial. For blacks, by contrast, 68 percent of those polled that March believed Simpson innocent, and the percentage expressing an opinion of actual guilt had declined from 15 percent in November to 8 percent four months later.[114] At the end of the trial 85 percent of blacks agreed with the verdict, while only 34 percent of whites did.[115] Between the public at large and the jury, however, there was obviously one important difference. The racial split on the outside was not reflected in the final verdict of those on the inside, although with nine blacks on the jury and the threat of another riot (implicitly made by Cochran), perhaps a simple desire for self- and public-preservation made unanimity inevitable.

Interviewed for a symposium in a September 1994 issue of *Ebony*, author Nikki Giovanni described the Simpson case as Scottsboro redux.[116] Johnnie Cochran, in the aftermath of the trial, also referred to the Scottsboro nine.[117] There was a similarity, but it is not one that either Giovanni or Cochran was likely to acknowledge. In both the Scottsboro and O.J. cases, jurors were asked to go beyond the evidence in the interest of broader societal purposes. "Show them, show them that Alabama justice cannot be bought and sold with Jew money from New York," was the 1933 "send a message" appeal.[118]

But there the similarity ended. Recall the Scottsboro facts: On a March morning nine black youths were rousted from a freight train in northern Alabama by a hastily assembled posse, and accused of rape by two white women. After a narrow escape from lynching, the nine, ranging in age from thirteen to twenty, were rushed to trial in a Scottsboro courtroom within two weeks of their arrest. Represented by an unprepared out-of-state counsel who had no more than a half hour consultation with his clients, eight of the defendants were summarily convicted and sentenced to death by all-white juries who deliberated within earshot of large crowds surrounding the court-house, cheering each guilty verdict. After seven subsequent trials, two rever-sals by the U.S. Supreme Court, and a recantation by one of the two women, five of the men served varying prison terms, the last released only in 1950.

No leisurely police escort, phone calls to Mom, calming sips of orange juice, black jurors, celebrated black attorney, or solicitous judge for the Scottsboro nine. In that case the duly authorized legal process was a travesty of justice. How have such ludicrous comparisons—part and parcel of the rhetoric of racial grievance—gained such currency in the current racial cli-mate? The sense of grievance infecting the criminal justice system—whatever its source—is not benign. The result is not only a heightened distrust of the law (and thus of the vital foundation upon which justice and order depends), but more fundamental doubts that blacks and whites share that equality of citizenship upon which a sense of community relies.

The O.J. acquittal was an exercise in jury nullification, an acquittal for reasons unrelated to the evidence—racial reasons, in this case. But it was not unique. No one knows how often black jurors have cast a racial protest vote in the face of overwhelming evidence that a black defendant is guilty. Courts do not keep records indicating the breakdown of juries by race. But in the Bronx, the *Wall Street Journal* reported in 1995, black defendants were ac-quitted in felony cases almost half the time—nearly three times the national rate. In Washington, D.C., in 1995, 95 percent of defendants were black, as were 70 percent of the jurors; in 29 percent of all felony trials, the accused went free, nearly double the national rate. In addition, postverdict letters and statements in a number of cases have drawn a clear picture of jury nullifica-tion. Thus, a Baltimore jury that included eleven blacks refused to convict Davon Neverdon of murder in July 1995, despite the presence of four eyewit-nesses; the lone Asian-American juror blew the whistle. In Washington in 1990 an all-black jury acquitted Darryl Smith of murder; a subsequent letter from an anonymous juror to the court said a minority on the panel who "didn't want to send any more Young Black Men to Jail" had swayed the rest. Other defendants acquitted for reasons of race include Larry Davis in 1988 on charges of attempting to murder nine police officers in the Bronx, and Lem-rick Nelson, a black teenager charged with the 1992 murder of Yankel Rosen-baum in Crown Heights. Damian M. Williams and Henry K. Watson, charged with beating Reginald Denny (and seven others) during the 1992 Los Angeles riots, got off on all the most serious charges.[119]

These are not isolated and inconsequential examples of black jurors taking the law into their own hands. Jury nullification has become an honorable means of what some scholars see as "black self-help."[120] In 1995, in fact, the *Yale Law Journal* put its stamp of respectability on the practice when it published an article by Paul Butler, a professor at the George Washington University Law School, entitled "Racially Based Jury Nullification: Black

Power in the Criminal Justice System."[121] Butler argued that "it is the moral responsibility of black jurors to emancipate some guilty black outlaws," although not those who have committed violent crimes. His goal, as he described it, was "the subversion of American criminal justice, at least as it now exists." Through jury nullification, he hoped "to dismantle the master's house with the master's tools." The law is an integral part of that house: "the traditional criminal justice process . . . is controlled by white lawmakers and white law enforcers." When a juror, against the evidence, votes not guilty, she "makes a decision not to be a passive symbol of support for a system for which she has no respect. . . . The black juror invokes the political nature of her role in the criminal justice system . . . [engaging] in an act of civil disobedience, except that her choice is better than civil disobedience because it is lawful."[122]

The academy is no "ivory tower"; as Jeffrey Rosen has pointed out, "the ideas of the seminar room trickle down, or up."[123] On the street Butler's voice could be heard in the aftermath of the Simpson verdict. "I think he did it," said a black Los Angeles musician. "But I don't think he's guilty. There is an unpaid debt in black history, and we [pulled] for O.J. because of past injustices to blacks."[124] His was a view that frequently made its way into the media from the very outset of the trial. "So many black men has been hung, lynched, and killed for things they didn't do, that it's time for a black man to get off for something he did do," a New York cabdriver told a *Village Voice* reporter almost two months before the trial started. "Whole lotta white people done killed black people and ain't served a day." The cabbie felt "deep down" in his heart that Simpson did it. But he didn't want to see him in jail. "Let them feel bad for once. . . . For years they been getting away with hurting black people."[125]

The problem was, of course, that whites were more likely to feel mad than bad when black jurors ignored the overwhelming evidence of guilt in the Simpson case. Nor could jury nullification dull the pain of those many years that whites got away with hurting black people. The outcome could only be a more racially divided nation.

Are we two nations or one? It was the question of the hour in the wake of the O.J. verdict. And it assumed still greater urgency when the Nation of Islam's Minister Louis Farrakhan—no friend of interracial brotherhood—led a Million Man March in Washington, D.C., just thirteen days later. On October 16, 1995, approximately 400,000 black men lined up to listen to a bizarre speech by Farrakhan, who kept his usual bigotry in check and instead indulged himself in lunatic numerology that went on for a mind-numbing two hours.[126] Although many—perhaps most—of those who turned out at the march may have been responding to Farrakhan's positive message that black men must accept greater responsibility for their own lives, it was not possible to divorce the message of the march from the messenger—a hate-filled demagogue who, as *New York Times* columnist A. M. Rosenthal put it, stood for "separation today, separation tomorrow, separation forever."[127]

BLACKS AND WHITES APART

"The wall between the black and white worlds is getting thicker and thicker every day. So the lens we look through the world is very different," Cornel West said, contemplating the racial divide over O.J.[128] (It is not coincidental that West was a supporter of the Million Man March.) Two nations, two perspectives, both defined by race. Blacks and whites both living closer and drifting apart.

In the preceding pages there is much that substantiates that view. And yet it is important not to get too carried away. "Forty years after the Supreme Court ordered the nation's schools integrated, 30 years after Congress passed the Voting Rights Act, white and black Americans—even successful blacks— live in the same country but in different worlds," *U.S. News & World Report* declared after the Simpson verdict.[129] In much the same vein the widely respected *Economist* two years earlier had reported that "for every middle class black making his way through a white corporation, going to a white college or mowing his lawn in a white suburb, many more are consciously seeking out black schooling and black culture." After the Rodney King verdict, it went on, "blacks *en masse* began to withdraw their money from the (white) commercial banks, putting it in black banks, and started a drive to support black businesses."[130] It was a profoundly misleading picture.

As we noted in Chapter 7, there is in fact no growing hunger for "black schooling." Only a quarter century ago, half of all black college students were enrolled in historically black institutions. By 1975 the proportion was down to 30 percent. It has continued to edge downward ever since, and was 16 percent at last report.[131] Some African Americans have been celebrating Kwanzaa, a December holiday invented in 1966 by the leader of a black nationalist group, but how many? And of those, for what proportion is it a substitute for Christmas? No one knows.[132] Some blacks undoubtedly make an effort to patronize black firms, but "it's not a major factor in their purchase decisions," according to Timothy Bates, an economist who studies black entrepreneurship. Undoubtedly more common is the view of one young black woman who told a reporter that she buys the shampoo that works.[133] In a 1995 *Washington Post* story about race relations on the Washington Redskins football team (almost 80 percent black), the reserve linebacker Terry Crews remarked that "it's always at this table, it's all black, and at one table there's all white, and when the workday's done, black guys go one place, or party at one place, and white guys go to another." But, the story went on, friendships between black and white players were not unusual.[134]

In fact, some survey data suggest an impressive commitment to integration on the part of both blacks and whites, despite the data on black pessimism about white racial attitudes and despite the considerable self-segregation on, for instance, college campuses. In accepting the Liberty Medal in 1992, Thurgood Marshall said: "As I look around I see that even educated whites and African-Americans have given up on integration. . . ."[135] But a December 1996 poll revealed that 84 percent of whites believed that the impact of the civil rights movement on American society had been positive. That made it the most popular social movement in modern times, ranking ahead of the environmental movement (81 percent), the women's movement (76 percent), the family-values movement (69 percent) and the right-to-life movement (50 percent).[136] When asked in 1995 whether the most effective way for black people to improve their situation was "to work less with whites and work more with other blacks," only a quarter of blacks thought so. Sixty-one percent of blacks and 70 percent of whites felt that racial progress required interracial cooperation.[137] The year before, a majority (54 percent) of blacks denied that there was "ever a circumstance in which it would be better for a black student to attend an all-black school."[138]

The majority of blacks and whites, then, seem still to be committed to integration. And, as Chapter 8 indicated, the majority of blacks are actually living in integrated neighborhoods. In 1992, Andrew Hacker claimed that "almost all residential areas" were still "entirely black or white."[139] It wasn't true even in 1964; it's not true now (Table 1). The year the great civil rights bill was passed, two-thirds of all blacks said some whites lived in their neighborhood; by 1994 the figure was five out of six. More than thirty years ago, it was less common for whites to live near blacks than vice versa—a reflection of the relative sizes of the two populations. But, while there are not enough blacks in the nation to provide neighbors for whites in Vermont and Utah, by 1994 three out of five whites were not racially isolated.

There is "a subtle part of racism that's very different from what our parents and grandparents experienced," Marcus L. Alexis II, a young New Yorker working in investment management, claimed in 1994. "The subtle part is unspoken," he went on. "It's inflection, it's body language, it's all the nuances people feel that suggest 'you're not welcome here.' And that's what a lot of my friends are feeling when they decide they don't want to participate in conversations and social gatherings with white folks."[140] Whatever Mr. Alexis and his friends feel, the picture that survey data draw is not of a blacks-only social life. The pattern of responses to questions asking whether respondents have friends of a different race very closely mirrors that which appears when blacks and whites are surveyed about the racial mix in their neighborhood.

Thus, in 1964, 62 percent of blacks but only 18 percent of whites reported having a friend of the other race; by 1989 (the date of the last survey to frame the question this way), five out of six black people could name a white person whom they considered a friend, while two out of three whites said their social circle included someone who was black. (Since at least a tenth of the population responds that they have *no* friends on such surveys, these figures would be even higher if calculated only for those people who have friends at all.)[141]

Table 1
Changes in Patterns of Black-White Social Contact Since the 1960s

	BLACK	WHITE
Percent of respondents who say that members of the other race		
Live in their neighborhood		
1964	66	20
1976	70	38
1982	69	46
1994	83	61
Are friends of theirs		
1964	62	18
1976	87	50
1989	82	66
Are "good friends" of theirs		
1975	21	9
1994	78	73
Have been dinner guests in their home		
1973	39	20
1994	53	34
Attend their church		
1978	37	34
1994	61	44

Sources: Neighborhood and friends data for 1964–1976 from Philip E. Converse et al., *American Social Attitudes Data Sourcebook, 1947–1978* (Cambridge: Harvard University Press, 1980), 71, 75; 1989 friends data from Lee Sigelman et al., "Making Contact? Black-White Social Interaction in an Urban Setting," *American Journal of Sociology* 101 (March 1996), 1314. Data for 1975 "good friends" from Mary R. Jackman and Marie Crain, " 'Some of My Best Friends are Black...': Interracial Friendship and Whites' Racial Attitudes," *American Journal of Sociology,* 50 (1986), 468; data for 1994 "good friends" from National Conference on Christians and Jews, *Taking America's Pulse: The National Conference Survey on Inter-Group Relations* (New York, 1994), B-7. All other figures tabulated from NORC General Social Survey tapes at the Harvard Data Center.

Of course there are friends and friends. Perhaps these interracial friendships are so superficial as to be meaningless. A 1975 national survey probed the matter more deeply by asking about "good friends," defined as people respondents got together with at least once a month or with whom they kept in close touch by calling or writing. Using this more restrictive criterion of friendship, the study found that two decades ago just over a fifth of blacks and 9 percent of whites had a good friend of the other race. The same question was not asked again in any national survey until 1994, and by then the extent of change was phenomenal. The proportion of African-American respondents who had one or more good friends who were white had soared from 21 to 78 percent. The change among whites was even more remarkable —from 9 percent to 73 percent.

Another measure of friendship comes from a survey question about whether respondents have ever entertained someone of the other race to dinner in their homes. In 1973, two-fifths of all blacks and one-fifth of whites said, yes. It is regrettable that we have no comparable evidence that precedes the civil rights revolution, but we can be sure that the figures would have been much lower—close to zero in the South, the region of the country that was still home to a majority of African Americans. By 1994, however, it was not the least bit unusual for blacks and whites to have brought someone of the other race home to dine, as Table 1 indicates. A third of white families and a majority of the black families had done so.

Some of the friendships that led to those dinner invitations were formed in the neighborhood, at school, or on the job. Others developed as a result of attending the same church. Separate churches for African Americans was the norm for most of American history, and the black church continues to play a central role in the black community today. But the color line in religion is no longer nearly as sharp as it was not long ago. We could not locate systematic national data before 1978, but a 1948 study of six leading Protestant denominations estimated that fewer than 0.1 percent of black Protestants belonged to racially mixed congregations.[142] By 1978, 37 percent of African Americans and 34 percent of whites were worshiping at churches attended by persons of the other race. Over the next sixteen years the figure for blacks has soared, and it now stands at over six out of ten, a remarkable development that has attracted virtually no comment. The fraction of whites belonging to racially mixed congregations has also climbed, though by much less—from 34 percent to 44 percent. A substantial majority of churchgoing African Americans and not much less than half of white Americans affiliated with a church, in other words, were sitting together on Sunday morning.

Religious values are often common ground for blacks and whites. In 1993 a black principal of Wingfield High School in Jackson, Mississippi, was dismissed for allowing a student to read a short prayer over the school intercom. His dismissal prompted a huge interracial protest, with teenagers praying outside the high schools and around the state, hundreds of students walking out of class, and thousands of people turning out at the State Capitol to hear Governor Kirk Fordice speak at one of the largest demonstrations in memory.[143]

Blacks and whites together—in the Deep South. The hopes of the 1960s have not been entirely dashed. With the voices of black anger and racial separatism so loud, and the racial division so sharp and clear over issues like the Simpson trial, it's easy to get discouraged. The racial landscape often does look bleak. But there's good news as well as bad. The one should not obscure the other.

GUESS WHO'S COMING TO DINNER

The good news includes a crumbling of the taboo on sexual relations between the two races that was at the very heart of the racial caste system. In the Jim Crow South, for a black man to become involved with a white woman was an invitation to a lynching. It was not uncommon for white men to have sexual relationships with black females, but these were strictly illicit. They could not lead to marriage, and the children of such unions were denied any claim to white being by the "one drop" rule. All the southern states and many in the North made black-white marriages illegal, and white public opinion was overwhelmingly negative even where the law was silent on the subject. Although the Supreme Court boldly attacked school segregation in 1954, it ducked the constitutional issue posed by antimiscegenation statutes for another thirteen years.[144]

This was prudent, as we argued in Chapter 4; to have declared these laws illegal in the early 1950s would have flouted public opinion far more than striking down dual school systems. Before 1958 no pollsters even bothered to ask about white attitudes with respect to interracial marriages; the consensus against them was so strong that it would have been like asking what fraction of the population believed in incest. The 1958 survey found that just 4 percent of whites approved of marriages between blacks and whites (Table 2). A decade later the figure had risen only to 17 percent. In 1963, when a question was first asked about support for laws banning intermarriage, 62 percent of whites were so opposed to mixed marriages that they wanted to outlaw them.

Hollywood thus showed some courage when it took up the issue in the 1967 film *Guess Who's Coming to Dinner.* Its "love will conquer all" approach to the question of whether Sidney Poitier should marry a white woman was far ahead of white opinion of the day. And black opinion, too, for that matter. Only 48 percent of African Americans in 1968 approved of mixed marriages, a year after the Supreme Court legalized them.

In the three decades since then, much has changed. Today the black basketball star Charles Barkley, who has a blond wife, talks of running for governor of Alabama when he retires from the NBA. In the 1960s the idea of a black athlete married to a white woman winning the governor's seat in George Wallace's home state would not even have been plausible fiction.

Table 2 shows that the proportion of whites who would like to see interracial marriages outlawed has dropped from over six out of ten to one in six, and the diehards on this issue are largely found in the South and among the elderly and those with the least education.[145] But a majority of whites, though

Table 2
The Crumbling of the Ultimate Taboo:
Shifting Attitudes About Marriages Across Racial Lines

	BLACK	WHITE
Percent favoring laws to make interracial marriages illegal		
1963	NA	62
1972	NA	39
1980	18	31
1994	3	16
Percent approving of marriages between blacks and whites		
1958	NA	4
1968	48	17
1978	66	32
1983	76	38
1991	71	44
1994	68	45

Sources: Data on antimiscegenation statutes: 1963 from Howard Schuman, Charlotte Steen, and Lawrence Bobo, *Racial Attitudes in America: Trends and Interpretations* (Cambridge: Harvard University Press, 1985), 74–75; 1972–1994 tabulated from the data files of the National Opinion Research Center's General Social Survey, obtained from the Harvard Data Center. On attitudes toward mixed marriages: 1958 from Schuman, *Racial Attitudes,* 74–75; 1968–1991 from George Gallup, Jr., *The Gallup Poll: Public Opinion, 1991* (Wilmington, Del.: Scholarly Resources Inc., 1992), 177; 1994 from *The Gallup Poll: 1994,* 142.

they no longer support *legal* bars to intermarriage, still do have their doubts about interracial weddings. Nevertheless, the proportion who say "no problem" has jumped impressively, from 4 percent in 1958 to almost a third in 1978 and 45 percent by today.

Other survey data—those on attitudes toward dating across racial lines—suggest this liberal trend is likely to continue (Table 3). In 1963 a bare 10 percent of whites had no objection to their teenage child dating an African American. In 1987, 43 percent of whites thought that interracial dating was okay. By 1994, only seven years later, it was 65 percent. What is more, most of the objections came from older white people. Approval among the young white people who were doing most of the dating stood at a stunning 85 percent. Although the earliest data on this question from blacks are from 1987, they reveal the same trend. The proportion with no objection to interracial dating jumped from 72 percent to 88 percent between 1987 and 1994. Journalist reports from campuses play up remarks like that of Malik Zulu Shabazz of the Howard University Law School, who said in 1994: "Brothers, don't ever let us catch you out there with a white woman." [146] Such

Table 3
Percent Who Think It's All Right for
Whites and Blacks to Date Each Other

	BLACK	WHITE
1963	NA	10
1987	72	43
1990	78	45
1994	88	65
Ages 18–24	NA	85
Age 65 or over	NA	36

Sources: Figures for 1963 from William Brink and Louis Harris, *Black and White: A Study of U.S. Racial Attitudes Today* (New York: Simon & Schuster, 1967), 132. Data for 1987–1994 from Times Mirror Center for the People and the Press, *The New Political Landscape* (Los Angeles: Times Mirror Center, 1994), 29–31.

tribalistic effusions perk up a story but appear to have little influence on student behavior.

Whether those who are romantically involved today will wed tomorrow depends of course on black as well as white attitudes toward interracial marriage. Few African Americans supported laws against mixed marriages when the question was first asked of a black sample, and virtually none do now. As to approval of intermarriage, blacks were far more positive than whites when the question was first posed to them, in 1968—about three times as likely to favor it. Until the early 1980s, their attitudes moved in a more liberal direction parallel with those of whites. But between 1983 and 1994 this gradual convergence in attitudes ended. The slow trend toward greater acceptance by whites continued, but black support for mixed marriages actually fell somewhat, from a high of 76 percent in 1983 to 68 percent in 1994.

Spike Lee's 1991 film *Jungle Fever,* which raised doubts about whether an honest romantic relationship is possible between blacks and whites, was thus in tune with the dropping black support for mixed marriages. It's the one area in which black separatist attitudes seem to be gaining support at the grassroots level. The most prominent African-American opponent of marriage between blacks and whites is Minister Louis Farrakhan. A March 1996 survey revealed that 52 percent of blacks gave Farrakhan a favorable rating, and 30 percent regarded him unfavorably.[147] Given his racist views, that is disheartening. It is impossible to think of any white leader with a comparable national following who makes opposition to mixed marriages one of his main issues.[148]

Attitudes are one question, behavior is another. And here the data are incomplete but suggestive. While the great majority of blacks and whites still marry someone of the same race, the rate of intermarriage has risen substantially over the past three decades. The evidence is scanty before 1963, but no one thinks that mixed marriages were anything but exceedingly rare then. In 1963 just 0.7 percent of all the new marriages that included a black partner were racially mixed (Table 4). The figure has multiplied more than seventeenfold since then.

Of course it can be said that 12 percent is still a small percentage of African-American marriages. But think of it this way: just 1.2 percent of the Jews marrying in New York City in 1908 had Gentile partners, and the rate was only 3 percent in 1940. According to the 1990 National Jewish Population Study, 8 percent of Jews who had married before 1965 had wed non-Jews. That picture rapidly changed. The Jewish rate of marriage with non-Jewish partners was 25 percent for those who wed between 1965 and 1974 and 57 percent for those who married from 1985 to 1990.[149]

No one thinks black intermarriage is likely to hit 57 percent in the next twenty years. But the rate of increase over the last thirty is impressive, and if it continues at the same pace, the proportions involved will be very significant indeed. One of the sharpest distinctions between the experience of African Americans and of that of the more than 50 million immigrants who came voluntarily to the United States in the nineteenth and twentieth centuries is that blacks were not allowed into the marital melting pot that did so much to blur immigrant group consciousness and foster assimilation. Although Louis Farrakhan and Spike Lee might not approve, that process has at last begun to affect African Americans in significant numbers.

Table 4

The Rising Rate of Interracial Marriage, 1963–1993: Racially Mixed Unions as a Percent of All New Marriages by African Americans

	Total
1963	0.7
1970	2.6
1980	6.6
1993	12.1

Sources: Based on National Center for Health Statistics data, available only since 1963. Figure for 1963 from David M. Heer, "Intermarriage," in Stephan Thernstrom, ed., *Harvard Encyclopedia of American Ethnic Groups* (Cambridge: Harvard University Press, 1980), 518; 1970–1993 data from Douglas J. Besharov and Timothy Sullivan, "One Flesh: America is Experiencing an Unprecedented Increase in Black-White Intermarriage," *New Democrat,* July-August 1996, 21. All of these figures may be biased downward, because states are not required to furnish them to the National Center for Health Statistics and several do not cooperate. It happens that four of the five states with the largest concentrations of interracial couples, according to the 1990 census (California, Oklahoma, Texas, and Washington), do not provide such information. Data from the Current Population Survey suggest, according to Besharov and Sullivan, that these estimates may be as much as one-fifth too low as a result.

Interracial dating and interracial marriage: a real increase in these most intimate of relationships between blacks and whites is bound to affect the racial climate. In the Jim Crow South, whites who fought so hard to maintain the old order knew that free and open sexual relationships across racial lines would strike at the heart of the system. What was the logic of strict segregation if it forced husbands and wives to sit apart on the same bus? And today, how long can the voices of black separation maintain their legitimacy as the lines of group identity begin truly to blur? Nathan McCall could write of coming to understand "that there were two distinct worlds in America," one white, one black, but both economic and demographic change along a variety of fronts threatens to complicate the picture he so starkly drew. McCall, Bell, the Nation of Islam, the Afrocentrists, the separatist voices on college campuses, among others, see whites as the enemy "without," but in a new and more fluid racial order, "within" or "without" could not retain the same exclusionary meanings.

ONE NATION, MANY INDIVIDUALS

It is startling that until 1989 our birth registration rules provided that the child of a white husband and black wife counted as "black," and so, too, did the child of a black husband and a white wife.[150] The offspring of such marriages simply expanded the size of the black population. As did the offspring of those offspring, even if they all married whites. It was the "one drop of blood" rule: a trace of black blood and you were black.[151]

The rule has been one of the last remnants of our once-pervasive caste society, and it may be on the way out. Golf superstar Tiger Woods is one-quarter black, one-quarter Chinese, one-quarter Thai, one-eighth white, and one-eighth Native American.[152] But while his "one drop" of black blood would have traditionally made him "black," and while Nike (as a corporate sponsor) has chosen to package him as black, he checked off Asian and African American on his college application form, and calls himself "Cablinasian"—a contraction of Caucasian, black, Indian, and Asian.[153] The Nike decision is, of course, telling in itself: as an Asian-American golf star, Woods would not have the same appeal, the company calculates. More important, however, is the simple fact of choice. The old genetic order—so important in shaping the racial climate—is at least fraying at the edges. "When I received my 1990 census form, I realized that there was no race category for my children," Susan Graham, a white woman married to a black man, told a congressional subcommittee in 1993. "My child," she said, "has been white on the United States census, black at school, and multiracial at home—all at the same time." Graham and other advocates wanted a "multiracial" category added to census forms.[154]

The practice of the Census Bureau has been, of course, to treat racial categories as mutually exclusive, and insist that every American belongs in one and only one. But a 1995 pilot study by the Current Population Survey found that 1.7 percent of the population would classify themselves as multiracial if given the opportunity.[155] It's a small fraction, but it works out to be over 4 million people, nearly double the total number of American Indians, for instance. Moreover, if a new category were actually to be created, the size of the group would surely grow. Just placing the "multiracial" option on the census "invites people to consider choosing it," journalist Lawrence Wright has noted. "When the census listed 'Cajun' as one of several examples under the ancestry question, the number of Cajuns jumped nearly two thousand percent. To remind people of the possibility is to encourage enormous change."[156]

Ironically, the main guardians today of the traditional and blatantly racist one-drop rule are the mainline civil rights organizations. They have much to lose by the institution of a multiracial category. If the number of Americans who check "black" drops off as a result, African-American claims to X number of executive jobs at Texaco and Y number of places at the University of Michigan Medical School will have to be modified. No wonder that advocates of a multiracial category—and those who would take the next logical step and abandon altogether the classifications upon which racism depends— have been quite bizarrely smeared as "pawns for racists."[157] The stakes are very high, and the rhetoric is correspondingly ugly. The civil rights groups, in fact, are generally opposed to any and all moves (for example, transracial adoption) that blur racial lines and thus potentially diminish the black head count.[158]

And so they hold fast to a system of racial classifications that sharply distinguishes blacks from whites. But those very classifications pit members of one group against the other, poisoning the racial atmosphere. As Lawrence Wright has written: "The use of racial statistics . . . creates a reality of racial divisions, which then require solutions, such as busing, affirmative action, and multicultural education, all of which are bound to fail, because they heighten the racial awareness that leads to contention."[159]

Why not abandon the classifications that help to make a bad situation worse, heightening racial divisions in a nation already deeply racially divided? The idea has surprising public support. No leading public figure has stood up to make the case for ending our obsession with counting by race, and yet close to half of the public favored such a move in a February 1995 poll. Although almost every national black organization opposes any modification of our current system of racial classifications, 48 percent of African Americans and 47 percent of whites believe that the census "should stop" collecting information on race and ethnicity.[160]

It was a central hope of the civil rights movement that blacks would come to be seen as individuals—"judged [not] by the color of their skin but by the content of their character," as Dr. King so famously put it. It is *the* change in the racial climate on which all else depends. It is on the ground of individuality that blacks and whites can come together. Large and important race-related problems still remain. Together blacks and whites can address them; as separate nations within our nation, they cannot—and will not.

Conclusion:
One Nation, Indivisible

In 1991, 13 percent of the whites in the United States said that they had generally "unfavorable" opinions about black Americans. In an ideal world, that number would be zero. But such a world is nowhere to be found. In Czechoslovakia that same year, 49 percent of Czechs had "unfavorable" attitudes toward the Hungarian ethnic minority living within the boundaries of their country (Table 1). Likewise, 45 percent of West Germans disliked the Turks living in Germany; 54 percent of East Germans regarded Poles negatively; 40 percent of Hungarians frowned on the Romanians who lived among them; and 42 percent of the French disdained Arab immigrants from North Africa. In only two of the dozen European countries surveyed—Britain and Spain—was the proportion of majority group members who expressed dislike for the principal minority group less than twice as high as in the United States.

Much of the animosity had deep historical roots. In 1991 a third of Poles still had an "unfavorable" opinion of Jews, for example. Gypsies had the most enemies, with unfavorable ratings ranging from a low of 50 percent in Spain to 91 percent in Czechoslovakia. "Ethnic, religious, and racial hatreds are thriving across Europe as the 20th Century draws to an end," noted two commentators on the study. As the movement toward European union increases the flow of labor across national boundaries, "the Continent could turn into a tinderbox," they warned.[1]

Against this yardstick the racial views of white Americans look remarkably good. But are seemingly tolerant whites simply more hypocritical than Czechs or French? Perhaps they have learned to keep their animus hidden from public view. We think not. Although different ways of framing questions about racial prejudice yield slightly different answers, the bulk of the evidence squares with the 1991 survey results: when it comes to intergroup tolerance, Americans rate high by international standards.

Table 1

**Majority Dislike for Ethnic Minorities in European Nations, 1991:
Percent with "Unfavorable" Attitudes Toward the Principal
Domestic Minority in Their Country**

COUNTRY	MINORITY GROUP	PERCENT DISLIKING
Bulgaria	Turks	39
Czechoslovakia	Hungarians	49
East Germany	Poles	54
France	North Africans	42
Great Britain	Irish	21
Hungary	Romanians	40
Lithuania	Poles	30
Poland	Ukrainians	42
Russia	Azerbaijanis	44
Spain	Catalans	22
Ukraine	Azerbaijanis	42
West Germany	Turks	45
United States	African Americans	13

Source: Times Mirror Center for the People and the Press, *The Pulse of Europe: A Survey of Political and Social Values and Attitudes* (Washington, D.C.: Times Mirror Center, 1991), sec. VIII.

AMERICA SINCE MYRDAL

This is a profound change. When Gunnar Myrdal first trained his microscope on the American racial scene in the closing years of the Great Depression, he was struck by the radical difference between the status of immigrants and that of African Americans. The United States stood out for its success in absorbing millions of immigrants from other lands into the melting pot. Myrdal believed that American social scientists were too preoccupied with "the occasional failures of the assimilation process" and the "tension" that immigration created in the society. They lacked the perspective available to "the outside observer," to whom the "first and greatest riddle to solve" was how "the children and grandchildren of these unassimilated foreigners" so quickly became "well-adjusted Americans." Part of the answer to the puzzle, Myrdal suggested, was "the influence upon the immigrant of a great national *ethos,* in which optimism and carelessness, generosity and callousness, were so blended as to provide him with hope and endurance."[2]

In those days, the "optimism" and "generosity" Myrdal found did not extend to the descendants of enslaved Africans, though the "callousness" certainly did. Blacks had not been coaxed or coerced into the American melting pot; they had been forcibly kept out of it. Everyone was eager to "American-ize" the immigrants, Myrdal noticed, and viewed "the preservation of their separate national attributes and group loyalties as a hazard to American insti-tutions." The recipe for African Americans was the reverse. They were "ex-cluded from assimilation," and advised "even by their best friends in the dominant white group" to "keep to themselves and develop a race pride of their own."[3]

In the South, where the large majority of African Americans lived, an elaborate legal code defined their position as a separate and inferior people. Poorly educated in segregated schools, and confined to ill-paid, insecure, menial jobs, they were a subordinate caste in a society dedicated to white supremacy. Moreover, in countless ways blacks were daily reminded of their status as a lesser breed; they entered only the back door of a white home, never shook hands with a white person, and grown men were habitually addressed as "boy" or simply by their first names. In the North, blacks could vote, and the color line was less rigid and lacked the force of law. But many of the semiskilled and skilled industrial positions that gave immigrants the chance to climb out of poverty were off-limits, and blacks lived for the most part in a world separate from whites. A color line in the housing market confined black families to black neighborhoods; swimming in the "white" part of a public beach was dangerous; and many restaurants would not serve black customers. As Myrdal found, nine out of ten of even the most liberal and cosmopolitan northerners whom he encountered in the 1940s blanched at the thought of interracial marriage.[4]

None of the public opinion surveys conducted in the Depression or World War II years included a specific question about whether whites had "favor-able" or "unfavorable" opinions about blacks. But there can be no doubt about the answer such an inquiry would have yielded. The polling data we reviewed in Part I of this book demonstrated that large majorities of whites held strongly racist sentiments. African Americans were a stigmatized group, assumed to be a permanent caste that would forever remain beyond the melting pot.

That world has now vanished. In the spring of 1995, in the wake of attacks on affirmative action, Georgia congressman and one-time civil rights hero John Lewis complained that he sometimes felt as if he were reliving his life. "Didn't we learn?" he asked. He felt "the need to . . . tell people we've got to do battle again."[5] But yesterday is not today, as many do recognize—includ-ing, we suspect, Lewis himself. "We black folk should never forget that our forefathers were slaves," Florida congresswoman Carrie P. Meek said in 1994. But then she added, "though my daughter says, 'Enough, Mom, enough of this sharecropper-slave stuff.' "[6] Meek was born in 1926, and in her own lifetime the rigidly oppressive caste system delineated in *An American Di-lemma* gave way to the far more fluid social order of today.

From rigid caste system to a more fluid social order: that was the story in Part I of this book. After the opening chapters on the Jim Crow South and life in the North, we reviewed decades of amazing change. In the 1940s and the 1950s, hundreds of thousands of blacks migrated North, the black poverty rate plunged, and black home ownership soared. From there we moved on to a discussion of the civil rights movement and the riots of the 1960s—the rise of SCLC, the psychological transformation of southern blacks, their mass mobilization, the genius and luck of Martin Luther King, Jr., the touch-and-go nature of the civil rights revolution, the tension between the leaders of a moral crusade and politicians such as John F. Kennedy, the emergence of racial separatism and black power, the four summers of rioting in which close to 300 Americans died and at least 8,000 were injured.

In Part II, we examined social, economic and political trends since the civil rights revolution, and in Part III we looked at the response of public and private institutions to the question of race. We did not neglect the bad news. In 1995 half of all the murder victims in the United States were African Americans, though they comprised just one-eighth of the population; more than half of those arrested for murder were also black. The black poverty rate that same year was still 26 percent; 62 percent of children in female-headed families were poor. Perhaps most ominously, in 1994, on average, blacks aged seventeen could read only as well as the typical white child just thirteen years old. The racial gap in levels of educational performance permanently stacks the deck against too many African American youngsters as they move on to work or further schooling.

To stress the bad news is to distort the picture, however. Equally important is the story of enormous change, of much more progress than many scholars have recognized. For instance, between 1970 and 1995 the proportion of African Americans living in suburban communities nearly doubled, and residential segregation decreased in almost all the nation's metropolitan areas with the largest black populations. One of the best kept secrets of American life today is that over 40 percent of the nation's black citizens consider themselves members of the middle class. The black male unemployment rate has gotten much press, but, in fact, of those who are in the labor force (working or looking for work), 93 percent had jobs in 1995. We have let the underclass define our notion of black America; it is a very misleading picture.

Over the last half century, the positions of African Americans thus improved dramatically by just about every possible measure of social and economic achievement: years of school completed, occupational levels, median incomes, life expectancy at birth, poverty rates, and homeownership rates. Much of the change took place before the civil rights movement. And while key decisions made by political and legal authorities in this early period were undeniably important (President Truman's order abolishing segregation in the armed forces, for example, and *Brown v. Board of Education*), the impersonal economic and demographic forces that transferred so many blacks from the southern countryside to the northern city were more fundamental.

In addition, white racial attitudes were gradually liberalized. Racist beliefs that were once firmly held by highly educated and uneducated whites alike lost all claim to intellectual respectability by the 1950s, and that changed racial climate finally opened doors. For instance, the door to the Brooklyn Dodgers' locker room. Had the visionary Branch Rickey believed Dodger fans were unreconstructed racists, he would not have put Jackie Robinson on the field and risked plunging ticket sales. As it was, his feel for changing racial attitudes brought championships to Brooklyn.

Social contact between the races has also increased enormously. By 1989, five out of six black Americans could name a white person whom they considered a friend, while two out of three whites said their social circle included someone who was black. By 1994 it had become not the least bit unusual for blacks and whites to have brought someone of the other race home to dine (a third of white families and a majority of the black families had done so), and most blacks and whites said someone of the other race lived in their neighborhood. When a sample of people in the Detroit metropolitan area were asked in 1992 whether they had contact on the job with people of the other race, 83 percent of blacks and 61 percent of whites said, yes. That same year, 72 percent of blacks and 64 percent of whites reported having interracial conversations on the job "frequently" or "sometimes." Even in the most intimate of relations, there had been substantial change. By 1993, 12 percent of all marriages contracted by African Americans were to a spouse of the other race.[7]

Two Nations: Black and White, Separate, Hostile, Unequal, Andrew Hacker called his best-selling book. Our book is in many ways an answer to Hacker. *One* nation (we argue), no longer separate, much less unequal than it once was, and by many measures, less hostile. Moreover, the serious inequality that remains is less a function of white racism than of the racial gap in levels of educational attainment, the structure of the black family, and the rise in black crime.

We quarrel with the left—its going-nowhere picture of black America and white racial attitudes. But we also quarrel with the right—its see-no-evil view. It seems extraordinarily hard for liberals to say we have come a long way; the Jim Crow South is not the South of 1997. But it seems very hard for conservatives to say, yes, there was a terrible history of racism in this country, and too much remains.

Conservatives seem to think that they concede too much if they acknowledge the ugliness of our racial history and the persistence of racism (greatly diminished but not gone)—that if they do so, they will be committed to the currently pervasive system of racial preferences and indeed to reparations. And liberals, from their different perspective, also fear concession. To admit dramatic change, they seem to believe, is to invite white indifference. As if everything blacks now have rests on the fragile foundation of white guilt.

EUROPEAN IMMIGRANTS, ASIANS, AND BLACKS

The foundation of progress for many blacks is no longer fragile. Progress is real and solid. But are blacks beginning to make the transition from stigmatized racial caste to ethnic group? The notion that blacks are permanently, indelibly, different is what political scientist Donald L. Horowitz has called "the figment of the pigment"—the myth that racial groups are sealed compartments, impervious to change.[8] In the opening decades of the twentieth century, most Americans regarded Italians, Greeks, Poles, and other "new immigrant" groups as separate "races," inferior, and unassimilable; hence the immigration quotas of the 1920s to keep them out.[9] Today no one considers Polish Americans an unmeltable racial group. Data from the 1980 census, in fact, reveal that only 7 percent of American Poles who married after 1950 chose a fellow Pole as their spouse.[10]

The experience of Asian Americans also illustrates the mutability of racial distinctions. Starting in 1860, Asian immigrants were classified as members of a separate, "Oriental" race by the U.S. Census, and figures about them were usually published under the umbrella category "Negro and other races."[11] Acute fear of "the Yellow Peril" led to restrictions on immigration from Asia in 1882, four decades before quotas were imposed on European immigrants. On the eve of World War II, Gunnar Myrdal found that prejudice against Asian Americans was intense and pervasive. They seemed to him, like African Americans, an unassimilable caste. "The Negroes are set apart, together with other colored people, principally the Chinese and Japanese," he said. "The *temporary* social disabilities of recent white immigrants" would be overcome in time, but not the "*permanent* disabilities of Negroes and other colored peoples."[12]

The "disabilities" of Chinese, Japanese, and other Asian immigrant groups were far from "permanent," we now see. Asian Americans have achieved spectacular economic and social mobility in recent decades. Though less than 4 percent of the population, they are currently 19 percent of the student body at Harvard and 11 percent of all the physicians in the United States. In 1992, 47 percent of Asian Americans aged twenty-five to forty-four were college graduates, a rate two-thirds higher than that for non-Hispanic whites. Some 63 percent held managerial, professional, technical, or administrative jobs in 1990, again well ahead of non-Hispanic whites. Average annual income for U.S.-born Asian families, according to the 1990 Census, was $47,840, more than a third above the national average. The median family income of Chinese Americans born in the United States was $56,762, 61 percent above the national average; native-born Japanese Americans had incomes 50 percent above the national average.[13]

The striking success of Asian Americans has obviously done nothing to alter their physical appearance. For the most part, they are still recognizably members of a "race" other than white, although the current very high rate of intermarriage means that an increasing fraction of their offspring will look less distinctive in the years to come. But it is hard to find anyone who cares much what their "race" is, and it has become anachronistic for the Census Bureau to continue (as it does) to put a racial label on people of Asian descent.

Indeed, if the ultimate measure of integration into a society is a high rate of ethnic intermarriage, then Asian Americans have been strikingly successful. In Los Angeles the proportion of Japanese marrying non-Japanese went from 2 percent in the 1920s to 14 percent in 1952 and 60 percent in 1977. And 50 percent of the Chinese Americans who wed in Los Angeles in 1977 took non-Chinese mates.[14] The trend has continued. The number of births to mixed Asian-white couples doubled between 1978 and 1992. In 1989, couples in which one parent was white and one Japanese outnumbered those in which both were Japanese-American by a 58:42 margin.[15] What once was seen by the vast majority of whites as a stark difference in racial identity has now become, for most, a modest difference in ethnic background—less important than social class as a barrier to social interaction.

There are parallels between blacks and Asian Americans, although they cannot be pushed too far. What it means to be black in American society in the 1990s is also far different from what it meant in the 1930s. Highly successful blacks like Franklin Delano Raines, Clinton's budget chief, Ann M. Fudge, the president of the Maxwell House Coffee Company, and Kenneth I. Chenault, chief operating officer for American Express, have become part of the country's economic and governing elite.[16] Countless others, who don't make the news, are all-American success stories. In addition, blacks are currently intermarrying with whites about as frequently as Jews married Gentiles or Japanese Americans married non-Japanese only fifty years ago.

On the other hand, at present blacks are far less successful than Asians, and their level of family disorganization in particular is conducive to high crime and poverty rates, as well as low educational achievement, obstacles to advancement and social integration that Asians did not face. Two other differences should be noted. Asian organizations like the Japanese American Citizens League took a strongly integrationist and assimilationist stance toward the larger culture. Few group leaders advocated racial separatism and indulged in racist antiwhite rhetoric of the kind that is too often heard today within the African-American community. In part because Asian immigrants came voluntarily rather than as slaves, there was no Asian Malcolm X to declare defiantly that his people were "not American."[17] In addition, Asians were well launched on their journey from caste to ethnic group before government began to pursue color-conscious policies to benefit racial minorities and hence to reward racial solidarity.

THE ROAD TO PROGRESS

Much racial progress has been made. And much has *yet* to be made. How to keep moving forward? It is a question that can be answered only by knowing the route by which African Americans have come to where they are today.

There is no mystery as to how they got from there to here, most writing on racial change in recent decades assumes. The story began with the civil rights movement, which, with a boost from *Brown v. Board of Education,* created turmoil in the nation and forced Congress and the White House to act. The civil rights and voting rights legislation of the mid-1960s destroyed Jim Crow institutions and gave equal legal status to African Americans. These color-blind measures, however, failed to remedy deeper economic and social inequalities rooted in race. Color-conscious policies that set specific numerical goals and timetables attacked the underlying problems. In fact, only the adoption of preferential policies could have created a black middle class and brought about other economic and educational gains.

From this account, a simple policy conclusion flows: preferential policies are the key to future progress. And thus Supreme Court decisions and other actions that constrain the use of racial classifications by public authorities are viewed by some as truly dangerous—a threat to black well-being comparable to the end of Reconstruction.

Such alarm ignores the historical record, we have argued, although the great strides forward have since been somewhat obscured by the gains and disappointments of subsequent years. The civil rights revolution reached a climax in a burst of legislation that destroyed the Jim Crow system, but that legislation promised more than it could quickly deliver. As Dr. King and others understood, the legal fix would not tomorrow solve the problem of economic and educational inequalities so long in the making. Blacks were understandably impatient. They had already waited much too long—almost a century since the passage of the great Reconstruction Amendments to the Constitution. It was tempting to seek shortcuts, ways of accelerating social change, and thus the demand for "freedom now" soon became a call for "equality as a fact and as a result," as Lyndon Johnson put it in 1965.[18]

That call for equality as a "fact" and "result" was the first step down the road to racial preferences. Much celebrated in the civil rights community for the benefits they have brought, preferences are in fact difficult to assess, as we suggested in Part II. In 1995 the historian Roger Wilkins described himself as the happy recipient of racial preferences. "I'd rather be an assistant attorney general who was a beneficiary of affirmative action than a GS 14," he said.[19] It's hard to believe Wilkins is really convinced he would have been languishing at the bottom of a bureaucratic heap had he not been rescued by preferential policies. His tale certainly does not square with the larger picture, as we understand it.

In a few respects the overall rate of black progress did accelerate after preferential policies were introduced. Rates of entry into law and medical schools are one example. But lawyers and doctors are a tiny fraction of the black middle class. And by many other measures progress slowed—and in some cases stopped altogether. One recent study found that the racial gap in median wages, labor-force participation, and joblessness was wider in 1992 than in 1967.[20] As a consequence of the huge rise in female-headed households among African Americans, the ratio of black to white family income has fallen somewhat since the 1960s. And the poverty rate for blacks in the 1990s is about as high as it was a generation ago.

Thus, on many counts the socioeconomic gains made by African Americans in the affirmative action era have been less impressive than those that occurred before preferential policies. On the basis of that historical record, however, we cannot conclude that affirmative action did nothing significant. In the 1940s and 1950s, big strides forward were relatively easy to take—blacks were so far behind whites. Thereafter, the rate of progress naturally slowed. Moreover, preferential policies may indeed have benefited some African Americans (those with better educational credentials) without dramatically improving the position of the group as a whole.[21]

The slower growth of the American economy since the early 1970s further complicates the task of assessment. Groups on the lower rungs of the socioeconomic ladder usually find it far easier to improve their position when the economy is booming, as it was to an extraordinary degree in the 1950s and 1960s. And perhaps without affirmative action, the slow economy would have been even harder on African Americans than it was. It's a what-might-have-been argument that cannot be settled. But those who assume that ending affirmative action will end black progress must reconcile the history of pre-1970s progress with their fear of a future that returns to the past.

Even assuming that affirmative action rescued Roger Wilkins and others from professional oblivion, an important question remains: have the benefits outweighed the costs? The issue was implicitly raised in a suprising 1993 letter. The mayors of Minneapolis and four other large American cities wrote to Attorney General Janet Reno, calling for an end to the collection and dissemination of any crime statistics broken down by race. "We believe," the mayors said, "that the collection and use of racial crime statistics by the federal government perpetuate racism in American society." Such data, the mayors went on, were "largely irrelevant" and conveyed the erroneous impression that race and criminality were causally linked. "Racial classifications," the letter continued, were "social constructs" and had "no independent scientific validity." An earlier letter from the Minneapolis mayor had expressed concern about the " 'we' vs. 'they' mentality" that racial classifications created.[22]

The crime statistics had wonderfully concentrated the mayors' minds. Momentarily, at least, they recalled what liberals had always believed until the late 1960s but had chosen to forget when they were converted to affirmative action: racial classifications perpetuate racism. The mayors did not object to racial body counts on principle, as liberals once had. They were simply troubled by the publication of statistics that made African Americans look bad. Racial statistics showing that black poverty and unemployment rates were higher than those of whites, that our colleges and universities did not have "enough" African American students, and that our corporations were short on black executives: these racial classifications apparently were not mere "social constructs" with "no scientific validity." They were essential to enlightened public policy. It was only the black crime rate to which the mayors objected.

But racial data used to distribute benefits inevitably creates the we-versus-they outlook that worried them. American society has paid, it seems to us, a very high price for well-intentioned race-conscious policies. Particularly those built into our law, for the law delivers messages that ripple through both the public and private sectors. And thus unlike the mayors, we hold to Justice Harlan's belief that "our Constitution is color-blind, and neither knows nor tolerates classes among citizens."[23]

In 1896, Justice Harlan was under no illusion that American *society* was color-blind; his was a statement about how to read the Constitution. Nor did Thurgood Marshall in 1947 suppose the country had become oblivious to race when he argued that "classifications based on race or color have no moral or legal validity in our society."[24] We're not naïve; we don't think Americans have to think twice about the color of someone they meet. And we do know that for many whites color still carries important connotations: a young black man on an urban street in the evening appears much more menacing than one who is white. Even middle-class black neighbors may still seem less appealing than white ones to too many white families. It is, in fact, precisely the problem of ongoing racism and just plain color-consciousness that makes race-blind public policy so imperative. Policies that work to heighten the sense of racial separatism spell disaster in a nation with an ugly history of racial subordination and a continuing problem, albeit dramatically diminished, of racial intolerance.

Race-conscious policies make for more race-consciousness; they carry American society backward. We have a simple rule of thumb: that which brings the races together is good; that which divides us is bad. Of course, which policies have what effect is a matter of deep contention. To tear down affirmative action "could start a race war that would make Bosnia look like a kindergarten party," Arthur Fletcher, a former assistant secretary for employment standards, said in 1995.[25] The Sniderman and Piazza research we have frequently cited suggests quite a different picture: a racial divide widened by preferences. Others argue that "diversity" strategies bring whites and blacks together; it is not our view. Only those policies that recognize differences among *individuals* can create a true community.

A nation in which individuals are judged as individuals: it was the dream of the 1960s, and we still cherish it. "There *is* a proper object for all the loathing in this country," *New Republic* literary editor Leon Wieseltier has said. "That object is: race. Instead of race hatred, the hatred of race. Instead of the love of what is visible about the person, the love of what is invisible about the person."[26] Does the Wieseltier view ask black Americans to turn their back on all things "black"—to deny all cultural differences associated with group membership? Of course not. Jews haven't; Armenians haven't; Ukrainians haven't. Many Americans arrange their private lives so as to spend much of their time with others of the same background. Purging all racial distinctions from our law and our public life would pose no threat to those who wish to live in a predominantly black neighborhood, attend an all-black church, and otherwise associate primarily or even exclusively with their fellow African Americans.

Racist Americans have long said to blacks, the single most important thing about you is that you're black. Indeed, almost the only important thing about you is your color. And now, black and white Americans of seeming good will have joined together in saying, we agree. It has been—and is—exactly the wrong foundation on which to come together for a better future. "There can be no empathy and persuasion across racial lines," the economist Glenn C. Loury has said, unless we understand "that the conditions and feelings of particular human beings are universally shared. Such an understanding can be had, but only if we look past race to our common humanity."[27] Ultimately, black social and economic progress largely depend on the sense that we are one nation—that we sink or swim together, that black poverty impoverishes us all, that black alienation eats at the nation's soul, and that black isolation simply cannot work.

We urge color-blind public policies. But how far would we go? It is tempting to halt the collection of all racial statistics by the Bureau of the Census, the Department of Justice, and other governmental bodies. But race has been such a crucial source of inequality and justice in American society that a strong case can be made for continuing to monitor group differences in education, employment, health, housing, and crime. It is precisely that information upon which much of the analysis in this book rests.

On the other hand, protecting citizens against discrimination does not require elaborate statistical data on the racial composition of the population. The government has never gathered information about religious affiliation or sexual orientation, and yet it is able to enforce laws forbidding discrimination against Jews and homosexuals.

Racial breakdowns of social and economic data are useful to monitor progress. The problem is that they are so easily abused. Statistical disparities—a situation, for example, in which only 10 percent of city contracts are awarded to black-owned firms although the city is 30 percent African American—are taken as proof of discrimination. Such disparities (as Chapter 15 indicated) can have numerous explanations. Uncritical use of racial statistics not only fails to identify true instances of continuing racism; it encourages color-conscious remedies that reduce the infinite diversity of individuals to a few racial categories—and thus actually perpetuates racism.

GROUP DIFFERENCES

The issue of group differences is actually enormously complicated. American society does not consist of two monolithic racial groups, blacks and whites. It is a complex mosaic of groups with different histories and different cultural traits that have led them to concentrate in different social niches. The complexities of the matter become evident when we notice that the socioeconomic gap between Jews and Christians today is greater than the gap between blacks and whites. Jewish per capita incomes are nearly double those of non-Jews, a bigger difference than the black-white income gap. Although Jews make up less than 3 percent of the population, they constitute more than a quarter of the people on the *Forbes* magazine list of the richest four hundred Americans. A remarkable 87 percent of college-age Jews are currently enrolled in institutions of higher education, as compared with 40 percent for the population as a whole.[28] Asian Americans similarly outrank whites on most measures, and the gap between Chinese and Japanese Americans born in the United States and whites is of the same order of magnitude as the black-white gap (Table 2).

Comparing America's ethnic groups clearly reveals their widely differing socioeconomic profiles. Consider the "Cajuns," who reside mainly in rural Louisiana.[29] They are indistinguishable from African Americans in their low rate of college graduation, and have incomes that are 19 percent below the national average. At the other end of the spectrum are Armenians, whose college completion rates are 88 percent above the national average, and who have incomes 45 percent above the average. Armenians, with Greeks and Latvians, are examples of allegedly unassimilable "new immigrant" groups who arrived on these shores less than century ago and have already moved ahead of earlier arrivals like the English, Germans, Irish, and Swedes.

"Whites" are not monolithic, and neither are the many groups sometimes described as "people of color." Note the large differences between Cubans on one side and Mexicans and Puerto Ricans on the other. And Chinese and Japanese Americans are "people of color" who have nevertheless climbed to the top rungs of the socioeconomic ladder. Groups differ from each other not

Table 2

Education and Family Incomes of Native-Born Members of Selected Ethnic Groups, 1990

	COLLEGE GRADUATES		FAMILY INCOME	
	Percent	*Index*	*Median*	*Index*
White	22.0	108	$35,975	101
Black	11.3	56	20,209	57
Armenian	38.1	188	51,614	145
Cajun	11.8	58	28,640	81
Chinese	51.0	251	56,762	160
Cuban	26.5	131	37,452	105
English	28.6	141	40,763	115
French Canadian	17.2	85	39,171	110
German	22.1	109	38,171	107
Greek	32.8	162	45,356	127
Irish	21.3	105	38,022	107
Italian	21.9	108	42,618	120
Japanese	34.2	168	52,728	148
Latvian	49.6	244	54,806	154
Mexican	8.6	42	26,766	75
Polish	23.4	115	41,943	118
Puerto Rican	9.4	46	21,945	62
Scottish	36.2	178	43,330	122
Slovenian	22.6	128	39,986	113
Swedish	27.5	135	40,518	114

Sources: White and black figures from U.S. Bureau of the Census, Current Population Reports, P-20-448, *The Black Population in the United States: March 1990 and 1989* (Washington, D.C.: U.S. Government Printing Office, 1991), tables 2 and 8. Data for all other groups are for native-born residents of the U.S. only, from U.S. Bureau of the Census, 1990 Census of the Population, *Ancestry of the Population in the United States,* 1990-CP-3-2 (Washington, D.C.: U.S. Government Printing Office, 1993), tables 3 and 5; U.S. Bureau of the Census, 1990 Census of the Population, *Ancestry of the Population in the United States,* 1990-CP-3-2 (Washington, D.C.: U.S. Government Printing Office, 1993), tables 3 and 5; U.S. Bureau of the Census, 1990 Census of the Population, *Asian and Pacific Islanders in the United States,* 1990-CP-3-5 (Washington, D.C.: U.S. Government Printing Office, 1993), tables 3 and 5; U.S. Bureau of the Census, 1990 Census of the Population, *Persons of Hispanic Origin in the United States,* 1990-CP-3-3 (Washington, D.C.: U.S. Government Printing Office, 1993), tables 3 and 5. Education for all persons 25 or older. The index for both education and income is the figure for the total population (20.3 percent college graduation, and $35,508 median family income) divided by the figure for the group in question.

only in education and incomes but in dozens of other ways, from life expectancy at birth to the age at which they choose to retire and accept lower incomes for greater leisure. Furthermore, they do not necessarily have precisely the same rank order on any two of these measures. For example, completion of higher education generally pays off in higher average incomes for a group, but not to the same degree for all. Americans of Scottish descent, for example, rank near the very top in education, but not nearly so far above average in income; many appear to have chosen careers that require lots of education but do not yield large financial rewards, such as the ministry and teaching. Italians have average incomes that are about as high as those of Scots, though many fewer of them possess college diplomas.

What explains why some of these groups have done so much better than others is very hard to say. Whatever the answer, the implications for thinking about black-white issues should be clear. Group differences are here to stay, whatever our public policies and however thoroughly we root out discrimination. James Farmer claimed in 1989 that affirmative action "will be needed until there are no longer any gaps between races in income, education, health, and housing."[30] But some racial gaps will undoubtedly remain. In a free society that contains many groups with differing cultural characteristics, it is impossible to ensure that all of those groups have identical socioeconomic profiles. Normal group differences, however, do not automatically mean "whites" ahead; in fact, the concept "white," as we have seen, is not meaningful—including, as it does, such disparate groups as Cajuns, Armenians, French Canadians, and Latvians. And thus, if today "white" socioeconomic status is by many measures higher than that of blacks, that is a picture that can and should change. If today college-educated black females earn more than white women with comparable education, there is no reason why tomorrow black males cannot also overtake white men.

One Nation, Indivisible

In 1942, George S. Schuyler, an iconoclastic columnist for a black newspaper published in Pittsburgh, attacked the nation's press for what he termed its "sinister policy of identifying Negro individuals as such." He argued that this was "a subtle form of discrimination designed to segregate those individuals in the mind of the public and thus bolster the national polity of bi-racialism." Thus, Paul Robeson was not identified as "a great baritone, he [was] a great 'Negro' baritone. . . . Langston Hughes [was] not a poet, merely, he [was] a 'Negro' poet." No other group in the country, Schuyler noted, was "so singled out for racial identification." None of the newspapers, after all, called Henry Morgenthau, Jr., President Roosevelt's "Jewish secretary of the treasury."[31]

Gunnar Myrdal was struck by Schuyler's insight, though he faulted him for failing to mention that black newspapers were "if possible, more unfailing in giving prominent Negroes their 'race label.'" Myrdal observed that "the Negro leader, the Negro social scientist, the Negro man of art and letters is disposed to view all social, economic, political, indeed, even esthetic and philosophical issues from the Negro angle." What is more, said Myrdal, "he is expected to do so. He would seem entirely out of place if he spoke simply as a member of a community, a citizen of America or as a man of the world." [32]

The Myrdal point suggests another. Whites could shed their racial identity. In the 1940s, when he wrote, they were not only demographically dominant; they had all the power. And thus they had the freedom to view themselves as doctor, lawyer, teacher. Part of the package of privileges that came with being white was the liberty to think in individual terms. Blacks—a segregated and subjugated caste—were always black. The black writer was thus a *black* writer.

Today most black writers are still *black* writers. A few celebrities do escape the confines of racial identification, but they are the exception. The prearrest O. J. Simpson and Colin Powell are obvious examples. In March 1995, when Powell was still contemplating a run for the presidency, *Time* magazine did a story on the former chairman of the Joint Chiefs of Staff entitled "The Candidate of Dreams." He was, the article stated, "the ideal candidate. . . . 'If he becomes President,' [said] Gaylord Stevens, a Vietnam vet who brought his son in a Boy Scout uniform to hear Powell speak in San Antonio, Texas, as his own father had brought him to hear J.F.K., 'we would have a dream again.'" [33]

In this extensive and extraordinary portrait, Powell's race was never directly mentioned. He could get elected, *Time* clearly believed, although—it is important to note—Jesse Jackson (contemplating a third try for the office) could not. Powell had made his race irrelevant. He seemed the fulfillment of Martin Luther King's dream: it was the content of his character, not the color of his skin, that people were ready to judge him by. The unelectable Jesse Jackson was a very different figure; he never let the American public forget his race. He was a voice from across the racial tracks—a spokesman for black rage, for emotions, he implied, only blacks could know. Men (and women) like Jackson are the more frequent presence on the American political and cultural stage. And thus, while Saul Bellow is rarely referred to as "the Jewish writer," Toni Morrison is almost always "the African-American writer." In this crucial respect, the world that Schuyler and Myrdal described has remained unchanged. We are far from being a society in which race is unimportant.

In a relatively short time, however, we have by many measures come a very long way, this book has argued. Just think: when W. E. B. Du Bois was born, in February 1868, the ink was hardly dry on the Thirteenth Amendment. Du Bois lived to the age of ninety-five; he died in August 1963. Thus, he barely missed living under slavery, and barely missed the passage of the great Civil Rights Act of 1964. One man's life: unimaginable change.

This is an optimistic book, but not more optimistic than *An American*

Dilemma. In 1944, Myrdal saw the North as "getting prepared for a fundamental redefinition of the Negro's status in America." And he believed that "the South has been, and is, changing rapidly."[34] Of course that process of change was greatly accelerated by a civil rights movement—informed by precisely that unshakable optimism that ran through Myrdal's great work. The men and women who made that movement possible, Andrew Young wrote fifty-two years later, "believed in this nation . . . believed in spite of it all, that as children of God and agents of history, we could redeem the soul of America." And to a degree unimaginable half a century ago, that is what they did. "We were thought to be naïve," Young has said, "but in truth we were visionary."[35] The vision of the movement to which Young himself contributed so much was a permanent gift to the nation. Its work is not yet finished, but it remains our guiding light.

Notes

INTRODUCTION

1. Whenever this introduction touches on matters to be explored in detail later in the book, we have chosen not to clutter it up with detailed citations to the sources. When no supporting note is provided, the information is included with full citations in later chapters.
2. Ralph Ellison, *Invisible Man* (New York: Random House, 1952; reprint, New York: Vintage Books, 1972), 292.
3. Jared Taylor, *Paved with Good Intentions: The Failure of Race Relations in Contemporary America* (New York: Carroll & Graf, 1992), 23.
4. Derrick Bell, *Faces at the Bottom of the Well: The Permanence of Racism* (New York: Basic Books, 1992), 18.
5. Retha Hill, "Scholarship Ruling Complicates U-Md. Efforts to Overcome Bias," *Washington Post*, 29 October 1994, A4.
6. "Store Closing Means the End of Civil Rights–era Battlefield, *Des Moines Register*, 22 October 1993, 7.
7. Michael K. Frisby, "Five Saluted for Aiding Blacks," *Boston Globe*, 17 October 1983, 19.
8. Gunnar Myrdal, *An American Dilemma: The Negro Problem and American Democracy* (New York: Harper & Row 1944), 559. We have used the Twentieth Anniversary paperback edition, published without the subtitle by McGraw-Hill in 1964. The pagination was the same in both.
9. Ibid., 65.
10. Irwin S. Kirsch et al., *Adult Literacy in America: A First Look at the Results of the National Adult Literacy Survey*, National Center for Education Statistics (Washington, D.C.: U.S. Government Printing Office, 1993), 36.
11. Peter T. Kilborn, "New York Police Force Lagging in Recruitment of Black Officers," *New York Times*, 17 July 1994, 1.
12. *U.S. v. Fordice*, 112 S.Ct. at 2727 (1992)
13. 112 S.Ct. at 2736
14. "Victory for Black Colleges," *Chronicle of Higher Education*, 9 March 1994, A20.
15. 112 S.Ct. at 2743.
16. Ibid.
17. Mary Jordan, "In Mississippi, an Integration Uproar," *Washington Post*, 17 November 1992, A1.

18. Patrick Healy, "At 'Valley,' Anxiety Remains over Lingering Threat to University," *Chronicle of Higher Education,* 17 March 1995, A25.
19. Mark Whitaker, "Whites v. Blacks," *Newsweek,* 16 October 1995, 28.
20. That was the question on the cover of *Time* ("O.J. and Race: Will the Verdict Split America?"), 9 October 1995.
21. DeNeen L. Brown and James Ragland, "Barry's Win Transcends City's Barriers," *Washington Post,* 15 September 1994, 1.
22. Gerald Early, ed., *Lure and Loathing: Essays in Race, Identity, and the Ambivalence of Assimilation* (New York: Penguin, 1993), xvii. Early is paraphrasing William James.

CHAPTER 1: JIM CROW

1. Colin L. Powell, *My American Journey* (New York: Random House, 1995), 72.
2. The phrase "the new slavery" is that of political scientist Andrew Hacker, and it was used on the CNN television program *Both Sides with Jesse Jackson* on July 30, 1995. "Segregation" and "hypersegregation" are terms frequently used in discussions of residential clustering; see, e.g., Douglas S. Massey and Nancy Denton, *American Apartheid: Segregation and the Making of the Underclass* (Cambridge: Harvard University Press, 1993). "Jim Crow" was originally an invidious term for blacks, believed to be derived from a character in a pre–Civil War minstrel song; it was subsequently used to refer to statutes and customs that imposed segregation on blacks.
3. See, e.g., Jim Sidanius and Felicia Pratto, "The Inevitability of Oppression and the Dynamics of Social Dominance," in Paul M. Sniderman, Philip E. Tetlock, and Edward G. Carmines, eds., *Prejudice, Politics, and the American Dilemma* (Stanford, Calif.: Stanford University Press, 1993), 208.
4. The quotation is from the Rev. T. J. Jemison, head of the National Baptist Convention, in the *Durham Morning Herald,* 7 September 1990, A9, but the sentiment has been expressed by many.
5. Linton Weeks, "The Continuing Hurt of History," *Washington Post,* 22 December 1995, C1.
6. On this point, see David Nicholson, "The Costs of Cultural Blackmail," *Washington Post,* 24 December 1995, C2.
7. Clarence Waldron, "Staged Slave Auction Sparks Debate on Slavery And Racism," *Jet,* 31 October 1994, 12.
8. Michael Janofsky, "Mock Auction of Slaves: Education or Outrage?" *New York Times,* 8 October 1994, 7.
9. "Emotions Flow at Slave Sale Re-enactment," *Houston Chronicle,* 11 October 1994, 8.
10. James Baldwin, *Notes of a Native Son* (Boston: Beacon Press, 1955), 8.
11. U.S. Bureau of the Census, *Historical Statistics of the United States: Colonial Times to 1970* (Washington, D.C.: U.S. Government Printing Office, 1975), 22–36.
12. Gerald David Jaynes and Robin M. Williams, Jr., eds., *A Common Destiny: Blacks and American Society,* National Research Council (Washington, D.C.: National Academy Press, 1989), 62; U.S. Bureau of the Census, *Statistical Abstract of the United States: 1996* (Washington, D.C.: U.S. Government Printing Office, 1996), 44–46.
13. *Historical Statistics of the U.S.,* 22–36.
14. In 1860 nine out of ten of the 4.4 million African Americans were enslaved, and 94 percent of all those living in the South; U.S. Bureau of the Census, Current Popula-

tion Reports, Special Studies, P-23-80, *The Social and Economic Status of the Black Population in the United States: An Historical View, 1790–1978* (Washington, D.C.: U.S. Government Printing Office, 1979), 11.

15. C. Vann Woodward, *American Counterpoints: Slavery and Racism in the North-South Dialogue* (Boston: Little, Brown, 1964), 160.

16. The 42 percent is as of 1860, calculated from *Historical Statistics of the U.S.*, 24–36.

17. Stephan Thernstrom, *A History of the American People*, vol. 1 (New York: Harcourt Brace Jovanovich, 1984), 424.

18. Herbert Shapiro, *White Violence and Black Response: From Reconstruction to Montgomery* (Amherst: University of Massachusetts Press, 1988), 15.

19. V. O. Key, *Southern Politics in State and Nation* (New York: Knopf, 1950), 10.

20. Ibid.

21. C. Vann Woodward, *The Strange Career of Jim Crow* (New York: Oxford University Press, 1957), 68.

22. Steven F. Lawson, *Black Ballots: Voting Rights in the South, 1944–1969* (New York: Columbia University Press, 1976), 15.

23. Quoted in Morton Keller, *Regulating a New Society: Public Policy and Social Change in America, 1900–1933* (Cambridge: Harvard University Press, 1994), 377 n. 16.

24. Quoted in Keller, *Regulating a New Society*, 255.

25. Woodward, *Strange Career*, 82, 87.

26. This connection is traced in George M. Frederickson, *White Supremacy: A Comparative Study in American and South African History* (New York: Oxford University Press, 1980), and John W. Cell, *The Highest Stage of White Supremacy: The Origins of Segregation in South Africa and the American South* (New York: Cambridge University Press, 1982).

27. The sole exception to this generalization was New Orleans, where for a period of six years during Reconstruction parents were free to choose where to send their children, and about a third of the city's schools had students of both races. White resistance brought an end to integrated schools in 1875. Louis R. Harlan, "Desegregation in New Orleans Public Schools During Reconstruction," *American Historical Review* 67 (April 1962), 663–675.

28. *Plessy v. Ferguson*, 163 U.S. 537, 551–552.

29. 163 U.S. at 558–559, 563.

30. On the other hand, as Andrew Kull points out, after *Plessy* the Supreme Court did not use the "separate but equal" doctrine permissively to uphold segregation with no regard for the "equal" part of the formula. In fact, in only one post-*Plessy* case— *Berea College v. Kentucky* (1908)—did the Court employ the doctrine to defend segregation against a constitutional challenge. As early as *McCabe v. Atchison, Topeka, and Santa Fe Railway* (1914), it held that the segregated facilities in question were not equal, and continued down the same road for another forty years, until *Brown;* see Kull, *The Color-Blind Constitution* (Cambridge: Harvard University Press, 1992), chap. 8.

31. *Historical Statistics of the U.S.*, 458, 462, 464.

32. Gunnar Myrdal, *An American Dilemma* (New York: Harper & Row, 1944), 205.

33. James P. Smith, "Poverty and the Family," in Gary Sandefur and Marta Tienda, eds., *Divided Opportunities: Minorities, Poverty, and Social Policy* (New York: Plenum Press, 1988), 142. For other similar estimates, see Christine Ross, Sheldon Danziger, and Eugene Smolensky. "The Level and Trend of Poverty in the United States, 1939–1979," *Demography* 24 (November 1987), 587–600; and Elizabeth Evanson, "Social

and Economic Change Since the Great Depression: Studies of Census Data, 1940–1980," *Focus* 11 (Fall 1988), 1–11.

34. Myrdal, *American Dilemma*, 365. Comprehensive and detailed breakdowns of regional differences in family income by race were not produced by the Current Population Survey until 1953, unfortunately. Although the southern economy had become notably more prosperous by then, and the huge population of black tenants, sharecroppers, and farm laborers had shrunk dramatically, the median income of black families in the South in 1953 was only 49 percent that of white families, while in the North the figure was 75 percent; *Social and Economic Status of the Black Population in the U.S.*, 36–37.

35. The exact figure was 47 percent; Robert Higgs, "Black Progress and the Persistence of Racial Economic Inequalities, 1865–1940," in Steven Shulman and William Darity, Jr., eds., *The Question of Discrimination: Racial Inequality in the U.S. Labor Market* (Middletown, Conn.: Wesleyan University Press, 1989), 15. Some 34 percent of southern blacks were urban residents in 1940, vs. 37 percent of whites. Robert A. Margo, *Race and Schooling in the South, 1880–1950: An Economic History* (Chicago: University of Chicago Press, 1990), 88, estimates that 47 percent of southern black males aged 20–64 were employed in agriculture in 1940, vs. 33 percent of whites.

36. Sixty-eight percent of black males in Mississippi in 1940 were employed in agriculture; Neil R. McMillen, *Dark Journey: Black Mississippians in the Age of Jim Crow* (Urbana: University of Illinois Press, 1990), 156.

37. Higgs, "Black Progress," 36. The incomes of tenants in the cotton South were about an eighth of the national average of $575 per person; *Historical Statistics of the U.S.*, 243. The national average, of course, includes the third of the population living in southern states who were well below the average for the rest of the country.

38. Thomas Sowell, *Race and Economics* (New York: David McKay, 1975), passim.

39. Margo, *Race and Schooling*, 103. Margo computes an index of black occupational segregation, which ranges from 0—a complete lack of occupational segregation—to 100, complete segregation. It was 26 in 1910 and 39 in 1940, 50 percent higher. Calculating segregation not by occupational category but by industry yields the same result. The index for segregation by industry rose from 15 in 1910 to 22 in 1940, 45 percent higher. Between 1910 and 1940 the proportion of white men holding white-collar or skilled manual jobs rose from 32 percent to 40 percent. In those three decades the proportion of blacks in these more desirable jobs increased only a hair, from 7.5 percent to 8.0 percent.

40. Ibid., 90.

41. Stanley Lebergott, *Manpower in Economic Growth: The United States Record Since 1800* (New York: McGraw-Hill, 1964), 519.

42. *Social and Economic Status of Black Population*, 102.

43. The exact figure was 61 percent in the South and 17 percent in the North; Myrdal, *American Dilemma*, 1084.

44. Myrdal, *American Dilemma*, 1085.

45. Estimated from consumer price indexes before 1970 in *Historical Statistics of the U.S.*, 210; from 1970 on in *Statistical Abstract of the U.S.: 1996*, 483.

46. *Historical Statistics of the U.S.*, 382.

47. National Center for Educational Statistics, *Digest of Educational Statistics: 1990* (Washington, D.C.: U.S. Government Printing Office, 1991), 17.

48. Gavin Wright, *Old South, New South: Revolutions in the Southern Economy Since the Civil War* (New York: Basic Books, 1986), 80.

49. Jaynes and Williams, *Common Destiny*, 59.

50. Myrdal, *American Dilemma*, 341.

51. *School Money in Black and White*, pamphlet issued by the Committee on Finance of the National Conference on Fundamental Problems in the Education of Negroes, May 1934, quoted in Paula Fass, *Outside In: Minorities and the Transformation of American Education* (New York: Oxford University Press, 1989), 131.

52. Myrdal, *American Dilemma*, 902–903.

53. Horace Mann Bond, *The Education of the Negro in the American Social Order* (Englewood Cliffs, N.J.: Prentice-Hall, 1934; rev. ed., Octagon Books, Chicago, 1966), 267.

54. Ibid., 275–277.

55. Margo, *Race and Schooling*, 44.

56. Charles S. Johnson, *Patterns of Negro Segregation* (New York: Harper & Brothers, 1943), 18–19.

57. James D. Anderson, *The Education of Blacks in the South, 1860–1935* (Chapel Hill: University of North Carolina Press, 1988), 174.

58. McMillen, *Dark Journey*, 84, 345. Charles S. Johnson, *The Negro in American Civilization: A Study of Negro Life and Race Relations in the Light of Social Research* (New York: Henry Holt, 1930), 230, reports that for the years 1914–1928, $20 million were expended on Rosenwald schools. The fund contributed $3 million of this, black individuals and organizations $4 million, and individual whites $1 million. The remaining $12 million was from public funds.

59. Johnson, *Negro in American Civilization*, 250, tabulates donations to this cause down to the late 1920s. Of the $28 million whose source he identifies, $19 million came from the General Education Board, $3 million from the Rosenwald Fund, and $2 million from the John F. Slater Fund.

60. John Dollard, *Caste and Class in a Southern Town* (New Haven: Yale University Press, 1937; reprint, Madison: University of Wisconsin Press, 1988), 201.

61. Anderson, *Education of Blacks*, 97.

62. Ibid., 101.

63. Ibid., 96.

64. Earl Black and Merle Black, *Politics and Society in the South* (Cambridge: Harvard University Press, 1987), 88.

65. McMillen, *Dark Journey*, 8.

66. Key, *Southern Politics*, 633.

67. Johnson, *Patterns*, 49–51.

68. Dollard, *Caste and Class*, 174.

69. Myrdal, *American Dilemma*, 611.

70. Dollard, *Caste and Class*, 181.

71. Johnson, *Patterns*, 139.

72. Ibid., 141.

73. Ibid., 280.

74. Ibid., 279.

75. Myrdal, *American Dilemma*, 65.

76. Johnson, *Patterns*, 39; Dollard, *Caste and Class*, 181.

77. Myrdal, *American Dilemma*, 608.

78. Walter A. Jackson, *Gunnar Myrdal and America's Conscience: Social Engineering and Racial Liberalism, 1938–1987* (Chapel Hill, N.C.: University of North Carolina Press, 1990), 122.

79. The phrase is Paul Lewinson's, quoted in Myrdal, *American Dilemma*, 603.
80. Thomas Brady, *Black Monday* (1954), as quoted in David R. Goldfield, *Black, White, and Southern: Race Relations and Southern Culture, 1940 to the Present* (Baton Rouge: Lousiana State University Press, 1990), 76.
81. Rev. James P. Dees in T. Robert Ingram, ed., *Essays on Segregation* (1960), quoted in Neil R. McMillen, *The Citizens' Council: Organized Resistance to the Second Reconstruction, 1954–64* (Urbana: University of Illinois Press, 1971), 179.
82. McMillen, *The Citizens' Council*, 185.
83. Johnson, *Patterns*, 128–132.
84. Reported by anthropologist Hortense Powdermaker, as quoted in Richard Polenberg, *One Nation Divisible: Class, Race, and Ethnicity in the United States Since 1938* (New York: Penguin, 1980), 25.
85. Myrdal, *American Dilemma*, 66.
86. Richard Wright, *Black Boy*, in Wright, *Later Works* (New York: Library of America, 1991), 236.
87. Johnson, *Patterns*, chap. 2.
88. McMillen, *Dark Journey*, 11.
89. Arthur Ashe, *Days of Grace: A Memoir* (New York: Knopf, 1993), 137.
90. Johnson, *Patterns*, 55.
91. Myrdal, *American Dilemma*, 172
92. Johnson, *Patterns*, 124–128; McMillen, *Dark Journey*, 11.
93. Johnson, *Patterns*, 251.
94. Charles Angoff and H. L. Mencken, "The Worst American State," *American Mercury* 24 (1934), 182–183.
95. McMillen, *Dark Journey*, 234.
96. Ibid., 227.
97. Ibid., 237.
98. Ibid., 236.
99. Myrdal, *American Dilemma*, 529.
100. Ibid., 559.
101. Ibid., 530.
102. Johnson, *Patterns*, 33–34.
103. Myrdal, *American Dilemma*, 543.
104. Johnson, *Patterns*, 35.
105. Myrdal, *American Dilemma*, 540–541.
106. Johnson, *Patterns*, 299.
107. August Meier and Elliot M. Rudwick, *Along the Color Line: Explorations in the Black Experience* (Urbana: University of Illlinois Press, 1976), 130–131.
108. Myrdal, *American Dilemma*, 549–550.
109. Johnson, *Patterns*, 30.
110. Dollard, *Caste and Class*, 280.
111. McMillen, *Dark Journey*, 204.
112. Ibid., 204.
113. Dollard, *Caste and Class*, 282.
114. Myrdal, *American Dilemma*, 551.
115. Edgar G. Murphy, *Problems of the Present South* (1904), quoted in Myrdal, *American Dilemma*, 1192.
116. Dollard, *Caste and Class*, 281–282.
117. The usual crime data that scholars analyze are always an imperfect measure of the

actual incidence of crime. They register the number of people who were identified as offenders at some stage of the criminal justice process. "Crime rates" are actually rates of arrests, indictments, convictions, or punishments. Not only was the South's criminal justice system deeply biased against blacks; its standards of record keeping were very low, so that all such evidence must be approached with great caution and skepticism. For a judicious discussion of how to assess the historical data on black crime, see Johnson, *The Negro in American Civilization,* chap. 22, esp. 316, and Thorsten Sellin's comments on 443–452 of that volume.

118. Guy B. Johnson, "The Negro and Crime," *Annals of the American Academy of Political and Social Science* 217 (September 1941), 99. The racial composition of the population of the communities studied, not given in the article, was calculated from Charles S. Johnson, *Statistical Atlas of Southern Counties* (Chapel Hill: University of North Carolina Press, 1941), 97, 177, 179, 182, 183, 188, 252.

119. Myrdal, *American Dilemma,* 927–928.

120. Richard Kluger, *Simple Justice: The History of Brown v. Board of Education and Black America's Struggle for Equality* (New York: Vintage, 1977), 316.

121. Most American social scientists who studied race and race relations at the time, including Myrdal, adhered to what has been called the "damage school." The revealing title of another work of the day written from this vantage point was Abram Kardiner and Lionel Ovesey's *Mark of Oppression* (1951). The scholarly reviews of *An American Dilemma,* including those by leading black scholars, failed to criticize the book for its unrelieved stress on the damage done to blacks by white oppression. Perhaps the most distinguished African-American sociologist of the time, E. Franklin Frazier, endorsed Myrdal's portrait of African-American culture as pathological, and praised him for not indulging in "a lot of foolish talk about the peculiar 'contributions' of the Negro and his deep 'spirituality.' " Two other leading black sociologists, St. Clair Drake and Horace Cayton, agreed that Myrdal was to be congratulated for focusing so sharply on the damage done to blacks by poverty and racial oppression.; Jackson, *Myrdal,* 246–247; David W. Southern, *Gunnar Myrdal and Black-White Relations: The Use and Abuse of An American Dilemma, 1944–1969* (Baton Rouge: Louisiana State University Press, 1987), 90–93.

122. Wright, Introduction to St. Clair Drake and Horace R. Cayton, *Black Metropolis: A Study of Negro Life in a Northern City* (New York: Harcourt Brace, 1945; New York: Harper Torchbook, 1962), xxix.

123. Wright shaped his novel to fit the environmental determinism outlined in his essay "How Bigger Was Born"; Richard Wright, *Early Works* (New York: Library of America, 1991), 853–881. Wright maintained that "Bigger Thomas was not black all the time; he was white, too, and there were literally milions of him, everywhere." Whites, too, "had their own kind of Bigger Thomas behavioristic pattern which grew out of a more subtle and broader frustration." Just as one could see "in a medical research laboratory jars of alcohol containing abnormally large or distorted portions of the human body, just so did I see and feel that the conditions of life under which Negroes are forced to live in America contain the embryonic emotional prefigurations of how a large part of the body politic would react under stress" (860, 862, 867). Specifically black cultural elements were not allowed to intrude into Wright's laboratory.

124. Ralph Ellison, *Shadow and Act* (New York: Signet, 1966), 301.

125. Ibid., xiv.

126. See, for instance, Roy L. Brooks, *Rethinking the American Race Problem* (Berkeley: University of California Press, 1990), 13–14: "Racial integration helps to open a

cultural and economic abyss in communities already suffering from the lingering effects of slavery and Jim Crow, creating an underworld of disfunction and self-destruction into which millions of African Americans have fallen." This "lingering effects" argument is often made by judges in the context of justifying affirmative action and other race-based programs.

127. John Edgar Wideman, *Brothers and Keepers* (New York: Penguin, 1985), 57, 72.
128. Nathan McCall, *Makes Me Wanna Holler* (New York: Random House, 1994), 93.
129. Robert S. Boynton, "Professor Bell, Sage of Black Rage," *New York Observer,* 10 October 1994, 1.

CHAPTER 2: THE PROMISED LAND

1. Richard Wright, *Black Boy,* in Wright, *Later Works* (New York: Library of America, 1991), 880. *Black Boy* was initially the first section of a longer autobiographical work, *American Hunger,* but the second part of it was not published until 1977, long after the author's death. The work appears in full as *Black Boy (American Hunger)* in Wright, *Later Works.* The remark about "dignity" was not in *American Hunger* as originally written; it was part of several pages written as a new conclusion after Harper agreed to drop Part II and to publish *Black Boy* alone, which the Book-of-the-Month Club insisted upon. Part II is a savage account of Wright's long involvement with the Communist Party and his profound disillusionment with it. According to Arnold Rampersad, Wright was convinced that the book club had insisted on the change as a result of pressure from Communist sympathizers; see "Note on the Texts" in *Later Works,* 868–869.
2. Sarah L. Delany and A. Elizabeth Delany, *Having Our Say* (New York: Dell, 1993), 145.
3. Wright, *Later Works,* 245.
4. Ibid., 249.
5. Ibid., 258.
6. U.S. Bureau of the Census, Current Population Reports, Special Studies P-23, No. 80, *The Social and Economic Status of the Black Population in the United States: An Historical View, 1790–1978* (Washington, D.C.: U.S. Government Printing Office, 1979), 15.
7. Harvard Sitkoff, *A New Deal for Blacks: The Emergence of Civil Rights as a National Issue,* vol. 1, *The Depression Decade* (New York: Oxford University Press, 1978), 90–91.
8. Allan H. Spear, *Black Chicago: The Making of a Negro Ghetto, 1890–1920* (Chicago: University of Chicago Press, 1967), 12; Kenneth L. Kusmer, *A Ghetto Takes Shape: Black Cleveland, 1870–1930* (Urbana: University of Illinois Press, 1976), 10; Sitkoff, *New Deal for Blacks,* 90–91.
9. Nicholas Lemann, *The Promised Land: The Great Black Migration and How It Changed America* (New York: Knopf, 1991), 16.
10. Gunnar Myrdal, *An American Dilemma* (New York: Harper & Row, 1944), 529–530.
11. Charles S. Johnson, *Patterns of Negro Segregation* (New York: Harper & Brothers, 1943), 124.
12. Wright, *Later Works,* p. 219.
13. "More Letters of Negro Migrants of 1916–1918, Collected Under the Direction of Emmet J. Scott," *Journal of Negro History* 4 (October 1919), 461.

14. See the interesting responses to a questionnaire given to black migrants to Chicago in 1920, supplied in St. Clair Drake and Horace R. Cayton, *Black Metropolis: A Study of Negro Life in a Northern City* (New York: Harcourt Brace, 1945; reprint, New York: Harper Torchbook, 1962), 99–100.

15. "More Letters of Negro Migrants," 461.

16. Wright, *Later Works,* 249.

17. "More Letters of Negro Migrants," 461.

18. Drake and Cayton, *Black Metropolis,* 342.

19. Myrdal, *American Dilemma,* 493.

20. Drake and Cayton, *Black Metropolis,* 348–349.

21. The only negative references to the police in this two-volume work are one comment in a note about police hassling racially mixed couples in public places (132, unnumbered note), the inclusion of "rough treatment by the police" on a long laundry list of complaints presented at the 1944 Mayor's Conference on Race Relations (202), and a mention of a 1939 meeting that protested, among other things, a case of alleged police brutality (742).

22. David L. Cohn, *Where I Was Born and Raised* (Boston: Houghton Mifflin, 1948), 343–344.

23. Spear, *Black Chicago,* 157.

24. Ibid., 152–153.

25. Drake and Cayton, *Black Metropolis,* 227.

26. Spear, *Black Chicago,* 151; Drake and Cayton, *Black Metropolis,* 227.

27. Stephan Thernstrom, *The Other Bostonians: Poverty and Progress in the American Metropolis, 1880–1970* (Cambridge: Harvard University Press, 1973), chap. 6.

28. Ibid., chap. 8.

29. This view is elaborated persuasively in Thomas Sowell, *Race and Economics* (New York: David McKay, 1975), chaps. 6 and 7. Employees will not have an incentive to hire the best person for the job regardless of color if community pressures force *all* employers to hire only whites, or to hire only whites for the more demanding and best-paid jobs. This was the case in the South until the 1960s. The same goes for an industry whose labor market is dominated by a well-entrenched all-white union. Nor does this logic influence employers who are not subject to the discipline of market forces, such as government agencies, nonprofit organizations like colleges and universities and hospitals, and regulated monopolies like local bus, electric, and gas companies.

30. Sterling D. Spero and Abram L. Harris, *The Black Worker: The Negro and the Labor Movement* (New York: Columbia University Press, 1931), passim.

31. James R. Grossman, *Land of Hope: Chicago, Black Southerners, and the Great Migration* (Chicago: University of Chicago Press, 1991), chap. 8, "The White Man's Union."

32. This is the title of David Katzman's study of blacks in nineteenth-century Detroit (Urbana: University of Illinois Press, 1973).

33. Kusmer, *A Ghetto Takes Shape,* 43–44.

34. Kathleen N. Conzen, "Immigrants, Immigrant Neighborhoods, and Ethnic Identity: Historical Issues," *Journal of American History* 79 (1979), 603–625.

35. Spear, *Black Chicago,* 22.

36. See the two pioneering studies by Stanley Lieberson: *Ethnic Patterns in American Cities* (New York: Free Press, 1963) and *A Piece of the Pie: Blacks and White Immigrants Since 1880* (Berkeley: University of California Press, 1980).

37. Spear, *Black Chicago,* 211–216.

38. Eugene L. Horowitz, " 'Race' Attitudes," in Otto Klineberg, ed., *Characteristics of the American Negro* (New York: Harper, 1944), 204.

39. Drake and Cayton, *Black Metropolis,* 103.

40. Louis Wirth and Herbert Goldhamer, "The Hybrid and the Problem of Miscegenation," in Klineberg, *Characteristics of the American Negro,* 360–363.

41. Howard Shuman, Charlotte Steeh, and Lawrence Bobo, *Racial Attitudes in America: Trends and Interpretations* (Cambridge: Harvard University Press, 1985), 74.

42. Johnson, *Patterns,* 61.

43. Ibid., 58.

44. Ibid., 24, 178. When Gary, Indiana, decided in 1927 to merge its separate black and white schools, white students staged a massive protest strike, with the result that a new school was built in a black section of the town; Ronald D. Cohen, *Children of the Mill: Schooling and Society in Gary, Indiana, 1906–1960* (Bloomington: Indiana University Press, 1990), 92–100.

45. *Social and Economic Status of the Black Population,* 94–95. The figures are for persons 25 to 34. These figures likely understate the magnitude of the regional difference, because they are based on where individuals were living in 1940, not where they lived when they were attending school. Some of the blacks aged 25 to 34 who were living in the North in 1940 were doubtless educated in the South, and received less schooling than their northern counterparts. Including these migrants with northern-born blacks, as the Census Bureau figures do, thus underestimates the benefits of growing up in the North and attending its public schools.

46. George S. Schuyler, quoted in Gilbert S. Osofsky, *Harlem: The Making of a Ghetto: Negro New York, 1890–1930* (New York: Harper & Row, 1966), 149.

47. Warren C. Whatley, "Labor for the Picking: The New Deal in the South," *Journal of Economic History* 43 (December 1983), 905–929; Jack Temple Kirby, *Rural Worlds Lost: The American South, 1920–1960* (Baton Rouge: Louisiana State University Press, 1987), 60–62.

48. Bruce J. Schulman, *From Cotton Belt to Sunbelt: Federal Policy, Economic Development, and the Transformation of the South, 1938–1980* (New York: Oxford University Press, 1991), 31.

49. Lee J. Alston and Joseph P. Ferrie, "Labor Costs, Paternalism, and Loyalty in Southern Agriculture: A Constraint on the Growth of the Welfare State," *Journal of Economic History* 45 (March 1985), 95–117. For an excellent critique of the view that such racial considerations were the primary determinant of the decision, see Gareth Davies and Martha Derthick, "Race and the Social Security Act of 1935," *Political Science Quarterly,* forthcoming. Including agricultural and domestic workers would have created many problems, and most other nations that had adopted such plans had not covered farm labor at the outset.

50. The failure to cover most black workers led both the National Association for the Advancement of Colored People and the National Urban League to testify in opposition to the bill; Ralph J. Bunche, *The Political Status of the Negro in the Age of FDR,* Dewey Grantham, ed. (Chicago: University of Chicago Press, 1973), 610–611; Richard Sterner, *The Negro's Share: A Study of Income, Consumption, Housing, and Public Assistance* (New York: Harper & Brothers, 1943), 214–215; Dona C. and Charles V. Hamilton, "The Dual Agenda of African American Organizations Since the New Deal: Social Welfare Policies and Civil Rights," *Political Science Quarterly* 107 (1992), 440–441.

51. Schulman, *From Cotton Belt,* 26–31. The South experienced virtually no increase in

industrial employment between 1929 and 1939; Gavin R. Wright, *Old South, New South: Revolutions in the Southern Economy Since the Civil War* (New York: Basic Books, 1986), 237.

52. Wright, *Old South*, 236; Alston and Ferrie, "Labor Costs," 95–117. Schulman, *From Cotton Belt*, 72–73, suggests that these regulations might have resulted in "economic catastrophe for southern industry" but for the completely fortuitous economic boom brought about by mobilization for World War II, which expanded manufacturing employment in the South by 50 percent and drove wages up well above the minimum levels specified in the Fair Labor Standards Act.
53. Schulman, *From Cotton Belt*, 29.
54. Wright, *Old South*, 214–216; it is impressive that Gunnar Myrdal, despite his ardent support for the New Deal, clearly perceived the negative effect upon blacks of New Deal economic reforms; *American Dilemma*, 297.
55. Wright, *Old South*, 245.
56. *Social and Economic Status of the Black Population in the U.S.*, 75.
57. Elliot M. Rudwick, *W. E. B. Du Bois: Propagandist of the Negro Protest* (New York: Atheneum, 1968), 160–164.
58. Sitkoff, *New Deal for Blacks*, 41; Bunche, *Political Status of the Negro*, 575.
59. Walter A. Jackson, *Gunnar Myrdal and America's Conscience: Social Engineering and Racial Liberalism, 1938–1987* (Chapel Hill: University of North Carolina Press, 1990), 6; Sitkoff, *New Deal for Blacks*, 95.
60. Bunche, *Political Status of the Negro*, 88, 97.
61. Morton Sosna, *In Search of the Silent South: Southern Liberals and the Race Issue* (New York: Columbia University Press, 1977), 95.
62. Michael Barone, *Our Country: The Shaping of America from Roosevelt to Reagan* (New York: Free Press, 1990), 160.
63. Sitkoff, *New Deal for Blacks*, 67.
64. Ibid., 76.
65. George B. Tindall, *The Emergence of the New South, 1913–1945* (Baton Rouge: Louisiana State University Press, 1967), 544.
66. Myrdal, *American Dilemma*, 475.
67. V. O. Key, *Southern Politics in State and Nation* (New York: Knopf, 1949), 620.
68. Barone, *Our Country*, 122.
69. Key, *Southern Politics*, 665.
70. Myrdal, *An American Dilemma*, 565.
71. Frank Freidel, *Franklin D. Roosevelt: A Rendezvous with Destiny* (Boston: Little, Brown, 1990), 246.
72. Ibid., 246–247.

CHAPTER 3: REMARKABLE CHANGE

1. W. E. B. Du Bois, *Dusk of Dawn: An Essay Toward an Autobiography of a Race Concept* (New York: Schocken, 1968), 199, 304, 309, 321.
2. W. E. B. Du Bois, *Writings* (New York: Library of America, 1986), 359.
3. Geoffrey Perrett, *Days of Sadness, Years of Triumph: The American People, 1939–1945* (New York: Penguin, 1974), 321.
4. Quoted in Harvard Sitkoff, *A New Deal for Blacks* (New York: Oxford University Press, 1978), 301.

5. Quoted in Richard M. Dalfiume, *Desegregation of the U.S. Armed Forces: Fighting on Two Fronts, 1939–1953* (Columbia: University of Missouri Press, 1969), 110.

6. Dalfiume, *Desegregation*, 107–108.

7. Ibid., 13.

8. Ibid., 26.

9. He named a black general (the first in American history) and appointed the first black federal judge, William Hastie, as special aide on Negro affairs to the secretary of war; Ulysses Lee, *United States Army in World War II: Special Studies: The Employment of Negro Troops* (Washington, D.C.: U.S. Government Printing Office, 1966), 79.

10. Quoted in John Hope Franklin and Isidore Starr, eds., *The Negro in Twentieth Century America: A Reader on the Struggle for Civil Rights* (New York: Vintage Books, 1967), 140.

11. Jervis Anderson, *A. Philip Randolph: A Biographical Portrait* (Berkeley: University of California Press, 1988), 248–250.

12. Ibid., 258.

13. Ibid., 259.

14. Richard M. Dalfiume, "The 'Forgotten Years' of the Negro Revolution," *Journal of American History* 60 (June 1968), 99.

15. Bruce J. Schulman, *From Cotton Belt to Sunbelt: Federal Policy, Economic Development, and the Transformation of the South, 1938–1980* (New York: Oxford University Press, 1991), 82–83.

16. The Gallup poll first asked "What do you regard as the most vital issue before the American people today?" in 1935, and has repeated the question at regular intervals ever since. It is striking that responses related to race were mentioned so infrequently that they were not even assigned a separate code until 1944; Paul B. Sheatsley, "White Attitudes Toward the Negro," *Daedalus* 95 (Winter 1966), 237. Until 1956 no more than 4 percent of the population ever rated racial problems as the most important ones confronting the nation; Mildred A. Schwartz, *Trends in White Attitudes Toward Negroes*, Report No. 119 (Chicago: National Opinion Research Center, 1967), 7.

17. A detailed survey of white opinion about racial matters was conducted by the National Opinion Research Center in 1942. The decision that it was important to gather evidence about what whites thought about blacks was a product of the war; this survey was financed by the Office of War Information. The broad support whites gave to segregation, even northern whites, reflected widespread doubt that blacks possessed the same innate capacities as whites. Hence the perceived need for protection from unnecessary contact. Given the prevalence of such racist beliefs, an order desegregating the armed forces would doubtless have provoked fierce opposition from a large majority of whites. The figures are given in Herbert H. Hyman and Paul B. Sheatsley, "Attitudes Toward Desegregation," *Scientific American* 195 (December 1956), 36–37, with more detailed breakdowns in Schwartz, *Trends in White Attitudes*, passim.

18. Samuel A. Stouffer et al., *The American Soldier: Adjustment During Army Life* (Princeton: Princeton University Press, 1949), 506.

19. Dalfiume, *Desegregation*, 130.

20. Lee, *U.S. Army in World War II*, 136–141.

21. Richard O. Hope, "Blacks in the U.S. Military: Trends in Participation," in Institute on Race and Ethnicity, University of Wisconsin System, *Race: Twentieth Century Dilemmas—Twenty-first Century Board Prognoses*, vol. 8, Ethnicity and Public Pol-

icy Series (Madison: Board of Regents, University of Wisconsin System, 1989), 190; U.S. Bureau of the Census, *The Social and Economic Status of the Black Population in the United States: An Historical View, 1790–1978,* Current Population Reports, Special Studies, Series P-23, no. 80 (Washington, D.C.: U.S. Government Printing Office, 1979), 160.

22. Stouffer, *American Soldier,* 495.
23. Lee, *U.S. Army in World War II,* 244.
24. Stouffer, *American Soldier,* 493.
25. Lee, *U.S. Army in World War II,* 245.
26. Stouffer, *American Soldier,* 501.
27. Ibid.
28. Dalfiume, *Desegregation,* 66.
29. For an example of this suggestion from an organ of liberal opinion, see "Negroes in the Armed Forces," special section on "The Negro: His Future in America," *New Republic,* 18 October 1943, 543.
30. Lee, *U.S. Army in World War II,* chap. 22. Many fewer blacks served in the U.S. Navy. In 1945, 4.8 percent of its enlisted men and none of its officers were black, as compared with 9.3 percent of the enlisted men and 0.8 percent of the officers in the Army; Hope, "Blacks in the U.S. Military," 190.
31. Calculated from data in Stouffer, *American Soldier,* 528, 568.
32. Ibid., 494; Dalfiume, *Desegregation,* 99–100.
33. Jules Tygiel, *Baseball's Great Experiment: Jackie Robinson and His Legacy* (New York: Vintage, 1984), 59.
34. Stouffer, *American Soldier,* 528.
35. Ibid., 515, 520.
36. U.S. Bureau of the Census, *Historical Statistics of the United States: Colonial Times to 1970* (Washington, D.C.: U.S. Government Printing Office, 1975), 131, 1140.
37. Stanley Lebergott, *Manpower in Economic Growth: The United States Record Since 1800* (New York: McGraw-Hill, 1964), 512.
38. David R. Goldfield, "The City as Southern History: The Past and the Promise of Tomorrow," in Joe P. Dunn and Howard L. Preston, eds., *The Future South: A Historical Perspective for the Twenty-first Century* (Urbana: University of Illinois Press, 1991), 26.
39. Schulman, *From Cotton Belt,* 72–73.
40. Howard Odum, *Race and Rumors of Race: Challenge to American Crisis* (Chapel Hill: University of North Carolina Press, 1943), 171.
41. Ibid., 95.
42. Jack D. Bloom, *Class, Race, and the Civil Rights Movement* (Bloomington: Indiana University Press, 1987), 69.
43. Odum, *Race,* chapters 9 and 10, explore the fantasy of "Eleanor Clubs" in rich detail.
44. Ibid., chap. 12.
45. Lebergott, *Manpower in Economic Growth,* 512.
46. Dudley L. Poston, Jr., and Robert H. Weller, eds., *The Population of the South: Structure and Change in Demographic Context* (Austin: University of Texas Press, 1981), chap. 7; Gavin Wright, *Old South, New South: Revolutions in the Southern Economy Since the Civil War* (New York: Basic Books, 1986), chap. 8.
47. Poston and Weller, *Population of the South,* 205.
48. Reynolds Farley and Walter R. Allen, *The Color Line and the Quality of Life in America* (New York: Russell Sage Foundation, 1987), 302.

49. Wright, *Old South*, 241–249.

50. Ibid., 245; T. Lynn Smith, "The Redistribution of the Negro Population of the United States, 1910–1960," *Journal of Negro History* 51 (July 1966), 171.

51. Robert A. Margo, *Race and Schooling in the South, 1880–1950: An Economic History* (Chicago: University of Chicago Press, 1990), 90–91. The index of segregation between black and white male workers calculated by Margo for occupational categories was 39.2 in 1940 and 37.0 in 1950. A similar index for distribution among ten industrial groups was 21.7 in 1940 and 19.5 in 1960. Both calculations point to the same conclusion: despite striking economic growth and many major social changes in the larger society, job segregation for southern blacks remained at the same very high level as before. See also Wright, *Old South*, 255.

52. U.S. Commission on Civil Rights, *The Economic Progress of Black Men in America*, Clearinghouse Publication 91, (Washington, D.C.: 1986), 168. Figures are for men with less than twelve years of education—a majority of blacks in the age group at the time.

53. *Social and Economic Status of the Black Population*, 36.

54. Ibid., 15.

55. James P. Smith and Finis R. Welch, "Black Economic Progress After Myrdal," *Journal of Economic Literature* 17 (June 1989), 544. These figures, and those in the next sentence of the text as well, are for black males, since the economic position of black men was the focus of both of the studies cited. Black females, however, migrated out of the South in about the same proportions as males, as can be seen from the detailed state-by-state tabulations in Everett S. Lee et al., *Population Redistribution and Economic Growth in the United States 1870–1950*, vol. 1, *Methodological Considerations and Reference Tables* (Philadelphia: American Philosophical Society, 1957), table P-1.

56. U.S. Civil Rights Commission, *Economic Progress of Black Men*, 169.

57. Donald J. Bogue, *The Population of the United States: Historical Trends and Future Projections* (New York: Free Press, 1985), 94–95.

58. *Social and Economic Status of the Black Population*, 14.

59. 1940 Census of Population, Subject Reports, *Occupational Characteristics* (Washington, D.C.: U.S. Government Printing Office, 1943), table 6; 1960 Census of Population, Subject Reports, *Occupational Characteristics*, PC(2)-7A (Washington, D.C.: U.S. Government Printing Office, 1962), table 3; Farley and Allen, *The Color Line*, 264.

60. Gerald David Jaynes and Robin M. Williams, Jr., eds., *A Common Destiny: Blacks and American Society* (Washington, D.C.: National Research Council, National Academy Press, 1989), 273.

61. Smith and Welch, "Black Economic Progress," 521. The article gives figures in 1987 dollars; they were adjusted to 1995 dollars with the price indexes given in *Statistical Abstract of the U.S.: 1996*, 483. These remarks on wage gains may seem to contradict what we said a few pages earlier about southern blacks failing to catch up with southern whites in the 1940s and 1950s. Two points explain the seeming contradiction. The earnings gains in this paragraph involve comparisons with black incomes earlier, not with whites. Whites were doing very well in these decades as well. Second, these are national figures, and huge numbers of black workers were leaving the South, where the racial gap in income was very large, to go to the North, where it was much narrower.

62. Jaynes and Williams, *Common Destiny*, 295.

63. Smith and Welch, "Black Economic Progress," 521.

64. Jaynes and Williams, *Common Destiny*, 295.

65. Since the 1950s, the racial gap in income between white and black males and between white and black females has narrowed dramatically, but the racial gap in family income has not. That is because of changes in the structure of the black family that have depressed income levels—mainly the proliferation of female-headed households. This development will be explored in chap. 9.

66. James P. Smith and Finis R. Welch, *Closing the Gap: Forty Years of Economic Progress for Blacks* (Santa Monica, Calif.: The Rand Corporation, 1986), 104.

67. *Social and Economic Status of the Black Population*, 103.

68. *Historical Statistics of the U.S.*, 55.

69. *Social and Economic Status of the Black Population*, 137.

70. Smith and Welch, *Closing the Gap*, 103; figures are for families whose heads were aged 26–55.

71. Richard K. Vedder and Lowell E. Galloway, *Out of Work: Unemployment and Government in Twentieth-Century America* (New York: Holmes & Meier, 1993), 272.

72. Back in 1930, indeed, when four out of five black Americans lived in the Jim Crow South, the jobless rate for blacks was actually 21 percent *lower* than it was for whites; Vedder and Galloway, *Out of Work*, 274. To say that blacks were thereby economically better off than whites in 1930 would obviously be ridiculous.

73. Farley and Allen, *The Color Line*, 303.

74. Margo, *Race and Schooling*, 24–25.

75. Wright, *Old South*, 245.

76. *Missouri ex rel. Gaines v. Canada*, 305 U.S. 337 (1938), held that the State of Missouri violated the constitutional rights of black students when it barred them from attending the University of Missouri Law School and offered instead to pay their expenses to attend law school in another state.

77. The question was not whether the Sojourner Truth project should be open to all on a color-blind basis. Since the inception of the Federal Public Housing Program in 1937, the agency had required racial separation in all the projects it financed, whether in the South or in the North. Congress would never have appropriated funds for the agency if its policies had fostered racial integration. Detroit's elected public officials would not have chosen to integrate the project even if federal officials had allowed it. The Detroit electorate, more than 90 percent white, strongly backed residential segregation; August Meier and Elliot M. Rudwick, *Black Detroit and the Rise of the UAW* (New York: Oxford University Press, 1979), 176–184; and Alan Clive, *State of War: Michigan in World War II* (Ann Arbor: University of Michigan Press, 1979), 144–151. As late as 1952, a survey of the Detroit white population found a solid majority in favor of racially segregated neighborhoods; Arthur Kornhauser, *Detroit as the People See It* (Detroit: Wayne State University Press, 1952), 85, 199.

78. Clive, *State of War*, 156–162.

79. Douglas McAdam, *Political Process and the Development of Black Insurgency, 1930–1970* (Chicago: University of Chicago Press, 1982), 80. In the 1940s these seven states together had 195 electoral votes, more than 70 percent of the 270 needed to elect a president; *Historical Statistics of the U.S.*, 1075. As a result of the decline of the Rustbelt and the rise of the Sunbelt in the past half century, all of these states except California have lost seats in the House of Representatives and votes in the Electoral College, with New York (− 14) and Pennsylvania (− 12) the biggest losers; *Statistical Abstract of the U.S.: 1996*, 270.

80. *Historical Statistics of the U.S.*, 1077
81. Quoted in Bernard Taper, *Gomillion versus Lightfoot: The Tuskegee Gerrymander Case* (New York: McGraw-Hill, 1962), 68.
82. Ralph J. Bunche, *The Political Status of the Negro in the Age of FDR*, Dewey Grantham, ed. (Chicago: University of Chicago Press, 1973), 389.
83. Earl Black and Merle Black, *Politics and Society in the South* (Cambridge: Harvard University Press, 1987), 85.
84. Neil R. McMillen, *The Citizens' Council: Organized Resistance to the Second Reconstruction, 1954–1964* (Urbana: University of Illinois Press, 1971), 215.
85. David R. Goldfield, *Black, White, and Southern: Race Relations and Southern Culture, 1940 to the Present* (Baton Rouge: Louisiana State University Press, 1990), 48.
86. *Grovey v. Townsend*, 321 U.S. 49 (1935).
87. Dalfiume, *Desegregation*, 123.
88. *Historical Statistics of the U.S.*, 178.
89. Meier and Rudwick, *Black Detroit*, 125–132, 162–172.
90. Donald R. McCoy and Richard T. Ruetten, *Quest and Response: Minority Rights and the Truman Administration* (Lawrence: University Press of Kansas, 1973), 9.
91. Nathan Glazer and Reed Ueda, "Prejudice and Discrimination, Policy Against," in Stephan Thernstrom, ed., *Harvard Encyclopedia of American Ethnic Groups* (Cambridge: Harvard University Press, 1980), 854.
92. Arnold R. Hirsch, *Making the Second Ghetto: Race and Housing in Chicago, 1940–1960* (New York: Cambridge University Press, 1983), 42.
93. Walter A. Jackson, *Gunnar Myrdal and America's Conscience: Social Engineering and Racial Liberalism, 1938–1987* (Chapel Hill: University of North Carolina Press, 1990), 275–277.
94. President's Committee on Civil Rights, *To Secure These Rights: The Report of the President's Committee on Civil Rights* (New York: Simon & Schuster, 1947), 139.
95. V. O. Key, *Southern Politics in State and Nation* (New York: Knopf, 1949), 329–344, nicely sums up the story of the Dixiecrat revolt.
96. Anderson, *Randolph*, 76.
97. Dalfiume, *Desegregation*, 172.
98. Ibid., 175–200.
99. Tygiel, *Baseball's Great Experiment*, 30.
100. Ibid., chap. 2.
101. How the logic of free markets undermines efforts to segregate the races is lucidly expounded in Thomas Sowell, *Race and Economics* (New York: David McKay, 1975), and Richard A. Epstein, *Forbidden Grounds: The Case Against Employment Discrimination Laws* (Cambridge: Harvard University Press, 1992).
102. Tygiel, *Baseball's Great Experiment*, 60.
103. Ibid., 59.
104. Ibid., 168–179.
105. Steve Sailer, "How Jackie Robinson Desegregated America," *National Review*, 8 April 1996, 40.
106. Jaynes and Williams, *Common Destiny*, p. 66.
107. Roger Kahn, *The Boys of Summer*, as quoted in Tygiel, *Baseball's Great Experiment*, 344.
108. The term-limits charge was made by Willie Brown, then Speaker of the California Assembly; "American Notes; Term Limits," *Time*, 23 March 1992, 31. Opposition to busing was equated with cross-burnings in Tenafly, New Jersey, in 1995; see Robert

Hanley, "Island in a Sea of White Resistance," *New York Times,* 21 December 1995, B1.

109. Kevin Sack, "Atlanta Leaders See Racial Goals as Olympic Ideal," *New York Times,* 10 June 1996, A1.

CHAPTER 4: AMAZING PATIENCE

1. Charlayne Hunter-Gault, *In My Place* (New York: Random House, 1993), 2, 169.
2. Walter Dellinger, "A Southern White Recalls a Moral Revolution," *Washington Post,* 15 May 1994, C1.
3. Ibid.
4. *Brown v. Board of Education of Topeka,* 347 U.S. 483, 493, 495 (1954).
5. In 1950, 32.5 percent of the nation's whites and 70.7 percent of its blacks lived in states with dual school systems; U.S. Bureau of the Census, *Historical Statistics of the United States: Colonial Times to 1970* (Washington, D.C.: U.S. Government Printing Office, 1975), 9, 22, 24, 28, 30, 32, 37. The 40 percent estimate is from Anthony Lewis and the New York Times, *Portrait of a Decade: The Second American Revolution* (New York: Bantam Books, 1965), 19.
6. Mark V. Tushnet, *The NAACP's Legal Strategy Against Segregated Education, 1925–1950* (Chapel Hill: University of North Carolina Press, 1987), chaps. 4–7.
7. Richard Kluger, *Simple Justice: The History of Brown v. Board of Education and Black America's Struggle for Equality* (New York: Vintage Books, 1977), 260–261, 282; *Sweatt v. Painter,* 339 U.S. 629, 634 (1950).
8. Kluger, *Simple Justice,* 266–269, 283; *McLaurin v. Oklahoma State Regents for Higher Education,* 339 U.S. 637 (1950).
9. 347 U.S. 483, 492 (1954).
10. 347 U.S. at 495.
11. Andrew Kull, *The Color-Blind Constitution* (Cambridge: Harvard University Press, 1992), 156–158.
12. Kull, *Color-Blind Constitution,* 153.
13. Howard Schuman, Charlotte Steen, and Lawrence Bobo, *Racial Attitudes in America: Trends and Interpretations* (Cambridge: Harvard University Press, 1985), 74.
14. This criticism is developed in Kull, *Color-Blind Constitution,* chap. 9.
15. Mildred A. Schwartz, *Trends in White Attitudes Toward Negroes,* Report No. 119 (Chicago: National Opinion Research Center, University of Chicago, 1967), 31. The percentages given above differ slightly from those provided in Schwartz because they were recalculated excluding "don't know" answers.
16. David J. Garrow, "Hopelessly Hollow History: Revisionist Devaluing of *Brown v. Board of Education,*" *Virginia Law Review* 80 (February 1994), 156. Whether *Brown* was truly an indispensable catalyst for the civil rights movement is the subject of intense and continuing debate. The controversy began with Gerald N. Rosenberg, *The Hollow Hope: Can Courts Bring About Social Change?* (Chicago: University of Chicago Press, 1991), a stimulating revisionist challenge to the conventional view that *Brown* was crucial. Other grounds for skepticism are offered by Michael J. Klarman in "How *Brown* Changed Race Relations: The Backlash Thesis," *Journal of American History* 81 (June 1994), 81–118, and "*Brown,* Racial Change, and the Civil Rights Movement," *Virginia Law Review* 80 (February 1994), 7–150. Klarman follows Rosenberg on most points, but differs in arguing that *Brown* did play a vital role in the

civil rights revolution by increasing southern white backlash against the decision to extremes that enraged northern whites and led them to support federal intervention in support of black rights. The February 1994 issue of the *Virginia Law Review* contains not only Klarman's long article but critical comments about it from David Garrow, Gerald Rosenberg, and Mark Tushnet, and a rejoinder from Klarman.

17. Twenty years before *Brown,* W. E. B. Du Bois had argued that integration would do more harm than good if it meant putting black children into schools in which they faced unremitting hostility from white teachers and students. He insisted that integration was the ultimate, long-term goal, but thought that some steps designed to bring about integration were counterproductive; "Does the Negro Need Separate Schools?" *Journal of Negro Education* 4 (July 1935), 328–335.

18. George H. Gallup, Jr., *The Gallup Poll: Public Opinion, 1935–1971* (New York: Random House, 1972), 1401. This result is consistent with the conservative attitudes of southern black soldiers about military segregation during World War II, discussed in chap. 3, p. 75. One might worry about biases in the results stemming from the fact that Gallup's interviewers were white. Southern blacks responding to white interviewers in places like Mississippi in 1955 might have been tempted to tell the pollsters what they thought the pollsters wanted to hear rather than the truth. However, another Gallup poll a few weeks later found that 82 percent of southern blacks approved the Interstate Commerce Commission's ban on segregation in trains, buses, and public waiting rooms; *The Gallup Poll,* 1402. The difference in responses to the two queries suggests that many blacks had real doubts about *Brown.* It is hard to see why they would claim to oppose *Brown* when they really favored it but not similarly claim to oppose the ICC's integration ruling.

19. See the discussion in chap. 3, p. 75.

20. Gallup provided no urban-rural breakdown for responses to this question, but the point made in the text follows from the undoubted fact that black migration from southern rural areas to cities in both the North and South was strongly selective of the young and the better-educated.

21. Robert Frederick Burk, *The Eisenhower Administration and Black Civil Rights* (Knoxville: University of Tennessee Press, 1984), 144–145, 192–194.

22. Walter Johnson, ed., *The Papers of Adlai E. Stevenson,* vol. 4, *"Let's Talk Sense to the American People,"* 1952–1955 (Boston: Little, Brown, 1974), 48, 520, 528; *The Papers of Adlai E. Stevenson: Vol. VI, Toward A New America, 1955–1957* (Boston: Little, Brown, 1976), 64–67. Stevenson's efforts to placate southern whites led him to denounce "the reckless assertions that the South is a prison in which half the people are prisoners and the other half are wardens," and to boast that his grandfather, as a congressman from Illinois, had voted against Republican proposals to use troops to protect black voters during Reconstruction; *Papers of Adlai Stevenson,* vol. 4, 111, 156.

23. Klarman, *"Brown,* Racial Change, and the Civil Rights Movement," 14.

24. *Brown v. Board of Education of Topeka,* 349 U.S. 294 (1955).

25. Harvard Sitkoff, *The Struggle for Black Equality, 1954–1980* (New York: Hill & Wang, 1981), 27.

26. Rosenberg, *Hollow Hope,* 50.

27. J. Harvie Wilkinson III, *From Brown to Bakke: The Supreme Court and School Integration, 1954–1978* (New York: Oxford University Press, 1979), 102.

28. Rosenberg, *Hollow Hope,* 127.

29. Ibid., 78; David R. Goldfield, *Black, White, and Southern: Race Relations and Southern Culture, 1940 to the Present* (Baton Rouge: Lousiana State University Press, 1990), 84–86.

30. Goldfield, *Black, White, and Southern*, 75–76. A lengthy excerpt from *Black Monday* is conveniently available in Clayborne Carson et al., eds., *Eyes on the Prize Civil Rights Reader: Documents, Speeches, and Firsthand Accounts from the Black Freedom Struggle, 1954–1990* (New York: Penguin, 1991), 83–94.

31. Goldfield, *Black, White, and Southern*, 77.

32. Neil R. McMillen, *Dark Journey: Black Mississippians in the Age of Jim Crow* (Urbana: University of Illinois Press, 1989), 17–18; Goldfield, *Black, White, and Southern*, 75–76.

33. Neil R. McMillen, *The Citizens' Council: Organized Resistance to the Second Reconstruction, 1954–1964* (Urbana: University of Illinois Press, 1971), 209–211.

34. Klarman, "How *Brown* Changed Race Relations," 97.

35. Martin Luther King, Jr., *Stride Toward Freedom: The Montgomery Story* (New York: Harper & Row, 1958), 193.

36. Goldfield, *Black, White, and Southern*, 87.

37. Even V. O. Key's magisterial study *Southern Politics in State and Nation* (New York: Knopf, 1949), published just six years before the Montgomery boycott began, completely ignores the possibility of a black mass movement. Key did not see the southern social order as impervious to change of any kind, as Dollard seemed to, but he believed it would happen very gradually, as increasing numbers of educated blacks won the franchise and made alliances with whites who would benefit from progressive change; Earl Black and Merle Black, *Politics and Society in the South* (Cambridge: Harvard University Press, 1987), 102.

38. Mrs. Parks recounts the incident in an interview in Howell Raines, *My Soul Is Rested: Movement Days in the Deep South Remembered* (New York: Putnam, 1977), 40–42.

39. J. Mills Thornton, "Challenge and Response in the Montgomery Bus Boycott of 1955–1956," *Alabama Review* 33 (July 1980), 191–197; David J. Garrow, ed., *The Montgomery Bus Boycott and the Women Who Started It: The Memoir of JoAnn Gibson Robinson* (Knoxville: University of Tennessee Press, 1987), 34–35.

40. Taylor Branch, *Parting the Waters: America in the King Years, 1954–1963* (New York: Simon & Schuster, 1988), 124–125, 128–129.

41. Aldon D. Morris, *The Origins of the Civil Rights Movement: Black Communities Organizing for Change* (New York: Free Press, 1984), 51. Given her history of political involvement, and given the fact that activists in the Women's Political Council and the NAACP had been searching for several months for someone to violate the bus segregation statute as a test case, it is hard to believe that on 1 December, Rosa Parks was not courting arrest as a test case. It seems to be the case, though. After her arrest she was asked if she was willing to back a legal challenge to the law under which she was arrested, and she apparently agonized before deciding to go ahead; Branch, *Parting the Waters*, 129–131.

42. The newcomer was Martin Luther King, Jr.; *Stride Toward Freedom*, 34–35. The collapse of the Citizens Coordinating Committee was so thoroughly dispiriting to King that it led him to conclude that "the tragic division in the Negro community could be cured only by some divine miracle" (69).

43. Branch, *Parting the Waters*, 129–133; Garrow, *Montgomery*, 39.

44. Ironically, the leader of the Montgomery bus boycott had apparently never himself ridden on one of the city's buses. Not because of the recency of his arrival but because he came from a prosperous middle-class family—his father was one of the leading preachers in Atlanta—and had owned his own car since college days.

45. Garrow, *Montgomery*, 60.

46. King, *Stride Toward Freedom*, 126–130.

47. Ibid., 61–62.
48. Two additional demands were included in the resolutions passed at the mass meeting on December 5. One was a vague plea that bus drivers treat black passengers more courteously, and the other was that black drivers be employed on four routes serving predominantly black neighborhoods; King, *Stride Toward Freedom*, 63–64. The call for first-come, first-served seating aroused the greatest opposition from local white officials.
49. Mobile was not an isolated example; a similar form of segregation was also used on the buses in Atlanta, Savannah, and Macon, Georgia; Goldfield, *Black, White, and Southern*, 94.
50. Thornton, "Challenge and Response," 205; Branch, *Parting the Waters*, 139–141. Ironically, this battle had already been fought in Montgomery half a century before. The city's first transportation segregation ordinance, adopted in 1900, had provoked a black boycott of the trolley lines (buses had not yet come into use), a boycott that only ended when the City Council amended the ordinance to provide that no black would have to abandon a seat except when there was a vacant one closer to the back. This ordinance was no longer controlling in Montgomery, though, because a 1945 state statute had overridden it. The boycott was initially an effort to restore the compromise that had been struck in 1900; Thornton, "Challenge and Response," 188–189.
51. David J. Garrow, *Bearing the Cross: Martin Luther King, Jr. and the Southern Christian Leadership Conference* (New York: Morrow, 1986), 52.
52. Kull, *Color-Blind Constitution*, 160–161; Catherine A. Barnes, *Journey from Jim Crow: The Desegregation of Southern Transit* (New York: Columbia University Press, 1981), 94. As Kull argues, the *Brown* decision failed to provide an adequate rationale for this extension, because it placed so much stress on the harmful psychological effects of segregation in schools, and stated that its central conclusion was "that in the field of public education the doctrine of 'separate but equal' has no place"; 347 U.S. at 495. That would seem to suggest that "separate but equal" might still have a "place" in other arenas of American life. What the Court had to say about the evils of segregated schools did not necessarily apply very well—or apply at all—to the issues raised by segregated housing projects, buses, municipal swimming pools, and the like. The Court struck down Jim Crow practices in those realms without further explanation, thus shirking its job of articulating constitutional principles to the American people.
53. Barnes, *Journey from Jim Crow*, chap. 6.
54. King, *Stride Toward Freedom*, 142–150; Thornton, "Challenge and Response," 221–227; Branch, *Parting the Waters*, 168, 173–178, 184–186.
55. Barnes, *Journey from Jim Crow*, 242.
56. Thornton, "Challenge and Response," 235.
57. Clayborne Carson, "The Boycott that Changed Dr. King's Life," *New York Times Magazine*, 7 January 1996, 38.
58. King, *Stride Toward Freedom*, 136.
59. Ibid., 137–138, 141.
60. A photograph of this ride is provided in King, *Stride Toward Freedom*, 168.
61. Garrow, *Bearing the Cross*, 83–87.
62. Morris, *Origins of the Civil Rights Movement*, 18–25.
63. King, *Stride Toward Freedom*, 70.
64. Rosenberg, *Hollow Hope*, 114–115.
65. E. D. Nixon, for example, felt very resentful about the press focus on King. He

eventually resigned as treasurer of the MIA in a letter that complained that he had been "treated as a child" by King; Branch, *Parting the Waters*, 200–201.

66. Ibid., 203.

67. King, *Stride Toward Freedom*, 80–81.

68. Ibid., 190.

69. Morris, *Origins of the Civil Rights Movement*, 82–84.

70. Ibid., 87.

71. Ibid., 77, 115.

72. Quotation from one of the position papers prepared for the meeting at which SCLC was founded; Morris, *Origins of the Civil Rights Movement*, 85.

73. Ibid., 29–35.

74. Earl Black, *Southern Governors and Civil Rights: Racial Segregation as a Campaign Issue in the Second Reconstruction* (Cambridge: Harvard University Press, 1976), 52. The runner-up in that gubernatorial race was George C. Wallace, who won the contest the next time around. In 1958, Wallace had run as a strict segregationist but did not focus on the race issue as much as the man who defeated him. Legend has it that after his defeat Wallace vowed that "I'm not goin' to be outniggered again," or, in some versions, "outsegged" again. Although the story appears in many secondary sources, there is no reliable evidence to establish that Wallace ever used these words; Stephan Lesher, *George Wallace: American Populist* (Reading, Mass.: Addison-Wesley, 1994), 128–129. In his successful 1962 race, though, Wallace did play the race card for all it was worth.

75. Black, *Southern Governors*, 52, 54, 300; Branch, *Parting the Waters*, 186–187.

76. Morris, *Origins of the Civil Rights Movement*, 29–35. This repressive effort reversed a very important trend that had been at work since the 1930s—that most of the growth in NAACP strength was occurring in the South, and especially in southern cities; Douglas McAdam, *Political Process and the Development of Black Insurgency, 1930–1970* (Chicago: University of Chicago Press, 1982), 103–105. The anti-NAACP crusade that began in 1956 rolled back most of these earlier gains.

77. Lesher, *Wallace*, 102–104.

78. Goldfield, *Black, White, and Southern*, 106–111; Black, *Southern Governors*, 100; Lesher, *Wallace*, 107–109; Burk, *Eisenhower Administration*, chap. 9.

79. Wilkinson, *From Brown to Bakke*, 88–95.

80. President Roosevelt's July 5, 1938, letter to the Conference on Economic Conditions of the South, quoted in David L. Carlton and Peter Coclanis, eds., *Confronting Southern Poverty in the Great Depression: "The Report on Economic Conditions in the South" with Related Documents* (New York: St. Martin's, 1996), 42. The term "Sunbelt" was not coined until 1969, and did not come into common usage until several years later, but the idea was there as early as the 1950s; David R. Goldfield, "The City as Southern History: The Past and the Promise of Tomorrow," in Joe P. Dunn and Howard L. Preston, eds., *The Future South: A Historical Perspective for the Twenty-first Century* (Urbana: University of Illinois Press, 1991), 29.

81. This transformation is persuasively analyzed in Gavin Wright, *Old South, New South: Revolutions in the Southern Economy Since the Civil War* (New York: Basic Books, 1986); and Bruce J. Schulman, *From Cotton Belt to Sunbelt: Federal Policy, Economic Development, and the Transformation of the South, 1938–1980* (New York: Oxford University Press, 1991).

82. Schulman, *From Cotton Belt*, 135.

83. Wright, *Old South*, 265.

84. Dunn and Preston, *The Future South*, 29.

85. Racial moderates were elected with increasing frequency outside of the Deep South in the early 1960s. This pattern appeared in the Deep South only after 1965; Black, *Southern Governors*, chap. 10.

86. The phrase is George Wallace's, from his first inaugural address as governor of Alabama in January 1963; Lesher, *Wallace*, 174.

87. Senate Rule 22 provided that two-thirds of the members had to agree to cut off debate on a subject; James L. Sundquist, *Politics and Policy: The Eisenhower, Kennedy, and Johnson Years* (Washington, D.C.: Brookings Institution, 1968), 515–518. Proponents of civil rights legislation, blocked by a filibuster, never succeeded in getting the necessary two-thirds support for cloture until the Civil Rights Act of 1964, and then it was only after fifty-seven days, the longest filibuster in American history; Mark Stern, *Calculating Visions: Kennedy, Johnson, and Civil Rights* (New Brunswick, N.J.: Rutgers University Press, 1992), 4, 182. The Senate reduced the margin of votes required for cloture from two-thirds to three-fifths in 1975.

88. Stern, *Calculating Visions*, 131.

89. Sundquist, *Politics and Policy*, 222–238; Goldfield, *Black, White, and Southern*, 150–151; Burk, *Eisenhower Administration*, chap. 10.

90. Gerald David Jaynes and Robin M. Williams, Jr., eds., *A Common Destiny: Blacks and American Society*, National Research Council (Washington, D.C.: National Academy Press, 1989), 233; Goldberg, *Black, White, and Southern*, 151.

91. Sundquist, *Politics and Policy*, 243–250.

92. One of the four, Franklin McCain, tells his story in an interview in Raines, *My Soul Is Rested*, 75–82. See also Goldfield, *Black, White, and Southern*, 118–120; and William H. Chafe, *Civilities and Civil Rights: Greensboro, North Carolina and the Black Struggle for Freedom* (New York: Oxford University Press, 1980), 114–120.

93. McCain met this woman fifteen years later—ironically, at a reunion commemorating the Greensboro sit-in. She explained then that she had feared for the personal safety of the four youths and worried that racial strife might cost her her job; Raines, *My Soul Is Rested*, 78.

94. Chafe, *Civilities*, 119.

95. Rosenberg, *Hollow Hope*, 142.

96. Goldfield, *Black, White, and Southern*, 120; Rosenberg, *Hollow Hope*, 134.

97. Goldfield, *Black, White, and Southern*, 121.

98. August Meier and Elliot M. Rudwick, *CORE: A Study in the Civil Rights Movement, 1942–1968* (Urbana: University of Illinois Press, 1975), 13–14.

99. John Morton Blum, *V Was for Victory: Politics and American Culture During World War II* (New York: Harcourt Brace Jovanovich, 1976), 217–218.

100. Morris, *Origins of the Civil Rights Movement*, 188–193.

101. Goldfield, *Black, White, and Southern*, 123.

102. Morris, *Origins of the Civil Rights Movement*, 196.

103. Reported in Associated Press Online, September 1, 1994.

CHAPTER 5: WE SHALL OVERCOME

1. Rick Bragg, "Emotional March Gains a Repentant Wallace," *New York Times*, 11 March 1995, 1.

2. Edward G. Carmines and James A. Stimson, *Issue Evolution: Race and the Transfor-

mation of American Politics (Princeton: Princeton University Press, 1989), 37; Robert Frederick Burk, *The Eisenhower Administration and Black Civil Rights* (Knoxville: University of Tennessee Press, 1984), 20; Mark Stern, *Calculating Visions: Kennedy, Johnson, and Civil Rights* (New Brunswick, N.J.: Rutgers University Press, 1992), 39. It should be noted that these and all other figures about how particular groups voted are merely estimates, and are susceptible to substantial error. Ballots are secret in the United States. To estimate how blacks voted, social scientists typically look at how the vote for a particular candidate or party fluctuated with the black proportion in different electoral units. Another method is to survey voters after they have left the polling place and to ask them about the choices they had made. Exit polls based upon a nationally representative sample large enough to yield reliable estimates of African-American voting patterns have only been conducted within the past two decades or so.

3. Carmines and Stimson, *Issue Evolution,* 38–39.
4. This remarkable statement, made to *New York Times* reporter and old Kennedy family friend Arthur Krock, remained private until long after JFK's death, when Krock reported it in an oral history interview for the John F. Kennedy Library. It would have been political dynamite if it had come out while Kennedy was in office; James N. Giglio, *The Presidency of John F. Kennedy* (Lawrence: University Press of Kansas, 1991), 160.
5. Harris Wofford, *Of Kennedys and Kings: Making Sense of the Sixties* (New York: Farrar, Straus & Giroux, 1980), 47–48.
6. Stern, *Calculating Visions,* 33.
7. Wofford, *Of Kennedys,* 58.
8. Stern, *Calculating Visions,* 33.
9. Taylor Branch, *Parting the Waters: America in the King Years, 1954–1963* (New York: Simon & Schuster, 1988), 349–350.
10. Branch, *Parting the Waters,* 354–378; Stern, *Calculating Visions,* 33–39.
11. Stern, *Calculating Visions,* 39.
12. U.S. Bureau of the Census, *Historical Statistics of the United States: Colonial Times to 1970* (Washington, D.C.: U.S. Government Printing Office, 1975), 1073, 1077. Many historians believe that Nixon likely did carry Illinois in fact, but was counted out by officials of the Chicago Democratic Party machine. There is also some question about the honesty of the count in Texas, where a shift of 24,000 votes would have put Nixon in the winner's column.
13. Stern, *Calculating Visions,* 42.
14. Ibid., 45–48.
15. Ibid., 40.
16. *Historical Statistics of the U.S.,* 1075; Michael J. Klarman, "*Brown,* Racial Change, and the Civil Rights Movement," *Virginia Law Review* 80 (February 1994), 139–140.
17. Wofford, *Of Kennedys,* 151.
18. Branch, *Parting the Waters,* 412–413; Catherine A. Barnes, *Journey from Jim Crow: The Desegregation of Southern Transit* (New York: Columbia University Press, 1981), 150–156.
19. August Meier and Elliot Rudwick, *CORE: A Study in the Civil Rights Movement, 1942–1968* (Urbana: University of Illinois Press, 1975), 135–137; Barnes, *Journey from Jim Crow,* 157.
20. David R. Goldfield, *Black, White, and Southern: Race Relations and Southern Culture, 1940 to the Present* (Baton Rouge: Louisiana State University Press, 1990), 124.

21. Barnes, *Journey from Jim Crow*, 160; Wofford, *Of Kennedys*, 152; Goldfield, *Black, White, and Southern*, 124–127.
22. Wofford, *Of Kennedys*, 125, 153.
23. Goldfield, *Black, White, and Southern*, 127.
24. Ibid., 127–128.
25. Giglio, *Presidency of John Kennedy*, 165
26. Barnes, *Journey from Jim Crow*, 163–165; Meier and Rudwick, *CORE*, 139.
27. Barnes, *Journey from Jim Crow*, 166–168; Wofford, *Of Kennedys*, 157.
28. Barnes, *Journey from Jim Crow*, 168.
29. Wofford, *Of Kennedys*, 157.
30. Barnes, *Journey from Jim Crow*, 168.
31. Meier and Rudwick, *CORE*, 172–175; Stern, *Calculating Visions*, 64–65; Abigail M. Thernstrom, *Whose Votes Count: Affirmative Action and Minority Voting Rights* (Cambridge: Harvard University Press, 1987), 12–14.
32. Arthur M. Schlesinger, Jr., *Robert Kennedy and His Times* (Boston: Houghton Mifflin, 1978), 301.
33. Branch, *Parting the Waters*, 479–482.
34. Gerald David Jaynes and Robin M. Williams, Jr., eds., *A Common Destiny: Blacks and American Society*, National Research Council (Washington, D.C.: National Academy Press, 1989), 233; Stern, *Calculating Visions*, 66.
35. Schlesinger, *Robert Kennedy*, 301.
36. Ibid., 301–302; Carl M. Brauer, *John F. Kennedy and the Second Reconstruction* (New York: Columbia University Press, 1977), 114; Clayborne Carson, *In Struggle: SNCC and the Black Awakening of the 1960s* (Cambridge: Harvard University Press, 1981), 39.
37. Branch, *Parting the Waters*, 509–523, 921; Stern, *Calculating Visions*, 67–68.
38. Branch, *Parting the Waters*, 540–550; Clayborne Carson, et al., eds., *Eyes on the Prize Civil Rights Reader: Documents, Speeches, and Firsthand Accounts from the Black Freedom Struggle, 1954–1990* (New York: Penguin, 1991), 133–134.
39. Pritchett describes his handling of the Albany Movement protests in Howell Raines, *My Soul is Rested: Movement Days in the Deep South Remembered* (New York: Putnam, 1977), 361–366.
40. Branch, *Parting the Waters*, 550; Robert Weisbrot, *Freedom Bound: A History of America's Civil Rights Movement* (New York: Norton, 1990), 66.
41. Branch, *Parting the Waters*, 600–607.
42. Ibid., 621–629.
43. Ibid., 615–618; Weisbrot, *Freedom Bound*, 64.
44. Branch, *Parting the Waters*, 620.
45. Stephan Lesher, *George Wallace: American Populist* (Reading, Mass.: Addison-Wesley, 1994), 164–166; Stern, *Calculating Visions*, 70–73; Branch, *Parting the Waters*, 434, 647–665.
46. Michael Barone, *Our Country: The Shaping of America from Roosevelt to Reagan* (New York: Free Press, 1990), 352.
47. Harvard Sitkoff, *The Struggle for Black Equality, 1954–1980* (New York: Hill & Wang, 1981), 130.
48. Sitkoff, *Struggle for Black Equality*, 128–130.
49. David J. Garrow, *Protest at Selma: Martin Luther King, Jr., and the Voting Rights Act of 1965* (New Haven: Yale University Press, 1978), 221–223. One of the first observers to call attention to this important shift was Howard Hubbard, in a perceptive

essay, "Five Long Hot Summers and How They Grew," *The Public Interest,* no. 12 (Summer 1968), 5–7.

50. Aldon B. Morris, *The Origins of the Civil Rights Movement: Black Communities Organizing for Change* (New York: Free Press, 1984), 68–73, 251–253.

51. David J. Garrow, *Bearing the Cross: Martin Luther King, Jr., and the Southern Christian Leadership Conference* (New York: Morrow, 1986), 226–227.

52. Branch, *Parting the Waters,* 708–711.

53. Ibid., 725–731.

54. James M. Washington, ed., *A Testament of Hope: The Essential Writings and Speeches of Martin Luther King, Jr.* (New York: HarperCollins, 1986), 289–302.

55. Dennis Chong, *Collective Action and the Civil Rights Movement* (Chicago: University of Chicago Press, 1991), 184.

56. Barone, *Our Country,* 354.

57. Eric Sevareid of CBS, quoted in James L. Sundquist, *Politics and Policy: The Eisenhower, Kennedy, and Johnson Years* (Washington, D.C.: Brookings Institution, 1968), 260.

58. Branch, *Parting the Waters,* 756–764.

59. Goldfield, *Black, White, and Southern,* 139–140; Branch, *Parting the Waters,* 764–771.

60. Sitkoff, *Struggle for Black Equality,* 141–142; Branch, *Parting the Waters,* 776–791.

61. Lesher, *Wallace,* 193–196; Branch, *Parting the Waters,* 792–800.

62. Branch, *Parting the Waters,* 825.

63. Ibid., 822; Richard Reeves, *President Kennedy: Profile of Power* (New York: Simon & Schuster, 1993), 501–502.

64. Sitkoff, *Struggle for Black Equality,* 144–145, 149.

65. The six leading organizations were the NAACP, the Legal Defense and Education Fund, the National Urban League, SCLC, CORE, and SNCC; Gerald N. Rosenberg, *The Hollow Hope: Can Courts Bring About Social Change?* (Chicago: University of Chicago Press, 1991), 151.

66. Lesher, *Wallace,* 174, chap. 9 passim; Reeves, *President Kennedy,* 517–519.

67. Stern, *Calculating Vision,* 84.

68. Sundquist, *Politics and Policy,* 261–262.

69. Branch, *Parting the Waters,* 807.

70. "Radio and Television Report to the American People on Civil Rights," June 11, 1963, in *Public Papers of the Presidents of the United States: John F. Kennedy, Containing the Public Messages, Speeches, and Statements of the President January 1 to November 22, 1963* (Washington, D.C.: U.S. Government Printing Office, 1964), 468–471.

71. Branch, *Parting the Waters,* 824–825.

72. Rosenberg, *The Hollow Hope,* 129–130; George H. Gallup, *The Gallup Poll: Public Opinion, 1935–1971* (New York: Random House, 1972), 1447.

73. Gallup, *Gallup Poll,* 1539.

74. Ibid., 1812.

75. The October 1963 figure is from Gallup, *Gallup Poll,* 1842. A July 1963 figure is not given in *The Gallup Poll,* for some reason, but the question was definitely asked that month. Rosenberg's *Hollow Hope,* 130, includes a graph that indicates a figure of 47–48 percent for July but does not specify the source. Paul B. Sheatsley, "White Attitudes Toward the Negro," *Daedalus* 95 (Winter 1966), 217–218, 237, notes that "since mid-summer, 1963, the question of race relations has been consistently cited by Americans as 'the most important problem facing the United States,' " and cites a

Gallup poll release of 21 July 1963. Sheatsley does not give a precise figure for July 1963, however.

76. Gallup, *Gallup Poll,* 1827, 1837–1838, 1863.

77. Hugh Davis Graham, *The Civil Rights Era: Origins and Development of National Policy* (New York: Oxford University Press, 1990), 79; Paul Burstein, *Discrimination, Jobs, and Politics: The Struggle for Equal Employment Opportunity in the United States Since the New Deal* (Chicago: University of Chicago Press, 1985), 64.

78. John Shelton Reed and Merle Black, "How Southerners Gave Up Jim Crow," *New Perspectives* 17 (Fall 1985), 15–19. For further evidence on this point, see Earl Black and Merle Black, *Politics and Society in the South* (Cambridge: Harvard University Press, 1987), chap. 9. The proportion of southern whites who favored what Black and Black define as "strict segregation" declined from 65 percent to 46 percent in just the three years from 1961 to 1964 (estimated from graph on p. 200). A few years earlier than 1961, they suggest, support for "strict segregation" would have been even higher than that.

79. Mildred A. Schwartz, *Trends in White Attitudes Toward Negroes,* Report No. 119 (Chicago: National Opinion Research Center, University of Chicago, 1967), 109.

80. Gallup, *Gallup Poll,* 1829–1830.

81. Sheatsley, "White Attitudes," 231. The notion that the civil rights movement was Communist-inspired, or at least was being influenced and manipulated by Communists was shared by some in positions of power in Washington, especially J. Edgar Hoover, the director of the FBI. In the early days of the Kennedy administration, Hoover warned Attorney General Robert Kennedy that one of King's closest advisors, Stanley Levison, was a key member of the Communist Party. A year later the FBI reported that another Communist, Jack O'Dell, had been hired in the SCLC's New York office, and the Bureau obtained permission to put bugs and wiretaps in King's office at the SCLC. Later, with the approval of the Kennedy and Johnson administrations, Hoover would subject every aspect of King's life to the most intense scrutiny, including bugging every hotel room he occupied until his death in 1968. Hoover sought to destroy King, and went to the lengths of having information about his habitual marital infidelities leaked to the press. The story of this disgraceful abuse of power is told in David J. Garrow, *The FBI and Martin Luther King, Jr.: From "Solo" to Memphis* (New York: Norton, 1981), and in the various biographies of King, the best of which are those by Garrow and by Taylor Branch. None of these writers, though, adequately place this matter in the context of the deadly struggle between the United States and Soviet totalitarianism in the period, a struggle in which the Communist Party USA consistently played the role of public relations agent for the Soviet Union and was controlled by the Kremlin. Anyone who doubts that harsh judgment should contemplate the documents from the Soviet archives that became available after the collapse of the USSR; see Harvey Klehr, John Earl Haynes, and Fridrikh Igorevich Firsov, *The Secret World of American Communism* (New Haven: Yale University Press, 1995). The FBI was apparently mistaken in thinking that Levison and O'Dell were still party members in the early 1960s, but they certainly had been members only a few years before, and their CP involvement raised serious questions about their loyalty to the United States. Communists were not just liberals with slightly stronger convictions; the party itself, though by no means all of its members, served as the agent of a hostile foreign power. It was no more unreasonable to have been worried about CP influence upon an important social movement than it would have been to have been worried about the influence of people who had been

active in the KKK or the American Nazi Party not long before. It was more reasonable, in fact, since Nazism was not a threat to the world in the 1960s and Communism
was. Richard Gid Powers, *Not Without Honor: The History of American Anticom-
munism* (New York: Free Press, 1995) is a thoughtful recent study by an author who
understands the moral issues involved in the battles between anti-Communists and
"anti-anti-Communists" in the Cold War era. The December 1996 revelation that
Thurgood Marshall had cooperated with the FBI in its efforts to monitor civil rights
activists it suspected of being under Communist influence should not have been
surprising and disturbing to anyone who understood the issues of the period; David
J. Garrow, "Marshall, Hoover, and the NAACP," *Newsweek*, 16 December 1996, 37.
Having cooperated with J. Edgar Hoover was far more morally defensible than having
served Lenin, Stalin, and their successors. Ronald Radosh, *Divided They Fell: The
Demise of the Democratic Party, 1964–1996* (New York: Free Press, 1996), chap. 1,
includes a perceptive discussion of the Communist Party and the civil rights movement of the early 1960s.

82. Sundquist, *Politics and Policy*, 262–265.
83. David B. Filvaroff and Raymond E. Wolfinger, "The Origin and Enactment of the
Civil Rights Act of 1964," Working Paper 95–23 (Berkeley: Institute of Government
Studies, University of California, Berkeley, 1995), 11.
84. Graham, *Civil Rights Era*, 77–87.
85. Filvaroff and Wolfinger, "Origin and Enactment," 12.
86. Chong, *Collective Action*, 202.
87. Giglio, *Presidency of John Kennedy*, 185; Stern, *Calculating Visions*, 93–105.
88. Stern, *Calculating Visions*, 103.
89. Reeves, *President Kennedy*, 580–581.
90. Branch, *Parting the Waters*, 873–874, 878–880; Reeves, *President Kennedy*, 582.
91. Washington, *Testament of Hope*, 217–220.
92. The 1960 Census classified 88.6 percent of the population as white, 10.5 percent as
black, and 0.9 percent as being of "other race," chiefly American Indians, Chinese
Americans, or Japanese Americans; *Historical Statistics of the U.S.*, 14. Hispanics,
who were then 3.9 percent of the population, were classified as white; Frank D.
Bean, and Marta Tienda, *The Hispanic Population of the United States* (New York:
Russell Sage Foundation, 1987), 59. In 1963, 5 out of 435 members of the House of
Representatives and none of the 100 senators were African-American.
93. Sundquist, *Politics and Policy*, 237, 263–264.
94. Stern, *Calculating Visions*,104.
95. Sundquist, *Politics and Policy*, 268; Filvaroff and Wolfinger, "Origin and Enactment,"
31.
96. Reeves, *President Kennedy*, 599–600.
97. Sundquist, *Politics and Policy*, 265.
98. Giglio, *Presidency of John Kennedy*, 183.

CHAPTER 6: COMING TOGETHER—AND APART

1. James M. Washington, ed., *A Testament of Hope: The Essential Writings and Speeches
of Martin Luther King, Jr.* (New York: HarperCollins, 1986), 218–219.
2. Quoted in Steven F. Lawson, *Black Ballots: Voting Rights in the South, 1944–1969*
(New York: Columbia University Press, 1976), 312.

3. Mark Stern, *Calculating Visions: Kennedy, Johnson, and Civil Rights* (New Brunswick, N.J.: Rutgers University Press, 1992), chap. 5.

4. Ibid., 160–167.

5. Ibid., 171.

6. James L. Sundquist, *Politics and Policy: The Eisenhower, Kennedy, and Johnson Years* (Washington, D.C.: Brookings Institution, 1968), 267; David B. Filvaroff and Raymond E. Wolfinger, "The Origin and Enactment of the Civil Rights Act of 1964," Working Paper 95–23 (Berkeley: Institute of Government Studies, University of California, Berkeley, 1995), 26, 33.

7. The constitutional legitimacy of a federal statute that reached Ollie's Barbecue was the question in *Katzenbach v. McClung,* 379 U.S. 294 (1964).

8. U.S. Bureau of the Census, *Historical Statistics of the United States: Colonial Times to 1970* (Washington, D.C.: U.S. Government Printing Office, 1975), 1077, 1083; Donald R. Kinder and Lynn M. Saunders, *Divided by Color: Racial Politics and Democratic Ideals* (Chicago: University of Chicago Press, 1996), 206.

9. Bayard Rustin, "From Protest to Politics: The Future of the Civil Rights Movement," *Commentary,* February 1965, reprinted in Rustin, *Down the Line: The Collected Writings of Bayard Rustin* (Chicago: Quadrangle Books, 1971), 117, 120–122.

10. Sundquist, *Politics and Policy,* 265.

11. Everett C. Ladd, Jr., *Transformations of the American Party System: Political Coalitions from the New Deal to the 1970s* (New York: Norton, 1975), 158.

12. Stern, *Calculating Visions,* 191. This figure is for 1962. Only 23,920 of the 514,589 African Americans of voting age were registered then.

13. Harvard Sitkoff, *The Struggle for Black Equality, 1954–1980* (New York: Hill & Wang, 1981), 169–178; Nicolaus Mills, *Like a Holy Crusade: Mississippi 1964—The Turning of the Civil Rights Movement in America* (Chicago: Ivan R. Dee, 1992), 16–17, 94–101. Three years later the deputy sheriff and six other men were convicted by a federal court for violating the civil rights of the three victims, and were sent to prison, with the longest sentence being for ten years. The state of Mississippi never filed murder charges against anyone in the case; David R. Goldfield, *Black, White, and Southern: Race Relations and Southern Culture, 1940 to the Present* (Baton Rouge: Lousiana State University Press, 1990), 159.

14. Mills, *Like a Holy Crusade,* 134.

15. Stern, *Calculating Visions,* 191, 270. About 17,000 African Americans completed voter registration forms with the help of the volunteers, but 90 percent of the applications were rejected on one pretext or another.

16. Stern, *Calculating Visions,* 186–187, 191–192, 197–209; Ronald Radosh, *Divided They Fell: The Demise of the Democratic Party, 1964–1996* (New York: Free Press, 1996), chap. 1.

17. Clayborne Carson, *In Struggle: SNCC and the Black Awakening of the 1960s* (Cambridge: Harvard University Press, 1981), 123–129 and pt. 3, passim.

18. In fact, the Voting Rights Act seems to have done the Democrats more harm than good in the South. Although it lifted the rate of southern black political participation to roughly the white level, thus adding to the Democratic total, it also contributed to the massive flight of southern whites from the Democratic Party. Southern whites have not cast a majority of their ballots for a Democratic presidential candidate since 1964. In 1968, just 18 percent of them supported the Democratic nominee; in 1972 it was an even more pathetic 14 percent; Stern, *Calculating Visions,* 232; Ladd, *Transformations,* 158. Democratic presidential candidates have done somewhat bet-

ter since then, but none has come close to winning a majority; Marjorie Connelly, "The Numbers: Portrait of the Electorate," *New York Times,* 10 November 1996, 28.

19. Abigail Thernstrom, *Whose Votes Count? Affirmative Action and Minority Voting Rights* (Cambridge: Harvard University Press, 1987), 17–18.

20. Sitkoff, *Struggle for Black Equality,* 188.

21. Goldfield, *Black, White, and Southern,* 163–165; Sundquist, *Politics and Policy,* 273.

22. Goldfield, *Black, White, and Southern,* 166–167. Reeb's killers were never apprehended. Liuzzo was murdered by four members of the Klan. Despite eyewitness testimony as to their guilt from an FBI informant, an all-white jury refused to convict them of murder.

23. Thernstrom, *Whose Votes Count?,* 15.

24. George H. Gallup, *The Gallup Poll: Public Opinion, 1935–1971* (New York: Random House, 1972), 1933.

25. Stern, *Calculating Visions,* 230; Vaughn Davis Bornet, *The Presidency of Lyndon B. Johnson* (Lawrence: University Press of Kansas, 1983), 232.

26. Thernstrom, *Whose Votes Count?,* 18.

27. Sundquist, *Politics and Policy,* 275.

28. Rustin, "From Protest to Politics," 111.

29. Dennis Chong, *Collective Action and the Civil Rights Movement* (Chicago: University of Chicago Press, 1991), 194.

30. Robert Conot, *Rivers of Blood, Years of Darkness* (New York: Bantam, 1967), is a vivid and detailed narrative.

31. Kinder and Saunders, *Divided by Color,* 103.

32. Dennis E. Gale, *Understanding Urban Unrest: From Reverend King to Rodney King* (Thousand Oaks, Calif.: Sage Publications, 1996), 17–18.

33. Howard Hubbard, "Five Long Hot Summers and How They Grew," *Public Interest,* no. 12 (Summer 1968), 13; John David Skrentny, *The Ironies of Affirmative Action: Politics, Culture, and Justice in America* (Chicago: University of Chicago Press, 1996), 72.

34. Robert M. Fogelson, *Violence as Social Protest: A Study of Riots and Ghettos* (Garden City, N.Y.: Doubleday, 1971), 3.

35. James W. Button, *Blacks and Social Change: Impact of the Civil Rights Movement in Southern Communities* (Princeton: Princeton University Press, 1989), 7. Different studies offer somewhat different estimates of how many riots there were, because of variations in the time period examined and in the definition of what constituted a "riot." A Johnson administration official identified 225 "hostile outbursts" in the 1964–1968 period; Bournet, *Presidency of Lyndon Johnson,* 228–229. Sidney Fine uses the figure of 341 riots in 265 cities from 1963 to 1968; Fine, *Violence in the Model City: The Cavanaugh Administration, Race Relations, and the Detroit Riot of 1967* (Ann Arbor: University of Michigan Press, 1989), 288. Donald L. Horowitz offers the estimate of "more than 500 disturbances, major and minor," for a somewhat longer period—1963–1970; "Racial Violence in the United States," in Nathan Glazer and Ken Young, eds., *Ethnic Pluralism and Public Policy: Achieving Equality in the United States and Great Britain* (Lexington, Mass.: Lexington Books, 1983), 192.

36. Horowitz, "Racial Violence," 192; David Steigerwald, *The Sixties and the End of Modern America* (New York: St. Martin's, 1995), 187.

37. Fine, *Violence in the Model City,* 1. Although the author's prose does not sparkle, this is the most perceptive and illuminating historical study of any of the sixties riots; chaps. 7–9 cover the actual events of the Detroit riot from hour to hour.

38. Ibid., 1, 32–34.

39. Ibid., 165–166; 173–181. The police in Watts, too, were under the impression that they should not fire their weapons unless they came under direct attack. As a result, looters ignored their orders to drop stolen property they were carrying, saying "Go to hell, you motherfuckers, they won't let you shoot"; Conot, *Rivers of Blood,* 242–243.

40. Fine, *Violence in the Model City,* 171–173.

41. Ibid., 249, 291, 299.

42. Peter H. Rossi, "Urban Revolts and the Future of American Cities," in David Boesel and Peter H. Rossi, eds., *Cities Under Seige: An Anatomy of the Ghetto Riots, 1964–1968* (New York: Basic Books, 1971), 413, 425 n 1; Fogelson, *Violence as Social Protest,* 5–8; Arthur I. Wascow, *From Race Riot to Sit-In: 1919 and the 1960s* (Garden City, N.Y.: Doubleday, 1966), chap. 10.

43. Fogelson, *Violence as Social Protest,* 113, derives the estimate that about a fifth of all participants were arrested from a comparison of arrest statistics with personal interviews conducted in Los Angeles, Newark, and Detroit. The calculation could be refined further by taking into account the fact that some whites joined in the looting and were arrested. Whites were 11.9 percent of the adults arrested in the Detroit riot, for example; Fine, *Violence in the Model City,* 249. It we apply that figure to the national totals, the estimate of black riot participants would drop to about 264,000.

44. Fogelson, *Violence as Social Protest,* 97, notes that the total number of whites killed in all of the 1960s riots was lower than the number of blacks killed in the East St. Louis race riots a generation ago, in which thirty-nine African Americans died.

45. Skrentny, *Ironies of Affirmative Action,* 73.

46. Ibid., 70.

47. Bayard Rustin, "The Watts 'Manifesto' and the McCone Report," *Commentary,* March 1966, reprinted in Rustin, *Down the Line,* 140–153. The remark quoted appears on 141–142.

48. National Advisory Commission on Civil Disorders [Kerner Commission] *Report* (New York: Bantam, 1968), 10. It should be noted that the full report did not develop this analysis systematically. In fact, the report did not present a coherent interpretation at all. The "white racism" theme, as Rossi points out, was mentioned only once in the text and once in the "Summary Report" that took up the first twenty-nine pages, and no definition of "white racism" was provided. Tom Wicker's introduction to the Bantam paperback, the edition most readers saw, stressed the concept more but did nothing to clarify its meaning. As Rossi observes, attributing the riots to something as ambiguous as "white racism" makes it impossible to know what policies might prevent future disorders. It could, for example, have the fatalistic implication that no significant racial progress could be made until every white was magically purged of negative racial attitudes toward blacks; Peter H. Rossi, "Urban Revolts and the Future of American Cities," in Boesel and Rossi, *Cities Under Seige,* 416–418, 425.

49. August Meier and Elliot Rudwick, *CORE: A Study in the Civil Rights Movement, 1942–1968* (Urbana: University of Illinois Press, 1975), 400.

50. Ibid.

51. Manning Marable, *Race, Reform, and Rebellion: The Second Reconstruction in Black America, 1945–1982* (London: Macmillan, 1984), 103.

52. Fine, *Violence in the Model City,* 57, 71, 91.

53. Edward C. Banfield, *The Unheavenly City; The Nature and Future of Our Urban*

Crisis (Boston: Little, Brown, 1970), 195. Although the Urban League study treated Los Angeles as a whole, not Watts alone, a large fraction of the Los Angeles black population resided in Watts, and the favorable generalizations the study made about Los Angeles in general applied to Watts in particular.

54. This is Horowitz's judicious summary of what the literature establishes; "Racial Violence," 193.

55. Fine, *Violence in the Model City*, 354, summarizing the findings of a paper by Seymour Spilerman.

56. In his essay on Watts, Bayard Rustin contended that "clearly it was no accident that the riots proceeded along an almost direct path to City Hall." If so, they never come close to it, and there is no evidence that this was anyone's aim. Nor was City Hall a target in the other riots; Rustin, *Down the Line*, 142.

57. Some writers simply take estimates of total damage to businesses and assume that all businesses that were harmed were owned by whites. Thus, Marable, *Race, Reform, and Rebellion*, 101–103, declares that "2700 white-owned ghetto businesses" in Detroit were looted without providing any source for the figure. Twenty-seven hundred is a somewhat inflated estimate of the total number of businesses that were hit, and is certainly not correct for white-owned businesses alone. Sidney Fine calculates that a quarter of the stores destroyed in the Detroit riot had black owners; *Violence in the Model City*, 292–293. The Kerner *Report*, 116, claims that "white-owned businesses are widely-believed to have been damaged much more frequently than those owned by Negroes." This is an oddly evasive formulation. What is "widely-believed" is often wrong, especially in the area of race relations. In this case it was definitely wrong.

58. Fine, *Violence in the Model City*, 132–133, 165, 293.

59. Richard Alan Berk, "The Role of Ghetto Retail Merchants in Civil Disorders," (Ph.D. diss., Johns Hopkins University, 1970), as summarized in Fine, *Violence in the Model City*, 292–293.

60. Angus Campbell and Howard Schuman, "Racial Attitudes in Fifteen American Cities," in *Supplemental Studies for the National Advisory Commission on Civil Disorders* (New York: Praeger, 1968), 16. The fifteen cities, the same ones covered in the Berk dissertation mentioned in the previous note, were selected for intensive study by the Kerner Commission. They were Baltimore, Boston, Brooklyn, Chicago, Cincinnati, Cleveland, Detroit, Gary, Milwaukee, Newark, Philadelphia, Pittsburgh, San Francisco, St. Louis, and Washington, D.C.

61. Campbell and Schuman, "Racial Attitudes," 27. It should be noted that blacks in the survey were questioned by black interviewers, eliminating one possible source of bias in the answers.

62. Ibid., 27, 48. This report gives figures broken down by sex without group totals. We have averaged the male and female figures to arrive at these totals, weighting female responses a little more heavily because the male-female balance in the sample for the fifteen-city study was 42-58 (see appendix A).

63. Kerner *Report*, 42–47. The Kerner Commission presented a table (114) showing that only 16 percent of the disorders in 1967 occurred in southern or border states, but failed to grasp the significance of that distribution. The only interpretation offered was the fatuous comment that "the violence was not confined to any one section of the country," which is literally true but far from the most interesting point to be made about this pattern.

64. David Paul Boesel, *The Ghetto Riots, 1964–1968* (Ph.D. diss., Cornell University; Ann Arbor, Mich.: University Microfilms, 1973), 128. The opposite view, purportedly

based upon an investigation of the Watts riot but in fact an expression of liberal ideology, may be seen in a comment by Deputy Attorney General Ramsey Clark: "It is no more possible to suppress rioting where its causes are fermenting than it is to hold the lid on a boiling pot"; quoted in James W. Button, *Black Violence: Political Impact of the 1960s Riots* (Princeton: Princeton University Press, 1978), 107. Clark to the contrary notwithstanding, "causes" for rioting could be found in abundance in southern cities. At least one important difference was that law enforcement officials were freer to do whatever it took to hold the lid on the pot.

65. Carson, *In Struggle*, 219.
66. Conot, *Rivers of Blood*, 16.
67. We are indebted to Horowitz, "Racial Violence," 196–198 for this analysis.
68. Fogelson, *Violence as Social Protest*, 130–133; Conot, *Rivers of Blood*, 193.
69. Fine, *Violence in the Model City*, 169.
70. David J. Garrow, *Bearing the Cross: Martin Luther King, Jr. and the Southern Christian Leadership Conference* (New York: Morrow, 1986), 496.
71. Ibid., 570–571.
72. Ibid., 484–485, 487–490, 533–534.
73. William L. Van Deburg, *New Day in Babylon: The Black Power Movement and American Culture, 1965–1975* (Chicago: University of Chicago Press, 1992), 134.
74. The sad story of Huey Newton's revolutionary delusions and descent into thuggery and murder is told unflinchingly by Hugh Pearson in *The Shadow of the Panther: Huey Newton and the Price of Black Power in America* (Reading, Mass.: Addison-Wesley, 1994). The Panthers also figure prominently and tragically in Peter Collier and David Horowitz's passionate memoir, *Destructive Generation: Second Thoughts about the 60s* (Los Angeles: Second Thoughts Books, 1989; 1995 ed.). The authors were editors of the leftist San Francisco magazine *Ramparts* in the late 1960s, and helped publicize the Panther cause until they became disillusioned.
75. Carson, *In Struggle*, 238.
76. Ibid., 216.
77. Sitkoff, *Struggle for Black Equality*, 216–217; Carson, *In Struggle*, 221.
78. Sitkoff, *Struggle for Black Equality*, 217; Allen J. Matusow, *The Unraveling of America: A History of Liberalism in the 1960s* (New York: Harper & Row, 1984), 365; Carson, *In Struggle*, 255.
79. Bruce Perry, *Malcolm: The Life of a Man Who Changed Black America* (Barrytown, N.Y.: Station Hill Press, 1991), 207, 239–240; Peter Goldman, *The Death and Life of Malcolm X* (Urbana: University of Illinois Press, 1979), 99, 118–119. Malcolm's account of the "chickens coming home to roost" incident in his autobiography is distorted. He denies that he was expressing pleasure at Kennedy's assassination, and claims that he was only saying that "America's climate of hate" was responsible. He fails to mention that the original remark drew applause and laughter, and that he then went on to say that the news didn't make him sad but glad; Malcolm X, *The Autobiography of Malcolm X* (New York: Grove Press, 1965), 301.
80. Goldman, *Death and Life of Malcolm X*, 101, 105.
81. Perry, *Malcolm*, 318.
82. Rossi, "Urban Revolts," 411.
83. Malcolm X, *Autobiography*, 367, 371.
84. Goldman, *Death and Life of Malcolm X*, 15.
85. Ibid., 71.
86. Ibid., 157. Malcolm, ironically, lifted the Plymouth Rock metaphor from a Broadway

song—Cole Porter's "Anything Goes" an amusing source for an assertion of black cultural separatism.

87. W. J. Weatherby, *James Baldwin: Artist on Fire* (New York: Donald I. Fine, 1989), 262.

88. Tom Wolfe, *Radical Chic and Mau-mauing the Flak Catchers* (New York: Farrar, Straus & Giroux, 1970).

89. Gary T. Marx, *Protest and Prejudice: A Study of Belief in the Black Community* (New York, Harper & Row, 1967), 26–27. Even after making full allowance for the likelihood that the subjects interviewed failed to include some of the poorest and most transient elements of the black community, whose views may have been different on some of these questions, the results are very clear.

90. Campbell and Schuman, "Racial Attitudes," 21.

91. William Brink and Louis Harris, *Black and White: A Study of U.S. Racial Attitudes Today* (New York: Simon & Schuster, 1967), 260, 262.

92. Campbell and Schuman, "Racial Attitudes," 52.

93. Ibid., 16.

94. Ibid., 48. Zero percent did not mean absolutely no one. A few of the 2,814 blacks in the sample may have picked that answer, but the number worked out to be less than 0.5 percent and it rounded off to 0 percent. The absolute number cannot have been more than fourteen people, since it was less than 0.5 percent, and 0.5 percent of 2,814 is 14.07.

95. Ibid., 47–48.

96. Ibid., 49, 55.

97. Ibid., 47–48.

98. Ibid., 48–49, 55.

99. The text of the report, an analysis of the controversy it provoked, and many of the key documents bearing on it have been conveniently assembled in Lee Rainwater and William Yancey, *The Moynihan Report and the Politics of Controversy* (Cambridge: MIT Press, 1967).

100. Ibid., 43.

101. Ibid., 4.

102. Lyndon B. Johnson, Speech at Howard University, June 4, 1965, reprinted in Rainwater and Yancey, *Moynihan Report*, 126.

103. See the penetrating analysis of this speech by Shelby Steele in his essay "White Guilt," *American Scholar* 59 (Autumn 1990), 497–506. Throughout the speech, Steele notes, whites are the actors; blacks are passive. Johnson was exhorting the former victimizers of African Americans to become their patrons, without blacks themselves doing anything. As Steele observes, "This is really a statement to and about white people, their guilt, their responsibility, their road to redemption." It includes "the two ever-present signposts of white guilt—white self-preoccupation and black invisibility" (504).

104. The language was lifted verbatim from an earlier executive order issued by President Kennedy (see chap. 15). The complicated history of these executive orders and their relationship to one another is sorted out in Hugh Davis Graham, *The Civil Rights Era: Origins and Development of National Policy* (New York: Oxford University Press, 1990), chap. 7. Executive Order 11246 superseded and abolished all preceding antidiscrimination orders.

105. Skrentny, *Ironies of Affirmative Action*, 18–19; Button, *Black Violence*, 37.

106. Sundquist, *Politics and Policy*, 284.

107. Robert Weisbrot, *Freedom Bound: A History of America's Civil Rights Movement* (New York: Norton, 1990), 266.

108. U.S. Department of Justice, Bureau of Justice Statistics, *Sourcebook of Criminal Justice Statistics: 1990* (Washington, D.C.: U.S. Government Printing Office, 1991), 353.

109. Gerald David Jaynes and Robin M. Williams, Jr., eds., *A Common Destiny: Blacks and American Society,* National Research Council (Washington, D.C.: National Academy Press, 1989), fig. 9-2, 459; Charles E. Silberman, *Criminal Violence, Criminal Justice* (New York: Random House, 1978), chap. 5.

110. Sundquist, *Politics and Policy,* 285.

111. Campbell and Schuman, "Racial Attitudes," 51.

112. *Historical Statistics of the U.S.,* 1083. The forty-nine-seat loss by the Democrats was comparable to the Republican loss of fifty-three seats in 1930, thanks to the onset of the Great Depression, and to the Republican loss of forty-eight seats in 1974, due to Watergate.

113. Thomas Byrne and Mary D. Edsall, *Chain Reaction: The Impact of Race, Rights and Taxes on American Politics* (New York: Norton, 1991) 59–61.

114. Weisbrot, *Freedom Bound,* 271.

115. Matusow, *Unraveling of America,* 395–396.

116. James L. Sundquist, *Dynamics of the Party System,* 382, quoted in Edsall, *Chain Reaction,* 71.

117. Button, *Black Violence,* 134.

118. *Historical Statistics of the U.S.,* 1073.

119. Matusow, *Unraveling of America,* 422–426.

120. Ladd, *Transformations,* 227–234.

121. Bettye K. Eidson, "White Public Opinion in an Age of Disorder," in Boesel and Rossi, *Cities Under Seige,* 403; Ladd, *Transformations,* 229.

122. Ladd, *Transformations,* 234–235.

123. Graham, *Civil Rights Era,* 271.

124. Campbell and Schuman, "Racial Attitudes," 37.

125. Eugene Robinson, "Black and White and Getting By," *Washington Post,* 15 July 1996, 1.

126. Unpublished tabulation of a 1994 NORC poll supplied to us by Glenn Loury.

127. *Reader's Digest* poll taken c. June 1994, as given in Robert J. Samuelson, "America, the Caricature," *Washington Post,* 4 July 1995, A23.

128. Mary Jordan, "In Mississippi, an Integration Uproar," *Washington Post,* 17 November 1992, A1.

129. Emily Yellin, "New Film Recollects Old Pain of Racism," *New York Times,* 15 November 1995, A18.

130. Peter Applebome, "Race Issues in Schools Roil Dallas," *New York Times,* 27 June 1996, A14.

131. Colbert I. King, "Meir Kahane as Malcolm X," *Washington Post,* 25 December 1990, C7.

132. The best brief account is Thomas Sowell, *Civil Rights: Rhetoric or Reality?* (New York: Morrow, 1984).

CHAPTER 7: THE RISE OF THE BLACK MIDDLE CLASS

1. Remarks on National Public Radio program on the fortieth anniversary of *Brown v. Board of Education,* 17 May 1994.

2. *Newsweek* poll of 23–25 April 1991, Gallup Organization World Headquarters, 26 April 1991. In 1991 only 55.7 percent of blacks lived in central cities; 35.3 percent of them—6,163,000 persons—had incomes below the poverty line. The 6,163,000 impoverished city-dwellers amounted to just 19.7 percent of the total African-American population; U.S. Bureau of the Census, Current Population Reports, P-20-471, *The Black Population in the United States: March 1992* (Washington, D.C.: U.S. Government Printing Office, 1993), table 15. The public estimate is off the mark in part because many people who are not officially classified as poor nonetheless have quite low incomes, and it is unrealistic to expect the general public to have a lot of detailed information on this subject. Nevertheless, the evidence supports our point about the stereotyped view that blacks are mostly poor.

3. Gunnar Myrdal, *An American Dilemma* (New York: Harper & Row, 1944), 309–310. Black undertakers constituted a tenth of all the undertakers in the United States, virtually the only business enterprise in which they were represented in proportion with their share of the population. The explanation is that white-owned funeral homes in the South refused to handle black corpses.

4. Seventy-eight percent of black public school teachers in 1940 were women, and 85 percent of black female teachers resided in the South; 1940 Census of Population, *Subject Reports, Occupational Characteristics* (Washington, D.C.: U.S. Government Printing Office, 1943), table 6; and U.S. Bureau of the Census, Current Population Reports, Special Studies, Series P-23, no. 80, *The Social and Economic Status of the Black Population in the United States: An Historical View, 1790–1978* (Washington, D.C.: U.S. Government Printing Office, 1979), 76. On salary discrimination in teaching, see Robert A. Margo, *Race and Schooling in the South, 1880–1950: An Economic History* (Chicago: University of Chicago Press, 1990), chap. 4.

5. E. Franklin Frazier, *Black Bourgeoisie: The Rise of a New Middle Class in the United States* (New York: Collier, 1962) 47.

6. We are dependent here upon evidence from the 1990 Census. Although more current occupational data are gathered regularly for the Current Population Survey, the size of the samples used is not large enough to permit accurate racial breakdowns for particular occupations.

7. As early as 1960, blacks were overrepresented in government jobs by 11 percent. By 1970 their edge was up to 36 percent; in 1982 it was 44 percent, and in 1994 it was 60 percent. Computed from data in Sharon M. Collins, "The Making of the Black Middle Class," *Social Problems* 30, no. 4 (April 1983), 373–374, and U.S. Bureau of the Census, Current Population Reports, PPL-45, *The Black Population in the United States: March 1995* (Washington, D.C.: U.S. Government Printing Office, 1996), table 2.

8. *Black Population in the U.S.: 1995,* table 2.

9. Steven Erie, "Public Policy and Black Economic Polarization," *Policy Analysis* 6 (1980), 305–317.

10. *Black Population in the U.S.: 1995,* table 2.

11. Kofi Lomotey, ed., *Going to School: The African-American Experience* (Albany: State University of New York Press, 1990), 1–2.

12. Eddie N. Williams and Milton D. Morris, "Racism and Our Future," in Herbert Hill and James E. Jones, Jr., eds., *Race in America: The Struggle for Equality* (Madison: University of Wisconsin Press, 1993), 417.

13. U.S. Bureau of the Census, *Statistical Abstract of the United States: 1984* (Washington, D.C.: U.S. Government Printing Office, 1984), 144. Most of the census data used in the following discussion, it should be noted, indicates how many people completed four years of high school, not whether they actually graduated. Likewise, figures on the college population only indicate how many spent four or more years in college, not how many received diplomas. Of the numbers we give here, only those from the 1995 Current Population Survey provide actual high school and college graduation rates. In January 1992 the Current Population Survey changed its educational question to identify specific degree completion levels rather than years of school completed; for a discussion, see U.S. Bureau of the Census, Current Population Reports, P-20-464, *The Black Population in the United States: March 1991* (Washington, D.C.: U.S. Government Printing Office, 1992), 17–21. Having finished four years of high school is a fairly good proxy for the high school graduation rate, and finishing four years of college correlates strongly with receiving a degree. But the 1995 data are not perfectly comparable to the earlier evidence, alas.

14. Note the striking fact that as late as 1960 no less than 85 percent of the black adults in the United States were southern-born; James P. Smith and Finis R. Welch, "Black Economic Progress After Myrdal," *Journal of Economic Literature* 17 (June 1989), 540.

15. The white figure for median years of school completed in 1960 was 10.8; the black figure was 8.0; National Center for Education Statistics, U.S. Department of Education, *Digest of Educational Statistics: 1995* (Washington, D.C.: U.S. Government Printing Office, 1995), 17; *Statistical Abstract of the U.S.: 1984*, 143. It is important to note that even if *Brown v. Board of Education* had brought about the immediate dismantling of separate and unequal schools—which it of course did not—it would have taken many more years for the change to affect the basic picture. Evidence about schooling includes many people who left school long ago, so changes take a long time to affect the educational characteristics of the population as a whole. When it is possible to examine a younger age group, like persons 25–29, change will become evident sooner, but even then there is a lag.

16. For random examples from the daily newspaper and the nightly news respectively, see, for Washington, D.C., Sally Quinn, "Childhood's End," *Washington Post*, 20 November 1994, C1, and the *MacNeil-Lehrer News Hour*, 23 November 1994.

17. The figures on high school dropout rates employed here include persons who have earned high school equivalency credentials with regular graduates. This is misleading for some purposes; alternative credentials seem to have considerably less market value than normal high school diplomas; Stephen Cameron and James Heckman, "The Non-Equivalence of High School Equivalents," *Journal of Labor Economics* 11 (1993), 1–47. This does not call into question our conclusions here. The number of people who receive alternative certification is not very large—5 percent in 1993. Most important for our purposes, there are "no significant differences" between racial and ethnic groups in the proportion taking alternative routes to a degree; National Center for Education Statistics, U.S. Department of Education, *Dropout Rates in the United States: 1993*, NCES 94-669 (Washington, D.C.: U.S. Government Printing Office, 1994), 53.

18. In 1994, 37 percent of white students in higher education were enrolled in two-year

institutions, and 42 percent of black students. Hispanics were considerably more concentrated in two-year schools, with a 56 percent figure; U.S. Department of Education, National Center for Education Statistics, *Enrollment in Higher Education: Fall 1986 Through Fall 1994*, NCES 96–851 (Washington, D.C.: U.S. Department of Education, 1996), table 2.

19. *Black Population in the U.S.: 1995*, table 7.

20. Donald J. Bogue, *The Population of the United States: Historical Trends and Future Projections* (New York: Free Press, 1985), 413.

21. Gordon LaVern Berry and Joy Keiko Asamen, eds., *Black Students: Psychosocial Issues and Academic Achievement* (Newbury Park, Calif.: Sage Publications, 1989), 198.

22. Reynolds Farley, *Blacks and Whites: Narrowing the Gap?* (Cambridge: Harvard University Press, 1984), 23.

23. The latest available figures are for fall 1993, and they show 231,198 black students enrolled in historically black colleges and universities, out of a total of a little over 1.4 million; *Digest of Educational Statistics: 1995*, 208, 225.

24. Grant Mindle, Kenyon Bunch, and Carolyn Nickolas, "Diversity on Campus: A Reassessment of Current Strategies," *Policy Studies Review* 12 (Spring-Summer 1993), 377.

25. *Digest of Educational Statistics: 1995*, 224, 283. The figure has dropped by a quarter since 1976, when it was 37 percent; Antoine M. Garibaldi, "Blacks in College," in Charles V. Willie, Antoine M. Garibaldi, and Wornie L. Reed, eds., *The Education of African-Americans* (New York, Auburn House, 1991), 95.

26. U.S. Bureau of the Census, Current Population Reports, P-60-194, *Poverty in the United States: 1995* (Washington, D.C.: U.S. Government Printing Office, 1996), table 1.

27. Calculated from U.S. Bureau of the Census, Current Population Reports, P-60-193, *Money Income in the United States: 1995* (Washington, D.C.: U.S. Government Printing Office, 1996), table 5.

28. U.S. Bureau of the Census, Current Population Reports, P-20-488, *Household and Family Characteristics: March 1995* (Washington, D.C.: U.S. Government Printing Office, 1996), table A.

29. It is important to note that white female-headed households have incomes nearly 50 percent higher than those of similar black households. Why? The lower proportion of black women with college degrees and their greater concentration in the South help explain the gap. Much more important is that seven out of ten black babies are currently born out of wedlock, nearly triple the proportion among whites (see chap. 9 for the evidence). Black women accordingly are far less likely to be collecting child support or alimony from the fathers of their children.

30. James P. Smith and Finis R. Welch, *Closing the Gap: Forty Years of Economic Progress for Blacks* (Santa Monica, Calif.: Rand Corporation, 1986), 104.

31. U.S. Bureau of the Census, Current Population Reports, Household Economic Studies, Series P-70-47, *Asset Ownership of Households: 1993* (Washington, D.C.: U.S. Government Printing Office, 1995), table F.

32. *Asset Ownership: 1993*, table D.

33. U.S. Bureau of the Census, Current Population Reports, P-20-480, *The Black Population in the United States: March 1994 and 1993* (Washington, D.C.: U.S. Government Printing Office, 1995), table 1.

34. U.S. Bureau of the Census, Current Population Reports, Household Economic Stud-

ies, Series P-70–22, *Household Wealth and Asset Ownership: 1988* (Washington, D.C.: U.S. Government Printing Office, 1990), table L.

35. "Black Household Income Leads Whites' in Queens," *New York Times*, 6 June 1994, A1, B7.

36. Two studies of the 1990 Census data, by Andrew Beveridge of Queens College and Joseph Salvo of New York City's Planning Department, are summarized in the *New York Times* story cited in the previous note. Both studies focused on household income, which differs from family income because it includes income from all people sharing a residential unit, including nonrelatives. The racial gap in the incomes of households and families, however, is just about the same; for evidence, cf. table 2 (household income) and table 14 (family income) of U.S. Bureau of the Census, Current Population Reports, Series P-60-184, *Money Income of Households, Families, and Persons in the United States: 1992* (Washington, D.C.: U.S. Government Printing Office, 1993).

37. U.S. Bureau of the Census, *Statistical Abstract of the United States: 1996* (Washington, D.C.: U.S. Government Printing Office, 1996), 48. These figures are especially impressive because a large proportion of the black population is concentrated in central cities whose housing markets have more rental than owner-occupied units.

38. Calculated from U.S. Bureau of the Census, 1990 Census of the Population, *Characteristics of the Black Population*, 1990-CP-3-6 (Washington, D.C.: U.S. Government Printing Office, 1994), table 60.

39. If Queens were a legally independent city, though, it is logical to assume that Brooklyn also would be, in which case Queens would be the fifth-largest city in the U.S., ahead of Houston but behind Brooklyn.

40. Otis Dudley Duncan, "Inheritance of Poverty or Inheritance of Race?" in Daniel P. Moynihan, ed., *On Understanding Poverty* (New York: Basic Books, 1969), 85–110.

41. Michael Hout, "Occupational Mobility of Black Men, 1962 to 1973," *American Sociological Review* 49 (1984), 308–322. Hout follows in the tradition of research into occupational mobility both in focusing solely on the career patterns of males and in using the occupation of the father as the basis for determining the social class of the family of origin. Both of these decisions seem increasingly anachronistic. They are particularly limiting in dealing with the black population, given the vital economic role that black women have long played. But this is the best evidence we have, despite this severe limitation.

42. Richard B. Freeman, "Black Economic Progress after 1964: Who Has Gained and Why?" in Sumner Rosen, ed., *Studies in Labor Markets* (Chicago: National Bureau of Economic Research, University of Chicago Press, 1981), 254–268.

43. Yankelovich Partners, *African-American Study: Topline Report*, prepared for the *New Yorker*, March 1996, 48.

44. Susan Saulney, "On the Inside and Looking Out," *Washington Post*, 8 July 1996, A1.

CHAPTER 8: CITIES AND SUBURBS

1. Don Terry, "Neighborhoods Try to Raze a Racial Wall," *New York Times*, 10 October 1993, 18.

2. U.S. Bureau of the Census, *Statistical Abstract of the United States: 1996* (Washington, D.C.: U.S. Government Printing Office, 1996), 14. The precise 1995 percentages that may be calculated from this table are 83.0 white, 12.6 African American, 3.7

percent Asian, and 0.8 percent American Indian. Hispanics are not classified as a race. They made up 10.3 percent of the total. If all of them are considered to be white, the non-Hispanic white population was 72.7 percent of the total. Since a small minority of Hispanics identify themselves as black, the 72.7 non-Hispanic white estimate errs on the low side. A March 1995 Current Population Survey offers a non-Hispanic white estimate of 73.5 percent; U.S. Bureau of the Census, *Current Population Reports*, PPL-45. *The Black Population in the United States: March 1995* (Washington, D.C.: U.S. Government Printing Office, 1996), table 1.

3. Paul Glastris, "A New City-Suburbs Hookup," *U.S. News & World Report*, 18 July 1994, 28.

4. National Advisory Commission on Civil Disorders [Kerner Commission], *Report* (New York: Bantam Books, 1968), 1, 10.

5. Ibid., 1.

6. Ibid., 398, 245, 389.

7. Ibid., 1, 10, 400.

8. One example is Fred R. Harris and Roger W. Wilkins, eds., *Quiet Riots: Race and Poverty in the United States: Twenty Years After the Kerner Report* (New York: Pantheon, 1988). The editors claimed that their work showed that the commission's predictions were "coming true" (xii). *Quiet Riots*, though, carefully avoided examining the specific, testable predictions contained in the report. Exactly what claims made in the Kerner report were "coming true"? Did the editors mean to assert that the demographic projections offered by the Kerner Commission had proven to be on target, and that "our large central cities" had indeed become "mainly Negro" by 1988? Had they found solid evidence that black people were still rarely to be found living in suburban America, as the commission predicted? Large portions of Douglas S. Massey, "The New Geography of Inequality in Urban America," in Aspen Institute, *Surburbs and Cities: Changing Patterns of Metropolitan Living*, Report of the 20–24 August 1994 Domestic Strategy Group Meeting in Aspen, Colorado, 27–36, read as if they were lifted verbatim from the Kerner report. For another instance, see Douglas S. Massey and Nancy Denton, *American Apartheid: Segregation and the Making of the Underclass* (Cambridge: Harvard University Press, 1993), 211: "Almost every problem defined by the Kerner Commission has become worse." A 1994 volume, Charles Bullard, J. Eugene Grigsby III, and Charles Lee, eds., *Residential Apartheid: The American Legacy* (Los Angeles: UCLA Center for Afro-American Studies, 1994) is in the same vein. The editors make the expected genuflection to the Kerner report, saying that "two and a half decades ago the National Advisory Commission on Civil Disorders implicated white racism in creating and maintaining the black ghetto and the drift toward two 'separate and unequal' societies. These same conditions exist today." In fact, according to them, "residential apartheid is the dominant housing pattern for most African Americans" (1–2). In the foreword to the volume, Congressman John Lewis asserts that "the majority of the thirty million African Americans are as segregated now as they were at the height of the Civil Rights Movement in the 1960s" (xii).

9. Kerner Commission, *Report*, 245, 389.

10. If instead of looking only at the 20 largest cities we broaden the base and consider all 195 American cities with populations of 100,000 or more in 1990, we find that only 13—less than 7 percent of the total—had black majorities in 1990. In addition to the four major cities listed in table 1—Detroit, Baltimore, Washington, and New Orleans —they are as follows, in order of size:

	Rank	Percent Black
Atlanta	36	67
Newark	56	59
Birmingham	60	63
Richmond, Va.	76	55
Jackson, Miss.	78	56
Savannah, Ga.	129	51
Gary, Ind.	154	81
Inglewood, Cal.	169	52
Macon, Ga.	179	52

Source: Statistical Abstract of the U.S.: 1996, 44–46.

11. Reynolds Farley and Walter R. Allen, *The Color Line and the Quality of Life in America* (New York: Russell Sage Foundation, 1987), 113–118.

12. Most of these references were in chap. 9, which was entitled "Comparing the Immigrant and Negro Experience." It was only five pages long.

13. The immigration total for the 1980s was the second highest for any decade in American history. The record decade was 1901–1910, when 8,795,000 immigrants entered. Although the total number for the 1980s was not too far below that, immigration in the 1980s was much less than for 1901–1910 when viewed in terms of the *rate* per 1,000 residents. The immigration rate for 1981–1990 was 3.1 per 1,000; for 1901–1910 it was more than triple that—10.4. *Statistical Abstract of the U.S.: 1996, 10.*

14. In 1990 the black population outnumbered the Hispanic population by more than a third (37 percent). The most recent projection suggests that by 2010 there will be more Hispanics than blacks in the United States. African Americans currently outnumber Asian Americans four to one; by 2025 it is expected that the ratio will be down to two to one; *Statistical Abstract of the U.S.: 1996, 25–26.* These population projections, of course, may prove to be no more accurate than those developed by the Kerner Commission. For some skeptical observations about projections that generated the conclusion that a "minority-majority" would emerge in the United States by the middle of the next century, see Stephan Thernstrom, "American Ethnic Statistics," in Donald L. Horowitz and Gerard Noiriel, eds., *Immigrants in Two Democracies: French and American Experience* (New York: New York University Press, 1992), 102–106.

15. U.S. Bureau of the Census, *Statistical Abstract of the United States: 1976* (Washington, D.C.: U.S. Government Printing Office, 1976), 16; U.S. Bureau of the Census, Current Population Reports, PPL-45. *The Black Population in the United States: March 1995* (Washington, D.C.: U.S. Government Printing Office, 1996), table 3.

16. Nineteen-ninety is our point of reference here rather than 1995 because data on the racial composition of individual metropolitan areas is not available since 1990. The Current Population Survey, from which the 1995 figures given above were drawn, does not employ a large enough sample to break down the results city by city. Atlanta figures from William P. O'Hare and William H. Frey, "Booming, Suburban, and Black," *American Demographics* 14 (September 1992), 38.

17. *Wall Street Journal*, 7 September 1994, "Greatest Threat to Washington, D.C.'s Health May be Growing Exodus of Black Middle Class," A16.

18. O'Hare and Frey, "Booming, Suburban, and Black," 32.

19. Not included in table 4 because they did not rank in the fifteen largest metropolitan areas. In Indianapolis the proportion of African Americans living in suburbs rose only from 2 percent to 4 percent between 1970 and 1990; in Milwaukee it went from 1 to 3 percent.

20. John F. Kain, "Black Suburbanization in the Eighties: A New Beginning or a False Hope?" in John M. Quigley and Daniel L. Rubinfeld, eds., *American Domestic Priorities: An Economic Appraisal* (Berkeley: University of California Press, 1985), 260; 1990 figures calculated from U.S. Bureau of the Census, 1990 Census of Population, *General Population Characteristics: United States,* 1990-CP-1-1 (Washington, D.C.: U.S. Government Printing Office, 1992), tables 266 and 276. The thirty-one metropolitan areas were those with a million or more residents in 1980.

21. "Wave of Suburban Growth Is Being Fed by Minorities," *New York Times,* 15 August 1994, A12.

22. E.g., Massey, "The New Geography of Inequality in Urban America."

23. "Often black 'suburbanization' only involves the expansion of an urban ghetto across a city line and does not reflect a larger process of racial integration"; Massey and Denton, *American Apartheid,* 70. The Kerner Commission expressed the same view without the qualifying "often"; "Negro settlements expand almost entirely through 'massive racial transition' at the edges of existing all-Negro neighborhoods, rather than by a gradual dispersion of population throughout the metropolitan area"; Kerner Commission, *Report,* 245.

24. Only 13.3 percent of blacks lived outside of metropolitan areas, in small towns and rural areas, in 1995, as compared with 21.6 percent of whites; *Black Population in the U.S.: 1995,* tables 3 and 16.

25. John F. Jakubs, "Recent Residential Segregation in U.S. SMSAs," *Urban Geography* 7 (1986), 151. The unit of analysis in this study was the census tract.

26. Reynolds Farley and William H. Frey, "Changes in the Segregation of Whites from Blacks During the 1980s: Small Steps Toward a More Integrated Society," *American Sociological Review* 59 (1994), 30. Precise comparison between the findings of Jakubs for the 1970s and Farley and Frey for the 1980s is not possible, because Jakubs calculated segregation indexes for census tracts, while Farley and Frey used data aggregated by "block group." Block groups are about a fifth the size of the typical census tract, typically having 1,000 to 1,200 people in them. The smaller the unit of analysis, the higher the segregation score will tend to be. The bottom line of both studies, though, is the same: residential segregation was declining modestly but appreciably in the vast majority of the nation's metropolitan areas.

27. Data for 1970 from John F. Kain, "Housing Market Discrimination and Black Suburbanization in the 1980s," in Gary A. Tobin, ed., *Divided Neighborhoods: Changing Patterns of Residential Segregation,* vol. 32 of *Urban Affairs Annual Review* (Newbury Park, Calif.: Sage Publications, 1987), 87–92; 1990 Census data from Courtenay M. Slater and George E. Hall, eds., *Places, Towns, and Townships: First Edition 1993* (Lanham, Md.: Bernan Press, 1993), Illinois sections of Tables A and B. Inspection of the same tables for Massachusetts reveals that not a single suburb in the Boston Metropolitan Area had no black residents, which would not have been the case a generation ago.

28. Gary Orfield and Carol Ashkinaze, *The Closing Door: Conservative Policy and Black Opportunity* (Chicago: University of Chicago Press, 1991), 234.

29. Three percent objected to living next door to a Catholic, 5 percent to a Jew; Stephen

Bates, *Battleground: One Mother's Crusade, the Religious Right, and the Struggle for Control of Our Classrooms* (New York: Simon & Schuster, 1993), 64.

30. The drop was from $49,000 to $26,000, in constant 1989 dollars; Reynolds Farley et al., "Stereotypes and Segregation: Neighborhoods in the Detroit Area," *American Journal of Sociology* 100 (1994), 777.

31. W. A. V. Clark, "Residential Preferences and Residential Choices in a Multi-Ethnic Context," *Demography* 29 (August 1992), 451–466.

32. David Harris, "Racial and Nonracial Determinants of Neighborhood Satisfaction Among Whites, 1975–1993," unpublished paper, Department of Sociology, Northwestern University, 1995.

33. "Wave of Suburban Growth Is Being Fed by Minorities," *New York Times,* 15 August 1994, A12. For a suggestive portrait of white residents of a section of Brooklyn who express similar sentiments in the face of racial change in their community, see Jonathan Rieder, *Canarsie: The Jews and Italians of Brooklyn Against Liberalism* (Cambridge: Harvard University Press, 1985). A careful study of residential change in St. Louis in the 1950s and 1960s stresses the desire of middle-class blacks to escape neighborhoods that lower-class blacks were entering. The authors conclude that "except for the genuinely poor, all people—white and black, rich and not-so-rich—are willing to pay, and substantially, to avoid class integration"; Charles L. Leven et al., *Neighborhood Change: Lessons in the Dynamics of Urban Decay* (New York: Praeger, 1976), 203.

34. Steven A. Holmes and Karen De Witt, "Black, Successful, and Safe and Gone from the Capital," *New York Times,* 27 July 1996, A1.

35. Richard P. Taub, D. Garth Taylor, and Jan D. Dunham, *Paths of Neighborhood Change: Race and Crime in Urban America* (Chicago: University of Chicago Press, 1984), 68, 113–118.

36. The most recent example is Farley's study of metropolitan Detroit, using 1990 Census data. The segregation index (computed for block groups) was 80 for black and white households with annual incomes under $5,000; for those with incomes over $100,000 it was 83; Farley, et al., "Stereotypes and Segregation,": 751.

37. W. A. V. Clark, "Residential Segregation in American Cities: A Review and Interpretation," *Population Research and Policy Review* 5 (1986), 105.

38. Massey and Denton, *American Apartheid,* 97.

39. John Yinger, *Closed Doors, Opportunities Lost: The Continuing Costs of Housing Discrimination* (New York: Russell Sage Foundation, 1995), 49. Although Yinger presents useful information on the housing market, much of his analysis is simplistic and ideologically driven. The author habitually attributes differences in socioeconomic status to discrimination without considering other explanations. The most egregious example is his discussion of Hispanic patterns of homeownership. Starting from the bizarre assumption that Hispanic households today would have the same homeownership rate as non-Hispanic whites but for "past and present discrimination" (107), Yinger estimates that discrimination has reduced the "housing wealth" of Hispanics by $200 billion. This ludicrous calculation completely overlooks the point that much of the huge recent increase in the Hispanic population has been due to immigration, and that the typical Latino immigrant to the United States arrives with little education and no command of English, both serious handicaps in the labor market. Almost half of the Hispanic adults counted in the 1990 Census had been born outside the U.S., and a majority of these immigrants had only arrived within the preceding decade; U.S. Bureau of the Census, 1990 Census of the Population, *Persons of Hispanic Origin in the United States,* 1990-CP-3-3, (Washington, D.C.: U.S.

Government Printing Office, 1993), table 1. Yinger apparently believes that if a 22-year-old Mexican immigrant with eight years of schooling and no English who arrived in San Diego three years ago does not own a home and a 50-year-old native-born white college graduate does, that is proof of discrimination against Hispanics in the housing market. Yinger also discerns what he takes to be further evidence of bias against "minorities" in the fact that the value of the average white-owned home in 1990 was $116,570, while the figure was only $73,415 for black homeowners and $111,376 for homes owned by Hispanics. Both the Hispanic and black figures were below that for whites, of course, but surely the remarkable thing here is the glaring difference between blacks and Hispanics, and the fact that the value of Hispanic homes was a mere 4.5 percent less than that for white homes. This is quite amazing when you consider that barely half of Hispanic adults have a high school diploma, and that 44 percent of them do not speak English "very well"; *Persons of Hispanic Origin*, tables 1 and 3. Why Hispanic-owned homes were nearly as valuable as those of whites is a puzzle that the author does not even notice.

40. Yinger, *Closed Doors*, 54. When the property had been advertised, steering was obviously more difficult. It is awkward to deny customers the opportunity to view an advertised property, even if they are of a race the realtor seeks to steer elsewhere.

41. David J. Armor, *Forced Justice: School Desegregation and the Law* (New York: Oxford University Press, 1995), 143–144.

42. Thomas F. Pettigrew, "Attitudes on Race and Housing: A Social-Psychological View," in Amos H. Hawley and Vincent P. Rock, eds., *Segregation in Residential Areas: Papers on Socioeconomic Factors in Choice of Housing* (Washington, D.C.: National Academy of Sciences, 1973), 44–45.

43. Calculated from the General Social Survey files, National Opinion Research Center, obtained through the Harvard Data Center. The question was framed, "If you could find housing that you would want and like, would you rather live in a neighborhood that is: all black, mostly black," etc. This question, unfortunately, was only asked of blacks in 1982.

44. Percentages can add up to more than 100 percent because both a first choice and a second choice were tabulated.

45. Reynolds Farley, et al., "Chocolate City, Vanilla Suburbs: Will the Trends toward Racially Separate Communities Continue?" *Social Science Research* 7 (1978), 331.

46. Yinger, *Closed Doors*, 118.

47. Clark, "Residential Preferences," passim.

48. On the other hand, we should note that by another measure of segregation we have relied upon—the proportion of the black population living in blocks that were at least 90 percent black—our hypothetical metropolis has no segregation at all, as compared with an average of 44 percent for blacks in a long list of major urban centers today (cf. table 6).

49. Nathan Kantrowitz, "Racial and Ethnic Residential Segregation in Boston, 1830–1970," *Annals of the American Academy of Political and Social Science* 441 (January 1979), 49–51.

50. Karen De Witt, "Housing Voucher Test in Maryland Scuttled by a Political Firestorm," *New York Times*, 28 March 1995, B10.

51. John Simons, "Paid to Leave, but Wanting to Stay," *U.S. News & World Report*, 11 July 1994, 21.

52. Joseph Berger, "Housing Plan Opens Doors to New Lives," *New York Times*, 12 June 1994, 41.

53. Ibid.

54. Howard Husock, "Mocking the Middle Class: The Perverse Effects of Housing Sub-sidies," *Policy Review* 56 (Spring 1991), 65–69. See also Husock's essay, "We Don't Need Subsidized Housing," *City Journal* 7 (Winter 1997), 50–58.

CHAPTER 9: POVERTY

1. Katherine Boo, "A City Divided, Even Where the Races Meet," *Washington Post,* 21 October 1994, 1.
2. *1996 Kids Count Data Sheet* (Washington, D.C.: Population Reference Bureau, 1996).
3. David Lamb, "How the Capitol Has Crumbled," *Los Angeles Times,* 26 June 1996, 1.
4. U.S. Bureau of the Census, Current Population Reports, P-60-194, *Poverty in the United States: 1995* (Washington, D.C.: U.S. Government Printing Office, 1996), table A. Although the federal government computes an official poverty line to the exact dollar each year, the precision of the figures is deceptive. The definition of poverty that is employed is arbitrary and subjective. The poverty line was first devel-oped by the Social Security Administration in 1964; it was based on Agriculture Department estimates of the annual cost of a mimimum nutritionally adequate diet for families of various sizes, which were then multiplied by three on the hardly objective and scientific assumption that food expenditures should represent one-third of a family's total expenditures! That is the shaky foundation upon which the whole poverty-line edifice rests. Poverty estimates for years before and since 1964 were computed by adjusting the 1964 poverty threshold for changes in the Consumer Price Index. The poverty threshold for a family of four was $3,169 in 1964; by 1995 it had risen to $15,569, almost five times the 1964 dollar figure; *Poverty in the U.S.: 1995,* table A-1. For an illuminating critical discussion of the method, see Patricia Ruggles, *Drawing the Line: Alternative Poverty Measures and Their Implications for Public Policy* (Washington, D.C.: Urban Institute Press, 1990), 33–38. Despite its inescapably arbitrary character, the poverty line is a simple and useful tool for judging how the situation of people on the bottom of the economic ladder has changed over time.
5. U.S. Bureau of the Census, Current Population Reports, Special Studies, P-23-80, *The Social and Economic Status of the Black Population in the United States: An Historical View, 1790–1978* (Washington, D.C.: U.S. Government Printing Office, 1979), 49; *Poverty in the U.S.: 1995,* table C-1. Poverty figures for the early 1960s are for "black and other races" rather than blacks alone, and are a little lower than the black poverty rate. However, 1965 figures are available for both groups, and the ratio between them was used to estimate black rates before that.
6. *Poverty in the U.S.: 1995,* table A.
7. Ibid., table C-2.
8. The 87 percent poverty rate for black families in 1940 was calculated by James P. Smith, "Poverty and the Family," in Gary Sandefur and Marta Tienda, *Divided Opportunities: Minorities, Poverty, and Social Policy* (New York: Plenum Press, 1988), 143–144. Another estimate, based on data for households headed by a person aged 25–64, puts the poverty rate at 91 percent for black married-couple families in 1940 and 95 percent for black female-headed families; Christine Ross, Sheldon Dan-ziger, and Eugene Smolensky, "The Level and Trend of Poverty in the United States, 1939–1979," *Demography* 24 (November 1987), 590–591.

We focus on family poverty levels in this section, because the earliest estimates are for families only. Poverty rates for individuals are closely correlated with family poverty rates but tend to be a few points higher. The proportion of individuals in poverty tends to be higher than the proportion of families in poverty because families in poverty tend to have more children than those not in poverty. Only 20 percent of the families in some group might be poor, but they could contain 30 percent of all the children in the group, and each child would count when the individual poverty rate was calculated.

9. Herbert Stein and Murray Foss, *The New Illustrated Guide to the American Economy,* 2nd ed. (Washington, D.C.: American Enterprise Institute Press, 1995), 12.

10. John Bound and George Johnson, "Wages in the United States During the 1980s and Beyond," in Marvin H. Kosters, ed., *Workers and Their Wages: Changing Patterns in the United States* (Washington, D.C.: American Enterprise Institute Press, 1991), 77. This generalization has been widely accepted, but it has now been seriously questioned by a December 1996 report of the Congressional Advisory Commission on the Consumer Price Index, chaired by Stanford economist Michael Boskin. The report concludes that the CPI currently in use overstates the rise in the cost of living by 1.1 percentage points per year. If so, it means that real median family income did not rise by a mere 4 percent between 1973 and 1995, as the official figures indicate. With a better correction for inflation, it rose by 36 percent. If Boskin's committee is correct, poverty has likewise declined much more than the official figures would suggest; Michael Boskin, "Prisoners of Faulty Statistics," *Wall Street Journal,* 5 December 1996, A20. Even if we use a substantially revised Consumer Price Index, though, the economy still looks considerably less buoyant after 1970 than it was in the preceding period.

11. George E. Peterson and Wayne Vroman, eds., *Urban Labor Markets and Job Opportunity* (Washington, D.C.: Urban Institute Press, 1992), 4. Other useful discussions of this development are to be found in Kosters, *Workers and Their Wages,* and Sheldon H. Danziger and Peter Gottschalk, eds., *Uneven Tides: Rising Inequality in America* (New York: Russell Sage Foundation, 1993). Current research by Kevin Murphy of the University of Chicago suggests that this development has run its course, and that the wage premium for college graduates began to decline in the early 1990s; Michael M. Phillips, "Wage Gap Based on Education Levels Off," *Wall Street Journal,* 22 July 1996, A2.

12. U.S. Bureau of the Census, Current Population Reports, P-20-484, *Marital Status and Living Arrangements: March 1994* (Washington, D.C.: U.S. Government Printing Office, 1996), table 6.

13. David Ellwood and Jonathan Crane, "Family Change Among Black Americans: What Do We Know?" *Journal of Economic Perspectives* 4 (Fall 1990), 81.

14. The full text of "the Moynihan Report," which appeared officially as U.S. Department of Labor, *The Negro Family: The Case for National Action* (Washington, D.C.: U.S. Government Printing Office, 1965), is conveniently available in Lee Rainwater and William Yancey, *The Moynihan Report and the Politics of Controversy* (Cambridge: MIT Press, 1967). Rainwater and Yancey offer a useful analysis of the controversy, and reprint key documents.

15. In "Restoring the Black Family," *New York Times Magazine,* 2 June 1985, 43. Norton deplored the fact that the attack on Moynihan resulted in "driving the issue from the public agenda and delaying for a generation the search for workable solutions." Savage criticism of the Moynihan Report is still appearing; for one example, see Carl

Ginsberg, *Race and Media: The Enduring Life of the Moynihan Report* (New York: Institute for Media Analysis, 1989).

16. That the proportion of black women who were divorced, separated, or widowed did not rise but actually declined between 1960 and 1994 is somewhat misleading, though. The figures are for *all* women aged 15–44, not just those who were ever married, and only those who ever married, of course, are eligible to become divorced, separated, or widowed. The sharp decline in the proportion of African-American women who have been marrying at all has meant a steep fall in the number of those who *could* experience a broken marriage. If we look only at the rate of divorce, separation, or widowhood for *ever-married* black women, it has risen substantially— from 28 percent in 1960 to 41 percent in 1992; Ellwood and Crane, "Family Change Among Black Americans," 67; U.S. Bureau of the Census, Current Population Reports, P-20-471, *The Black Population in the United States: March 1992* (Washington, D.C.: U.S. Government Printing Office, 1993), table 4. The divorce rate is currently higher for black women than white women; U.S. Bureau of the Census, Current Population Reports, P-23-180, *Marriage, Divorce, and Remarriage in the 1990s* (Washington, D.C.: U.S. Government Printing Office, 1992), 5. Nevertheless, the declining marriage rate for African Americans is a more important source of family change than the increase in the rate of breakup of marriages that have already been formed.

17. *Marital Status and Living Arrangements: 1994*, table 1.

18. Ellwood and Crane, "Family Change Among Black Americans," 68; U.S. Bureau of the Census, *Statistical Abstract of the U.S.: 1996* (Washington, D.C.: U.S. Government Printing Office, 1996), 75, 77.

19. Andrew Hacker, *Two Nations: Black and White, Separate, Hostile, Unequal* (New York: Scribner 1992), 68, 80.

20. The journalist Michael Lind has recently dismissed concern about the spectacular rise in out-of-wedlock births by black mothers as "one of the great conservative hoaxes of our time"; Lind, *Up from Conservatism: Why the Right Is Wrong for America* (New York: Free Press, 1996), 167. According to Lind, the crucial fact about black unwed births is that the typical unwed mother today is *not* having more children than was the case a generation ago; the huge rise in the proportion of African-American births that occur outside of marriage is due mainly to the fact that the fertility of black married women has gone down very sharply. This point derives from Christopher Jencks's calculation that if married black women had continued to have babies between 1960 and 1987 at the same rate as they did in 1960, the proportion of black out-of-wedlock births would have risen much less—from 23 percent to 29 percent rather than from 23 percent to 62 percent; *Up from Conservatism*, 167–170. There would have been just as many babies born out of wedlock, but they would have been a much smaller proportion of all African-American births. Jencks's estimate seems a useful footnote that clarifies the demographic mechanisms responsible for the current pattern. That is all it was intended to be. Jencks did not use it to support the tendentious claim that it is therefore a "hoax" to speak of a crisis of illegitimacy in the black community. That is Lind's unique contribution to the dialogue, and it seems to us like arguing that "if my grandmother had wheels she'd be a bus." The fertility of married black women did in fact decline very sharply in the post–Baby Boom period, while that of unmarried black women did not. The fact that seven in ten black children are born out of wedlock is what merits attention, not what the family circumstances of a hypothetical black baby might have been today if black

married women had continued to bear children at the same rate that they did in the Baby Boom years. It does not really matter what particular combination of changes in marital and nonmarital fertility produced the current mess. What's important is the kind of family that a great many of the next generation of African-American children will grow up in. Lind does acknowledge (feebly) that "it may be that any number of out-of-wedlock births is a problem"; *Up from Conservatism,* 169. But if "any number" is a problem, then surely seven out of ten is a very big problem indeed. Denying that elementary point seems the real "hoax."

21. Stephanie Crockett, "Single Mother and Proud," *Washington Post,* 14 July 1996, C5.
22. David Whitman, "The War over 'Family Values,' " *U.S. News & World Report,* 8 June 1992, 35.
23. U.S. Bureau of the Census, Current Population Reports, P-60-193, *Money Income in the United States: 1995* (Washington, D.C.: U.S. Government Printing Office, 1996), table 3.
24. Much of the evidence is summarized in Sara McLanahan and Gary Sandefur, *Growing Up With a Single Parent: What Hurts, What Helps* (Cambridge: Harvard University Press, 1994).
25. Lawrence M. Mead, *The New Politics of Poverty: The Nonworking Poor in America* (New York: Basic Books, 1992), 7–10, 49–55.
26. U.S. Bureau of the Census, Current Population Reports, P-60-194, *Poverty in the United States: 1995* (Washington, D.C.: U.S. Government Printing Office, 1996), table 2. Until only quite recently, black women have had distinctly higher rates of employment than white women. This is evidence not of their liberation but of their desperation—they were more likely to be in mother-child families, and if they did have a spouse, his earnings were lower than those of white males. In 1955, 46 percent of black women aged 16 or more were in the labor force, and 35 percent of white women; in 1970, the figure was 48 vs. 43 percent, in 1980 53 vs. 51 percent. The gap didn't disappear until the 1980s; Donald J. Bogue, *The Population of the United States: Historical Trends and Future Projections* (New York: Free Press, 1985), 488.
27. Quoted in Brian Dumaine, "Blacks on Blacks," *Fortune,* 2 November 1992, 119.
28. The unemployment rate is defined as the proportion of men and women who have attempted to find work within the past month but have not found it. People who have given up on the search—discouraged workers—are thus left out of consideration. The labor-force participation rate is a broader measure; it is the proportion of the population of working age that is either employed or seeking work.
29. U.S. Commission on Civil Rights, *The Economic Progress of Black Men in America* (Washington, D.C.: U.S. Commission on Civil Rights Clearinghouse Publication 91, 1986), 44.
30. The evidence of change is supplied in abundance in Part I of the present work. A good deal of it is conveniently summarized in Howard Schuman, Charlotte Steen, and Lawrence Bobo, *Racial Attitudes in America: Trends and Interpretations* (Cambridge: Harvard University Press, 1985). For some reservations about the analysis in this work, see Abigail Thernstrom in *The Public Interest,* no. 85 (Fall 1986), 96–101j.
31. The employment/population ratio is a simple measure that takes into account the joint effects of labor-force participation and unemployment. It shows what proportion of a particular age group is in the labor force and working. The figure is always less than 100, because some members of the labor force will be jobless and some members of the age group will not be in the labor force at all. The figures in this and the next two paragraphs are from Richard T. Gill, Nathan Glazer, and Stephan Thern-

strom, eds., *Our Changing Population* (Englewood Cliffs, N.J.: Prentice-Hall, 1992), 265; *Economic Report of the President: February 1995* (Lanham, Md.: Bernan Press, 1995), 319; *Statistical Abstract of the U.S.: 1995*, 407, and *Black Population in the U.S.: 1994*, table 1.

32. Clifford J. Levy, "Paterson, Used to Struggling, Struggles for Control," *New York Times*, 26 February 1995, 1.

33. The most influential proponent of the spatial mismatch theory is William Julius Wilson. For his fullest and most recent statement of the argument, see *When Work Disappears: The World of the New Urban Poor* (New York: Knopf, 1996). Harry J. Holzer and Wayne Vroman, "Mismatches and the Urban Labor Market," chap. 3 of Peterson and Vroman, *Urban Labor Markets*, is a useful review of the literature on the spatial mismatch issue. The authors conclude that the theory does help to explain some—though by no means all—of the employment difficulties of African Americans.

34. Sidney Fine, *Violence in the Model City: The Cavanaugh Administration, Race Relations, and the Detroit Riot of 1967* (Ann Arbor: University of Michigan Press, 1989), 71.

35. Three of the neighborhoods on the South Side of Chicago that William J. Wilson has studied intensively are a good example. They were home to 250,000 people in 1950 and only 86,000 by 1990, a stunning 66 percent drop; Wilson, *When Work Disappears*, 45. The total population of Chicago's Black Belt declined by almost half between 1970 and 1990 alone (16). Wilson's main point is that rates of joblessness, poverty, and associated pathologies have mushroomed in Black Belt neighborhoods in the past quarter century. But if the people moving from the Black Belt to better neighborhoods tended to be those who were faring best economically, which is surely the case, the concentration of social problems among those left behind would rise by definition. Wilson has trained his high-powered microscope on a fraction of the black urban population that has been shrinking precipitously, a point that he sometimes seems to forget and that must be kept constantly in mind in drawing larger conclusions from his work.

36. Donald J. Bogue, *The Population of the United States* (New York: Free Press, 1959), chap. 3; Bogue, *Population of the U.S.: Historical Trends*, 118–135.

37. U.S. Bureau of the Census, *Statistical Abstract of the United States: 1974* (Washington, D.C.: U.S. Government Printing Office, 1974), 21; *Statistical Abstract of the U.S.: 1996*, 40.

38. David E. Hayes-Bautista, et al., *No Longer a Minority: Latinos and Social Policy in California* (Los Angeles: UCLA Chicano Studies Research Center, 1992), passim.

39. Wilson, *When Work Disappears*, 250. One of the virtues of this work is that the author includes such evidence, even though it runs counter to his theory that black joblessness is due to large structural changes in the economy. Part of the reason for the greater job success of Hispanic inner-city residents in Chicago is that they have much more positive attitudes toward work and are more eager to please their employers (139–141, 251). Another indication of the importance of cultural rather than structural forces is that Mexican workers in Chicago manage to organize car pools to get out to suburban jobs, while blacks do not, for some reason (223).

40. Roger Waldinger, *Still the Promised City? African-Americans and New Immigrants in Post-Industrial New York* (Cambridge: Harvard University Press, 1996), chap. 5. Waldinger shows that one reason that native-born blacks fared much less well in the job competition in New York City than immigrants (including black immigrants from

the Caribbean) is that they disdained the unskilled, low-paid jobs that immigrants were happy to accept, and that employers correctly perceived them as having a weaker work ethic. Commenting on Waldinger's book, Nathan Glazer argues that it refutes the "spatial mismatch" theory and identifies a different mismatch as the problem—a mismatch between "black expectations regarding what constituted suitable work and suitable wages and what was available" to them; Glazer, "Help Wanted," *New Republic,* 16 December 1996, 29.

41. Richard B. Freeman, "Crime and the Employment of Disadvantaged Youths," in Peterson and Vroman, *Urban Labor Markets,* 207.

42. Marc Mauer and Tracy Huling, *Young Black Men and the Criminal Justice System: Five Years Later* (Washington, D.C.: Sentencing Project, 1995), 3–4.

43. The data are for Cook County, which is virtually coterminous with the city of Chicago; Gary Orfield, "Urban Schooling and the Perpetuation of Job Inequality in Metropolitan Chicago," in Peterson and Vroman, *Urban Labor Markets,* 181. Given these striking figures, it is remarkable that Wilson's intensive study of the poor black neighborhoods of Chicago has so little to say about crime. Wilson may downplay the subject because of his faith that the chief cause of crime is lack of employment. He is impressed with a study that found that *employed* black and white men had similarly low violent crime rates, and that the huge overall racial difference was attributable to crime committed by men who had no jobs (22). But what was causing what? Were employed black males not committing criminal acts because of the accident that they have a job? Or did they have a job because they had traits that made them attractive to employers, and that people without those traits were both less likely to get jobs and more likely to commit crimes? Wilson calls for a massive public job-creation program, and predicts that "as more people become employed, crime, including violent crime, and drug use will subside" (238). If the causal relation were this simple, crimes by African Americans should have declined sharply during the economic boom of the Kennedy-Johnson years; instead, they rose (see chap. 10). "Do many young people engage in crime because of weak opportunities in the regular market," asks Holzer, "or do their illegal activities lower their interest in (by providing alternative income) and ability to obtain regular jobs?"; Harry J. Holzer, "Can We Solve Black Youth Unemployment?" *Challenge,* November-December 1988, 48.The issue of causation is discussed perceptively in two reviews of Wilson's book; see Marvin Kosters, "Looking for Jobs in All the Wrong Places," *Public Interest* 125 (Fall 1996), 125–131, and Glenn Loury, review of *When Work Disappears, Wilson Quarterly,* (Fall 1996), 89–92.

44. Michael Tonry, *Malign Neglect: Race, Crime, and Punishment in America* (New York: Oxford University Press, 1995), 29–30.

45. Daniel Fusfield and Timothy Bates, *The Political Economy of the Urban Ghetto* (Carbondale: Southern Illinois University Press, 1984), 168–169.

46. Michael E. Porter, "The Competitive Advantage of the Inner City," *Harvard Business Review* 73 (May-June 1995), 63–64.

47. Freeman, "Crime and the Employment of Disadvantaged Youths," 217–220.

48. John Bound and Richard B. Freeman, "What Went Wrong? The Erosion of Relative Earnings and Employment Among Young Black Men in the 1980s," *National Bureau of Economic Research Working Paper,* no. 3778 (Cambridge, Mass.: National Bureau of Economic Research 1991), 24.

49. Joleen Kirschenman and Kathryn M. Neckerman, " 'We'd Love to Hire Them, but . . . ': The Meaning of Race for Employers," in Christopher Jencks and Paul E.

Peterson, eds., *The Urban Underclass* (Washington, D.C.: Brookings Institution, 1991), 202–232.

50. Orfield, "Urban Schooling and Job Inequality," 181.

51. Robert P. Hey, "Minorities: Congress Studies Aid to Black Males," *Christian Science Monitor,* 1 August 1989, 7.

52. Freeman, "Crime and the Employment of Disadvantaged Youths," 229–230.

53. See the sources cited in n. 31 above.

54. Joel Kotkin, "Black Economic Base in L.A. Erodes as Demographics Change," *Washington Post,* 1 October 1989, H2.

55. U.S. Department of Education, National Center for Education Statistics, *NAEP 1994 Reading Report Card for the Nation and the States* (Washington, D.C.: U.S. Department of Education, 1996), 48.

56. William Julius Wilson, *The Truly Disadvantaged: The Inner City, the Underclass, and Public Policy* (Chicago: University of Chicago Press, 1987), 84–89. Wilson has modified his position somewhat in the light of subsequent research; see *When Work Disappears,* 94–97. Again, this recent work includes information difficult to square with the main argument that joblessness and poverty are the main source of the disintegration of the black family. Wilson has no economic explanation as to why "inner-city black single parents, unlike their Mexican-immigrant counterparts, feel little pressure to commit to a marriage" (105.)

57. Robert I. Lerman, "Employment Opportunities of Young Men and Family Formation," *American Journal of Economics* 79 (1989), 62–66.

58. Carl Husemoller Nightingale, *On the Edge: A History of Poor Black Children and Their American Dream* (New York: Basic Books, 1993), 61–62.

59. Ellwood and Crane, "Family Change Among Black Americans," 75–78; Robert D. Mare and Christopher Winship, "Socioeconomic Change and the Decline of Marriage for Blacks and Whites," in Jencks and Peterson, *Urban Underclass,* 175–203.

60. In 1980, for example, the weekly wages of married black males aged 25–34 were 17 percent higher than those of their unmarried peers. For married African-American men aged 35–44, the differential was 16 percent, and for those 45–54 it was 21 percent; U.S. Commission on Civil Rights, *Economic Progress of Black Men,* 85.

61. For a regression analysis of data from 1940 to 1980 that suggests that "lower marriage rates among blacks may be a reason for the low relative earnings of black males" instead of the other way around, see U.S. Commission on Civil Rights, *Economic Progress of Black Men,* 95–96.

62. Ellwood and Crane, "Family Change Among Black Americans," 81.

63. The description of Ward 8 is based on Don Terry and Karen De Witt, "Toll is Even Greater in Forgotten Anacostia," *New York Times,* 26 July 1996, 1; and Sabra Chartrand, "A Washington District That's a World Apart," *New York Times,* 8 October 1992, A20.

64. Katha Pollitt, "Unwed Mothers Aren't the Cause of Poverty," *Boston Globe,* 19 May 1994, 19.

65. Kai Erikson, review of Ruth Sidel, *Keeping Women and Children Last, Washington Post Book World,* 11 August 1996, 5.

66. For a sophisticated demonstration of the impressive upward mobility achieved by Asian and Hispanic immigrants in Southern California during the 1980s, see Dowell Myers, *The Changing Immigrants of Southern California,* Research Report No. LCRI-95-04R, Lusk Center Research Institute (Los Angeles: University of Southern

California, 1995). Roger Waldinger's *Still the Promised City?* shows that New York City has similarly afforded great opportunities to the immigrants who have come to it since World War II.

67. Joe Klein, "There Are Jobs in Chicago," *Newsweek,* 20 December 1993. Wilson's *When Work Disappears* includes Chicago evidence to the same effect. See the passages cited in n. 39 above. A *New York Times* article on moving welfare recipients into the world of work also makes the point that the problem might not be an absence of jobs but the lack of basic life and literacy skills on the part of those who have never held down a steady job; Jon Nordheimer, "Welfare-to-Work Plans Show Success Is Difficult to Achieve," *New York Times,* 1 September 1996, 1.

68. Paul Duke, Jr., "Urban Teen-Agers, Who Often Live Isolated from the World of Work, Shun the Job Market," *Wall Street Journal,* 14 August 1991, A10.

69. Quoted in David Whitman, "How Much Effect Do Middle-Class Mores Have in the Ghetto?," *U.S. News & World Report,* 8 June 1992, 35.

70. Albert J. Reiss, Jr., and Jeffrey A. Roth, eds., *Understanding and Preventing Violence,* vol. 3, *Social Influences* (Washington, D.C.: National Academy Press, 1994), 73.

71. Erick Eckholm, "Solutions on Welfare: They All Cost Money," *New York Times,* 26 July 1992, 1.

72. Douglas J. Besharov with Timothy S. Sullivan, "Welfare Reform and Marriage," *Public Interest* 15 (Fall 1996), 81–94.

73. Bob Herbert, "Death at an Early Age," *New York Times,* op-ed, 2 December 1996, A15.

CHAPTER 10: CRIME

1. Jay Carr, "Spike and Malcolm," *Boston Globe,* 15 November 1992, 89.

2. T. Deon Warner on *Nightline* (ABC), October 16, 1995.

3. Letter, *Wall Street Journal,* 28 May 1992, A21.

4. Jordana Hart, "Cab Drivers Balance Fears, Obligations," *Boston Globe,* 21 December 1992, 1.

5. National Opinion Research Center survey described in Thomas Edsall, "Recalling Lessons of the '60s," *Washington Post,* 3 May 1992, A25.

6. George Gallup, Jr., *The Gallup Poll: Public Opinion, 1993* (Wilmington, Del.: Scholarly Resources, 1994), 271. This dovetails with the results of a 1992 poll commissioned by the Anti-Defamation League, which found that 38 percent of Americans (of all races) thought that black Americans were "more prone to violence"; *Highlights from an Anti-Defamation League Survey on Racial Attitudes in America* (New York: Anti-Defamation League, 1992), unpaginated.

7. "Polling in Black and White," *Washington Post,* November 5, 1989, C5. The proportion of whites who said that it was "common sense" to avoid black neighborhoods dropped from 50 percent to 40 percent when they were interviewed by blacks.

8. *Time*/Yankelovich Clancy Shulman survey January 19–21, 1987, obtained from the Roper Center for Public Opinion Research.

9. Paul M. Sniderman and Thomas Piazza, *The Scar of Race* (Cambridge: Harvard University Press, 1993), 45.

10. *Los Angeles Times,* 17 November 1992, JJ2 (special supplement evaluating issues raised by the riots); poll conducted October 9–14. The figure for whites wasn't much better (43 percent), suggesting that urban residents of all races are highly fearful.

11. Katherine McFate and David A. Bositis, *Joint Center for Political and Economic Studies 1996 National Opinion Poll: Social Attitudes* (Washington, D.C.: Joint Center for Political and Economic Studies, 1996), table A-2.

12. Larry Hugick, "Blacks See Their Lives Worsening," *Gallup Poll Monthly*, April 1992, 26. It should be said, though, that responses to questions like what are the "most important" or "most urgent" problems fluctuate a great deal without necessarily revealing anything very important. Between 1981 and 1993, for example, the proportion of Americans citing crime as the most important problem never hit double digits. It then jumped to 37 percent in January 1994 and to 52 percent by August 1994 before slumping to 27 percent by January 1995; U.S. Department of Justice, Bureau of Justice Statistics, *Sourcebook of Criminal Justice Statistics: 1994* (Washington, D.C.: U.S. Government Printing Office, 1995), 140.

13. Larry Hugick and Linda Saad, "Before L.A. Riots: Race Issue Campaign 'Sleeper,' " *Gallup Poll Monthly*, May 1992, 10.

14. George Gallup, Jr., and Frank Newport, "Major U.S. Cities Seen as Unsafe Places to Live and Work," *Gallup Poll Monthly*, September 1990, 41–43.

15. As of 1995, 54.9 percent of black Americans were living in central cities; U.S. Bureau of the Census, Current Population Reports, PPL-45, *The Black Population in the United States: March 1995* (Washington, D.C.: U.S. Government Printing Office, 1996), table 3.

16. John Greenwald, "L.A.'s Open Wounds," *Time*, 8 February 1993, 35.

17. Felicity Barringer, "Washington's Departing Police Chief Laments the Sleep of Murderers," *Washington Post*, 20 September 1992, E7.

18. Jonathan Rieder, *Canarsie: The Jews and Italians of Brooklyn Against Liberalism* (Cambridge: Harvard University Press, 1985), 75.

19. Survey conducted in 1989 by the City of Atlanta, Department of Public Safety, cited in Adele V. Harrell and George E. Peterson, eds., *Drugs, Crime, and Social Isolation: Barriers to Urban Opportunity* (Washington, D.C.: Urban Institute Press, 1992), 23.

20. Dennis Hevesi, "Couple Are Found Slain in their Manhattan Home," *New York Times*, 11 November 1992, B3.

21. Susan Sward, "Community Policing," *San Francisco Chronicle*, 20 November 1992, A10.

22. Alex Kotlowitz, *There Are No Children Here* (New York: Doubleday, 1991), 26, 263, 302.

23. George James, "Caught in Crossfire," *New York Times*, 19 April 1991, B1

24. Michael Marriott, "Teen-Agers Describe Repeated Harassment," *New York Times*, 12 June 1992, B7.

25. David Gonzales, "Seeking Security, Many Retreat Behind Bars and Razor Wire," *New York Times*, 17 January 1993, A1.

26. Patrice Gaines and DeNeen L. Brown, "Where Despair and Defeat Reign," *Washington Post*, 30 September 1993, 1.

27. Roger Lane, *The Roots of Violence in Black Philadelphia* (Cambridge: Harvard University Press, 1986), 141–143.

28. U.S. Bureau of the Census, *Historical Statistics of the United States: Colonial Times to 1970* (Washington, D.C.: U.S. Government Printing Office, 1975), 414.

29. Christopher Jencks, *Rethinking Social Policy: Race, Poverty, and the Underclass* (Cambridge: Harvard University Press, 1992), 185–187, is highly critical of the FBI data, but he does not appear to doubt that the 1960s witnessed a very major rise in crime. The appendix, "Notes on Criminal Statistics," in Charles E. Silberman, *Crimi-*

nal Violence, Criminal Justice (New York: Random House, 1978) concludes that "there can be little doubt about the essential accuracy of the overall trends depicted in the *Uniform Crime Reports* during the last fifteen to twenty years" (610). It should be noted that the index of violent crimes in the FBI reports is unweighted; each crime counts equally. That means that it is dominated by changes in the level of the most common and least serious crimes. The murder rate has gone up much less than the rate for aggravated assault. On the other hand, forcible rape is a very serious crime, and since 1960 it has risen at a rate almost identical to the rate for all violent crimes.

30. James Q. Wilson, "Crime and Public Policy," in James Q. Wilson and and Joan Petersilia, eds., *Crime* (San Francisco: Institute for Contemporary Studies Press, 1995), 489–491 and James Lynch, "Crime in International Perspective" in the same volume, 21–26.

31. U.S. Bureau of the Census, *Statistical Abstract of the United States: 1984* (Washington, D.C.: U.S. Government Printing Office, 1984), 180; U.S. Department of Justice, Federal Bureau of Investigation, *Crime in the United States 1995: Uniform Crime Reports* (Washington, D.C.: U.S. Government Printing Office, 1996), 16.

32. *Sourcebook of Criminal Justice Statistics: 1994*, 232.

33. The generalization that black victimization for violent crime is up does not depend upon the somewhat suspect base of the FBI data; the pattern shows up in the victimization surveys, too; U.S. Department of Justice, Bureau of Justice Statistics, *Criminal Victimization in the United States: 1973–1992 Trends*, NCJ-151657 (Washington, D.C.: U.S. Department of Justice, 1994), pp. 1, 5, 13.

34. As quoted in Michael Tonry, *Malign Neglect: Race, Crime, and Punishment in America* (New York: Oxford University Press, 1995), 50.

35. *Crime in the U.S.: 1995*, 17.

36. *Sourcebook of Criminal Justice: 1994*, 535, 546.

37. AP Wire Service, "Guns Take Ever-Higher Toll Among Young Blacks," *New York Times*, 17 March 1991, 31.

38. Alfred Blumstein, "Prisons," in Wilson and Petersilia, *Crime*, 398–401, 412–413; Children's Defense Fund, *The State of America's Children: Yearbook, 1994* (Washington, D.C.: Children's Defense Fund, 1994), 65.

39. *Crime in the U.S.: 1995*, 276.

40. William J. Bennett, John J. DiIulio, Jr., and John P. Walters, *Body Count: Moral Poverty . . . and How to Win America's War Against Crime and Drugs* (New York: Simon & Schuster, 1996), 22.

41. The radio and sneakers examples are from Paul M. Barrett, "Epidemic, Killing of 15-Year-Old Is Part of Escalation of Murder by Juveniles," *Wall Street Journal*, 25 March 1991, A1. The earrings example is from Joseph B. Treater, "Teen-Age Murders: Plentiful Guns, Easy Power," *New York Times*, 24 May 1992, A1.

42. Lee A. Daniels, "Brooklyn Youth, 15, Slain on Crowded Subway," *New York Times*, 7 March 1992, 29.

43. David Gonzalez, "Where Coffins Come in Size Young," *New York Times*, 10 March 1992, B1.

44. "Life at 'Jeff': Tough Students Wonder Where Childhood Went," *New York Times*, 7 March 1992, 28.

45. Ibid.

46. Celia W. Dugger, "Boy in Search of Respect Discovers How to Kill," *New York Times*, 15 May 1994, A1.

47. "Boston Teen-Ager Gives Motive for a Rape and a Murder: Boredom," *New York Times*, 27 May 1991, 6.

48. Nancy Lewis, "Suspect in Interstate 295 Slaying Charged in 2nd Random Shooting," *Washington Post*, 14 December 1991, D1.

49. "Young people aren't taught the value of life," a youth outreach worker for the Boston Community Schools, explained to a reporter. "You have to take them by the hand and teach them to live normally"; Anthony Flint, "Youths at Congress Talk of Urban Violence," *Boston Globe*, 29 April 1991, 13.

50. Joseph B. Treaster and Mary B. W. Tabor, "Teen-Age Gunslinging Rises, Seeking Protection and Profit," *New York Times*, 17 February 1991, A1.

51. "After MIT Slaying, a Search for Answers," *Boston Globe*, 23 September 1992, 27. Many kids—at least many interviewed by newspaper reporters—say that either they themselves or their peers treat death casually. Thus, a sixteen-year-old boy from the Roxbury section of Boston told a *Globe* reporter that gang members often don't think about the consequences of ending someone else's life. "If he dies, so what? He dies. That's how people think," he said; Flint, "Youths at Congress."

52. Treaster, "Teen-Age Murderers," *New York Times*, 24 May 1992, A1.

53. Claude Brown, *Manchild in the Promised Land* (New York: Signet, 1965), 17.

54. The reference to "righteous-doing folks" is on p. 169 of *Manchild*. The phrase "going the crime way" comes from p. 173.

55. Susan Chira, "Conversations/Johnnetta B. Cole," *New York Times*, 10 January 1993, E7.

56. Ibid.

57. Brown, *Manchild*, 127.

58. Barrett, "Epidemic."

59. Bob Hohler, "Classmates' Deaths Take Toll on City's Students," *Boston Globe*, 28 June 1993, 1.

60. Raymond Hernandez, "Armed with Knives, Youths Stalk Safety," *New York Times*, 23 May 1993, 1. In August 1996, the *New York Post* reported that knives and other weapons had come to be favored over guns in that city because the use of other weapons reduced the chance that the perpetrator would do serious time if busted; Rocco Parascandola, "Cutting Edge of Crime," *New York Post*, 18 August 1996, 3.

61. *Sourcebook of Criminal Justice Statistics: 1994*, 251, 275.

62. Treaster and Tabor, "Teen-Age Gunslinging Rises."

63. Barrett, "Epidemic."

64. Treaster and Tabor, "Teen-Age Gunslinging Rises."

65. Ibid.

66. Bennett et al., *Body Count*, 36.

67. Quoted in Howard Kurtz, "Some Journalists Link Crime Coverage, Racism," *Washington Post*, 29 July 1994, 11.

68. Marc Mauer and Tracy Huling, *Young Black Men and the Criminal Justice System: Five Years Later* (Washington, D.C.: Sentencing Project, 1995), 3–4.

69. Speech of Willie L. Brown, Jr., at Howard University Law School, October 20, 1992, 9–10. Photocopy obtained from Speaker Brown's office.

70. Seth Mydans, "Homicide Rate Up for Young Blacks," *New York Times*, 7 December 1990, A26.

71. Seth Mydans, "The Courts on Trial," *New York Times*, 7 April 1993, A14.

72. Lynda Gorov, "Blacks Charge Police Brutality," *Boston Globe*, 30 October 1992, 21.

73. Pamela Warrick, "What Next for Detroit?" *Los Angeles Times*, 25 November 1992, E1.

74. *Beyond Rodney King: Police Conduct and Community Relations,* a report prepared by the Criminal Justice Institute, Harvard Law School, and the William Monroe Trotter Institute, University of Massachusetts at Boston for the NAACP, March 1993, unpublished draft copy, 10.

75. Ibid., 11, 15, 21, 20.

76. Thus, for example, in January 1991, the president of the Springfield, Massachusetts, chapter of the NAACP said: "There are young minorities being brutalized and victimized by police on a regular basis"; *Boston Globe,* 25 January 1991, 27.

77. Don Terry, "For Los Angeles Residents, Police Badge Tarnishes," *New York Times,* 25 March 1991, 1.

78. Marc Mauer, *America Behind Bars: One Year Later* (Washington, D.C.: Sentencing Project, 1992), 11–12.

79. Seth Mydans, "After the Riots," *New York Times,* 15 May 1992, 1.

80. Peter S. Canellos, "Mission Hill Residents Say Justice Not Served," *Boston Globe,* 3 November 1992, 1.

81. Marc Mauer, *America Behind Bars: A Comparison of International Rates of Incarceration* (Washington, D.C.: Sentencing Project, 1991), 9.

82. *Imprisoned Generation: Young Men Under Criminal Justice Custody in New York State,* a report by the Correctional Association of New York and New York State Coalition for Criminal Justice, September 1990.

83. Editorial, *New York Times,* 7 May 1992, A26.

84. Bob Blauner, *Black Lives, White Lives: Three Decades of Race Relations in America* (Berkeley: University of California Press, 1989), 223.

85. Furious Styles, the father, as quoted in Clarence Page, "Genocide Theories Can Blind Blacks to the Real Culprits," *Chicago Tribune,* 14 August 1991, C17.

86. Ze'ev Chafets, *Devil's Night and Other True Tales of Detroit* (New York: Vintage Books, 1991), 65.

87. Bruce Weber, "Students Confront Officials on Race, Anger, and Rodney King," *New York Times,* 4 May 1992, B1.

88. Edsall, "Recalling Lessons of the '60s."

89. Andrew Hacker, *Two Nations: Black and White, Separate, Hostile, Unequal* (New York: Scribner, 1992), 188.

90. U.S. Bureau of the Census, *Statistical Abstract of the United States: 1996* (Washington, D.C.: U.S. Government Printing Office, 1996), 220.

91. *Sourcebook of Criminal Justice Statistics: 1994,* 554; U.S. Bureau of the Census, *Statistical Abstract of the United States: 1994* (Washington, D.C.: U.S. Government Printing Office, 1994), 14.

92. U.S. Department of Justice, Bureau of Justice Statistics, *Criminal Victimization in the United States, 1993,* NCJ-151657 (Washington, D.C.: U.S. Department of Justice, 1996), 45, 49. Figures for particular crimes like burglary are only for victimizations involving a single offender. On top of that, there were an additional 2,438,000 violent victimizations involving multiple offenders in 1993. Information about these was not broken down in enough detail to compute offenses by race, but multiple-offender crimes are included in all the analysis of violent crimes totals.

93. Ibid. It is possible that the whites in the survey lied about the race of the criminals they encountered, but it is difficult to see why. One could imagine—though it seems far-fetched—that significant numbers of whites were so biased that they wanted to defame African Americans by exaggerating their involvement in crime. But one could speculate with equal plausibility that many blacks in the survey lied, falsely claiming that their assailants were white to avoid reinforcing stereotypes

about black crime. Neither line of speculation should be taken very seriously, in our view.

94. We borrow the method employed here from John J. DiIulio, Jr., "My Black Crime Problem and Ours," *City Journal* 6 (Spring 1996), 25. DiIulio fails to include crimes by multiple offenders, and uses population figures for age groups that differ substantially from those in *Statistical Abstract of the U.S.: 1995*, 21. His estimated ratio of 57.5 may be the result of errors in his base figures. But he notes that using different age brackets brings the estimate down to about 50 to 1. Our figure was 49.8.

95. See Tonry, *Malign Neglect*, chap. 2, "Racial Disproportion in the Criminal Justice System," for an excellent review of the literature. The quotation is from p. 79. Tonry's bottom line is that "for nearly a decade there has been a near consensus among scholars and policy analysts that most of the black punishment disproportions result not from racial bias or discrimination within the system but from patterns of black offending and of blacks' criminal records" (49). Tonry makes an exception for drug offenses, a matter we take up later in this chapter. Key items in this literature include Michael Hindelang, "Race and Involvement in Common Law Personal Crimes," *American Sociological Review* 43 (1978), 93–109; Michael Hindelang, "Variations in Sex-Race-Age Specific Rates of Offending," *American Sociological Review* 46 (1981), 461–474; Gary Kleck, "Racial Discrimination in Criminal Sentencing: A Critical Evaluation of the Evidence," *American Sociological Review* 46 (1981), 783–805; Alfred Blumstein, "On the Racial Disproportionality of United States Prison Populations," *Journal of Criminal Law and Criminology* 73 (1982), 1259–1281; Joan Petersilia, *Racial Disparities in the Criminal Justice System* (Santa Monica, Calif.: Rand Corporation, 1983); Patrick A. Langan, "Racism on Trial: New Evidence to Explain the Racial Composition of Prisons in the United States," *Journal of Criminal Law and Criminology* 76 (1985), 666–683; Stephen P. Klein, Susan Turner, Joan Petersilia, *Racial Equity in Sentencing* (Santa Monica, Calif.: Rand Corporation, 1988); Stephen P. Klein et al., *Predicting Criminal Justice Outcomes: What Matters* (Santa Monica, Calif.: Rand Corporation 1991).

96. The D.C. police force is 67.8 percent black, while the population of the city is 65.8 percent African American; DiIulio, "My Black Crime Problem," 22.

97. U.S. Department of Justice, *Felony Defendants in Large Urban Counties, 1990* (Washington, D.C.: Bureau of Justice Statistics, 1993). For a brief summary, see Patrick A. Langan, "No Racism in the Justice System," *Public Interest* 117 (Fall 1994), 48–51.

98. Langan, "No Racism in the Justice System."

99. Randall Kennedy, "Blacks and Crime," *Wall Street Journal*, 8 April 1994, A16.

100. Brent Mitchell, "Bill Takes Aim at Racism in Death Penalty," *Washington Post*, 14 July 1991, A5.

101. *Sourcebook of Criminal Justice Statistics: 1994*, 587.

102. Ibid., 486. Of course there are different degrees of murder, and the death penalty is only awarded for first-degree murders, usually for particularly heinous first-degree murders. These distinctions need to be taken into account is assessing whether the death penalty is administered fairly, and we shall do so below.

103. For a brief favorable evaluation of this study, conducted by David C. Baldus, see Randall Kennedy, "History: Unequal Protection," draft chapter from a book in progress, Harvard Law School, May 1996, 88–95. A more critical view is provided in Stanley Rothman and Stephen Powers, "Execution by Quota?" *Public Interest* 116 (Summer 1994), 10–12. A 1987 Supreme Court opinion—*McCleskey v. Kemp*, 481

U.S. 279—dismissed a Georgia death penalty appeal that rested upon the Baldus study. Justice Powell's opinion for the Court comments on the study in considerable detail.

104. The figures in Table 5—11 percent vs. 2 percent—suggest a larger disparity than the 4.3:1 figure given in the text. But the tabular percentages are rounded off; the ratio in the text is from unrounded percentages and is correct.

105. Bryan Stevenson, director of Alabama's Capital Representation Resource Center, quoted in *Time*, 29 April 1991, 68.

106. If those who murder blacks get off disproportionately easy, one logical answer would be more executions for those convicted in homicide cases in which an African American was the victim. The racial disparity could be eliminated by executing a larger number of criminals convicted of murdering blacks. Treating all killers more leniently is not the obvious solution to excessive leniency with some. If executing the murderers of whites demonstrates the value society places on white life, why not show in the same fashion that an equal value is placed on black life? To do that would change the racial mix on Death Row, however, thus raising anew the old question of whether black defendants are getting fair treatment. Since whites rarely kill blacks, imposing the death penalty on more killers of blacks means putting more African Americans on Death Row. The NAACP-commissioned study found that the killers of blacks in Georgia did not receive their "fair share" of death sentences, but if an additional 145 of them in the years 1973–1979 had been executed, the racial disparity would have been eliminated. It happens, though, that 96 percent of the people who were convicted of murdering blacks in that state in those years were themselves black; capital punishment, therefore, would have been awarded to an additional 139 blacks and just 6 more whites. The proportion of white killers getting the death penalty would have risen only slightly—to 8.1 percent—while the black rate would have gone from 4.1 to 12.2 percent. The result would have been whites condemned to death at a rate 50 percent lower than black defendants, as opposed to a rate 80 percent higher. It seems unlikely that critics would have taken this as evidence the system had become more equitable.

107. Since many states do not have a death penalty at all, or others apply it more sparingly than Georgia, the national rate is much lower than 5 percent. In 1990 just 244 of the 11,028 people who were convicted of murder in a state or federal court in the nation were sentenced to death, a mere 2.2 percent of the total; *Sourcebook of Criminal Justice: 1994*, 485; *Statistical Abstract of the U.S.: 1995*, 220.

108. Rothman and Powers, "Execution by Quota?" 11.

109. Ibid.

110. See Kennedy's thoughtful comments on "racially selective sympathy and indifference" in "History," 94–96.

111. "Hobbling a Generation: Young African American Males in the Criminal Justice System of America's Cities: Baltimore, Maryland," News Release of the National Center on Institutions and Alternatives, Alexandria, Va., 1992, 1.

112. Allan Ellis, "Of Race and Incarceration," *American Lawyer*, 5 December 1991, 6.

113. Quoted in Mauer and Huling, *Young Black Men*, 16.

114. Mauer and Huling, *Young Black Men*, 9.

115. At the time the law was passed, the prevailing scientific opinion was that crack cocaine had more dangerous pharmacological properties than the powdered form. This may not be the case. In a recent report in the *Journal of the American Medical Association*, two psychologists specializing in drug addiction concluded that the dif-

ferences between the two forms were negligible. "Topics of the Times: Unfair Sentencing," *New York Times*, 6 February 1997, A24.

116. DiIulio, "My Black Crime Problem," 19–20.
117. Kennedy, "Blacks and Crime." The argument summarized in this op-ed piece is worked out in detail in Kennedy's "The State, Criminal Law, and Racial Discrimination," *Harvard Law Review* 104 (April 1994), 1255–1278.
118. Mauer, *Young Black Men*, 9.
119. DiIulio, "My Black Crime Problem," 19; *Sourcebook of Criminal Justice Statistics: 1994*, 546, 558.
120. *Sourcebook of Criminal Justice: 1994*, 553.
121. Ibid., 559.
122. Quoted in Silberman, *Criminal Violence*, 222.
123. For a brief summary, see Stephen J. Markman, "Foreword: The 'Truth in Criminal Justice' Series," *Journal of Law Reform* 22 (Spring-Summer 1989), 430–436.
124. Bennett et al., *Body Count*, 54–55. This estimate, of course, does not include prosecutions that never proceeded in the absence of confessions that might have been obtained in the pre-*Miranda* era.
125. Evidence supporting these findings is summarized in Robert J. Sampson and Janet L. Lauritsen, "Violent Victimization and Offending: Individual-, Situational-, and Community-Level Risk Factors," in National Research Council, *Understanding and Preventing Violence*, vol. 3, *Social Influences* (Washington, D.C.: National Academy of Sciences, 1994), 1–114. The authors suggest that poverty and unemployment "have had weak or inconsistent effects on violence rates in past research" because they "may not have direct effects on crime," but instead exert an influence through their tendency to increase family disruption, which is a "strong predictor of variations in urban black violence." They also cite evidence that family disruption has similarly negative impact on whites (72–73).
126. For excellent discussions of the problem of disorder, see Wesley G. Skogan, *Disorder and Decline: Crime and the Spiral of Decay in American Neighborhoods* (Berkeley: University of California Press, 1990) and George L. Kelling and Catherine M. Coles, *Fixing Broken Windows: Restoring Order and Reducing Crime in Our Communities* (New York: Free Press, 1996).
127. Skogan traces the impact of neighborhood disorder on the lives of responsible residents; see especially chap. 4.
128. Lee A. Daniels, "Black Crime, Black Victims," *New York Times Magazine*, 16 May 1982, 38.
129. Mark Thompson, "Violence and the Verdict," *Wall Street Journal*, 19 April 1993, A12.
130. Kenneth B. Noble, "Los Angeles Losing Allure for Blacks," *New York Times*, 8 January, 1995, A1; Miles Corwin, "Black Flight," *San Francisco Chronicle*, 30 August 1992, 13.
131. Susan McHenry quoted in Drian Dumaine, "Blacks on Blacks," *Fortune*, 2 November 1992, 119.
132. Steven A. Holmes and Karen De Witt, "Black, Successful, and Safe and Gone from the Capital," *New York Times*, 27 July 1996, 1.
133. Gunnar Myrdal, *An American Dilemma* (New York, Harper & Row, 1945), 655. Emphasis is Myrdal's.
134. The Washington, D.C., buzzer system was defended by *Washington Post* columnist Richard Cohen in a very controversial piece; Cohen, "Closing the Door on Crime,"

Washington Post, 7 September 1986, W13. On the Dee Brown story, see the *Boston Globe,* editorial, 26 September 1990, 18.

135. Chrisena Coleman, "Railroad Apology to Black Mag Exec," *New York Daily News,* 9 May 1995, 4. See also: Lena Williams, "When Blacks Shop, Bias Often Accompanies Sale," *New York Times,* 30 April 1991, 1; Carol Stocker and Barbara Carton, "Guilty . . . of Being Black," *Boston Globe,* 7 May 1992, 85.

136. Brent Staples, *Parallel Time* (New York: Pantheon Books, 1994), 202–204, 194.

CHAPTER 11: POLITICS

1. Denise Goodman, "Blacks Emerge from Sea of White Votes," *Boston Globe,* 2 February 1994, 36.

2. U.S. Bureau of the Census, 1990 Census of Population, *General Population Characteristics: United States,* 1990-CP-1-1 (Washington, D.C.: U.S. Government Printing Office, 1992), table 262.

3. Calculated from a list of all blacks elected mayor of cities with populations of 50,000 or more, compiled from the Joint Center for Political and Economic Studies' invaluable series of volumes, *Black Elected Officials: A National Roster,* and supplemented with cases gleaned from newspapers and other periodicals.

4. Lani Guinier, "Keeping the Faith: Black Voters in the Post-Reagan Era," *Harvard Civil Rights–Civil Liberties Law Review* 24 (1989), 429.

5. Remark made on televised program moderated by Tracy Larkin, University of Alabama, March 13, 1991.

6. Earl Black and Merle Black, *Politics and Society in the South* (Cambridge: Harvard University Press, 1987), 302.

7. Stephan Lesher, *George Wallace: American Populist* (Reading, Mass: Addison-Wesley, 1994), 504–506.

8. Phil Duncan, ed., *Congressional Quarterly's Politics in America 1994* (Washington, D.C.: Congressional Quarterly, 1994), 1367.

9. U.S. Bureau of the Census, 1990 Census of the Population, *Characteristics of the Black Population,* 1990-CP-3-6 (Washington, D.C.: U.S. Government Printing Office, 1994), table 1.

10. For the 1968 numbers, see David Campbell and Joe R. Feagin, "Black Politics in the South: A Descriptive Analysis," *Journal of Politics* 37 (1975), 141. The 1973 figure is from the Joint Center for Political and Economic Studies, *Black Elected Officials: A National Roster: 1973. 3rd edition.* (Washington, D.C.: Joint Center for Political and Economic Studies. 1974), xvii. For 1996, see National Conference of Black Mayors, *Program of 22nd Annual Convention* (Atlanta, 1996), unpaginated.

11. David Bositis, *Black State Legislators: A Survey and Analysis of Black Leadership in State Capitols* (Washington, D.C.: Joint Center for Political and Economic Studies, 1992), 6; U.S. Bureau of the Census, *Statistical Abstract of the United States: 1995* (Washington, D.C.: U.S. Government Printing Office, 1995), 287.

12. Joint Center for Political and Economic Studies, *Black Elected Officials: A National Roster, 1993. 21st edition* (Washington, D.C.: Joint Center for Political and Economic Studies, 1974), xl.

13. Everett Carll Ladd, ed., *America at the Polls, 1994* (Storrs, Conn.: Roper Center for Public Opinion Research, University of Connecticut, 1995), 159.

14. Rep. Gary Franks of Connecticut, one of the two black Republican members of

Congress, was defeated, and Rep. Cleo Fields of Louisiana did not run for reelection after the lines of his district were redrawn by court order, sharply reducing the proportion of blacks within it. Four other black incumbents whose districts were similarly redrawn chose to run nevertheless, and all four were elected from white-majority districts. In addition, Julia Carson won a congressional seat in an Indianapolis district that was only 27 percent black. Thus, the net loss of black seats was just one. For further discussion of these contests, see chap. 16.

15. Harold W. Stanley and Richard G. Niemi, *Vital Statistics on American Politics* (Washington, D.C.: Congressional Quarterly Press, 1994), 402–403.
16. U.S. Bureau of the Census, *Statistical Abstract of the United States: 1993* (Washington, D.C.: U.S. Government Printing Office, 1993), 283; Joint Center, *Black Elected Officials: 1993*, xxiii.
17. David Bositis, *The Congressional Black Caucus in the 103rd Congress* (Washington, D.C.: Joint Center for Political and Economic Studies, 1993), 3; Bositis, *Blacks and the 1996 Democratic National Convention,* (Washington, D.C.: Joint Center for Political and Economic Studies, 1996), 10.
18. Bositis, *Black State Legislators,* 7.
19. In the sixteen states in which the black voting-age population, as of 1990, was above the national average of 11.3 percent, black legislators in 1992 made up an average of 19.3 percent of the Democrats in the state Houses and 15.9 percent of the Democrats in the state senates. Calculations based on tables contained in Bositis, *Black State Legislators,* 23–24.
20. U.S. Bureau of the Census, 1990 Census of Population, *General Population Characteristics: United States,* 1990-CP-1-1 (Washington, D.C.: U.S. Government Printing Office, 1992), tables 3 and 6.
21. National Conference of Black Mayors, *Program of 22nd Annual Convention.*
22. U.S. Bureau of the Census, Current Population Reports, PPL-45. *The Black Population in the United States: March 1995* (Washington, D.C.: U.S. Government Printing Office, 1996), tables 3 and 16. The precise figures for 1995 are 32.7 percent of whites and 55.5 percent of blacks.
23. We are grateful to Professor Charles Bullock III, for first suggesting this point. Phone conversation, June 8, 1994.
24. Lesher, *George Wallace,* 104.
25. Voter News Service exit-polling data, as given in Marjorie Connelly, "The Numbers: Portrait of the Electorate," *New York Times,* 10 November 1996, A28. The Hispanic vote also went Democratic in all of these contests, but it made much less of a difference, for two reasons. First, Hispanics have not voted Democratic by such lopsided margins. Second, the Hispanic electorate has been much smaller than that of blacks because a substantial fraction of the voting-age population consists of immigrants who have not become citizens. The Asian-American vote was too small for exit poll estimates until 1992, but in both 1992 and 1996 it went Republican. Asian Americans preferred Bush to Clinton by 24 points in 1992 and Dole to Clinton by 5 points in 1996.
26. The three senators were Breaux (Louisiana), Fowler (Georgia), and Shelby (Alabama). The figures for the black share of the Clinton vote are taken from David Bositis, *Blacks and the 1996 Republican National Convention* (Washington, D.C.: Joint Center for Political Studies, 1996), table 2. See also Matthew Rees, *From the Deck to the Sea: Blacks in the Republican Party* (Wakefield, N.H.: Longwood Academic Press, 1991), 422; and Jack E. White, "The Limits of Black Power," *Time,* 11 May 1992, 38.

27. Bositis, *Blacks and the 1996 Republican National Convention*, 1, notes that in 1996 "the level of black turnout, and even a minimal shift in the allegiances of black voters, could determine the outcome of the presidential and congressional vote in several important states."

28. U.S. Bureau of the Census, Current Population Reports, P-20-155, *Negro Population: March, 1965* (Washington, D.C.: U.S. Government Printing Office, 1966), 1; U.S. Bureau of the Census, Current Population Reports, Special Studies, P-23-80, *The Social and Economic Status of the Black Population in the United States: An Historical View, 1790–1978* (Washington, D.C.: U.S. Government Printing Office, 1979), 145, 150; U.S. Bureau of the Census, *Statistical Abstract of the U.S.: 1996* (Washington, D.C.: U.S. Government Printing Office, 1996), 14, 286.

29. *Statistical Abstract of the U.S.: 1996*, 286.

30. Bositis, *Blacks and the 1996 Republican National Convention*, 9.

31. Counting registrants and voters is surprisingly hard, and there are questions about the reliability of the data. Only two states—Louisiana and South Carolina—keep official turnout rates broken down by race, and eight compute registration rates by race. Thus, scholars rely on estimates derived from the Current Population Survey, conducted by the U.S. Bureau of the Census. The survey depends on self-reporting, and respondents may not give accurate answers. Some scholars have argued that blacks are more likely than whites to claim to have voted when they did not, and that there is thus a larger gap between black and white turnout than census figures would suggest; Paul R. Abramson and William Claggett, "Racial Differences in Self-Reported and Validated Turnout in the 1988 Presidential Election," *Journal of Politics* 53 (February 1991), 186–197; and Abramson and Claggett, "The Quality of Record Keeping and Racial Differences in Validated Turnout," *Journal of Politics* 54 (August 1992), 871–880. Katherine Tate, *From Protest to Politics: The New Black Voters in American Elections* (Cambridge: Harvard University Press, 1993) dismisses the problem. Michael Traugott basically splits the difference—acknowledging some over-reporting by African Americans, but arguing that it is less than Abramson, Claggett, and others have asserted. See his expert witness report in *NAACP v. Austin*, 14 July 1994, U.S. Dist. Court. for the E. Dist. of Mich. 857 F. Supp. 560, no. 92-CV-72696-DT.

32. *Statistical Abstract of the U.S.: 1995*, 289.

33. Bositis, *Blacks and the 1996 Republican National Convention*, 9–10.

34. Sidney Verba, Kay Lehman Schlozman, and Henry E. Brady, *Voice and Equality: Civic Voluntarism in American Politics* (Cambridge: Harvard University Press, 1995), chap. 8.

35. Jonathan P. Hicks, "Disappointed Black Voters Could Hurt Mayor's Chances," *New York Times*, 4 October 1993, 1. The 66 percent figure is from the fourteen predominantly black Assembly districts.

36. Tate, *From Protest to Politics*, 7, 78, 110.

37. Bositis, *Blacks and the 1996 Republican National Convention*, 10.

38. Bositis, *Blacks and the 1992 Democratic National Convention*, 5.

39. Ronald Smothers, "Ex-Mayor's Son Wins a Run-Off in New Orleans," *New York Times*, 7 March 1994, A10.

40. William J. Grimshaw, *Bitter Fruit: Black Politics and the Chicago Machine, 1931–1991* (Chicago: University of Chicago Press, 1992), 162–163.

41. Paul Kleppner, *Chicago Divided: The Making of a Black Mayor* (DeKalb: Northern Illinois University Press, 1985), 146.

42. Ibid., 47.

43. Ibid., 149. Higher estimates of black registration and turnout are presented in Michael B. Preston, "The Election of Harold Washington," in Preston, Lenneal J. Henderson, Jr., and Paul L. Puryear, eds., *The New Black Politics* (New York: Longman, 1987), 153. See also Robert T. Starks and Michael B. Preston, "Harold Washington and the Politics of Reform in Chicago: 1983–1987," in Rufus P. Browning, Dale Rogers Marshall, and David H. Tabb, eds., *Racial Politics in American Cities* (New York: Longman, 1990), 97.

44. Preston, "The Election of Harold Washington," table 7.10, 168.

45. Charles E. Jones and Michael L. Clemons, "A Model of Racial Crossover Voting: An Assessment of the Wilder Victory," in Georgia A. Persons, ed., *Dilemmas of Black Politics: Issues of Leadership and Strategy* (New York: HarperCollins, 1993), 141.

46. Harold W. Stanley, "Assessing the Presidential Candidacies of Jesse Jackson," in Paul M. Sniderman, Philip E. Tetlock, and Edward G. Carmines, eds., *Prejudice, Politics, and the American Dilemma* (Stanford, Calif.: Stanford University Press, 1993), 265. See also Adolph L. Reed, Jr., *The Jesse Jackson Phenomenon* (New Haven: Yale University Press, 1986), 17–22. Reed argues that the Jackson campaign had an uncertain impact on registration, but a clear effect on turnout in the primaries. Stanley cautions the reader that Jackson's campaign is not the only possible explanation for the voter mobilization that took place.

47. William E. Nelson, Jr., "Cleveland: The Rise and Fall of the New Black Politics," in Preston, *The New Black Politics*, 200–201. Thomas F. Pettigrew estimates overall turnout of registered voters in the Stokes election for both races at "over 70%," and for the Hatcher election that same year at "well over 80%"; Thomas F. Pettigrew, "When a Black Candidate Runs for Mayor: Race and Voting Behavior," in Harlan Hahn, ed., *People and Politics in Urban Society*, Urban Affairs Annual Reviews 6 (Beverly Hills, Calif.: Sage Publications, 1972), 97, 100.

48. Tate, *From Protest to Politics*, 81.

49. Preston, "The Election of Harold Washington," 160.

50. Carol M. Swain, *Black Faces, Black Interests: The Representation of African Americans in Congress* (Cambridge: Harvard University Press, 1993), 131.

51. The 1994 voting-age population was calculated from *Statistical Abstract of the U.S.: 1996*, 286; black turnout from Ladd, *America at the Polls*, 159.

52. Connelly, "The Numbers: Portrait of the Electorate." Whether the difference between the 8.5 percent in 1994 and the 10 percent (no more precise figure is given) in 1996 is statistically significant cannot be determined from the information supplied by Ladd and Connelly, but it seems doubtful.

53. Joint Center for Political and Economic Studies, *Black Elected Officials A National Roster: 1976, 6th edition* (Washington, D.C.: Joint Center for Political and Economic Studies, 1977), 6, xxxv.

54. Joint Center, *Black Elected Officials: 1993*, 247–248.

55. National Conference of Black Mayors, *Program of 22nd Annual Convention*.

56. Gerald David Jaynes and Robin M. Williams, Jr., eds., *A Common Destiny: Blacks and American Society*, National Research Council (Washington, D.C.: National Academy Press, 1989), 62–63; *Statistical Abstract of the U.S.: 1996*, 44–46.

57. This is true whether the setting is majority- or minority-black. Thus, in 1983, Harold Washington got 99 percent of Chicago's black vote; 95 percent of New York's African-American electorate went for David Dinkins in 1993; Freeman Bosley, Jr., got 93 percent of the vote in St. Louis's predominantly black wards that same year. None of those cities had a black majority. On Chicago, see Kleppner, *Chicago Divided*, 218;

on New York, Peter Applebome, "Mayoral Elections: Results Hint at Secondary Role for Race," *New York Times,* 4 November 1993, A24; on St. Louis, Joe Holleman, "Mayoral Vote Reflects Divisions," *St. Louis Post-Dispatch,* 8 April 1993, 1A.

58. Peter Applebome, "Racial Divisions Persist 25 Years After King Killing," *New York Times,* 4 April 1993, 16.
59. Ze'ev Chafets, *Devil's Night and Other True Tales of Detroit* (New York: Vintage, 1991), 179.
60. Applebome, "Mayoral Elections: Results."
61. Holleman, "Mayoral Vote Reflects Divisions."
62. On this point, see James M. Vanderleeuw, "A City in Transition: The Impact of Changing Racial Composition on Voting Behavior," *Social Science Quarterly* 71 (June 1990), 332. Vanderleeuw argues that "incumbency affects electoral outcomes by providing the officeholder with increased voter support and, relatedly, reduced competition. The vote in contests with an incumbent, then, is expected to be less racially divided than the vote in open-seat elections." Furthermore, "black mayoral incumbents typically encounter less resistance among white voters in their reelection attempts." Since "blacks have traditionally been a highly cohesive voting group, and in biracial contests . . . tend to bloc vote to a greater extent than do whites," there is more "racial crossover voting for black incumbents than for white incumbents." See also Charles S. Bullock III, "Racial Crossover Voting and the Election of Black Officials," *Journal of Politics* 46 (1984) 243–244: "Incumbents attract more crossovers than do challengers or candidates for open positions. . . . Black incumbents poll almost half of the white vote . . . , while black challengers and contestants for open seats average 18.5 pecent white crossovers."
63. Greg Freeman, "A Modern Tale of Two Cities," *St. Louis Post-Dispatch,* 22 September 1992, 1C.
64. Alan Bernstein, "Dallas Sets Pace for the Notion of a Black Houston Mayor," *Houston Chronicle,* 14 May 1995, 30.
65. Calculated from the list of mayors in National Conference of Black Mayors, *Program of 22nd Annual Convention* and demographic data from Courtenay M. Slater and George E. Hall, eds., *Places, Towns, and Townships: First Edition, 1993* (Lanham, Md.: Bernan Press, 1993).
66. R. H. Melton, "Wilder's Demographic Strategy Led to Win," *Washington Post,* 12 November 1989, A1.
67. Thomas B. Edsall, "A Big Day for Black Politicians," *Washington Post National Weekly Edition,* 13–19 November 1989, 6.
68. Coleman Warner, "Racial Concerns Swung Key Votes," *New Orleans Times-Picayune,* 6 March 1994, A1.
69. Those fliers may have had a marked impact on the level of racial polarization. Just two weeks before the election, polls showed the white candidate with nearly 20 percent of black voters; Warner, "Racial Concerns."
70. As University of Rochester political scientist Harold Stanley points out, such a definition allows plaintiffs to find polarization in every jurisdiction in which whites and blacks do not vote identically—even when the majority of blacks and nonblacks support the same candidate. It's too sweeping a definition. At the very least, polarization should mean majorities of black and nonblack voters backing different candidates, not simply preferring the same candidate but with different levels of enthusiasm. See Harold W. Stanley, "A Report on Polarization and Political Participation," submitted in the case of *NAACP v. Austin,* April 14, 1994, 2–3. Moreover,

racially polarized voting is not necessarily a sign of something wrong; whites and blacks can back different candidates for legitimate political reasons.

71. Michael Barone, "Why Don't Blacks Run in White Districts?" *Washington Post,* 23 November 1984, A26.

72. As a *New York Times* reporter wrote a few months before Dinkins's unsuccessful bid for reelection in 1993, "race helped elect Dinkins in the first place—and anxieties about depriving him of his job may ultimately help keep him in office." Todd S. Purdum, "Buttoned Up," *New York Times Magazine,* 12 September 1993, 45.

73. Sam Roberts, "Race and Politics: Issues that Most Still Sidestep," *New York Times,* 19 July 1993, B3.

74. "Dinkins campaigned as the man who could heal racial wounds after Koch's abrasive 12-year tenure, and his candidacy gathered steam after the August 23 slaying of a black teenager in Brooklyn's predominantly white Bensonhurst section"; Howard Kurtz, "Dinkins Vows to Resist 'Reactionary Republican,' " *Washington Post,* 14 September 1989, A3. "In 1989, Mr. Dinkins was elected Mayor as much to heal as to lead." Sam Roberts, "Given New York Today, Could Anyone Lead it?" *New York Times,* 29 December 1991, sec. 4, p. 10. The 23 August racially motivated slaying was that of Yusif Hawkins in Brooklyn's predominantly white Bensonhurst section, discussed further in chap. 17.

75. *Economist,* 24 October 1992, 25. Freeman Bosley, Jr., elected in 1993 as the first black mayor of St. Louis, seems also to have benefited from the desire of some whites to vote for an African American. As one Democratic committeeman put it (speaking after the March primary), some whites "would say simply that it's time for St. Louis to have a black mayor. That clearly played a part." Tim O'Neil, "White Votes Gave Edge to Bosley," *St. Louis Post-Dispatch,* 4 March 1993, 1A.

76. Michael K. Frisby, "Blacks, Money, and Politics," *Focus* 20 (August 1992), 3–4.

77. Juan Williams, "Carolina Gothic," *Washington Post Magazine,* 28 October 1990, 21; Kenneth Terrell, "Support for Helms' Rival Pours Into North Carolina, *New Orleans Times-Picayune,* 4 August 1996, A19; Nancy E. Ronan, "Gantt Has Twice Helms' War Chest," *Washington Times,* 23 October 1996, A4.

78. Stephen Casmier et al., "Black Mayors Expanding Their Ranks," *St. Louis Post-Dispatch,* 7 March 1993, 1A.

79. Sam Howe Verhovek, "Dallas Is First Big Texas City to Elect a Black to Be Mayor," *New York Times,* 8 May 1995, 11.

80. Reynolds Farley, *The New American Reality: Who We Are, How We Got There, Where We Are Going* (New York: Russell Sage Foundation, 1996), 270.

81. Richard Stengel, "Riding the Backlash," *Time,* October 16, 1995, 70.

82. Ben Wattenberg, "In the Realm of Race, the Trend Is to Blend," *Baltimore Sun,* 29 November 1996, 27A.

83. Quoted in Martin Kilson, "Problems of Black Politics: Some Progress, Many Difficulties," *Dissent* 36 (Fall, 1989), 529.

84. Charles Bullock, "Minorities in State Legislatures," in Gary F. Moncrief and Joel A. Thompson, eds., *Changing Patterns in State Legislative Careers* (Ann Arbor: University of Michigan Press, 1992), 39–58.

85. Michael Abramowitz, "P.G.'s Political Shift," *Washington Post,* 18 February 1994, A1.

86. Dana Milbank, "Cleveland's Mayor Shuns Black Themes to Court White Votes," *Wall Street Journal,* 11 October 1993, 1.

87. Rice, White, and Bosely all challenged the scope of court-ordered busing programs in their campaigns for mayor. Thomas B. Edsall, "Conflicting Trends Seen in Whites' Willingness to Vote for Blacks," *Washington Post,* 19 December 1993, A27.

88. Chafets, *Devil's Night*, 177.

89. Rogers Worthington, "Black Voters Look Beyond Race Politics," *Chicago Tribune*, 7 November 1993, 21.

90. Peter Applebome, "Mayoral Elections: Results."

91. Ronald Smothers, "Councilman's Victory in Atlanta Mayoral Runoff Signals New Era," *New York Times*, 25 November 1993, A16; Edsall, "Conflicting Trends."

92. On the reparations issue, see Lena Williams, "Group of Blacks Presses the Case for Reparations for Slavery," *New York Times*, 21 July 1994, B10.

93. Philip D. Duncan and Christine C. Lawrence, *Congressional Quarterly's Politics in America, 1996* (Washington, D.C.: CQ Press, 1995), 682.

94. Calculations for black members of the House of Representatives were made from data in Michael Barone and Grant Ujifusa, *The Almanac of American Politics, 1996* (Washington, D.C.: National Journal, 1996); data on mayors from National Conference of Black Mayors, *Program of 22nd Annual Convention;* demographic information from Courtenay M. Slater and George E. Hall, eds., *1996 County and City Extra: Annual Metro, City, and County Data Book* (Lanham, Md.: Bernan Press, 1996).

95. David Hedge, James Button, and Mary Spear, "Accounting for the Quality of Black Legislative Life: The View from the States," *American Journal of Political Science* 40 (February 1996), 82–98, suggests that black legislators "who represent white majority and more affluent districts frequently share a common political base and political profile with many of their white colleagues" (94).

96. "Voting Integration," *Wall Street Journal*, 2 December 1996, A20. Before the elections civil rights leaders had issued dire predictions that these redistricting decisions would dramatically reduce black representation in Congress, because black candidates could not win without black-majority districts, claims that proved entirely misguided. For further discussion, see chap. 16.

97. Southern whites have been drifting into the Republican Party for some time, as their voting in presidential elections indicates. "Not since [Lyndon B.] Johnson's presidential campaign have a majority of white southerners voted Democratic, and only once since then—in Carter's 1976 candidacy—has a Democratic nominee won as much as 45 percent of the white vote"; Earl Black and Merle Black, *Politics and Society in the South* (Cambridge: Harvard University Press, 1987), 269–270. Subsequent contests have done nothing to alter the pattern. Michael Dukakis got 32 percent of the southern white vote in 1988. Despite the fact that Bill Clinton is a son of the South, he did only slightly better than Dukakis, receiving 34 percent in 1992 and 36 percent in 1996; Connelly, "The Numbers."

98. Quoted in Jones and Clemons, "A Model of Racial Crossover Voting," 133. In the 1996 campaign, black incumbents in majority-white southern districts that had previously been majority-black were, as one reporter put it, "polishing their moderate credentials"; Charles Oliver, "Goodbye to Minority Districts," *Investor's Business Daily*, 27 August 1996, 1. Forced to court white voters, as a consequence of Supreme Court decisions that declared unconstitutional their former, racially gerrymandered districts, they ran much more centrist campaigns, and were rewarded with victories in each case.

99. Thomas B. Edsall, "Amid Detroit's Climate of Change, Rep. Conyers Faces a Challenge," *Washington Post*, 27 June 1994, A6.

100. Karen Schneider, "Blacks Face New Hurdles in Congress: Caucus Now More Diverse, Divided," *Houston Chronicle*, 12 September 1993, A21.

101. Howard Fineman, " 'Malcolms' and Dealmakers," *Newsweek*, 5 July 1993, 26.

102. *Almanac of American Politics, 1996*, 1096.

103. Kenneth J. Cooper, "The Black Caucus's Odd Man In," *Washington Post*, 1 September 1993, C1. The "eat but not meet" phrase is Cooper's. No Democratic member of the CBC objected to the effort to bar Franks from the deliberations of the caucus, and Cleo Fields, considered one of its more conservative members, introduced the motion to expel him. David Bositis, *The Congressional Black Caucus in the 103rd Congress* (Washington, D.C.: Joint Center for Political and Economic Studies, 1993), 24.

104. "Open Letter" to Rep. Gary Franks from Rep. William Clay, July 25, 1993, obtained from Congressman Clay's office.

105. Wattenberg, "In the Realm of Race."

106. Bositis, *Blacks and the 1996 Republican National Convention*, 14.

107. Hugh Pearson, *The Shadow of the Panther* (Reading, Mass.: Addison-Wesley, 1994), 63.

108. Eric Harrison, "Race Emerges as Top Chicago Mayoral Issue," *Los Angeles Times*, 28 February 1989, 14.

109. Dana Milbank, "Cleveland's Mayor Shuns Black Themes to Court White Votes," *Wall Street Journal*, 11 October 1993, 1; Jack E. White, "Bright City Lights," *Time*, 1 November 1993, 30.

110. Larry Rohter, "Ethnic Politics Fall by Wayside in a Miami Race," *New York Times*, 1 November 1993, B9.

111. Edsall, "Conflicting Trends"; Edward Walsh, "As Detroit Prepares to Elect His Successor, Mayor Weighs In," *Washington Post*, 24 October 1993, A6.

112. Connelly, "The Numbers."

113. Surveys by the Joint Center indicate that by 1992 only 8.8 percent of African Americans were calling themselves Republicans, and that number has not changed since then. In 1996 the percentage was 8.7, with 4 percent solidly in the GOP camp and 4.7 percent leaning in that direction; Bositis, *Blacks and the 1996 Republican National Convention*, 2.

114. Bositis, *Blacks and the 1996 Republican National Convention*, 5, and table 3. The Thad Cochran story is in Milton Coleman, "Dixie Rising: Changing Politics of the South," *Washington Post*, 21 May 1986, A1; see also Michael Barone and Grant Ujifusa, *The Almanac of American Politics, 1984* (Washington, D.C.: National Journal, 1984). 640.

115. Peter Kerr, "Pleased with Past, Kean Looks to Future," *New York Times*, 12 January 1990, B1.

116. Bositis, *Blacks and the 1996 Republican National Convention*, table 3.

117. Robert Woodson, "The Independent Black Voter," *Wall Street Journal* 15 November 1993, A12.

118. "Race in the United States," *Public Perspective* 7 (February–March 1996), 32.

119. Bositis, *Blacks and the 1996 Republican National Convention*, 5–7.

120. "Race in the United States," 26–27.

121. This is a topic to which we will return, but it should be noted that there is much polling data documenting white opposition to preferences. See, e.g., the surveys taken by the Gallup Organization, 1977–1991, in which the same question on preferential treatment was repeated six times, summarized in Seymour Martin Lipset, *American Exceptionalism: A Double-Edged Sword* (New York: Norton, 1996), 125. See also Paul M. Sniderman and Thomas Piazza, *The Scar of Race* (Cambridge: Harvard University Press, 1993), 97–104; and "Race in the United States," 26. Furthermore, the Joint Center's 1996 survey indicated very high (62.8 percent) support among

blacks for revising affirmative action programs; only 27.5 percent wanted them maintained in their current form. Bositis, *Blacks and the 1996 Democratic National Convention,* 6.

122. Michael C. Dawson, *Behind the Mule: Race and Class in African-American Politics* (Princeton: Princeton University Press, 1994), 55 and passim.

123. Rep. Melvin L. Watts (D-N.C.), quoted in Harvey Berkman, "Black Caucus Tackles Crime," *National Law Journal,* 28 March 1994, 1.

124. *Time*/CNN survey, 13–14 July 1994, in George J. Church, "Threat and Defiance," *Time* 25 July 1994, 20.

125. On the Daley, Rendell, and other related mayoral stories, see Jim Sleeper, "The End of the Rainbow," *New Republic,* 1 November 1993, 20.

126. On Rep. Lindy Boggs, see Swain, *Black Faces, Black Interests,* 170–179. New Jersey representative. Peter Rodino, Jr., a member of the U.S. House of Representatives for twenty years, also held on to his office running in a district that became majority black and in which a serious black candidate ran in 1986 (see Swain, *Black Faces* 179–189).

127. Coleman Warner, "Race Still Influences Mayoral Vote," *New Orleans Times-Picayune,* 27 January 1994, A1.

128. The differences in the skin color of Jefferson and Barthelemy and their supporters was frequently mentioned in the press. See, for example, Frances Frank Marcus "Morial Rival Wins Mayoral Race," *New York Times,* 3 March 1986, B6.

129. Georgia A. Persons, "Black Mayoralties and the New Black Politics: From Insurgency to Racial Reconciliation," in Persons, ed., *Dilemmas of Black Politics: Issues of Leadership and Strategy* (New York: HarperCollins, 1993), 51–53.

130. Rene Sanchez, "Barry Evokes Chasm in Electorate," *Washington Post,* 18 July 1994, 1. In 1989 the journalist Juan Williams predicted that "the defining fear of the '90s [was] more likely to be economic than racial, with affluent blacks, whites and browns fearing the poverty, violence, drugs and disease of impoverished blacks, whites and browns"; Williams, "The '90s: The New Mosaic of Race," *Washington Post,* 19 November 1989, D1. Politics, he was suggesting, will soon be shaped more by social class than by race. This seems to be happening, albeit gradually.

131. Malcolm Gladwell, "New York City Plays the New Ethnic Politics," *Washington Post,* 15 October 1993, 1. The "post black-white" phrase quoted by Gladwell comes from political scientist John Mollenkopf.

132. Jonathan P. Hicks, "For Black Politicians, a Debate of Strategy and Leadership," *New York Times,* 2 February 1994, B1.

133. Grimshaw, *Bitter Fruit,* chap. 9.

134. So called by Carl Holman, leader of the Urban Coalition; cited in Kilson, "Problems of Black Politics," 529.

135. Jay Mathews, "Massive Conservative Turnout Cited; Race Discounted as Factor in Defeat of Bradley," *Washington Post,* 6 November 1982, A2. How Willie Brown could have considered Deukmejian a WASP is difficult to grasp. As an American of Armenian background, Deukmejian was neither Anglo-Saxon nor Protestant. For another claim that it was Bradley's race that cost him the election, see Thomas E. Cavanagh, *Race and Political Strategy: A JCPS Roundtable* (Washington, D.C.: Joint Center for Political Studies, 1983), 33.

136. Much of this discussion is based on Jack Citrin, Donald Philip Green, and David O. Sears, "White Reactions to Black Candidates: When Does Race Matter?" *Public Opinion Quarterly* 54 (1990), 74–96, and Thomas F. Pettigrew and Denise A. Alston,

Tom Bradley's Campaigns for Governor: The Dilemma of Race and Political Strategies (Washington, D.C.: Joint Center for Political Studies, 1988). Pettigrew and Alston, however, see much more racism in the outcome than we do—or than Citrin et al. do. See also: Kilson, "Problems of Black Politics," 529.

137. In the wake of his defeat Deukmejian's campaign aide said it was "important that people understand that Tom Bradley lost because he's a liberal, not because he's black"; Mathews, "Massive Conservative Turnout." In part, Bradley was seen as a liberal because—as Pettigrew and Alston note—he could not avoid some degree of identification with the incumbent Democratic governor, Jerry Brown. His support of handgun control also cast him as soft on crime.

138. Sniderman and Piazza, *The Scar of Race*, passim. It is precisely the distinction between policy positions and hostility to blacks that got lost in the Pettigrew and Alston analysis of the role of racism in Bradley's defeat.

139. Todd S. Purdum, "Supporting Dinkins, Clinton Worries about Role of Race," *New York Times*, 27 September 1993, A1. Lani Guinier was quick to concur. If the mayor "were a white Democrat," she said in early October, the loyalty of voters "to the party and to the broader social agenda he represents would be more important than his race." Sam Roberts, "Metro Matters" column, *New York Times*, 4 October 1993, B7.

140. Applebome, "Mayoral Elections: Results."

141. Edsall, "Conflicting Trends."

142. Felicia R. Lee, "For Blacks, Loss by Dinkins Spotlights Painful Racial Gap," *New York Times*, 4 November 1993, 1.

143. A. M. Rosenthal, "On Civil Respect," *New York Times*, 26 October 1993, A21.

144. Jim Sleeper, "The End of the Rainbow," *New Republic*, 1 November 1993, 20. See also: Sleeper, "Attn: Gray Ladies and Guilty White Libs," *New York Daily News*, 28 September 1993, 8.

145. For the claim that Dinkins had been held to an unfairly high standard, see, for instance, Felicia R. Lee, "In St. Albans, Black Voters Express Faith in Dinkins," *New York Times*, 25 October, 1993, B3; Sam Roberts, "Mayor Dinkins: Every Day a Test," *New York Times Magazine*, 7 April 1991, 28; and Felicia Lee, "The 1993 Elections: The Supporters: Viewing a Verdict as Based on Race," *New York Times*, 3 November 1993, B2.

146. Edsall, "Conflicting Trends."

147. Mark Shields, "Abortion: So Long, 'Silver Bullet' Theory," *Washington Post*, 31 July, 1990, A25; Peter Applebome, "Road Still Rough for Black Candidates," *New York Times*, 14 August 1990, A16.

148. On the reliance of voters on cues such as race, see Bullock, "Racial Crossover Voting," 239–240.

149. Paul Glastris, "Second City Race Baiting," *U.S. News & World Report*, 2 January 1989, 36.

150. Ronald Smothers, "Ex-Mayor's Son Wins."

151. Michael Barone and Grant Ujifusa, *The Almanac of American Politics, 1992* (Washington, D.C.: National Journal, 1992), 914; "Gantt's Day," *Economist*, 9 June 1990, 29; Paul Taylor, "In North Carolina a Try at Leaping Another Hurdle," *Washington Post*, 5 May 1990 A4. "The real killer" is Barone's and Ujifusa's description of the third ad.

152. Mark Russell and Richard Perry, "Race a Subtle Election Issue," *Cleveland Plain Dealer*, 2 December 1992, 8A.

153. The argument has become a staple not only of political and media discourse, but in

the academy as well. "The new rules governing public discussion of race require not the abandonment of racism, but rather that appeals to prejudice be undertaken carefully, through indirection and subterfuge. . . . Racial codewords make appeals to prejudice electorally profitable even when . . . prejudice is officially off limits," Donald R. Kinder and Lynn M. Sanders *Divided by Color: Racial Politics and Democratic Ideals* (Chicago: University of Chicago Press, 1996) 223 have written. See also Martin Gilens, " 'Race-Coding' and White Opposition to Welfare," *American Political Science Review* 90 (September 1996), 593–604. Gilens, like Kinder and Sanders and others in the "symbolic racism" school, claims that discussions of welfare, crime, affirmative action, and the like constitute an illegitimate subterranean discourse on race. If you don't take the liberal view on these matters, you are by definition racist. We find this assumption obnoxious.

154. The ads and the press response are perceptively analyzed in Carl M. Cannon, "The Return of Willie Horton, *Forbes Media Critic,* Summer 1996, 49–55. Kinder and Sanders, *Divided by Color,* 233–239, discuss the Willie Horton ad at some length from a different vantage point. The phrase "rhetorical wink" is that of another scholar quoted by Kinder and Sanders, 223.

155. Ralph Ellison, *Invisible Man* (New York: Random House, 1952; New York: Vintage Books 1972), 3.

156. George Gallup, Jr. and Frank Newport, "Americans Ignorant of Basic Census Facts," *Gallup Poll Monthly,* no. 294 (March 1990), 2.

157. The 1994 survey was based on replies from 2,313 employers; Stuart Silverstein, "Workplace Diversity Efforts Thrive Despite Backlash," *Los Angeles Times,* 2 May 1995, 1.

158. Kevin Fedarko, "The Joyful Power Broker," *Time,* April 15, 1996, 68.

159. "He moved between the still largely separate black and white worlds with seeming ease and grace," the *New York Times* reported after his death; Steven A. Holmes, "So Visible, but from Which Angle?," 7 April 1996, E1.

160. Sniderman and Piazza, *The Scar of Race,* 8.

CHAPTER 12: WITH ALL DELIBERATE SPEED

1. Sam Fulwood III, *Waking from the Dream: My Life in the Black Middle Class* (New York: Anchor Books, 1996), 25.

2. The court-ordered and voluntary programs together added up (in the survey) to 78 percent of all districts and 72 percent of large districts currently having racial-balancing/desegregation programs in place; Council of Urban Boards of Education, *Still Separate, Still Unequal? Desegregation in the 1990s* (Alexandria, Va.: National School Boards Association, 1995), 19, 26–27.

3. "NAACP Sets Advanced Goals," *New York Times,* 18 May 1954, 16, as quoted in Gerald N. Rosenberg, *The Hollow Hope: Can Courts Bring About Social Change?* (Chicago: University of Chicago Press, 1991), 43.

4. Christine H. Rossell, "The Convergence of Black and White Attitudes on School Desegregation Issues During the Four Decade Evolution of the Plans," *William and Mary Law Review* 36 (January 1995), 615.

5. Rosenberg, *Hollow Hope,* 50.

6. Hugh Davis Graham, *The Civil Rights Era: Origins and Development of National Policy* (New York: Oxford University Press, 1990), 372–373.

7. J. Harvie Wilkinson III, *From Brown to Bakke: The Supreme Court and School Integration, 1954–1978* (New York: Oxford University Press, 1979), 102.
8. Andrew Kull, *The Color-Blind Constitution* (Cambridge: Harvard University Press, 1992), 173.
9. *Brown v. Board of Education of Topeka* [*Brown II*], 349 U.S. 294 (1955) at 300–301.
10. Kull, *Color-Blind Constitution*, 173.
11. Ibid. The student-assignment law adopted by Alabama in 1955 declared that it would be unduly "disruptive" for local authorities to assign pupils "according to any rigid rule of proximity of residence," and specified sixteen other factors that school boards were to consider in making individual assignments; Mark V. Tushnet, *Making Civil Rights Law: Thurgood Marshall and the Supreme Court, 1936–1961* (New York: Oxford University Press, 1994), 244.
12. Zora Neale Hurston, "Court Order Can't Make Races Mix," *Orlando Sentinel*, 11 August 1955, reprinted in Hurston, *Folklore, Memoirs, and Other Writings* (New York: Library of America, 1995), 956–958. Hurston was not the only eminent black intellectual to express skepticism about school integration. For a similar view two decades earlier, see W. E. B. Du Bois, "Does the Negro Need Separate Schools?" *Journal of Negro Education* 4 (July 1935), 328–335.
13. November 1955 poll, in George H. Gallup, *The Gallup Poll: Public Opinion, 1935–1971* (New York: Random House, 1972), 1402. It is tempting to dismiss this evidence on the grounds that blacks in the South in those days were probably unwilling to state their true opinions to pollsters, most of whom were white. Although this hypothesis is plausible, it cannot be squared with the results of another Gallup poll just a few weeks later, which showed that 82 percent of southern blacks approved of a recent Interstate Commerce Commission ruling against segregation in transportation; Gallup, *Gallup Poll*, 1402. If so many southern blacks were willing to admit to holding views about segregated transportation that were contrary to those of most southern whites, it is hard to see why they would dissemble when questioned about segregation in education. The roughly fifty-fifty split in opinion among southern blacks is probably as accurate as most polling results.
14. Robert A. Margo, *Race and Schooling in the South, 1880–1950: An Economic History* (Chicago: University of Chicago Press, 1990), 24–28, 54–56, 64–67.
15. The U.S. Commission on Civil Rights seemed resentful when it reported in 1967 that "improvements in facilities and equipment . . . in all-Negro schools in some districts" had helped to "discourage Negroes from selecting white schools"; cited in *Green v. School Board of New Kent County*, 391 U.S. 430, n. 5. Presumably the commission would have preferred that as little as possible be spent on the traditionally black schools, so that parents would be more strongly motivated to enroll their children in the formerly white schools. Gary Orfield, a scholar writing from the same vantage point, noted in 1969 that in more than one hundred districts with freedom-of-choice plans approved by a court, "community attitudes were so strong that not a single Negro student chose to enroll in any white school," and in "hundreds of others only an insignificant fraction" did so. Orfield attributed the negative attitudes of black parents toward integration to "fear" or "apathy"; Orfield, *The Reconstruction of Southern Education* (New York: Wiley, 1969), 120. How Orfield determined that black parents kept their children in black schools out of "fear" or "apathy" rather than out of a feeling that such schools would provide a better education for their children is not evident. Orfield was so sure of the superiority of integrated schools that he never entertained the latter possibility.

16. 377 U.S. 218 (1964).

17. Raymond Wolters, *The Burden of Brown: Thirty Years of School Desegregation* (Knoxville: University of Tennessee Press, 1984), pt. II.

18. 377 U.S. at 229.

19. Wilkinson, *From Brown to Bakke,* 102–105.

20. Rosenberg, *Hollow Hope,* 97–100.

21. Kull, *Color-Blind Constitution,* 177–181; Wilkinson, *From Brown to Bakke,* pp. 106–107. For a full discussion of the differences between the two sets of guidelines and the reasons for the shift, see Steven C. Halpern, *On the Limits of the Law: The Ironic Legacy of Title VI of the 1964 Civil Rights Act* (Baltimore: Johns Hopkins University Press, 1995), chap. 3.

22. The bizarre circumstances surrounding the promulgation of the 1965 guidelines did not inspire confidence that its authors were enforcing the law in a methodical and fair-minded manner. Guidelines that were supposed to inform local school boards how to proceed in conformity with the law were not officially released by the Department of Health, Education, and Welfare. Instead, they were published in an article by G. W. Foster, a law professor who worked as a consultant to HEW, in the March 20, 1965, issue of the *Saturday Review of Literature!* Amazingly, HEW never did decide to formally issue these guidelines with its imprimatur. Furthermore, the guidelines were never actually signed by President Johnson, as required by law. Although LBJ had given the 1964 act his full backing, leaving his signature off the controversial guidelines was thought to be a way of sheltering him from criticism from southern whites. This remarkable story is told in Halpern, *On the Limits of the Law,* 48–50.

23. 391 U.S. at 441; Halpern, *On the Limits of the Law,* 48–50. Fifteen percent of the county's blacks attended the formerly white school; they comprised 17 percent of the student body there, so 83 percent of the student body was white.

24. 391 U.S. at 437.

25. 391 U.S. at 437, n. 4, citing *Louisiana v. United States,* 380 U.S. 145 (1965) at 154.

26. Concurring opinion in *Missouri v. Jenkins* (1995), 132 L Ed.2d 63 at 103.

27. *Swann v. Charlotte-Mecklenburg Board of Education,* 402 U.S. 1 (1971).

28. 402 U.S. at 15.

29. 402 U.S. at 24.

30. 402 U.S. at 25. Involuntary busing was not the only tool used to racially balance the county's schools, but it was the most important element in the court order.

31. Rosenberg, *Hollow Hope,* 50.

32. Finis Welch and Audrey Light, *New Evidence on School Desegregation* (Washington, D.C.: U.S. Commission on Civil Rights Clearinghouse Publication 92, 1987), tables 8 and 9.

33. John Shelton Reed and Merle Black, "How Southerners Gave Up Jim Crow," *New Perspectives* 17 (Fall 1985), 15–19.

34. Earl Black and Merle Black, *Politics and Society in the South* (Cambridge: Harvard University Press, 1987), 200.

35. A few lower-court decisions involving segregation in the schools of northern cities like Kansas City, Cincinnati, and Gary, Indiana, were appealed to the Supreme Court in the 1960s, but the court found no constitutional issues in need of adjudication in northern jurisdictions without a history of de jure segregation, and it denied certiorari in those cases; Wilkinson, *From Brown to Bakke,* 341, n. 14.

36. Clark as quoted in Wolters, *Burden of Brown,* 5.

37. For the history of this "harm and benefit thesis" and an assessment of the relevant

empirical evidence, see David J. Armor, *Forced Justice: School Desegregation and the Law* (New York: Oxford University Press, 1995), chap. 2.

38. On the district court decision, see Kull, *Color-Blind Constitution*, 195–196.

39. *Keyes v. School District No. 1*, 413 U.S. 189 (1973); see also Kull, *Color-Blind Constitution*, 198–199.

40. 413 U.S. at 208.

41. 413 U.S. at 205.

42. 413 U.S. at 220–221, 225–226.

43. *Milliken v. Bradley*, 418 U.S. at 717 (1974).

44. 413 U.S. at 197–198.

45. Figures for 1973 from Justice White's dissent in *Milliken*, 418 U.S. at 765; 1993–1994 figures from U.S. Department of Education, *Digest of Educational Statistics: 1995* (Washington, D.C.: U.S. Government Printing Office, 1995), table 91.

46. Armor, *Forced Justice*, 38, 41.

47. Residents of the suburban districts that were included in the metropolitan plan ordered by the lower court had good reason to feel that they had not gotten a fair shake from the judge. In the first phase of the case, in which the issue was whether a constitutional violation had taken place, the suburbs were not allowed to offer evidence or argument. When, during the penalty phase of the proceeding, they were finally allowed to comment on the legal propriety of the metropolitan desegregation plan under consideration, they were given only a week to prepare their responses. The court appeared to have sentenced fifty-one suburban school districts without benefit of a trial. Further doubt about the fairness of the lower court was raised by the fact that the new superdistict created by the judge was to be governed by a four-person desegregation panel. Three of the four would be from the Detroit school board and only one from a suburban district. Detroit thus had a 75 percent representation on the governing body, even though Detroit's students comprised only 35 percent of the pupils in the new district; 418 U.S. at 730–733.

48. The minority in *Milliken* argued that an interdistrict remedy was justified because the villain in the piece was not only Detroit but the Michigan state government. Since all school districts in the state were subdivisions of the state, proof of culpability on the part of the state could logically justify a remedy that involved any or all of its school districts. The majority of the justices, though, were not persuaded that the evidence established that the Detroit Board of Education had been acting as a tool of the state when it pursued segregative policies. The argument turned on whether or not one thought that the state of Michigan had an "affirmative duty" to see to it that its subdivisions consistently acted to maximize racial integration in the schools.

49. 391 U.S. at 439.

50. Armor, *Forced Justice*, pp. 46–47; Wilkinson, *From Brown to Bakke*, 242–245.

51. Armor, *Forced Justice*, 49–50.

52. Howard Schuman, Charlotte Steen, and Lawrence Bobo, *Racial Attitudes in America: Trends and Interpretations* (Cambridge: Harvard University Press, 1985), 88–89.

53. Schuman et al., *Racial Attitudes*, 144–147. These are figures from the National Opinion Research Center. Polls by another leading organization, the Institute for Social Research, in 1972, 1974, 1976, and 1980 showed that only in 1976 did a majority of blacks (57 percent) approve busing. In the other three of these years, the results were 46 percent, 43 percent, and 49 percent. Not very impressive backing from a group in whose name the litigation that resulted in the busing orders was undertaken.

54. Ronald P. Formisano, *Boston Against Busing: Race, Class, and Ethnicity in the 1960s and 1970s* (Chapel Hill: University of North Carolina Press, 1991), 192.

55. The story is vividly told through the history of three families caught up in the struggle in J. Anthony Lukas, *Common Ground: A Turbulent Decade in the Lives of Three American Families* (New York: Knopf, 1985). For less of the human drama but more on the political and social context, see Formisano's *Boston Against Busing*.

56. Formisano, *Boston Against Busing*, 70.

57. Ibid., 75–83.

58. Ibid., 174.

59. Ibid., 198–199.

60. Rossell, "The Convergence of Black and White Attitudes," 634–635, 640.

61. Christine H. Rossell and Peggy Davis-Mullen, "A Proposal for Transitioning the Boston Public Schools from the Current Controlled Choice Desegregation Plan to Community/Neighborhood Schools," unpublished paper (Boston, 1994), table 1; Boston School Committee, *Boston Public Schools—School Profiles, 1994–1995* (Boston: City of Boston, 1995), 1. Figures for 1970 include Hispanics in the white population, while later ones are for non-Hispanic whites only. In 1970, though, Boston's Hispanic population was very small, so this would have little effect on the results. In this discussion we refer to non-Hispanic whites simply as whites, for simplicity's sake. It should not be forgotten, though, that most Hispanics in the United States consider themselves white, and are so classified by the Census Bureau; see the discussion in Stephan Thernstrom, "American Ethnic Statistics," in Donald L. Horowitz and Gerard Noiriel, eds., *Immigrants in Two Democracies; French and American Experience* (New York: New York University Press, 1992), 91, 98–100. For further evidence on Hispanic racial identification, see U.S. Bureau of the Census, Current Population Reports: Special Studies, P-23-182, *Exploring Alternative Race-Ethnic Comparison Groups in Current Population Surveys* (Washington, D.C.: U.S. Government Printing Office, 1992); U.S. Bureau of Labor Statistics, "A CPS Supplement for Testing Methods of Collecting Racial and Ethnic Information: May, 1995" (Washington, D.C.: U.S. Department of Labor, 1995); Peter Skerry, "Many American Dilemmas: The Statistical Politics of Counting by Race and Ethnicity," *Brookings Review*, Summer 1996, 36–39.

62. Rossell and Davis-Mullen, "A Proposal," table 1. Of course there were reasons other than busing for parents to abandon the Boston public schools. But fig. 1 of the Rossell paper suggests that busing greatly accelerated the pace of white dropout from the system. If, after the court order, non-Hispanic white enrollment in the Boston schools had continued to drop only at the rate it had fallen in the five years *before* the court order, there would have been about 37,000 white students left in the system in 1993, when in fact there were fewer than 12,000.

63. Abigail Thernstrom, *School Choice in Massachusetts* (Boston: Pioneer Institute for Public Policy Research, 1991), 16–17, 23–30, 57–58.

64. Rossell and Davis-Mullen, "A Proposal," 1. The 91 percent rule was arrived at when whites were 19 percent and minority pupils 81 percent of total enrollment. The system allows individual schools to have enrollments that deviate by 10 points but no more than 10 points from the citywide average. A school could thus be as much as 29 percent white or as little as 19 percent white—and thus 91 percent minority. Presumably the definition has changed again in response to the further decline in white enrollment.

65. Ibid., 12.

66. A busing proponent trying to make the case that the policy was not as unpopular as we argue here declares that "by the mid-1980s, the vast majority of both white and black families who had been undergoing busing for desegregation purposes reported that they were satisfied with the experience"; Gary Orfield, "School Desegregation After Two Generations," in Herbert Hill and James E. Jones, Jr., eds., *Race in America: The Struggle for Equality* (Madison: University of Wisconsin Press, 1993), 243. There is a glaring flaw in the reasoning here. This is a bit like administering a dangerous experimental drug to a thousand subjects, discovering that eight hundred of them died from it, and concluding that the drug worked well because "the vast majority" of the two hundred survivors felt that it was beneficial. In Boston and Denver white enrollment has fallen by 70–80 percent since the beginning of busing, and many middle-class blacks left as well. The studies Orfield refers to are not based on samples of all the people exposed to the stimulus of busing; they only inspect a sample of those who responded to the stimulus in a certain, distinctly atypical way— that is, by continuing to enroll their children in the city public schools.

67. "Denver Will Trade Busing for Neighborhood Schools," *New York Times,* 17 September 1995, 30; U.S. Department of Education, *Digest of Educational Statistics: 1995* (Washington, D.C.: U.S. Government Printing Office, 1995), table 91.

68. Formisano, *Boston Against Busing,* 230–232.

69. Ibid., 72.

70. Pam Belluck, "Case Story in Brooklyn," *New York Times,* 23 September 1996, B1.

71. Welch and Light, *New Evidence on School Desegregation,* 23, 45.

72. Brian C. Mooney, "Bus Costs Ride an Upward Spiral," *Boston Globe,* 21 May 1991, 13.

73. "Off the Buses," *Economist,* 29 January 1994, 30.

74. To call this a measure of their "expected share" is slightly oversimplified, because the population figures are for persons of all age groups, not just children of school age. It is possible that disproportionate numbers of the whites living in Boston or the other cities in table 3 are single persons or married couples without children. The index figure is affected by this factor as well as by parental decisions to use private schools. That whites without children of school age are more drawn to Boston than those with children, though, likely has a lot to do with perceptions of the quality of the public schools.

75. 413 U.S. at 199.

76. The Bureau of the Census classifies persons of Hispanic origin as a separate group, but not as a racial group. Tables containing data on Hispanics always specify that "persons of Hispanic origin may be of any race." Most Hispanics in fact identify as white; see the sources cited in n. 61 above. However, many do not fit comfortably into the two-race model we are criticizing here.

77. *Digest of Educational Statistics: 1995,* 60.

78. It may seem as if we are indulging ourselves in an argument reductio ad absurdum, but a desegregation order that currently governs the San Francisco public schools does distinguish specific national origin groups in precisely this fashion. The decree included a maximum cap of 45 percent enrollment for any group at a given school. In special schools, like the city's elite Lowell High School, the cap was 40 percent for any group. To keep Chinese-American students from taking more than 40 percent of the places, they were required to have higher scores on the entrance examination than students from other groups; Elaine Woo, "Caught on the Wrong Side of the Line?" *Los Angeles Times,* 13 July 1995, A1. A legal challenge from Chinese-

American parents led to some relaxation of the quotas, but the issue remains alive. Chinese-American parents are currently complaining that the desegregation decree maintains an unconstitutional "scheme of racial classification," and are insisting on "the right to be judged as an individual"; Caroline Hendrie, "S.F. Reforms Put on the Line in Legal Battle," *Education Week,* 11 December 1996, 1, 30.

79. It is regrettable that similar tabulations are not available for concentrations of African Americans in schools 90 percent or more black, rather than "minority." Nearly all-black schools arguably would have a quite different character than ones that are 40 percent Hispanic, say, 30 percent black, and 20 percent Asian.

80. Randall Kennedy, "The State, Criminal Law, and Racial Discrimination," *Harvard Law Review* 104 (April 1994), 1273, n. 79.

81. Peter Schmidt, "Policies Using Race to Assign Pupils Attacked," *Education Week,* 27 September 1995, 1. See also Michael Dabney, "Parents Sue School District over Racial Quota System," *Philadelphia Tribune,* 15 September 1995, 3A.

82. Lisa Frazier, "P.G. Braces for Major Change in Schools," *Washington Post,* 24 June 1996, B1. On the P.G. County story, see also Lisa Frazier, "Some Black Parents in P.G. Say Busing is Hurting Children," *Washington Post,* 30 October 1995, 1; Lisa Frazier, "P.G. Struggle with Racial Plan," *Washington Post,* 2 April 1996, C1; Lisa Frazier, "Pr. Georges' Schools Vote to End Racial Quotas," *Washington Post,* 19 June 1996, 1; Lisa Frazier, "School Desegregation Faces Review in P.G.," *Washington Post,* 19 July 1996, 1; Lisa Frazier, "P.G. Magnet Quotas Suspended," *Washington Post,* 10 August 1996, 1.

83. *Board of Ed. of Oklahoma City Pub. Schools v. Dowell,* 498 U.S. 237, 249 (1991).

84. 498 U.S. at 243, 247–248.

85. *Freeman v. Pitts* (1992), 118 L Ed 2d 108 at 134. Justice Clarence Thomas did not participate in the decision, since he arrived on the Court after the other members had already heard the oral argument.

86. Frazier, "P.G. Braces for Major Change."

87. Frazier, "Some Black Parents in P.G."

88. Lisa Frazier, "P.G. Brakes on Busing Plan," *Washington Post,* 24 August 1995, 1.

89. "Cleveland Board Adopts Plan for Reducing Busing," *Education Week,* 4 August 1993, 4. A similar plan to end busing was drawn up in Prince Georges County, but derailed due to lack of funding for the improved schools. See Frazier, "P.G. Brakes on Busing Plan."

90. Peter Schmidt, "40 Years After Brown, Integration Is an Elusive Goal," *Education Week,* 25 May 1994, 1.

91. Katherine Kerstin, "NAACP Lawsuit Could Force a Proven Failure on Schools," *Minneapolis Star Tribune,* 26 September 1995, 13A.

92. This list of amenities is taken from *Missouri v. Jenkins* (1995), 132 L Ed 63 at 74–75; "The Cash Street Kids," *Economist,* 28 August 1993, 23.

93. Appendix to the petition to the Supreme Court for certiorari, quoted in *Missouri v. Jenkins,* 132 L Ed at 75.

94. Dennis Farney, "Integration Is Faltering in Kansas City Schools as Priorities Change," *Wall Street Journal,* 26 September 1995, 1.

95. *Missouri v. Jenkins,* 132 L Ed at 77.

96. Caroline Hendrie, "Racial Quotas Are Ordered for Rockford," *Education Week,* 19 June 1996, 1, 17.

97. Peter Schmidt, "Judge Orders Steps to Spur Integration in Phila.," *Education Week,* 7 December 1994, 7.

98. 132 L Ed 2d 63 at 96.
99. Dennis Farney, "Integration Is Faltering in Kansas City Schools as Priorities Change," *Wall Street Journal,* 26 September 1995, 1.
100. Michael deCourcy Hinds, "Judge Orders Desegregation of Schools in Philadelphia," *New York Times,* 5 February 1994, 6.
101. See Robert Hanley, "N.A.A.C.P. Ousts Official for Criticism," *New York Times,* 18 July 1996, B1.
102. James Brooke, "Court Says Denver Can End Forced Busing," *New York Times,* 17 September 1995, 16.

CHAPTER 13: SKILLS, TESTS, AND DIVERSITY

1. Shelby Steele, "The Race Not Run," *New Republic,* October 7, 1996, 23. See also Steele, *The Content of Our Character: A New Vision of Race in America* (New York: St. Martin's, 1990), passim, where he spells out the argument at much greater length. We have slightly restated Steele's point, without, we hope, distorting it.
2. National Center for Education Statistics, *Digest of Educational Statistics: 1995,* NCES 95–029 (Washington, D.C.: U.S. Department of Education, 1995), 150.
3. Debra J. Saunders, "More Dumb Teachers," *San Francisco Chronicle,* 6 June 1996, 7. See also, for quite an extensive list of the test questions: editorial, "Can You Pass the State Teacher Exam? Test Yourself," *San Francisco Chronicle,* 19 September 1996, A19.
4. Albert Shanker, "Will CBEST Survive?" *New York Times* (in space purchased by the American Federation of Teachers), 7 March 1996, E7.
5. Joseph Perkins,"There Is No Bias in Requiring the Basics," *Rocky Mountain News,* 25 February 1996, 36A.
6. Nanette Asimov, "Beyond Teacher Test Controversy," *San Francisco Chronicle,* 8 February 1996, A1.
7. The answer became clear in December 1996, when the Oakland Alliance of Black Educators pressured the Oakland school board to declare that the native tongue of African Americans is not English but "ebonics," a recently concocted label for what in the past was described as "black English." (The term comes from a mating of "ebony" with "phonics.") The board complied with this demand; Peter Applebome, "School District Elevates the Status of Black English," *New York Times,* 20 December 1996, A18. Although intended mainly as a ploy to acquire federal bilingual education money for black pupils in the district, this assertion has disturbing cultural implications we will comment on later in this chapter. Whatever the merits of the claim with respect to lower class inner-city pupils from Oakland, it seems quite a stretch to suggest that African-American *teachers* in California live in families in which the sentence "He be rich" is regarded as proper English. And even if they do, that is hardly a sufficient excuse for being unable to *read* English at the tenth-grade level.
8. David Hill, "Minorities Challenge Basic Skills Test for Teachers," *Sacramento Bee,* 6 June 1996, FO1. This article suggests that the California Teachers Association later came to accept the CBEST, but we have found that information nowhere else.
9. Letter by Steve Phillips, president of the San Francisco Board of Education and Dr. Leland Yee, board member, *San Francisco Chronicle,* 17 February 1996, A18.
10. John Chandler, "Cal State to Consider Tightening Admissions," *Los Angeles Times,* 17 July 1995, A3.

11. David Hill, "Minorities Challenge Basic Skills Test for Teachers," *Sacramento Bee,* 6 June 1996, FO1.

12. Shanker, "Will CBEST Survive?"

13. Richard Lee Colvin, "Suit Challenges Basic Skills Test for Teachers as Biased," *Los Angeles Times,* 5 February 1996, A1.

14. Dan Walters, "Logic Clear in Decision on Skills Test for Teachers," *Fresno Bee,* 21 September 1996, A3. If the California plaintiffs had been victorious and the tests had been struck down, similar suits were likely to be brought in other states. In Florida, 63 percent of blacks but only 12 percent of whites failed the basic skills test for teacher licensing upon their first try during the 1980s, an even bigger racial gap than in California. In Texas, 27 percent of whites but 72 percent of blacks did not pass the state examination for admission to educational school. In New York, 65 percent of blacks and 17 percent of whites flunked the general-knowledge section of the teacher-licensing examination in 1987; Thomas Toch, *In the Name of Excellence: The Struggle to Reform the Nation's Schools, Why It's Failing, and What Should be Done* (New York: Oxford University Press, 1991), 164. For a table giving pass rates on teacher competency tests in ten states for the year 1982–1983, all of which show a large racial gap, see Gerald David Jaynes and Robin M. Williams, Jr., eds., *A Common Destiny: Blacks and American Society* (Washington, D.C.: National Research Council, National Academy Press, 1989), 364. The authors cite evidence that black performance on these tests improved dramatically in some states after teacher-training institutions made an effort to address the problem (363).

15. *Digest of Educational Statistics: 1995,* 74, 163; National Center for Education Statistics, *The Condition of Education: 1996* (Washington, D.C.: U.S. Government Printing Office, 1996), 160. Some of the shift, though, is arguably due to the proliferation of "special education," bilingual, and other special programs that tend to have smaller than average classes.

16. *Digest of Educational Statistics: 1995,* 380.

17. See, for example, Jonathan Kozol, *Savage Inequalities* (New York: Crown, 1991.)

18. National Center for Education Statistics, *Disparities in Public School District Spending, 1989–1990,* NCES 95–300 (Washington, D.C.: U.S. Government Printing Office, 1995), 15.

19. *Digest of Educational Statistics: 1995,* table 91; David D. Boaz, "How Much Does D.C. Really Spend Per Pupil?" *Washington Post,* 3 August 1995, A31.

20. U.S. Department of Education, National Center for Educational Statistics, *Youth Indicators 1988: Trends in the Well-Being of American Youth* (Washington, D.C.: U.S. Government Printing Office, 1988), 52.

21. A 1994 review of New York City's schools concluded that students were apparently promoted "solely on the basis of their age." Any youth who reached the age of 15 was placed in high school, even if he or she could only read at the third-grade level; Ray Kerrison, "We're Promoting Kids Who Can't Even Read Their Diplomas," *New York Post,* 28 December, 1994, 4. In 1996, Chicago's new school administration announced that it was abandoning its previous policy of not holding any child back a grade more than once between kindergarten and grade 8; Michael Martinez, "Schools May Get Tough on Promotions," *Chicago Tribune,* 27 March, 1996, 1.

22. Paul E. Peterson and Jay R. Girotto, "Do Hard Courses and Good Grades Enhance Cognitive Skills?" Occasional Paper 96–2, April 1996, Program in Educational Policy and Governance, Harvard University, 5, 25.

23. Theodore R. Sizer, *Horace's Hope: What Works for The American High School* (Boston: Houghton Mifflin, 1996), 158–159.

24. Language of a resolution passed by the NEA in 1995, as quoted in Thomas Toch, "The Case for Tough Standards," *U.S. News & World Report*, April 1, 1996. 36.

25. Sara Mosle, "Scores Count," *New York Times Magazine*, 8 September 1996, 42.

26. Richard J. Herrnstein and Charles Murray, *The Bell Curve: Intelligence and Class Structure in American Life* (New York: Free Press, 1994). The most judicious critical assessment of this volume, in our view, was provided by James J. Heckman in "Cracked Bell," *Reason*, March 1995, 49–55.

27. This is the central point of Richard J. Murnane and Frank Levy, *Teaching the New Basic Skills: Principles for Educating Children to Thrive in a Changing Economy* (New York: Free Press, 1996). For an influential earlier analysis that also stressed the failure of our schools to produce enough graduates with the cognitive skills demanded in this phase of economic development, see W. B. Johnston and A. Packer, *Workforce 2000: Work and Workers for the Twenty-First Century* (Indianapolis: Hudson Institute, 1987). We comment further on the link between race, cognitive skills, and income in chap. 15.

28. *Digest of Educational Statistics: 1995*, 115.

29. Ibid.

30. Sol H. Pelavin and Michael Kane, *Changing the Odds: Factors Increasing Access to College* (New York: College Entrance Examination Board, 1990), 10–11; National Center for Education Statistics, *The Condition of Education: 1995* (Washington, D.C.: U.S. Government Printing Office, 1995), 42.

31. For an even more negative reading of the NAEP evidence and the argument that spending more money on schooling usually cannot be shown to have improved student performance, see Erik Hanushek, "School Resources and Student Performance," in Gary Burtless, ed., *Does Money Matter? The Effect of School Resources on Student Achievement and Adult Success* (Washington, D.C.: Brookings Institution Press, 1996), 43–73. Of course it can always be argued, as Larry Hedges and Rob Greenwald do in this volume (77–80) that the positive results we might have expected from increased spending and reduced class size were offset by other unfavorable social trends, such as the decline in the time mothers spend with their children because of their increased employment, and the rise in the number of homes with no father present.

32. Between 1971 and 1980 the racial gap in reading scores declined by 12 points for students aged 9, and by 7 points for those aged 13. In mathematics the gap narrowed by 6 points for 9-year-olds between 1973 and 1982, and by 12 points for 13-year-olds. In science, between 1970 and 1982 the gap dropped by 15 points for students aged 9, and by 8 points for those aged 13.

33. National Center for Educational Statistics, *Trends in Academic Progress: Achievements of American Students in Science, 1969–70 to 1990, Mathematics, 1973 to 1990, Reading, 1971 to 1990, and Writing, 1984 to 1990* (Washington, D.C.: U.S. Government Printing Office, 1991), 287, 333. A similar, though weaker, pattern appeared among whites. Those reading at the 5th percentile gained 13 points, and those at the 25th percentile 8 points. Those at the 95th percentile, by contrast, lost 7 points. Whatever was benefiting the most disadvantaged black students in those years also was helping disadvantaged whites perform better.

34. National Center for Education Statistics, *NAEP 1994 Reading Report Card for the Nation and the States* (Washington, D.C.: U.S. Department of Education, 1996), 27, 48.

35. Looking at the actual scores given in Table 1 may make it seem that this claim is

exaggerated. The mean reading score for African Americans fell only from 274 to 266 between 1988 and 1994, and the math score fell just 3 points between 1990 and 1994. These seemingly small changes are in fact large ones, given the way the test scores are scaled. A few points on the scale can amount to a difference of a full grade level or more.

36. Published by the Education Trust, Washington, D.C.

37. Peter Applebome, "Minorities Falling Behind in Student Achievement," *New York Times,* 29 December 1996, A12.

38. David J. Armor, *Forced Justice: School Desegregation and the Law* (New York: Oxford University Press, 1995), 92–98.

39. David J. Armor, "Why Is Black Educational Achievement Rising?" *Public Interest* 108 (Summer 1992), 65–80.

40. It was prescient of Marshall S. Smith and Jennifer O'Day, writing before the 1990 NAEP results were in, to have suggested that "the achievement gap may increase again in the future, rather than continuing its steady decline"; see their essay, "Educational Equality: 1966 and Now," in D. Verstegen and J. Ward, eds., *Spheres of Justice in Education: The 1990 American Education Finance Association Yearbook* (New York: HarperCollins, 1991), 85.

41. We have no NAEP tests for these earlier decades, though. It is certainly possible that the decline in black poverty in the 1940s, 1950s, and 1960s was accompanied by learning gains on the part of African-American children. On the other hand, the racial gap registered in the 1965 Coleman report and the first NAEP tests was so wide that it is difficult to imagine that it could have been much wider in earlier decades.

42. U.S. Bureau of the Census, Current Population Reports, P-60-189, *Income, Poverty, and Valuation of Noncash Benefits: 1994* (Washington, D.C.: U.S. Government Printing Office, 1996), table B-6.

43. The large body of recent research that demonstrates this is summarized in Sara McLanahan and Gary Sandefur, *Growing Up with a Single Parent: What Hurts, What Helps* (Cambridge: Harvard University Press, 1994).

44. Smith and O'Day argue that expanding opportunities for preschool education were particularly important; "Educational Equality: 1966 and Today," 80. An intricate analysis of the evidence from NAEP, the National Longitudinal Survey of Youth, and the National Education Longitudinal Survey concludes that "some combination of increased public investment in education and social programs and changing social policies aimed at equalizing educational opportunities" were important causes of minority gains; David W. Grissmer et al., *Student Achievement and the Changing Family,* MR-488-LE (Santa Monica, Calif.: Rand Corporation, 1994), 100. The authors unfortunately concentrated on differences between scores on the earliest tests and those in 1990, and failed to notice the backsliding that began in the late 1980s.

45. Janet Currie and Duncan Thomas, "Does Head Start Make a Difference?" *American Economic Review* 85 (June 1995), 341–361; Mark Pitsch, "Chapter 1 Fails to Spur Gains, Data Indicate," *Education Week,* 24 November 1993. Armor, "Why is Black Educational Achievement Rising?" 75–77, refers to studies of Chapter 1 programs that are a little more positive, but not dramatically so.

46. *The Condition of Education: 1996,* 98, 255. For further discussion of this change, see Diane Ravitch, *National Standards in American Education* (Washington, D.C.: Brookings Institution, 1995), 94–97.

47. Barbara Lerner, "Aim Higher," *National Review,* 6 March 1995, 57. Peterson and

Girotto, "Do Hard Courses and Good Grades Enhance Cognitive Skills?" is an excellent case study of three Iowa high schools that provides an affirmative answer to the question posed in its title. Students learn more, they demonstrate, when they take harder courses and put more effort into their studies.

48. One bit of evidence on the question of whether courses were in fact dumbed down: A 1993 study by the Wisconsin Center for Education Research examined math and science courses in eighteen schools in six states that raised educational standards and found that the contents remained as rigorous after the standards were increased; described in Jeffrey Mirel and David Angus, "High Standards for All? The Struggle for Equality in the American High School Curriculum, 1890–1990," *American Educator* 18 (Summer 1994), 40.

49. This educational culture has been explored in a number of excellent books, the most recent of which is E. D. Hirsch, Jr., *The Schools We Need and Why We Don't Have Them* (New York: Doubleday, 1996).

50. Ibid., 43, 54.

51. Diego Ribadeneira, "Data: 40% of Hub Seniors Can't Read at 8th Grade Level," *Boston Globe*, 16 December 1989, 1; Brian C. Mooney and Renee Loth, "Silber Explains School Board Attack," *Boston Globe*, 4 May 1990, 25.

52. V. Dion Haynes and Michael Martinez, "City Schools Dropping Iowa Skills Tests," *Chicago Tribune*, 15 February 1996.

53. *Debra P. v. Turlington*, 564 F. Supp. 177 (1983); aff'd 11th Circuit, 730 F2nd 1405.

54. Bob Zelnick, *Backfire: A Reporter's Look at Affirmative Action* (Chicago: Henry Regnery, 1996), 268–269. In Boston, too, in 1996, city-wide academic goals were once again set. Under the new guidelines third-graders, for instance, were expected to recite memorized poems as well as add and subtract basic fractions. But while the standards, according to the *Boston Globe*, "triggered doubt among teachers about whether they [were] achievable," they were not legally challenged and have remained in place. Karen Avenoso, "New School Standards Stir Doubts," *Boston Globe*, 12 March 1996, 1.

55. Quoted in Mark Tushnet, *Making Civil Rights Law: Thurgood Marshall and the Supreme Court, 1936–1961* (New York: Oxford University Press, 1994), 225.

56. Hugh Davis Graham, *The Civil Rights Era: Origins and Development of National Policy* (New York: Oxford University Press, 1990), 149–150.

57. *Griggs v. Duke Power Company*, 401 U.S. 427, 430 (1971); this case is discussed at length in chap. 15.

58. *Hobson v. Hansen*, 269 F. Supp. 401, 485 (D.D.C. 1967).

59. Myron Lieberman, *Public Education: An Autopsy* (Cambridge: Harvard University Press, 1993), 188.

60. *Larry P. v. Riles*, 495 F. Supp. 926 at 957 (1979).

61. 495 F. Supp. at 959.

62. Lieberman, *Public Education*, 188.

63. Charles V. Willie, "The Unfair Effects of Standardized Testing on Blacks and Other Minorities," in Judah L. Schwartz and Katherine A. Viator, eds., *The Prices of Secrecy: The Social, Intellectual, and Psychological Costs of Current Assessment Practice* (Cambridge: Harvard Graduate School of Education, Educational Technology Center, 1990), 24.

64. 495 F. Supp. at 958.

65. In 1986, Judge Peckham extended his ban on IQ tests to their use in placing black children in special education classes; by that date the EMR track had been abolished.

But when a group of *black* parents challenged that order, he reversed his own ban in a 1992 decision—over the objection of the state of California, which continued to call the tests racially biased; Mark Walsh, "Appeals Court Upholds Black Parents' Rights to Learn Child's I.Q.," *Education Week,* 12 October 1994, 12. By 1992, however, Peckham himself had backed away from the racial bias argument. In granting the black parents relief, the judge claimed that the essence of his original ruling had not been that IQ tests were innately discriminatory but that in that instance they had been used to place disproportionate numbers of black children in a particular "dead-end" program; *Crawford v. Hoenig,* No. C-89–0014-RFP, "Memorandum and Order," August 1992, 23.

66. Portland Public Schools, *African-American Baseline Essays* (Portland, Oreg.: Portland Public Schools, 1987; rev. ed., Spring 1990), LA-32. For background, see David Nicholson, "Afrocentrism and the Tribalization of America," *Washington Post National Weekly Edition,* 8–14 October 1990, 23; Leon Jaroff, "Teaching Reverse Racism," *Time,* 4 April 1994, 74. For further discussion, see our section on "Afrocentric Delusions" later in this chapter.

67. Carol Chomsky, "Language and Language Arts Assessment," in Schwartz and Viator, *The Prices of Secrecy,* 74.

68. D. Monty Neill and Noe J. Medina, "Standardized Testing: Harmful to Educational Health," *Phi Delta Kappan* 70 (September 1988), 691–692.

69. Applebome, "School District Elevates the Status of Black English"; Jacob Heilbrum, "Speech Therapy," *New Republic,* 20 January 1997, 17. As we write, there is great uncertainty about the educational implications of this decision in Oakland. One of the arguments for deciding officially that "African Americans have a different language system" was that it might somehow help in devising better strategies for teaching them standard English. But the board's resolution was mainly aimed at "destigmatizing" black English and encouraging teachers to "respect" the Ebonics "language" spoken by their students; "Black English Plan Baffles Some Students in Oakland," *New York Times,* 21 December 1996, A8. The resolution even claimed that "studies" had shown that "African Language systems are genetically based," which presumably means having melanin in your skin makes it only natural for you to say "I be tired" and "He axed me a question"; Joseph Boyce, "Oakland's Insult to Blacks and Equality," *Wall Street Journal,* 26 December 1996, A6. Teachers who criticize students for using constructions like this will be vulnerable to the charge that they failed to show the proper "respect" for the "native language" of the students. It seems likely that the policy will make it even more difficult to develop a command of standard English. Mainstream black leaders, including Jesse Jackson and Maya Angelou, have denounced the idea of "making slang a language," and the U.S. Department of Education has rejected the idea that Ebonics is a distinct language eligible for bilingual education funds; Eric Stirgus, "Al and Jesse: Black Slang is No Way to Speak," *New York Post,* 23 December 1996, 6; James Bennet, "Administration Rejects Black English as a Second Language," *New York Times,* 25 December 1996, A22; Cathy Young, "They Be All Wrong about 'Ebonics,' " *Detroit News,* 24 December 1996, A7.

70. Janice Hale-Benson, in Gordon L. Berry and Joy K. Asamen, eds., *Black Students: Psychosocial Issues and Academic Achievement* (Newbury Park, Calif.: Sage Publications, 1989), 91. It is astonishing to hear anyone seriously suggest that American schools today place undue emphasis upon academic subjects, and that young people need more encouragement to develop their athletic and musical skills. It might have

been true of American schools a century ago; it might be true of the schools in Japan today. But in the present-day United States?

71. Dirk Johnson, "Milwaukee Creating 2 Schools Just for Black Boys," *New York Times,* 30 September 1990, 1.

72. Mark A. Uhlig, "Learning Style of Minorities to Be Studied," *New York Times,* 21 November 1987, 29.

73. Neill and Medina, "Standardized Testing," *Phi Delta Kappan,* 692. The assumption that African-American children learn differently pervades the widely used Portland *Baseline Essays,* discussed later in this chapter.

74. Carol Innerst, "Definition of 'Intelligence' Grows in the Name of Diversity," *Washington Times,* May 28, 1990, 1A.

75. Quoted in Florence King, "The Goading of America," *Chronicle,* May 1991, 26.

76. Innerst, "Definition of 'Intelligence.' "

77. This is certainly the implication contained in Peckham's approving citation of the Asa Hilliard testimony arguing that blacks and whites disagree over the meaning of common words. For the views of other critics, see, e.g., Michelle Guido, "Californians Debate Halting Use of IQ Test," *Chicago Tribune,* 18 August 1991, C5.

78. Nicholson, "Afrocentrism and the Tribalization of America," 23.

79. Guido, "Californians Debate Halting Use."

80. Jeannie Oakes, *Keeping Track: How Schools Structure Inequality* (New Haven: Yale University Press, 1985), 11.

81. Kenneth J. Cooper, "Exams Opposed over Potential Harm to Minorities," *Washington Post,* 12 June 1991, A 21.

82. *Larry P. v. Riles,* 343 F. Supp. 1306, 1310 (1972).

83. 495 F. Supp. at 944 (1979).

84. Lieberman, *Public Education,* 188.

85. Calculated from the College Entrance Examination Board, *1995 National Ethnic/Sex Data,* unpaginated.

86. Michael T. Nettles and Arie L. Nettles, eds., *Equity and Excellence in Educational Testing and Assessment* (Boston: Kluwer Academic Publishers, 1995), 354.

87. Howard Odum, *Social and Mental Traits of the Negro: Research into the Conditions of the Negro Race in Southern Towns; A Study of Race Traits, Tendencies, and Prospects* (New York: Columbia University Press, 1910).

88. FairTest: National Center for Fair and Open Testing, "K-12 Testing Fact Sheet," brochure (Cambridge, Mass.: n.d.).

89. *Locked In/Locked Out: Tracking and Placement Practices in Boston Public Schools* (Cambridge: Massachusetts Advocacy Center, 1990), 11.

90. The charge has been made by many commentators. See, e.g., Eva Wells Chun, "Sorting Black Students for Success and Failure: The Inequity of Ability Grouping and Tracking," in "Black Education: A Quest for Equity and Excellence," a special edition of the *Urban League Review* 11 (Spring 1987/Winter 1987–1988), 93–106.

91. 343 F. Supp. at 1309–1310.

92. ABC News, 4 September 4 1990. The reporter quoting Oakes was Bill Blakemore. See also Chun, "Sorting Black Students," 100: "Even high-achieving blacks tend to be placed in low-ability groups or tracks, while low-achieving white, middle-class students tend to be placed in high tracks or ability groups."

93. *Washington Post,* 14 February 1990, A3.

94. Jonathan Eig, "Black Parents Decry Remedial Program," *Dallas Morning News,* 19 February 1991, TK.

95. Asian Americans make up almost identical proportions of the public school populations in Boston and New York—9.5 percent in Boston, 9.6 percent in New York. But Asian Americans are only 17 percent of the student body at Boston Latin and 51 percent of the students at the New York equivalent of Boston Latin—Stuyvesant High School. One reason for this puzzling difference is that there are no racial quotas at Stuyvesant, and blacks and Hispanics together—72 percent of total city enrollment —have only 9 percent of the places. At Boston Latin there are nearly four times as many African-American and Hispanic students, thanks to the quota, and some of the places they take up would otherwise have gone to Asian Americans in all likelihood; "The Long Arm of the Tongs," *Newsday*, 12 May 1994, 4; Boston School Committee, *Boston Public Schools—School Profiles, 1994–1995* (Boston, 1995), 1, 240.

96. Adrian Walker and Jordana Hart, "Menino Denies Offering Deal to Drop School Lawsuit," *Boston Globe*, 16 August 1995, A1, A25.

97. *McLaughlin v. Boston School Committee*, Civil Action No. 95-11803-WAG, "Complaint," 1.

98. *McLaughlin v. Boston School Committee*, "Memorandum and Order for a Preliminary Injunction," August 22, 1996, B1. At the end of 1996, the Boston School Committee—presumably to avert a class action suit—agreed to admit to Boston Latin 154 white or Asian-American students who, like Julia McLaughlin, would have been accepted but for the racial quota. Another 145 would be admitted to the Boston Latin Academy, another examination school, on the same grounds; Karen Avenoso, "Payzant: Admit 300 More to Top Schools," *Boston Globe*, 19 December 1996, A1. However, the system adopted in place of the 35 percent quota will admit only half of the Boston Latin applicants on the basis of merit, and will allocate the other half of the entrance spots in accord with the racial composition of the applicant pool. It is likely that it, too, will be legally challenged; Tim Cornell, "McLaughlin Eyes Another Suit vs. Exam School Plan," *Boston Herald*, 20 December 1996, 22.

99. Diane Ravitch. "Multiculturalism: E Pluribus Plures," *American Scholar* 59 (Summer 1990), 339.

100. Ibid., 340–341.

101. The best brief critical introduction to Afrocentrism is John J. Miller, ed., *Alternatives to Afrocentrism* (Washington, D.C.: Center for the New American Community, Manhattan Institute, 1994). For an extended critique by a classicist, see Mary Lefkowitz, *Not Out of Africa: How Afrocentrism Became an Excuse to Teach Myth* (New York: Basic Books, 1996). The list of cities comes from C. Vann Woodward, "The Disuniting of America: Reflections on a Multicultural Society," *New Republic*, 15 July 1991, 41. It would be much longer today, but no one has compiled an up-to-date one.

102. David C. Butty, "Afrocentrism Generates Mixed Results in Detroit and Debate Across the Nation," *Detroit News*, 19 May 1996; Charles Hurt, "Afrocentric Education: Kids Are Learning, but Can They Read and Write?" *Detroit News*, 23 April 1996. *Education Week*, 16 October 1996, 29, reported that Detroit had "three full-fledged African-centered academies and 18 other schools with African-centered themes of one sort or another."

103. For a perceptive account of the nineteenth-century and early-twentieth century origins, see Wilson Jeremiah Moses, *The Golden Age of Black Nationalism, 1850–1925* (New York: Oxford University Press, 1978). The next chapter of the story is well told in James O. Young, *Black Writers of the Thirties* (Baton Rouge: Louisiana State University Press), chap. 4. Carter G. Woodson, the founder of the *Journal of Negro History* and of National Negro History Month, was an ardent Afrocentrist; see, for

example, his *Miseducation of the American Negro* (Washington, D.C.: Associated Publishers, 1933). Kwame Anthony Appiah, "Illusions of Race," chap. 2 of *In My Father's House: Africa in the Philosophy of Culture* (New York: Oxford University Press, 1992), is an excellent critique of romantic racialism, focused on W. E. B. Du Bois but with broader implications.

104. Sari Horowitz, "Unlicensed College Provided D.C. Afrocentric Training," *Washington Post,* 14 August 1993, 1.

105. Sari Horowitz, "Participants Laud Afrocentric Program, Blast Media," *Washington Post,* 23 September 1993, B1; Sari Horowitz, "District to Expand Afrocentric Classes," *Washington Post,* 25 August 1994, B1.

106. Sari Horowitz, "From K to 12, Afrocentrism Has Made the Grade in Atlanta," *Washington Post,* 17 October 1993, B1; Gary Putka, "Curricula of Color," *Wall Street Journal,* 1 July 1991, 1.

107. Portland Public Schools, Foreword, *Baseline Essays,* 11. Why Portland, a city that was only 7.7 percent black at the time of the most recent census? A judicial desegregation order started Portland down the Afrocentric road. In response to the ruling, the school district hired a "multicultural coordinator," who in turn retained Georgia State University professor Asa Hilliard, known for his Afrocentric views; Hilliard selected the authors of the seven essays. Chester E. Finn, Jr., "Not Out of Africa," *Commentary,* June 1996, 71.

108. Walter F. Rowe, "School Daze: A Critical Review of the 'African-American Baseline Essay' for Science and Mathematics," *Skeptical Inquirer,* September-October, 1995, 27–32. For another sharp and persuasive demolition, see Irving M. Klotz, "Multicultural Perspectives on Science Education: One Prescription for Failure," *Phi Delta Kappan* 75 (November 1993), 266–269.

109. Portland Public Schools, *Baseline Essays,* S-13, S-21, S-86. An instructive example of the author's scientific logic is that to support the proposition that Egyptians flew around in gliders he quotes an engineer who remarked that "if the Egyptians could build pyramids and dam the Nile, it's not too difficult to imagine them having the ingenuity to make gliders out of papyrus and glue" (S-53). If it's "not too difficult to imagine," then it must be true.

110. Ibid., S-14.

111. David Nicholson, "D.C.'s African-Center Curriculum; What Will the New Program Really Teach?" *Washington Post,* 23 September 1990, B4.

112. Rowe, "School Daze," 32.

113. Speech by Jeffries at Second Annual Conference on Afrocentric Education, Atlanta, 1 November l990; tape recording in possession of the authors.

114. Molefi Kete Asante, *Afrocentricity* (Trenton, N.J.: Africa World Press, 1988), vii–viii.

115. Ibid., 81, 87, 89.

116. The infamous anti-Semitic tract *The Protocols of the Elders of Zion* was featured in the book display at the Second Annual Conference on Afrocentric Education, which Abigail Thernstrom attended.

117. Andrew Sullivan, "Racism 101," *New Republic,* 26 November 1990, 18.

118. Butty, "Afrocentrism Generates Mixed Results"; Hurt, "Afrocentric Education."

119. Butty, "Afrocentrism Generates Mixed Results."

120. Jerry Adler, "African Dreams," *Newsweek,* 23 September 1991, 42.

121. Butty, "Afrocentrism Generates Mixed Results."

122. Debra Viadero, "A School of Their Own," *Education Week,* 16 October 1996, 27.

123. Horowitz, "From K to 12, Afrocentrism Has Made the Grade," B1.

124. Ralph Ellison, *The Collected Essays of Ralph Ellison* (New York: Modern Library, 1995), 164.

125. C. Vann Woodward, "The Disuniting of America: Reflections on a Multicultural Society," *New Republic*, 15 July 1991, 41.

126. Political scientist James Jennings quoted in Diego Ribadeneira, "Tracking Cheats Needy Students in City, Study says," *Boston Globe*, 27 March 1990, 1.

127. *Morgan v. Hennigan*, 379 F. Supp. 410, 460.

128. Thomas Grillo, "Effort in Hiring Minority Teachers on the Cape Praised," *Boston Globe*, 30 June 1996, 39.

129. Joanna Richardson, "Talent Scouts," *Education Week*, 17 May 1995, 23.

130. Ronald F. Ferguson, "Paying for Public Education: New Evidence on How and Why Money Matters," *Harvard Journal on Legislation* 28 (Summer 1991), 465–498.

131. Data on teachers and principals from National Center for Education Statistics, *Schools and Staffing in the United States: A Statistical Profile, 1993–94*, NCES 96-124 (Washington, D.C.: U.S. Government Printing Office, 1996), 48. Black share of college graduates aged 40–44 in 1993 from U.S. Bureau of the Census, Current Population Reports, P-20-476, *Educational Attainment in the United States: March 1993 and 1992* (Washington, D.C.: U.S. Government Printing Office, 1994), table 1. Racial composition of public school population from National Center for Education Statistics, *Digest of Educational Statistics: 1995*, 60.

132. National Center for Education Statistics, *Schools and Staffing*, 50.

133. Bob Hotakainen, "Incentives Urged to Attract Minority Students to State," *Minneapolis Star Tribune*, 14 August 1991, 1.

134. Richardson, "Talent Scouts," 25.

135. Tracie Reddick, "Labels Stick," *Tampa Tribune*, 15 May 1995, 1.

136. Rene Sanchez, "Urban Schools Face Teacher Shortage, Study Finds," *Washington Post*, A14.

137. Kenneth J. Cooper, "Seeking Better Teachers," *Washington Post Education Review*, 18 November 1990, 20–21.

138. G. Pritchy Smith, Martha Miller, and Janice Joy, "A Case Study of the Impact of Performance-Based Testing on the Supply of Minority Teachers," *Journal of Teacher Education*, July-August 1988, 45–53.

139. Quoted in Sullivan, "Racism 101," 18.

140. National Center for Education Statistics, *Digest of Educational Statistics: 1995*, 275.

141. Oversight Hearings on School Discipline Before the Subcommittee on Elementary, Secondary, and Vocational Education of the Committee on Education and Labor, House of Representatives, 98th Cong., 2nd sess., 23 and 24 January 1984, 19, 30, testimony of Gary D. Gottfredson.

142. Teacher Victimization graph in *Education Week*, 7 April 1993, 7; National Center for Education Statistics, *The Condition of Education: 1993* (Washington, D.C.: U.S. Government Printing Office, 1993), 115. In another 1991 survey city teachers reported feeling quite safe during the instructional hours, but 15 percent said they felt unsafe after school—triple the rate for suburban teachers. The Council of the Great City Schools, *National Urban Education Goals: Baseline Indicators, 1990–91* (Washington, D.C.: Council of Great City Schools, 1992), 66.

143. Jonetta Rose Barras, "Students Threaten, Bring Arms, Teachers Say," *Washington Times*, 13 February 1993, A9. The survey results were issued in a document by the Washington Teachers' Union entitled "Report from the Trenches."

144. The study was the January 1978 report to Congress entitled *Violent Schools–Safe*

Schools, published by the National Institute of Education. For a careful analysis of the findings, see Jackson Toby, "Crime in American Public Schools," in Nathan Glazer, ed., *The Public Interest on Crime and Punishment* (Cambridge, Mass.: Apt Books, 1984), 219–243.

145. Phone conversation with Jackson Toby, 23 June 1993.

146. Gerald Grant, *The World We Created at Hamilton High* (Cambridge: Harvard University Press, 1988); Robert Sam Anson, *Best Intentions: The Education and Killing of Edmund Perry* (New York: Vintage, 1987), 46.

147. Jackson Toby, "Violence in School," in National Institute of Justice, *Research in Brief* (Washington, D.C.: U.S. Department of Justice, 1983), 3. Black students may well have been more than 29 percent of the public school population, of course; that figure is not given. But in 1974–1975 many urban whites were still to be found in big-city public schools; busing and white flight were just beginning.

148. Jackson Toby, "The Victims of School Violence," in Timothy F. Hartnagel and Robert A. Silverman, eds., *Critique and Explanation: Essays in Honor of Gwynne Nettler* (New Brunswick, N.J.: Transaction Books, 1986), 177–179.

149. National Center for Education Statistics, *Schools and Staffing, 1993–94,* 12, 112.

150. National Center for Education Statistics, "How Safe Are the Public Schools: What Do Teachers Say?" *Issue Brief,* April 1996.

151. Douglas Martin, "Teachers Strive to Rise Above the Grip of Despair," *New York Times,* 29 February 1992, 25.

152. Patricia Mangan, "Parents Demand End to School Violence," *Boston Herald,* 26 March 1992, 1.

153. DeNeen L. Brown, "Simple Things Turn Violent When Students Move to New School," *Washington Post,* 1 October 1993, A1.

154. David Montgomery, "Area Teachers Losing More Time to Fighting Violence," *Washington Post,* 25 April 1994, 1.

155. Emily Sachar, *Shut Up and Let the Lady Teach: A Teacher's Year in a Public School* (New York: Simon & Schuster, 1991), 150.

156. Ibid., 67, 69, 75, 98, 148. Sachar's experience was not unique. Cf. DeNeen L. Brown, "It's About Respect, Say Students Who Curse Teachers," *Washington Post* 18 April 1993, 1.

157. Sachar, *Shut Up,* 52.

158. See Jackson Toby, "To Get Rid of Guns in Schools, Get Rid of Some Students," *Wall Street Journal,* 3 March 1992, A14.

159. Douglas Martin, "Teachers Strive to Rise Above the Grip of Despair," *New York Times,* 29 February 1992, 25.

160. National Center for Education Statistics, *The Condition of Education, 1975–1990* (Washington, D.C.: U.S. Department of Education, 1991), 116. For similar figures a few years later, see "Oversight Hearings on School Discipline," 19, 30, testimony of Gary D. Gottfredson. It is striking that the standard reference works published annually by the U.S. Department of Education—the *Digest of Educational Statistics,* and *The Condition of Education,* used to include evidence on this point, but no longer do so. The explanation is not that the problem has been solved.

161. Jean Johnson and Steve Farkas, *Getting By: What American Teenagers Really Think About Their Schools: A Report from Public Agenda* (New York: Public Agenda, 1997), 31.

162. Quoted in Jackson Toby, "The Politics of School Violence," *Public Interest,* 116 (Summer 1994), 42–43.

163. Ibid., 43.

164. Michael Casserly, Executive Director of the Council of Great City Schools to Albert Shanker, 2 October 1995; Shanker to Casserly, 10 October 1995; Ellen Roe, Chair of the Board of the Council of Great City Schools and other officers to Shanker, 15 October 1995; Shanker to Casserly, 5 December 1995; copies made available to authors by Mr. Shanker.

165. William Raspberry, "Safety, Discipline, Standards," *Washington Post* 1 September 1995, A23.

166. Donna V. Ford, *Reversing Underachievement Among Gifted Black Students: Promising Practices and Programs* (New York: Teachers College Press, 1996), 87.

167. Oversight Hearings on School Discipline, 100, testimony of Gary L. Bauer, U.S. Department of Education.

168. Lynn Olson, "Atlanta Plans Shows Benefits, Drawbacks of Private School Choice," *Education Week*, 11 November 1992, 1.

169. Raspberry, "Safety, Discipline, Standards."

170. Nick Ravo, "Court Overturns Suspension of Bronx Student with Handgun," *New York Times*, 18 September 1996, B1; editorial, "Keeping Guns Out of School," *New York Times*, 21 September 1996, 18.

171. Lynda Richardson, "Student Anonymity Fuels the Truancy," *New York Times*, 19 June 1994, 23.

172. Study by Julian Betts, Professor of Economics at the University of California, San Diego; Jonathan Marshall, "How Homework Really Pays Off," *San Francisco Chronicle*, 20 May 1996, C 2.

173. For example, on the 1992 International Assessment of Educational Progress, American 9- and 13-year-olds ranked behind their counterparts in South Korea, Taiwan, Russia, and France in both math and science; National Center for Education Statistics, *Condition of Education: 1996*, 88–91. Ravitch, *National Standards in American Education*, 83–89, briefly summarizes the large literature on this. For evidence on time spent doing homework and watching television, by students in other countries, see Lawrence Steinberg, *Beyond the Classroom: Why School Reform Has Failed and What Parents Need to Do* (New York: Simon & Schuster, 1996), 19, and National Center for Education Statistics, *Condition of Education; 1993*, 356–357.

174. Jon Jeeter, "Alarm Over TV Time Highlights Viewing Habits of Black Children," *Washington Post*, 23 June 1996, A8.

175. National Center for Education Statistics, *Digest of Educational Statistics: 1995*, 138.

176. Steinberg, *Beyond the Classroom*, 86–87, 156–157, 184–186.

177. Ibid., 155–156; chaps. 7 and 8, passim.

178. Ibid., 90–92.

179. Ibid., 158–162. For a similar description of the "acting white" phenomenon but with a very different political spin, see Signithia Fordham and John Ogbu, "Black Students' School Success: Coping with the Burden of 'Acting White,' " *Urban Review* 18 (1986), 187–206.

180. That was the description given by Charles J. Ogletree, Jr., a Harvard University Law School professor who cochaired the task force overseeing the change. Karen Avenoso and Patricia Nealon, "Exam School Plan Alters Race Policy," *Boston Globe*, 14 November 1996, 1.

181. "Why, After 15 Years of Gains, Are Black SAT Scores Now Losing Ground on White Scores?" *Journal of Blacks in Higher Education* 9 (Autumn 1995), 10–11.

182. Diane Ravitch, "Testing Catholic Schools," *Wall Street Journal*, 1 October 1996, A22.

Part of the secret is doubtless that students at Catholic schools are self-selected. But Paul T. Hill, Gail E. Foster, and Tamar Gendler, *High Schools with Character* (Santa Monica, Calif.: Rand Corporation, 1990), demonstrates that minority children from extremely disadvantaged backgrounds who were selected more or less at random to have their way paid to Catholic schools performed far better than their peers who remained in the public schools. Since it was not a strictly randomized selection procedure, the problem of selectivity cannot be dismissed altogether, but it is very hard to believe that it was the only factor at work.

183. A good brief review of the literature on minority achievement in the Catholic schools is provided in Sol Stern, "Why Catholic Schools Work," *City Journal*, Summer 1996, 14–26. Course-taking is obviously not the only secret to their success, as Stern argues.

184. Ford, *Reversing Underachievement*, 3, 22.

CHAPTER 14: THE HIGHER LEARNING

1. Laird Townsend, "Is Diversity Taking a Back Seat at Stanford?" *Journal of Blacks in Higher Education* 6 (Winter 1994–1995), 110. The Stanford decision was also discussed in Elwood Watson, "In Higher Education, Grade Inflation Has Not Helped Blacks," *Michigan Chronicle*, 27 June 1995, 6-A.

2. John H. Bunzel, *Race Relations on Campus: Stanford Students Speak Out* (Stanford, Calif.: Stanford Alumni Association, 1992).

3. SAT data for 1994 as given in Theodore Cross, "What If There Was No Affirmative Action in College Admissions? A Further Refinement of Our Earlier Calculations," *Journal of Blacks in Higher Education* 5 (Autumn 1994), 55.

4. Shelby Steele, *The Content of Our Character: A New Vision of Race in America* (New York: St. Martin's, 1990), 134. The two paragraphs that essentially summarize Steele are all based on chap. 7; without, we hope, putting words in his mouth, we have slightly reworded much of his discussion in order to make it fit better with our Stanford story.

5. Christopher Jencks and David Riesman, *The Academic Revolution* (Garden City, N.Y.: Doubleday, 1968), 428–433. For telling evidence about the quality of students in the southern black colleges in the mid-1960s, see James S. Coleman, *Equality of Educational Opportunity*, U.S. Department of Health, Education, and Welfare, Office of Education (Washington, D.C.: U.S. Government Printing Office, 1966), 345. In tests of verbal competence, nonverbal reasoning, mathematics, and science, no more than 5 to 15 percent of seniors in these schools had scores that were above the mean score for whites. Furthermore, on each of the tests black freshmen in southern colleges were at least a few points closer to the white mean than they were four years later, which suggests that these schools provided a learning environment inferior to that in the institutions attended by the typical white student.

6. Coleman, *Equality of Educational Opportunity*, 443.

7. Sar A. Levitan, William B. Johnston, and Robert Taggart, *Still a Dream: The Changing Status of Blacks Since 1960* (Cambridge: Harvard University Press, 1975), 84, 102; National Center for Education Statistics, *Historically Black Colleges and Universities, 1976–1990*, NCES 92–640 (Washington, D.C.: U.S. Government Printing Office, 1992), table 5.

8. It may not seem very surprising that the trends of the previous two decades have continued, but the point needs to be underscored because a myth that the rate of

black college attendance has declined gained considerable currency. That myth is based on the relatively brief downturn in just one of several possible measures of college attendance; in fact, the decline bottomed out in 1983 and black college attendance rates have been rising more or less steadily ever since. The primary source of the belief that black college attendance rates were declining is Gerald David Jaynes and Robin M. Williams, Jr. eds., *A Common Destiny: Blacks and American Society,* National Research Council, (Washington, D.C.: National Academy Press, 1989), 338–345. The discussion there relied entirely upon changes in the rates at which black high school graduates entered college directly, in the fall following graduation. This ignored all who took out time for work or military service before going back to school, a distorting influence unless it could be shown that the proportion of students who went to college later was the same for all racial groups. Further, the denominator in the rate was the number of high school graduates, not the entire age group, and this complicates intergroup comparisons. The proportion of blacks who were graduating from high school in these years was growing more rapidly than the proportion of whites graduating, arguably because "social promotions" were becoming more common. That many more black youths were acquiring high school diplomas meant that more of them were technically "eligible" to go to college. But that did not necessarily mean a corresponding increase in the number who were good college material, which the measure assumes. The rate of college attendance for the entire age group, not high school graduates alone, is in our view a better measure. See table 2 for these figures, which do not show any significant reversal of black prospects in the early 1980s. For a much more comprehensive discussion of these issues, which does not endorse the simple and alarmist conclusion that opportunities for blacks were plunging, see Daniel Koretz, *Trends in the Postsecondary Enrollment of Minorities* (Santa Monica, Calif.: Rand Corporation, 1990). Thomas J. Kane, *Black Educational Progress Since 1970: Policy Lessons,* Malcolm Wiener Center for Social Policy, Working Paper Series #H-90-8 (Cambridge: John F. Kennedy School of Government, Harvard University, 1990), 3–4, noted that the decline in black college entry in the early 1980s had been exaggerated, and argued correctly that the main problem for African Americans is not entry into college but persistence in college and completion of degree requirements. For more details, see Kane's *College Entry by Blacks Since 1970: The Role of Tuition, Financial Aid, Local Economic Conditions, and Family Background,* Malcolm Wiener Center for Social Policy Working Papers: Dissertation Series #D-91-3 (Cambridge: John F. Kennedy School of Government, Harvard University, 1991). Robert M. Hauser, "The Decline in College Entry Among African-Americans: Findings in Search of Explanations," in Paul M. Sniderman, Philip E. Tetlock, and Edward G. Carmines, eds., *Prejudice, Politics, and the American Dilemma* (Stanford, Calif.: Stanford University Press, 1993), 271–312, offers a more detailed and nuanced version of the analysis in *A Common Destiny.*

The argument that the rate of black college attendance has declined is still being advanced. See, e.g., a 1994 volume by economist Martin Carnoy; *Faded Dreams: The Politics and Economics of Race in America* (New York: Cambridge University Press), 149, which speaks in the present tense of "falling college enrollment levels" for blacks and other minorities. The author's discussion of "declining minority college enrollment" rests upon the authority of *A Common Destiny,* whose conclusions on this point were glaringly out of date by the time Carnoy's manuscript went to press. In an essay, "Why Aren't More African Americans Going to College?" *Journal of Blacks in Higher Education* 6 (Winter 1994–1995), 56, Carnoy claims that "the proportion of young blacks enrolled in college fell in the late 1970s, as it did for whites. But white enrollment rates recovered in the 1980s and black rates did not." This claim is quite mistaken. College attendance numbers bounce around too much from year to year for short-term changes to be very meaningful. But in 1983 only 38.2 percent of recent black high school graduates went directly on to college, as compared with 55 percent of whites, for a black/white ratio of 69. Over the most recent three years for which data are available—1992–1994—the average figure for African Americans has been 51.5 percent, notably higher than in the early 1980s. The white average has been higher, too—63.9 percent—but that gives a black/white ratio of 81. Even by this imperfect measure, the negative trend of the late 1970s and early 1980s has been reversed; National Center for Education Statistics, *The Condition of Education, 1996* (Washington, D.C.: U.S. Department of Education, 1996), 52.

9. Strictly speaking, the evidence, except that for 1995, has to do with completion of four or more years of college, not with the attainment of a degree, but the two are so closely related that it seems justifiable to speak as if completing four years was the same as graduating with a bachelor's degree. Until 1992 the Census and Current Population Survey questions about educational attainment were in terms of years of schooling completed. In 1992 the question was changed to one about degrees obtained. For a discussion of the relatively minor difference this made, see U.S. Bureau of the Census, Current Population Reports, P-20-476, *Educational Attainment in the United States: March 1993 and 1992* (Washington, D.C.: U.S. Government Printing Office, 1994), xii–xv.

10. U.S. Bureau of the Census, Current Population Reports, P-60–193, *Money Income in the United States: 1995* (Washington, D.C.: U.S. Government Printing Office, 1996), table 7.

11. Kane, *Black Educational Progress Since 1970,* 6.

12. The data are for the 301 NCAA Division I institutions, as given in "Graduation Rates of African-American College Students," *Journal of Blacks in Higher Education* 5 (Autumn 1994), 44–46. Some of those who had not taken their degree within six years may have still been enrolled and plugging away at it, but it cannot have been very many. The NCAA's assumption that a six-year span is long enough to measure completion and dropout rates seems sound.

13. National Collegiate Athletic Association, *1996 NCAA Division I Graduation-Rates Report* (Overland Park, Kans., 1996), 622.

14. John S. Brubacher and Willis Rudy, *Higher Education in Transition: A History of American Colleges and Universities, 1636–1976* (New York: Harper & Row, 1976), 236; National Center for Education Statistics, *Digest of Educational Statistics: 1995* (Washington, D.C.: U.S. Government Printing Office, 1995), 368, 381, 387.

15. *Digest of Educational Statistics: 1995,* 321.

16. Coleman, *Equality of Educational Opportunity,* 274–275.

17. Richard A. Lester, *Antibias Regulation of Universities: Faculty Problems and Their Solutions,* Report for the Carnegie Commission on Higher Education (New York: McGraw-Hill, 1974), 3–4; John E. Fleming, Gerald R. Gill, and David H. Swinton, *The Case for Affirmative Action for Blacks in Higher Education* (Washington, D.C.: Howard University Press, 1978), 118–119. The obligation was as a result of their status as a federal contractor, making them subject to executive order 11246; see chap. 15.

18. This statute made it an "unfair educational practice" for any educational institution to make "any written or oral inquiry concerning the race, religion, color, or national

origins of a person seeking admission"; *Massachusetts General Laws Annotated,* vol. 22A (St. Paul, Minn.: West Publishing Co., 1996), 440.

19. Brian McGrory, "Affirmative Action: An American Dilemma," pt. 3, *Boston Globe,* 23 May 1995, 1.

20. Lyndon B. Johnson, Speech at Howard University, 4 June 1965, in Lee Rainwater and William Yancey, *The Moynihan Report and the Politics of Controversy* (Cambridge: MIT Press, 1967), 126.

21. Commission on Higher Educational Opportunity in the South, *The Negro and Higher Education in the South* (Atlanta: Southern Regional Education Board, 1967), 25–26.

22. Thomas Sowell, "The Plight of Black Students," a searching 1974 essay reprinted in *Education: Assumptions vs. History: Collected Papers* (Stanford, Calif.: Hoover Institution Press, 1986), 136. The flood of criticism of affirmative action in higher education that has appeared since the publication of this paper and Sowell's 1972 volume, *Black Education: Myths and Tragedies* (New York, David McKay), offers nothing more than minor variations on what Sowell perceived when preferential policies were still taking shape.

23. Grant Mindle, Kenyon D. Bunch, and Carolyn Nickolas, "Diversity on Campus: A Reassessment of Current Strategies," *Policy Studies Review* 12, (Spring-Summer 1993), 25–46.

24. "Pursuing Diversity," *Boston Globe,* 1 February 1995, 1, 4. The *Globe* story, a typical puff piece supporting the university's plan, failed to include the population figures we provide, though one would think them highly relevant to the issue at hand. They are taken from U.S. Bureau of the Census, 1990 Census of Population, *General Population Characteristics: United States,* 1990-CP-1-1 (Washington, D.C.: U.S. Government Printing Office, 1992), table 253.

25. David W. Murray, "Racial and Sexual Politics in Testing," *Academic Questions* 9 (Summer 1996), 10–17. In 1995 the College Board began to "recenter" the scores on its verbal and mathematics tests, which meant adding 76 points to the average verbal score and making other adjustments. Although the Board offered various technical reasons for the change, Murray argues that resulting compression of the scale will obscure distinctions in performance that are currently visible, and that this may have been the primary motivation. For outstanding students, as Diane Ravitch has put it, the change is like moving the fences in the baseball park 76 feet closer to home plate. There will be many more home-run hitters, and the great long-ball hitters will be indistinguishable from mediocre ones who presently hit a lot of long fly balls that are easy outs. For students who are below average, the lower your score the more you benefit from the recentering. Those with an old-scale score of 380 in math get 430 on the new scale, a nice 50-point gain; see Murray, "Racial and Sexual Politics," 14–16. All the scores we make use of in the present chapter are of the older, pre-recentered, type. Similar analysis of long-term trends in SAT scores will be impossible unless the Board continues to release detailed breakdowns using the old scale.

26. Some 34 percent of high school graduates took the SATs in 1972; in 1995 it was 42 percent; National Center for Education Statistics, *The Condition of Education, 1996,* 239. If the rising participation rate meant that more students who were average or below average were taking the SATs, as seems likely, it becomes difficult to interpret changes in mean scores over the period.

27. The 1995 SAT scores are somewhat inflated. The test was made easier in three ways: (a) students were given an extra half hour in which to do it; (b) they were allowed to

use a calculator; (c) the vocabulary test supplied contextual information that had not been given in previous SATs.

28. Theodore Cross, the editor of the *Journal of Blacks in Higher Education*, reports that a telephone survey by his staff found that the mean combined SAT score of freshmen in these twenty-five schools was 1,291; "What if There Was No Affirmative Action in College Admissions? A Refinement of Our Earlier Calculations," *Journal of Blacks in Higher Education* 5 (Autumn 1994), 53.

29. "College-Bound Black Students are Slowly Advancing in Advanced Placement Tests," *Journal of Blacks in Higher Education*, 11 (Spring 1996), 6–9.

30. Calculated from the relevant pages of *1996 NCAA Report*.

31. This should be self-evident, but it may not be these days. If the Asian-American share of enrollments at an institution is six times their share of the population at large, as it is today at Columbia and Stanford, for example, other groups must inevitably have considerably less than their share, because admissions is a zero-sum game. Diversity and meritocracy, in this instance and many others, are conflicting goals.

32. Theodore Cross, "Why the *Hopwood* Ruling Would Remove Most African Americans From the Nation's Most Selective Universities," *Journal of Blacks in Higher Education* 11 (Spring 1996), 66–70. Cross calculated racial distributions for those scoring 650 or better on either the verbal or math tests. He also made some allowance for economic disadvantage and for "strong personal qualities," but is unclear about precisely how this was done. The calculation seems essentially of the same kind as that provided in table 4.

33. "College Presidents Reply to *The Wall Street Journal*," *Journal of Blacks in Higher Education* 11 (Spring 1996), 12.

34. Cross, "What If There Was No Affirmative Action?," 53n. And there is a wealth of evidence that SATs are accurate predictors of black college performance. See, for example, Robert Klitgard, *Choosing Elites* (New York: Basic Books, 1985), 160–165, 187–188. "One might wish that standardized tests underestimated the later performance of blacks," Klitgard concludes, but at elite institutions black students "typically do worse" than "whites do with the same test scores, perhaps one to two thirds of a standard deviation worse." Klitgard estimates that to make the prediction of black college grades precisely correct it is necessary to *subtract 240 points* on the combined SAT. Among black and white students with the same high school grades, blacks will perform as well in college as whites with an SAT score that is 240 points lower. No college in the country demands higher test scores of black applicants; most accept black applicants with scores as much as 240 points *below* those of whites and Asian Americans. SAT scores are better predictors of college performance than high school grades for black students but not for whites or Asians; Stanley Sue and Jennifer Abe, *Predictors of Academic Achievement Among Asian Students and White Students* (New York: College Entrance Examination Board, 1988), 1. For data indicating that standardized tests predict the performance of African-American students enrolled in historically black colleges even more accurately than they do in the case of black students in predominantly white institutions, see Jaqueline Fleming, "Standardized Test Scores and the Black College Environment," in Kofi Lomotey, ed., *Going to School: The African-American Experience* (Albany: State University of New York Press, 1990), 143–152. It is particulary striking that these supposedly biased instruments, allegedly devised by whites to keep blacks down, work so well for African-American students at predominantly black institutions. It is also striking that an experimental program designed to improve the performance of minority freshmen at

the University of Michigan was deemed successful because the first-semester grades of blacks "did not fall behind those earned by white students with similar standard-ized test scores," as had usually been the case in the past. That black students needed a special program to perform as well as whites with comparable SAT scores plainly indicates that such tests are not biased against blacks, as is commonly charged. They are rather biased in favor of blacks, in the sense that they lead us to expect them to peform better in college than in fact they do without programs like that at Michigan; Denise K. Magner, "Professor Takes Aim at Blacks' Racial Vulnerability," *Chronicle of Higher Education,* 1 April 1992, A5.

35. National Center for Education Statistics, "Making the Cut: Who Meets Highly Selec-tive College Entrance Criteria?" *Statistics in Brief,* NCES 95–732 (Washington, D.C.: U.S. Government Printing Office, 1995), table 1.

36. "College Presidents Reply to *Wall Street Journal,*" 12.

37. Thus, there was a national stir in 1991, when Timothy McGuire, a law student employed part-time in the admissions office at the Georgetown University Law School, used his inside knowledge to write an article charging that African-American students at his school had notably weaker academic qualifications than their white classmates. It created national news. Defenders of the policy claimed that McGuire was disseminating "incomplete and distorted information" that would "renew the long-standing and intellectually dishonest myth" that black students were "less quali-fied than their white counterparts to compete in school . . ."; "Degrees of Success," *Washington Post,* 8 May 1991, A31. None of those who complained of McGuire's allegedly "incomplete and distorted" information offered any data to contradict his double-standards point, however. Of course the policy could have been defended in a variety of ways, but the first step should have been a candid acknowledgment that McGuire had his facts right.

38. Bob Zelnick, *Backfire: A Reporter's Look at Affirmative Action* (Chicago: Henry Regnery, 1996), chap. 9.

39. These data are for 1989 rather than 1988 freshmen, but that seems close enough; "Affirmative Action Under Attack on Campus Where It Worked," *New York Times,* 4 June 1995, A22.

40. Robert Lerner and Althea K. Nigai, *Racial Preferences in Undergraduate Enrollment at the University of California, Berkeley, 1993–1995: A Preliminary Report* (Washing-ton, D.C.: Center for Equal Opportunity, 1996), charts 4 and 5.

41. Thus, at the University of Virginia in 1994, the average alumni child who was admit-ted had a combined SAT score that was just 25 points below that of nonalumni children; blacks had scores that were 196 points below those of whites. Alumni preference was stronger at William and Mary, a private school with a presumably greater need to encourage alumni loyalty to enhance fund-raising. But even at Wil-liam and Mary alumni status counted for only 58 points, while the premium given to black applicants amounted to 197 points. At Virginia, being an African American helped your chances of admission eight times as much as having a parent who had attended the school; at William and Mary it increased them more than three times as much; Philip Walzer, "Diversity's Cost on Campus," *Hampton Roads Ledger-Star,* 6 June 1995, A1, A6. At Harvard, the sons and daughters of alumni who are admitted have average scores just 35 points below those of nonalumni children, so alumni preference is about a third of the magnitude of the affirmative action preference for blacks; Zelnick, *Backfire,* 142. Klitgard reports that in the early 1980s being from a disadvantaged minority group increased the chances of admission, holding other

variables constant, by 53 percent at Williams, 51 percent at Bucknell, and 46 percent at Colgate. No other factor came close to race in importance, except having an alumni parent at Bucknell, which improved admission chances by 47 percent; Klitgard, *Choosing Elites,* 46.

42. These and other figures cited in the paragraph are from "Black Graduation Rates at Second-Tier Public Universities, *Journal of Blacks in Higher Education,* 5 (Autumn 1994), 45. The pages of the journal are a treasure trove for anyone seeking information and a wide range of opinions on this topic.

43. Ibid.; "The Status of Black Faculty at the Flagship State Universities," *Journal of Blacks in Higher Education,* 12 (Summer 1996), 15.

44. J. Harvie Wilkinson III, *From Brown to Bakke: The Supreme Court and School Integration, 1954–1978* (New York: Oxford University Press, 1979), 256–258.

45. Allan P. Sindler, *Bakke, DeFunis, and Minority Admissions: The Quest for Equal Opportunity* (New York: Longman, 1978), 63–67.

46. Ibid., 214–215.

47. Ibid., 222–235.

48. Ibid., 241–245.

49. *Regents of the Univ. of Calif. v. Bakke,* 438 U.S. 265, 407 (1978).

50. 438 U.S. at 355.

51. 438 U.S. at 325, 365.

52. 438 U.S. at 307, 313, 323.

53. 438 U.S. at 316–317.

54. Guidelines given to interviewers for the Harvard Medical School stated that "the minimum goal should be representation of minority groups in the student body at least equal to the proportion of those minority groups in the population of the U.S.A. at large"; quoted in Klitgard, *Choosing Elites,* 40. In 1969 the Harvard Business School voted to admit all minority applicants whose records indicated that they had no more than one chance in four of flunking out. After a few years this practice was abandoned and replaced with a goal of 10–12 percent minority representation, partly out of a fear that the business world would come to think that Harvard Business School awarded two kinds of degrees—white degrees and black degrees; Klitgard, *Choosing Elites,* 43–44. Bernard D. Davis, "Academic Standards in Medical Schools," *New England Journal of Medicine* 294 (13 May 1976), 1118–1119, points to the negative consequences of lowered standards at the Harvard Medical School.

55. 438 U.S. at 378, 323–324.

56. 438 U.S. at 318.

57. 438 U.S. at 375.

58. 438 U.S. at 402.

59. 438 U.S. at 412–414, 418.

60. 438 U.S. at 319, n. 53.

61. The phrasing of a typical notice was given to the *Los Angeles Times* by Professor Stephen R. Barnett, who had been on the Boalt Hall faculty since the early 1970s. Jean Merl and William Trombley, "UC Law School Violates Civil Rights, U.S. Says," *Los Angeles Times,* 29 September 1992, A1.

62. Ruben Navarrette, Jr., "Berkeley's Awkward Two-Step to Ensure a Racially Diverse Campus," *Los Angeles Times,* 11 October 1992, 8.

63. The quotations are from William Trombley, "Colleges Fear Affirmative Action Setback," *Los Angeles Times,* 30 September 1992, A3.

64. *Hopwood v. Texas,* 78 F. 3d 932, 932–937 (1996).

65. *Hopwood v. Texas,* 78 F. 3d at 937.
66. *Hopwood v. Texas,* 78 F. 3d at 962.
67. 438 U.S. at 402.
68. U.S. Department of Justice, Brief Supporting Petition for a Writ of Certiorari in *Hopwood v. Texas.*
69. Scott Jaschik and Douglas Lederman, "Appeals Court Bars Racial Preference in College Admissions," *Chronicle of Higher Education,* 29 March 1996, A27.
70. Jeffrey Rosen, "Is Affirmative Action Doomed?" *New Republic,* 17 October 1994, 25.
71. Marc Fisher, "Equal and Opposite Reaction," *Washington Post,* 29 October 1996, E1.
72. Chang-Lin Tien, "Perspective on Affirmative Action," *Los Angeles Times,* 18 July 1995, B9.
73. Robert Bruce Slater, "Why Socioeconomic Affirmative Action in College Admissions Works Against African Americans, *Journal of Blacks in Higher Education* 8 (Summer 1995), 59.
74. Brian McGrory, "Affirmative Action: An American Dilemma," pt. 3, *Boston Globe,* 23 May 1995, 1. The director of student search services for the Educational Testing Service told the *Globe* that more than 1,280 of the country's 1,600 public and private four-year colleges and universities request minority-specific lists.
75. Elena Newman, "Harvard's Sins of Admission," 9 October 1995.
76. Suzanne Espinosa Solis, "Teens' Strong Views on UC Regents' Vote," *San Francisco Chronicle,* 26 July 1995, A1. Jesley Zambrano was a Latino student, but her point obviously applies to any minority student currently protected by affirmative action admissions.
77. Steele, *Content of Our Character* 138.
78. Ibid., 147.

CHAPTER 15: JOBS AND CONTRACTS

1. Louis Freedberg, "The Enforcer," *San Francisco Chronicle,* 4 June 1995, 1. The Office of Federal Contract Compliance Programs (OFCCP) has the power to conduct a "compliance review"—an investigation into a corporation's hiring record—which can be either a random audit or the consequence of a complaint. The settlements in the Marriott Hotel and UC–San Diego cases were the result of just such compliance reviews. In congressional testimony in 1995, OFCCP director Shirley Wilcher stated that the agency was then finding violations in 73 percent of the more than 4,000 compliance reviews it conducted each year; James Bovard, "Here Comes the Goon Squad," *American Spectator,* July 1996, 36. Our research assistant, Kevin Marshall, prepared a first draft of portions of this chapter.
2. Christopher Edley, Jr., and George Stephanopoulos, "Affirmative Action Review: Report to the President," 19 July 1995, 67, n. 85.
3. "Minority Enterprise: Fat White Wallets," *Economist,* 27 November 1993, 29.
4. Quoted in Justice William Rehnquist's dissent in *United Steel Workers of America v. Weber,* 443 U.S. 193 (1979) at 242, n. 20.
5. Alfred W. Blumrosen, *Black Employment and the Law* (New Brunswick, N.J.: Rutgers University Press, 1971), 53.
6. Ibid., 58.
7. Alfred W. Blumrosen, "Strangers in Paradise: *Griggs v. Duke Power Co.* and the

Concept of Employment Discrimination," *Michigan Law Review* 71 (November 1972), 95.

8. Ibid. EEOC chairman Clifford Alexander said in 1968: "We . . . here at EEOC believe in numbers . . . our most valid standard is in numbers . . . in a variety of categories, not just total numbers. . . . The only accomplishment is when we look at all those numbers and see a vast improvement in the picture"; quoted in Herman Belz, *Equality Transformed: A Quarter-Century of Affirmative Action* (New Brunswick, N.J.: Transaction Publishers, 1991), 28–29.

9. Blumrosen, *Black Employment*, 71–73. Terry Eastland, *Ending Affirmative Action: The Case for Colorblind Justice* (New York: Basic Books, 1996), 92, sets the figure in early 1996 at 94 million.

10. Blumrosen, "Strangers in Paradise," 69–71.

11. Quoted in Belz, *Equality Transformed*, 10. Much of the following discussion draws on Belz's excellent account. Also useful are Terry Eastland, *Ending Affirmative Action: The Case for Colorblind Justice* (New York: Basic Books, 1996) and Clint Bolick, *The Affirmative Action Fraud: Can We Restore the American Civil Rights Vision?* (Washington, D.C.: Cato Institute, 1996). For a penetrating broader critique of current employment law, see Walter Olson, *The Excuse Factory: How Employment Law Is Paralyzing the American Workplace* (New York: Free Press, 1997).

12. Hugh Davis Graham, *The Civil Rights Era: Origins and Development of National Policy* (New York: Oxford University Press, 1990), 33.

13. Belz, *Equality Transformed*, 20.

14. Graham, *Civil Rights Era*, 111–113. This proposal never became official Urban League policy, because the League's trustees were convinced that "seeking special privileges" for African Americans instead of color-blind treatment would cause a disastrous loss of public support for the organization.

15. Belz, *Equality Transformed*, 20–21.

16. Ibid., 22.

17. Ibid., 18–19.

18. Graham, *Civil Rights Era*, 197.

19. Belz, *Equality Transformed*, 40.

20. Graham, *Civil Rights Era*, 343.

21. The history of these executive orders and their relationship to one another is comprehensively reviewed in Graham, *Civil Rights Era*, chap. 7. E.O. 11246 superseded and abolished all preceding antidiscrimination orders.

22. Laurence Silberman, "The Road to Racial Quotas," *Wall Street Journal*, 11 August 1978; Graham, *Civil Rights Era*, 278–297.

23. Graham, *Civil Rights Era*, 342. For criticism of the crucial "underutilization" concept by an economist, see Farrell Bloch, *Antidiscrimination Law and Minority Employment* (Chicago: University of Chicago Press, 1994), 71.

24. Quoted in Belz, *Equality Transformed*, 31.

25. For a stinging criticism of the methods of the OFCCP and the costs of refusing to cave in to pressure from it, see Bovard, "Here Comes the Goon Squad."

26. Title VII, sec. 703 (h).

27. *Griggs v. Duke Power Company*, 401 U.S. 424 at 427, 430 (1971).

28. 401 U.S. at 431–432.

29. 401 U.S. at 429–430. In discussing the statute, Burger failed to mention much of the relevant language. And that which he did cite was at one point pulled from its context and severed from its statutory history. Burger quoted from sec. 703(h), which

authorizes the use of "any professionally developed ability test" that is not "designed, intended *or used* to discriminate" (433). But the italics were added by him, and the phrase was not, in 1964, meant to suggest the legitimacy of a disparate-impact test, as other statutory language makes clear. See Richard A. Epstein, *Forbidden Grounds: The Case Against Employment Discrimination Laws* (Cambridge: Harvard University Press, 1992), 197–199.

30. 401 U.S. at 433–434.
31. More specifically, Title VII, sec. 706(g), empowered courts to "enjoin" an employer from continuing an unlawful employment practice, and to "order such affirmative action as may be appropriate, which may include reinstatement or hiring of employees with or without back pay." Congress added "but is not limited to" after "which may include" and "or any other equitable relief as the court deems appropriate" after "back pay."
32. 411 U.S. 792 (1973).
33. 411 U.S. at 802, 805.
34. Epstein, *Forbidden Grounds*, 200.
35. 422 U.S. 405, 421 (1975). The case also accepted the EEOC guidelines on employment testing—guidelines that spelled out what "job-related" (the *Griggs* test) meant.
36. 422 U.S. at 449.
37. 422 U.S. at 425.
38. 443 U.S. 193 (1979). The decision was 5 to 2; Justices Powell and Stevens did not participate.
39. 443 U.S. at 201, 204.
40. 443 U.S. at 209, n. 9, and at 222–223 (Justice Rehnquist dissenting). Those race-conscious hiring and promotion policies for federal contractors were demanded by Executive Order 11246; see the discussion of 11246 on pages 427–429.
41. 443 U.S. at 200, n. 9, and 222–223.
42. 443 U.S. at 220, 241.
43. 443 U.S. at 244–245.
44. 448 U.S. 448 (1980). The decision had no majority opinion, but two pluralities combined to uphold the set-aside.
45. 448 U.S. at 481, 484. As Justice Stevens noted, writing in dissent, despite the rhetoric about barriers to minority entry, the law removed no such barriers, nor did its "sparse legislative history detail any insuperable or even significant obstacles to entry into the competitive market" (543).
46. *Texas Dept. of Community Affairs v. Burdine,* 450 U.S. 248 (1981) followed in the line of *McDonnell Douglas,* emphasizing that the burden of proof in disparate treatment cases is ultimately the plaintiff's. This case becomes prominent in *Wards Cove,* a disparate impact case, discussed below. *Connecticut v. Teal,* 457 U.S. 440 (1982), applied disparate impact to each stage of a hiring process, not allowing an employer to justify his process by its final result. *Firefighters Local Union No. 1784 v. Stotts,* 467 U.S. 561 (1984) prevented a consent decree governing new hiring from overriding seniority in layoff decisions, and struck down an affirmative action program as exceeding the judicial remedial authority. It was superseded just two years later, though, by *Local 28 Sheet Metal Workers International Association v. EEOC,* 478 U.S. 421 (1986).
47. 480 U.S. 616 (1987).
48. 480 U.S. at 639, and at 641, n. 17.
49. *Griggs v. Duke Power Company,* 401 U.S. at 430.

50. 480 U.S. at 658, 659, 673.

51. When this case was decided, in 1989, the *Washington Post* reported that at least 36 states and more than 190 local governments had programs of this type; Al Kamen, "High Court Voids Minority Contract Set-Aside Program," *Washington Post,* 24 January, 1989, A1.

52. *Richmond v. J. A. Croson,* 488 U.S. 469, 480, (1989).

53. 488 U.S. at 487–492.

54. 488 U.S. at 491. The distinction between congressional and state power was in fact weak, since, unless O'Connor wished to overrule *Bolling v. Sharpe,* the equal protection clause applied to Congress every bit as much as to a state entity, a point that Justice Marshall picked up in dissent.

55. 488 U.S. at 491, 493.

56. 488 U.S. at 499.

57. 488 U.S. at 505–506.

58. *Wards Cove v. Atonio,* 490 U.S. 642 (1989), at 652.

59. 490 U.S. at 659.

60. 490 U.S. at 660.

61. 490 U.S. at 662.

62. Editorial, "Coyly, the Court Turns 180 Degrees," *New York Times,* 12 June 1989, A18.

63. Roger Clegg, "Introduction: A Brief Legislative History of the Civil Rights Act of 1991," in Clegg et al., eds., "The Civil Rights Act of 1991: A Symposium," *Louisiana Law Review,* 54 (1994), 1463.

64. The statute contained other provisions as well. For instance, it overturned another 1989 decision, *Patterson v. McLean Credit Union,* which had held that racial harassment did not violate the 1866 Civil Rights Act since the act applied to making contracts, not to conduct after the contract was made that did not interfere with its enforcement. And it allowed an employee to challenge an employer's hiring process as a whole if he or she could show its parts to be inseparable.

65. The example comes from Steven A. Holmes, "Adjusting of Test Scores Inflames Rights Debate," *New York Times,* 17 May 1991, A12.

66. The cooking-the-books reference was in Holmes, "Adjusting of Test Scores." Although John A. Hartigan and Alexandra K. Wigdor, eds., *Fairness in Employment Testing: Validity Generalizations, Minority Issues, and the General Aptitude Test Battery* (Washington, D.C.: National Academy Press, 1989), demonstrates that the leading employment test is not racially biased, the authors offer an unconvincing defense of race-norming.

67. Jeffrey Rosen, "Is Affirmative Action Doomed?" *New Republic,* 17 October 1994, 25.

68. Different accounts give slightly different dollar amounts. Neil Munro, "Clinton Set-Aside Plan Becomes Election-Year Pawn," *Washington Technology* sets the figure at $4.8 billion. The *Wall Street Journal* says $5.2 billion; Stephanie N. Mehta, "SBA Program For Minorities Is Under Attack," 18 April 1996, B2. The $5.8 billion comes from Steven A. Holmes, "U.S. Retreats on Contracts for Minorities," *New York Times,* 23 May 1996, A26.

69. These are the actual facts in a case: *Dynalantic Corp. v. United States Department of Defense and United States Small Business Administration,* U.S. District Court for the District of Columbia, C.A. No 95CV02301 (filed December 15, 1995).

70. That is the figure the SBA gave to the *Wall Street Journal.* Mehta, "SBA Program For Minorities." In the case of the contract for the flight simulator, the amount of money involved was actually too high to avoid competitive bidding, but, again, that is

the exception. The law, as amended in 1988, requires competition among 8(a) firms for manufacturing contracts in excess of $5 million and all other contracts in excess of $3 million. On the other hand, small contracts with minority firms can, over time, cease to be small, which has not stopped the SBA from renewing them. See Edley, and Stephanopoulos, "Affirmative Action Review," 67.

71. 20 U.S.C.S., sec. 1112d.

72. The following discussion of the Energy Policy Act of 1992 is taken from Michael A. Carvin, "Attacking the Constitutionality of Federally Enacted Minority Set-Aside Programs," in Roger Clegg, ed., *Racial Preferences in Government Contracting* (Washington, D.C.: National Legal Center for the Public Interest, 1993). See also Thomas W. Lippman, "Energizing Minorities' Objectives," *Washington Post,* 1 December 1992, A17; and Terry Eastland, "The Set-Aside Set," *American Spectator,* March 1993.

73. Paul M. Barrett, "Successful, Affluent, but Still 'Disadvantaged,' " *Wall Street Journal,* 13 June 1995, B1.

74. Edley and Stephanopoulos, "Affirmative Action Review," 65–66. The authors do not give a year for the 40 percent figure.

75. Jeffrey Rosen, "The Day the Quotas Died," *New Republic,* 22 April 1996, 21. A challenge to this practice was rejected by a federal district court in *McCrossan v. Cook* 1996 U.S. Dist. LEXIS 14721.

76. Patrick Healy, "Ohio State U. Agrees to Stop Minority Set-Aside Program . . . ," *Chronicle of Higher Education,* 5 April 1996, A28.

77. Tim W. Ferguson, "Race (etc.) Preferences on the Line," *Wall Street Journal,* 14 March 1995, A16.

78. Peter Behr, "Crucial Break or Unjustified Crutch?" *Washington Post,* 10 March 1995, 1.

79. The media covered the Viacom story extensively; see, e.g., Jeffrey H. Birnbaum, "Turning Back the Clock," *Time,* 20 March 1995, 36; Terry Eastland, "Powell Preferred," *National Review,* 12 February 1996, 20.

80. Jonathan Rauch, "Color TV," *New Republic,* 19 December 1994, 9.

81. Selwyn Raab, "12 Charged in Minority Businesses Scheme," *New York Times,* 19 May 1995, B2.

82. Speech by President Clinton at the National Archives, 19 July 1995, extended excerpts from which were reprinted in the *Washington Post,* 20 July 1995, A12.

83. U.S. Bureau of the Census, Current Population Reports, P-20-480, *The Black Population in the United States: March 1994 and 1993* (Washington, D.C.: U.S. Government Printing Office, 1995), table 7.

84. George Farkas and Keven Vicknair, "Appropriate Tests of Racial Wage Discrimination Require Controls for Cognitive Skills: Comment on Cancio, Evans, and Maume," *American Sociological Review* 61 (August 1996), 557–560. This is a critique of A. Silvia Cancio, T. David Evans, and David J. Maume, "Reconsidering the Declining Significance of Race: Racial Differences in Early Career Wages" in the same issue of the *American Sociological Review,* 541–556, which had measured education crudely by levels of schooling completed. The authors' rejoinder to this critique in the same issue, 561–564, argues that it is inappropriate to control for education by using tests of cognitive skills because those tests are biased, and really only test "exposure to the values and experiences of the White middle class" (561). Employers are apparently guilty of class and racial bias if they want employees to be able to read a training manual or to calculate how many bags of grass seed and fertilizer the customer will need to make a lawn that is 60 feet long and 40 feet wide.

85. This approach grows out of James S. Coleman's pioneering work suggesting that researchers should assess the effects of education not in terms of "inputs" (how many years spent in school?) but in terms of "outputs" (how much do students know when they come out of school?). This insight of Coleman's was appealing to economists, most of them associated with the University of Chicago, who were interested in the role of "human capital"—investment in education and training—in economic growth. The first systematic examination of racial differences in income that controlled for cognitive skills, by Eric Hanushek in 1978, used the 1965 Coleman report results and 1970 census data from the Public Use Sample; it found, like the Farkas study cited in the previous note, that black males were actually better paid than white males with comparable education—they received "higher returns per year of quality-equivalent schooling [years of schooling adjusted by test scores] than comparable whites"; Eric Hanushek, "Ethnic Income Variations: Magnitudes and Explanations," in Thomas Sowell, ed., *Essays and Data on American Ethnic Groups* (Washington, D.C.: Urban Institute, 1978), 139–166. More than a decade elapsed before other researchers pursued these issues, but several important studies pointing in the same direction have appeared in the 1990s. These include June O'Neill, "The Role of Human Capital in Earnings Differences Between Black and White Men," *Journal of Economic Perspectives* 4 (Fall 1990), 25–45; Ronald F. Ferguson, "New Evidence on the Growing Value of Skill and Consequences for Racial Disparity and Returns to Schooling" (Cambridge: Malcom Wiener Center for Social Policy, H-93-10, Harvard University, 1993); Ferguson, "Shifting Challenges: Fifty Years of Economic Change Toward Black-White Earnings Equality," *Daedalus* 124 (Winter 1995), 37–76; Derek A. Neal and William R. Johnson, "The Role of Pre-Market Factors in Black-White Wage Differences," *Journal of Political Economy* 104 (October 1996), 869–896. Not all of these studies showed an earnings advantage for black males. In O'Neill's sample the hourly earnings of black men in their twenties were 17.1 percent below those of whites in 1987 without adjusting for any characteristics. When she controlled for region, years of schooling, and test scores, the differential shrank by three-quarters, to 4.5 percent, and it virtually disappeared when years of work experience were controlled. Ferguson's point of departure was the growth in the racial wage gap for 18-to-28-year-old males from 6 percent in 1976 to 16 percent in 1989. He found that the reason was an increase in the value of basic reading and math skills. Had the value of skills to employers not increased as it did, "the long-term patterns of convergence toward parity between young black and white males would have continued through the 1980s." The one exception was in the case of men with twelve or fewer years of schooling living in the North Central Region after the mid-1980s. Neal and Johnson found that applying an educational control that included test scores cut the wage gap between black and white males by three-quarters, to just 27 cents per hour in 1990–1991, and reversed it among women, so that black women earned 3 cents more per hour. No studies of this type can measure the extent of discrimination with much precision, but together they certainly challenge the premise upon which current preferential policies rest—that racial discrimination in employment is severe and pervasive.

86. Richard J. Murnane and Frank Levy, *Teaching the New Basic Skills: Principles for Educating Children to Thrive in a Changing Economy* (New York: Free Press, 1996), 32. A more detailed technical version of the analysis is available in Richard Murnane, John Willett, and Frank Levy, "The Growing Importance of Cognitive Skills in Wage Determination," *Review of Economics and Statistics* 77 (1995), 251–266.

87. Murnane and Levy, *Teaching the New Basic Skills,* 41–44.

88. Ibid., 34–35; National Center for Education Statistics, *Data Compendium for the NAEP 1992 Mathematics Assessment of the Nation and the States,* Report No. 23-ST04 (Washington, D.C.: U.S. Government Printing Office, 1993), 744 [percent above 300 anchor level]; National Center for Education Statistics, *NAEP 1994 Reading Report Card for the Nation and the States* (Washington, D.C.: U.S. Department of Education, 1996), 48 [percent reading at or above proficient level].

89. The findings of the Urban Institute Washington and Chicago studies are reported in Margaret Turner, Michael Fix, and John Yinger, *Opportunities Denied, Opportunities Diminished: Discrimination in Hiring* (Washington, D.C.: Urban Institute Press, 1991). The Denver study is described in Franklin L. James and Steve W. DelCastillo, "Measuring Job Discrimination by Private Employers Against Young Black and Hispanic Males Seeking Entry Level Work in the Denver Metropolitan Area," unpublished report (Denver: University of Colorado, 1991). The key findings of the three studies are conveniently summarized in James J. Heckman and Peter Siegelman, "The Urban Institute Audit Studies: Their Methods and Findings," in Michael Fix and Raymond J. Struyk, eds., *Clear and Convincing Evidence: Measurement of Discrimination in America* (Washington, D.C.: Urban Institute Press, 1993), tables 5.1 and 5.3. Justice Ginsberg cites this research approvingly in her dissent in *Adarand Constructors, Inc. v. Pena,* 115 S.Ct 2097 (1995) at 2135.

90. The special character of the District of Columbia could have skewed the results for another reason as well. Private employers in a labor market so dominated by a single employer known to follow strong preferential policies in hiring might as a result have been inclined to be suspicious of black job applicants who looked attractive, reasoning that "if they're as good as they seem, why aren't they applying for a better-paid, more secure post in the Department of Transportation?"

91. For example, whether the "matched" pairs were truly matched in every important respect can be debated. Did the researchers have sufficient knowledge of the cognitive skills and other traits employers value most in making hiring decision? People who seemed a perfect match to the researchers might not have appeared so to employers. The difference in perception would not be chalked up as an error by the researchers; it would be interpreted as employer bias. Heckman and Siegelman provide a searching and, we think, quite devastating critique in *Clear and Convincing Evidence,* 187–258. A rejoinder by John Yinger and a further set of comments by Heckman and Siegelman appear on 259–275.

92. Heckman and Siegelman in *Clear and Convincing Evidence,* 216, 272.

93. Farai Chideya, "Equality? I'm Still Waiting," *New York Times,* op-ed, 11 March 1995, 23.

94. "Affirmative Action," *Economist,* 15 April 1995, 21.

95. Kevin Sack, "Atlanta Leaders See Racial Goals as Olympic Ideal," *New York Times,* 10 June 1996, 1.

96. John J. Donahue and James Heckman, "Continuous vs. Episodic Change: The Impact of Civil Rights Policy on the Economic Status of Blacks," *Journal of Economic Literature* 29 (December 1991), 1603–1643.

97. Ibid., 1610.

98. Bloch, *Antidiscrimination Law,* 101–109; Bob Zelnick, *Backfire: A Reporter's Look at Affirmative Action* (Chicago: Henry Regnery, 1996), 31–41.

99. Timothy Bates and Darrell Williams, "Preferential Procurement Programs and Minority-Owned Businesses," *Journal of Urban Affairs* 17 (1995), 1–17.

100. "Affirmative Action," *Economist*, 15 April 1995, 21.

101. Louis Uchitelle, "Union Goal of Equality Fails the Test of Time," *New York Times*, 9 July 1995, 1.

102. Morton M. Kondracke, "Pennsylvania Avenue," *Roll Call*, 29 May 1995, 8. The survey by Organization Resources Counselors, Inc., was also cited in "Progressing Beyond Affirmative Action: A Course for the Future," National Planning Association and Joint Center for Political and Economic Studies Affirmative Action Task Force draft report, 15 May 1996, 20.

103. Holly Idelson, "Pressure Builds for Retreat on Affirmative Action," *Congressional Quarterly*, 3 June 1995, 1578.

104. Jonathan D. Glater and Martha M. Hamilton, "Affirmative Action's Corporate Converts," *Washington Post*, 19 March 1995, B1.

105. Ibid.

106. "Company's EEO Efforts Pay Off," *USA Today*, 27 April 1990, 8A.

107. Peggy Schmidt, "Women and Minorities: Is Industry Ready?" *New York Times*, 16 October 1988, Careers Supplement 25.

108. Amy Stevens, "Lawyers and Clients," *Wall Street Journal*, 19 June 1995, B6.

109. The description of "white male culture" comes from Pam Fomalont, a Los Angeles diversity consultant, quoted in Matthew Robinson, "Diversity's Double-Edged Sword," *Investor's Business Daily*, 20 February 1997, A1. On diversity training in general, see Heather MacDonald, "The Diversity Industry," *New Republic*, 5 July 1993, 22; Frederick R. Lynch, *The Diversity Machine: The Drive to Change the 'White Male Workplace'* (New York: Free Press, 1996). In 1992, the *New York Times* reported that 40 percent of American companies had instituted some sort of diversity training. Lena Williams, "Companies Capitalizing on Worker Diversity," *New York Times*, 15 December 1992, 1.

110. Udayan Gupta, "Minority Suppliers Get More Aid from Big Customers," *Wall Street Journal*, 21 November 1995, B2.

111. Spencer S. Hsu, "Minority Business Leaders Uneasy over Disney Hiring," *Washington Post*, 25 July 1994, B1.

112. *Adarand Constructors, Inc. v. Pena*, 115 S.Ct 2097 (1995) at 2117.

113. Statement of John R. Schmidt, Associate Attorney General, Before the Subcommittee on the Constitution, Committee on the Judiciary, U.S. House of Representatives, and Subcommittee on the Constitutution, Committee on the Judiciary, U.S. Senate, concerning *Adarand Constructors Inc. v. Pena*, 22 September 1995. The decision had come down on June 12, 1995.

114. The evidence is well summarized in Seymour Martin Lipset, "Affirmative Action and the American Creed," *Wilson Quarterly*, Winter 1992, 52–62.

115. Ann Devroy, "Clinton Orders Affirmative Action Review," *Washington Post*, 24 February 1995, 1.

116. Knight-Ridder Newspapers, "Anti-bias Programs Fall Review," New Orleans *Times-Picayune*, 25 February 1995, A3.

117. Devroy, "Clinton Orders Affirmative Action Review."

118. "Clinton Orders Affirmative Action Review," *Chicago Tribune*, 25 February 1995, 1.

119. "Memorandum to General Counsels" from Walter Dellinger, assistant attorney general, U.S. Department of Justice, Office of Legal Counsel, June 28, 1995.

120. 488 U.S. at 493.

121. Speech by President Clinton at the National Archives, 19 July 1995, extended excerpts of which were reprinted in the *Washington Post*, 20 July 1995, A12.

122. See, for instance, Todd S. Purdum, "Broad Group Visits President on Affirmative Action's Future," *New York Times*, 15 March 1995, 1.

123. John R. Schmidt, "Post-*Adarand* Guidance on Affirmative Action in Federal Employment," Office of the Associate Attorney General, U.S. Department of Justice, 29 February 1996.

124. Department of Justice, "Proposed Reforms to Affirmative Action in Federal Procurement," 22 May 1996. We have labeled this a Schmidt memo. His name is not on the document itself, but he was credited in the press with directing the process of drafting the memo. See, for instance, Ann Devroy, "Administration Memo Outlines Limited Affirmative Action Contracting," *Washington Post*, 7 March 1996, A8.

125. Ann Devroy, "Administration Memo."

126. Ann Devroy, "Rule Aiding Minority Firms to End," *Washington Post*, 22 October 1995, 1.

127. Deval Patrick quoted in Neil Munro, "Clinton Set-Aside Plan Becomes Election-Year Pawn," *Washington Technology*, 11 April 1996, 1.

128. Calculated from U.S. Bureau of the Census, 1990 Census of the Population, *Asian and Pacific Islanders in the United States*, 1990 CP-3-5 (Washington, D.C.: U.S. Government Printing Office, 1993), table 4.

129. Thomas Sowell has devoted much of his long and immensely productive career to tracing out the connections between the cultural attributes of ethnic and racial groups and their economic success, particularly in the realm of business enterprise. See, among many other items, his *Race and Economics* (New York: David McKay, 1975); *Ethnic America: A History* (New York: Basic Books, 1981); and *Race and Culture: A World View* (New York: Basic Books, 1994). For a fascinating portrait of a very small ethnic group—Chaldean Christian Arabs—that has largely displaced the Jews as merchants in Detroit's ghetto neighborhoods, see Ze'ev Chafets, *Devil's Night and Other True Tales of Detroit* (New York: Random House, 1990).

130. Jeffrey Rosen, "The Day the Quotas Died," *New Republic*, 22 April 1996, 21. The points in this paragraph are basically Rosen's, somewhat reworked.

131. "[A]n amorphous claim that there has been past discrimination in a particular industry cannot justify the use of an unyielding quota." *Richmond v. J. A. Croson*, 488 U.S. 469, 499.

132. Edley and Stephanopoulos, "Affirmative Action Review." These points can all be found in the introduction, which is also a summary; see esp. p. 3.

133. Statement of Deval L. Patrick, before the Subcommittee on the Constitution, 7 December 1995, 3, 13, 19.

134. Herbert H. Hyman and Paul B. Sheatsley, "Attitudes Towards Desegregation," *Scientific American* 211 (July 1964), 16–23.

CHAPTER 16: VOTING RIGHTS

1. The advertisement was carried on local radio and paid for by the Get Out to Vote Committee; the election was on 4 August 1981. Abigail Thernstrom came across it in the course of a research trip to Mobile. Much of this account of the history of the Voting Rights Act up through 1986 is taken from Abigail Thernstrom, *Whose Votes Count? Affirmative Action and Minority Voting Rights* (Cambridge: Harvard University Press, 1987).

2. Hearings before the Subcommittee on Civil and Constitutional Rights of the Com-

mittee on the Judiciary, U.S. Senate, 94th Cong., 1st sess., Extension of the Voting Rights Act, April-May 1975 (hereafter cited as 1975 Senate Hearings), 237.

3. Ibid., 536.

4. Washington Research Project, *The Shameful Blight: The Survival of Racial Discrimination in Voting in the South* (November 1972), 2.

5. *South Carolina v. Katzenbach,* 383 U.S. 301, 315 (1966). 1975 House Hearings), 167.

6. Thus, Frank Parker likened the results of election-related violence in Mississippi in 1964 to those that flowed from the retention of an at-large electoral system in the state capital ten years later. Jackson's black citizens had finally acquired their Fifteenth Amendment rights, but citywide voting in that 60 percent white city did mean that black candidates could not win without white support. The absence of majority-black, single-member districts, Parker said, was much "the same as continuing to prevent blacks from voting at all"; 1975 Senate Hearings, 162. Arthur Flemming of the U.S. Commission on Civil Rights, looking back to the bloody days of Selma, saw the disfranchisement imposed by police with nightsticks and electric cattle prods as only more "spectacular" than that which resulted from districting and other electoral arrangements; 1975 House Hearings, 26.

7. 1975 Senate Hearings, 3.

8. Hearings Before Subcommittee no. 5 of the Committee on the Judiciary, U.S. House of Representatives, 89th Cong., 1st sess., on H.R. 6400 and other proposals to enforce the Fifteenth Amendment to the Constitution of the United States, March-April 1965 (hereafter cited as 1965 House Hearings), 43.

9. Ibid., 21.

10. That the initial purpose of sec. 5 was to stop states from instituting novel devices that violated basic Fifteenth Amendment rights was evident in the 1965 congressional hearings. References to the preclearance provision were sparse, but Attorney General Katzenbach did briefly explain it. "Our experience in the areas that would be covered by this bill," he said, "has been such as to indicate frequently on the part of state legislatures a desire in a sense to outguess the courts of the United States." But for proposed new voting procedures to be rejected, Katzenbach went on, they would have to have the effect of denying the rights guaranteed by the Fifteenth Amendment; 1965 House Hearings, 60. And numerous witnesses at the hearings reassured their audience that those rights, which it was the entire purpose of the act to secure, were expected to be narrowly defined. The provision was viewed as so minor as to not merit even a mention in the summary of the bill contained in the Senate Judiciary Committee report, and the House report gave it only a cursory and unilluminating glance.

11. *Allen v. State Board of Elections,* 393 U.S. 544 (1969).

12. Or, after 1975, nine majority black and Hispanic districts. We refer in this chapter only to the protection provided blacks, but the statute actually covered four other protected groups, Hispanics being the only demographically important one.

13. Very few cases involving sec. 5 have reached the High Court; jurisdictions have seldom gone to the court to obtain preclearance for a proposed change in electoral procedure, since they have had another option: the relatively speedy Department of Justice process. The latter does not offer the same full-scale hearing; on the other hand, if they are dissatisfied with the outcome, they can start again in the D.C. court.

14. For an extended discussion of the annexation and other sec. 5 decisions, see Thernstrom, *Whose Votes Count?,* chap. 7.

15. *Beer v. United States,* 425 U.S. 130 (1976). See also *City of Lockhart, Texas v. United States,* 460 U.S. 125 (1983). *Shaw v. Reno* and other constitutional cases discussed below underscored the continuing validity of *Beer.*

16. *Beer v. United States,* 425 U.S. at 141.
17. The annexation cases were not alone in promising something more than the protection from "retrogression"—backsliding—promised by *Beer.* See, most notably, *City of Rome, Georgia v. United States,* 446 U.S. 156 (1980), involving changes to the city charter that included a majority-vote requirement, as well as thirteen annexations. The assumptions running through Justice Marshall's majority opinion were that only black officeholders could represent black voters, and that the point of the statute had become to promote black officeholding. See Thernstrom, *Whose Votes Count?,* 153–155.
18. See *City of Petersburg, Virginia v. United States,* 354 F. Supp. 1021 (D.D.C., 1972), aff'd 410 U.S. 962 (1973).
19. The annexation decision was *City of Richmond, Virginia v. United States,* 422 U.S. 358 (1975).
20. *Miller v. Johnson,* 132 L. Ed 2d 762 (1995). It is important to note that, in reality, as Timothy G. O'Rourke has pointed out, racially gerrymandered single-member districts do not necessarily ensure proportionate black officeholding. The operative standard has thus been a qualified proportional representation. O'Rourke, "The 1982 Amendments and the Voting Rights Paradox," in Bernard Grofman and Chandler Davidson, eds., *Controversies in Minority Voting: The Voting Rights Act in Perspective* (Washington, D.C.: Brookings Institution, 1992), 104. It is for this reason that Lani Guinier and Rep. Cynthia McKinney, among others, have called for methods of election that are designed to guarantee true proportionality. See Guinier, *The Tyranny of the Majority: Fundamental Fairness in Representative Democracy* (New York: Free Press, 1994), chap. 4.
21. *Johnson v. Miller,* (864 F. Supp. 1354 S.D. Ga. 1994 at 1377).
22. *Miller v. Johnson* (132 L. Ed. at 774, quoting from 864 F. Supp. at 1389. In her dissent Justice Ginsburg argues that "[e]vidence at trial . . . shows that considerations other than race went into determining the Eleventh District's boundaries" (798). Her denial that race was the overwhelming consideration in the configuration of that district is—given the evidence—truly puzzling.
23. For a discussion of the negotiating process, see Thernstrom, *Whose Votes Count?,* chap. 8; she had access to voting section files in the mid-1980s.
24. 864 F. Supp. at 1363.
25. 864 F. Supp. at 1386.
26. Quoted in Hiroshi Motomura, "Preclearance Under Section Five of the Voting Rights Act," *North Carolina Law Review,* 61 (January 1983), 191, n. 15. The full quotation ran: "In the conduct of our preclearance function under section 5 of the Voting Rights Act, we traditionally have considered ourselves to be a surrogate of the district court, seeking to make the kind of decision we believe the court would make if the matter were before it." DOJ regulations made the same point (28 C.F.R. 51.39).
27. 864 F. Supp. at 1368.
28. 115 S.Ct. at 2494.
29. *City of Mobile, Alabama v. Bolden,* 446 U.S. 55 (1980).
30. The report of the House Judiciary Commitee itself adopted the smoking-gun image. "Efforts to find a 'smoking gun' to establish racial discriminatory purpose or intent are not only futile, but irrelevant . . . ," it said. Report no. 97-227, Voting Rights Act Extension, Committee on the Judiciary, U.S. House of Representatives, 97th Cong., 1st sess., 15 September 1981, 29.
31. *Whitcomb v. Chavis,* 403 U.S. 124 (1971); *White v. Regester,* 412 U.S. 755 (1973).
32. *Baker v. Carr,* 369 U.S. 186 (1962), dissenting opinion.

33. *Johnson v. De Grandy,* 114 S.Ct. 2647 (1994) 2660.
34. These were basically the facts in *Whitcomb,* which involved vote dilution in Marion County, Indiana. Since blacks were Democrats in a largely Republican county, the dilution of their voting strength, the Court said, was a "mere euphemism for political defeat." It was not race but party that had determined the electoral outcome. 403 U.S. at 153 (1971).
35. *Holder v. Hall,* 114 S.Ct. 2581 (1994).
36. 114 S.Ct. 2581.
37. 114 S.Ct. 2586 (Thomas, J., concurring in judgment).
38. The Report of the Subcommittee on the Constitution to the Senate Committee on the Judiciary, reprinted in the 1982 Senate Judiciary Committee Report, S. Rep. no. 417, 97th Cong, 2nd sess. (1982) (hereafter cited as 1982 Senate Report), 148–149.
39. Ibid., 32. Emphasis added.
40. Hearings before the Subcommittee on the Constitution of the Committee on the Judiciary, U.S. Senate, 97th Cong., 2nd sess., Bills to Amend the Voting Rights Act, January–March 1982 (hereafter cited as 1982 Senate Hearings), testimony of Armand Derfner, 803 and 810. Some of Derfner's commentary was directed to the question of vote dilution in an at-large scheme, but there is no logical reason to distinguish at-large voting from single-member districting plans in dealing with the question of sec. 2 standards.
41. Ibid., 803.
42. Residential patterns are relevant to the availability of a remedy if a sec. 2 violation is found. They are thus, as the Court has said, a "threshold" question; *Thornburg v. Gingles,* 478 U.S. 30 (1986). A method of election in a racist context may impermissibly dilute black voting strength, but the remedy of a districting plan that provides for majority-black districts will be unavailable if black voters are too residentially dispersed to make feasible the drawing of such a plan.
43. Again, it was a process encouraged by the Supreme Court. In *Thornburg v. Gingles* the Court held that a violation of the revised sec. 2 had occurred where whites voting as a bloc were "*usually* . . . able to defeat candidates supported by a politically cohesive, geographically insular minority group"; 478 U.S. at 48–49. Where, "usually," less than a majority of whites had supported black candidates and where black officeholding was disproportionately low, plaintiffs were thus well on their way to prevailing. At least that is how almost every lower court read the decision.
44. 1982 Senate Hearings, 340.
45. Ibid., 1340 and 1335.
46. Deval L. Patrick, remarks, NAACP National Convention, Chicago, Illinois, July 12, 1994, unpublished transcript, on file with authors, 2.
47. In the sentences leading up to the point that voting rights were not yet secure, Mr. Patrick referred to the "blood," "toil," and "sacrifice" of (presumably) the 1960s, making no distinction between the two eras.
48. Not even a reenactment of the March 1965 Selma-to-Mongomery march brought out much of a crowd, despite the warning by Deval Patrick that "[t]he Voting Rights Act itself is under direct attack." Jim Yardley, "March of Remembrance Ends in Alabama," *Atlanta Constitution,* 12 March 1995, 5A.
49. All contemporary cases in which plaintiffs challenge districting and other electoral arrangements fit this description. A few of these cases are discussed below. As in previous chapters, by "affirmative action" we mean race-conscious action to secure equal outcomes for certain designated groups. We do not mean outreach, or aggres-

sive recruiting, which was how the term was defined when it was first used in President Lyndon B. Johnson's 1965 Executive Order 11246, as noted in chap. 6.

50. No. 92 C 1683, 1996 WL 34432 (N.D. Ill., 28 August 1995). Our discussion of the Chicago case is based upon the documents generated by the litigation, in possession of the authors. We have used *Barnett* to illustrate the point, but the practice of bringing—and indeed winning—voting rights suits in settings in which there has been a strong record of black electoral success began immediately after the revision of sec. 2 in 1982. Thus, a suit was filed in 1983 challenging Norfolk, Virginia's at-large election of a seven-member city council; plaintiffs won despite the fact that two blacks held seats on the council. Since they had to run citywide, and blacks were only 35 percent of the city's population, they inevitably depended on and received considerable white support. For a discussion of the case, see Timothy G. O'Rourke, "The 1982 Amendments and the Voting Rights Paradox," in Bernard Grofman and Chandler Davidson, eds., *Controversies in Minority Voting: The Voting Rights Act in Perspective* (Washington, D.C.: Brookings Institution, 1992), 101–103.

51. *De Grandy v. Wetherell,* 794 F. Supp. 1076 (1992) (U.S. District Court for the Northern District of Fla.).

52. The frequency of sec. 2 suits and their high degree of success has been widely acknowledged by voting rights experts. See, e.g., Chandler Davidson and Bernard Grofman, "The Voting Rights Act and the Second Reconstruction," in Davidson and Grofman, eds., *Quiet Revolution in the South: The Impact of the Voting Rights Act, 1965–1990* (Princeton: Princeton University Press), 385: "The number of section 2 cases between 1982 and 1989 dwarfed the number of constitutional challenges brought during the 1970s in the pre-*Bolden* period." The authors go on to detail the level of success, which is demonstrated in other essays in the volume.

53. Chandler Davidson, "The Recent Evolution of Voting Rights Law Affecting Racial and Language Minorities," in Davidson and Grofman, *Quiet Revolution in the South,* 35–36. Davidson readily acknowledges the number of jurisdictions that have not bothered to defend their method of voting in the wake of the revision to sec. 2. "Many dilution cases were filed in the 1980s, some of which were settled out of court in a manner favorable to plaintiffs. . . . Many at-large jurisdictions in the South (and to a lesser extent in the Southwest), having seen the handwriting on the wall, decided to adopt at least some single-member districts before someone filed a section 2 case in their locale, just to be on the safe side" (35).

54. Bernard Grofman, "*Shaw v. Reno* and the Future of Voting Rights," *PS: Political Science and Politics* 28 (March 1995), 27.

55. *Shaw v. Reno,* 509 U.S. 630, 649 (1993). *Shaw* did no more than recognize the right of voters to challenge districting maps on equal-protection grounds. The case was remanded to a three-judge federal court, which looked again at the contours of the majority-black first and twelfth districts, and held that, although they were racial classifications, they met the demanding Fourteenth Amendment standard of strict scrutiny; *Shaw v. Hunt,* 861 F. Supp. 408 (E.D. N.C. 1994). But the Supreme Court subsequently reversed in what is referred to as *Shaw II; Shaw v. Hunt,* 116 S.Ct. 1894 (1996).

56. 509 U.S. at 646. An astonishing number of articles on *Shaw* have distorted its holding. To take an exreme example, Dianne M. Pinderhughes, professor of political science and director of the Afro-American Studies and Research Program at the University of Illinois, Urbana-Champaign, has written that "the Court's ruling raises the question of whether it is constitutional for African Americans to be represented by an offi-

cial of their own race." Dianne M. Pinderhughes, "The Voting Rights Act—Whither History?" *PS Political Science and Politics* 28 (March 1995), 56. That, of course, was not the question; no court or scholar or other commentator has suggested that (for example) Rep. Charles Rangel's election by black voters in New York City —from a district that is majority-black but not racially gerrymandered—is unconstitutional. And in *Shaw* the issue was not the constitutionality of the representation but that of the race-driven contours of the districts.

57. *Regents of the University of California v. Bakke,* 438 U.S. 265, 407 (1978) (Blackmun, J., concurring).

58. 132 L. Ed 2d, 776–778 115 S.Ct. 2475, 2483 (1995).

59. *Shaw v. Reno,* 113 S.Ct. 2816, 2824 (1993) (emphasis added).

60. 113 S.Ct. at 2824.

61. 113 S.Ct. at 2827.

62. *Hays v. Louisiana,* 115 S.Ct. 2431 (1995). Abigail Thernstrom wrote an amicus brief submitted by the Institute for Justice in this case. The Supreme Court, in 1995, threw the case out on the ground that the plaintiffs, who lived outside the district, lacked standing to sue.

63. 862 F. Supp. 119, 122, and 121. (W.D. La. 1994).

64. *Johnson v. Miller,* 864 F. Supp, 1354, 1377 (S.D. Ga. 1994).

65. *Vera v. Richards,* 861 F. Supp. 1304 (S.D. Tex. 1994) at 1336. In the case of North Carolina, Timothy O'Rourke (who was an expert witness) has reported, the database used by the General Assembly included split blocks, which meant the total number of "blocks" was 229,563, which allowed districting "to be conducted at a level much more proximate to the individuals within a state rather than distal units that represent groups of people aggregated across large geographical areas." Carmen Cirincione, Thomas Darling, and Timothy G. O'Rourke, "Race and Congressional Redistricting: A Computer-Intensive Evaluation of the 1992 North Carolina Plan," paper prepared for delivery at the 1996 annual meeting of the American Political Science Association, 1996, 2.

66. 861 F. Supp. at 1336.

67. 861 F. Supp. at 1345.

68. See, for instance, the Brief for the Congressional Black Caucus as Amicus Curiae, 19–20, in the Louisiana case.

69. T. Alexander Aleinikoff and Samuel Issacharoff, "Race and Redistricting: Drawing Constitutional Lines After Shaw v. Reno," *Michigan Law Review* 92 (1993), 588, 630–631. Whites in majority-black districts, the authors write, "should not be expected to compete in any genuine sense for electoral representation" in those districts, "lest they undo the preference given to the specified minority group (631).

70. It is hardly a coincidence that the occupant of the Congressional seat from the fourth district after the 1992 election was the chairman of the Louisiana State Senate reapportionment committee that drew its convoluted boundaries. The district he mapped out was designed as a safe black seat—for him. Phil Duncan, ed., *Congressional Quarterly's Politics in America 1994* (Washington, D.C.: Congressional Quarterly Inc., 1994), 650.

71. David Lublin, "Gerrymander for Justice? Racial Redistricting and Black and Latino Representation," unpublished Ph.D. dissertation, 1994, Harvard University Archives, 48, 90.

72. 115 S.C. 2475, 2487 (1995): "Our observation in *Shaw* of the consequences of racial stereotyping was not meant to suggest that a district must be bizarre on its face

before there is a constitutional violation. . . . Shape is relevant not because bizarreness is a necessary element of the constitutional wrong or a threshold requirement of proof, but because it may be persuasive circumstantial evidence that race for its own sake, and not other districting principles, was the legislature's dominant and controlling rationale in drawing its districting. . . . Parties may rely on evidence other than bizarreness to restablish race-based districting." In her dissent, Justice Ginsburg argues that "our Nation's cities are full of districts identified by their ethnic character —Chinese, Irish, Italian, Jewish, Polish, Russian, for example." What can be wrong, then, with black districts? The analogy doesn't hold. No legislature has strung Polish voters together from widely dispersed residential pockets in order to ensure Polish officeholding; nor has the Justice Department ever suggested that any legislature should. Ginsburg, J., dissenting (115 S.Ct. at 2505).

73. *Smith v. Beasely,* C.A. No 3:95-3235-0, U.S. District Court, District of South Carolina, slip opinion, 39–40.

74. 132 L. Ed 2d at 779. The Court in *Miller* made it very clear that plaintiffs must prove that "the legislature subordinated traditional race-neutral districting principles . . . to racial considerations." It was thus not sufficient to assert that a legislature was "aware of racial demographics"; such awareness should be no more than part of "the complex interplay of forces that enter a legislature's redistricting calculus."

75. *Shaw v. Reno,* 113 S.Ct. at 2821.

76. 113 S.Ct. at 2821.

77. Stuart Taylor, Jr., "Voting Rights Redux: A Racial Spoils System?" *Legal Times,* 13 September 1993, 23. Joe Klein, whose liberal credentials were also strong, was equally alarmed. He saw the race-conscious districting as resegregating electoral districts in the South, which he viewed as having a "disastrous impact on civil society"; "The End of Affirmative Action," *Newsweek,* 13 February 1995, 36.

78. Timothy M. Phelps, "Court Test for Minority Seats," *Newsday,* 4 December 1995, A15.

79. David G. Savage, "High Court Rejects Voter Districts Drawn Only on Basis of Race," *Los Angeles Times,* 30 June 1995, A1.

80. Kevin Sack, "Victory of 5 Redistricted Blacks Recasts Gerrymandering Dispute," *New York Times,* 23 November 1996, 1.

81. Richard Carelli, "Racial Maps Given a Blow," *Chattanooga Times,* 14 June 1996, A4.

82. Pamela S. Karlan, "Minority Reps," editorial, *The Nation,* 8 March 1993, 292. Others sounded much the same note. See, e.g., Paul D. McClain and Joseph Stewart, Jr., "W(h)ither the Voting Rights Act After *Shaw v. Reno:* Advancing to the Past?" *PS: Political Science and Politics,* 28 (March 1995), 26: "It does not seem to us a manifestation of paranoia to see the attack on the creation of majority-minority districts . . . as a veiled attack on the Voting Rights Act."

83. These results were summarized in numerous articles. See, e.g., Sack, "Victory of 5 Redistricted Blacks."

84. Peter Applebome, "The 1994 Campaign," *New York Times,* 19 September 1994, B8.

85. Jim Sleeper, "The Rainbow Coalition," *New Republic,* 2 December 1996, 24. A Michael Fletcher, "New Tolerance in the South or Old Power of Incumbency?" *Washington Post,* 23 November 1996, A1.

86. Representative Cynthia McKinney claimed after the fact that her victory said "more about the power of incumbency than anything else"; McKinney, "Why Minority Districts Matter," *Washington Times,* 5 December 1996, A-17.

87. It is possible, of course, that the lines of causation have been running the other way.

Perhaps the racial composition of the districts didn't promote racial militance; instead, blacks attracted to congressional races were more left-leaning because the job of congressman is more ideological than that of mayor.

88. Estimates vary as to how many seats in Congress Democrats lost as a consequence of racial redistricting, "I've warned the Black Caucus for years that this was coming. Over the last two elections, the Democrats have lost as many as 15 seats because of majority black redistricting," said the respected analyst for the Joint Center for Political and Economic Studies, David Bositis, in 1995; John J. Miller, "Race to Defeat," *Reason,* February 1995, 23. Writing before the 1996 elections, the political scientist Charles S. Bullock III noted that the 1992 and 1994 Republican gains were made by a combination of redistricting and the general nationwide changes in voter allegiance. "After two rounds of congressional elections in the new districts, Republicans had won all 20 seats where redistricting reduced the percent black by more than ten percentage points, for a gain of six seats. In 1994, Republicans won the open seats in which the black percentage decreased even modestly or held constant during redistricting"; Bullock, "The South and the 1996 Elections," *PS* 29 (September 1996), 453. The NAACP disputed these conclusions; NAACP Legal Defense and Education Fund, *The Effect of Section 2 of the Voting Rights Act on the 1994 Congressional Elections,* unpublished ms., 30 November 1994. For further discussion of this issue, see A. Thernstrom and Andrew Hazlett, "Endangered Species: Their Habitats Destroyed, White Southern Democrats are a Vanishing Breed," *New Democrat,* January-February 1995, 17–18; Mark F. Bernstein, "Racial Gerrymandering," *Public Interest,* Winter 1996, 59–69; and Charles S. Bullock III, "Winners and Losers in the Latest Round of Redistricting," *Emory Law Journal,* 44 (Summer 1995), 943–977.

89. Thernstrom, *Whose Votes Count?,* 234. A year earlier, in four South Carolina state legislative districts, conservative Republicans replaced incumbent liberal Democrats as a consequence of race-conscious redistricting. In *Thornburg,* the important sec. 2 case that reached the Supreme Court in 1987, North Carolina state Republican leaders acknowledged the "happy coincidence" between the interests of blacks and Republicans, and indeed they had much to celebrate. The political scientist Charles S. Bullock III examined partisan shifts in state legislatures as a consequence of redistricting subsequent to the 1970 census, and concluded that the GOP did better in the preclearance states than elsewhere. Bullock, "The Election of Blacks in the South: Preconditions and Consequences," *American Journal of Political Science* 19 (November 1975), 727–739. See also Carol M. Swain, *Black Faces, Black Interests: The Repesentation of African Americans in Congress* (Cambridge: Harvard University Press, 1993), 205.

90. Steven A. Holmes, "For Very Strange Bedfellows, Try Redistricting," *New York Times,* 23 July 1995, 16. On the trade-off between electoral arrangements that ensure minority officeholding and the representation of black interests, see Charles Cameron, David Epstein, and Sharyn O'Halloran, "Do Majority-Minority Districts Maximize Substantive Black Representation in Congress" *American Political Science Review* 90 (December 1996), 794–812.

91. Steven A. Holmes, "Majority Rules; But, Will Whites Vote for a Black?" *New York Times,* 16 June 1996, sec. IV, 1.

92. Even sophisticated voting rights scholars closed their eyes to changing white racial attitudes—and kept them shut. Thus, in a 1994 essay, political scientists Lisa Handley and Bernard Grofman wrote: "there is little evidence for a widespread increase in

the willingness of white voters to cast their ballots for black candidates." Handley and Grofman, "The Impact of the Voting Rights Act on Minority Representation: Black Officeholding in Southern State Legislatures and Congressional Delegations," in Davidson and Grofman, eds., *Quiet Revolution in the South,* 335. That view had long been a mantra in the literature on voting rights.

93. We are indebted to Professor Timothy O'Rourke of the University of Missouri–St. Louis for a number of points in this paragraph; phone conversation with Abigail Thernstrom, 5 January 1997.

94. Holmes, "Majority Rules."

95. Pinderhughes, "The Voting Rights Act—Whither History?" 55.

96. Don J. DeBenedictis, "A.G.: Lone Black District OK," *American Lawyer,* 10 December 1996. The case was *Abrams v. Johnson,* and the plaintiffs asked the Court to reject the congressional districts drawn the previous year by a federal district court. The lower court had taken on the mapmaking task after members of the Georgia General Assembly had failed to agree on one themselves.

97. See, for instance, Pamela S. Karlan and Thomas C. Goldstein, "On a Collision Course," *Legal Times,* 17 April 1995, 24. Grofman, "*Shaw v. Reno,*" 31, also raises the "collision course" point.

98. 113 S.Ct. at 2831.

99. "Nonretrogression [was] not a license for the State to do whatever it deems necessary to insure [the] continued electoral *success*" of black candidates, the Court said. Section 5, the majority opinion continued, "merely mandates that the minority's *opportunity* to elect representatives of its choice not be diminished, directly or indirectly, by the State's actions." And quoting from *Shaw I,* it reaffirmed its position that "a reapportionment plan would not be narrowly tailored to the goal of avoiding retrogression if the State went beyond what was reasonably necessary to avoid retrogression." *Bush v. Vera,* 116 S.Ct. 1941 (1996) at 1963. Abigail Thernstrom wrote an amicus brief filed by the Institute for Justice in this case.

100. 132 L. Ed. 2d at 785. In the North Carolina case the DOJ had not insisted on the totally bizarre twelfth district as it was eventually drawn, but it had objected to a plan with only one majority-black district and thus made clear the necessity for creating another—an order that did not square with the law, since the state's one district map went beyond the demands of the retrogression test.

101. As the memo put it, since blacks in Barbour County, Alabama, "constitute 40.5 percent of the voting age population, they would be entitled to 2.8 districts"—which meant two that were safe for black candidates and one that had less than the magic number of 65 percent black population. Abigail Thernstrom, *Whose Votes Count?,* 172; this was information from the internal files of the Department of Justice to which A.T. had partial access for a brief period of time.

102. Remarks of John R. Dunne before the National Institute of Municipal Law Officers Concerning 'Reapportionment," 29 October 1991, Sheraton Hotel, San Diego, Calif., on file with authors.

103. The Louisiana story is actually a bit complicated and involved correspondence over an earlier districting plan for the state board of education, which the Department of Justice refused to preclear because an allegedly better one could have been drawn. That "better" one contained another, bizarrely shaped majority-black district, and the failure to draw that district was viewed as evidence of discriminatory intent. Louisiana thus logically assumed that the same rules would apply to congressional redistricting —that the Justice Department would refuse to preclear a proposed plan as long as

another majority-black constituency could still be created; *Bossier Parish School Board v. Reno,* 907 F. Supp. 434 (D.D.C. 1995), 438–440. In the case of Georgia, too, the state's allegedly inadequate explanation for "its refusal in the first two submissions [of districting plans] to take the steps necessary to create a third majority-minority district" was read by the federal government as a violation of sec. 5's prohibition against purposefully discriminatory plans; 132 L. Ed 2d at 773.

104. See, for instance, *New York v. United States,* 874 F. Supp. 394, 401 (D.D.C. 1994); *Georgia v. Reno,* 881 F. Supp. 7, 14 (D.D.C. 1995).

105. This is not to say, of course, that there can be no circumstantial evidence of invidious purpose. As Katharine Butler has pointed out, if a state has failed to recognize concentrations of minority voters that would naturally produce majority-minority districts using standard districting criteria, it could legitimately be said to have failed to carry its burden of proving an absence of discriminatory intent. But unless a rejected plan clearly meets the state's own stated redistricting criteria and is superior in that regard to the plan actually adopted, the argument that rejection itself is a sign of unacceptable purpose amounts to nothing more than an insistence on a maximum number of majority-minority districts; Katharine Inglis Butler, "Affirmative Racial Gerrymandering: Fair Representation for Minorities or a Dangerous Recognition of Group Rights?" *Rutgers Law Journal* 26 (1995), 498, 510–511.

106. Brief for the United States, 19; amicus brief for the DNC, 20. Both on file with authors.

107. A state that strings together black residential pockets in order to create majority-black districts "is akin to a manufacturer paying punitive damages to potential purchasers of its product prior to anyone suffering an injury or establishing a defect in the product," Katharine Butler has written. "Affirmative Racial Gerrymandering," 613. This is obviously our reading of sec. 2 as well.

108. This summary of the Bossier Parish case is taken from 907 F. Supp. 434 (D.D.C. 1995). The identical plan that had been precleared was for the "policy jury," Louisiana's name for a county council. The Supreme Court heard argument in the case on 9 December 1996; as we write, no decision has been handed down.

109. 907 F. Supp. at 441. The district court decision in *Bossier* was not the first to recognize the distinction between secs. 2 and 5. The two provisions "differ in structure, purpose, and application," the Supreme Court noted in *Holder v. Hall* (114 S.Ct. 2581, 2587 [1994]). See also *New York v. United States,* 874 F. Supp. 394, 401 (D.D.C. 1994); *Georgia v. Reno,* 881 F. Supp. 7, 14 (D.D.C. 1995).

110. See Thernstrom, *Whose Votes Count?,* 300, n. 10, for a fuller history of the "incorporation" of sec. 2 into sec. 5.

111. See, e.g., 128 *Congressional Record* 14,938 (1982) (exchange between Reps. Don Edwards and Elliott H. Levitas).

112. See Procedures for the Administration of Section 5 of the Voting Rights Act, 28 C.F.R., § 51.55: "In those instances in which the Attorney General concludes that, as proposed, the submitted change is free of discriminatory purpose and retrogressive effect, but also concludes that a bar to implementation of the change is necessary to prevent a clear violation of amended Section 2, the Attorney General shall withhold Section 5 preclearance."

113. That footnote states that "[i]n light of the amendment to section 2, it is intended that a section 5 objection also follow if a new voting procedure itself so discriminates as to violate section 2." 1982 Senate Report, 12, n. 31.

114. *White v. Regester,* 412 U.S. 755, 769 (1973).

115. The Justice Department itself, in its "comments" introducing the new 1987 guidelines, admitted that administrative review did not remotely resemble a judicial proceeding. Procedures for the Adminstration of Section 5, 28 C.F.R. § 51.55(b).

116. Voting rights specialist Pamela S. Karlan has argued that "*Shaw* repesented an extraordinary feat of judicial intrusion into the political process." Pamela S. Karlan, "Apres *Shaw* le deluge?" *PS* 28 (March 1995), 50. Given the degree to which Karlan has applauded administrative intrustion into those same political processes, the argument seems a bit odd.

117. Richard L. Engstrom, "Preliminary Report," October 27, 1995 and Allan J. Lichtman, "Preliminary Report," October 26, 1995, *Barnett* documents on file with authors. Indeed, they implied that in a majority-black ward where black turnout had been low and a white alderman elected, whites exercised pernicious "control" of an unspecified but disfranchising nature. Defendant-Intervenors' Answer to the Barnett Plaintiffs' Third Amended Complaint, 24–25.

118. The success of black candidates in majority-white settings has been routinely dismissed as aberrational by civil rights advocates. An ACLU attorney, referring to Gov. Wilder's election, called it exceptional, and questioned whether it illustrated white racial tolerance, since Wilder did not get a majority of the white vote; O'Rourke, "The 1982 Amendments," 109. As chap. 11 noted, however, neither had Charles Robb, his Democratic predecessor in office. And for that matter, neither did President Bill Clinton in either 1992 or 1996—a fact that did not taint the election returns. The view that exceptions to white racism are rare regularly crops up in voting rights briefs. See, for instance, the Brief for the Congressional Black Caucus in *Hays v. Louisiana:* Black candidates cannot get elected in majority-white settings; that, it claims, is "contemporary reality" (1).

119. Ronald Walters, "Two Political Traditions: Black Politics in the 1990s," in Lucius Barker, ed., *Ethnic Politics and Civil Liberties* (New Brunswick, N.J.: Transaction, 1992), 198.

120. Defendant City of Chicago's Answer and Defenses to the Barnett Plaintiffs' Third Amended Complaint, 17; Defendant-Intervenors' Answer to the Barnett Plaintiffs' Third Amended Complaint, 15. Only in the nineteen majority-black wards, plaintiffs had asserted, did "African-Americans have sufficient population to elect candidates of their choice." See also Defendant City of Chicago's Answer and Defenses to the Barnett Plaintiffs' Third Amended Complaint, 23: blacks are only "able" to elect the candidates of their choice in heavily black districts. Throughout the redistricting process, the plaintiffs and their attorney insisted on a black concentration of at least 70 percent in the wards drawn to create black electoral "opportunity." Defendant-Intervenors' Answer to the Barnett Plaintiffs' Third Amended Complaint, 27.

121. Defendant-Intervenors' Answer to the Barnett Plaintiffs' Third Amended Complaint, 21.

122. The issue has cropped up regularly in voting rights disputes. Thus in *NAACP v. Austin,* a case involving redistricting for the Michigan state legislature, a lengthy report by Professor Edward J. Littlejohn reviewed "Official Discrimination in Michigan History," and attributed contemporary economic inequality to alleged discrimination in the past. But, as chap. 6 pointed out, the unemployment rate for blacks in Detroit in 1965 was 3.4 percent, while in 1992 it was up to 19.3 percent. Likewise, median black family income in Detroit in 1965 was a remarkable 94 percent that of whites. Discrimination, before 1965, the focus of the Littlejohn report, obviously cannot explain the deteriorating position of Detroit blacks since 1965.

123. Defendant City of Chicago's Answer and Defenses to the Barnett Plaintiffs' Third Amended Complaint, 17.

124. Flynn McRoberts, "Kenwood, Oakland Reject CHA Plan," *Chicago Tribune,* 16 November 1995, MetroChicago sec., 1.

125. Karen M. Thomas, "Parents in Class Conflict," *Chicago Tribune,* 28 March 1989, 1; "One School, Different Worlds," *Chicago Tribune,* 13 August 1990, C1.

126. That scholarship had been contained in Richard P. Taub, D. Garth Taylor, and Jan D. Dunham, *Paths of Neighborhood Change: Race and Crime in Urban America* (Chicago: University of Chicago Press, 1984).

127. 509 U.S. at 657. Justice O'Connor's concern had been stated by Justice William O. Douglas as early as 1964—a year before the passage of the Voting Rights Act—in a case involving districting in New York. "When racial or religious lines are drawn by the State," Douglas said, "the multiracial, multireligious communities that our Constitution seeks to weld together as one become separatist; antagonisms that relate to race or to religion rather than to political issues are generated; communities seek not the best representative but the best racial or religious partisan." *Wright v. Rockefeller,* 376 U.S. 52 (1964) at 67. (Douglas, J., dissenting). His view in 1964 was civil rights orthodoxy; Douglas was a clear and much celebrated voice of American liberalism on the Court. His views—quoted above—have by now acquired the label "conservative."

128. *Hays v. Louisiana,* 862 F. Supp. 119 (1994) at 125.

CHAPTER 17: THE RACIAL CLIMATE

1. Notes taken by Abigail Thernstrom, who was a participant, at the initial taping on January 25, 1996, Washington, D.C. The "white" group included one Hispanic (Linda Chavez) and one Southeast Asian (Dinesh D'Souza).

2. Roger Wilkins, "Howard Beach Started 200 Years Ago," *New York Times,* 5 January 1987, A17.

3. "Fighting Racism," *USA Today,* 21 January 1991, 9A.

4. Carl Rowan, *The Coming Race War in America: A Wake-up Call* (Boston: Little, Brown, 1996), 4.

5. Remark made on *Both Sides with Jesse Jackson,* CNN, July 30, 1995.

6. Toni Morrison, "On the Backs of Blacks," *Time,* Special issue, Fall 1993, 57.

7. Remark made on *Both Sides with Jesse Jackson,* CNN, July 30, 1995.

8. Robert Hanley, "Island in a Sea of White Resistance," *New York Times,* 21 December 1995, B1.

9. "American Notes; Term Limit; Nothing Is Forever," *Time,* 23 March 1992, 31.

10. Linton Weeks, "The Continuing Hurt of History," *Washington Post,* 22 December 1995, C1. A month later the exhibit did find another home: the Martin Luther King Memorial Library.

11. Remark made on *Both Sides with Jesse Jackson,* CNN, July 30, 1995.

12. Joe Klein, "Deadly Metaphors," *New York Magazine,* 9 September 1991, 28.

13. "Black Like Whom?" *Newsweek,* 14 November 1994, 64.

14. Jim Sleeper, *The Closest of Strangers: Liberalism and the Politics of Race in New York* (New York: Norton, 1990), 247.

15. "The White Negro" was reprinted in Mailer's *Advertisements for Myself* (New York: Putnam, 1960), 302–322. Wolfe's classic essay is in *Radical Chic and Mau-mauing*

the Flak Catchers (New York: Farrar, Straus and Giroux, 1970). For the story of the Black Panthers, see Hugh Pearson, *The Shadow of the Panther: Huey Newton and the Price of Black Power in America* (Reading, Mass.: Addison-Wesley, 1994).

16. Brent Staples, *Parallel Time: Growing Up in Black and White* (New York: Pantheon Books, 1994), 259.

17. Derrick Bell *Faces at the Bottom of the Well: The Permanence of Racism* (New York: Basic Books, 1992), 45.

18. Ibid., chap. 5.

19. Ibid., chap. 7.

20. Ibid., chap. 9.

21. Nathan McCall, *Makes Me Wanna Holler: A Young Black Man in America* (New York: Random House, 1994), 3–4.

22. Ibid., 58, 78–79.

23. Ibid., 196.

24. Ibid., 236.

25. Ibid., 254.

26. Robert Pear, "Attacks Begin on Proposal to Cut Social Programs," *New York Times*, 10 December 1994, 30.

27. David Seifman, "Hold on to Your Seat," *New York Post*, 21 October 1995, 2.

28. The definitive account of the case has been written by six members of the *New York Times* staff—Robert D. McFadden et. al., *Outrage: The Story Behind the Tawana Brawley Hoax* (New York: Bantam Books, 1990).

29. Steve Pfarrer, "Many Say Issues Raised Are Still Valid," *Daily Hampshire Gazette*, 28 September 1994, 1.

30. Nancy Newcombe, "Assault Tale, Racist Notes Said a Hoax," *Daily Hampshire Gazette*, 28 September 1994, 1.

31. Colman McCarthy, "The Harm of Taking Cover in Racial Rift," *Washington Post*, 13 September 1994, C10.

32. Coretta Scott King, "Dream Rocks But Survives," *Cleveland Plain Dealer*, 20 January 1995, 11B.

33. David Nicholson, "Driving Old Dixie Down," *Washington Post*, 24 April 1994, C1.

34. Howard Schuman, Charlotte Steen, and Lawrence Bobo, *Racial Attitudes in America: Trends and Interpretations* (Cambridge: Harvard University Press, 1985; rev. paperback ed., 1988) 74, 106, 118.

35. Schuman et al., *Racial Attitudes*, 75, 107, 118.

36. Ibid., xii-xiii. This generalization is also supported by the findings of two recent analyses of polling data—Benjamin I. Page and Robert Y. Shapiro, *The Rational Public: Fifty Years of Trends in Americans' Policy Preferences* (Chicago: University of Chicago Press, 1992), 67–81; William G. Mayer, *The Changing American Mind: How and Why American Public Opinion Changed Between 1960 and 1988* (Ann Arbor: University of Michigan Press, 1993), 22–28, 365–374.

37. Paul M. Sniderman and Thomas Piazza, *The Scar of Race* (Cambridge: Harvard University Press, 1993), 7–8.

38. Ibid., 4, 76, 25.

39. Ibid., 109.

40. Ibid.

41. Lance Morrow, "The Cure for Racism," *Time*, 5 December 1994, 106.

42. Cindy Skrzycki, "AT&T Apologizes for 'Racist Illustration,'" *Washington Post*, 17 August 1993, 1.

43. AP wire story, "2 Convicted of Setting Black Tourist Afire in Tampa," *Washington Post,* 8 September 1993, 1.

44. Jacques Steinberg, "Racist Message Reveals Rift," *New York Times,* 21 June 1995, B4.

45. The Denny's story is told in detail in Howard Kohn, "Service with a Sneer," *New York Times Magazine,* 6 November 1994, 43–47, 58, 78, 81.

46. "The Killing of Carol Stuart: An Implausible Truth," *Economist,* 13 January 1990, 31. The story was written by Abigail Thernstrom, then a stringer for the magazine, and this account thus lifts some sentences from that one.

47. The quotations are taken from Don Terry, "False Accusation in South Carolina Hurts Blacks," *New York Times,* 6 November 1994, 22; the story was widely covered, however.

48. "Board Member Resigns," *Education Week,* 25 October 1995, 4.

49. Retha Hill and Pierre Thomas, "Anti-Bias Message Sent, in Big Letters," *Washington Post,* 25 May 1994, D1.

50. See n. 45.

51. "Shifting Racial Climate," *Washington Post,* 25 October 1989, A1.

52. Viva Hardigg, "Dream in the Desert," *U.S. News & World Report,* 18 January 1993, 19.

53. Rick Bragg, "Just a Grave for a Baby . . . ," *New York Times,* 31 March 1996, 14.

54. The original story was Kurt Eichenwald, "Texaco Executives, On Tape, Discussed Impeding a Bias Suit," *New York Times,* 4 November 1996, A1. "Hate on Tape at Texaco" and "Surreptitious Tapes Betray Texaco's Outrageous Racism" were from the *Cleveland Plain Dealer,* 10 November 1996, 2H and the *Columbus Dispatch,* 7 November 1996, 13A respectively.

55. Kurt Eichenwald, "Investigation Finds No Evidence of Slur on Texaco Tapes," *New York Times,* 11 November 1996, A1; Sharon Walsh, "Texaco Says Tape Analysis Refutes Slurs," *Washington Post,* 12 November 1996, 1.

56. "Excerpts from Tapes in Discrimination Lawsuit," *New York Times,* 4 November 1996, D4.

57. Sam Zagoria, "What Jesse Jackson Said," *Washington Post,* 22 February 1984, A20.

58. "If the executives at the top demonstrate a concrete commitment to workplace diversity by tying the diversity effort to the performance evaluations of managers and supervisors—that is, to their promotions and pay—diversity is far more likely to become part of the social and economic fabric of the corporation"; Walter C. Farrell, Jr., and James H. Johnson, Jr., "Toward Diversity, and Profits," *New York Times,* 12 January 1997, F14. Managers who have any regard for their self-interest will promote a slate of candidates with the correct racial and gender mix, not the individuals who seem to them the best qualified, period. This is calculated to produce an organization riddled with discrimination in the old-fashioned sense of the term—that the individuals within it are treated differently according to irrelevant ascribed characteristics like race and gender. Readers who see nothing wrong with this might ask themselves how they would view the matter if a corporate board of directors decided that "too many" Jews were being promoted, and that Christians should be given their fair share of opportunities to ensure sufficient diversity.

59. Kurt Eichenwald, "Texaco Plans Wide Program for Minorities," *New York Times,* 19 December 1996, D1; Thomas S. Mulligan, "Texaco Disciplines Executives in Scandal," *Los Angeles Times,* 7 November 1996, D3. See also Sharon Walsh, "Texaco Settles Bias Suit," *Washington Post,* 16 November 1996, 1. The employment discrimi-

nation suit that the company was forced to settle apparently rested on statistical disparities: the disproportionately small number of black Texaco executives making over $106,000 a year. No one has as yet answered two glaringly obvious questions. What proportion of the people holding these jobs at Texaco were trained in geology, petroleum engineering, and related fields? How many blacks have the relevant professional training to be eligible for such jobs?

60. Richard Cohen, "The Texaco Story (Cont'd.)," *Washington Post*, 12 November 1996, A17. Michael Kelly made much the same point in the *New Republic*, "TRB," 9 December 1996, 6.

61. Fox Butterfield, "Old Fears and New Hope," *New York Times*, 21 July 1996, 12.

62. Melissa Fay Greene, "The Fire Last Time," *Newsweek*, 24 June 1996, 34.

63. Michael Kelly, "Playing with Fire," *New Yorker*, 15 July 1996, 35.

64. Henry Allen, "Black Unlike Me: Confessions of a White Man Confused by Racial Etiquette," *Washington Post*, 29 May 1994, C1.

65. Quoted in Joyce Purnick, "Metro Matters," *New York Times*, 21 December 1995, B1.

66. Orlando Patterson, "The Paradox of Integration," *New Republic*, 6 November 1995, 24.

67. Larry Hugick, "Blacks See Their Lives Worsening," *Gallup Poll Monthly*, April 1992, 28; "An American Dilemma (Part II)," *Public Perspective* 7 (February-March 1996), 22.

68. Anti-Defamation League, *Highlights from an Anti-Defamation League Survey on Racial Attitudes in America* (New York: Anti-Defamation League, 1993), 36–37, 40–41.

69. C. Gray Wheeler, "30 Years Beyond 'I Have A Dream,' " *Gallup Poll Monthly*, October 1993, 5.

70. Richard Lacayo, "We, Too, Sing America," *Time*, 30 October 1995, 35.

71. "American Dilemma (Part II)," 20–21.

72. Sniderman and Piazza, *Scar of Race*, 45–46. For example, 52 percent of whites believed that "it was a very good description" of "most blacks" to say that they were "aggressive or violent." But even more African Americans—59 percent—thought that was true. Likewise, 21 percent of whites believed that blacks are "irresponsible," but twice that many black respondents—40 percent—accepted that stereotype. It is also significant that a 1994 Harris poll found that Asian and Hispanic Americans were considerably more likely than whites to have negative views of blacks, and that African Americans were in turn more negative about those groups than were whites; blacks were also twice as likely as non-Jewish whites to hold anti-Semitic views; National Conference of Christians and Jews, *Taking America's Pulse: The National Conference Survey on Inter-Group Relations"* (New York: National Conference of Christians and Jews, 1994), appendix B.

73. Patterson, "The Paradox of Integration."

74. McCall, *Makes Me Wanna Holler*, 17, 93.

75. Ellis Cose, *The Rage of a Privileged Class* (New York: HarperCollins, 1993), 73–74.

76. Ibid., chap. 1.

77. Robert J. Samuelson, "The Triumph of the Psycho-Fact," *Washington Post*, 4 May 1995, A25.

78. Cose, *Rage*, 160, quoting sociologist Joe Feagin.

79. Ronald Sullivan, "Brutality of Rape Detailed as Jogger Trial Opens," *New York Times*, 26 June 1990, B1.

80. These examples are from John Cassidy, "American Nightmare," *Sunday Times* (Lon-

don), 22 July 1990, Features section. But the coverage of the case was extensive, and the point could be made on the basis of any one of dozens of articles. *The New American,* a black weekly newspaper, was among those that spread the story that the jogger's (white) boyfriend was the perpetrator.

81. The publisher was Wilbert A. Tatum, and the newspaper is the *Amsterdam News;* quoted in David Evanier, "Invisible Man: The Lynching of Yankel Rosenbaum," *New Republic,* 14 October 1991, 21. Rev. Calvin O. Butts III is the prominent black minister, quoted in William Glaberson, "In Jogger Case, Once Viewed Starkly, Some Skeptics Side with Defendants," *New York Times,* 8 August 1990, B3.

82. The word "murder" was used often in response to the death of Gavin Cato. See, for instance, "Side By Side, Apart," *U.S. News & World Report,* 4 November 1991, 44, statement of Henry Rice, a Crown Heights resident.

83. Sharpton's remarks were widely reported; a good summary is contained in Philip Gourevitch, "The Crown Heights Riot and Its Aftermath," *Commentary,* January 1993, 29–34.

84. Melinda Beck and Bruce Shenitz, "Bonfire in Crown Heights," *Newsweek,* 9 September 1991, 48. The *Amsterdam News* carried a banner headline at the height of the crisis that read "Many Blacks, No Jews Arrested in Crown Heights." Again, the clear implication was of racial bias on the part of the authorities—a refusal to recognize criminal acts on the part of Jews; Klein, "Deadly Metaphors," 28.

85. Ronald Smothers, "Victim of Attack Ties Car's Driver to Gang in Queens," *New York Times,* 27 December 1986, 1.

86. Quoted in Michael Meyers, "Black Extremists and Howard Beach," *New York Times,* 13 January 1987, 27.

87. Ronald Smothers, "23 Black Leaders and Koch Attack 'Pervasive' Racism," *New York Times,* 1 January 1987, 1.

88. Dennis Hevesi, "Black Protesters March in Brooklyn Communities," *New York Times,* 13 May 1990, 24.

89. Sam Roberts, "Can Politics Get to the Roots of Racial Strife?" *New York Times,* 20 May 1990, sec. 4, 1.

90. Phone conversation with Sleeper, 10 October 1993. See also Sleeper, *The Closest of Strangers,* chap. 7, for a good discussion of these cases and the politics of racial resentment.

91. Robert McFadden, "Television Crews Hit with Bricks from Protesters," *New York Times,* 19 May 1990, 27.

92. Klein, "Deadly Metaphors."

93. Herbert Daughtry, "Who Really Killed Yusef Hawkins," op-ed, *New York Times,* 29 August 1989, 19. Daughtry was the pastor of the House of the Lord Pentacostal Church in Brooklyn.

94. David Streitfeld, "Bernie Goetz's Trial by Ire," *Washington Post,* 21 November 1986, B5.

95. *New York Newsday,* 28 June 1987, 3. Goetz got a substantial sympathy vote from blacks as well; 45 percent applauded the verdict, suggesting that in this instance the voices of racial grievance were not able to smother law-and-order sentiment within the black community.

96. The degree to which the LAPD had treated Simpson's wife-beating with kid gloves has been fully documented in Jeffrey Toobin, *The Run of His Life: The People v. O. J. Simpson* (New York: Random House, 1996). Early in the book (p. 12) Toobin noted that "the defense cleverly obscured the one actual police conspiracy that was

revealed over the course of the case—that of the starstruck cops who in 1989 tried to minimize and excuse O. J. Simpson's history of domestic violence."

97. This account of the Simpson case owes much to Henry Fetter, who coauthored the article from which this discussion is largely taken. See Abigail Thernstrom and Henry D. Fetter, "From Scottsboro to Simpson," *Public Interest* 122 (Winter 1996), 17–27. The basic story of the Simpson case has appeared in so many places that we footnote only quotations and the less widely known facts.

98. Details in this and the next paragraph are from David Whitman's perceptive account "The Untold Story of the LA Riot," *U.S. News & World Report*, 31 May 1993, 35–39, 44–47, 50–59. A full-scale scholarly study of the 1992 Los Angeles riot is sorely needed. Raphael J. Sonenshein, *Politics in Black and White: Race and Power in Los Angeles* (Princeton: Princeton University Press, 1993), provides useful background on racial politics, but devotes little attention to the riot, which occurred when the book was clearly nearing completion. The topic addressed in Nancy Abelmann and John Lie, *Blue Dreams: Korean Americans and the Los Angeles Riot* (Cambridge: Harvard University Press, 1995), is important and neglected, but the authors' attempt to make the story conform to the "people of color" orthodoxy is unconvincing.

99. Jack Miles, "Blacks vs. Browns: The Struggle for the Bottom Rung," *Atlantic Monthly*, October 1992, 41–68.

100. Stephen Battaglio, "Simpson Made TV History, Nielsen Says," *Hollywood Reporter*, 5 October 1995, 1.

101. Toobin, *The Run of His Life*, 431.

102. Reuters, "Model Was Called on Night of Slayings," *Chicago Tribune*, 14 May 1995, 8.

103. The story of the redecorating job is in Lawrence Schiller and James Willwerth, *American Tragedy: The Uncensored Story of the Simpson Defense* (New York: Random House, 1996), 371–372; "stagecraft" is their term.

104. Remark in a 1968 interview with Robert Lipsyte of *The New York Times;* quoted in Toobin, *The Run of His Life*, 49.

105. Toobin, *The Run of His Life*, 72. Jackson made the remark on CNN.

106. Miles Corwin, "Location of Trial Can Be Crucial to Outcome," *Los Angeles Times*, 27 November 1995, A3.

107. Maura Dolan, "Demographics Favor Racial Parity for O. J. Simpson Jury," *Los Angeles Times*, 25 September 1994, A22; "The Simpson Report," *Atlanta Constitution*, 16 October 1994, A13.

108. "The Verdict's Aftermath," *U.S. News & World Report*, 16 October 1995, 38. Toobin pointed out that Marcia Clark thought of black women jurors, with whom she had worked in previous trials, as her special fan club. In fact, in the mock juries before the trial, black women thought of her as "shifty," "strident," and a "bitch." Black women were thus O.J.'s strongest supporters, even believing physical force was appropriate in a marriage. Toobin, *The Run of His Life*, 189, 193.

109. Vincent Schodolski, "The Verdict: Not Guilty," *Chicago Tribune*, 4 October 1995, 1. There was irony in that complaint from Shapiro, who was the first to have the idea of building the case around the theme of a racist police frame-up; Toobin, *The Run of His Life*, 152–157.

110. Jim Newton et al., "Jury Urged to Free Simpson," *Los Angeles Times*, 29 September 1995, 1.

111. Robert Weisbrot, *Freedom Bound: A History of America's Civil Rights Movement* (New York: Norton, 1990), 93.

112. Toobin, *The Run of His Life*, 171, 180. "Because of the overwhelming evidence of Simpson's guilt, his lawyers could not undertake a defense aimed at proving his innocence," Toobin has argued (11). "Instead, in an astonishing act of legal bravado, they sought to create for the client . . . the mantle of victimhood. Almost from the day of Simpson's arrest, his lawyers sought to invent a separate narrative, an alternative reality, for the events of June 12, 1994."

113. Jennifer L. Hochschild, *Facing Up to The American Dream: Race, Class, and the Soul of the Nation* (Princeton: Princeton University Press, 1995), table 5.1, 106.

114. AP Wire Service, "Racial Split Grows on Guilt," *Memphis Commercial Appeal*, 11 February 1995, 2A.

115. Richard Morin, "Poll Reflects Division over Simpson Case," *Washington Post*, 8 October 1995, A31. Since the verdict in the criminal trial the proportion of both whites and blacks who believed that Simpson was guilty has risen, but the racial gap has remained roughly the same. As of May 1996, 34 percent of blacks thought the charges were true, as compared with 80 percent of whites; Frank Newport, "Americans Still Think O. J. Simpson Guilty," *Gallup Poll Monthly*, May 1996, 16.

116. "The O. J. Simpson Case: Prominent Blacks Discuss Race, Sex, Crime, and 'The Case of the Century,'" *Ebony*, September 1994, 29. (Nikki Giovanni was one of the participants.)

117. Cochran remarks on CNN's "Burden of Proof," 28 November 1996, Transcript 9611280, IV 38, 12:30 a.m. EST; Cheryl Lavin "Well Acquitted: Q's and A's with Johnnie Cochran," *Chicago Tribune*, 5 January 1996, C1.

118. Dan T. Carter, *Scottsboro: A Tragedy of the American South* (New York: Oxford University Press, 1971), 235.

119. "Race Seems to Play An Increasing Role in Many Jury Verdicts, *Wall Street Journal*, 4 October 1995, 1. See also Center for Equal Opportunity, *Race and the Criminal Justice System: How Race Affects Jury Trials* (Washington, D.C.: Center for Equal Opportunity, 1996). In 1996 Lemrick Nelson was convicted in federal court of violating Yankel Rosenbaum's civil rights.

120. See Jeffrey Rosen, "The Bloods and the Crits," *New Republic*, 9 December 1996, for a discussion of "self-help" as a justification for jury nullification.

121. Paul Butler, "Racially Based Jury Nullification: Black Power in the Criminal Justice System," *Yale Law Journal* 105 (December 1995), 677. Butler makes an explicit link between "self-help" and nullification, although he does not encourage jurors to ignore the evidence of guilt in cases involving violent crime or property crime against the black community itself.

122. Ibid., 679, 714.

123. Rosen, "The Bloods and the Crits," 33.

124. Kenneth J. Garcia, "Jury United, but Nation Remains Divided," *San Francisco Chronicle*, 4 October 1995, 1.

125. Nick Charles, "O.J. Papers: Nobility Savaged," *Village Voice*, 1 November 1994, 23.

126. Thus, Farrakhan dwelt on the fact that the statues of Lincoln and Jefferson at their memorials in the capital were both nineteen feet high, that Jefferson was the third and Lincoln the sixteenth president, and that three plus sixteen, amazingly, equals nineteen. Furthermore, "when you have a 9 you have a womb that is pregnant, and when you have a 1 standing by the 9, it means there is something secret that has to be unfolded." No national newspaper printed enough of the text to convey the flavor of this bizarre speech. The quotation is from Richard Cohen, "What Was Jesse Jackson Thinking?" *Washington Post*, 18 October 1995, A19. Although the march

organizers claimed that as many as 1.5 million African-American men attended, the Park Police put the figure at 400,000; Steven A. Holmes, "After March, Lawmakers Seek Commission on Race Relations," *New York Times,* 18 October 1995, A1.

127. A. M. Rosenthal, "Farrakhan Owned The Day," *New York Times,* 17 October 1995, A19.

128. Lorraine Adams, "180 Degrees Separate Black, White Views of O. J. Simpson Case," *Washington Post,* 30 July 1995, A3.

129. Jerelyn Eddings, "Black and White in America," *U.S. News & World Report,* 16 October 1995, 33.

130. Editorial, *Economist,* 10 July 1993, 14.

131. Reynolds Farley, *Blacks and Whites: Narrowing the Gap?* (Cambridge: Harvard University Press, 1984), 23; U.S. Department of Education, National Center for Education Statistics, *Digest of Educational Statistics: 1994* (Washington, D.C.: U.S. Government Printing Office, 1994), 208, 224.

132. Estimates of the number of black families (worldwide) who celebrate the holiday run from 5 to 18 million, with the majority of them middle- or upper-middle-class; Anna Day Wilde, "Mainstreaming Kwanzaa," *Public Interest,* Spring 1995, 69. There is of course a big difference between the two numbers, and if "celebrating" means more than buying one Hallmark card, even the 5 million figure may be much too high.

133. Leon E. Wynter, "Business and Race" column, *Wall Street Journal,* 17 August 1994, B1.

134. David Aldridge, "Inside the Color Lines," *Washington Post,* 16 December 1995, 1.

135. "Marshall Receives Award," *Houston Chronicle,* 5 July 1992, 10.

136. Ellen Graham and Cynthia Crossen, "God, Motherhood, and Apple Pie," *Wall Street Journal,* 13 December 1996, R1.

137. "American Dilemma (Part II)," 41.

138. Leslie McAneny and Lydia Saad, "America's Public Schools: Still Separate? Still Unequal?" *Gallup Poll Monthly,* May 1994, 24.

139. Andrew Hacker, *Two Nations: Black and White, Separate, Hostile, Unequal* (New York: Scribner, 1992), 35.

140. Charisse Jones, "Years on Integration Road: New Views of an Old Goal," *New York Times,* 10 April 1994, 1.

141. The opposite-race friends that the people surveyed had in mind were not necessarily the neighbors of the opposite race that they reported having, but the two sets of figures track each other very closely, suggesting that the trend toward neighborhood integration was the driving force behind the impressive growth in the number of interracial friendships.

142. Gerald David Jaynes and Robin M. Williams, Jr., eds., *A Common Destiny: Blacks and American Society,* National Research Council (Washington, D.C.: National Academy Press, 1989), 93.

143. "Mississippi Fights Ban on Prayers in Schools," *New York Times,* 7 December 1993, B8.

144. *Loving v. Virginia,* 388 U.S. 1 (1967). See Kull's penetrating discussion of the Court's handling of the interracial marriage question in Andrew Kull, *The Color-Blind Constitution* (Cambridge: Harvard University Press, 1992), 159–160, 162, 168–171. Myrdal reported that "even a liberal-minded Northerner of cosmopolitan culture . . . will, in nine cases out of ten, express a definite feeling against" interracial marriage. This "consecrated taboo," he argued, was "the center in the complex of attitudes which can be described as 'the common denominator' in the problem. It defines the Negro

group in contradistinction to all the non-colored minority groups in America and all other lower class groups. The boundary between Negro and white is not simply a class line which can be successfully crossed by education, integration into the national culture, and individual economic advancement. The boundary is fixed" and "erected with the intention of permanency"; Gunnar Myrdal, *An American Dilemma* (New York: Harper & Row, 1944), 57–58; see also 606–608 and 1208–1209.

145. Mayer, *The Changing American Mind*, 201, 217–221.

146. Quoted in Allen, "Black Unlike Me."

147. Yankelovich Partners, Inc., *African-American Study: Topline Report,* prepared for the *New Yorker,* March 1996, 29. African Americans surveyed in January 1996, however, were considerably less supportive; 36 percent approved of Farrakhan and 41 percent opposed him; David A. Bositis, *Joint Center for Political and Economic Studies 1996 National Opinion Poll: Political Attitudes* (Washington, D.C.: Joint Center for Political and Economic Studies, 1996), table 19. Support for Farrakhan was not largely confined to the least-educated inner-city residents. In the Joint Center poll, blacks with college degrees were actually slightly more favorable to him than others (38 percent), and high school dropouts (28 percent) were the least favorable.

148. Farrakhan follows in the tradition of the most important black nationalist leader of the early twentieth century, Marcus Garvey, who argued that W. E. B. Du Bois and other NAACP leaders of mixed racial ancestry were not true blacks and threatened to expel from his organization, the Universal Negro Improvement Association, anyone who married a white; F. James Davis, *Who Is Black? One Nation's Definition* (University Park: Pennsylvania State University Press, 1991), 134. Even Du Bois warned of the dangers of miscegenation in 1960, arguing that the loss of "physical evidence of color and racial type" would result in a loss of "our memory of Negro history"; Arthur Herman, *The Idea of Decline in Western History* (New York: Free Press, 1997), 209.

149. Arthur Goren, "Jews," in Stephan Thernstrom, ed., *Harvard Encyclopedia of American Ethnic Groups* (Cambridge: Harvard University Press, 1980), 596; Seymour Martin Lipset and Earl Raab, *Jews and the New American Scene* (Cambridge: Harvard University Press, 1995), 72.

150. Until 1989 the National Center for Health Statistics guidelines for classifying newborns on birth certificates prescribed, amazingly, that the children born to mixed couples were always to be assigned the race of the nonwhite parent. Nonwhite blood, it was assumed, trumped white blood. Only in 1989 did the NCHS alter these guidelines and recommend instead that registration officials assign children born of mixed marriages to the race of their mothers; Christopher A. Ford, "Administering Identity: The Determination of 'Race' in Race-Conscious Law," *California Law Review* 82 (October 1994), 1257–1259. Until 1970, racial determinations on the U.S. Census were made by the enumerators, and persons of mixed white and other parentage were classified as being of "other" race, in accord with the one-drop rule. The 1970 Census shifted to making self-identification the basis of racial classification. It broke from the one-drop rule by putting "a person of mixed white and other parentage who was in doubt as to his classification" into the racial category of his father; U.S. Bureau of the Census, *Historical Statistics of the United States: Colonial Times to 1970* (Washington, D.C.: U.S. Government Printing Office, 1975), 3.

151. Judge Jose Cabranes has drawn an intriguing contrast between the United States and Puerto Rico at the beginning of the twentieth century: "On the mainland a drop of Negro blood makes a white man a Negro; while in Puerto Rico a drop of white blood

makes a Negro a white man"; Cabranes, *Citizenship and the American Empire* (1979), 98, quoted in Ford, "Administering Identity," 1244–1245.

152. Clarence Page, "Grappling with the 'One-Drop' Rule," *Chicago Tribune,* 27 April 1997, C19.

153. Martin F. Nolan, "Tiger's Racial Multiplicity," *Boston Globe,* 26 April 1997, A11 (op-ed).

154. Lawrence Wright, "One Drop of Blood," *New Yorker,* 25 July 1994, 47. See also Susan Kalish, "Multiracial Births Increase as U.S. Ponders Racial Definitions," *Population Today* 23 (April 1995), 1–2; Kalish, "U.S. Ponders Retooling Its Race and Ethnic Categories for 2000 Census," *Population Today* 24 (January 1996), 1–2; Peter Skerry, "Many American Dilemmas: The Statistical Politics of Counting by Race and Ethnicity," *Brookings Review,* Summer 1996, 36–39.

155. Bureau of Labor Statistics, *A CPS Supplement for Testing Methods of Collecting Racial and Ethnic Information: May, 1995* (Washington, D.C.: U.S. Department of Labor, 1995), table 2.

156. Wright, "One Drop of Blood," 47, 53.

157. Michael K. Frisby, "Black, White, or Other," *Emerge,* December-January 1996, 48–51, 54. "American blacks now feel they have a vested interest in a rule [the one-drop rule] that has for centuries been a key instrument in their oppression"; Davis, *Who Is Black?* 180. For an academic defense of this tribalistic perspective on racial classification by a lawyer, see Luther Wright, Jr., "Who's Black, Who's White, and Who Cares: Reconceptualizing the United States's Definition of Race and Racial Classification," *Vanderbilt Law Review* 48 (March 1995), 513–569. Wright argues that we need a stricter racial classification system so as to recognize the "permanent importance" of racial divisions. Since he ardently supports racial preferences in education and hiring, he worries about how to prevent "racial fraud"—whites attempting to pass as black to secure affirmative action entitlements. This is indeed a problem if you grant meaningful preferences to people on the basis of the group they claim to belong to. If being considered an X will increase your chances of law school admission by 50 percent, what is to prevent many non-X's from claiming to be X's? The more that benefits are attached to group membership, the more the need for gatekeepers who keep pretenders out. Wright would deal with such "racial fraud" by imposing "fines and immediate job or benefit termination if they falsified their racial identity." We have had such statutes before. A 1924 Virginia law required statewide racial registration and provided a year in jail as the penalty for making a "false" report of one's race; Ford, "Administering Identity," 1275. The white legislators who put this into the Virginia Jim Crow code were not, of course, seeking to stop whites who were falsely claiming to be African-American. Presumably Wright would have no objection to this attempt to make the color line bright and clear, nor should he find any fault with the Nuremberg Laws. Critical race theory and the KKK join hands.

158. Very few ordinary citizens have any objections to adoptions across racial lines. Just 12 percent of blacks and 15 percent of whites surveyed in 1995 disapproved of a white married couple adopting an African-American baby, and attitudes toward a black couple adopting a white baby were almost identical; "American Dilemma (Part II)," 41. But transracial adoptions have been made difficult or impossible because of political pressure from groups presuming to speak for African Americans, most notably the National Association of Black Social Workers.

159. Wright, "One Drop of Blood," 54.

160. Kalish, "Multiracial Births Increase," 2.

CONCLUSION: ONE NATION, INDIVISIBLE

1. Robert C. Toth and Stanley Meisler, "Ethnic Tensions at a Dangerous Simmer," *Los Angeles Times*, 17 September 1991, H1. See also "Old Hatreds Emerge in Europe," *Chicago Tribune*, 16 September 1991, 5.

2. Gunnar Myrdal, *An American Dilemma* (New York: Harper & Row, 1944), 51.

3. Ibid., 54.

4. Ibid., 57.

5. "Marching to a New War," *U.S. News & World Report*, 6 March 1995, 32.

6. Ana Puga, "Capitol Gains," *Boston Globe Magazine*, 20 March 1994, 38.

7. Figures from Tables 1 and 4 of chap. 8 and Lee Sigelman, et al., "Making Contact? Black-White Social Interaction in an Urban Setting," *American Journal of Sociology* 101 (March 1996), 1313.

8. Donald L. Horowitz, *Ethnic Groups in Conflict* (Berkeley: University of California Press, 1985), 46. Horowitz persuasively attacks the common view that "race" is fundamentally different from "ethnicity." His section on "The Indicators of Ethnic Identity" (41–51) offers a subtle analysis of a wide range of indicators, placed on a continuum from the most immutable to the most superficial and most easily altered. Color and other distinctive physical features, he shows, vary greatly in significance not only from society to society but over time within particular societies.

9. Stephan Thernstrom, "Ethnic Groups in American History," Lance Liebman, ed., *Ethnic Relations in America* (Englewood Cliffs, N.J.: Prentice-Hall, 1982), 13–18. Yankee fears of the various European "races" are vividly expressed in Madison Grant, *The Passing of the Great Race* (New York: Scribner, 1916).

10. The endogamy rate was similarly low for most other ethnic groups; Richard Alba, *Ethnic Identity: The Transformation of White America* (New Haven: Yale University Press, 1990), 13.

11. Stephan Thernstrom, "American Ethnic Statistics," Donald L. Horowitz and Gerard Noiriel, eds., *Immigrants in Two Democracies; French and American Experience* (New York: New York University Press, 1992), 90.

12. Myrdal, *American Dilemma*, 53–54, 667. Emphasis in original.

13. National Collegiate Athletic Association, *1996 NCAA Division I Graduation-Rates Report* (Overland Park, Kans.: National Collegiate Athletic Association, 1996), 203; U.S. Bureau of the Census, 1990 Census of the Population, Supplementary Reports, *Detailed Occupation and Other Characteristics from the EEO File for the United States* 1990 CP-S-1 (Washington, D.C.: U.S. Government Printing Office, 1992), table 1; William P. O'Hare, "America's Minorities: The Demographics of Diversity," *Population Bulletin* 47 (December 1992), 29, 33–34; U.S. Bureau of the Census, 1990 Census of the Population, *Asian and Pacific Islanders in the United States*, 1990-CP-3-5 (Washington, D.C.: U.S. Government Printing Office, 1993), table 5.

14. Harry H. L. Kitano and Roger Daniels, *Asian Americans* (Englewood Cliffs, N.J.: Prentice-Hall, 1988), 176–180.

15. Susan Kalish, "Multiracial Births Increase as U.S. Ponders Racial Definitions," *Population Today* 23 (April 1995), 1–2; Susan Kalish, "Interracial Baby Boomlet in Progress?" *Population Today* 20 (December 1992), 1; Thernstrom, "Ethnic Groups," 23.

16. Richard W. Stevenson, "Moving from Big Money to Power," *New York Times*, 13 April 1996, 8; Judith H. Dobrzynski, "Way Beyond the Glass Ceiling," *New York Times*, 11 May 1995, D1; Saul Hansell, "American Express Names Apparent Successor to Chief," *New York Times*, 28 February 1997, B2.

17. Peter Goldman, *The Death and Life of Malcolm X* (Urbana: University of Illinois Press, 1979), 15, 71.

18. Lyndon B. Johnson, Speech at Howard University, June 4, 1965, reprinted in Lee Rainwater and William Yancey, *The Moynihan Report and the Politics of Controversy* (Cambridge: MIT Press, 1967), 126.

19. Ann Scales, "Affirmative Action: An American Dilemma," pt. 2, *Boston Globe,* 22 May 1995, 1.

20. Lawrence Buron, Robert Haveman, and Owen O'Donnell, *Recent Trends in U.S. Male Work and Wage Patterns: An Overview,* Discussion Paper #1060-95 (Madison: Institute for Research on Poverty, University of Wisconsin-Madison, 1995).

21. Few proponents of preferential policies frankly defend them in these terms, though. Instead, they typically refer to matters like the racial gap in unemployment, and ignore the point that affirmative action does nothing whatever to ameliorate that problem.

22. "Should Crime Be Color-Blind?" *Law Enforcement News,* 15 December 1993, 1; letter of October 21, 1993 to Attorney General Janet Reno from Mayors Donald M. Fraser (Minneapolis), Glenda E. Hood (Orlando), Sharpe James (Newark), Kurt Schmoke (Baltimore), and Wellington Webb (Denver), on file with authors.

23. *Plessy v. Ferguson,* 163 U.S. 537, at 558.

24. Andrew Kull, *The Color-Blind Constitution* (Cambridge: Harvard University Press, 1992), 146.

25. "Preference Programs under Fire . . . ," Special Report no. 34, C-1, Bureau of National Afffairs, Washington D.C., February 21, 1995.

26. Leon Wieseltier, "Washington Diarist," *New Republic,* 6 November 1995, 46.

27. Glenn C. Loury, "Individualism Before Multiculturalism," *Harvard Journal of Law and Public Policy,* 19 (Spring 1996), 726. The second sentence quoted is from the original lecture to the Federalist Society, copy on file with authors.

28. Seymour Martin Lipset and Earl Raab, *Jews and the New American Scene* (Cambridge: Harvard University Press, 1995), 26; Edward S. Schapiro, "Blacks and Jews Entangled," *First Things,* 45 (August-September 1994), 34.

29. The data given here for various groups of European origin are from Census data based on answers to a question about the "ancestry" of respondents. How many of those who mention a particular ancestry can be considered to be members of that ethnic group is questionable; mentioning that one is of Norwegian ancestry, say, is only a very weak indicator of ethnic identification. For discussions of this data, see Stanley Lieberson and Mary Waters, *From Many Strands: Ethnic and Racial Groups in Contemporary America* (New York: Russell Sage Foundation, 1990) and Stephan Thernstrom, "Counting Heads: New Data on the Ethnic Composition of the American Population," *Journal of Interdisciplinary History* 20 (Summer 1989), 107–114.

30. Michele Collison, "One of the 'Big Four' Civil-Rights Leaders Keeps History Alive," *Chronicle of Higher Education,* 22 February 1989, A3.

31. *Pittsburgh Courier,* 13 June 1942, as quoted in Myrdal, *American Dilemma,* I, lxxxviii, n 2.

32. Ibid., 28, lxxxviii, n. 2.

33. J. F. O. McAllister, "The Candidate of Dreams," *Time,* 13 March 1995, 88.

34. Myrdal, *American Dilemma,* 1010, 1014.

35. Andrew Young, *An Easy Burden: The Civil Rights Movement and the Transformation of America* (New York: HarperCollins, 1996), 2–3.

List of Tables

PART I: HISTORY

PART II: OUT OF THE SIXTIES: RECENT SOCIAL, ECONOMIC, AND POLITICAL TRENDS

Chapter 10: Crime

Chapter 11: Politics

PART III: EQUALITY AND PREFERENCE:
THE CHANGING RACIAL CLIMATE

Chapter 12: With All Deliberate Speed

Index